Why do you need this new edition?

8 good reasons why you should buy this new Second Edition of *Visions of America*!

1. New with this Second Edition: *Visions of America* works in tandem with the innovative website, *MyHistoryLab*, helping you learn more in your history course (www.myhistorylab.com). *MyHistoryLab* icons connect the main narrative in each chapter of the book to a powerful array of resources, including primary source documents, analytical video segments, multi-media tutorials, and more. A *MyHistoryLab Connections* feature now appears at the end of each chapter, capping off the study resources for each chapter. *MyHistoryLab* also includes both an eText and Audio Book of *Visions of America*, so that you can read or listen to your textbook any time you have access to the Internet. For even greater flexibility, you may download the eText to an iPad® using the free Pearson eText app.

2. New with this Second Edition: *Visions of America* now uses the latest *New MyHistoryLab*, which offers the most advanced Study Plan ever. You get personalized study plans for each chapter, with content arranged from less complex thinking—like remembering facts—to more complex critical thinking—like understanding connections in history and analyzing primary sources. Assessments and learning applications in the Study Plan link you directly to the *Visions of America* eBook for reading and review.

3. New with this Second Edition: the *New MyHistoryLab* course for *Visions of America* offers more than 100 powerful Closer Look learning applications developed by the authors of the textbook. These engaging on-line applications will help you learn to think critically about the past, which is essential to doing well in your history class.

4. Also in the *New MyHistoryLab* course for *Visions of America*, the text authors have created Critical Visions videos for each chapter of the book. In these videos the author highlights the most important themes and questions explored in the chapter. View the videos to get more out of your reading of each chapter, and watch them later to refresh your understanding of the material before classes and exams.

5. A new feature in this Second Edition of *Visions of America* is the Envisioning Evidence sections that appear in fifteen of the chapters. Each Envisioning Evidence uses charts, graphs, maps, or illustrations to discuss and highlight the kind of materials that historians use to illuminate and analyze the past. Among the topics covered in this new feature are: the eighteenth-century slave trade (Chapter 3), a comparison of military strength of the North and South during the Civil War (Chapter 13), and interpreting public opinion polls during the Great Depression (Chapter 22).

6. The pedagogical framework of the Second Edition of *Visions of America* has also been strengthened by the addition of Learning Objective Questions at the start of each chapter. These questions help you identify the most important themes and topics as you work through the chapter.

7. The Second Edition of *Visions of America* covers numerous new topics in the thematic features that appear in every chapter–Competing Visions, Images as History, and Choices and Consequences. Among these new topics are: reactions to the French Revolution in the early Republic (Chapter 6), the freeing of slaves during the Civil War (Chapter 13), and the annexation of the Philippines in 1898 after the Spanish-American War (Chapter 19).

8. To improve the narrative presentation of the Second Edition of *Visions of America*, the authors and editors have reviewed each line of the text and made numerous significant changes to enhance the strengths of the First Edition.

PEARSON

VISIONS of AMERICA

SECOND EDITION

VISIONS *of* AMERICA

A History of the United States

VOLUME 1 • TO 1877

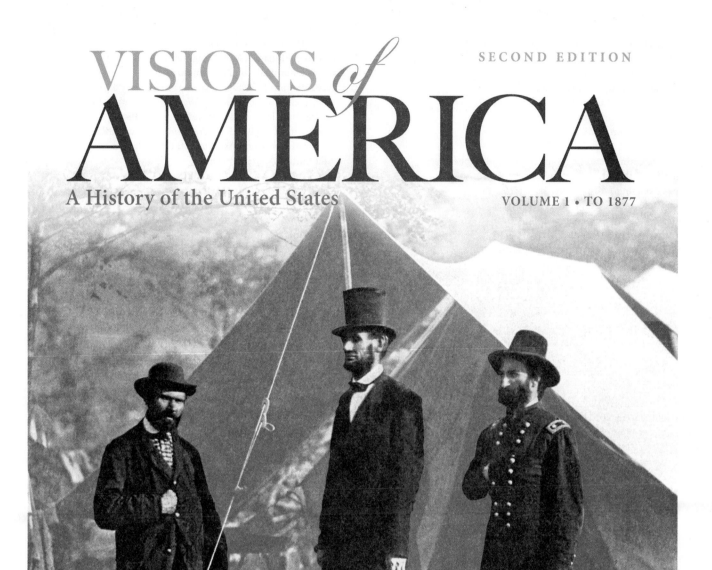

Jennifer D. Keene
Chapman University

Saul Cornell
Fordham University

Edward T. O'Donnell
College of the Holy Cross

PEARSON

Boston Columbus Indianapolis New York San Francisco Upper Saddle River
Amsterdam Cape Town Dubai London Madrid Milan Munich Paris Montréal Toronto
Delhi Mexico City São Paulo Sydney Hong Kong Seoul Singapore Taipei Tokyo

Editorial Director: Craig Campanella
Editor in Chief: Dickson Musslewhite
Executive Editor: Ed Parsons
Development Editor: Gerald Lombardi
Editorial Project Manager: Alex Rabinowitz
Supplements Editor: Emsal Hasan
Editorial Assistant: Emily Tamburri
Director of Marketing: Brandy Dawson
Senior Marketing Manager: Maureen E. Prado Roberts
Marketing Assistant: Samantha Bennett
Senior Managing Editor: Ann Marie McCarthy
Senior Project Manager: Debra A. Wechsler
Senior Operations Manager: Mary Fischer
Operations Specialist: Alan Fischer
Cover Design: Laura Gardner and John Christiana

Interior Designer: Laura Gardner
AV Project Manager: Mirella Signoretto
Cartographer: Peter Bull Art Studio
Cover Art: Lincoln: © Ivy Close Images/Alamy; Pocohantas: ©Bettmann/CORBIS; George Washington: National Portrait Gallery, Smithsonian Institution/Art Resource, NY; Progress of the Century: ©Bettmann/CORBIS; First Vote: ©Bettmann/CORBIS
Director of Media and Assessment: Brian Hyland
Media Editor: Andrea Messineo
Media Project Manager: Tina Rudowski
Full-Service Project Management: Melissa Sacco
Composition: PreMediaGlobal USA, Inc.
Printer/Binder: Quad/Graphics
Cover Printer: Lehigh-Phoenix Color/Hagerstown
Text Font: Minion Pro Regular

Credits and acknowledgments borrowed from other sources and reproduced, with permission, in this textbook appear on appropriate page within text (or on page C-1).

Many of the designations by manufacturers and seller to distinguish their products are claimed as trademarks. Where those designations appear in this book, and the publisher was aware of a trademark claim, the designations have been printed in initial caps or all caps.

Library of Congress Cataloging-in-Publication Data

Keene, Jennifer D.
   Visions of America : a history of the United States / Jennifer D. Keene, Saul Cornell, Edward T. O'Donnell. — 2nd ed.
      p. cm.
   Includes bibliographical references and index.
   ISBN-13: 978-0-205-09266-6 (combined vol.)
   ISBN-10: 0-205-09266-7 (combined vol.)
   ISBN-13: 978-0-205-09267-3 (v. 1)
   ISBN-13: 978-0-205-09268-0 (v. 2)
   1. United States—History—Textbooks.   I. Cornell, Saul.   II. O'Donnell, Edward T.
III. Title.
   E178.1.K24 2012
   973—dc23

                                                2011041966

10 9 8 7 6 5 4 3 2 1

Combined Volume
ISBN 10: 0-205-09266-7
ISBN 13: 978-0-205-09266-6
Instructor's Review Copy
ISBN 10: 0-205-19244-0
ISBN 13: 978-0-205-19244-1
Volume 1
ISBN 10: 0-205-09267-5
ISBN 13: 978-0-205-09267-3

Volume 1 à la carte
ISBN 10: 0-205-19327-7
ISBN 13: 978-0-205-19327-1
Volume 2
ISBN 10: 0-205-09268-3
ISBN 13: 978-0-205-09268-0
Volume 2 à la carte
ISBN 10: 0-205-19329-3
ISBN 13: 978-0-205-19329-5

Dedication

To our parents, who imbued us with a love of history; our spouses, who have learned to share this passion; and our children, present and future students of American history.

Brief Contents

CHAPTER

1 People in Motion: The Atlantic World to 1590   2

2 Models of Settlement: English Colonial Societies, 1590–1710   34

3 Growth, Slavery, and Conflict: Colonial America, 1710–1763   64

4 Revolutionary America: Change and Transformation, 1764–1783   96

5 A Virtuous Republic: Creating a Workable Government, 1783–1789   128

6 The New Republic: An Age of Political Passion, 1789–1800   156

7 Jeffersonian America: An Expanding Empire of Liberty, 1800–1824   188

8 Democrats and Whigs: Democracy and American Culture, 1820–1840   220

9 Workers, Farmers, and Slaves: The Transformation of the American Economy, 1815–1848   252

10 Revivalism, Reform, and Artistic Renaissance, 1820–1850   282

11 "To Overspread the Continent": Westward Expansion and Political Conflict, 1840–1848   316

12 Slavery and Sectionalism: The Political Crisis of 1848–1861   340

13 A Nation Torn Apart: The Civil War, 1861–1865   374

14 Now That We Are Free: Reconstruction and the New South, 1863–1890   404

Contents

Maps **xxii**
Charts, Graphs, and Tables **xxiii**
Envisioning Evidence **xxiv**
Images as History **xxv**
Competing Visions **xxvi**
Choices and Consequences **xxvii**
About the Authors **xxix**
Supplements for Instructors and Students **xxx**

CHAPTER 1 People in Motion: The Atlantic World to 1590 2

The First Americans **4**
- Migration, Settlement, and the Rise of Agriculture **4**
- The Aztec **6**
- Mound Builders and Pueblo Dwellers **7**
- Eastern Woodlands Indian Societies **8**
- American Societies on the Eve of European Contact **9**

European Civilization in Turmoil **10**
- The Allure of the East and the Challenge of Islam **10**
- Trade, Commerce, and Urbanization **10**

Competing Visions
EUROPEAN AND HURON VIEWS OF NATURE **12**

- Renaissance and Reformation **13**
- New Monarchs and the Rise of the Nation-State **14**

Columbus and the Columbian Exchange **16**
- Columbus Encounters the "Indians" **16**
- European Technology in the Era of the Columbian Exchange **17**
- The Conquest of the Aztec and Inca Empires **17**

West African Worlds **20**
- West African Societies, Islam, and Trade **20**
- The Portuguese-African Connection **20**
- African Slavery **21**

Choices and Consequences
BENIN, PORTUGAL, AND THE INTERNATIONAL SLAVE TRADE **23**

European Colonization of the Atlantic World **24**
- The Black Legend and the Creation of New Spain **24**
- Fishing and Furs: France's North Atlantic Empire **26**
- English Expansion: Ireland and Virginia **28**

Images as History
MARKETING THE NEW WORLD: THEODORE DE BRY'S ENGRAVINGS
OF THE AMERICAS **31**

CHAPTER REVIEW **32**

CHAPTER 2 Models of Settlement: English Colonial Societies, 1590–1710 **34**

The Chesapeake Colonies 36
- The Founding of Jamestown **36**
- Tobacco Agriculture and Political Reorganization **37**

Choices and Consequences
THE ORDEAL OF POCAHONTAS **38**
- Lord Baltimore's Refuge: Maryland **40**
- Life in the Chesapeake: Tobacco and Society **41**

New England 42
- Plymouth Plantation **42**

Images as History
CORRUPTION VERSUS PIETY **43**
- A Godly Commonwealth **44**

Envisioning Evidence
PATTERNS OF SETTLEMENT IN NEW ENGLAND AND THE
CHESAPEAKE COMPARED **46**
- Challenges to Puritan Orthodoxy **47**
- Expansion and Conflict **48**

Competing Visions
ANTINOMIANISM OR TOLERATION: THE PURITAN DILEMMA **49**

The Caribbean Colonies 50
- Power Is Sweet **50**
- Barbados: The Emergence of a Slave Society **50**

The Restoration Era and the Proprietary Colonies 52
- The English Conquest of the Dutch Colony of New Netherland **52**
- A Peaceable Kingdom: Quakers in Pennsylvania **53**
- The Carolinas **54**

The Crises of the Late Seventeenth Century 55
- War and Rebellion **55**
- The Dominion of New England and the Glorious Revolution **57**
- The Salem Witchcraft Hysteria **58**

The Whig Ideal and the Emergence of Political Stability 60
- The Whig Vision of Politics **60**
- Mercantilism, Federalism, and the Structure of Empire **61**

CHAPTER REVIEW **62**

CHAPTER 3 Growth, Slavery, and Conflict: Colonial America, 1710–1763 **64**

Culture and Society in the Eighteenth Century 66
- The Refinement of America **66**
- More English, Yet More American **68**

Images as History
A PORTRAIT OF COLONIAL ASPIRATIONS **69**
- Strong Assemblies and Weak Governors **70**

Enlightenment and Awakenings 72
- Georgia's Utopian Experiment **73**

- American Champions of the Enlightenment **73**
- Awakening, Revivalism, and American Society **74**
- Indian Revivals **76**

African Americans in the Colonial Era   77
- The Atlantic Slave Trade **77**

Envisioning Evidence
THE EIGHTEENTH-CENTURY ATLANTIC SLAVE TRADE   **78**

- Southern Slavery **79**
- Northern Slavery and Free Blacks **80**
- Slave Resistance and Rebellion **81**
- An African American Culture Emerges under Slavery **81**

Immigration, Regional Economies, and Inequality   83
- Immigration to the Colonies **83**
- Regional Economies **83**
- New England **84**
- The Mid-Atlantic **84**
- The Upper and Lower South **85**
- The Back Country **85**
- Cities: Growth and Inequality **86**
- Rural America: Land Becomes Scarce **86**

War and the Contest over Empire   87
- The Rise and Fall of the Middle Ground **87**
- The Struggle for North America **88**

Competing Visions
SIR WILLIAM JOHNSON AND THE IROQUOIS: INDIAN VISIONS VERSUS
BRITISH ARMS   **91**

Choices and Consequences
QUAKERS, PACIFISM, AND THE PAXTON UPRISING   **93**

CHAPTER REVIEW   **94**

CHAPTER **4** Revolutionary America: Change and Transformation, 1764–1783   **96**

Tightening the Reins of Empire   98
- Taxation without Representation **98**

Envisioning Evidence
A COMPARISON OF THE ANNUAL PER CAPITA TAX RATES IN BRITAIN AND THE
COLONIES IN 1765   **99**

- The Stamp Act Crisis **100**
- An Assault on Liberty **101**
- The Intolerable Acts and the First Continental Congress **103**
- Lexington, Concord, and Lord Dunmore's Proclamation **105**

Patriots versus Loyalists   107
- The Battle of Bunker Hill **107**

Images as History
TRUMBULL'S *THE DEATH OF GENERAL WARREN AT THE BATTLE OF BUNKER HILL*   **108**

- *Common Sense* and the Declaration of Independence **110**
- The Plight of the Loyalists **111**

Choices and Consequences
A LOYALIST WIFE'S DILEMMA   **113**

America at War 114
- The War in the North **114**
- The Southern Campaigns and Final Victory at Yorktown **117**

The Radicalism of the American Revolution 119
- Popular Politics in the Revolutionary Era **119**
- Constitutional Experiments: Testing the Limits of Democracy **120**
- African Americans Struggle for Freedom **122**
- The American Revolution in Indian Country **122**
- Liberty's Daughters: Women and the Revolutionary Movement **123**

Competing Visions
REMEMBER THE LADIES **125**

CHAPTER REVIEW **126**

CHAPTER **5** A Virtuous Republic: Creating a Workable Government, 1783–1789 **128**

Republicanism and the Politics of Virtue 130
- George Washington: The American Cincinnatus **130**
- The Politics of Virtue: Views from the States **131**

Images as History
WOMEN'S ROLES: TRADITION AND CHANGE **134**
- Democracy Triumphant? **135**
- Debtors versus Creditors **137**

Life under the Articles of Confederation 138
- No Taxation with Representation **138**
- Diplomacy: Frustration and Stalemate **138**
- Settling the Old Northwest **140**
- Shays's Rebellion **141**

The Movement for Constitutional Reform 143
- The Road to Philadelphia **143**
- Large States versus Small States **143**
- Conflict over Slavery **145**
- Filling out the Constitutional Design **146**

The Great Debate 148
- Federalists versus Anti-Federalists **148**

Competing Visions
BRUTUS AND THE PUBLIUS DEBATE THE NATURE
OF REPUBLICANISM **149**
- Ratification **150**

Choices and Consequences
TO RATIFY OR NOT **152**
- The Creation of a Loyal Opposition **153**

CHAPTER REVIEW **154**

CHAPTER **6** The New Republic: An Age of Political Passion, 1789–1800 **156**

Launching the New Government 158
- Choosing the First President **158**
- The First Federal Elections: Completing the Constitution **158**
- Filling Out the Branches of Government **159**

Hamilton's Ambitious Program **160**
- Hamilton's Vision for the New Republic **160**
- The Assumption of State Debts **161**
- Madison's Opposition **162**
- The Bank, the Mint, and the Report on Manufactures **164**
- Jefferson and Hamilton: Contrasting Visions of the Republic **165**

Partisanship without Parties **166**
- A New Type of Politician **166**
- The Growth of the Partisan Press **166**
- The Democratic-Republican Societies **167**

Conflicts at Home and Abroad **168**
- The French Revolution in America **168**
- Adams versus Clinton: A Contest for Vice President **169**
- Diplomatic Controversies and Triumphs **169**
- Violence along the Frontier **170**

Competing Visions
JEFFERSON'S AND HAMILTON'S REACTIONS TO THE FRENCH REVOLUTION **171**

Choices and Consequences
WASHINGTON'S DECISION TO CRUSH THE WHISKEY REBELLION **174**

Cultural Politics in a Passionate Age **175**
- Political Fashions and Fashionable Politics **175**
- Literature, Education, and Gender **175**
- Federalists, Republicans, and the Politics of Race **176**

Images as History
LIBERTY DISPLAYING THE ARTS AND SCIENCES **178**

The Stormy Presidency of John Adams **179**
- Washington's Farewell Address **179**
- The XYZ Affair and Quasi-War with France **181**
- The Alien and Sedition Acts **182**
- The Disputed Election of 1800 **183**
- Gabriel's Rebellion **185**

CHAPTER REVIEW **186**

CHAPTER 7 Jeffersonian America: An Expanding Empire of Liberty, 1800–1824 **188**

Politics in Jeffersonian America **190**
- Liberty and Small Government **190**
- The Jeffersonian Style **190**
- Political Slurs and the Politics of Honor **191**

Envisioning Evidence
THE WORLD OF SLAVERY AT MONTICELLO **192**

An Expanding Empire of Liberty **194**
- Dismantling the Federalist Program **194**
- The Courts: The Last Bastion of Federalist Power **194**
- The Louisiana Purchase **195**

Choices and Consequences
JOHN MARSHALL'S PREDICAMENT **196**

- Lewis and Clark **197**
- Indian Responses to Jeffersonian Expansionism: Assimilation or Revivalism **198**

Dissension at Home   200
- Jefferson's Attack on the Federalist Judiciary   **200**
- The Controversial Mr. Burr   **200**

America Confronts a World at War   201
- The Failure of Peaceable Coercion   **201**
- Madison's Travails: Diplomatic Blunders Abroad and Tensions on the Frontier   **201**
- The War of 1812   **203**

Competing Visions
WAR HAWKS AND THEIR CRITICS   **204**
- The Hartford Convention   **206**

The Republic Reborn: Consequences of the War of 1812   208
- The National Republican Vision of James Monroe   **208**
- Diplomatic Triumphs   **209**
- Economic and Technological Innovation   **210**

Images as History
SAMUEL MORSE'S *HOUSE OF REPRESENTATIVES* AND THE NATIONAL REPUBLICAN VISION   **211**
- Judicial Nationalism   **212**

Crisis and the Collapse of the National Republican Consensus   213
- The Panic of 1819   **213**
- The Missouri Crisis   **213**
- Denmark Vesey's Rebellion   **215**
- Jeffersonian America and the Politics of Compromise   **217**

CHAPTER REVIEW   **218**

CHAPTER **8** Democrats and Whigs: Democracy and American Culture, 1820–1840   **220**

Democracy in America   222
- Democratic Culture   **222**
- Davy Crockett and the Frontier Myth   **222**

Competing Visions
SHOULD WHITE MEN WITHOUT PROPERTY HAVE THE VOTE?   **224**

Andrew Jackson and His Age   225
- The Election of 1824 and the "Corrupt Bargain"   **225**
- The Election of 1828: "Old Hickory's" Triumph   **227**
- The Reign of "King Mob"   **229**
- States' Rights and the Nullification Crisis   **230**

White Man's Democracy   233
- Race and Politics in the Jacksonian Era   **233**
- The Cherokee Cases   **236**
- Resistance and Removal   **236**

Choices and Consequences
ACQUIESCE OR RESIST? THE CHEROKEE DILEMMA   **237**

Democrats, Whigs, and the Second Party System   239
- Third Party Challenges: Anti-Masonic and Workingmen's Parties   **239**
- The Bank War and the Rise of the Whigs   **241**
- Andrew Jackson, the Whigs, and the Bank War   **242**
- Economic Crisis and the Presidency of Martin Van Buren   **242**

Images as History
KING ANDREW AND THE DOWNFALL OF MOTHER BANK **244**

Playing the Democrats' Game: Whigs in the Election of 1840 **246**
- The Log Cabin Campaign **246**
- Gender and Social Class: The Whig Appeal **247**
- Democrats and Whigs: Two Visions of Government and Society **248**

CHAPTER REVIEW **250**

CHAPTER **9** Workers, Farmers, and Slaves: The Transformation of the American Economy, 1815–1848 **252**

The Market Revolution **254**
- Agricultural Changes and Consequences **254**
- A Nation on the Move: Roads, Canals, Steamboats, and Trains **255**

Images as History
NATURE, TECHNOLOGY, AND THE RAILROAD: GEORGE INNESS'S
THE LACKAWANNA VALLEY (1855) **257**
- Spreading the News **258**

The Spread of Industrialization **260**
- From Artisan to Worker **260**
- Women and Work **260**
- The Lowell Experiment **261**
- Urban Industrialization **262**

Competing Visions
THE LOWELL STRIKE OF 1834 **263**

The Changing Urban Landscape **264**
- Old Ports and the New Cities of the Interior **264**
- Immigrants and the City **266**
- Free Black Communities in the North **266**
- Riot, Unrest, and Crime **267**

Envisioning Evidence
THE ECONOMICS AND GEOGRAPHY OF VICE IN MID-NINETEENTH
CENTURY NEW YORK **269**

Southern Society **270**
- The Planter Class **270**
- Yeoman and Tenant Farmers **271**
- Free Black Communities **272**
- White Southern Culture **273**

Life and Labor under Slavery **274**
- Varied Systems of Slave Labor **274**
- Life in the Slave Quarters **276**
- Slave Religion and Music **276**
- Resistance and Revolt **277**
- Slavery and the Law **278**

Choices and Consequences
CONSCIENCE OR DUTY? JUSTICE RUFFIN'S QUANDARY **279**

CHAPTER REVIEW **280**

CHAPTER 10 Revivalism, Reform, and Artistic Renaissance, 1820–1850 **282**

Revivalism and Reform 284
• Revivalism and the Market Revolution **284**
• Temperance **285**
• Schools, Prisons, and Asylums **287**

Abolitionism and the Proslavery Response 290
• The Rise of Immediatism **290**

Images as History
THE GREEK SLAVE **292**

• Anti-Abolitionism and the Abolitionist Response **293**
• The Proslavery Argument **293**

The Cult of True Womanhood, Reform, and Women's Rights 295
• The New Domestic Ideal **295**
• Controlling Sexuality **296**
• The Path toward Seneca Falls **296**

Religious and Secular Utopianism 298
• Millennialism, Perfectionism, and Religious Utopianism **298**

Competing Visions
REACTIONS TO SHAKER GENDER ROLES **300**

• Secular Utopias **301**

Choices and Consequences
MARY CRAGIN'S EXPERIMENT IN FREE LOVE AT ONEIDA **302**

Literature and Popular Culture 304
• Literature and Social Criticism **304**
• Domestic Fiction, Board Games, and Crime Stories **305**
• Slaves Tell Their Story: Slavery in American Literature **306**
• Lyceums and Lectures **307**

Nature's Nation 308
• Landscape Painting **308**
• Parks and Cemeteries **309**
• Revival and Reform in American Architecture **311**

CHAPTER REVIEW **314**

CHAPTER 11 "To Overspread the Continent": Westward Expansion and Political Conflict, 1840–1848 **316**

Manifest Destiny and Changing Visions of the West 318
• The Trapper's World **318**
• Manifest Destiny and the Overland Trail **319**
• The Native American Encounter with Manifest Destiny **321**
• The Mormon Flight to Utah **322**

Images as History
GEORGE CATLIN AND MAH-TO-TOH-PA: REPRESENTING INDIANS FOR AN AMERICAN AUDIENCE **323**

American Expansionism into the Southwest **325**
- The Transformation of Northern Mexico **325**
- The Clash of Interests in Texas **326**
- The Republic of Texas and the Politics of Annexation **327**
- Polk's Expansionist Vision **328**

The Mexican War and Its Consequences **330**
- A Controversial War **330**

Choices and Consequences
HENRY DAVID THOREAU AND CIVIL DISOBEDIENCE **331**
- Images of the Mexican War **332**

The Wilmot Proviso and the Realignment of American Politics **334**
- The Wilmot Proviso **334**
- Sectionalism and the Election of 1848 **334**

Competing Visions
SLAVERY AND THE ELECTION OF 1848 **337**

CHAPTER REVIEW **338**

CHAPTER **12** Slavery and Sectionalism: The Political Crisis of 1848–1861 **340**

The Slavery Question in the Territories **342**
- The Gold Rush **342**
- Organizing California and New Mexico **343**
- The Compromise of 1850 **344**
- Sectionalism on the Rise **347**

Choices and Consequences
RESISTING THE FUGITIVE SLAVE ACT **349**

Political Realignment **350**
- Young America **350**
- The Kansas–Nebraska Act **351**
- Republicans and Know–Nothings **353**
- Ballots and Blood **354**

Images as History
THE "FOREIGN MENACE" **355**
- Deepening Controversy **358**

Two Societies **360**
- The Industrial North **360**

Envisioning Evidence
THE RISE OF KING COTTON **362**
- Cotton Is Supreme **363**
- The Other South **363**
- Divergent Visions **364**

A House Divided **366**
- The Lincoln-Douglas Debates **366**
- John Brown's Raid **366**
- The Election of 1860 **367**
- Secession **369**

Competing Visions
SECESSION OR UNION? **371**

CHAPTER REVIEW **372**

CHAPTER 13 A Nation Torn Apart: The Civil War, 1861–1865 374

Mobilization, Strategy, and Diplomacy 376
- Comparative Advantages and Disadvantages 376
- Mobilization in the North 377
- Mobilization in the South 378
- The Struggle for the Border States 379
- Wartime Diplomacy 380

The Early Campaigns, 1861–1863 381
- No Short and Bloodless War 381
- The Peninsular Campaign 382
- A New Kind of War 383
- Toward Emancipation 384

Images as History
WHO FREED THE SLAVES? 385
- Slaughter and Stalemate 386

Behind the Lines 387
- Meeting the Demands of Modern War 387
- Hardships on the Home Front 387
- New Roles for Women 388
- Copperheads 389
- Conscription and Civil Unrest 389

Competing Visions
CIVIL LIBERTIES IN A CIVIL WAR 390

Toward Union Victory 392
- Turning Point: 1863 392
- African Americans under Arms 392

Choices and Consequences
EQUAL PERIL, UNEQUAL PAY 394
- The Confederacy Begins to Crumble 395

Envisioning Evidence
HUMAN RESOURCES IN THE ARMIES OF THE CIVIL WAR 396
- Victory in Battle and at the Polls 397
- War Is Hell 399

CHAPTER REVIEW 402

CHAPTER 14 Now That We Are Free: Reconstruction and the New South, 1863–1890 404

Preparing for Reconstruction 406
- Emancipation Test Cases 406
- Lincoln's Ten Percent Plan 408
- Radical Republicans Offer a Different Vision 408

The Fruits of Freedom 409
- Freedom of Movement 409
- Forty Acres and a Mule 409
- Uplift through Education 410
- The Black Church 411

The Struggle to Define Reconstruction 412
- The Conservative Vision of Freedom: Presidential Reconstruction **412**

Competing Visions
DEMANDING RIGHTS, PROTECTING PRIVILEGE **414**

- Congressional Reconstruction and the Fourteenth Amendment **415**
- Republicans Take Control **417**

Implementing Reconstruction 418
- The Republican Party in the South **418**
- Creating Reconstruction Governments in the South **419**
- The Election of 1868 **420**
- The Fifteenth Amendment **421**
- The Rise of White Resistance **422**

Reconstruction Abandoned 423
- Corruption and Scandal **423**
- Republican Disunity **423**
- The Election of 1872 **424**
- Hard Times **424**
- The Return of Terrorism **424**

Images as History
POLITICAL CARTOONS REFLECT THE SHIFT IN PUBLIC OPINION **425**

- The End of Reconstruction **426**

The New South 428
- Redeemer Rule **428**
- The Lost Cause **428**
- The New South Economy **429**
- The Rise of Sharecropping **431**
- Jim Crow **432**

Choices and Consequences
SANCTIONING SEPARATION **434**

CHAPTER REVIEW **436**

Appendix **A-1**
Glossary **G-1**
Credits **C-1**
Index **I-1**
Maps **M-1**

Maps

1.1 Migration from Asia to America **4**

1.3 Early American Civilizations **6**

1.11 Internal African Trade Routes and Portuguese Trade with Africa **21**

1.13 Major European Explorations of the Atlantic **24**

2.6 Caribbean Colonies **50**

2.8 Seventeenth-Century English Mainland Colonies **52**

2.10 King Philip's War **56**

3.2 The Triangle Trade **67**

3.16 Map of Colonial Regions **84**

3.19 British Conquest of New France **89**

3.21 Proclamation of 1763 **92**

4.2 Stamp Act Protests **100**

4.12 Northern Campaigns **116**

4.13 Southern Campaigns **117**

5.9 Border Disputes in Old Northwest and Southwest **139**

5.11 Court Closings and Major Battles in Shays's Rebellion **142**

5.18 Geographical Distribution of the Vote on Ratification **153**

6.7 Map of Spanish Interests in America **170**

6.13 Electoral Map 1796 **181**

6.17 Electoral Map of 1800 **185**

7.4 Louisiana Purchase **197**

7.9 Major Battles of the War of 1812 **205**

7.15 The Missouri Compromise **214**

8.1 Changes in Suffrage Requirements between 1800 and 1828 **223**

8.4 Electoral Votes and Popular Votes 1824 **227**

8.12 Indian Removal **238**

9.3 Time Lag for News 1800–1841 **258**

10.11 Utopian Communities **303**

11.2 Western Trails **319**

11.9 Mexican War **329**

12.4 The Compromise of 1850 **346**

12.9 The Kansas-Nebraska Act **352**

12.19 The Election of 1860 and Secession **368**

13.5 The Vital Border States **379**

13.7 Major Battles in the West, 1862–1863 **382**

13.8 Major Battles in the Eat, 1861–1862 **383**

13.16 The Final Battles in Virginia Campaign, 1864–1865 **398**

13.17 Sherman's March to the Sea, 1864–1865 **398**

14.19 The Readmission of Southern States and Return of White Rule **427**

14.23 Moving from Slavery to Freedom: The Barrow Plantation, Oglethorpe County, Georgia, 1860 and 1861 **432**

Charts, Graphs, and Tables

1.8 Columbian Exchange   17

3.15 Eighteenth-Century Immigration to the Colonies   83

3.18 Poor Relief, Boston   86

4.7 British Policies and their Consequences for Relations with the American Colonies   105

5.7 The Democratization of the State Legislatures   137

5.8 Continental Paper Currency   138

5.13 Comparison of the Articles of Confederation, Virginia, and New Jersey Plans   145

5.14 Comparison of the Articles of Confederation and the Constitution   147

5.16 Anti-Federalist versus Federalist Ideas   151

6.4 Political Views: Hamilton versus Jefferson   165

8.17 Democrats and Whigs: Major Beliefs   249

9.6 Average Height of Native-Born American Men by Year of Birth   262

9.9 Sources of European Immigration   266

9.12 Schematic Map of Hermitage Plantation   270

12.7 The Election of 1852   350

12.13 The Election of 1856   358

12.19 The Election of 1860 and Secession   368

13.1 Union Advantages on the Eve of War, 1861   376

14.14 The Election of 1868   421

14.16 The Election of 1872   424

14.18 The Election of 1876   427

Envisioning Evidence

CHAPTER

2 Patterns of Settlement in New England and the Chesapeake Compared   **46**

3 The Eighteenth-Century Atlantic Slave Trade   **78**

4 A Comparison of Annual Per Capita Tax Rates in Britain and the Colonies in 1765   **99**

7 The World of Slavery at Monticello   **192**

9 The Economics and Geography of Vice in Mid-Nineteenth Century New York   **269**

12 The Rise of King Cotton   **362**

13 Human Resources in the Armies of the Civil War   **396**

Images As History

CHAPTER

  1 Marketing the New World: Theodore De Bry's Engravings of the Americas   **31**

  2 Corruption versus Piety   **43**

  3 A Portrait of Colonial Aspirations   **69**

  4 Trumbull's *The Death of General Warren at the Battle of Bunker Hill*   **108**

  5 Women's Roles: Tradition and Change   **134**

  6 *Liberty Displaying the Arts and Sciences*   **178**

  7 Samuel Morse's *House of Representatives* and the National Republican Vision   **211**

  8 King Andrew and the Downfall of the Mother Bank   **244**

  9 Nature, Technology, and the Railroad: George Inness's *Lackawanna Valley* (1855)   **257**

 10 *The Greek Slave*   **292**

 11 George Catlin and Mah-to-toh-pa: Representing Indians for an American Audience   **323**

 12 The "Foreign Menace"   **355**

 13 Who Freed the Slaves?   **385**

 14 Political Cartoons Reflect the Shift in Public Opinion   **425**

Competing Visions

CHAPTER

1 European and Huron Views of Nature   **12**

2 Antinomianism or Toleration: The Puritan Dilemma   **49**

3 Sir William Johnson and the Iroquois: Indian Visions versus British Arms   **91**

4 Remember the Ladies   **125**

5 Brutus and the Publius Debate the Nature of Republicanism   **149**

6 Jefferson's and Hamilton's Reactions to the French Revolution   **171**

7 War Hawks and their Critics   **204**

8 Should White Men without Property Have the Vote?   **224**

9 The Lowell Strike of 1834   **263**

10 Reactions to Shaker Gender Roles   **300**

11 Slavery and the Election of 1848   **337**

12 Secession or Union?   **371**

13 Civil Liberties in a Civil War   **390**

14 Demanding Rights, Protecting Privilege   **414**

Choices and Consequences

CHAPTER

1 Benin, Portugal, and the International Slave Trade   **23**

2 The Ordeal of Pocahontas   **38**

3 Quakers, Pacifism, and the Paxton Uprising   **93**

4 A Loyalist Wife's Dilemma   **113**

5 To Ratify or Not   **152**

6 Washington's Decision to Crush the Whiskey Rebellion   **174**

7 John Marshall's Dilemma   **196**

8 Acquiesce or Resist? The Cherokee Dilemma   **237**

9 Conscience or Duty? Judge Ruffin's Quandary   **279**

10 Mary Cragin's Experiment in Free Love at Oneida   **302**

11 Henry David Thoreau and Civil Disobedience   **331**

12 Resisting the Fugitive Slave Act   **349**

13 Equal Peril, Unequal Pay   **394**

14 Sanctioning Separation   **434**

About the Authors

Jennifer D. Keene

Saul Cornell

Edward T. O'Donnell

Jennifer D. Keene is a Professor of History and chair of the History Department at Chapman University in Orange, California. Dr. Keene has published three books on the American involvement in the First World War: *Doughboys, the Great War and the Remaking of America* (2001); *The United States and the First World War* (2000); and *World War I: The American Soldier Experience* (2011). She has received numerous fellowships for her research, including a Mellon Fellowship, a National Research Council Postdoctoral Award, and Fulbright Senior Scholar Awards to Australia and France. Her articles have appeared in the *Annales de Démographie Historique*, *Peace & Change*, *Intelligence and National Security*, and *Military Psychology*. Dr. Keene served as an associate editor for the *Encyclopedia of War and American Society* (2005), which won the Society of Military History's prize for best reference book. She works closely with the Gilder-Lehrman Institute, offering Teaching American History workshops for secondary school teachers throughout the country.

Saul Cornell is the Paul and Diane Guenther Chair in American History at Fordham University in New York. Professor Cornell has also taught at the Ohio State University, the College of William and Mary, Leiden University in the Netherlands, and has been a visiting scholar at Yale Law School. He is the author of *A Well Regulated Militia: The Founding Fathers and the Origins of Gun Control* (Langum Prize in Legal History) and *The Other Founders: Anti-Federalism and the Dissenting Tradition in America, 1788–1828* (Society of the Cincinnati Book Prize), both of which were nominated for the Pulitzer Prize. His articles have appeared in the *Journal of American History*, the *William and Mary Quarterly*, *American Studies*, *Law and History Review*, and dozens of leading law reviews. His work has been cited by the U.S. Supreme Court and several state Supreme Courts. He lectures widely on topics in legal and constitutional history and the use of visual materials to teach American history.

Edward T. O'Donnell is an Associate Professor of History at the College of the Holy Cross in Worcester, Massachusetts. He taught previously at Hunter College, City University of New York. He is the author of *Ship Ablaze: The Tragedy of the Steamboat General Slocum* (Random House, 2003) and the forthcoming *Talisman of a Lost Hope: Henry George and Gilded Age America* (Columbia University Press). His articles have appeared in *The Journal of Urban History*, *The Journal of the Gilded Age and Progressive Era*, and *The Public Historian*. He is also very active in the field of public history, curating exhibits and consulting at institutions such as the Lower East Side Tenement Museum and the New York Historical Society. Since 2002, he has worked with more than fifty Teaching American History grant programs across the country, offering lectures and workshops for middle and high school teachers.

Supplements for Instructors and Students

FOR QUALIFIED COLLEGE ADOPTERS

Name of Supplement	Supplements for Qualified College Adopters
MyHistoryLab	MyHistoryLab (www.myhistorylab.com) **The moment you know** Educators know it. Students know it. It's that inspired moment when something that was difficult to understand suddenly makes perfect sense. Our MyLab products have been designed and refined with a single purpose in mind: to help educators create that moment of understanding with their students.
Instructor's Resource Manual with Test Bank	Available at the Instructor's Resource Center, at **www.pearsonhighered.com/irc**, the Instructor's Resource Manual with Test Bank contains chapter overviews, key points and discussion questions, suggested assignments and information on audio-visual resources that can be used in developing and preparing lecture presentations. The Test Bank includes multiple choice and essay questions that are both general and text specific. It also contains brief answers to all the questions in the textbook—learning objective questions, crawl questions, review questions, and questions for analysis.
Annotated Instructor's eText	Contained within MyHistoryLab, the *Annotated Instructor's eText for Visions of America (Second Edition)* leverages the powerful Pearson eText platform to make it easier than ever for teachers to access subject-specific resources for class preparation. The *AI eText* serves as the hub for all instructor resources, with chapter-by-chapter links to PowerPoint slides, content from the Instructor's Manual, and to MyHistoryLab's ClassPrep engine, which contains a wealth of history content organized for classroom use.
PowerPoint Presentation	Available at the Instructor's Resource Center, at **www.pearsonhighered.com/irc**, the PowerPoint presentations are text specific and available for download. The PowerPoint slides to accompany Visions of America (Second Edition) include an outline of each chapter and full-color images, maps, and figures from the textbook. All images from the textbook have corresponding teaching notes that provide background information about the image and teaching strategies.
MyTest	Available at **www.pearsonmytest.com**, MyTest contains a diverse set of over 2,300 multiple choice, true-false, and essay questions, with a test bank that supports a variety of assessment strategies. The large pool of multiple choice questions for each chapter includes factual, conceptual, and analytical questions, so that instructors may assess students on basic information as well as critical thinking. The MyTest program helps instructors easily create and print quizzes and exams. Questions and tests can be authored online, allowing instructors ultimate flexibility and the ability to efficiently manage assessments anytime, anywhere! Instructors can easily access existing questions and edit, create, and store using simple drag-and-drop and Word-like controls.
Retrieving the American Past	Available through the Pearson Custom Library (**www.pearsoncustom.com, keyword search | rtap**), the *Retrieving the American Past* (RTAP) program lets you create a textbook or reader that meets your needs and the needs of your course. RTAP gives you the freedom and flexibility to add chapters from several best-selling Pearson textbooks, in addition to *The American Nation, 14/e*, and/or 100 topical reading units written by the History Department of Ohio State University, all under one cover. Choose the content you want to teach in depth, in the sequence you want, at the price you want your students to pay.

Name of Supplement	Supplements for Students
MyHistoryLab	MyHistoryLab (**www.myhistorylab.com**) **The moment you know** Educators know it. Students know it. It's that inspired moment when something that was difficult to understand suddenly makes perfect sense. Our MyLab products have been designed and refined with a single purpose in mind: to help educators create that moment of understanding with their students.
CourseSmart	**www.coursemart.com** CourseSmart eTextbooks offer the same content as the printed text in a convenient online format—with highlighting, online search, and printing capabilities. You **save 60% over the list price** of the traditional book.
Books à la Carte	Books à la Carte editions feature the exact same content as the traditional printed text in a convenient, three-hole-punched, loose-leaf version at a discounted price—allowing you to take only what you need to class. You'll **save 35% over the net price** of the traditional book. **Vol. 1 - ISBN: 0205193277; ISBN-13: 9780205193271; Vol. 2 - ISBN: 0205193293; ISBN-13: 9780205193295**
Library of American Biography Series	**www.pearsonhighered.com/educator/series/Library-of-American-Biography/10493.page** Pearson's renowned series of biographies spotlights figures who had a significant impact on American history. Included in the series are Edmund Morgan's *The Puritan Dilemma: The Story of John Winthrop*, B. Davis Edmund's *Tecumseh and the Quest for Indian Leadership*, J. William T. Youngs, *Eleanor Roosevelt: A Personal and Public Life*, John R. M. Wilson's *Jackie Robinson and the American Dilemma and Sandra* Opdycke's *Jane Addams and her Vision for America*.
Penguin Valuepacks	**www.pearsonhighered.com/penguin** A variety of Penguin-Putnam texts is available at discounted prices when bundled with *Visions of America*, 2/e. Texts include Benjamin Franklin's *Autobiography and Other Writings*, Nathaniel Hawthorne's *The Scarlet Letter*, Thomas Jefferson's *Notes on the State of Virginia*, and George Orwell's *1984*.
A Short Guide to Writing About History, 7/e	Written by Richard Marius, late of Harvard University, and Melvin E. Page, Eastern Tennessee State University, this engaging and practical text helps students get beyond merely compiling dates and facts. Covering both brief essays and the documented resource paper, the text explores the writing and researching processes, identifies different modes of historical writing, including argument, and concludes with guidelines for improving style. **ISBN-10: 0205118607; ISBN-13: 9780205118601**
Longman American History Atlas	This full-color historical atlas designed especially for college students is a valuable reference tool and visual guide to American history. This atlas includes maps covering the scope of American history from the lives of the Native Americans to the 1990s. Produced by a renowned cartographic firm and a team of respected historians, the Longman American History Atlas will enhance any American history survey course. ISBN: **0321004868; ISBN-13: 9780321004864**

MyHistory Lab

The Moment You Know

Educators know it. Students know it. It's that inspired moment when something that was difficult to understand suddenly makes perfect sense. Our MyLab products have been designed and refined with a single purpose in mind—to help educators create that moment of understanding with their students.

The new MyHistoryLab delivers **proven results** in helping individual students succeed. It provides **engaging experiences** that personalize, stimulate, and measure learning for each student. And, it comes from a **trusted partner** with educational expertise and a deep commitment to helping students, instructors, and departments achieve their goals.

A **personalized study plan** for each student, based on Bloom's Taxonomy, promotes critical-thinking skills, and helps students succeed in the course and beyond.

Assessment tied to every video, application, and chapter enables both instructors and students to track progress and get immediate feedback—and helps instructors to find the best resources with which to help students.

The **Pearson eText** lets students access their textbook anytime, anywhere, and any way they want. Just like the printed text students can highlight relevant passages and add their own notes. For even greater flexibility, students can download the eText to an iPad® using the free Pearson eText app. And, students can even listen to their text, streaming **full chapter audio** on their computers.

Closer Look tours walk students through maps, images, and key primary sources in detail, helping them to uncover their meaning and understand their context.

Author Video Lectures with Pearson history authors help students achieve a deeper understanding of key topics and themes. These narrated clips feature documentary images that capture students' attention.

Class Prep collects the very best class presentation resources in one convenient online destination, so instructors can keep students engaged throughout every class.

Key Supplements

Annotated Instructor's eText

Contained within MyHistoryLab, the *Annotated Instructor's eText* for *Visions of America, Second Edition*, leverages the powerful Pearson eText platform to make it easier than ever for teachers to access subject-specific resources for class preparation. The *AI eText* serves as the hub for all instructor resources, with chapter-by-chapter links to PowerPoint slides, content from the Instructor's Manual, and to *MyHistoryLab's* ClassPrep engine, which contains a wealth of history content organized for classroom use.

Instructor's Manual

The Instructor's Manual contains chapter overview, lecture supplements, discussion questions, suggested assignments, and research resources for each chapter, including both general and text-specific content. It also contains brief answers to all the questions in the textbook—learning objective questions, question crawl, review questions, and questions for analysis—along with the text of the questions themselves.

PowerPoint Presentation

The PowerPoint slides to accompany *Visions of America, Second Edition,* include an outline of each chapter and full-color images, maps, and figures from the textbook. All images from the textbook have corresponding teaching notes that provide background information about the image and teaching strategies.

MyTest Test Bank

Containing a diverse set of over 2,300 multiple choice, true-false, and essay questions, the MyTest test bank supports a variety of assessment strategies. The large pool of multiple choice questions for each chapter includes factual, conceptual, and analytical questions, so that instructors may assess students on basic information as well as critical thinking.

The First Americans p. 4

Why did Paleo-Indians migrate to the Americas?

European Civilization in Turmoil p. 10

How did economic and political changes in Europe facilitate overseas expansion?

Columbus and the Columbian Exchange p. 16

What was the Columbian Exchange, and how did it affect societies in the Americas and Europe?

West African Worlds p. 20

What were the chief similarities and differences between the civilizations of Africa and the Americas?

European Colonization of the Atlantic World p. 24

How did the different labor systems employed by the Spanish, French, and English affect the indigenous populations of the Americas?

People in Motion
The Atlantic World to 1590

To the people who had lived in the Americas for millennia, the idea that theirs was a "New World" would have seemed strange. Scientists continue to debate when the first people arrived in the Americas from Asia, but estimates range from between 40,000 and 14,000 years ago. In the millennia that followed, the peoples of the Americas fanned out and established a range of societies.

Yet to the Europeans who arrived in the Americas toward the end of the fifteenth century, America was indeed a "brave new world," as William Shakespeare wrote, inhabited by exotic plants, animals, and peoples. In images and words Europeans portrayed this extraordinary land in the most fantastic terms. Some accounts spoke of America as an Eden-like earthly paradise inhabited by good-natured, but primitive, peoples. Others emphasized themes like those featured in this engraving, *Amerigo Vespucci Awakens a Sleeping America*. Vespucci, an Italian-Spanish navigator from whose first name the New World came to be called the Americas, gazes upon a naked native woman rising from her hammock. Her nudity symbolizes the wild sexuality Europeans believed characterized the native inhabitants of the Americas. The cannibals behind her, devouring human flesh, represent savagery, a second prominent element of the European vision of the New World. Neither vision of the Americas was accurate, but both would greatly complicate Europeans' understanding of the American civilizations they encountered, leading to a legacy of violence, exploitation, and conquest.

The European arrival in the Americas was part of a process of exploration and colonization pursued primarily by Portugal, Spain, France, and England. This impulse was driven both by a hunger for riches as well as by profound changes in European society, religion, economics, and politics brought on by the Renaissance and Reformation. Africa was eventually drawn into this vast trading network encompassing the entire Atlantic world. Colonization almost always involved the severe exploitation of native peoples, including dispossession of land and coerced labor. Eventually Europeans turned to the international slave trade and the labor of enslaved Africans to draw the wealth from the mines and fields of the New World.

"Your Magnificence must know that herein they are so inhuman that they outdo every custom (even) of beasts; for they eat all their enemies whom they kill or capture . . . and are libidinous beyond measure."

AMERIGO VESPUCCI, 1497

The First Americans

In one sense America was the New World—or at least a newer one in terms of human habitation. The oldest traces of human life have been found in Africa, where the earliest human fossil remains unearthed date to somewhere between 190,000 and 160,000 years ago. In contrast the oldest human fossils found in North America are roughly 14,000 years old, far more recent than those found in Europe, Asia, or Australia. The ancient inhabitants of America, **Paleo-Indians**, were an Ice Age people who survived largely by hunting big game and to a lesser extent by fishing and collecting edible plants. Within a few thousand years of their arrival in America from Asia, they had fanned out across the Americas.

1.1 Migration from Asia to America Most scholars believe the first inhabitants of America migrated from Asia across the Bering Strait by way of the land bridge that once connected Asia and North America.

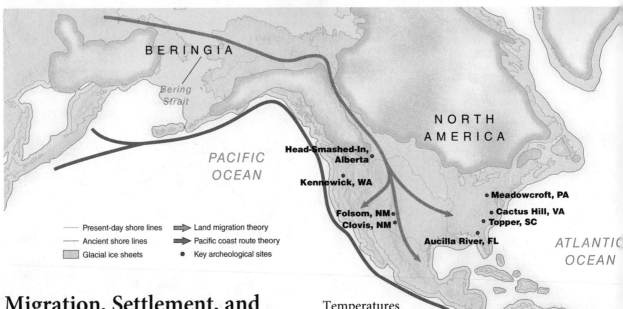

Migration, Settlement, and the Rise of Agriculture

Most scholars agree that humans first migrated to North America from Asia across a land bridge that formed during the Ice Age (**1.1**) about 20,000 years ago. This land bridge lasted from about 28,000 to 10,000 BCE before melting glacial waters submerged it below rising sea levels. An alternative theory holds that humans may have traveled to the New World by boat even earlier; this has attracted some support, but most scholars favor the land bridge theory. With much of the world's oceans frozen in massive glaciers, ocean levels during the Ice Age were almost 360 feet lower than present-day levels, resulting in dry land where the Bering Strait is now. Nomadic hunters simply crossed what to them appeared an endless 600-mile wide tundra in pursuit of migratory big game animals like the woolly mammoths—huge, long-tusked members of the elephant family that provided furs for warm clothing and ample stocks of meat.

Temperatures slowly warmed as the Ice Age passed, causing the great glaciers to melt and sea levels to rise. The rising waters covered the Bering Strait land bridge, cutting off migration from Asia. But the recession of the glaciers also opened the way for human migration southward and eastward into what is now Canada and the United States. Over time this migration reached the very tip of South America.

Armed with spears tipped with flint, a hard, dark stone, Paleo-Indians roamed in search of big game. These spear heads, called Clovis points, named after the New Mexico town in which scientists first discovered them, were one of the Stone Age tools used by the ancient inhabitants of America. Clovis point arrowheads like those shown in (**1.2**) were lashed to poles to make simple spears. Paleo-Indians also used other simple stone tools such as stone axes and scrapers for hunting and preparing meat, a variety of bone tools such as antler harpoons for fishing, and bone needles for sewing hides. These ancient peoples generally hunted in small bands of perhaps 20 to 30 people in cooperative kin groups. Hunting parties pursued a wide range of prey, including primitive horses and the oversized ancestors of many modern species, such as beaver, bison, caribou, and forerunners of the camel. Hunting, gathering, and other activities among Stone Age peoples were probably divided along gender lines. Men hunted and fished, while women reared children, gathered nuts and berries, and made clothing.

Many of the mammals that Paleo-Indians hunted, including horses and camels, eventually became extinct (the Spanish reintroduced modern horses from Europe thousands of years later). Three competing scientific theories attempt to explain the mass extinctions of large mammals in the Americas. Some scientists believe overhunting led to the demise of the large mammals. Others argue that dramatic climate change—the rising temperatures that accompanied the passing of the Ice Age—killed off animals that were unable to adapt to the new warmer environments. The most recent explanation focuses on diseases that may have been brought to the New World by humans and the animals that accompanied them, most notably dogs and possibly rats. Whatever the cause of the mass extinctions, the decline in large game eventually led Paleo-Indians to search for new food sources and develop new modes of providing food and other necessities.

Approximately 9,000 years ago, a period known as the **Archaic Era** began. Lasting approximately 6,000 years, it ushered in significant social changes that began with increased efforts by native peoples to shape the environment to enhance food production. At first these efforts were primitive. Archaic Era Indians, for example, burned forest underbrush to provide better habitats for smaller mammals such as deer, which they hunted. They also relied increasingly on gathering nuts and berries and, in some cases, on harvesting shellfish from lakes, streams, or coastal waters. The gendered division of labor found in Stone Age societies persisted into the Archaic Era: women cared for children and did much of the gathering and preparing of food while men hunted and fished.

Some Archaic Era Indians even took the first steps toward agriculture. At first they encouraged the growth of edible plants, such as sunflowers and wild onions, by simply weeding out inedible plants around them. Over time Archaic Era Indians learned how to collect and plant seeds and developed basic ideas about irrigation. These primitive cultivation techniques led to increased food supplies and diminished reliance on hunting.

By about 5000 BCE fixed agricultural settlements appeared in what is now Mexico. There native people learned how to grow maize (corn), squash, and beans, leading to the development of food surpluses and consequently large increases in population. Planting, tending, and defending crops necessitated the creation of larger permanent settlements, leading to urbanization, the creation of towns and cities. Increased food surpluses allowed the ancient peoples of the Americas to devote more resources to a variety of cultural, artistic, and engineering projects. The combination of agriculture, urbanism, and increasing social complexity set the foundation for the emergence of the first great civilizations of the southern region of North America, an area stretching from modern Mexico to Nicaragua known as Mesoamerica.

The most advanced societies in Mesoamerica included the Olmecs (1150 BCE to about 800 BCE), Maya (peaked in 300 BCE–900 CE), and Toltecs (900 CE–1200 CE). These complex societies developed written languages, systems of mathematics, sophisticated irrigation techniques, and

1.2 Clovis Point The range of tools available to Paleo-Indians was limited, but included stone tools, such as arrowheads, axes, scrapers, bone needles, and harpoons. Clovis point arrowheads were attached to spears for hunting.

What impact did agriculture have on the evolution of the societies of the Americas?

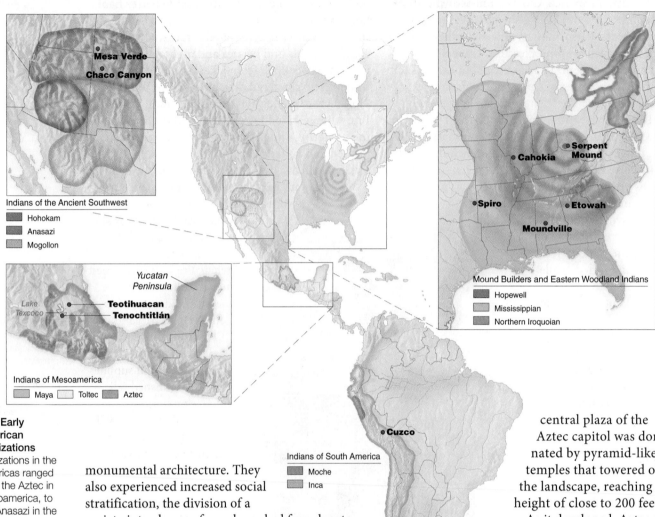

Indians of the Ancient Southwest
- Hohokam
- Anasazi
- Mogollon

Indians of Mesoamerica
- Maya   Toltec   Aztec

Mound Builders and Eastern Woodland Indians
- Hopewell
- Mississippian
- Northern Iroquoian

Indians of South America
- Moche
- Inca

1.3 Early American Civilizations
Civilizations in the Americas ranged from the Aztec in Mesoamerica, to the Anasazi in the Southwest, and the Mound builders of the Midwest.

monumental architecture. They also experienced increased social stratification, the division of a society into classes of people ranked from low to high according to status, wealth, and power. One of the most important of these societies, the Aztec (1300 CE to 1521 CE), created a powerful empire in what is now Mexico (**1.3**).

The Aztec

The rise of the immensely powerful Aztec Confederacy transformed Mesoamerica. By the time the Spanish arrived in the early sixteenth century, the Aztecs controlled a vast empire of between 10 and 20 million people. The **Aztec** Empire's capital, the great city of Tenochtitlán, was built on an island in Lake Texcoco in 1325 on the site of today's Mexico City. Causeways connected the city to the mainland. An elaborate system of dams controlled the water level of the lake, while aqueducts carried fresh water to the city. A sophisticated system of floating gardens produced food to feed the large urban population, which swelled to almost 300,000 over the next two centuries. The

central plaza of the Aztec capitol was dominated by pyramid-like temples that towered over the landscape, reaching a height of close to 200 feet.

As it developed, Aztec society became extremely stratified. At the top of the social pyramid sat a powerful emperor. Below the emperor were a class of nobles, a priestly class, a warrior class, and an administrative class that collected taxes and tributes. The foundation of this vast pyramid comprised merchants, artisans, and farmers. At the very bottom were slaves. Some were Aztec-born and became slaves temporarily as punishment for crime. Prisoners of war also added to the slave population, and human chattel was provided as part of tax debts owed to the Aztec Empire by its many conquered peoples.

Gender roles were sharply defined among the Aztec. Women helped men tend the fields but were primarily responsible for child rearing, cooking, weaving cloth, and shopping in the markets. Although the priests were invariably men, Aztec religion accorded women an important role in the family, including making religious offerings to the gods.

Trade and commerce were crucial to the Aztec economy. In the smaller towns daily markets provided a wide array of goods, but these markets were miniscule compared to the great open-air market in Tenochtitlán. Countless foods, textiles, ceramics, and other goods were available for trade, illustrating the richness and complexity of the Aztec economy.

The Aztecs were a war-like society. Conquered peoples were forced to pay tribute in the form of textiles, agricultural products, precious stones, and ceramics, and even provide slaves for human sacrifices. For the Aztecs human sacrifice was a central religious ritual necessary to appease the gods, especially the gods of rain and war.

> "Begin with the dealers in gold, silver, precious stones, feathers, mantles, and embroidered goods . . . . But why waste so many words in recounting what they sell in their great market? If I describe everything in detail I shall never be finished."
>
> BERNAL DIAZ DEL CASTILLO,
> Spanish historian of the conquest of Mexico, 1568

years ago, Cahokia's population ranged between 20,000 and 40,000. The city was protected by a huge wooden palisade and featured at its center a massive terraced earthwork mound that covered 16 acres and rose over 100 feet above the ground. Capping this mound was a wooden temple that would have been among the tallest human-made structures in the Americas, exceeded only by the pyramids of Mesoamerica. Other Mississippian communities developed in present-day Alabama, Georgia, and Oklahoma.

In the American Southwest, the Anasazi peoples created another complex civilization marked by a sophisticated urban culture that included a series of towns inter-connected by roads (1.3). To survive in the arid climate of the Southwest, the Anasazi developed impressive engineering skills to build their cities and construct complex irrigation systems to supply water for drinking and agriculture. Using adobe (clay) bricks, they built large dwellings later known by their Spanish name, *pueblos*. At Chaco Canyon in what is now northwest New Mexico, the Anasazi built Pueblo Bonito. This dwelling contained hundreds of rooms including dozens of kivas, or circular rooms intended for religious ceremonies. Until the development of modern apartment buildings in the late nineteenth century, this was the largest human dwelling in history.

The Anasazi also developed skills in making pottery and textiles, some of which they used in a vast trade network that stretched hundreds of miles to the south. The most valuable commodity they traded was turquoise, a bright blue-green stone used to make jewelry. In exchange for it, the Anasazi acquired prized luxuries such as sea shells from as far away as the Gulf of California to the west and carved images and feathers from Mesoamerica.

Mound Builders and Pueblo Dwellers

Urban settlements also appeared in other regions of North America (1.3). One group, the mound-building societies, created monumental earthen burial mounds as part of their religious practices. Some 2,000 years ago, the Adena of what is now southern Ohio built The Great Serpent Mound. Still visible, it resembles a giant snake. Excavations of this and other mounds have unearthed a host of artifacts used for religious purposes and personal adornment. We can also conclude that these inland people acquired the conch shells and shark teeth found at their sites from other cultures, as part of a trade network that extended to the Atlantic coast.

The most complex mound-building society, the Mississippian, developed in the Mississippi Valley (1.3). The central city of this civilization, Cahokia, arose in what is now southern Illinois near St. Louis. Cahokia developed a stratified society with a chief at the top, followed by an elite class and a lower class that provided labor for agriculture and building projects. At its height about 700–1,000

1.4 John White's Painting of Secoton
John White's painting of the Eastern Woodlands Indian village of Secoton includes images of wigwams, the Algonquian word for "dwelling place." (Europeans sometimes described these dwellings as longhouses.)

Eastern Woodlands Indian Societies

A different type of society developed in a region encompassing what is now the Eastern United States and Canada. In contrast to the native societies of the Southwest and Mesoamerica, Eastern Woodlands societies were neither highly urban nor stratified. Organized into tribes, these Eastern Woodlands Indian peoples lived as hunters and gatherers as well as agriculturalists. Most spoke a dialect of one of two major Indian languages, Iroquois and Algonquian.

Instead of living in urban settlements, Eastern Woodland Indians moved with the seasons to take advantage of different food sources, tracking animals in forest regions or fishing in lakes, streams, and rivers. Consequently as this painting, one of the earliest European views of an actual Indian village (**1.4**), shows, their villages were composed of wood and bark structures that were easily disassembled and reassembled to make seasonal movement possible. Dwelling in small villages rather than settled urban areas, Eastern Woodlands Indians avoided many of the sanitation problems and diseases that periodically afflicted ancient cities such as Tenochtitlán and Cahokia.

The complex religious life of Eastern Woodlands Indians embraced the concept of a supreme being, the great Manitou, but also included animism, or the belief that everything in nature possessed a spirit that had to be respected. Rather than seeking to own land and subdue the world around them in the manner of European societies, Eastern Woodlands Indians sought to inhabit the land and to live in dynamic relationship with it. These beliefs, however, did not keep them from actively altering or managing their environments to their advantage. Indians adopted strategies such as controlled burning of brush, a technique that encouraged the growth of habitats for the deer they hunted. This type of strategy contrasted with European agriculture, which used clear cutting to make land available for farming.

The tribal societies of the Eastern seaboard had a relatively egalitarian political and social structure. Apart from the chief and a religious figure known as a shaman, most members of a tribe enjoyed a rough equality. While many indigenous societies in the Americas, particularly the more hierarchical ones of Mesoamerica, were patrilineal, with inheritance and decision making residing in the male line, some Eastern Woodlands societies were matrilineal, tracing descent and determining inheritance from ancestors on the female side. In some tribes women enjoyed significant roles in tribal governance. When captives were taken in war, for example, women often decided whether to adopt or execute them. Nonetheless Woodland Indians divided labor along gender lines, with women consigned to the fields, planting beans, corn, and squash, while men tracked and hunted animals for food, hides, and pelts.

> "They are not delighted in baubles, but in useful things.... I have observed that they will not be troubled with superfluous commodities."
>
> THOMAS MORTON,
> English lawyer, 1637

Eastern Woodland Indians were more communal than individualistic in outlook. Although trade was important and individuals might own some goods, accumulating material wealth was not an important goal, as it was in the more stratified Mesoamerican societies. Individual tribes controlled territory, but the notion of owning land as private property was alien to most of these tribal societies.

Warfare among many Eastern Woodlands tribes was intermittent but common. They often fought over control of tribal territory or hunting rights. Warfare typically consisted of skirmishes between rival war parties, a style of combat that usually kept casualties low. Casualties suffered in war, however, might trigger further military actions, or "mourning wars," intended to replenish the population reduced by fighting. In such a war some prisoners taken captive might be tortured and killed, while others deemed suitable were adopted by the tribe.

The persistent warfare among tribes led to the creation of the powerful Iroquois League of Five Nations, an organization that sought to reduce conflict among its members: the Seneca, Mohawk, Onondaga, Cayuga, and Oneida nations. Women played a significant role in the governance of the league. Female elders from each of the individual nations selected the men who formed the league's Great Council, a body that met to discuss matters of common concern, especially war and peace.

American Societies on the Eve of European Contact

American Indian societies were socially and culturally diverse, ranging from the highly stratified and urban Aztec in Mesoamerica to the relatively egalitarian hunter-farmer Iroquois in the Northeast. The peoples of the Americas spoke a host of different languages, developed distinctive religious traditions, and created different political models to govern themselves.

These societies shared many characteristics among themselves and with peoples in other parts of the world. Like their Asian and European contemporaries, the societies of the Americas were pre-modern, with limited scientific knowledge and widespread belief in magic. Most people worked the land, struggling to provide the basics needed to support life. Except for the privileged few, life was hard, sometimes brutal, and short.

In the Andes Mountains of South America, alpaca and llamas were domesticated, providing wool or food and, in the case of the llama, serving as a pack animal. But in contrast to Africa, Asia, or Europe, in North America and Mesoamerica there were no large domesticated animals, such as horses (extinct after the Paleo-Indian period), cattle, or camels. Without such animals the people of these regions lacked the mobility and power that horses afforded Europeans, Africans, and Asians and that camels provided for North Africans and Asians.

American societies on the eve of contact with Europeans were distinctive in another way. While African and Asian societies had developed considerable trade with Europe, the peoples of the Americas had remained largely cut off from contact with other parts of the world for thousands of years. This isolation had prevented their exposure to a host of diseases. By the time of the first contact between Europe and America in the late 1400s, many of the inhabitants of Asia, Africa, and Europe, long exposed to a common pool of diseases because of their extensive trade contacts, had developed immunity to many virulent pathogens. In their relative isolation, however, the indigenous societies of the Americas were highly susceptible to the microbial invaders introduced by Europeans.

What were some of the distinctive characteristics shared by all of the societies of the Americas?

European Civilization in Turmoil

As the Aztec Empire was reaching the height of its power at the close of the fifteenth century, European society was in the midst of a profound transformation. This period of cultural, intellectual, scientific, and commercial flourishing is known as the Renaissance. The revival of interest in ancient Greek and Latin not only led to renewed interest in the civilizations of Greece and Rome but also caused Renaissance thinkers to re-examine the early history of the church and its teachings. Reformers drawing on these traditions and reacting to the corruption of the Roman Catholic Church challenged the authority of the church. The rise of a new strain of Christian thought, Protestantism, led to creation of a host of new Christian sects. Amid this tumult powerful monarchs across Europe forged new nation-states out of the relatively weak decentralized governments of Europe. Modern nations such as England, France, and Spain were born in this era. State building required money, and the monarchs of these nations were eager to increase their wealth and power, a desire that ultimately led to the colonization and exploration of Africa and the Americas.

The Allure of the East and the Challenge of Islam

The leading European powers' decision to explore, conquer, and exploit lands in the Atlantic world was facilitated by a host of economic, technological, and cultural changes. Contact with Asia led to major changes in taste and patterns of consumption during the early modern period, from the fifteenth through the seventeenth centuries. Europeans looked beyond their borders, particularly to China and the Far East, for spices to enrich their bland foods and for luxury goods, especially exotic textiles such as silk and cotton, to enliven their fashions. These commodities, not native to Europe, had to be obtained from Asia.

The overland trade routes to the East were controlled by Muslims, adherents of Islam, a monotheistic faith shaped by the teachings of the Prophet Muhammad. Since its emergence in the seventh century Middle East, Muslim influence spread, stretching from Europe to parts of Africa and Asia. Europeans resented the economic power of Muslim rulers who controlled the lucrative trade routes to the East.

European antagonism toward the Muslim world also sprang from an intense religious animosity. For almost 300 years, Christian Europe had waged a holy war against Islam, launching Crusades to regain control of Jerusalem, a city sacred to Jews, Christians, and Muslims. Islam's influence in Europe was most pronounced in the Ottoman Empire, whose power eventually spread across the Eastern Mediterranean and Balkans.

Trade, Commerce, and Urbanization

Among the important changes in Europe during this period was the dramatic growth of the economy. The Black Death (1347–1352 CE), a pandemic that spread to Europe between 1347 and 1352, wiped out about half of Europe's population. In the centuries following the Black Death, Europe's population began to expand again, eventually becoming larger than it had been before the epidemic. The economies of Europe also recovered. By 1400, the Italian city-states, especially Venice, dominated trade and finance, particularly trade with the East. In part, Venice's dominance resulted from its proximity to the lucrative eastern trade routes. Italy also dominated textile production, and Florence became Europe's leading producer of woolen cloth. Slowly the economic center of Europe shifted west and north. By about 1500, the city of Antwerp in what is today Belgium had become the leading commercial center of Europe but was eventually surpassed by the Dutch port of Amsterdam.

As trade and commerce expanded, innovative financial practices and services facilitated continued economic growth. New accounting methods helped merchants keep track of inventories and profits and losses. Marine insurance reduced the risks of maritime trade. A more elaborate banking system also helped finance trade. The growth of deposit banking, a system in which merchants could deposit funds with bankers and then draw on written checks instead of presenting gold or silver coins for payment of goods, greatly bolstered trade and commerce. All these developments made economic ventures more secure and encouraged investment, some of which was directed toward overseas trade and exploration. Together the new commercial and financial practices were key elements in the growth of capitalism. Simply put, **capitalism** is an economic system in which a market economy, geared toward the maximization of profit, determines the prices of goods and services. This new, profit-driven capitalist ethos slowly transformed European life beginning in the fifteenth century.

Capitalism also transformed rural Europe. European culture had always viewed nature as something to be tamed and exploited (see *Competing Visions: European and Huron Views of Nature*, page 12.) Rather than simply produce food for themselves, the new capitalist ethos led some farmers to seek the maximum yield from their land and plant crops that would fetch a higher price at market. In other cases landowners evicted farmers from their lands, so that they could graze sheep on the land and produce wool that would be turned into cloth. This latter change in agriculture forced many to leave the countryside and seek employment in towns and cities.

Migration from the countryside and commercial development led to greater urbanization in Europe. In the two centuries after the Black Death, the population of London increased from 50,000 to more than 200,000. Outside of London, England's changes were less dramatic, but no less significant. Populations mushroomed in ports such as Bristol, regional market towns such as Cambridge, and the new textile centers such as Norwich.

Technological improvements and new inventions also spurred economic growth. The printing press transformed the way knowledge was produced and disseminated. While a scribe hand-copying a book onto parchment might turn out two or three books a year, the typical print run of a book produced on paper by a printing press was between 100 and 1,000. Printed books not only made it easier to preserve knowledge but also encouraged advances in science and in geographic exploration by making it easier to collect, organize, and analyze information. Printed texts and engraved images also whet the appetites of Europeans for exploration by making accounts of exotic places such as India and China more accessible. Marco Polo's (1254?–1324) influential text about his adventures in China, *The Travels of Marco Polo*, circulated widely in manuscript form for more than a century before a printed edition appeared in 1477.

Printing created an entire new industry for the production, dissemination, and sale of books. The new technology also transformed visual culture, making it possible to create cheap images. The new technique of engraving (**1.5**) was a multistep process. On the right a skilled craftsman gouges out an image on a copper plate. In the center the plates are inked and then wiped clean. On the left the final stages in the engraving process are demonstrated, including the giant press used to create the final image.

1.5 Copper Engraving
The many steps used to make an engraving, from the artist's hand to the final drying of the printed page, are illustrated in this early image.

Competing Visions
EUROPEAN AND HURON VIEWS OF NATURE

European capitalism was built on deeply rooted beliefs, including the notion of private property and the belief that nature existed as a resource for humans to tame and exploit. European and Eastern Woodlands Indian cultures had starkly different attitudes toward the natural world. Following a mandate laid down in the biblical Book of Genesis, Europeans believed that they had a God-given right to rule over nature. The Huron, an Eastern Woodlands Indian tribe from Canada, approached nature in a radically different way that reflected their animist belief that all living things had spiritual power. What ecological consequences flowed from the Huron view of nature? How might this view have shaped the European impression of Indians? What ecological consequences follow from the Western view?

In Genesis God gave humans complete control over nature. According to this view humanity was not simply enjoined to "subdue nature" but to make sure that the "fear of you and the dread of you shall be upon every beast of the earth."

And God blessed them, and God said unto them, Be fruitful, and multiply, and replenish the earth, and subdue it: and have dominion over the fish of the sea, and over the fowl of the air, and over every living thing that moveth upon the earth.
King James Bible, Genesis 1:28 (1611)

Lucas Cranach, *Adam and Eve*

One of the best sources for understanding Indian views of nature can be found in the writings of Jesuit missionaries, a Catholic order active in the French colonization of Canada. In this selection a Jesuit recounts his exchange with a Huron Indian about the proper treatment of animal bones, which Hurons believed had to be treated with respect to avoid angering the animal spirits that might take offense and make hunting more difficult.

It is remarkable how they gather and collect these bones, and preserve them with so much care, that you would say their game would be lost if they violated their superstitions. As I was laughing at them, and telling them that Beavers do not know what is done with their bones, they answered me, "Thou dost not know how to take Beavers, and thou wishest to talk about it." Before the Beaver was entirely dead, they told me, its soul comes to make the round of the Cabin of him who has killed it, and looks very carefully to see what is done with its bones; if they are given to the dogs, the other Beavers would be apprised of it and therefore they would make themselves hard to capture. (*Paul le Jeune*, 1633)
The Jesuit Relations and Allied Documents: Travels and Explorations of the Jesuit Missionaries in New France 1610–1791 (1896–1901) 6: 211.

John White, *Indians Fishing*

How does this painting of Adam and Eve reflect European views of nature?

View the **Closer Look** *Competing Visions: European and Huron Views of Nature*

Renaissance and Reformation

A revival of interest in the cultures of Greek and Roman antiquity, arising first in Italy, spread across Europe at the end of the fifteenth century. This rebirth of classical learning, the Renaissance, transformed the way Europeans thought about art, architecture, science, and political philosophy. The most significant change was the shift from theology, the primary scholarly subject in the Middle Ages, to the study of the liberal arts, including poetry, history, and philosophy. Much like the ancient Greeks, Renaissance scholars emphasized the human capacity for self-improvement and exalted the beauty of the human body in painting and sculpture. For these scholars, known as **humanists**, humans were the masters of their world and obligated to study it. These Renaissance values, in particular the spirit of exploration, would soon inspire explorers to seek out new lands and trade routes.

In contrast to medieval Europe, with its cloistered monasteries where monks prayed and copied texts for their own libraries, the Renaissance placed a high value on public art, architecture, and philosophical thought aimed at civilizing humanity. Civic humanism, the new philosophy of the Renaissance, encouraged artists and philosophers to participate in public life, especially in cities, which replaced monasteries as the ideal place to encourage learning and glorify God.

The study of ancient languages fostered a new interest in the early church and inspired some religious figures to call for reforms in the Roman Catholic Church. One church practice that drew intense criticism was the sale of indulgences. In essence money donated to the Church could buy forgiveness for sin in this life and after death. In 1517 a young German monk named Martin Luther attacked the sale of indulgences and other key elements of Catholic doctrine and practice. Luther eventually developed a new theological alternative to Catholicism. Rejecting the Catholic Church's focus on good works as the key to achieving salvation, Luther argued that only faith could bring salvation. Luther also argued that ordinary people did not need to depend on the clergy to gain access to God's word; they could and should read the Bible themselves. Luther translated the Bible from Greek and Latin to German, and the newly invented printing press made it widely accessible. Anyone who could read could now receive the word of God in his or her own home. Luther championed the idea of the priesthood of all true believers—the notion that everyone could experience salvation directly. Priests would continue to preach the word of God and perform rituals such baptizing infants and marriage ceremonies, but Luther would dispense with the Catholic ritual of going to a priest for confession, penance, and absolution for sins. Luther also rejected monasticism. The place for the committed Christian was in this world, not cloistered away in a monastery.

Luther also urged Christian monarchs to take up the cause of religious reform and reject the authority of the Pope. His attack on the political power of the Roman Catholic Church appealed to some European rulers eager to strengthen their power. Luther was summarily excommunicated by the Church, but his calls for reform had wide appeal, especially in what is now Germany and Scandinavia. His supporters, known as Protestants, began a movement for religious reform known as the **Reformation**.

Protestantism found an especially receptive home in Geneva, a French-speaking city in Switzerland. Here the French reformer John Calvin (1509–1564) articulated a new variant of Protestantism with a different theological emphasis from Luther's version. Calvin's theology stressed the doctrine of pre-destination, the notion that God had destined people to salvation or damnation prior to their birth no matter how righteously or wickedly they lived. He also maintained that the true church was not embodied in any official organization, including the Roman Catholic Church, but rather in a group of the "elect," or those chosen by God for salvation. According to this ideal the elect could continue to act as a reformed church even if they had no physical place of worship or formal ministry to serve their spiritual needs. With the Bible and personal faith, argued Calvin, Protestants could constitute a true church wherever they lived, including, eventually, a wilderness like America.

Calvinists in Switzerland and elsewhere took their critique of Catholic worship a step further than Lutherans, becoming iconoclasts, or image breakers. They took the biblical injunction in Exodus to avoid "graven," or carved images literally: decrying them as sacrilegious and a form of idolatry, Calvinists smashed the stained glass windows and religious carvings that adorned churches. One Catholic nun described a Protestant rampage in Geneva in these terms: "Like enraged wolves, they destroyed those fine images with great axes, and hammers, especially going after the blessed crucifix, and the image of Our Lady [Mary]." This contemporary image of one such rampage shows Protestants pulling down sculptures and smashing stained glass

What were the essential teachings of Calvinism?

1.6 Protestants Stripping a Church of Images
This image depicts Calvinist iconoclasm, the destruction of "graven" images such as religious statues and stained glass windows.

windows (**1.6**). Once purged of all such Catholic images, religious worship, Calvinists believed, could focus on the words of the Bible alone. In 1560 English Calvinists published the Geneva Bible, a text that would become the most important text for English-speaking Protestants.

New Monarchs and the Rise of the Nation-State

By 1500, the kingdoms of France, England, Portugal, and Spain had evolved into sovereign nation-states. Powerful monarchs consolidated their power, eliminated rivals to their thrones, created administrative bureaucracies to rule, and built larger, more effective armies. Paying for these required huge sums of money, and if they could not raise what they needed at home, some monarchs began to look

abroad. Territorial expansion and exploration of new regions, they reasoned, would increase both trade and revenues.

In England Henry VII (r. 1485–1509) established the House of Tudor as the ruling family of England. His son, Henry VIII (r. 1509–1547), expanded the power of the monarchy. His most important act as king of England was his break with Rome when the Pope refused to dissolve his marriage to the Spanish princess Catherine of Aragon. After failing to obtain a divorce, Henry declared himself head of his own independent English church. He rejected the authority of the Roman Catholic Church, confiscated the monastic lands, and sold them for a handsome profit or gave them to favored supporters. The intensity of Henry's anti-Catholic feeling (and his particular hostility to the Pope) is evident in this portrait painted by an unknown artist in 1570 (**1.7**). Henry VIII lies in bed, pointing to his son and successor Edward VI (r. 1547–1553). The Pope collapses in the foreground and two monks flee the scene, while a monastery is sacked in the background.

Perhaps the most ambitious of the new monarchies was Spain's, created by the marriage of Ferdinand of Aragon and Isabella of Castile in 1469. When they became joint rulers of Spain, Ferdinand and Isabella followed a strategy common to all the new monarchs: they reduced the power of the nobility and strengthened their own control over the military. They also boosted crown revenue by raising taxes and making tax collection more efficient.

As part of their effort to transform Spain into a world power, Ferdinand and Isabella sought to strengthen the power of the Roman Catholic Church and ally its interests with the state. In 1478 the Spanish monarchy sought the Pope's approval to create the **Spanish Inquisition**, a religious tribunal charged with finding and punishing heresy, or unorthodox beliefs among Christians, and for eliminating non-Christians, most notably Muslims and Jews, from Spain. Thousands of suspected heretics were arrested, tortured, and imprisoned. Hundreds were executed. Eventually in 1492 the government ordered all Jews, except those who converted to Christianity, expelled from Spain. That same year Ferdinand and Isabella achieved another goal in their effort to strengthen Church and state by conquering Granada, the last remaining Islamic state in Spain.

The conquest of the last Muslim kingdom in Spain, in 1492 was the final phase of this *reconquista* ("re-conquest"). Spain's holy war united state and Church in a single purpose. This partnership between a militant clergy and an equally aggressive military would serve Spain well when its attention moved beyond Europe to the wider Atlantic world.

1.7 Henry VIII and Edward the VI
In this unfinished painting England's Henry VIII passes on his authority to his son Edward VI, including his role as head of the new Church of England. In the upper right English Protestant iconoclasts attack a monastery. At the bottom of the image the Pope collapses and monks flee from the "worde of the Lorde."

View the **Map** *Western Europe During the Renaissance and Reformation*

How was the English Reformation different than the Continental Reformation?

Columbus and the Columbian Exchange

In 1492, Queen Isabella agreed to outfit a small expedition to find a quicker route to Asia. The expedition's leader, an Italian sailor named Christopher Columbus, was an experienced mariner who had worked in the Portuguese seagoing trade to Africa and the Atlantic islands. Familiar with Marco Polo's written accounts of China, Columbus believed he could find a faster and more direct route to Asia than traveling around the tip of Africa by simply crossing the Atlantic. He first asked the King of Portugal to fund the voyage, but the king's advisors warned Columbus that he had greatly underestimated the circumference of the Earth and would certainly perish long before he reached Asia. Undeterred Columbus turned to Queen Isabella, who consented to fund his expedition.

Columbus Encounters the "Indians"

After sailing for 33 days, Columbus reached the Caribbean islands, most likely the Bahamas. Mistakenly convinced that he had arrived in India, he called the native peoples "Indians." Columbus claimed all the lands he visited for Spain. Concluding that the native people were savages, he believed that they were "fit to be ordered about, and made to work, plant, and do everything else that may be needed, and build towns and be taught our customs." Returning to Spain with captive Indians, exotic plants, and gold, Columbus was greeted as a hero and secured funding for additional voyages of exploration.

Columbus was not the first European to cross the Atlantic, nor was he the first to create a small European outpost in America. The Vikings had sailed from Iceland almost 400 years earlier, establishing small fishing outposts in what is now Newfoundland, Canada. Nevertheless Columbus's voyage to the Americas brought the two worlds together in ways that Viking ventures had not. Europe's printing presses would make accounts of his voyage widely available, providing a model for later explorers, conquerors, and settlers. Columbus's voyage also began one of the most complex ecological changes in modern history. The worlds on both sides of the Atlantic were suddenly reconnected, a development that would have far-reaching biological consequences for Europe, Africa, and America.

Modern scholars have described the biological encounter between the two sides of the Atlantic as the **Columbian Exchange (1.8)**, a name that acknowledges the crucial role that Columbus played in instigating this transformation. This exchange involved a range of foods, plants, animals, and diseases. Moving from the Americas to Europe by way of Columbus and the Europeans who followed him were a host of foods now closely identified with European cuisine. Before Columbus Italian cuisine had no tomatoes, Irish and German food no potatoes, and Switzerland no chocolate. Moving in the other direction were animals, including the horse, long extinct in the Americas but reintroduced by the Spanish, sheep, cattle, and swine.

"As soon as I arrived in the Indies, in the first island which I found, I took by force some of them, in order that they might learn and give me information."

CHRISTOPHER COLUMBUS, 1493

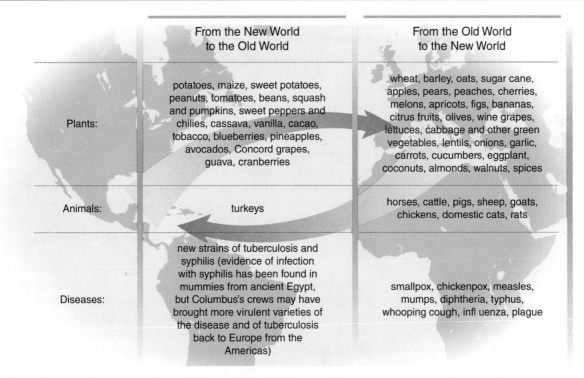

	From the New World to the Old World	From the Old World to the New World
Plants:	potatoes, maize, sweet potatoes, peanuts, tomatoes, beans, squash and pumpkins, sweet peppers and chilies, cassava, vanilla, cacao, tobacco, blueberries, pineapples, avocados, Concord grapes, guava, cranberries	wheat, barley, oats, sugar cane, apples, pears, peaches, cherries, melons, apricots, figs, bananas, citrus fruits, olives, wine grapes, lettuces, cabbage and other green vegetables, lentils, onions, garlic, carrots, cucumbers, eggplant, coconuts, almonds, walnuts, spices
Animals:	turkeys	horses, cattle, pigs, sheep, goats, chickens, domestic cats, rats
Diseases:	new strains of tuberculosis and syphilis (evidence of infection with syphilis has been found in mummies from ancient Egypt, but Columbus's crews may have brought more virulent varieties of the disease and of tuberculosis back to Europe from the Americas)	smallpox, chickenpox, measles, mumps, diphtheria, typhus, whooping cough, infl uenza, plague

1.8 Columbian Exchange

This table shows the most important crops and animals involved in the Columbian Exchange. A host of pathogens, mostly of Old World origin, were also part of the Columbian Exchange.

Diseases also crossed the Atlantic. Europeans may have brought back a plague in the form of a more deadly strain of the sexually transmitted disease syphilis that sailors picked up on the Caribbean islands. Far more devastating were the diseases like smallpox brought to the New World. These diseases killed huge numbers of Indian men, women, and children.

European Technology in the Era of the Columbian Exchange

Columbus and the Europeans who led the exploration of the Atlantic world benefited from technological changes developed in Europe in the fifteenth century. Improvements in map making and the introduction of navigational devices that allowed mariners to calculate latitude more accurately aided exploration. Europeans borrowed technology from the Islamic world and Asia to improve their ships. The Portuguese also made important strides in ship-building with the caravel, a vessel whose lateen (triangular) sails were better suited to catching wind than were those of traditional European ships.

Europeans enjoyed a clear technological and military advantage over the peoples of America, a disparity that would profoundly affect European interactions with the Aztec, and later with Eastern Woodlands Indian peoples. Foremost among these advantages were the metallurgical techniques that allowed Europeans to forge iron weapons that were stronger than those of the Aztec and other Indians. Domesticated horses allowed Europeans to support their armies with swift-moving cavalry. Through trade with China, Europeans had learned about gunpowder and developed powerful cannons and firearms such as the arquebus, a forerunner of the musket and rifle. Among the inventions depicted in this engraving, "Nova Reperta," ("New Discoveries") (1584), by artist Johannes Stradanus, are the compass, the mechanical clock, cannons and gunpowder, and a saddle with stirrups (**1.9**).

The Conquest of the Aztec and Inca Empires

Columbus's successful voyage in 1492 was followed by waves of Spanish explorers and conquerors (*conquistadores* in Spanish), who soon seized control of the islands of the Caribbean. The harsh labor

1.9 Nova Reperta
In this drawing, the artist links new scientific and technological discoveries with the exploration of the "New World." A printing press stands between a map of the Americas and a compass. The image is anchored by a cannon and casks of gunpowder, symbolic of European military technology.

regime and the deadly diseases the Spanish brought nearly wiped out these indigenous populations. On the island of Hispaniola (present-day Haiti and the Dominican Republic), 95 percent of the native peoples died within 25 years. Faced with the loss of this indigenous labor force, the Spanish turned to the African slave trade to supply the labor they demanded for the production of lucrative cash crops such as sugar.

Spanish *conquistadores*, lured by rumors of a fabulous empire possessing great wealth, eventually turned their attention to the mainland of what is now Mexico. In 1519, eager to acquire this wealth for himself and Spain, Hernán Cortés, a brash and ambitious protégé of the Spanish governor of Hispaniola, embarked on an expedition to find the famed capital of the Aztec Empire and conquer it. Landing on Mexico's southeast coast with over 500 men and 16 horses, he burned his ships, depriving his men of any opportunity to retreat. He forced his men to push forward to conquer or die in the attempt.

Although vastly outnumbered by the Aztecs, Cortés and his men had military advantages. First they possessed horses, firearms, and steel weapons. Second they quickly gained allies among the peoples conquered by the Aztecs. After years of subjugation in which they were forced to provide the Aztecs with victims for human sacrifice, these exploited peoples now willingly sided with the Spanish. Finally the Spanish unknowingly carried with them a host of diseases, in particular the deadly smallpox virus that infected and killed vast numbers of Aztecs. By 1521,

What technological advances facilitated European expansionism?

View the **Map** *Native American Population Loss, 1500–1700*

just two years after his arrival, Cortés had subdued the once mighty Aztec Empire. A decade later other Spanish conquistadors led by Francisco Pizarro toppled the similarly powerful Inca Empire which stretched from present-day Ecuador to what is now Chile.

To many people of the Americas, who had never seen anything like firearms before, the Spanish *did* seem to have god-like power. European firearms left an indelible impression on South American cultures. Created centuries after European contact, this Peruvian painting (**1.10**) shows an angel carrying an arquebus, the type of firearm used by the Spanish during their conquest of Central and South America.

The Spanish took advantage of the existing systems of tribute and taxation created by the Aztec to extract the maximum amount of wealth from the region. Spanish America yielded a glittering array of valuable items from gold to pearls. The Spanish also began exporting prized dyes such as the brilliant red cochineal and indigo. The latter blue dye became closely associated with a type of cloth associated with the Italian city of Genoa. The French name for this cloth "bleu de Gênes" is the origin of the modern word blue jeans.

Among the agricultural products exported, cacao, the key ingredient in chocolate, helped spur a Spanish obsession with drinking chocolate. In contrast to the Aztecs, the Spanish preferred to drink their chocolate with an added sweetener, such as honey and eventually sugar.

In the 1540s, the discovery of silver in what is now Peru generated what became the most profitable American commodity for export. Silver would become the cornerstone of Spain's new-found wealth. Silver was a mixed blessing for the Spanish economy. The influx of large amounts of silver into the Spanish economy helped some become rich, but others suffered as prices were inflated as more and more of the precious metal was introduced into the economy.

1.10 Heavenly Militia
This South American painting done hundreds of years after the conquest shows an angel with an arquebus, a precursor of the modern rifle. The image shows the awesome power that Spanish weaponry had on the consciousness of the conquered peoples of Central and South America.

"Cacao by itself, largely being eaten raw, causes all this harm of which we spoke, but that toasted and incorporated with warm spices, as it is mixed in chocolate, it has great benefits for everything."

JUAN DE CÁRDENAS, *Marvelous Problems and Secrets of the Indies,* 1591

What role did disease play in the Spanish conquest of the Aztecs?

West African Worlds

 Africa, the world's second largest continent in terms of land mass, is home to some of the most ancient civilizations in the world. The range of societies in Africa in the sixteenth century rivaled those of the Americas in social complexity and cultural and religious diversity. Africa featured class-stratified urban civilizations alongside more simple egalitarian societies. Monotheistic faiths, including Christianity and Islam, flourished in parts of Africa, as did religions closer in principle to the animist beliefs of Eastern Woodlands Indians.

The North African states on the Mediterranean had been trading with Europe since the founding of the great ancient port of Carthage (814 BCE) near modern Tunis. Africans possessed many commodities sought by Europeans, including salt, gold, ivory, and exotic woods. But the development of a direct sea route from Europe to West Africa in the fifteenth century greatly increased trade and contact between Europeans and Africans. The most profound consequence of the sea routes to West Africa was the development of the international slave trade, a process that changed virtually every society in the Atlantic world.

West African Societies, Islam, and Trade

The civilizations of Africa south of the Sahara Desert, including those with Atlantic ports, were socially and culturally diverse. The powerful Songhai Empire (1370–1591) extended from the Atlantic inward to the Sudan. Primarily agricultural, the empire included urban centers and a highly organized military and administrative bureaucracy. In the great city of Timbuktu, an Islamic university rivaled many European centers of learning.

Other peoples, such as the Igbos of West Africa, lived in smaller, autonomous villages. These simpler, more egalitarian societies were organized mainly around kinship, more like America's Eastern Woodlands Indians than the empires of Mesoamerica or the rising nation-states of Europe. Local rulers consulted with a council of elders before making decisions affecting the community. Societies such as the Igbos were matrilineal, whereas other African societies traced descent and organized inheritance through the paternal line.

Before the seventh century most societies of West Africa practiced animist religions. These polytheistic faiths considered aspects of nature, such as the sun, wind, and animals, to be gods and spirits. Ancestor worship also played a prominent role in many West African religious traditions. But beginning in the mid-seventh century, the faith of Islam, first established in Arabia by Muhammad in 622 CE, began spreading via trade routes through northern, western, and eastern Africa. Islam eventually became the dominant religion in these areas, especially in trading centers.

Trade played a key role in the economic life of both North and West Africa. Trade goods included salt, ivory, and precious metals. While salt was an essential ingredient for cooking and preserving food, the other items were sought by artists and artisans who fashioned them into luxury goods such as jewelry. An extensive network of caravan routes linked West Africa to the North African ports of Tangier, Tunis, Tripoli, and Alexandria. But Portuguese exploration of the African coast in the late 1400s soon led to the development of direct trade between Europeans and Africans (**1.11**).

The Portuguese-African Connection

Portugal took the lead in exploring an Atlantic route to Asia, which provided Europe with spices and exotic fabrics such as silk and cotton. Prince Henry the Navigator (1394–1460), a member of the Portuguese royal family, used his wealth and power to encourage exploration of the West African coast. Even after his death Portugal continued to explore the West African coast, leading to Vasco da Gama's voyage (1497–1499) around the Horn of Africa and arrival on the southwest

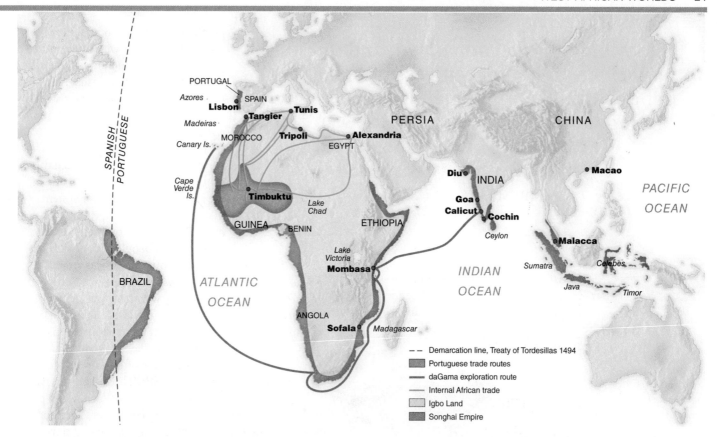

1.11 Internal African Trade Routes and Portuguese Trade with Africa
West African kingdoms were linked by several different inland trade routes to
North Africa and the Mediterranean. The Portuguese traded with the Atlantic
islands and the west coast of Africa.

coast of India (1.11). Portuguese traders then established a lucrative trade with India and began to
explore trading possibilities with Africa, seeking such
prized goods as ivory and gold. After 1470, Portuguese
trade with West Africa increased, and within a decade
the Portuguese had established forts along the African
coasts to facilitate further trading opportunities.

At approximately the same time that the Portuguese were exploring the African coast, they were
embarking on an ambitious but ruthless plan of conquest and colonization in the Atlantic island groups
of the Madeiras, Azores, and Cape Verde, (1.11).
These Atlantic outposts were converted into sugar-
producing plantation economies. The Portuguese
also vied with the Spanish for pre-eminence in the
Canary Islands. The Pope eventually brokered a
treaty between these two Iberian powers, giving
control to the Spanish. The biggest losers were the
indigenous populations of the Canary Islands, the
Guanche—a North African people who had settled
the islands thousands of years earlier. The semitropi-
cal climate of the Canaries was ideal for sugar cultivation. The Pope blessed the Guanche enslavement,

which was entirely justified because the Guanche
were, in his words, "infidels and savages." The model
developed in the Canaries foreshadowed European
interactions with the peoples of the Americas.

With no previous exposure to the diseases carried by Europeans, thousands of Guanche people
became ill and died. Unable to rely on an indigenous
source of labor, Europeans eventually turned to
Africa for slaves to provide the back-breaking labor
they demanded for cultivating, harvesting, and
processing sugar.

African Slavery

Slavery was widely practiced in Africa long before
the arrival of the Portuguese. Rival tribes usually
took slaves as spoils of war; but some prisoners
attained privileged positions as petty officials,
military leaders, and, in rare cases, political advisors to rulers. In Africa slavery was not always a
permanent or hereditary condition, and slaves
were sometimes absorbed into the societies that
held them.

> "[T]hey kidnap even noblemen, and the sons of noblemen, and our relatives, and take them to be sold to the white men who are in our Kingdoms . . . and as soon as they are taken . . . they are immediately ironed and branded with fire."
>
> NZINGA MBEMBA (King Afonso of the Kongo, Central Africa), 1526

Initially controlled by Muslim traders, the slave trade after 1600 came increasingly under European domination. The ever-rising demand for labor in the Americas, fueled by extraordinary profits from slave-based sugar plantations, prompted rival European powers to compete with one another for a share of this lucrative trade. As the value of slaves increased, Africans began raiding neighboring territories with the express purpose of obtaining slaves.

European involvement in the African slave trade transformed this centuries-old institution into one of the most exploitative labor systems in world history. Europeans developed a racist conception of slavery that declared people of dark skin to be inferior beings for whom slavery was a natural and proper condition. As a consequence Europeans treated slaves as property with few legal rights or protections. Masters were free to extract the maximum amount of labor from them with minimal regard for their humanity. Slaves taken by Europeans to the Americas were often worked literally to death in the sugar fields. Those who survived found that slavery in the New World was a permanent and hereditary condition. They and their descendants faced a lifetime of slavery with no hope of ever obtaining freedom.

Some West African nations managed to fend off the ravages of the slave trade. Benin, a well-organized nation-state ruled by a powerful monarch, traded slaves captured during war to the Portuguese in the fifteenth century but gradually withdrew from the slave trade (see *Choices and Consequences: Benin, Portugal, and the International Slave Trade*, page 23). Benin continued to trade with the Portuguese on its own terms. Among the goods sought by the Portuguese were a type of pepper and ivory; the Benin sought bronze from the Portuguese. Among the most visually impressive uses of this bronze were the finely crafted panels created for the walls of the royal palace. In the panel pictured here (**1.12**), a Portuguese soldier with a pike is surrounded by five "manilas," the bronze bars that were among the most important trade goods brought by the Portuguese.

1.12 Benin Bronze Panel
The artists of Benin were widely admired for their finely crafted bronze plaques and sculptures which decorated the walls of the royal palace. The panel depicts a Portuguese soldier and the bronze bars used as a common trade item.

What roles did slaves play in African societies?

View the **Map** Benin Empire

Choices and Consequences

BENIN, PORTUGAL, AND THE INTERNATIONAL SLAVE TRADE

The Portuguese took advantage of ethnic and tribal rivalries and the traditional African practice of taking captured opponents as slaves. Africans were eager to trade with the Portuguese who offered highly prized goods such as bronze, cloth, horses, and in limited cases, firearms. The Kingdom of Benin, one of the more powerful West-African kingdoms initially participated in this trade, but by 1516 the Oba (King) faced a momentous decision about whether to continue the slave trade.

Choices

1 Cut off all trade with the Portuguese	**2** Continue to trade with the Portuguese, and participate fully in the expanding international slave trade	**3** Continue to trade with the Portuguese, but end their involvement in the international slave trade

Decision

Benin's king continued to trade with the Portuguese but restricted the trade in male slaves, the most sought after slaves for heavy agricultural labor. Benin allowed women to be traded (eventually prohibiting this trade too) and continued to tolerate slavery within its own kingdom.

Consequences

Benin's decision allowed it to prosper and preserve its political autonomy far longer than many neighboring states. Benin obtained the benefits of trade by selling cloth instead of slaves. By refusing to become a major supplier of slaves, Benin avoided the costly and potentially destabilizing warfare needed to obtain large numbers of slaves.

Continuing Controversies

What does the kingdom of Benin's experiences with the slave trade reveal about the nature of African slavery?

Few scholars believe Benin's actions were motivated by humanitarian concerns about the evils of slavery, which the African kingdom continued to tolerate. Scholars disagree over Benin's motivation for ending its involvement in the slave trade. Some argue that Benin's economy required a large supply of labor, which meant it could ill afford to export slaves. Others argue that Benin's rulers wisely calculated that continued expansion and warfare would only weaken their power and lead to political instability.

City of Benin

What theories account for Benin's ability to resist involvement in the international slave trade?

European Colonization of the Atlantic World

By the early sixteenth century, Portugal, Spain, and France had established permanent outposts in the Atlantic world, with England soon to follow. Each of these nations concentrated on a particular region of the Atlantic world (**1.13**). Portugal focused primarily on West Africa and Brazil, where trade in slaves and production of sugar generated enormous profits. Spain's massive empire in the Atlantic extended from the tip of South America to southwestern North America. The Spanish Empire's chief export was silver. Meanwhile France directed its attention northward toward Canada, where the fur trade produced a lucrative commodity for export, and south to the Caribbean islands where plantations could produce sugar and tobacco. Finally England, a relative latecomer to colonization, established its first outposts on the east coast of North America, in present-day North Carolina and Virginia.

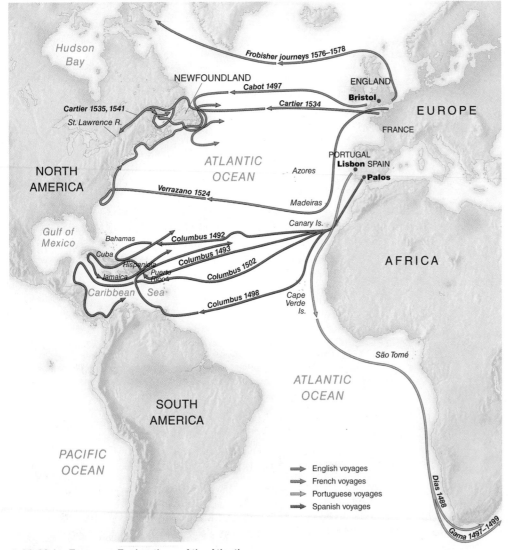

1.13 Major European Explorations of the Atlantic
The European nations that explored the Atlantic took different arcs. The Portuguese turned toward Africa, the Spanish explored Central and South America, and the English and French focused on the North Atlantic.

The Black Legend and the Creation of New Spain

The Spanish had used images of Aztec human sacrifice to justify their conquest and Spain's rivals, particularly Protestant nations such as England, used the power of images for their own political advantage. Tales of Spanish brutality during the conquest of the Americas gave rise to the "Black Legend." This indictment of Spanish cruelty toward the native peoples of the Americas first appeared in the writings of the Spanish bishop, Bartolomé de Las Casas, in the 1550s. The new medium of print allowed copies of his scathing critique of Spanish colonialism to be distributed throughout Europe; it was soon translated into French, Dutch, and English. Some of these translations contained gruesome wood-cut images such as those that appeared in the English edition, *The Tears of the Indians* (1656). The four scenes depicted on the front cover of the book, the "massacre and slaughter" of the Indian inhabitants of the

Americas, are described in Las Casas's narrative. The title page shows scenes of torture and punishment, including being hacked to death and burnt alive (**1.14**).

Within two decades the Spanish had conquered much of Central and South America. Inspired by tales of fabulously wealthy civilizations to the north, they launched expeditions to explore the vast continent of North America. Hernando de Soto's expedition to Florida explored much of the southeastern United States in 1539. Another expedition in 1540, under the command of Francisco Vasquez de Coronado, traversed a huge swath of western America from what is now Kansas to Colorado. Subsequent settlements in Florida and the Southwest greatly extended the Spanish Empire. Within 60 years of conquering the Aztecs and Incas, Spain's North American colonial empire extended from Santa Fe (present-day New Mexico) in the west, to St. Augustine (present-day Florida) in the east, and then all the way south to what are now Chile and Argentina—an area larger than ancient Rome's vast empire. The Spanish crown had taken an active role in colonizing these regions, and the government it created to rule its American empire reflected the investment of time, money, and resources. The empire was divided into a series of administrative units and was staffed by a large number of bureaucrats and administrative officials. Of crucial importance was Spain's board of trade, headquartered in the Spanish port of Seville. It granted licenses for trade with Spain's colonies, enforced commercial laws, and collected customs taxes and any revenues due the crown.

Along with the colonial government, the Roman Catholic Church exercised enormous power and influence in Spanish America. Spain granted the Church sizeable amounts of land and money, and priests and church officials enjoyed a privileged status. They also bore responsibilities such as establishing churches, schools, and hospitals, converting native people to the faith, and enforcing religious conformity through the Inquisition.

The Spanish established a network of interconnected urban centers to aid them in the administration of the peoples and territories they conquered. In part this policy reflected the relatively high degree of urbanization the Spanish found among the civilizations of Mesoamerica and South America. However, this model of organization also reflected Spanish values and interests, allowing them to project the power of the church and state in highly visible ways. By 1600, there were 225 towns in Spanish America, all laid out according to Renaissance models of urban

1.14 Illustration from Bartolomé de Las Casas, *The Tears of the Indians*
This illustration from *The Tears of the Indians,* the English translation of Las Casas's work, portrays Spanish cruelty toward Indians. The spread of these images gave credence to the "Black Legend" of Spanish conquest and violence.

planning in a grid-like pattern. The grand central plazas in the larger towns and cities afforded both a place for commerce and a symbolic space for monumental civic and church architecture. This painting of the central plaza in Mexico City (**1.15**) captures the use of urban planning and monumental architecture to reinforce the power of the state and the church. The cathedral and the viceroy's (local governor) and archbishop's palaces tower over the central square, vivid reminders of the dominance of church and state.

What does the architecture of the central Plaza of Mexico City tell us about Spain's approach to colonization?

1.15 Central Square of Mexico City
Spanish urban planners sought to project imperial power onto the colonial landscape. In this painting of the town square in Mexico City, the buildings most closely identified with church and state, the cathedral and the headquarters of the government, tower over the central plaza.

Much of the economy of New Spain was based on a highly exploitive system of labor. Ensuring an adequate labor supply for the arduous mining and agricultural work became a top economic priority of Spanish colonial officials. Rather than enslave the inhabitants of Central and South America as they had done to the native peoples in the Caribbean islands, the Spanish developed a system of forced labor, the *encomienda,* that was only marginally less exploitive than slavery itself. The crown declared Indians "vassals" who owed their labor to noblemen who in turn were required to provide for the Indians' spiritual welfare. The system provided labor and in theory demonstrated the Spanish commitment to saving the souls of the Indians by converting them. In reality it led to the brutal exploitation of Indians. Criticism of the system by religious reformers such as Las Casas, combined with high mortality among the indigenous population, which easily succumbed to diseases brought by the Spanish, eventually led to the use of other types of labor, including conscript (enrolled by compulsion) labor, wage labor, and slavery.

Fishing and Furs: France's North Atlantic Empire

In 1493, the Pope had settled a colonial dispute between Spain and Portugal by dividing the Atlantic world between them, a decision later ratified by a treaty between both countries in 1494. France rejected the authority of the treaty and sent fleets to take advantage of the abundant cod fisheries in the waters off what is now Newfoundland. In 1524 France dispatched Giovanni da Verrazano, an Italian mariner working for the king of France, to find the so-called Northwest Passage that would allow ships to sail through the waterways of the Americas to Asia. Although Verrazano failed to find such a route (it did not exist), his mapping of the North American coast aroused the interest of the French monarch, who decided to commit additional resources for further exploration of North America. In the 1530s French explorer Jacques Cartier made a more extensive and detailed investigation of the North Atlantic, eventually traveling up the St. Lawrence River, where he encountered a group of Micmac Indians (an Algonquian-speaking Eastern Woodlands Indian nation). Their offer of furs in exchange for European goods such as

knives, kettles, and beads led the French to recognize the potential of furs as a lucrative commodity. Furs could be sold to Europeans who valued their warmth and treated them as a high-status luxury item.

In 1604, the French established Port Royal in Nova Scotia and four years later founded the city of Quebec, now the capital of the province of Quebec, on the banks of the St. Lawrence River. Located on a high ridge at a strategic bend in the river, Quebec was well placed to allow the French to trade with the local Indians, who were skilled fur trappers. The beaver pelts traded to the French fetched a good price in the European markets.

The French encounter with Native Americans differed from that of the Spanish and Portuguese in three significant ways. First, the relatively small size of the settlement in New France and the dependence of the French on Indians to provide furs necessitated maintaining good relations with local tribes. Second, the predominantly male French population intermarried with local Indians. Eventually the French government even encouraged intermarriage, believing it would lead to the gradual assimilation of the Indian population into the French culture of New France.

Third, the French like the Spanish were committed to converting the Indians to their Catholic faith, but rather than trying to impose Catholicism by force, French Jesuit missionaries lived among Indians and learned their languages and customs. The French Jesuits were just as eager as the Spanish to convert the Indians, but they recognized the need to understand the culture of those they wished to convert. The French also took advantage of religious art and images to help convert the Indians. This early account of life in New France includes an image that shows how religious painting was used to introduce Indians to Christian ideas (**1.16**).

1.16 *Two Europeans Show a Religious Painting to A Group of Native Americans*
This image from an early French traveler account of New France underscores the way in which images were used to help Indians understand Christianity.

What were the most important differences between New France and New Spain?

English Expansion: Ireland and Virginia

Although England took advantage of the rich opportunities for fishing provided by the Atlantic Ocean, its exploration of the Americas was a relatively low priority for most of the sixteenth century. Three factors explain this lack of interest. First England faced less economic pressure to find export markets because its primary export—wool—was in high demand on the European continent. Second England faced a crisis of leadership after the death of Henry VIII in 1547. He was succeeded by his sickly ten-year-old son, Edward VI, who died in 1553 only six years into his reign. Next came Henry's daughter Mary I, who tried to reestablish Catholicism, a campaign that included the intense persecution of Protestants. Her reign was also short; she died in 1558. Finally England was bogged down in a colonial venture closer to home, the subjugation of Ireland. Spain easily conquered the last Moors in Spain before moving on to Atlantic exploration in 1492. Irish resistance to English colonization, by contrast, tied up English resources for decades.

Yet even as the English struggled to colonize Ireland, these experiences provided a distinctive model for future colonial policy in the New World. While the Spanish set out to conquer and convert the inhabitants of the Americas, absorbing them into Spanish society as a subordinate class at the bottom of the social order, the English took a different approach. Rather than attempt to incorporate the Irish, the English expelled them from their land. They then repopulated the land with colonists from England and Scotland, creating **plantations**, or fortified outposts dedicated to producing agricultural products for export. Originally the term plantation simply meant any English settlement in a foreign land, but it later became synonymous with a distinctive slave-based labor system used in much of the Atlantic world.

One source of this policy of exclusion can be traced to the intense religious animosity between Protestants and Catholics. The English not only detested the Catholic faith of the Irish but they also feared the Irish would support efforts to reimpose Catholicism on England and would assist Catholic nations like France and Spain if they went to war with England. Expelling the Irish and transplanting loyal Protestant farmers from England and Scotland, therefore, promised to boost the English economy

and secure control of a potentially troublesome neighboring island. This colonial model developed in parts of Ireland—expulsion and plantation—would shape subsequent English experiments in colonization.

Economic pressures eventually impelled England to follow its European rivals and engage in the exploration and colonization of the Atlantic. The profitable wool trade with the continent began to decline in the 1550s, prompting English merchants to seek new commercial opportunities. These merchants founded scores of new companies devoted to overseas trade with Europe, Africa, and the Mediterranean.

In 1558 England's entry into exploration and colonization was also helped when another of Henry VIII's daughters, Elizabeth I succeeded "Bloody Mary," as Protestants called her, and quickly established herself as a strong leader determined to project English power overseas. She eagerly pursued an aggressive policy of expansion, challenging Spain's dominance in the Atlantic. A committed Protestant, Elizabeth viewed Spanish power as a threat to her realm. Her religious convictions and foreign policy objectives eventually brought England into direct conflict with Spain.

England's support for Spain's enemies on the continent, including the Protestant Dutch, the raids of English pirates, and English anti-Catholicism, finally drove King Philip II of Spain to take decisive action. In 1588, Spain launched a mighty Armada, or fleet of warships, to invade England and destroy Europe's most powerful Protestant monarchy. The Spanish considered their ships invincible, but the Armada was routed by the smaller, faster ships of the English navy. (Weather conditions at sea favored the English and hampered the Spanish fleet.) The defeat of the Armada shifted the balance of power in the Atlantic, as England eventually emerged as the major force in the Atlantic world. To commemorate the stunning victory, Queen Elizabeth commissioned a portrait that symbolized England's rise to power in the Atlantic world. In the painting Elizabeth's hand rests prominently on a globe and the crown, a symbol of the monarchy, sits perched above the globe (**1.17**). In the background the artist includes two scenes depicting the defeat of the Armada, a further reminder of England's power and naval supremacy.

Among the most ardent supporters of expanding England's role in the Atlantic world were former **privateers**. These were Englishmen who engaged in

What lessons did the English learn from their experiences in Ireland?

🔲◖┤**Read** the **Document** *Thomas Hariot*, A Briefe and True Report of the New Found Land of Virginia *(1590)*

state-sanctioned piracy in the Atlantic against Spanish treasure fleets returning from South America. A number of them had grown rich and influential from their successes. John Hawkins, for example, earned himself a fortune and a knighthood for his daring seizures of Spanish ships. One of the most dashing of these buccaneers, Sir Walter Raleigh, had participated in the English conquest of Ireland and became a favorite of Queen Elizabeth. Raleigh sought support for a more ambitious plan of colonization in the lands north of Spanish America and south of French Canada. Queen Elizabeth bestowed her blessing on the enterprise, but not money. As a result Raleigh and the colonial ventures that followed had to turn to private capital to finance his plan.

In contrast to France and Spain's state-financed model of exploration and colonization, England adopted a more capitalist model, with private investors forming companies and issuing stock to finance exploration and settlement. Having raised the funds to outfit two ships, Raleigh's expedition arrived in the outer banks regions of what is now North Carolina in July 1585. Naming the new settlement Virginia, in honor of Elizabeth, known widely as the "Virgin Queen" because she never married, England had finally established its first colony in the New World. Unfortunately for Raleigh and the original colonists, the first colony at Roanoke (an Algonquian Indian name for shell money) ended in disaster. To begin with, although the location near the treacherous region of Cape Hatteras protected the settlement from possible Spanish raids, it also deterred passing ships from stopping, which made reprovisioning the colony difficult. Then conflict with local Indians erupted when the colonists accused them of stealing a silver cup. All the while relief for the colonists was delayed by the outbreak of war with Spain. The English required every available ship to repulse the Spanish Armada. When a ship finally arrived three years later, the new settlers found the colony deserted. All

1.17 **Elizabeth's Armada Portrait**
In this portrait commemorating England's victory over the Spanish Armada, Queen Elizabeth's hand rests on the globe, reaching out to cover much of what is now North America. In the upper left the Spanish fleet sets out toward England, while in the upper right the defeated Spanish Armada flounders.

What is the symbolic importance of the position of Queen Elizabeth's hand in the Armada portrait?

1.18 John White's Painting
White's depiction of an Indian religious ritual, involving an elaborate dance is one of the first visual representations of Indian religious practices.

the residents had disappeared, leaving behind only one clue: the word "CROAT-OAN" carved into a door-post. The fate of Roanoke remains a mystery, but scholars suspect that the term *croatoan* was a vague reference to an Indian village some 50 miles south of the settlement that may have been the colonists' destination before they disappeared.

Although the first English attempt to create a fixed settlement was a dismal failure, the information gained by the colonists about the Algonquian tribes who inhabited North Carolina proved invaluable. The governor of the colony, John White, was an accomplished artist who captured scenes from Indian life in vivid paintings (**1.18**). In his visual representation of the village of Secoton, John White included a scene of Indians engaged in a religious ritual. White includes a brief description in the painting, noting that it was "A Ceremony in their prayers with strange iesturs and songs dansing about post carved on the topps lyke mens faces."

A number of his images were popularized by the Flemish engraver Theodore de Bry, who in some cases made subtle but important alterations to make them more appealing to European tastes. In the case of the village of Secoton, these changes were fairly minor. In other cases, de Bry altered the images in significant ways. Representing America posed a number of challenges for de Bry, for a more detailed discussion of these issues, see *Images as History: Marketing the New World: Theodore de Bry's Engravings of the Americas.*

> "In respect to us they are a people poore, and for want of skill and juegement in the knowledge and use of our things, doe esteeme our trifles before things of greater value: Nothwithstanding, in their proper maner (considering the want of such meanes as we have), they seeme to be very ingenious. For although they have no suche tooles, nor any such crafts, Sciences and Artes as wee, yet in those things they doe, they shew excellence of wit. . . . [and] in short time bee brought to civilitie, and the imbracing of true Religion"
>
> THOMAS HARIOT, *A Briefe and True Report of the Newfound Land of Virginia,* 1588

How did the English model of financing colonial projects differ from the Spanish model?

View the **Closer Look** *An Early European Image of Native Americans*

Images as History

MARKETING THE NEW WORLD: THEODORE DE BRY'S ENGRAVINGS OF THE AMERICAS

Theodore de Bry, an engraver and printer from the city of Antwerp in what is today Belgium, published a multi-volume series, entitled *America* (1590–1634) that provided many Europeans with their first glimpse of the exotic New World. The first volume of this series was published in English, French, German, and Latin. Subsequent volumes were published only in German and Latin. Although a Calvinist, de Bry cut out material that he believed would offend Catholics to make the Latin edition truly universal and appealing to both Catholics and Protestants. In particular, he eliminated portrayals of Catholic explorers as brutally exploitive of the indigenous populations of the Americas. Given the expense of producing copper plate engravings, de Bry concluded it was simply too costly to create separate images for the Latin and German editions of his later volumes in the series. Instead he tried to make the images appealing to Catholics and Protestants by exaggerating the "otherness" of the indigenous populations. The most striking example of this strategy occurred in an engraving in which de Bry conjured up an exotic pagan ritual in which half-naked Indians parade before a grotesque five-headed, two-tailed deer god, an image that would have struck his audience as the epitome of an unholy and demonic religious practice.

A monstrous pagan sculpture dominates the image, a visible reminder that the inhabitants of the New World were un-Christian savages.

The natives' lack of clothing demonstrates that they are primitive peoples, who lack the most basic attributes of a civilized society.

The Latin text underscores the barbarism of the New World. The author describes the pagan idol as "a horrible effigy made in the form of a misshapen evil-demon."

Der Indianer Religion oder Gottesdienst.   XXII

How did de Bry represent the religious beliefs of the Americas?

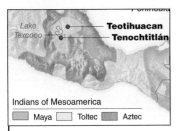

1325

Founding of Tenochtitlán
Aztec Empire becomes dominant
power in Mesoamerica

1440

**Gutenberg invents
printing press**
Print revolution transforms the
way knowledge is organized and
spread

1519–1521

Hernán Cortés conquers Aztecs
Founding of Spanish empire in what
is now Mexico

1534

Henry VIII breaks with Rome
Henry becomes the leader of a new
English Church

Review Questions

1. What were the chief advantages of fixed agriculture, and how did it contribute to the rise of more complex civilizations?

2. How did new technology affect European overseas expansion in the fifteenth and sixteenth centuries?

3. What were the most important ideas associated with the Renaissance?

4. What role did food and animals play in the Columbian Exchange?

5. Compare the impact of Spanish, French, and English approaches to colonization on the indigenous populations of the Americas.

Key Terms

Paleo-Indians The name given by scientists to the first inhabitants of the Americas, an Ice Age people who survived largely by hunting big game, and to a lesser extent by fishing and collecting edible plants.   **4**

Archaic Era Period beginning approximately 9,000 years ago lasting an estimated 6,000 years. It was marked by more intensive efforts by ancient societies to shape the environment to enhance food production.   **5**

Aztec Led by the Mexica tribe, the Aztec created a powerful empire whose capital, the great city of Tenochtitlán, was built on an island in Lake Texcoco in 1325 CE.   **6**

Capitalism An economic system in which the market economy determines the prices of goods and services.   **11**

Humanists Individuals who advocated a revival of ancient learning, particularly ancient Greek and Roman thought, and encouraged greater attention to secular topics including a new emphasis on the study of humanity.   **13**

Reformation The movement for religious reform started by Martin Luther.   **13**

Spanish Inquisition A tribunal devoted to finding and punishing heresy and rooting out Spain's Jews and Muslims.   **15**

Columbian Exchange The term used by modern scholars to describe the biological encounter between the two sides of the Atlantic, including the movement of plants, animals, and diseases.   **16**

Plantation An English settlement or fortified outpost in a foreign land dedicated to producing agricultural products for export. (Later the term would become synonymous with a distinctive slave-based labor system used in much of the Atlantic world.)   **28**

Privateer A form of state-sponsored piracy, usually directed against Spanish treasure fleets returning from the Americas.   **28**

CHAPTER REVIEW

1560

Publication of the Geneva Bible
English Protestant exiles living in Switzerland publish the Geneva Bible, which becomes the central text for English Calvinists.

1585

English establish colony of Roanoke on North Carolina's Outer Banks
England's first permanent settlement in America fails, and no trace is found of the settlers when new supplies are brought to the colony

1588

English defeat Spanish Armada
England defeats Spain, challenging Spanish dominance of the Atlantic world

1608

Quebec founded
France's major settlement in North America established

MyHistoryLab Connections

Visit www.myhistorylab.com for a customized Study Plan that will help you build your knowledge of *People in Motion*.

Questions for Analysis

1. What role did human sacrifice play in Mesoamerican societies and how did Europeans view these practices?

View the **Closer Look** *Images as History: Blood of the Gods, p. 6*

2. How did European views of nature differ from those of Eastern Woodland Indians?

View the **Closer Look** *Competing Visions: European and Huron Views of Nature, p. 12*

3. What was Columbus's legacy?

Watch the **Video** *What is Columbus's Legacy?, p. 17*

4. What was the Black Legend?

View the **Image** *Torturing Native Amerindians, p. 24*

5. What do early European artistic representations of the Americas tell us about Europeans in the period after Columbus?

View the **Closer Look** *An Early European Image of Native Americans, p. 30*

Other Resources from This Chapter

Read the **Document**

- Iroquois Creation Story, *p. 9*
- *Thomas Hariot,* A Briefe and True Report of the New Found Land of Virginia *(1590), p. 28*

View the **Image** *Pueblo Indian Ruins, p. 7*

View the **Map**

- *Native American Peoples to 1450, p. 8*
- *Spread of Printing, p. 11*
- *Western Europe During the Renaissance and Reformation, p. 15*
- *Native American Population Loss, 1500–1700, p. 18*
- *Benin Empire, p. 22*
- *Spanish America to 1610, p. 26*

The Chesapeake
Colonies p. 36

How did tobacco agriculture shape the evolution of Chesapeake societies?

New England p. 42

How did the religious ideals of New England society shape its early history?

**The Caribbean
Colonies** p. 50

Why did slavery take root in the Caribbean earlier than in the mainland colonies of British North America?

**The Restoration Era
and the Proprietary
Colonies** p. 52

How did the Restoration colonies differ from earlier efforts at colonization in British North America?

**The Crises of the Late
Seventeenth Century**
p. 55

What does the outbreak of witchcraft accusations in Salem tell us about the crisis of the late seventeenth-century?

**The Whig Ideal and
the Emergence of
Political Stability** p. 60

What political and legal concepts defined Whig ideology?

((•─[**Hear** the **Audio File** on **myhistorylab.com**

◉─[**Watch** the **Video** *Critical Visions, Chapter 2*

Models of Settlement
English Colonial Societies, 1590–1710

Theodore de Bry's 1619 engraving, *The Chickahominy Become "New Englishmen,"* from his book *America*, portrays treaty negotiations between Virginia Indians and the English. Captain Samuel Argall, the Englishman negotiating the treaty, sits on a mat with a tribal elder. Another tribal leader addresses his people, informing them about the terms of the treaty, which was meant to promote trade and peace between the English and the Virginia Indians. As the engraving title, which refers to the Chickahominy as "New Englishmen," suggests, the English insisted that Indian tribes submit to English rule and accept the English king as their lord. By contrast the Indians believed that negotiating a treaty with the English did not mean that they had given up control of their own political affairs. These differing visions of diplomacy led to conflict between Native Americans and English settlers throughout the seventeenth century.

At the dawn of the 1600s, England trailed far behind Spain and France in the race to exploit the wealth of the Americas. By 1700, however, England had become a formidable colonial power in both North America and the Caribbean. In contrast to Spain and France, whose colonization efforts relied on active support from the monarchy and church, England's first efforts to colonize America relied on joint stock companies, which were privately financed commercial ventures. The two great early English experiments in colonization, in Virginia and New England, faced many challenges in their early years, including how to deal with local Indian populations. The solution for the English was not simply rendering the Indians politically subservient to the king but also segregating themselves from the Indians whenever possible.

Relations between settlers and Indians complicated colonial politics for most of the seventeenth century. Bacon's Rebellion (1676), a popular uprising in Virginia triggered by colonists' conflict over Indian policy, shook the foundations of the colony. In New England persistent conflict between Indians and settlers exacerbated existing social and economic tensions and contributed to the worst outbreak of witchcraft accusations in colonial America, the Salem witchcraft hysteria (1692). The reassertion of political control by England, whose Glorious Revolution (1688) contributed to the emergence of a new, more stable colonial world, helped facilitate the resolution of the witchcraft crisis. In the years to come, colonists would often invoke the political and constitutional ideas of the Glorious Revolution to defend their liberties.

> "Our first work is expulsion of the savages to gain the free range of the country . . . for it is infinitely better to have no heathen among us, who at best are but thorns in our side, than to be at peace and league with them."
>
> Virginia Governor FRANCIS WYATT, 1623–1624

The Chesapeake Colonies

 The failure of the Roanoke colony in Virginia (see Chapter 1) between 1585 and 1590 was only a temporary setback for English colonial projects in America. Less than two decades later, a new group of English settlers established a colony, Jamestown, in the Chesapeake Bay area of what is now Virginia. Although the early history of Jamestown was fraught with problems, the colony eventually began to prosper. Tobacco agriculture provided a strong financial incentive to expand into the wider Chesapeake region. By the 1630s, Lord Baltimore had developed an ambitious plan to found another colony in the region, Maryland.

The Founding of Jamestown

Joint stock companies charted by King James I (r. 1603–1625) funded the English colonial enterprises. Investors bought shares in the company and at the end of a specified period received their investment back plus a percentage of the profits. In April 1606, the king issued a charter to the Virginia Company of London to create a colony in America. In late December 1606, three ships set sail for the Chesapeake, arriving off the coast of Virginia in May 1607. The first settlers were a motley assortment of men; no women traveled on this first voyage. The settlers named the new settlement Jamestown, in honor of King James.

> ## "Our men were destroyed with cruel diseases, as swellings, Fluxes, Burning fevers and by wars, and some departed suddenly, but for the most part they died of mere famine."
>
> GEORGE PERCY, Colonist, 1607

The colonists scouted a location secure from possible Spanish attack, but still accessible to the sea. They built a fortified palisade to protect them from possible attacks by hostile Indians and Spanish ships. Unfortunately the site they chose turned out to be a public health disaster. On the edge of a swamp, Jamestown was a fertile breeding ground for mosquitoes and the pathogens they carried, including malaria. Salt water from the nearby estuary contaminated the wells the colonists dug to supply fresh drinking water. In addition poor drainage meant the colonists' own waste occasionally contaminated the water supply. Many settlers died within a year of disembarking.

The Virginia Company's promotional pamphlets (**2.1**) deceptively cast Virginia as an "earthly paradise" that would offer opportunities for the settlers to become rich. Almost one-third of the early settlers were gentlemen who were unprepared for the arduous life in Virginia and who viewed manual labor as undignified. Believing that vast troves of mineral wealth existed in the region, settlers wasted time searching for gold and silver instead of planting crops or repairing fortifications. Dissension and a lack of firm political leadership also undermined the colony.

Relations between the settlers and the powerful Powhatan Indian confederacy began amicably. Chief Powhatan, the ruler of the confederacy, was eager to trade with the English and acquire manufactured goods, especially firearms and metal tomahawks (a type of hatchet). Powhatan had also hoped to use the English as allies against rival Indian tribes. However once the Indians realized that the English were not temporary visitors merely interested in trade, but were intending to settle permanently in the region, relations between the two peoples deteriorated.

In dealing with the Indians, Virginians applied the same principles that the English had developed in the conquest of Ireland: expelling the local population and limiting contact with them as much as possible. The English failed to grasp basic rituals of hospitality and gift giving, essential to establishing cordial relations with Indian peoples. Whereas the French and Spanish encouraged marriage between male settlers and Indian women, the English discouraged such unions. This marriage taboo not only deprived the colony of a means of establishing friendly relations between the two peoples but also deprived the colonists of cultural go-betweens who could have smoothed out conflicts and misunderstandings.

Among the most enduring myths associated with Jamestown and the English settlers' relations with the Indians is the tale of Pocahontas. Settler-soldier John Smith's tale of how a beautiful Indian girl saved his life is a foundational myth in American history, one that later writers often cast in romantic terms: an American Romeo-and-Juliet story of love at first sight between a beautiful Indian "princess" (a term straight from English aristocratic culture) and a dashing English officer. Smith's published account of his time in Virginia helped create this mythology. Smith took considerable liberties with the truth, highlighting his role as a romantic hero who saved Jamestown from disaster.

The events Smith described in his account almost certainly did not take place as he described them. However, Smith was likely captured and eventually adopted into the tribe, and Pocahontas, then a young girl, may indeed have taken part in the adoption ritual. Among some Eastern Woodland Indian tribes, capture and in some cases ritual torture, followed by adoption into the tribe, was one means of conducting diplomacy. Once adopted into the tribe, prisoners became political intermediaries.

Although prone to inflate his achievements, Smith, an experienced soldier who had fought with the French and Dutch against Spain in the 1590s and then against the Muslim Turks in the early 1600s, played a decisive role in helping the colony avert disaster. In 1608, he negotiated an exchange of goods for food with Indians that helped stave off starvation. Smith's reforms may have staved off immediate catastrophe, but they did not prevent enormous suffering and high mortality during the difficult winter of 1609–1610, known as the "starving time." The colonists were so pressed for food that some even resorted to cannibalism to survive the winter. In his history of Virginia, Smith wrote about the "starving time." Smith reported, with a macabre sense of humor, that one man "did kill his wife, powdered her, and had eaten part of her before it was knowne," adding "but of such a dish as powdered wife I never heard of."

In 1609, Smith returned to England. After his departure the hostility between the English and the Indians intensified. In 1613, Captain Samuel Argall led a party of Virginians on a mission to capture

NOVA BRITANNIA.

OFFERING MOST

Excellent fruites by Planting in VIRGINIA.

Exciting all such as be well affected to further the same.

LONDON

Printed for SAMVEL MACHAM, and are to be sold at his Shop in Pauls Church-yard, at the Signe of the Bul-head.

1609.

2.1 Virginia Promotional Literature The Virginia Company produced pamphlets that promoted the riches to be had by planting in Virginia.

Pocahontas, whom Indians and Englishmen now knew by her adult name of Matoaka. The English hoped that by holding her hostage they could force her people to sign a peace treaty. For more on this episode, see *Choices and Consequences: The Ordeal of Pocahontas*, page 38.

Tobacco Agriculture and Political Reorganization

Jamestown had barely survived the "starving time," when the population dropped from between 500 and 600 to 60. Although the colony held on, it had not yet found a profitable commodity that could make it economically viable. John Rolfe solved this problem by introducing tobacco into the Virginia colony. Experimenting with various strains of tobacco, Rolfe finally settled on a variety that had been successfully cultivated in the Caribbean. Tobacco was all the rage

Choices and Consequences

THE ORDEAL OF POCAHONTAS

Desperate to force the local Powhatan Indians to negotiate a peace treaty, English settlers embarked on an audacious plan. They abducted a local Powhatan Indian woman they knew as Pocahontas, whose adult Indian name was Matoaka, hoping to force her people to accept a peace treaty. Her kidnappers took her to Henrico, a heavily fortified settlement upriver from Jamestown. The plan was to isolate her from her people. The English placed Matoaka in the household of a minister, who instructed her in the English language and customs and began indoctrinating her in Christianity. At the weekly prayer meetings hosted by the minister, she met John Rolfe, an influential Englishman recently widowed. Within a year of her abduction, Matoaka was baptized a Christian and had adopted a new English name, Rebecca. John Rolfe proposed marriage to the newly Christianized woman. Matoaka now faced three options.

Choices

1   Reject the offer of marriage and remain a captive among the English until her people rescued her or negotiated for her freedom.

2   Attempt to escape.

3   Marry Rolfe, and through that marriage help her people forge an alliance with the Virginians.

Decision

Matoaka chose the third option; she married John Rolfe. Two years after their marriage, the couple journeyed to England, where she became something of a celebrity and was even introduced at court.

Consequences

Marrying Rolfe gained Matoaka (Rebecca) her freedom. In her new role as the wife of a high-status Englishman, she became a mediator between her people and the English. Indeed, had she not become ill and died within a year after arriving in England, she might have been able to expand this important role.

Matoaks als Rebecka daughter to the mighty Prince Powhatan Emperour of Attanoughkomouck als Virginia converted and baptized in the Christian faith and Wife to the worll Mr Tho. Rolff.

Continuing Controversies

How do Indian conceptions of gender roles help explain Pocahontas's decision to marry?
Scholars have suggested different explanations for her decision. Some have seen it as an expression of romantic love; others, as sheer expedience. The most recent and perhaps most persuasive explanation of her conversion and marriage to John Rolfe acknowledges the key role of women as cultural intermediaries in Indian diplomacy. By creating ties of kin to bind potentially warring nations in a blood bond, marriage served an important diplomatic function. With this explanation, rather than viewing her decision as a slight to her Indian heritage, one can see her decision as likely having increased her status with her tribe by allowing her to assume an important diplomatic role

What role did women play in Indian diplomacy?

in Europe, a fact reflected in this humorous painting showing a group of monkeys in a tavern eagerly consuming tobacco (**2.2**). Playing on the popular notion that monkeys have a great capacity for imitation, the artist ridicules the consumption of tobacco as a bad habit all too easily emulated. Smoking tobacco for pleasure became popular among all classes in European society. Tobacco was also believed to have many medicinal uses; it was recommended as a cure for colds and an aid to digestion.

Rolfe sent his first consignment of tobacco to England in 1613. Tobacco proved to be the colony's economic salvation: Profits from its sale created a boom in the colony, which then led its inhabitants to devote nearly every acre of land to the "sot weed." Exports increased dramatically in the decades following the introduction of the crop. Although tobacco agriculture made some Virginians wealthy, the pursuit of profits diverted time and other resources from basic tasks, such as planting food crops and repairing buildings. As a result of this neglect, settlers in boom-time Virginia continued to die at an alarming rate.

Establishing political order in Virginia proved far more difficult than the founders of the colony had expected. In 1618, Sir Edwin Sandys became the Virginia Company of London's treasurer and instituted reforms to make the government of the colony more effective. A key reform was the creation of a representative body to make laws. The privilege of voting for representatives was extended to free men of property, who were to elect representatives who would then enact laws for the colony. Virginia's new legislative body, the House of Burgesses (representatives), first convened in July 1619. Rather than take orders from company officials, the colonists gained some control over their own political affairs, a milestone in the evolution of representative government in America.

Because laborers continued to be scarce in Virginia, Sandys also introduced a new system to

2.2 The Smoking Room with Monkeys
Artist Abraham Teniers mocked the popularity of smoking, substituting monkeys for humans. In European art, monkeys often symbolized the baser instincts of humankind.

What important reforms did Sir Edwin Sandys implement in 1618?

provide incentives to attract settlers. The **headright** system encouraged additional immigrants by giving 50 acres to anyone who would pay his own fare to Virginia and 50 additional acres for each person he brought with him. The year 1619 also marked the arrival of the first Africans in Virginia. An English pirate vessel flying under a Dutch flag sold the Africans, captured from a Portuguese slaving ship in the Caribbean, to the Virginia colonists.

Immigrants continued to arrive in Virginia despite the high mortality rates. Approximately two-thirds of the settlers died in the next three years. Deteriorating relations with local Indian communities reached a crisis point in 1622, when Powhatan's successor launched an assault on the colony that killed 347 colonists. The sensational attack inspired this engraving (**2.3**), which appeared in England six years later. To contrast the imagined civility of the colonists and the alleged barbarism of the Indians, the engraver included inaccurate details, including tablecloths and a European-style walled city in the distance.

2.3 Theodore de Bry Engraving of the "Massacre" of 1622
This engraving of the 1622 Indian attack on Virginia residents contains inaccuracies. To exaggerate the difference between Indian savagery and English "civilization," the artist included a European-style city in the background.

Two years after the attack, King James revoked the colony's charter. Now the king, not the Virginia Company of London, would appoint the governor. Eventually the king recognized the House of Burgesses, giving his royal sanction to the colonists' efforts at self-rule. Virginia had become England's first royal colony.

Lord Baltimore's Refuge: Maryland

James I died in 1625, and his son, Charles I (r. 1625–1649), came to the throne. Having married the French Catholic princess Henrietta Maria, Charles I resolved to make good on his marriage promise to ease the plight of England's Catholics. Most of England's aristocracy was Protestant, but a few had remained Catholic. One Catholic nobleman, George Calvert, Lord Baltimore, realized that he might be able to help his fellow Catholics and increase his own wealth by obtaining a royal charter for land in Virginia, making it a haven for English Catholics. After Calvert's death in 1632, his son Cecil, the second Lord Baltimore, obtained a charter for a colony from King Charles.

Maryland began as a proprietary colony under the legal authority of Lord Baltimore. The legal title of **proprietor** gave its possessor almost king-like authority over his domains. This early map of Maryland (**2.4**), not only contains the family's coat of arms in the top corner, but the text underneath proclaims Lord Baltimore "Absolute Lord and Proprietor." Calvert learned an important lesson from Jamestown: The lure of profits from tobacco agriculture could drive colonists to starve themselves to death to get rich quickly. To avoid this danger, he ordered that settlers first obtain a "sufficient quantity of corn and other provisions of victual" before producing tobacco or other commodities for export. Although he envisioned his colony as a haven for Catholics, Calvert knew that its

What was a proprietor?

economic success depended on attracting laborers, so the colony would need to be equally hospitable to Protestants. Maryland therefore afforded religious freedom to all Christians.

From the start the proprietors and the freemen battled over control of the colony. Colonists challenged Lord Baltimore. The Maryland assembly routinely voted down bills he introduced; Baltimore responded by blocking acts passed by the assembly. Exacerbating the discord was the continuing religious tension between the Catholic proprietor and the overwhelmingly Protestant assembly. Eventually the two sides accommodated each other, and by the 1640s, Maryland had a functional legislature.

Life in the Chesapeake: Tobacco and Society

The demands of an expanding tobacco economy in the Chesapeake, an area that included parts of Virginia and Maryland bordering Chesapeake Bay, produced a society that was driven by the profit motive. Tobacco production rose dramatically in the mid-seventeenth century, with exports from Virginia to England growing from over 10,000 pounds in the first years of production and export to well over a million pounds by the end of the 1630s. Attracting laborers to work in the tobacco fields proved difficult. Indentured servants, individuals who contracted to be servants for a specified number of years, usually four to seven years, provided an important source of labor. Employers paid for the voyage of their indentured servants to the colonies and clothed and fed them while they remained bound to their employer. At the end of the term of service, employers usually gave their indentured servants clothes and tools and allowed them to set out on their own. African slaves provided another source of labor, but slavery was not yet the dominant labor system in the region, and slavery had not yet hardened into a fixed status. A few slaves did eventually obtain their freedom.

Most planters preferred men for the arduous work of growing tobacco, so immigrants to the Chesapeake society were overwhelmingly male. Scholars estimate that before 1640, men

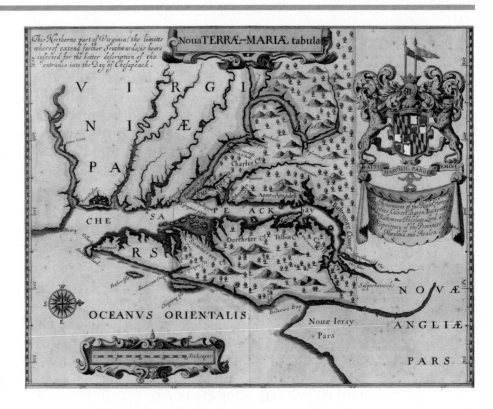

2.4 Early Map of Maryland
This early map of Maryland included the coat of arms of the Calvert family, a visible reminder that proprietor Lord Baltimore enjoyed almost monarchical authority over colonists.

out-numbered women by as much as six to one. The lopsided sex ratio meant that the few women who migrated to the region and managed to survive the high mortality rates enjoyed considerable control over their decision to marry. Since women often outlived their husbands, a fortunate woman could make several favorable matches during her life and create a sizeable estate. By 1700, as food supplies, sanitation, and shelter all improved, more children were born in the region, more women migrated there, and sex ratios became less lopsided.

Tobacco agriculture shaped the distinctive pattern of settlement in the Chesapeake. Rather than organize themselves into towns, colonists spread out in search of arable land to plant. They prized locations close to navigable rivers that fed into one of the major waterways in the area because that made shipping tobacco easier and cheaper. A few wealthy planters monopolized these choice locations. The demands of tobacco agriculture led to an almost insatiable need for additional land, which exacerbated the tensions with local Indians determined to prevent further encroachments on their territories.

How did the unbalanced sex ratio of the Chesapeake affect gender roles in this colonial region?

New England

The same year that the Virginia Company of London obtained a charter to settle what is now Virginia, another group of investors organized a rival company, the Virginia Company of Plymouth, intending to settle north of Virginia. Their charter included lands as far north as modern Bangor, Maine. In 1607, the company established a small plantation at the Sagadahoc River (known now as the Kennebec). The fierce Maine winter, however, proved too much for the colonists, who abandoned the settlement and returned to England.

Although the region's severe winters seemed to have doomed the prospects of settling this region, a group of Protestant religious dissenters known as Puritans expressed interest in migrating to New England. The ascension of Queen Elizabeth I (1558–1603), who had embraced the Protestant faith and supported the ideals of the Reformation, helped further the progress of the English Reformation.

The queen's support for Protestantism stopped well short of what the most zealous reformers had sought. Elizabeth opted to chart a middle path between traditional Catholicism and the most radical wing of the Protestant Reformation. Those who urged further reform earned themselves the name Puritans because of their desire to purify the Church of England of all vestiges of Catholic belief and practice.

Elizabeth never married and produced no heir, so the royal line passed to her cousin King James VI of Scotland who became James I of England when Elizabeth died in 1603. Although eager to assert his power, James was not particularly interested in pursuing the ideals of the Protestant Reformation. When his son Charles I ascended the throne in 1625 and took a French Catholic woman for his wife, proponents of reform feared the worst—a revival of Catholicism. In response to religious developments in England, two factions emerged within the reformation movement. Puritans continued to believe that reform was possible within the Church of England. Separatists, bent on further reformation, argued for complete separation from the established church.

> "The name Puritan is very aptly given to these men . . . because they think themselves . . . more pure than others . . . and separate themselves from all other churches and congregations as spotted and defiled."
>
> JOHN WHITGIFT,
> Elizabethan clergyman, 1573

Plymouth Plantation

In 1608, a large group of Separatists fled to Holland, renowned for its religious toleration and a haven for Protestant dissenters, including other Calvinists from France and England. Life there proved difficult for the English Separatists. The problem was not persecution, but rather the corrupting influences of the affluent urban culture of the Dutch Republic. Describing the Separatists' experience in the Dutch university town of Leiden, William Bradford recalled "the manifold temptations of the place" and expressed particular concern that the Separatists' children would be "drawn away by evil examples into extravagant and dangerous courses." Jan Steen, a Dutch painter who explored the theme of corruption in many of his paintings, captured these fears in his portrayals of Dutch urban life. *Images as History: Corruption versus Piety* examines one of Steen's moralizing paintings about the temptations of Dutch life.

Why were English reformers called Puritans?

Images as History
CORRUPTION VERSUS PIETY

In his painting *The Topsy-Turvy World*, Jan Steen conjures up a chaotic household that seems to be the exact opposite of the ideals of domestic tranquility, godliness, and order. The painting depicts a multitude of sins. The seated couple in the middle represents unbridled sensuality. The duck on the shoulder of the piously dressed man mocks the couple's commitment to religion. Neither man nor woman seems aware of the lewd behavior around them. What moral lessons does this painting teach, and how does the artist represent the vices of city life in Holland?

A small child, unattended, smokes a pipe, while another unsupervised youth steals a coin from a purse in the cupboard against the wall.

The duck on the shoulder of the man mocks his false piety. The man hides his face in his book rather than restore order to the chaos around him.

The immodestly dressed woman in the center of the painting leers at viewers. She rests a wine glass suggestively in the lap of the drunken man seated next to her.

Jan Steen, *The Topsy-Turvy World*

The animals represent vice and disorder. Instead of sitting obediently in the background, the dog scavenges for food on the table, while a pig roots around on the floor for a meal.

What does Jan Steen's painting tell us about the world English Separatists encountered in Holland?

English Separatists living in Leiden decided that life in tolerant, worldly Holland posed too many temptations. A group of the Leiden Separatists, resolving to leave sinful Holland, returned to England briefly before setting out for what they believed to be the unspoiled New World. Later called Pilgrims, a term traditionally used to describe Christians on a spiritual quest for salvation, they set sail for Virginia. After a harrowing two-month journey aboard their ship the *Mayflower*, the Pilgrims found themselves not off Virginia, but rather off the coast of Cape Cod, in what is now Massachusetts, in late fall 1620. William Bradford, their leader, described the experience of arriving safely in America in emotional terms. "Being thus arrived at safe harbor, and brought safe to land," the Pilgrims then "fell upon their knees and blessed the God of Heaven who had brought them over the vast and furious ocean."

Realizing that their company charter was not legally binding on a settlement outside Virginia, they drew up a new political document, the *Mayflower Compact* (1620), that stated the principles that would govern their community. The document asserted that its signers did "solemnly and mutually, in the Presence of God and one another, covenant and combine ourselves together into a civil Body Politick, for our better Ordering and Preservation, and Furtherance of the Ends aforesaid." The agreement also bound those non-Pilgrims traveling to America, including many servants, who promised to abide by the decisions of the community. The Pilgrims named their colony Plymouth after the English port they departed from. Their goal was not religious tolera-tion, but rather Protestant purity. The Pilgrims fled England to create a community purged of all taints of unreformed Catholic practice. Tolerance for what they considered religious error was inconsistent with the goal of creating a pure form of Christian worship.

The world the Pilgrims encountered in Massachusetts had been inhabited by Indians for millennia, but European contact had already irrevocably altered this world. The Indian population of the area had been largely wiped out by the end of the sixteenth century. Contact with European traders and fishing fleets had exposed the Indians of this region to smallpox and other devastating pathogens.

Life in America was hard for the Pilgrims. Half of their complement of just over one hundred men and women died within the first year. The Pilgrims would have all perished had not Squanto, a local Indian from the Patuxet, a tribe decimated by European diseases, befriended them. English traders had kidnapped Squanto years before and taken him to England, where he lived as a slave. Through harrowing events involving two further kidnappings, Squanto eventually returned to New England. His skills as an interpreter and knowledge of Indian agricultural practices proved to be indispensible to the Pilgrims.

A Godly Commonwealth

In 1629, Charles I dissolved Parliament and continued his plans to restore elements of Catholic ritual to the English church, a move that alarmed the Puritans. His disregard of Parliament, which included many Puritan leaders, and his elevation of anti-Puritan bishops in the Church of England struck many reformers as ominous. The same year that Charles I dismissed Parliament, John Winthrop, a member of the Puritan gentry, wrote to his wife that "I am verily persuaded God will bring some heavy affliction upon this land." A year later Winthrop led a group of Puritans to New England where they hoped to create a church and community freed from the corruption Winthrop saw everywhere in England. By the early 1630s, another twenty thousand Puritans would leave England for America. By 1650, the settlers from the Massachusetts Bay Colony had spread out into the Connecticut Valley.

> "For we must consider that we shall be as a city upon a hill. The eyes of all people are upon us. So that if we shall deal falsely with our God in this work we have undertaken, and so cause him to withdraw his present help from us, we shall be made a story and a by-word through the world."
>
> JOHN WINTHROP, Puritan leader, 1630

John Winthrop, who became the first governor of the Massachusetts Bay Colony, captured the Puritan vision of the world when he reminded immigrants to America that they must become "a city upon a hill," an example of true reformation that would guide others toward this holy ideal. Winthrop contrasted the holy purpose of New England's Puritans with earlier colonial efforts in Virginia, which had been driven more by a lust for gold than by love of God. The hardships and failures of Virginia were, according to Winthrop, a direct result of their goals, which were "Carnal and not Religious." Choosing the right type of colonists was also important. Rather than transport "a multitude of rude and misgoverned persons," the Puritans in New England would ensure their success by selecting godly persons and establishing "a right form of government" that would promote their religious mission.

The settlement of Puritan New England differed significantly from that of the Chesapeake. For one, in contrast to the settlers of Virginia, many immigrants to Puritan New England were married. For another, unlike many first Virginians, who were gentlemen, the Puritans came largely from the middling ranks of society, including farmers. In some cases whole Puritan congregations followed their ministers to America during the Great Migration (1630–1642). When these settlers arrived, they did not scatter in search of better lands or access to navigable waters, as did the colonists in the Chesapeake, but remained clustered in towns.

Putting a premium on building stable communities, Puritans settled in towns and villages so that communities would remain cohesive. Typically a Puritan village included a central meetinghouse and a town green. The geographical distribution of population explored in *Envisioning Evidence: Patterns of Settlement in New England and the Chesapeake Compared* shows the difference between Puritan patterns of settlement and those of the Chesapeake. In New England homes clustered close to the center of town, and fields were arranged at the outskirts of these town centers. The meetinghouse, literally the nucleus of the community, served both a religious and a civic function. A 1635 law required that new houses be built within half a mile of the meetinghouse.

Rather than expand the size of towns and allow settlers to spread out and weaken the bond of community, Puritans created new towns and villages. New England's town structure served two critical functions: It enhanced the colonists' ability to defend themselves against Indian attack, and it facilitated the enforcement of communal norms and beliefs. Deviance and misbehavior were easier to control in the small tight-knit towns of New England than in the Chesapeake. In 1630, New England boasted 11 towns. By 1647, the number had tripled to 33 and would rise to more than 100 by 1700.

The family was another building block of Puritan society. Puritans migrated to New England as families, and their conception of the family was designed to further their religious ideals. John Winthrop expressed this view when he noted that "A family is a little common wealth, and a common wealth is a great family." The foundation for this set of beliefs was the Fifth Commandment, which enjoined believers to honor their father and mother. Puritans saw this commandment extending well beyond the requirement of honoring parents. Minister John Cotton reminded his parishioners that the Fifth Commandment applied to "all our Superiors, whether in Family, School, Church, and Commonwealth." In Cotton's view honor meant more than reverence; it also mandated obedience. Taking these words to heart, in 1648 the Massachusetts colonists made disobedience to parents a crime punishable by death. Although this penalty was never applied, it signaled the seriousness with which the Puritans took the idea of patriarchal authority.

The government of the Massachusetts colony evolved out of the joint-stock company used to raise money to fund the Puritans' voyage to the New World. The charter for the company did not require the governing body to remain in England, so Puritan leaders simply set up their own governing body in America. In contrast to England, where property determined the right to vote, Massachusetts allowed all male church members this privilege. Since many of the first generation of settlers were church members, the franchise in Massachusetts was much more inclusive than that in England. Historians estimate that 40 percent of men may have qualified to vote in the 1630s.

Puritan law encouraged sobriety and a strong work ethic and discouraged frivolity. Folk customs that had been traditional parts of religious observances were banned from New England worship. Christmas too was purged of all non-religious

What does John Cotton's interpretation of the Fifth Commandment reveal about Puritan society?

Envisioning Evidence
PATTERNS OF SETTLEMENT IN NEW ENGLAND AND THE CHESAPEAKE COMPARED

Puritan towns were clustered around a meeting house. These buildings served as places of worship and as the political center of the community. The strong pull inward toward a town center with the meeting house at the core is illustrated in the diagram of a typical New England town and the map of Sudbury, Massachusetts (below left). Town ordinances actually forbade settlers from establishing homesteads too far from the meeting house. Settlement in towns helped Puritans preserve their religious mission by enhancing the ability of neighbors to watch one another and report anti-social or religiously disruptive behavior to legal or church authorities. Settlement in the Chesapeake followed a different model. Here the profit motive and the desire to find the most fertile lands and access to navigable rivers pulled settlers outward. The diagram of settlement in the Chesapeake and the map of St. Mary's County in Maryland shows how settlers in the Chesapeake scattered across the area in search of good land and access to waterways they could use to export their cash crops.

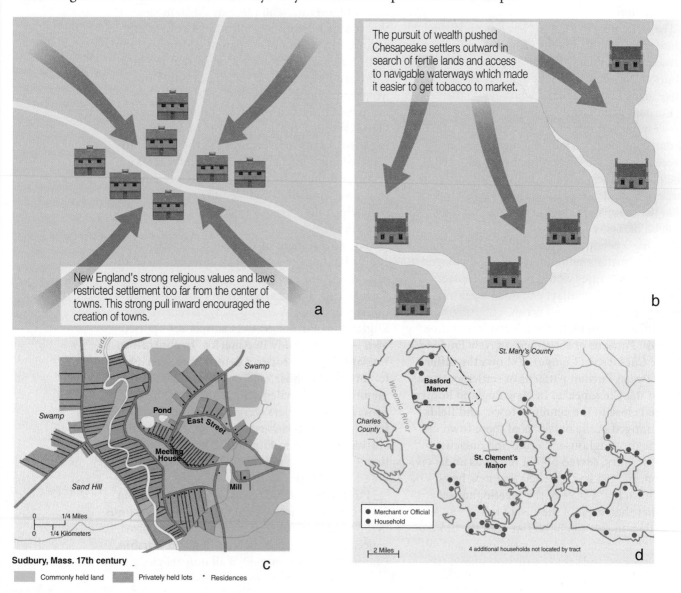

The pursuit of wealth pushed Chesapeake settlers outward in search of fertile lands and access to navigable waterways which made it easier to get tobacco to market.

New England's strong religious values and laws restricted settlement too far from the center of towns. This strong pull inward encouraged the creation of towns.

a

b

Sudbury, Mass. 17th century

c

Commonly held land   Privately held lots   · Residences

Swamp
Pond
East Street
Meeting House
Sand Hill
Mill
0   1/4 Miles
0   1/4 Kilometers

St. Mary's County
Basford Manor
Wicomic River
Charles County
St. Clement's Manor
● Merchant or Official
● Household
2 Miles
4 additional households not located by tract

d

What were the most important differences in the settlement patterns typical of the Chesapeake and New England?

The Vindication of
CHRISTMAS,
OR,
His Twelve Yeares Obſervations upon the
Times, concerning the lamentable Game called Sweep-
ſtake ; acted by General *Plunder*, and Major General *Tax*;
With his Exhortation to the people ; a deſcription of that
oppreſsing Ringworm called *Exciſe* ; and the manner how
our high and mighty Chriſtmas-Ale that formerly would
knock down *Hercules*, & trip up the heels of a Giant, ſtrook
into a deep Conſumption with a blow from *Weſtminſter*.

Keep out, you come not here,

Sir, I bring good cheere.

Old Chriſtmas welcome ; Do not fear.

Imprinted at London for G. Horton, 1653.

2.5 Puritans Chase Away Father Christmas
This anti-Puritan woodcut pokes fun at the Puritans' opposition
to traditional Christmas celebrations, which included drunkenness and too much "mad mirth."

trappings. In this anti-Puritan woodcut (**2.5**),
a Puritan chases away Father Christmas, a cultural figure similar to Santa Claus. Indeed, in the
1650s Puritans outlawed many popular Christmas
customs.

Challenges to Puritan Orthodoxy

Massachusetts sought to enforce orthodoxy
through its laws, the layout of its towns, and the
messages preached by its clergy. Yet, despite these
efforts to enforce conformity the Reformation
vision that animated Puritanism contained radical ideas that threatened the survival of the city
upon a hill. The first great challenge to orthodoxy
in Massachusetts came in 1635 from the devout
Separatist minister Roger Williams. He attacked

the government of Massachusetts Bay for using the
power of the state to enforce religious orthodoxy.
For Williams the goal of creating a purified church
led to the conclusion that government ought not to
meddle in religious affairs. Williams advocated the
complete separation of church and state. Whereas
many modern supporters of the separation of
church and state seek to prevent government from
being influenced by religion, Williams sought the
opposite—to protect religion from possible corruption by government. (For additional discussion, see
*Competing Visions: Antinomianism or Toleration:
The Puritan Dilemma*.) Williams also attacked the
colonists for unjustly seizing Indian lands, a position that proved almost as unpopular as his novel
religious views.

Although Governor John Winthrop of Massachusetts greatly respected Williams for his
intellect and piety, Massachusetts Bay could not
tolerate his direct challenge to the state's authority to enforce religious orthodoxy. Before he could
be arrested, Williams fled the colony and headed
south. He purchased land from the Narragansett
Indians and settled in what is now Rhode Island.
Thankful that God had rescued him from his enemies, Williams named his new settlement "Providence." Eventually he returned to England and in
1644 obtained a parliamentary charter for a new
colony, Rhode Island.

While the Massachusetts Bay Colony was still
reeling from the Williams controversy, a new
challenge to orthodoxy emerged. In 1634, Anne
Hutchinson, the wife of a prominent merchant,
began holding religious meetings in her home. A dynamic speaker and forceful personality, Hutchinson
was also a gifted thinker who did not accept the inferior status that Puritan theology accorded women.
Although she did not directly question the role prescribed for women, her actions implicitly challenged
accepted ideas about gender roles in Puritan society.
Hutchinson also openly questioned the theological
purity of the colony's leading ministers. In her view,
only one minister, John Cotton, was preaching the
true Calvinist idea that only God's grace alone could
bring about salvation. Hutchinson charged the other
ministers with sliding backward toward the notion
that good works could contribute to salvation. Attacking the religious views of the ministry was bad
enough, but for a woman to do so, especially one
who attracted a following among both sexes, was too
much.

The colony's leaders feared that Hutchinson and
her followers had succumbed to the Antinomian

heresy. Antinomians took the logic of Calvinism to its extreme: The elect, if possessed of true saving grace, need not follow earthly laws. If good works really had no connection to salvation then why follow earthly laws? Most Puritans feared that the Antinomian heresy would lead to moral anarchy. (For additional discussion, see *Competing Visions: Antinomianism or Tolerance: The Puritan Dilemma.*) The Puritans also charged Hutchinson with violating the Fifth Commandment by refusing to honor and obey the ministers who were the colony's patriarchs.

In 1637 Hutchinson was hauled before a special court and subjected to a grueling examination. During this ordeal she brilliantly parried virtually all of the questions posed. At the end of her examination, however, she made a serious mistake. When asked how she could be so sure of her actions, she claimed that God spoke directly to her by an immediate revelation. Puritans believed that God spoke to his chosen people only by his revealed word—the Bible—not by direct revelations. For Winthrop and others the claim that God spoke directly to Hutchinson exposed the dangerous Antinomian strain in her thinking. If this was true, anyone, including those who acted immorally, could simply claim to be acting according to a prophetic voice from God. Hutchinson was convicted and banished from Massachusetts Bay Colony. She headed south to Rhode Island, where she and several of her followers sought refuge before eventually settling on what is now Long Island, near the Dutch town of New Amsterdam in the colony of New Netherlands.

While Puritans in New England continued striving to build their city upon a hill and protect it from heresy, Puritans on the other side of the Atlantic had been locked in a protracted political struggle with King Charles I. This led to civil war in 1642. Emerging victorious, Parliament tried the king for crimes against his people and executed him in 1649. The commander of parliamentary forces, Oliver Cromwell, assumed the title of Lord Protector of England with nearly monarchical powers.

While raising an army against the king, Parliament had decided to lift censorship and allow freedom of the press for the first time in English history. To gain popular support and recruit soldiers for their army, Parliament also inaugurated a new policy of religious toleration for all Protestants. With censorship lifted a host of sectarian religious groups emerged during the Civil War. One of these sects, the Society of Friends, or **Quakers**, believed each individual possessed a divine spark

of grace, an inner light that could lead him or her to salvation. The origin of the word *Quaker* is complex. The leader of the Quakers, George Fox, had earned this name when he reminded a magistrate that the righteous ought to "tremble at the word of the Lord." The name stuck because of the nature of Quaker worship. As one contemporary noted, men, women, and children would "fall into quaking fits" in response to the workings of grace within themselves. Quakers rejected the need for any ministry at all. At their meetings anyone who felt the spirit move within them was entitled to preach.

Expansion and Conflict

In contrast to the disease-ridden Chesapeake, New England's environment was reasonably healthy, and the population expanded owing to natural increase. Infant mortality in New England was lower than in England. Although exact figures are difficult to obtain, historians estimate that just over 10 percent of the children born in colonial New England died before their first birthday. The comparable figure in England was about 15 percent. While few people in England lived past middle age, about 50 percent of New Englanders who survived to age 20 would have lived until their late 60s.

New England's growing population combined with the relative longevity of its inhabitants created enormous pressure to acquire additional land so that children could start their own families. Religious leaders played a prominent role in New England's early expansion. The Puritan minister Thomas Hooker led a group of Massachusetts settlers in 1636 and founded the town of Hartford, Connecticut; the Reverend John Davenport left Massachusetts and established the town of New Haven, Connecticut, a year later. In 1638, representatives from Connecticut towns drafted a frame of government, the Fundamental Orders of Connecticut.

Expansion into the Connecticut Valley brought New Englanders into direct conflict with the local Pequot Indians, who refused to submit to English authority. In the resulting fierce war against the Pequots, New Englanders exploited intertribal rivalries to gain an advantage over the Pequots. New Englanders aligned with tribes that sought to take advantage of the colonists' firearms to destroy a rival tribe. The ferocity of English warfare horrified the Narragansett and Mohegan Indians, traditional enemies of the Pequots, who joined forces with the English in the war against the Pequots.

Why was Ann Hutchinson such a threat to the Puritan elite?

Competing Visions
ANTINOMIANISM OR TOLERATION: THE PURITAN DILEMMA

During the English Civil War, English Puritans embraced the idea of religious toleration for all Protestants. New Englanders who continued to oppose such policies gained a reputation for intolerance. Nathaniel Ward, a Massachusetts Puritan, defended New England's polices against English criticism. In New England, Roger Williams, championed the new idea of toleration. For Williams, the religious and secular spheres were entirely separate. Freedom in one sphere had no necessary implications for actions in the other sphere.

In his pamphlet, *The Simple Cobbler of Aggwam*, Nathaniel Ward captured the views of Puritan New Englanders who opposed religious toleration. According to Ward, religious toleration invariably led to ethical relativism and moral anarchy. Without religion to guide behaviour, how could one avoid the temptation to indulge the basest passions?

Wee have beene reputed . . . wild Opinionists, swarmed into a remote wildernes to find elbow-roome for our phanatick Doctrines and practises: I trust our diligence past, and constant sedulity against such persons and courses, will plead better things for us. I dare take upon me, to bee the Herald of New-England so farre, as to proclaime to the world, in the name of our Colony, that all . . . Antinomians, Anabaptists, and other Enthusiasts shall have free Liberty to keepe away from us, and such as will come to be gone as fast as they can, the sooner the better.

That State that will give Liberty of Conscience in matters of Religion, must give Liberty of Conscience and Conversation in their Morall Laws, or else the Fiddle will be out of tune, and some of the strings crack.

Experience will teach Churches and Christians, that it is farre better to live in a State united, though a little Corrupt, then in a State, whereof some Part is incorrupt, and all the rest divided.

The Ranters, a true Antinomian sect that emerged in the chaos of the English Civil War, believed that salvation exempted one from all earthly law, including laws prohibiting sexual misconduct.

Roger Williams followed the logic of Puritanism in a different direction. In his zeal to purify the church, Williams came to believe it was impossible for any earthly power to rid itself of corruption and false piety. To avoid contaminating the purity of religion, he proposed separating church and state. Williams developed the metaphor of the state as a ship. Although passengers were free to worship as they saw fit, this did not exempt them from following the orders of the Captain. Is the metaphor of the ship of state an effective rebuttal to those who feared that liberty would become anarchy?

That ever I should speak or write a title, that tends to such an infinite liberty of conscience, is a mistake, and which I have ever disclaimed and abhorred. To prevent such mistakes, I shall at present only propose this case: There goes many a ship to sea, with many hundred souls in one ship, whose weal and woe is common, and is a true picture of a commonwealth, or a human combination or society. It hath fallen out sometimes, that both papists and protestants, Jews and Turks, may be embarked in one ship; upon which supposal I affirm, that all the liberty of conscience, that ever I pleaded for, turns upon these two hinges—that none of the papists, protestants, Jews, or Turks, be forced to come to the ship's prayers of worship, nor compelled from their own particular prayers or worship, if they practice any. I further add, that I never denied, that notwithstanding this liberty, the commander of this ship ought to command the ship's course, yea, and also command that justice, peace and sobriety, be kept and practiced, both among the seamen and all the passengers.

The Ranters Declaration, 2

WITH

Their new Oath and Protestation; their strange Votes, and a new way to get money; their Proclamation and Summons; their new way of Ranting, *never before heard of*; their dancing of the *Hey* naked, at the white *Lyon* in Peticoat-lane; their mad Dream, and Dr. *Porkridge* his Speech, with their Trial, Examination, and Answers: the coming in of 3000. their Prayer and Recantation, *to be in all Cities and Market-towns read and published*; the mad-Ranters further Resolution; their Christmas Carol, and blaspheming Song; their two pretended-abominable Keyes to enter Heaven, and the worshiping of his little-majesty, the late Bishop of *Canterbury*: A new and further Discovery of their black Art, with the Names of those that are possest by the Devil, having strange and hideous cries heard within them, *to the great admiration of all those that shall read and peruse this ensuing subject.*

Licensed according to order, and published by M. *Stubs*, a late fellow-Ranter

Imprinted at London, by J. C. MDCL. 1650

The Caribbean Colonies

 From England's point of view, the economic jewel in the Atlantic world was not the American mainland, but the Caribbean "sugar islands." Not long after Columbus landed in the Bahamas in 1492, the Spanish established a firm colonial presence in the Caribbean. By the early 1600s, Spain, France, England, and Holland had colonies in the area. The enormous wealth of the "sugar islands" encouraged warfare among these rival colonial powers that resulted in a continuous redrawing of the map, as islands traded hands between different colonial powers (**2.6**). During Cromwell's rule Admiral Sir William Penn seized Jamaica from Spain in 1655, and France took part of Hispaniola (Haiti) in 1664. France and England traded islands such as St. Kitts back and forth for much of the century. Spain conquered the English colony of Providence Island in 1641. The most profitable English sugar colonies were St. Kitts (1624), Barbados (1627), Nevis (1628), Montserrat (1632), Providence Island (1630), Antigua (1632), and eventually Jamaica.

2.6 Caribbean Colonies
The sugar islands of the Caribbean became the most profitable region of the Atlantic economy. Barbados became a major producer of sugar and an example for how slavery could be accommodated to English law.

Power Is Sweet

Although the amount of land that the English cultivated in the Caribbean was small, the region became the richest in the English Atlantic empire. Sugar generated enormous profits for Caribbean planters, exceeding the value of all exports from the mainland colonies. Because of the enormous wealth of the West Indies, roughly two-thirds of all English migrants headed for the Caribbean. By the mid-seventeenth century, the population of this region had reached approximately 44,000, while the population of the Chesapeake was about 12,000 and New England around 23,000.

The wealth produced by sugar could be substantial. Seventeenth-century Europe developed an appetite for sugar that seemed limitless. Besides its use in desserts, sugar was sprinkled on cooked food as a condiment, used to preserve food, and used as medicine to treat afflictions. The use of sugar could also broadcast wealth, social status, or power. Wealthy Europeans displayed lavish sugar sculptures with intricately carved figurines and scenes on banquet tables for guests to admire.

Producing sugar and preparing it for export required a labor force capable of surviving the brutal heat of the Caribbean. Sugar production also entailed backbreaking and dangerous agricultural labor. The multistage process that followed the cutting of the cane required additional labor at every phase. This French engraving (**2.7**) shows the multiple stages of sugar production, including milling and boiling.

Barbados: The Emergence of a Slave Society

The key island economically in the English Caribbean was Barbados. Far from the sea routes plied by Spanish fleets, Barbados avoided the European

Why did the Caribbean become the jewel in the crown of England's colonial empire?

View the **Closer Look** *Sugar and Slavery*

> "I consider the laws concerning Negroes to be reasonable, for by reason of their numbers they become dangerous, being a brutish sort of people and reckoned as goods and chattels [property] in the Island."
>
> Colonial English official, 1680

rivalry and warfare that embroiled other parts of the Caribbean. Visitors to the island often found it "more healthful than any of her neighbors." By 1660, 26,000 English immigrants had settled there, drawn by the promise of wealth through the sugar trade.

Because of the harsh conditions for laborers on Barbados and the high mortality of workers in the sugar fields, maintaining an adequate labor force was a serious problem. During the first decade of colonization, planters in Barbados emulated their countrymen in Virginia, relying heavily on indentured servants as a labor source. Some unfortunate individuals were actually "barbadosed," to use the seventeenth-century phrase that became a synonym for "kidnapped" but originally meant being abducted and transported to the Caribbean to work in the sugar fields. Desperate for workers, planters even tried convict labor. The need for agricultural labor eventually led English planters to emulate the Portuguese and Spanish and turn to slave labor. Within the first decade of turning to sugar production, Barbadian planters bought 20,000 African slaves. Within the colonies of the English Atlantic world, Barbados became the primary destination for African slaves, who outnumbered whites there by 1660.

Spanish and Portuguese law had easily accommodated the institution of slavery. But English law had no precedent upon which to draw in framing a law for slavery. The first efforts to deal with slavery occurred in a piecemeal fashion. Early laws dealt with slave theft and other practical problems, such as slaves wandering off their plantations. By 1661, Barbados had enacted a comprehensive set of laws to govern relations between masters and slaves. The Barbadian slave code created a system of legalized segregation in which race defined servitude. Harsh penalties prevented slaves from challenging the authority of their masters. The legal code also minimized penalties for masters' mistreatment of slaves. Murdering a slave incurred a modest fine, while accidentally killing a slave during punishment carried no legal penalty at all. The Barbadian slave code would provide a model for other areas of the English Atlantic where slavery took hold, including Virginia.

2.7 Sugar Production
This engraving of the various steps in the production of West Indian sugar shows the centrality of black slave labor for sugar agriculture.

Why did Barbados turn to slavery as its primary source of labor?

The Restoration Era and the Proprietary Colonies

2.8 Seventeenth-Century English Mainland Colonies This map shows the Restoration colonies of Carolina, New York, New Jersey, and Pennsylvania. By 1700, England had established its dominance on the eastern seaboard of North America. English control extended from northern New England to the Carolinas.

In 1660, Charles II (r. 1660–1685) reestablished the English monarchy. The **Restoration**, as this period was known, inaugurated a new phase in the evolution of English colonial America. The driving force behind colonization now came from a small group of courtiers, aristocrats close to the king who used their influence to secure colonial charters. In America, building on the model pioneered by Lord Baltimore, these new Restoration-era proprietors sought to increase their wealth while advancing their own particular political and religious ideals. The new colonies also experienced the same type of conflicts that had plagued Maryland. Proprietors struggled to impose their vision of government on settlers who demanded representation. Nevertheless, by 1700, England had cemented its control of the eastern seaboard of America from the Carolinas to northern New England (**2.8**).

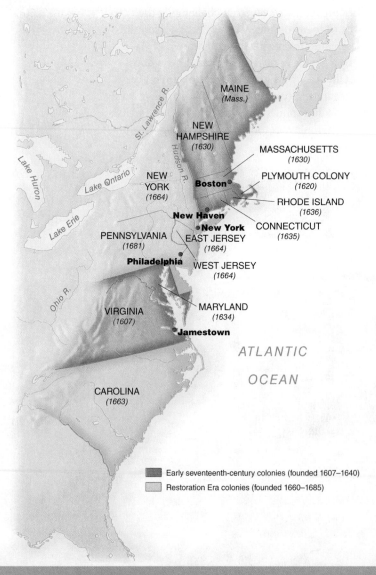

MAINE
(Mass.)

NEW HAMPSHIRE
(1630)

MASSACHUSETTS
(1630)

NEW YORK
(1664)

Boston

PLYMOUTH COLONY
(1620)

RHODE ISLAND
(1636)

New Haven

New York

CONNECTICUT
(1635)

PENNSYLVANIA
(1681)

EAST JERSEY
(1664)

Philadelphia

WEST JERSEY
(1664)

VIRGINIA
(1607)

MARYLAND
(1634)

Jamestown

ATLANTIC

OCEAN

CAROLINA
(1663)

St. Lawrence R.

Lake Huron

Lake Ontario

Lake Erie

Hudson R.

Ohio R.

■ Early seventeenth-century colonies (founded 1607–1640)
■ Restoration Era colonies (founded 1660–1685)

The English Conquest of the Dutch Colony of New Netherland

Along with England the other great Protestant nation in Europe was Holland (the Netherlands), which also engaged in trans-Atlantic trade, including sugar and slaves. Although Dutch merchants traveled the entire Atlantic world, the Dutch had established only a modest presence in North America. The Dutch exploration of the Hudson River (1609) laid the foundation for the colony of New Netherland. The Dutch East India Company established fur-trading outposts in present-day Albany (New York) in 1614. About a decade later the Dutch established a settlement at the tip of Manhattan Island that they called New Amsterdam in honor of Holland's most important city. The Dutch welcomed traders from across Europe and embraced religious toleration. The small but thriving city of New Amsterdam included Dutch, English, Scandinavians, Germans, and Portuguese. By the mid-century, a few Sephardic Jews (Portuguese and Spanish Jews), who had fled persecution in Portuguese Brazil, had also joined the community.

The centrality of the fur trade to the economy of New Amsterdam emerges in this early image of the city. Although the image (**2.9**) does not accurately depict the two Indians, it shows that the wealth of the city depended on the cooperation of Indian trappers. The Hudson River made it easy to ship beaver pelts downriver to New Amsterdam from the area around Albany. Merchants shipped these pelts to Europe, where their fur was prized for hats. This image also features the city's port, a key to its economic vitality.

Unhappy that Dutch merchants in New Netherland were getting rich in the fur trade, English merchants urged the crown to seize the Dutch stronghold. The thriving, long-lived communities of New England had faced the prospect of running out of land, and splinter communities had sprung up in Connecticut and as far south as Long Island, just southeast of New Amsterdam. The expansion of English settlers into the region claimed by the Dutch increased friction between England and Holland.

The prospect of eliminating the Dutch corridor between English settlements in the Chesapeake and New England also appealed to Charles II, and particularly to his brother, James, Duke of York. Charles II gave his brother a charter for the area and dispatched a fleet to seize New Netherland in 1664. Although Peter Stuyvesant, the Dutch governor, tried to rally opposition to the English invasion, Dutch merchants in the city decided that it was better to secure favorable terms from the superior English forces than fight. After their conquest of the Dutch, the English divided the region into two new colonies, New York and New Jersey.

James intended to take firm control of New York. He believed that his role as proprietor gave him almost absolute power over his dominions. Protesting their lack of adequate representation, New Yorkers refused to pay taxes. Eventually James relented, and the first New York assembly convened in 1683.

A Peaceable Kingdom: Quakers in Pennsylvania

After the capture of New Netherland, James granted land that would become New Jersey to courtiers who attracted settlers by promising representation and religious toleration for all Protestants. One of these men, the Quaker William Penn, saw an unprecedented opportunity for creating a religious refuge for members of his faith and others persecuted for their religious

beliefs. Penn's father, Admiral Sir William Penn, had helped wrest Jamaica from the Spanish. The king also owed him a large debt. The king paid this debt with a grant for a large tract of land near New Jersey that became known as Pennsylvania (Penn's woods). As a result of this enormous gift of land, Penn's ambitious plans for Pennsylvania, a colony inspired by his Quaker vision of religious toleration, soon overshadowed his involvement in New Jersey.

One of the few radical sects to survive the English Civil War, Quakers had been persecuted for their beliefs in the Restoration era. Quakers believed individual congregations could conduct their own worship without priests. The group also refused to abide by social customs that demanded individuals show deference to those who stood above them in society. Thus Quakers refused to doff their hats and refrained from using any form of honorific address, such as sir, lord, or lady. Quakers simply addressed each other as thee and thou, terms that sound odd to the modern ear but that signified their belief that everyone was equal before God.

Penn intended Pennsylvania to be a "holy experiment" in which Quakers would live in harmony with those of other faiths. Penn's "peaceable kingdom" also embraced Indians. True to his Quaker principles, Penn resolved to negotiate for Indian lands and submit disputes to arbitration by a committee composed of Indians and Quakers.

2.9 New Amsterdam In this image, a Europeanized-looking Indian man hands a small furry animal to a similarly unrealistic Indian woman. The image captures the importance of the fur trade to the economy of this region.

View the **Map** Atlas Map: Settlement in North America, c. 1660   How did Pennsylvania embody Quaker ideals?

> "Our worthy Proprietor treated the Indians with extraordinary humanity; they became very civil and loving to us, and brought in an abundance of venison."
>
> RICHARD TOWNSEND,
>
> Quaker, 1682

Penn desired to live beside the Indians as "Neighbors and Friends." Penn praised the local Leni-Lenape people for their eloquence and honor and tried to learn their language and customs. During the first generation of settlement, when land was plentiful and the immigrant population small, Pennsylvania upheld Penn's promise to treat the Indians with respect.

In formulating a government for his colony, Penn drew on a number of new ideas in English politics, including the writings of the English political philosopher James Harrington, who believed that a stable society depended on a relatively broad distribution of property. In Harrington's view owning property gave individuals a permanent stake in society and also allowed men to be independent, voting for representatives without being manipulated or intimidated.

The Carolinas

Influential English courtiers, the Lords Proprietors, founded Carolina as a joint effort, hoping to make money and create a buffer between Spanish Florida and other English settlements on the eastern seaboard. Although the Lords Proprietors sought to shape their dominion according to their own vision, the settlers who migrated there had other ideas. From the outset Carolina's fortunes were closely tied to those of the West Indies, Barbados in particular. Many of the colony's first settlers emigrated from the West Indies. Rather than produce goods for export to England, Carolina began as a colony of a colony, providing naval stores such as pine tar resins to waterproof ships and food such as cattle for the West Indian islands.

The Lords Proprietors had studied New England and Virginia and had concluded that New England-style towns were superior to the "inconvenience and Barbarisme of scattered Dwellings" that characterized settlement in the Chesapeake. The visions of Lords Proprietors and the interests and aspirations of the colonists clashed. Rather than settle in the New England-style nucleated villages (villages with a town center) as the proprietors had hoped, settlers followed the Chesapeake model, scattering to find the most productive land and, when available, access to navigable waterways. In 1712, the proprietors divided their holdings into two colonies, North Carolina and South Carolina. The crown took over South Carolina in 1719 and North Carolina a decade later.

The close economic ties between Carolina and Barbados meant that its early settlers were well acquainted with slavery. But the settlers who tried to impose the West Indies' slave system on the frontier environment of Carolina discovered problems they had not anticipated. The rude conditions of early Carolina history, its small population and simple economy, made it harder to maintain social distance between slaves and their masters. The Carolinas were at the edge of English America. Their proximity to Spanish-controlled Florida and hostile Indian tribes meant that slaves and masters had to work closely together, including defending settlements against attack. The location of the Carolinas also encouraged a less exploitive form of slavery, as slaves in the Carolinas had more opportunities to run away and might find refuge with Indian tribes. By contrast apart from a few mountainous regions on islands such as Jamaica, the West Indies afforded few sanctuaries for runaway slaves.

Relations with local Indian tribes were complex. Conflicts among Indian tribes provided early Carolina colonists with an unexpected economic boon: The sale of Indian slaves became a lucrative enterprise. Indians sold prisoners they had taken during intertribal warfare to the English, who then exported them to other British colonies. Carolinians also traded with Indian tribes for deer hides, which were exported to England. At the start of the eighteenth century these exports were surpassed by a new crop, rice, which was developed with help from agricultural knowledge brought to America by African slaves. Carolina began as a colony of a colony but soon became an integral part of the Atlantic economy, exporting slaves, deer hides, and eventually rice.

How did the Restoration-era colonies differ from earlier colonies on the issue of religious toleration?

View the **Closer Look** *Competing Visions: Lord Baltimore and William Penn: Two Visions of Religious Toleration*

The Crises of the Late Seventeenth Century

The last quarter of the seventeenth century was a period of unrest in colonial North America. Religious and ethnic tensions sometimes produced political volatility. In Spanish New Mexico, and in English New England and Virginia, Europeans were pitted against indigenous populations. In Maryland animosities between the Catholic proprietor and a largely Protestant population caused friction. In New York divisions between the Dutch and the English kept old wounds open. In New York and Maryland, the tensions triggered a crisis that led to government reorganization. Other forces were at work as well. Relations between the English and the Indians had settled into a pattern of mutual suspicion and antagonism. Colonial governors became entangled in mediating disputes between land-hungry settlers and tribes eager to fend them off. Seeing the brutality of Anglo-Indian warfare, many witnesses who testified at the Salem witchcraft trials envisioned the devil as a tawny-skinned tormentor whose tortures resembled those used by Indians on their enemies. Finally at the end of the seventeenth century, the political realignment associated with the Glorious Revolution in England helped usher in a new era of political stability in the colonies.

War and Rebellion

In New England relations with the Wampanoag Indians, who had helped the Pilgrims, had deteriorated since both groups sat down for their harvest feast in 1621. The Wampanoag leader, Metacom, whom the colonists sometimes called King Philip, grew frustrated with English expansion and eventually led the Wampanoags in King Philip's War against New Englanders. The fierce fighting spread across New England, with hardly a town escaping the conflict. Nearly 3,000 Indians died in the conflict and almost 1,000 colonists. This map shows the devastating impact of the war, which ravaged dozens of towns in New England (**2.10**).

Puritans interpreted the ferocity as a sign of God's displeasure. Increase Mather, a leading Puritan minister, reported that after the war ended, the government of Massachusetts appointed a committee to promote "a Reformation of those Evils which hath provoked the Lord to bring the sword upon us." Among the causes of God's displeasure, Mather listed drunkenness; the presence of "heretical" sects, such as the Quakers; an obsession with material profit; and a loss of modesty demonstrated by attention to fashion, especially "excesses in Apparel and hair."

In the Chesapeake tensions between colonists and Indians also led to violence. In Virginia, **Bacon's Rebellion**, a popular uprising named after its leader,

Nathaniel Bacon, erupted in 1676. The royal governor, Sir William Berkeley, had long played favorites, dealing out lucrative patronage positions and generous land grants to his cronies. The governor had also made a handsome profit from the fur trade with Indians. Frustrated by Berkeley's policies, Bacon, a relative newcomer to the colony and a distant relative of the governor, decided to challenge Berkeley's corruption and favoritism. Finding a common enemy, the area's Indians, Bacon attracted a broad range of Virginians to his cause.

He drew some support from planters frustrated with Berkeley's favoritism and landowners frustrated by the governor's refusal to adopt a more expansionist policy and acquire additional Indian land for settlement. He drew the bulk of his supporters, however, from the bottom ranks of Virginia society, including indentured servants and slaves. Promising to exterminate Indians and distribute land to all, Bacon exploited the deep class resentments that had smoldered for a long time in the Chesapeake region. The success of Bacon forced Berkeley to flee to the eastern shore of the Chesapeake. Buoyed by popular support, Bacon torched the colony's capital, Jamestown. Bacon's rising star faded almost as quickly as it rose when he died from fever, leaving the rebellion leaderless. Berkeley, returning with reinforcements, easily defeated the remnants of Bacon's followers.

A commission investigating the causes of the uprising concluded that the "giddy headed multitude"

What were the main causes of Bacon's Rebellion?

2.10 King Philip's War
This map suggests the scale of the conflict between Indians and Puritans during King Philip's War.

attracted to Bacon's Rebellion was largely composed of men "lately crept out of the condition of servants." For the colony's leaders an especially troubling aspect of the rebellion was the interracial solidarity among servants, including whites serving temporary indentures and Africans slaves. Indeed, one group of rebels was composed of 80 blacks and 20 whites.

Slavery in Virginia began as a legally amorphous category. Earlier in the century some slaves had managed to acquire their freedom, either through grants from their master or through their own resourcefulness. One slave who took advantage of the earlier laxity in the law was Anthony Johnson, who became a planter himself. By the eve of Bacon's Rebellion, Virginia's laws regarding slavery had hardened into an almost impenetrable barrier preventing slaves from

achieving what Anthony Johnson had attained— freedom. Bacon's Rebellion accelerated these changes, driving Virginia to invest more heavily in slaves. The danger posed by a "giddy multitude" of landless laborers, whose frustration so-called rabble-rousers such as Nathaniel Bacon could exploit, hastened the shift away from use of indentured servants to African slaves, who would remain a permanent underclass.

Economic and demographic forces also pushed Virginia toward a slave-based economy. Among these the number of immigrants into the Chesapeake declined during the late seventeenth century, reducing the available work-force. As the price of slaves decreased and the high levels of mortality in the region, including of slaves, dropped, purchasing slaves became more economical. Previously there had been little in-

What economic and demographic forces contributed to the emergence of slavery in the Chesapeake region?

Read the Document *Nathaniel Bacon's Declaration (1676)*

centive to purchase a slave for almost twice the price of an indentured servant if the slave was unlikely to live long enough to make the difference in price economically advantageous. At mid-century a mere 300 slaves resided in the Chesapeake. By 1700, there were 13,000.

England's colonies were not the only ones rocked by unrest at the end of the seventeenth century. Other parts of the Atlantic colonial world experienced similar unrest. In Spanish New Mexico disputes culminated in the Pueblo Revolt (1680). In New Spain Indians were pitted against the Roman Catholic Church. Dispirited by droughts and attacks by Apache and Navajo war parties, the Pueblo people sought solace in their traditional religious practices and turned away from the Catholicism of their Spanish conquerors. Fearing a challenge to their authority, the Spanish Catholic missionaries in New Mexico brought the full force of church and state power against these "heretics." Rather than accept the new wave of repression, Indians rose up against Spanish authority, killing most of the missionaries and more than 400 settlers. The rebellion drove the Spanish from New Mexico for more than a decade. However, divisions within the Pueblo community and continuing drought hampered the ability of the Pueblo people to resist Spanish power indefinitely. When the Spanish returned 13 years later, they easily reconquered New Mexico.

The Pueblo revolt forced the Spanish to be more tolerant, at least to Indians who accepted Christianity. They could retain elements of their traditional religious practices and culture, including the use of Shamans, or religious healers. The Spanish also reformed the system of forced labor, which improved the Indians' economic situation.

The Dominion of New England and the Glorious Revolution

Although the Pueblo Revolt demonstrated that even Spain's hierarchical colonial empire was not immune from strife, many close to King Charles II of England, including his brother James envied the Spanish model of empire. In 1685, Charles died without a legitimate son, and James II became England's first Catholic monarch in 127 years. As Duke of York, James had been closely involved in colonial affairs in New York,

and he hoped to consolidate the English colonies into larger administrative units with powerful governors similar to those in New Spain. He therefore revoked the colonial charters of New York and New Jersey, folding them into New England as a single new administrative and political entity, the Dominion of New England. A powerful English governor and a council appointed by the king would rule this Spanish-style dominion. Representative assemblies were abolished, and a reorganized legal system made it more difficult for colonists to have access to the courts. To extract additional wealth from the colonists, the colonial government raised taxes dramatically and revoked land deeds. To regain title to their own land, colonists would have to obtain new deeds and pay new taxes on land.

James II had a bold agenda to strengthen royal power at home as well. He sought to ally England with Catholic France. James supported religious toleration for Catholics and Dissenters, but sought to impose this policy by royal decree, thus alienating potential support among Dissenters who were sympathetic to these policies. Even more troubling was his attempt to weaken the militia and raise a standing army, which included appointing Catholic officers loyal to the crown. Finally, James attempted to bypass Parliament and raise revenues through taxation. When Parliament refused to accept his agenda, James dissolved it. In the autumn of 1688, English opponents of the king allied with the Protestant Dutch Prince William of Orange and ousted James from the throne. William, whose English wife, Mary, was James's daughter, reestablished a Protestant monarchy. The relatively bloodless revolution that led to the ascension of William III and Mary II was proclaimed a **Glorious Revolution** and a vindication of English liberty. Indeed, the association between the Glorious Revolution and English liberty was literally cast in metal. The commemorative medallion (**2.11**) produced for

2.11 Glorious Revolution Commemorative Medal
In this medal commissioned to commemorate the ascension of William and Mary to England's throne and the Glorious Revolution, Britannia, symbol of England, sits under an orange tree, which was the symbol of William of Orange. She grasps a liberty pole firmly in her hand, a reminder that William restored English liberty.

What was the Glorious Revolution?

the occasion depicts Britannia, symbol of England. She sits under an orange tree, the symbol of the Prince of Orange. Britannia grasps a liberty pole and has her hand on the Bible. The Latin inscription announces that "the Prince of Orange restores the law to us."

William and Mary accepted Parliament's "Act Declaring the Rights and Liberties of the Subject and Settling the Succession of the Crown," more generally known as the English Bill of Rights. This act excluded Catholics from the monarchy, affirmed the supremacy of Parliament, protected basic rights, and asserted "That excessive bail ought not to be required, nor excessive fines imposed, nor cruel and unusual punishments inflicted." It also affirmed that "the subjects which are Protestants may have arms for their defense suitable to their condition and as allowed by law." Restricted to Protestants, this particular right was further limited by social class and ultimately subject to Parliament's right to regulate arms. Taken together the various provisions became an important rallying point for those seeking to limit government power and protect liberty.

While official word of the Glorious Revolution took time to reach the colonies, rumors about the ascension of William and Mary arrived in spring 1689. In the colonies the right to have arms for self-defense was an absolute necessity and the militia was an important local institution. In April 1689, 2,000 militiamen, mostly from country towns, marched on Boston, arrested the governor, and restored their old charter. In late May New York's militia took control of that colony. In Maryland John Coode marched with 700 militiamen to "vindicate and assert the Sovereign Dominion and right of King William and Mary." Protestant resentment against the power of the Catholic proprietary government also fueled Coode's rebellion. The Glorious Revolution in America was a victory for representative government, and the notion that a well-regulated militia under local control was the best protection for liberty.

The Salem Witchcraft Hysteria

Within a decade of the close of King Philip's War (1675), New Englanders were again at war with their Indian neighbors, this time in Maine along the northern border of Massachusetts. Fighting was fierce, and Maine's proximity to French Quebec led English colonists to see their latest troubles as part of a French Catholic plot against Protestant New England. Colonists in Massachusetts even accused the Indians of using witchcraft against them. Complicating matters, the recent upheavals of the Glorious Revolution had not yet produced a stable government, and a new royal governor had yet to be appointed in Massachusetts.

Amid this heightened anxiety came the most serious outbreak of witchcraft accusations in colonial America. The center of the witchcraft hysteria was Salem, Massachusetts, but the accusations spread throughout Essex, the coastal county closest to Maine. Before the witchcraft prosecutions ended, 19 innocent men and women would be executed, and one man who refused to plead either innocent or guilty suffered an archaic penalty, heavy stones were piled on his chest to force him to plead. Rather than enter a plea, he was crushed to death.

The Puritans who inhabited this region thought themselves an especially attractive target for Satan, who would, they believed, have been eager to upset their effort to build a city upon a hill. New England's covenant with God was mirrored in Satan's own demonic contracts with witches. To seal these contracts, New Englanders believed, Satan made his disciples sign his book, a belief reflected in this seventeenth-century woodcut, which shows the devil offering his disciples his book to sign (**2.12**).

The witchcraft hysteria began in Salem Village, the outlying part of the port of Salem town. The first purported occurrence of witchcraft occurred in the home of Minister Samuel Parris, whose daughter and her cousin, Abigail Williams, began acting strangely. After consulting a physician, who could find no explanation for his daughter's illness, Parris concluded that the girls were victims of witchcraft. When questioned, the girls accused two Salem women and Tituba, a Caribbean Indian slave whom Parris owned, of practicing witchcraft. Parris forced a confession from Tituba. The accusations eventually engulfed the whole community. The scope of the witch hunt changed dramatically when the accusations spread to another local minister, George Burroughs, who had recently returned from Maine. Much of the testimony from that point forward concerned the Devil taking the shape of an American

New Englanders believed that the Devil made his minions sign a book or contract for what purpose?

2.12 Signing Satan's Book In this rough woodcut image, Satan presents his book to a witch. Puritans believed that the devil required individuals to renounce their covenant with God and sign a new contract with Satan.

Indian, creating another theme in the witchcraft hysteria. The Puritans even compared the suffering they believed that Satan inflicted on them with how Indians tortured settlers in the brutal frontier war in Maine.

Historians have identified a number of patterns in the web of accusations. Witches in New England were more likely to be women, particularly older women who did not live in male-headed households. Women who failed to fit the model of the pious, submissive female, ruled by a benevolent patriarch, an ideal that Puritans esteemed, were particularly at risk.

Pressure to stop the trials mounted, particularly after accusations were leveled at more prominent individuals from outside Salem. At the start of the trials, ministers had approved the use of spectral evidence—testimony that witches were using magic to torture victims. But as Rebecca Nurse argued during her trial, verifying such evidence was impossible. How, she asked the court, could one know if spectral evidence was genuine? Could not Satan appear at a trial to confound the court and trick them into accusing the wrong person? Doubts began to trouble leading ministers in the colony, including Increase Mather, who had been an early supporter of the prosecutions. Mather delivered a sermon stating a principle that became a bedrock of Anglo-American law: "It were better that ten suspected witches should escape, than that one innocent person should be condemned." The new royal governor, William Phips. replaced the court that had handled the witchcraft trials with a new court whose guidelines followed more recent English law and disallowed convictions based on spectral evidence.

What was spectral evidence?

The Whig Ideal and the Emergence of Political Stability

 The Massachusetts legal system that produced the Salem witchcraft trials was out of step with legal developments in England, and even more so in light of the events of the Glorious Revolution (1688). The English Bill of Rights adopted by Parliament (1689) not only weakened royal power but also provided stronger protections for individual liberty, including explicit prohibitions on cruel and unusual punishments and a more robust affirmation of the right to a jury trial.

In the long struggle between Parliament and the monarchy, Parliament had finally emerged as preeminent in the English political and constitutional system. The group that supported Parliamentary power after the Glorious Revolution became known as **Whigs**. Their opponents, the Tories, were proponents of monarchical authority. The period after the Glorious Revolution ushered in relative political stability in Anglo-American politics. This new era of stability did not end political debate, but it marked clear boundaries for future discussions.

The Whig Vision of Politics

Whig theory, put into place after the Glorious Revolution, put a premium on the ideal of civic virtue, placing the public good above personal interest. To promote such virtue, one needed a society in which property ownership was widespread. An agricultural nation, where farming was thought to encourage honesty, frugality, and independence, was less likely to become corrupt than a society dependent on commerce and manufacturing. In an agrarian society politics would be less fractious because everyone's interest would be similar. In such a society representatives would be equally affected by whatever laws they passed. This would prevent them from tyrannizing over the people by passing oppressive laws.

The Whig view of politics was not democratic. It assumed that only men who owned property had a sufficient permanent stake in society to be trusted with the vote. (The few women who owned property, mostly widows, were not allowed to vote.) According to Whig thought, only the best—most virtuous—men would serve as representatives. The notion of frequent elections became a cornerstone of Whig politics. The great danger, however, lay in the potential for electoral corruption, as reflected in this political cartoon (**2.13**), which shows voters being bribed outside a tavern. The fear of corruption became an important feature of Whig political culture, underscoring the need for a virtuous elite and an electorate that could not be manipulated by unscrupulous politicians.

The Glorious Revolution also affected English law. England had no written constitution, but the common law, the unwritten rules of law worked out over a centuries by English courts, embodied many of the essential liberties esteemed by Englishmen. To these protections Parliament had added the Bill of Rights of 1689, which would strongly influence the worldview of colonists in America. By asserting the ideal of the rule of law, the Glorious Revolution established the principle that no one, not even the king, was above the law. The revolution also lodged the right to tax firmly in the representative branch of government, Parliament, and it rejected the practice of raising a standing army, which was considered a serious threat to liberty, without the consent of the legislature. Among the other provisions protected by the Bill of Rights were the rights to petition government for redress of grievances, trial by jury, and bail, and a prohibition on cruel and unusual punishments. A century later, the U.S. Constitution's Bill of Rights codified and expanded these ideals.

Ready Mony the prevailing Candidate, or the Humours of an Election. 1727

2.13 English Whig Cartoon on Electoral Corruption
In this early political satire of an English election, the electorate mill about waiting to be bribed by a candidate. The text below the scene warned of the dangers of "flattery and gold" which cause men to be corrupted and "liberty sold".

Mercantilism, Federalism, and the Structure of Empire

In 1651, the Parliament passed the first navigation act designed to limit the profitable Dutch trade with the English colonies. The act required that all goods entering or leaving colonial ports be carried on English or colonial ships and that non-English goods be carried on English ships or ships of the country from which the goods originated. Parliament passed even more restrictive navigation acts in 1660, 1663, 1673, and 1696. These acts required that all goods be transported on American or English carriers, which meant goods from other parts of Europe had to transit through English ports before arriving in the colonies. In 1696, Parliament also created the Board of Trade to help coordinate policy toward the colonies. Three years later Parliament passed the Woolens Act, to protect the English woolen industry from competition from Ireland and the colonies. The act did not ban Americans from making and selling woolens within the colonies, but it prohibited them from exporting woolens to England.

The great eighteenth-century Scottish economist Adam Smith called this economic system **mercantilism**. According to mercantilist theory the wealth of the "mother" country England would be increased by heavy governmental regulation of imports and exports to the colonies. Colonies existed to generate wealth for their mother country by supplying it with raw materials and purchasing consumer goods from it. To enforce its mercantile policies, Parliament used legislation such as the navigation acts to control colonial behavior. It also created admiralty courts to try violations of the laws governing commerce.

In 1707, the Act of Union united the kingdoms of Scotland and England, creating the United Kingdom of Great Britain. The act also divided power in the new British Empire between local and imperial authority. Colonial assemblies continued to legislate on local matters, and Parliament exercised powers over the whole empire. In essence British government had created a federal system that divided power between a distant central authority and local governments. This system of divided authority paved the way for the modern U.S. division between national authority (seated in Washington, D.C.) and the individual state governments.

> "The encouragement of exportation and the discouragement of importation [of manufactured goods] are the two great engines by which the mercantile system proposes to enrich every country."
> ADAM SMITH, *The Wealth of Nations*, 1776

What was the theory of mercantilism?

1607

Founding of Jamestown
First successful English colony in America

1613

John Rolfe exports first tobacco crop from Virginia
The struggling Jamestown colony finally finds a cash crop for export

1620

***Mayflower Compact* signed**
Pilgrims arrive in Massachusetts without a legal title to the land and frame their own government

1634–1638

Colony of Maryland established
First proprietary colony

Roger Williams founds Providence
First colony founded on religious toleration established in colonial America

Anne Hutchinson banished to Rhode Island
Antinomian controversy ends

Review Questions

1. How do you account for the early failures of Jamestown and its eventual successes?

2. Why were the patterns of settlement in the Chesapeake and New England so different? What forces and ideas shaped the spatial organization of each region?

3. Why was the term *Puritan* an apt characterization of the Calvinists within the English church seeking further reformation?

4. What role did conflicts with Native Americans play in the crisis of the latter part of seventeenth century?

5. What ideas and values were most closely associated with Whig politics?

Key Terms

Headright An incentive system to encourage additional immigrants by giving 50 acres to any man who would pay his own fare to Virginia and 50 additional acres for each person brought with him.　**40**

Proprietor This English legal title carried with it enormous political power, giving its possessor almost king-like authority over his domains. Colonial proprietors carried similar powers.　**40**

Quakers The Society of Friends, who believed each individual possessed a divine spark of grace, an inner light that could lead to salvation.　**48**

Restoration In 1660 Charles II became king of England, restoring the monarchy to power after the Civil War and Cromwellian rule.　**52**

Bacon's Rebellion A popular uprising in Virginia in 1676 named after its leader, Nathaniel Bacon.　**55**

Glorious Revolution The relatively bloodless revolution that led to the ascension of William and Mary, which was widely seen as a vindication for English liberty.　**57**

Whigs (English, 17th Century) The group that supported parliamentary power after the Glorious Revolution.　**60**

Mercantilism Theory of empire that advocated strict regulation of trade between colonies and the mother country to benefit the latter.　**61**

CHAPTER REVIEW

1642

English Civil War
English Puritans under Oliver Cromwell take up arms against Charles I

1664–1681

England captures New Netherland, which is renamed New York
James, Duke of York, gains control of New York and New Jersey

William Penn obtains royal charter for Pennsylvania
Quaker William Penn founds Pennsylvania

1688

Glorious Revolution in England
William and Mary ascend to the throne, and Whig political ideals triumph

1692

Salem Witchcraft Trials
A witchcraft hysteria engulfs Salem Village and Salem town

MyHistoryLab Connections

Visit www.myhistorylab.com for a customized Study Plan that will help you build your knowledge of *Models of Settlement*.

Questions for Analysis

1. **Why did relations between the English and Indians deteriorate so quickly in the seventeenth century?**

   View the **Closer Look** The Chickahominy Become "New Englishmen", *p. 36*

2. **What were the most important differences between the Chesapeake colonies and New England?**

   Read the **Document** Profile: John Winthrop, *p. 45*

3. **Why did the Caribbean become the jewel in the crown of England's colonial empire?**

   View the **Closer Look** Sugar and Slavery, *p. 50*

4. **Why did the Restoration-era colonies adopt a more expansive view of toleration?**

   View the **Closer Look** Competing Visions: Lord Baltimore and William Penn: Two Visions of Religious Toleration, *p. 54*

5. **What legal ideas were associated with the Glorious Revolution?**

   Read the **Document** English Bill of Rights (1689), *p. 60*

Other Resources from This Chapter

Read the **Document**

- Mayflower Compact, *p. 43*
- *John Winthrop*, A Model of Christian Charity, *p. 44*
- *"John Calvin: On Predestination," p. 49*
- *Nathaniel Bacon's Declaration (1676), p. 56*

View the **Image** Powhatan in Longhouse, *p. 37*

View the **Map**

- *European Empires in 1660, p. 52*
- *Atlas Map: Settlement in North America, c. 1660, p. 53*

Culture and Society in the Eighteenth Century p. 66

In what ways did American colonial society become more English in the first part of the eighteenth century?

Enlightenment and Awakening p. 72

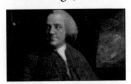

What were some of the main ideas of the Enlightenment?

African Americans in the Colonial Era p. 77

What forces contributed to the growth of the African American population of colonial America?

Immigration, Regional Economies, and Inequality p. 83

What role did economic forces play in the emergence of distinctive regional cultures in eighteenth-century America?

War and the Contest over Empire p. 87

How did the French and Indian War transform the map of North America?

Growth, Slavery, and Conflict

Colonial America, 1710–1763

Life in the seventeenth-century American colonies, even for the wealthiest, was crude and primitive. Beginning in the eighteenth century, however, a more cosmopolitan and refined culture began to emerge. Prosperous colonists sought out the latest British and European consumer goods, such as finely woven Turkish or English carpets, tea sets, and pattern books of English architectural and furniture styles.

Captain Archibald Macpheadris, a fur trader in Portsmouth, New Hampshire, built an elegant new house in 1716, complete with beautifully executed wall murals, signifying his wealth and refinement. One of the most striking murals depicted two Mohawk Indian chiefs. The unknown painter copied these images from an engraving of a group of Indians who had traveled to London to meet with Queen Anne (r. 1703–1714). The engraver and the painter included authentic elements, such as the tomahawk wielded by the Indian on the right. Yet the image of the Indians also reflected the conventions of European painting: The position of the Mohawk "Indian Kings' " hands at their hip resembled a common aristocratic pose found in English portraits from this period.

Books, newspapers, and letters all were part of the expanding commerce of the Atlantic world, This economy included a lively exchange of ideas on a wide array of subjects, including architecture, fashion, politics, religion, science, and philosophy. One highly influential set of ideas was associated with the **Enlightenment** and its ideals of reason and social progress. These ideas fostered new social experiments, such as the founding of the colony of Georgia.

Religious ideas also crossed the Atlantic. The English evangelical minister George Whitefield crisscrossed the colonies from New Hampshire to Georgia. His tour helped spread the ideas of the religious revival movement known as the **Great Awakening.** Enlightenment ideals of liberty, human dignity, and progress and new religious ideas led some Americans to question the institution of slavery, despite its growing importance to the colonial economy. The stark contrast between the wealthy planters and wretchedly housed slaves was not the only divide in American life. As the overall wealth of the colonies increased, so did the disparity between the wealthy and the poor.

Land itself became scarce by the mid-eighteenth century. Expansion westward was hampered by the Appalachian Mountains, and the French and a host of Indian tribes controlled the rich lands of what is now America's Midwest. Ultimately the balance of power in North America was decided by the French and Indian War.

> "In 1740, I don't remember [seeing] such a thing as a [Turkish] carpet in the country. . . . Now nothing are so common as [Turkish] or [English] Carpets, the whole furniture of the Roomes Elegant & every appearance of opulence."
>
> JOHN WAYLES, future father-in-law of Thomas Jefferson, 1766

Culture and Society in the Eighteenth Century

As trade expanded with Britain, colonists strove to emulate the culture and sophistication of the mother country. New and grander houses, filled with the latest European-style furnishings, testified to the growing sophistication of the colonies. Yet while the colonies were striving to become more British, they were also developing their own distinctly American political culture and institutions. A native-born elite emerged, an American gentry class whose wealth, confidence, and education inspired them to become leaders in the colonial assemblies. A distinctive American style of politics had begun to take shape.

The Refinement of America

At the end of the seventeenth century, even the homes of the most prosperous families in colonial America had few imported luxury goods. The sparse furnishing of the Hart Room (**3.1**), now in the Metropolitan Museum of Art in New York City, capture the primitive nature of late seventeenth-century American homes. Thomas Hart, a landowner in Ipswich, Massachusetts, built his house in 1639 and furnished it in the ensuing decades. This parlor, the best room in the house, usually served as both a bedroom and a communal living space. Information from probates, a list of goods assembled as part of a will, suggests that homeowners furnished even the best parlor rooms sparsely, with simple tables and cupboards. The furniture's simplicity and boxy look reflected prevailing styles and the scarcity of skilled craftsmen in the colonies at the time. The walls were generally whitewashed, with no ornamentation; the post and beams used to support the walls and the roof were clearly visible.

Colonial culture began to change with the expansion of commerce at the start of the eighteenth century. America became more fully integrated into the Atlantic economy, a huge triangle that stretched from Scotland to Africa to the interior of the British mainland colonies (**3.2**). Trade in the Atlantic world involved a staggering array of goods. Scottish merchants purchased Virginia tobacco, which was sold throughout Europe. Another side of the triangle tied New England merchants to West Indian sugar planters. West Indian sugar was distilled into rum by New Englanders. Some of this alcohol was traded to Indians in the lucrative beaver trade in upstate New York. These beaver furs were often used in hats and sometimes ended up in London or on the European continent.

By the early eighteenth century, expanding trade with the British Empire increased the number of wealthy colonists and brought a flood of new luxury goods into affluent American homes.

3.1 The Hart Room, Metropolitan Museum of Art
The simple whitewashed walls and exposed beams in this prosperous seventeenth-century room and the simple boxy style of its furniture were typical of the lack of ornamentation in this era.

Define Anglicization and give an example of an aspect of colonial life transformed by this process.

Acquiring such goods allowed individuals and families to demonstrate that they were not simple provincials; they were part of a wider cosmopolitan world. Rather than eat with simple earthenware ceramics, as their forebears had, the wealthiest Americans now aspired to dine on fine porcelain imported from England or Holland. Refined taste was proof of gentility, a term that became synonymous with the attributes associated with wealth and sophistication. American society underwent a process of **Anglicization** as colonists emulated English society, including its tastes in furniture, foods, clothing, and customs.

Nothing better captured the rise of gentility and the increasing Anglicization of colonial America than the rage for imported tea. As the consumption of tea increased dramatically between the end of the seventeenth century and the dawn of the eighteenth, the rituals of serving tea became more refined and complicated. Serving tea to one's guests became essential. Although tea drinking started among the wealthy, it gradually spread to all levels of American society. By the mid-eighteenth century, tea drinking had evolved from a luxury to a necessity, so much so that inmates in the Philadelphia poorhouse demanded that their meager rations include tea.

The Verplank Room (**3.3**) in the Metropolitan Museum of Art contains furniture from the New York City townhouse of Samuel Verplank and the country house of Cadwallader Colden Jr. in Orange, New York. In contrast to the simple whitewashed walls of the seventeenth-century Hart Room, the Verplank Room has painted wood paneling. The elegant card table in the Verplank Room is one of many specialized pieces of furniture likely to have adorned a prosperous home in the mid-eighteenth century. The Verplanks, Coldens, and other genteel families would each have owned an imported china set and tea table as well.

Changes in furnishing provide insights into deeper changes in colonial society. The rising popularity of writing desks and drop-leaf bookcases with writing surfaces (see detail in 3.3) reflected the expansion of trade networks in the British Empire. Merchants needed to keep better track of a variety of written documents as they broadened the range of their correspondence on business and political matters.

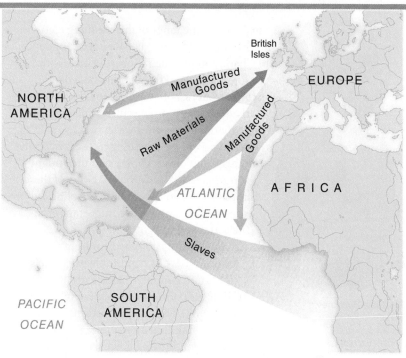

3.2 The Triangle Trade
The Atlantic economy can be visualized as a triangle. Goods from Europe were sold or traded in America or Africa. Raw materials from the Americas were sold in Europe. European goods were sold or traded for African slaves who were then shipped to the Americas.

3.3 The Verplank Room, Metropolitan Museum of Art
The highly specialized furniture reflected the growing wealth of many colonists and the Anglicization of colonial culture. In the inset image of a secretary bookcase, note the drop-leaf writing surface and cubbyholes that made this piece of furniture well adapted to the needs of merchants.

View the **Closer Look** *Images as History: A Portrait of Colonial Aspiration*

Why did new pieces of furniture like drop-leaf bookcases become popular in the eighteenth century?

An insight into the range of this far-flung commerce comes from the extensive correspondence of Charleston merchant Robert Pringle with business associates throughout the Atlantic world, from Lisbon, Portugal to London and Barbados to Boston. The entrepreneurial Pringle experimented with a variety of desirable agricultural imports, including pistachios, Seville oranges, and olives, hoping that they might be produced in the Carolinas. None of these imports took hold, but South Carolina did provide Europe with two important products, rice and indigo.

For wealthy colonists nothing was more effective at communicating one's riches and gentility than a formal portrait in the latest English style. Following the conventions of European portraits, men and women struck standard aristocratic poses; elegant ladies dressed in flowing gowns, mimicking the style of their monarch, Queen Anne. Men and even young boys were painted wearing elegant outfits that reflected their wealth, status, and power. The portrait of the young Henry Darnall III, one of the earliest done in the American South, testifies to the growing wealth and refinement of the colonial elite (see *Images as History: A Portrait of Colonial Aspirations*).

Eliza Lucas Pinckney, an affluent South Carolinian, exemplified the new ideal of refined female gentility. Born into a prosperous family of rice planters, Eliza helped introduce the profitable dye plant, indigo, into South Carolina (1738–

3.4 Eliza Pinckney's Dress
Silk produced on Pinckney's plantation was sent to England to be spun into fine fabric, dyed, and sewn into a dress that reflected the latest London fashions.

3.5 Westover Plantation
The doorway of Byrd's mansion was crafted in England and included the latest architectural details. Note the carved pineapple above the door.

1744), which became the colonies' second most important export crop in the eighteenth century. She eagerly consumed British fashions and ideas, and aspired to create a lifestyle that a visitor from London would have easily recognized. She studied French, was conversant in the ideas of the English philosopher John Locke, and participated in the management of her family's plantation. Her social life was equally busy. She regularly attended teas, dances, and concerts. Eliza's beautiful gold silk dress (**3.4**) was woven from silk produced on her own plantation. After the silk was harvested, she sent it to England to be dyed and woven into a fabric suitable for a gown that might be worn to the most elegant party in either London or Charleston.

For women the new customs of gentility were a mixed blessing. A wealthy woman might have servants or slaves to help her entertain in a suitable style, but it took additional time and effort to supervise these activities. Most women did not enjoy the luxury of additional help and had to handle these new responsibilities themselves.

More English, Yet More American

The exteriors of American houses also underwent a process of Anglicization. English-style manor houses such as William Byrd's Westover (1730–1734) (**3.5**), borrowed ideas from English pattern books (architectural guidebooks of the latest styles) (**3.6**). The main entrance of this elegant red brick mansion took guests through an impressive doorway that Byrd imported from England. The model for the door and its frame came from a London design. The classical columns and the swan-shaped broken pediment at the top of the doorframe include a carved pineapple. This exotic West Indian fruit created a sensation among the wealthy on both sides of the Atlantic, as both a culinary delicacy and a symbol of affluent hospitality. The pineapple soon became a common architectural motif in the mansions of wealthy Americans.

3.6 English Pattern Book
Byrd used this picture from an influential London design book when selecting a style for his doorway.

How does Westover Plantation illustrate the growing wealth of the colonies?

Read the **Document** *William Byrd II*, Diary: An American Gentleman *(1709)*

Images as History
A PORTRAIT OF COLONIAL ASPIRATIONS

Justus Engelhardt Kühn's portrait of the young Henry Darnall III (1710) reveals how the aspirations of colonists continued to exceed the bounds of the possible. Although the Darnalls lived a life of luxury compared with most colonists, surrounding themselves with goods that earlier generations of colonists would have envied, they did not quite live up to the standards of the typical British aristocrat.

The scene behind Darnall is pure fantasy. An elegant stone balustrade overlooking an elaborate formal garden projects an image of wealth, refinement, and power. Yet neither the fancy garden nor the stone balcony would have existed anywhere in the colonies at the time. Kühn's decision to include these imaginary elements in the background reflected the aspirations rather than the realities of life in the colonies. The picture symbolized the wealth, power, and gentility that the Darnalls sought to achieve, not their actual condition.

The work is also the first known painting of an African American in the colonies. Darnall's slave wears a silver yoke around his neck, a symbol of his inferior status. Although much younger, Darnall towers over his slave.

The slave, silver shackle around his neck, is situated below his master and looks up at him adoringly. The image of the docile slave clearly reflected the slave owner's point of view, not the slave's.

Darnall's elegant suit testifies to his family's wealth and cosmopolitan taste.

The imaginary garden in the background represents the Darnalls' desires, but this level of grandeur was not yet attainable in the colonies.

Henry Darnall III as a Child by Justus Engelhardt Kühn

How is slavery represented in this portrait?

Anglicization transformed churches and public architecture as well. Some of the grandest buildings erected in the colonies during the first half of the eighteenth century were public structures such as the Pennsylvania State House in Philadelphia, where Pennsylvania's assembly met. Constructed between 1732 and 1756, the State House's two-and-half-story red brick structure dominated the Philadelphia skyline. Built in the Palladian style (also known as Georgian, in honor of the British monarch, King George I (r. 1714–1727)), the Pennsylvania State House captured two seemingly opposing trends in the evolution of American society in the eighteenth century. Its architecture testified to the powerful influence of Anglicization. With its beautiful windows and impressive red brick exterior, the State House visibly symbolized the colonists' esteem for and knowledge of the latest English architectural styles (**3.7**). The actions inside the State House, however, the debates and votes of the Pennsylvania assembly, were emblematic of the growing power and assertiveness of an American-born colonial elite. The building was later renamed Independence Hall, reflecting its close association with the signing of the Declaration of Independence and the drafting of the U.S. Constitution.

3.7 Pennsylvania State House
The new Pennsylvania State House reflected the Anglicization of American tastes and the growing wealth of colonial Pennsylvania.

Strong Assemblies and Weak Governors

The Pennsylvania State House was a potent visual reminder of the power of the colonial assembly. The assemblies had become the preeminent political institutions in the colonies. American ideas about legislative power drew support from seventeenth-century English Whig ideas that triumphed during England's Glorious Revolution in 1688 (see Chapter 2).

Several developments in American colonial history helped reinforce the growth of legislative power. Although voting in America remained restricted to adult white male landholders, the percentage of such individuals in the colonies was larger than it was in Britain. The larger voting population meant that a higher percentage of Americans were politically active than Britons. Additionally none of the colonies had anything like an upper house comparable to Parliament's House of Lords. The governors' councils, the closest thing to a colonial upper house, had little power. America's native-born elites were not a titled British aristocracy, with a distinct legislative body, the House of Lords, to guard their privileges and powers. Ambitious young Americans from good families, like the young Thomas Jefferson, expected to enter politics by election to the lower house of the colonial assembly, not by inheriting a place in an aristocratic upper house.

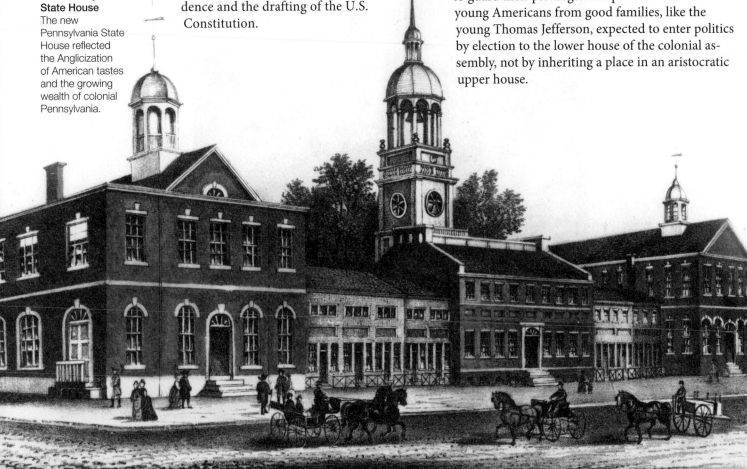

What does the design of the Pennsylvania State House reveal about colonial society?

In part the actions of colonial assemblies filled a void that the structure of the empire had created. In an age in which a letter could take months to travel from London to the colonies, it was imperative that local assemblies have the authority to deal with a host of governmental responsibilities, from organizing the militia to providing for the poor. Although colonists had gained the right to legislate on local matters, they were also part of the larger British Empire. Most colonies had agents who represented their interests in London and lobbied Parliament. Apart from these agents the colonies had no actual representation in Parliament: No member of Parliament was elected from the colonies or watched over their interests. In this regard the American colonies were no worse off than were other British colonies, including Barbados and Jamaica. Even within Britain newer cities such as Manchester and Birmingham had no representation in Parliament, and at least one town, Dunwich, continued to send two members to Parliament even though the town

to take a more active role in managing the empire and collecting greater revenues in the 1760s, the colonial practices and British theory collided.

Royal governors repeatedly complained that the colonial assemblies had exercised authority that did not belong to them and frustrated their plans. The royal governors' dependence on the assemblies for their salaries weakened their position with regard to the legislature. By controlling the power of the purse, colonial assemblies were able to frustrate the plans of the most ambitious royal governors: If they wished to collect their salaries, the governors dared not anger the assemblies. Colonial assemblies came to act like and think of themselves as mini-parliaments, with full legislative power over local matters. In 1728 the Massachusetts legislature reminded the governor that it was "the undoubted Right of all English men . . . to raise and dispose of Moneys for the publick Service of their own free accord without any Compulsion."

> "My Lord Cornbury has and dos still make use of an unfortunate Custom of dressing himself in Womens Cloaths and of exposing himself in that Garb upon the Ramparts to the view of the public; in that dress he draws a World of Spectators about him and consequently as many Censures."
>
> Letter spreading rumors of Lord Cornbury's cross-dressing, 1709

had literally crumbled into the North Sea. To cast their votes "legal residents" of Dunwich had to row out to the location of the former town hall, which was submerged.

According to traditional Whig political theory, members of Parliament were expected to represent the whole nation, not a particular locality. Rather than speak for any local interest, representatives were supposed to act in the larger public good. By the 1760s, the differences between American and British practices had become so great that they prompted a new theoretical defense. Thus, champions of the traditional British practice argued that all Britons, including the colonists, had **virtual representation** in Parliament, even if they had no actual representatives to guard their interests. As long as Parliament did not meddle much in colonial affairs, a policy of "salutary neglect," this theory caused few problems. When Parliament began

Colonial politics could be nasty, and most royal governors lacked the power to tame their legislatures. No governor was more ineffective and despised than Lord Cornbury, Royal Governor of New York and New Jersey (the two colonies shared the same royal governor until 1738). Enemies of Cornbury accused him of parading around the ramparts of New York's forts in women's clothing and used these rumors to undermine his authority, a strategy that was extremely effective. Sir Danvers Osborne, another New York governor, became so despondent over dealings with the colonial assembly that he hanged himself. To avoid the fate of Cornbury or Osborne, savvy royal governors understood the necessity of making strategic alliances with members of the assembly. The give-and-take between the governors and the assembly defined colonial politics for much of the eighteenth century.

Why were colonial governors so weak?

Enlightenment and Awakenings

By mid-century a British traveler to Philadelphia, the largest city in America, would have been impressed by the fine houses, elegant coaches, and other signs of America's refinement and gentility. The visitor would also have been struck by the signs of Enlightenment in the city: a fine lending library, the American Philosophical Society, and a new college. The city hosted scientists of international renown, such as Benjamin Franklin, the man who had tamed lightning. A visitor to the colonies might also have encountered the great evangelist George Whitefield, on one of his tours. Even if one missed hearing the "peddler in divinity," one could read about his exploits in the expanding press. The religious revival movement, known as the Great Awakening attacked traditional styles of worship in favor of a more emotional style of devotion. Communities across America were divided into those who favored the new style of religion and those opposed to it.

3.8 *The Gaols Committee of the House of Commons* In William Hogarth's painting, members of Parliament involved in prison reform, including James Oglethorpe (second from the left), examine a prisoner. His tattered clothes and shackles reveal the inhumanity of Britain's prisons.

How did Georgia reflect Enlightenment ideals?

Georgia's Utopian Experiment

One of the most ambitious Enlightenment endeavors was the new colony of Georgia, founded as an experiment to reform criminals and the poor by transplanting them from England to a more wholesome environment in America. James Oglethorpe, a spokesman in Parliament for humanitarian causes, secured parliamentary support for his plan to use colonization as an alternative to imprisonment. Georgia, named for King George II (r. 1727–1760), was strategically located as a buffer between the Carolinas and Spanish Florida.

Life in British prisons in the eighteenth century was harsh. At least half of the prisoners were debtors, whose crime was failing to pay their bills. Oglethorpe became a leading champion for prison reform and was appointed to a parliamentary committee charged with investigating the nation's jails. The committee's work attracted the interest of artist and social critic William Hogarth. In this painting of Oglethorpe's committee, Hogarth presents a stark contrast between the elegantly dressed members of Parliament and a prisoner in rags who was "clamped in irons," a painful form of physical restraint commonly used in British prisons (**3.8**).

For Oglethorpe, removing prisoners from debtors' prison and sending them to a colony in America meshed perfectly with his vision for dealing with crime and poverty in Britain. In America the poor would have a fresh opportunity to earn a living and avoid the impoverishment they faced in England. Oglethorpe's vision for Georgia reflected the views of Enlightenment thinkers such as John Locke, who rejected the notion that humans were born depraved and could not be rehabilitated if placed in a healthier environment.

The 1732 charter granted Oglethorpe and the trustees of the colony of Georgia enormous power. To prevent the colony from becoming just another slave society in which a few enjoyed great wealth and the majority were poor, the trustees banned slavery. To promote sobriety, the trustees also prohibited the importation of rum. Oglethorpe and the trustees soon confronted the same types of problems that earlier proprietary colonies had experienced (see Chapter 2). Settlers demanded a greater say in their affairs, including the right to import slaves. By 1738, the colony had abandoned much of its original vision, including its ban on importing both slaves and rum. Having begun as something of a utopian experiment, Georgia became another slave society in the lower South.

Although Enlightenment ideals helped shape the early history of Georgia, defense was never far from Oglethorpe's mind. His plan for the city of Savannah drew on the ideals of Renaissance city planning that had inspired the design of many other towns in the Americas (see Chapter 1). Reflecting the city's position on the frontier of Spanish America, the plan looked like a design for a military encampment, a model stretching back to ancient Rome (**3.9**). Oglethorpe had dreamed of using Georgia as the launching point for the conquest of Spanish America, but his attack on the Spanish town of St. Augustine in Florida in 1740 failed. Two years later when the Spanish retaliated, Oglethorpe repelled them. Georgia did not become a staging ground to root out the Spanish, but it was an effective barrier, protecting the colonies from Spanish attack.

American Champions of the Enlightenment

The Enlightenment championed the work of Sir Isaac Newton, the great English scientist and mathematician who explored the laws of motion, optics, and gravity. The Newtonian universe was radically different from the world that had produced the Salem witchcraft accusations (see Chapter 2). Rather than looking primarily to the invisible world of the supernatural, Newtonianism

3.9 Savannah, Georgia The layout of Savannah resembled a Roman military garrison, reflecting its strategic importance as a frontier outpost protecting the British colonies from Spanish America.

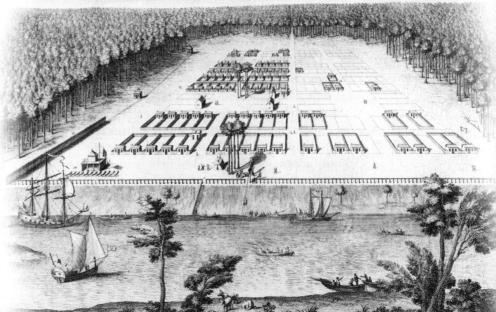

electrical current and theorized the possibility of creating a battery to store an electrical charge. Franklin also demonstrated that lightning was a form of electrical discharge. This insight led the practical-minded Franklin to develop the lightning rod. The device was designed to attract lightning and then conduct the current safely away from a building. American homes were generally built of wood, a plentiful material in most parts of the colonies that was extremely susceptible to damage by lightning. In a tribute to Franklin, John Adams wrote, "Nothing, perhaps, that ever occurred upon this earth was so well calculated to give any man an extensive and universal celebrity as the discovery of . . . lightning rods." Franklin's close association with electricity in general and the lightning rod in particular was captured in this 1762 painting (**3.10**), which depicts Franklin at his desk with a lightning storm raging in the background and a lightning rod prominently positioned on a building visible through a window.

Franklin helped found the American Philosophical Society (1743), a learned society committed to the advancement of knowledge; the College of Philadelphia (1751) (later the University of Pennsylvania); and the Library Company, a private lending library. In addition to these institutions that reflected the Enlightenment's emphasis on education and the spread of knowledge, Franklin helped found organizations dedicated to improving the lives of Philadelphians, including a fire company and the first public hospital in the colonies. Although Franklin owned slaves, as did many in Philadelphia, he eventually came to regard slavery as a great evil and vigorously opposed it.

Awakening, Revivalism, and American Society

From 1730 to 1770, the colonies experienced a series of religious revivals that historians group together as the Great Awakening. The resulting religious conflict divided families, split churches, and fragmented communities, forever altering the religious landscape of colonial America.

One of the early leaders of the revival movement, Gilbert Tennent, a New Jersey minister, attacked ministers for preaching an empty, "dead form of religion." Only by accepting the reality of sin and opening one's heart to grace could one hope to achieve salvation. Tennent also took aim

3.10 Benjamin Franklin and Electricity
This contemporary painting of Franklin links him with his work on electricity. In the background, lightning destroys one building while another, to which Franklin's lightning rod is attached, survives a strike.

focused on the visible world of nature, which functioned according to the rules discerned by observation and interpreted by reason. Newtonianism was not antithetical to religion, but the God of the Newtonian universe was different from the traditional Christian notion of God as a patriarch or king. In the Newtonian vision God was the great clockmaker who fashioned the universe to run according to predictable natural laws.

In contrast to Newton's grand theorizing, the Enlightenment in America took a distinctly practical approach. No figure in America more closely approximated this ideal than Benjamin Franklin. Printer, scientist, reformer, and statesman, Franklin became a symbol of the American Enlightenment on both sides of the Atlantic. His international fame derived from his scientific experiments with lightning and electricity, which he published in 1751. Franklin coined the terms positive and negative to describe the nature of

How does this portrait of Franklin reflect his reputation as a champion of the Enlightenment?

Read the **Document** *Profiles: Benjamin Franklin*

at America's expanding consumer society and the "covetousness" that society had encouraged.

The leading intellectual champion of the Awakening was New England minister Jonathan Edwards, who captured the spirit of this movement when he wrote that "Our people do not so much need to have their heads" filled, as much as "have their hearts touched." Edwards's fiery sermon, "Sinners in the Hands of an Angry God" (1741), offered his parishioners a vision of the eternal fires of hell that awaited the unconverted. To shake his parishioners out of their complacency and remind them of the necessity of grace for salvation, Edwards compared their fate to that of a spider dangling above the pit of eternal damnation, with only God's mercy preventing them from falling in.

In 1757, Edwards became the president of the College of New Jersey (which became Princeton University), one of several new colleges founded by supporters of the Awakening to train a new generation of ministers. Princeton, allied to the Presbyterian Church, also had close ties to Scottish universities that were leading centers of Enlightenment thought. Rhode Island College (Brown University) was founded by the Baptists in 1764; Queens College (later Rutgers), by the Dutch Reformed Church in 1766. Dartmouth College was founded by the Congregationalist Eleazar Wheelock in 1769, originally as an Indian mission school.

Edwards's account of his own Massachusetts revival inspired the English Anglican minister George Whitefield to take his evangelical crusade to the colonies. Whitefield's 1739–1740 tour was America's first genuinely inter-colonial event. The energetic English preacher traversed most of the eastern seaboard from New Hampshire to Georgia. His tour took advantage of improved roads and the expansion of inter-colonial shipping routes. He traveled the same routes as the merchants who hawked the latest English wares, and his gift for selling the gospel prompted one critic to describe him and other evangelical ministers as "Peddlers in Divinity." Whitefield attracted such large crowds that much of his preaching was outdoors because few churches were big enough to hold his audience.

The Great Awakening changed American society. The evangelical methods employed by gifted preachers implicitly challenged the hierarchical assumptions of colonial society about gender, race, and social status. Individuals exercised greater choice, many choosing to leave their own congregations and find one that better suited their spiritual needs. For some the Awakening provided opportunities to step forward as lay preachers. For the first time in American religious history, ordinary people were given a significant public voice. For those whose voices were seldom heard in public—women, blacks, artisans, or poor folk—the opportunity to testify about their spiritual life, often to mixed crowds that included people like themselves or even their social betters, challenged traditional ideas about hierarchy. Mary Cooper, a resident of Long Island, noted in her diary that she heard an astonishing assortment of individuals preach, including a Quaker woman, a "Black man," and even two Indian preachers. By giving a voice to many groups previously excluded from traditional preaching, the Great Awakening contributed to the growth of a more democratic culture.

> "The God that holds you over the pit of hell, much as one holds a spider, or some loathsome insect, over the fire, abhors you, and is dreadfully provoked; his wrath towards you burns like fire; he looks upon you as worthy of nothing else, but to be cast into the fire."
>
> JONATHAN EDWARDS, 1741

In a few cases women touched by the spirit began preaching, an action that prompted their own ministers to denounce them for flouting the accepted roles assigned to women in colonial society. Testifying to one's religious experiences was one thing, but assuming the role of preacher, a role traditionally reserved for men, was simply too radical. After Bathsheba Kingsley stole a horse and rode from community to community preaching the gospel, Jonathan Edwards denounced her for perverting the spirit of revival. Edwards, wed to traditional ideas about women's roles, was horrified that Kingsley interpreted the Awakening's message as an invitation to become a gospel preacher.

Not all ministers approved of the ideas and methods of the revivalist preachers. Opponents of the revival, dubbed **Old Lights**, attacked the revivalists, or **New Lights**, for their excessive emotionalism. Old Light ministers ridiculed the revivalists for telling their congregants that "they were damned! damned! damned!" Rather than

3.11 *Lamentation,* **Moravian Painting of Christ** Depictions of the "blood of the savior" in images such as this, made them highly effective tools for Moravian missionaries. Here the artist highlights physical pain and stoic endurance, two traits that appealed strongly to American Indian men.

embraced art as a means of promoting the gospels (see Chapters 1 and 2). In particular Moravians focused on the redemptive power of Christ's suffering as the foundation for religious salvation. Their most renowned artist in America, John Valentine Haidt, was well schooled in European styles of religious painting and used these techniques to translate the Moravians' Christian vision into visually rich images (**3.11**). The idea of Christ's suffering resonated with Indian converts, and the Moravians displayed images of the crucifixion to bring the gospel to the Indians. After viewing such pictures in the home of a Moravian missionary, two visiting Indians commented on "how many wounds he has, how much blood flows forth!" For American Indians Moravian religious imagery of Jesus suggested a brave spiritual warrior, an ideal that resonated in the minds of young male Indians, whose conception of masculinity was based on a martial ideal of physical strength, bravery, and the endurance of pain and suffering.

adopt the new, more emotional style, Old Lights continued to favor sermons based on learned explications of biblical texts. In response to this backlash against the Awakening, Gilbert Tennent accused his opponents of lacking "the Courage, or Honesty, to thrust the Nail of Terror into sleeping Souls." One New Light preacher, James Davenport, took the emphasis on emotionalism to an extreme, urging that books and sermons written by Old Light ministers be burned. As congregations divided between New Lights and Old Lights, many communities were pulled apart.

Indian Revivals

The Great Awakening also spilled over into Indian country. Indians won over by evangelical efforts often served as cultural mediators between their communities and the colonists. The Moravians, German-speaking evangelical Protestants, were particularly effective at evangelizing among Indian tribes. In 1740, many German Moravians migrated to Pennsylvania, where they settled in a town they named Bethlehem. Moravians also established communities in the Carolinas and Georgia.

Unlike the Calvinist faith of many English colonists, which shunned the use of images in their churches, the Moravians were Lutherans and

Although the Great Awakening touched a small but influential group of Indians, a different type of native religious renewal movement had an even greater impact on American Indians. As early as 1737, reports began filtering back from Indian country, the broad swath of territory from western Pennsylvania to French-controlled land in Illinois, that Indian religious leaders were preaching the need for a return to traditional ways and a complete separation from colonists. The alcohol that Europeans traded with Indians had contributed to rising levels of alcoholism among Indians. In the 1760s, the Delaware Indian prophet Neolin championed the revival of traditional beliefs and the rejection of European influences. He urged his people to "learn to live without any Trade or Connections with White people." In place of dependency and trade, he counseled "Clothing and Supporting themselves as their forefathers did." Neolin and other prophets of Indian revitalization traveled as itinerants through Indian territory preaching their message. Indian revivalists attacked Indian involvement with and dependence on the world of trade and commerce with Europeans.

Why was Moravian art so helpful to missionaries interested in converting American Indians?

African Americans in the Colonial Era

 By the eighteenth century, racial slavery had become a central feature of the Atlantic world, with firm roots in British North America. The greatest demand for slaves came from the sugar-producing regions of Brazil and the Caribbean. An additional 300,000 slaves arrived in the British mainland colonies, with the greatest demand for their labor in the upper and lower South. The highest proportion of slaves lived in the lower South, where Africans actually outnumbered Europeans. Slavery in British North America was not an exclusively southern phenomenon. Slaves were an important part of urban life in New York, Philadelphia, and Boston. Slavery was also significant in the economies of the mid-Atlantic and New England.

Slavery was a brutal and exploitative labor system, but the experience of individual slaves varied greatly from region to region. Regardless of where they were and under what circumstances they lived, slaves found ways to resist their masters' domination. Occasionally they turned to violent resistance, but more often they used economic sabotage—pretending sickness, destroying tools, mutilating livestock, or running away—to undermine the profitability of slavery. Perhaps even more significant were the slaves' attempts to assert their humanity and create lives beyond the reach of the master's dominion. Establishing families despite the ever-present threat of being torn from one's loved ones and sold, building a viable community, and practicing their own religion gave slaves the cultural resources to survive and denied their masters complete control over their lives.

The Atlantic Slave Trade

Slaves had been traded internally within Africa for centuries; indeed, it took hundreds of years for the Atlantic slave trade to surpass the internal African slave trade. The demand for agricultural labor in the Atlantic world created a strong market for African slaves and led to a dramatic increase in the trans-Atlantic slave trade in the late 1600s. The leading participants in the international slave trade in the seventeenth century had been Spain, Portugal, and Holland, but by the eighteenth century, Britain had become the preeminent slave-trading nation in the Atlantic world.

As the graphs and figures presented in *Envisioning Evidence: The Eighteenth-Century Atlantic Slave Trade* show, most slaves in the Atlantic trade ended up in one of the sugar colonies. Portuguese sugar production was centered in Brazil, while Dutch, French, and British sugar production was centered in the Caribbean. Less than 10 percent of the slaves imported from Africa were transported to the American colonies, but the significance of slavery to the British mainland American colonies was enormous.

The brutality of slavery began far from the Atlantic coast of Africa in the inland regions, where slave catchers acquired most slaves. The captive slaves were then bound by ropes or wooden yokes and marched to the coast, where they were housed in pens. To prevent communication among captives and reduce the chances of slaves organizing themselves to escape or challenge their captors, the slave catchers often separated individuals from the same ethnic or language groups. They also routinely separated family

> "The stench of the hold . . . became pestilential. The closeness of the place, and the heat of the climate, added to the number in the ship, which was so crowded that each had scarcely room to turn himself, almost suffocated us."
>
> OLAUDAH EQUIANO,
> *The Life of Olaudah Equiano* (London, 1789)

Which regions of the Atlantic world imported the greatest number of slaves?

Envisioning Evidence
THE EIGHTEENTH-CENTURY ATLANTIC SLAVE TRADE

In the eighteenth century, the slave trade was the economic cornerstone of the Atlantic economy. It supplied indispensable labor necessary to produce plantation cash crops such as sugar and tobacco in the New World, and transporting slaves provided huge profits for those engaged in the brutal, forced migration of Africans to the Americas.

The data presented in this map and the accompanying graph bring into focus an important fact about the Atlantic slave trade: Most of the slaves transported to the Americas ended up in the sugar islands of the Caribbean or in Brazil. Less than 10 percent of the slaves went to British North America.

The experience of the Middle Passage was horrific, a fact underscored by the mortality rates depicted in the pie chart above.

Where did most slaves end up and how high were mortality rates during the Middle Passage?

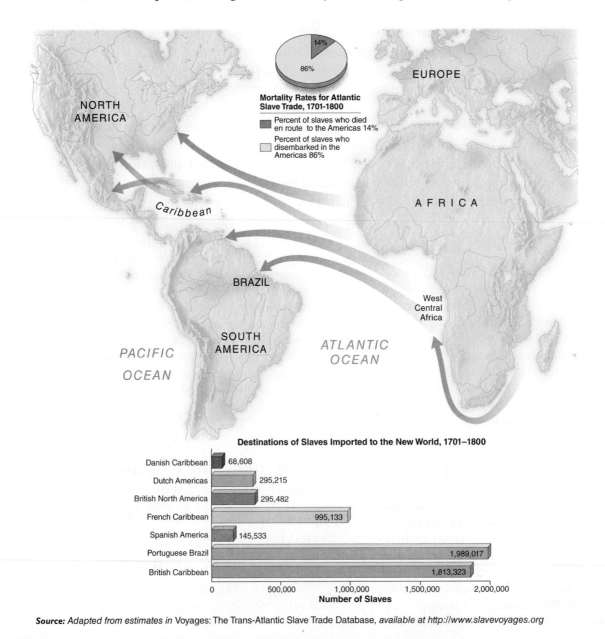

Mortality Rates for Atlantic Slave Trade, 1701-1800

■ Percent of slaves who died en route to the Americas 14%

□ Percent of slaves who disembarked in the Americas 86%

Destinations of Slaves Imported to the New World, 1701–1800

Destination	Number of Slaves
Danish Caribbean	68,608
Dutch Americas	295,215
British North America	295,482
French Caribbean	995,133
Spanish America	145,533
Portuguese Brazil	1,989,017
British Caribbean	1,813,323

Number of Slaves

Source: *Adapted from estimates in* Voyages: The Trans-Atlantic Slave Trade Database, *available at http://www.slavevoyages.org*

Which European nations were most heavily involved in the international slave trade?

⚲ View the Closer Look *African Slave Trade, 1451–1870*

members. Slaves might remain housed in these inhumane conditions for months before being boarded on slave ships bound for the Americas.

The voyage across the Atlantic from Africa to the Americas, known as the **middle passage**, was horrific. The cramped conditions on these voyages depicted in this antislavery petition barely convey the ordeal (**3.12**). Typically their captors forced the slaves to remain in shackles during the voyage. Slaves endured meager rations and unsanitary conditions, a situation that led those who preferred "death to such a life of misery" to drown themselves. Mortality rates during the middle passage exceeded 10 percent.

In the seventeenth century most slaves bound for the British mainland colonies in America came first to the Caribbean, where they were "seasoned," a process of physical and psychological adjustment to the rigors of slavery. Afterward they would make the final leg of the voyage to the American mainland. This pattern changed in the eighteenth century when the demand for slave labor increased dramatically, and many traders chose to bypass the seasoning process. Thus most slaves arriving in British North America in the eighteenth century were "saltwater slaves," coming directly from Africa. Most slaves arrived at Sullivan's Island in Charleston harbor, leading scholars to describe it as Black America's Ellis Island (page 500).

After being unloaded and quarantined on Sullivan's Island, slaves were typically transported for sale in the slave markets of the major ports and cities. This was often the last time family members would see each other. After being subjected to a humiliating inspection, similar to that used by livestock buyers, slaves were auctioned off to their new masters. Even if family members had managed to remain together, they now faced permanent separation from their loved ones. Thus the experience of the auction block further traumatized slaves who had already suffered a multitude of horrors on their perilous journey from Africa to America.

Southern Slavery

The two regional subcultures in the colonial South—the lower and upper South—had distinctive slave labor systems and cultures. Slavery in the lower South (parts of the Carolina and Georgia low country) had evolved as the region evolved from a frontier settlement to an integrated part of the Atlantic slave economy. In the upper South slavery had gradually replaced indentured servitude (p. 83) as the main source of labor by 1700.

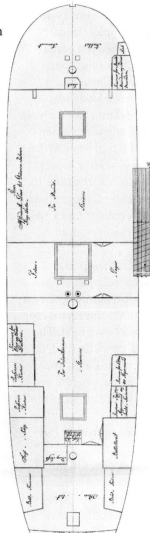
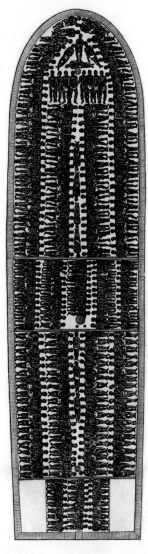

3.12 Tight Packing
This abolitionist depiction of tight packing shows the cramped conditions on slave ships, which maximized the number of bodies carried with no concern for the health of the slaves transported.

The lower South began as a colony of a colony. Carolina was first conceived as a base for supplying food to the Caribbean sugar islands. The colony also traded captured Indian slaves and deer hides. In the 1690s, rice was introduced into this region and eventually became its most profitable export. Many slaves had learned to cultivate rice in Africa, and their knowledge contributed to the increase in rice production from 10,000 pounds in 1698 to 20 million pounds in 1730.

In the 1740s, another important cash crop—indigo—was introduced into the region. By the 1730s, when the Carolinas had been divided into North and South Carolina, two-thirds of the region's population were African slaves. Most blacks worked under a task system that gave them considerable autonomy over their work. Once their tasks were completed, slaves might use the remaining time to hunt, fish, or tend their own gardens to supplement their meager diets.

What was tight packing?

The swampy regions of the Carolina low country were fertile breeding grounds for tropical diseases, including malaria. Africans had developed partial immunity to this disease, but whites of European descent were extremely susceptible. Given the unhealthy environment of the coastal lowlands, wealthy planters preferred to spend much of the year at their Charleston homes. The many white absentees and the continuous influx of slaves from Africa helped blacks living in this region preserve aspects of their African heritage despite the deprivations of slave life. The conical-shaped, thatched-roofed huts in the slave quarters on Mulberry plantation (**3.13**), South Carolina, reflect the influence of African architectural styles.

Slavery in the upper South, the Chesapeake region, differed markedly from its practice in the low country Carolinas. While the task system worked for rice cultivation, growing tobacco, the dominant crop in the Chesapeake, demanded more oversight. The plants were easily damaged if not properly tended, so planters preferred to organize their slaves into gangs that worked together under the watchful eye of a white overseer or a black slave driver chosen by the master.

Slaves in the Chesapeake were a minority, and they lived on plantations typically smaller than those in the lower South. Although slaves in this region preserved elements of traditional African culture, their smaller numbers and wider distribution made it more difficult to preserve their African cultural heritage.

3.13 Slave Quarters, Mulberry Plantation, South Carolina
The conical design of these slave cabins, including their thatched roofs, drew on West African architectural influences.

Northern Slavery and Free Blacks

Although slavery was less vital to the colonial economy outside of the South, it was important in some areas. For example, in parts of New York and New Jersey, the slave population might range from 15 to 30 percent. Typically slaves in the rural North worked as field hands on small family farms. There were also many urban slaves in the North, who generally worked as domestics in wealthier homes. In seaports, slaves worked in maritime occupations. In Pennsylvania slaves were so essential to iron manufacturing that their masters petitioned the assembly to lower tariffs on slave imports so that they could continue to produce iron.

A small community of free blacks emerged and settled in northern cities such as Philadelphia, New York, and Boston. Slaves gained their freedom by several means. Some were freed by masters who recognized the evil of slavery. One of the earliest groups to condemn slavery was the Quakers. Other slaves, particularly those who had learned a skill such as carpentry, might be able to strike a bargain with their owners and gain the right to work for themselves part time, eventually saving enough money to buy their freedom. Although a few freed slaves became farmers, many ended up in one of the thriving seaports where economic opportunities were greater.

Urban settings also provided African Americans in the North with many cultural opportunities. In both New York City and Albany, the African American communities adapted the Dutch religious holiday of "Pentecost" and turned it into a carnival-like festival they named "Pinkster." The holiday was presided over by an African American figure, "King Charles," who acted as the political leader of

What were the main differences between the task system and the gang system of labor?

his community during the holiday. During Pinkster African Americans participated in music, dancing, and festive meals; they also paraded as part of their African "different nations," an explicit demonstration of their African roots.

The Great Awakening helped spread Christianity to slaves across America and among free blacks in the North. The Moravians were particularly aggressive in preaching the gospel to slaves in North Carolina. Jonathan Edwards, himself a slave owner, reported that slaves in his own community had embraced the revival. Evangelical groups such as the Methodists encouraged free blacks to attend their revival meetings. The new more emotional style favored by so many Awakening preachers appealed to African Americans because it more closely resembled traditional African styles of religious practice.

Slave Resistance and Rebellion

The growth of slavery in the late 1600s led colonial governments to ensure that African slaves remained subservient to their white masters (see Chapter 2). Slave codes gave masters almost unlimited authority over their slaves. The codes also legally defined as slaves children born to slave mothers, even when fathered by free whites.

Although deprived of any legal means to protect themselves, slaves developed strategies for coping with the horrors of slavery and escaping the domination of their masters. Stealing, shirking responsibility, feigning illness, or breaking tools: all of these actions deliberately slowed the pace of their work and provided temporary relief. Some slaves ran away, simply hiding in the woods, seeking refuge with a family on nearby plantations in the slave quarters. Avoiding the white patrols that were always on the lookout for runaways made this a risky option. In those parts of the South closer to Indian country or Spanish territory, including parts of the Carolinas and Georgia, slaves might try to find refuge in a territory beyond the control of the English colonists.

Slaves who took part in South Carolina's Stono Rebellion of 1739 took advantage of the colonies' proximity to Spanish Florida. The rebels broke into a storehouse and seized arms, murdered whites, and torched the homes of slave owners. The rebels hoped that other slaves would rally to their standard, and some slaves from the

> "Many of the white people in these provinces take little or no care of Negro marriages . . . they often part men from their wives by selling them far asunder."
>
> JOHN WOOLMAN, Journal, 1774

surrounding countryside did join the rebellion, whose numbers rose to around 150. The slave rebels hoped to find refuge in Spanish Florida. But the Carolina militia intercepted the rebels before they could reach it, and the better organized and armed militia routed the Stono rebels, slaughtering them by the dozens and executing those who survived. In response to the Stono Rebellion, South Carolina passed harsher slave codes and temporarily blocked importation of slaves into the region, a ban that was soon lifted because of the economic importance of slave labor. The Stono Rebellion was the largest African American uprising in the colonial era, but it would not be the last in the history of American slavery.

An African American Culture Emerges under Slavery

Most slaves did not adopt rebellion as their primary strategy for challenging the authority of their masters. Simply establishing families, building an African American community, and practicing their own religion were more realistic goals for most slaves—but all were difficult to achieve given the constraints imposed by slavery. Forming a family under slavery was not easy. For one thing, the sex ratio among slaves during much of the colonial period was sharply skewed, with many more males than females. During the early years of the slave trade, slave owners preferred males for the backbreaking agricultural work required to produce, rice, tobacco, or sugarcane. So most slaves imported into the Americas were male; the odds of a male slave finding a wife were slim. During the eighteenth century, as more slaves were born in America, the sex ratio became more balanced because roughly comparable numbers of boys and girls were born. But even if the chances of a man finding a mate increased, slavery made

How did slaves resist the authority of their masters?

family formation difficult. Slave marriages had no legal standing. So slaves faced the constant threat of separation from their spouses. The decision to break up slave families rested entirely with the master, and many children were sold from their families. On relatively small plantations slaves usually sought a spouse on a neighboring plantation, which left couples at the mercy of masters who could withhold visiting privileges and prevent husbands and wives from seeing one another. Nevertheless, many slaves did manage to find partners and create stable families.

One of the many aspects of traditional African culture preserved by slaves was naming practices. As was customary in many parts of West Africa, slave parents might name their children after the day of the week on which they were born. Plantation records commonly show West African names like Cudjo (Monday) for boys or Cuba (Wednesday) for girls, evidence that slaves continued to honor their ancestral practices.

Slaves also drew on African traditions in shaping distinctive music and dance forms, which provided an outlet for cultural expression. Using African techniques they constructed musical instruments, including drums and stringed instruments. Masters typically found African styles of dancing and singing exotic and alien to their European sensibilities. One British visitor to Maryland noted that on Sundays, the one day that masters generally allowed slaves to rest, blacks met "to amuse themselves with Dancing," which was a "most violent exercise." This rare colonial-era painting of slaves dancing not only illustrates the intensity of African-inspired dance but also shows the importance of an African-style instrument that would become a fixture in American music—the banjo (**3.14**). Music could serve ulterior purposes as well. Shortly after the Stono Rebellion, South Carolina banned drumming, fearing that slaves could drum and communicate secret messages from one plantation to another.

3.14 Slaves Dancing and Playing Banjo
This image of slaves dancing in the slave quarters prominently features a banjo. The instrument was modeled on an instrument that was well known in Africa.

What evidence exists for the persistence of African cultural traits among American slaves?

Immigration, Regional Economies, and Inequality

 Although distinctions of wealth emerged almost immediately in American society, especially in the cities, the relative abundance of land in the seventeenth century allowed many rural colonists to own their own land, a goal almost unattainable in Europe, where the aristocracy owned most land. Even in cities, those without a farmstead generally earned higher wages than they would have in Europe because labor commanded a higher price in the colonies, where skilled craftsmen were rarer. Although all of these facts contributed to the prosperity of the colonists, population growth (natural increase and immigration) and the dwindling availability of land became serious problems by the mid-eighteenth century. In the colonies' expanding cities, the gulf between the rich and poor widened, and in rural areas young people faced the prospect that they might not be able to obtain land for their own farms.

Immigration to the Colonies

The population of British North America expanded rapidly in the eighteenth century. Between 1700 and 1750, the white population of the colonies rose from around 250,000 to more than a million. In contrast to America's first predominantly English colonists who arrived in the early 1600s, eighteenth-century immigrants varied in national origin and ethnic identity. As chart (**3.15**) illustrates, the colonies attracted settlers from elsewhere in Britain, including Scotland, Ireland, and Wales. Immigration from the European continent also included many Dutch and Germans.

The decision to immigrate to America was a momentous one. The financial and personal costs of immigration could demand heavy sacrifices. The trans-Atlantic crossing, which could take four months, meant enduring cramped conditions on a ship with few amenities. Additionally, the cost of the trans-Atlantic passage was well beyond the yearly wages of the average Englishman and even more expensive for those from the European continent. To finance their passage, many immigrants, men and women alike, contracted to work as **indentured servants**. In exchange for having their passage paid, indentured servants agreed to work for a specified number of years, usually seven. In some cases the indenture system separated family members, with husband and wife indenturing themselves to different families.

Regional Economies

By the mid-eighteenth century, the British had settled the eastern seaboard, from Georgia to New Hampshire. Although each of the thirteen colonies functioned as its own separate political unit, historians have grouped the colonies into five regions—New England, the mid-Atlantic, the upper South, the lower South, and the back country—reflecting their unique histories, distinctive patterns of settlement, and diverse economies (**3.16**). Race, ethnicity, and religious composition also lent a distinctive quality to each of the major regions of colonial America.

3.15 Ancestry of the Population of the British Mainland Colonies in the Eighteenth Century
During the eighteenth century, the number of non-English immigrants increased. Immigrants from other parts of the British Empire, including Scotland and Ireland, rose as well. Another major source of immigration was continental Europe, especially Germany and Holland. [*Source:* Adapted from Thomas L. Purvis, "The European Ancestry of the United States Population, 1790," *William and Mary Quarterly.* 3d series, 41 (1984), p, 98.]

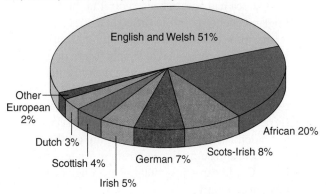

How did the ethnic composition of America change in the eighteenth century?

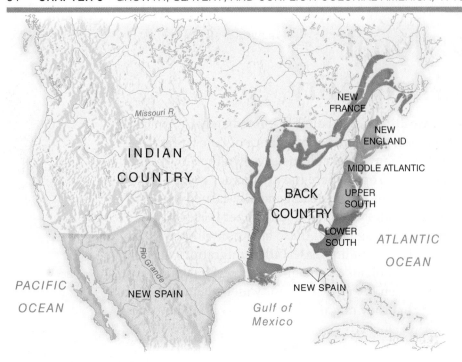

3.16 Map of Colonial Regions
By the mid-eighteenth century, colonial America had evolved into five distinctive regions: New England, mid-Atlantic, upper South, lower South, and the back country.

New England

New England (Connecticut, Massachusetts, New Hampshire, and Rhode Island) was the most ethnically homogenous region in colonial British America (see 3.17), overwhelmingly white and English. The Congregational Church, the heir of the Puritan tradition, was the dominant religion. New England also included other Protestant churches—Anglicans (Church of England), Presbyterians, Quakers, and Baptists. This lent some religious diversity to the region, particularly in Rhode Island, which had embraced religious toleration from its founding.

The sea had always been central to the New England economy, but in the eighteenth century, its maritime economy expanded dramatically. New England continued to supply fish to domestic and foreign markets, it became a major center of shipbuilding, and its merchants carried on a lively trade in a variety of commodities. Yankee trade in spirits—including the amber-colored dessert wine of Madeira, a Portuguese island group off the coast of Africa, and rum, distilled from molasses procured in the Caribbean—was vital to New England's commercial economy.

The ministerial elite continued to shape the affairs of the region, but the rising merchant class became increasingly powerful during the eighteenth century. Many of the region's leaders were educated at Harvard (1636), the oldest college in the colonies, or Yale (1701).

The Mid-Atlantic

The mid-Atlantic (New York, Pennsylvania, New Jersey, and Delaware) was the most ethnically diverse region in the colonies, and its hubs, New York and Philadelphia, were home to a wide range of ethnic and religious groups (see 3.16). Indeed as this engraving (**3.17**) of the eighteenth-century New York skyline illustrates, the spires and bell towers of the city's churches and lone synagogue proclaimed its religious diversity for miles around.

Philadelphia and New York became centers of commerce and finance. Each city boasted a thriving port, facilitating trade with Europe and coastal trade with other ports in the Atlantic world. Agricultural products from rural Pennsylvania and Delaware were sold in the markets of Philadelphia. New York's Hudson River carried agricultural products from upriver farms and furs from northern New York. The mid-Atlantic region also had small manufacturing enterprises, including flour milling, lumbering, mining, and metal foundries. The region depended on indentured servants for much of its labor. Between 1700 and 1775, about 100,000 servants came from the British Isles and another 35,000 from German-speaking regions on the European continent.

Although Quakers were powerful in Pennsylvania politics, the region's merchant class was even more influential. The mid-Atlantic region was slower to create colleges than either Massachusetts or Virginia, but by the mid-eighteenth century it boasted several new institutions of higher learning. The following colleges were created in this region: the College of Philadelphia was established in 1755 (now the University of Pennsylvania); in New York George II chartered Kings College (now Columbia University) in 1754; the College of New Jersey was founded in 1746 (now Princeton), and Queens College (now Rutgers) was established in New Jersey in 1766.

Which region of colonial America was the most culturally diverse?

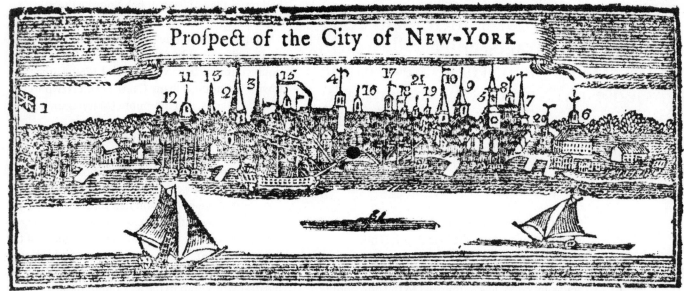

Prospect of the City of New-York

1 Fort George
2 Trinity Church
3 Presbyter. Meeting
4 North D. Church
5 St. George's Chapel

6 The Prison.
7 New Brick Meeting
8 King's College
9 St. Paul's Church
10 N. Dutch Cal, Church

11 Old Dutch Church
12 Jew's Synagogue
13 Lutheran Church
14 The French Church
15 New Scot's Meeting

16 Quaker's Meeting
17 Calvinist Church
18 Anabaptist Meeting
19 Moravian Meeting
20 N. Lutheran Church
21 Methodist Meeting

3.17 Engraving of New York Skyline This engraving of New York's skyline lists a score of churches and one synagogue whose spires dominated the skyline of the colonial town.

The Upper and Lower South

The South was most closely tied to slave labor. Actually it was two distinct regions: the upper South, or Chesapeake Region, and the lower South, including parts of South Carolina and the Georgia low country (see 3.16). Each produced different cash crops and employed slave labor in different ways. Immigration into the two regions varied, and the ethnic composition of the upper and lower South was also different.

Although more ethnically diverse than New England, the upper South, those areas of Virginia and Maryland tied to the Chesapeake, drew immigrants largely from England and Scotland. The planter elite who dominated this region built great fortunes from tobacco grown on plantations with slave labor. Many of the area's wealthiest citizens were educated at the College of William and Mary (1693) in Virginia, the nation's second-oldest college.

The lower South was settled later than the Chesapeake, and it benefited more from the growth of immigration and was more religiously diverse than the upper South. In addition to Anglicans the region included Presbyterians, German Moravians, Baptists, and Quakers.

The damp, hot climate of the low country bred diseases. To avoid these conditions, for much of the year, the wealthiest planters preferred their second

homes in Charleston, which became a major cultural and economic center of the region. Nevertheless, Charleston lacked an educational institution comparable to William and Mary, so the wealthiest Carolinians typically headed to England for their education.

The Back Country

In the early seventeenth century, colonists had hugged the coastline. By the eighteenth century they began pushing westward to areas such as the interior of the Carolinas, and western Pennsylvania, and Virginia (see 3.16). Many new immigrants headed directly for the back country. The Scots-Irish were particularly attracted to the back country of Pennsylvania and the Carolinas, where they settled in large numbers.

The back country lacked many of the refinements of the older, more settled regions of the colonies, leading travelers to compare back country colonists with Indians and describe both as savages.

Whatever their similarities, relations between back country whites and Indians were generally strained. Rather than seek to trade with Indians and learn their ways, the Scots-Irish wanted to create farmsteads, which required displacing Indians. The simmering tensions between residents of the back

Read the **Document** Of the Servants and Slaves in Virginia *(1705)*

What were the main cash crops produced by slave labor in the South?

> "They were as rude in their Manners as the Common Savages, and hardly a degree removed from them. Their Dresses almost as loose and Naked as the Indians, and differing in Nothing save Complexion."
>
> Minister CHARLES WOODMASON, observations on the back country, 1766

country region and the local Indians erupted into violence throughout the eighteenth century.

Back country settlers farmed, hunted, and raised livestock for their own consumption and local trade and were less connected to the burgeoning Atlantic economy. The economic realities of life in the back country encouraged independence and a strongly egalitarian culture. Courts were rare, and so were tax officials or other representatives of either the colonial or the British governments. A visitor to this region would also have noted a lack of churches, primary schools, and institutions of higher education.

Cities: Growth and Inequality

Although most Americans lived in the countryside during the eighteenth century, cities were growing. Philadelphia boasted 23,000 residents by 1760, making it the largest city in the colonies. Still America was far less urban than either Europe or the Spanish colonies to the south. Compared to London, with more than 700,000 people, Philadelphia was tiny, and Spanish America had half a dozen cities larger than Philadelphia. Mexico City, for example,

had more than 100,000 inhabitants by the mid-eighteenth century.

But the growth rates of the cities of colonial British America were impressive. Boston, for example, doubled in size between 1700 and 1760. Larger towns, including Albany (New York), Newport (Rhode Island), and Baltimore (Maryland), became regional centers.

Throughout these urban areas eighteenth-century society became polarized along economic lines. The percentage of wealth owned by the richest Americans increased. In Boston and Philadelphia 5 percent of the population had amassed almost half of their city's wealth by the last quarter of the eighteenth century. At the same time the number of the urban poor also rose dramatically in Boston, New York, and Philadelphia. The graph (**3.18**) illustrates the dramatic climb in the amount of money Boston devoted to poor relief from the mid-century onward. During this same period many trades and crafts established their own mutual benefit societies to help the poor. The stark inequality between the lives of the destitute and those of Boston's wealthiest merchants, who lived in fine new mansions and traveled around the city in elegant coaches, grew more pronounced, especially by the 1770s.

Rural America: Land Becomes Scarce

By the mid-eighteenth century, many Americans living in the countryside or in small towns in most of the settled regions of the colonies confronted a scarcity of land. The problem Connecticut's colonists faced illustrates the interconnected issues of population growth and land scarcity. Between 1720 and 1760, Connecticut's population more than doubled, from 59,000 to 142,000. Beginning in the 1740s, children faced the prospect that their parents would not have enough land to help them establish their own farms when they became adults.

Many sons and daughters delayed marriage until they could acquire a farmstead and establish their own independent household. Others moved to nearby towns. Many of Connecticut's young adults went as far as northern New Hampshire, and others headed to the most western parts of New York, Pennsylvania, Virginia, or the Carolinas. Finally, some families simply postponed their dreams of independence, working as tenants on another farmer's land as they struggled to save enough money to purchase their own farm.

3.18 Poor Relief, Boston
Poverty increased in colonial Boston in the late eighteenth century, as did the poor relief needed to deal with this problem.

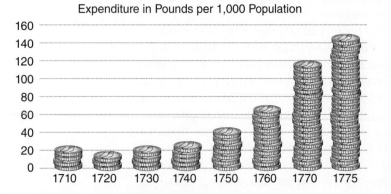

Poor Relief in Boston 1710-1775

Expenditure in Pounds per 1,000 Population

| 1710 | 1720 | 1730 | 1740 | 1750 | 1760 | 1770 | 1775 |

How was American society becoming more unequal toward the end of the eighteenth century?

View the **Closer Look** *Expanding Settlements c. 1750*

War and the Contest over Empire

By mid-century, nearly 1.2 million people lived in the British mainland colonies, making it far more densely populated than New France, which numbered well under 100,000. Britain and France had been almost constantly at war since the late seventeenth century. Although these wars generally originated in Europe, control of North America became important to both nations. The British were keen to eliminate French influence in Canada and the Great Lakes. Eliminating France also appealed to American colonists, who viewed the rich agricultural lands controlled by France as a means of alleviating the land shortage they faced. The struggle between the British and the French for control of North America would dramatically alter the map of North America.

The relatively small population of New France was spread across a vast territory, from Quebec in the north to New Orleans in the south, and as far west as Illinois (see map 3.19). In the Great Lakes region, French traders lived and worked among the Indians, often marrying Indian women. Unlike the British, who sought to displace the tribes and resettle the land with small farmers, the French developed a complex multiracial society that included Indians.

The Rise and Fall of the Middle Ground

In 1600, more than two million Indians lived in communities east of the Mississippi River. Lacking immunity to diseases brought by the Europeans, Indian populations who came into contact with Europeans were extremely vulnerable to infection. Tribes east of the Mississippi were repeatedly devastated by epidemics that reduced their numbers to less than 250,000 by 1700. One response to this dramatic decrease in population was "mourning wars," in which rival tribes raided each other's villages and took prisoners to bolster their own populations. In these wars men were often tortured and executed, but women and children were typically adopted into the conquering tribes.

Indians were also increasingly drawn into the trans-Atlantic economy, exchanging furs for European goods, including beads, fabric, alcohol, metal tools, and even firearms. The growing European demand for furs, and increased Indian desires for European goods, led to conflict among tribes for access to prime hunting and trapping grounds. Intertribal warfare changed as limited mourning wars evolved into "beaver wars," in which tribes fought one another for control of territory.

Further west in the Great Lakes region, France, not Britain, was the dominant power. Here the French and Indians created a **middle ground**, a cultural and geographical region in which Indians and the French negotiated with each other for goods, and neither side could impose its will on the other by force. Indians traded furs for guns, metal tools, and cloth.

Although the French colonial government had hoped to regulate and tax this lucrative trade by establishing a series of forts, or outposts, young, fiercely independent French traders, known as *coureurs des bois* ("runners of the woods"), established their own trading networks beyond the direct control of the French government. Many married Indian women, producing children who became a distinctive group called *métis*, or people of mixed French and Indian descent. Familiar with both Indian and French customs, and fluent in both Indian languages and French, the *métis* became critical intermediaries between Indian and French cultures, even when the gulf was difficult to bridge. Like other European societies, French culture was patriarchal: Inheritance passed from father to son, a practice that gave fathers enormous power over their sons. Thus it was natural for the French to cast themselves as fathers to their Indian children in the Great Lakes region. Indians accepted the notion of the French as fathers, but they understood the concept of fatherhood in radically different terms than Europeans. In the Indian cultures of the middle ground region, fathers were not powerful patriarchs. Indeed, one chief tried in vain to explain

Read the **Document** Cadwallader Colden, An Iroquois Chief Argues for his Tribe's Property Rights *(1742)*

What made the middle ground a distinctive region of colonial America?

"Go and see the forts our [French] Father has created, and you will see that the land beneath their walls is still hunting ground . . . whilst the English, on the contrary, no sooner get possession of a country than the game is forced to leave; the trees fall down before them, the earth becomes bare."

Contemporary Indian account of
the French and English settlement, late eighteenth century

to a French colonial official the different views of paternal authority in their respective cultures: "When you command, all the French obey and go to war. But I shall not be heeded and obeyed by my nation in such a manner." Although a gulf continued to exist between the two cultures, intermarriage between French traders and Indian women nevertheless promoted cultural exchange and mutual understanding.

The expansion of British settlement beyond the Appalachian Mountains threatened the middle ground created in the Great Lakes region. Rather than seek to preserve a middle ground, the British hoped to incorporate this region into their colonial empire. As had been true for so much of British colonization, the idea was to eliminate indigenous populations, transplant British agricultural practices, and establish permanent settlements.

The Struggle for North America

The great military powers of Atlantic Europe—Britain, France, and Spain—remained locked in a struggle for political supremacy. In 1739, European conflicts once more spilled over into North America when Britain again went to war, this time with Spain. British ships smuggled goods into Spanish America depriving Spain of valuable trade and tax revenues. Spain responded by capturing British ships, seizing their crews and cargos. British outrage over Spanish policy reached a critical moment when Captain Robert Jenkins testified before Parliament that after capturing his ship, the Spanish placed him in custody and cut off his ear as punishment for his alleged smuggling. Jenkins presented his ear in a pickle jar to an outraged Parliament. The resulting conflict between Britain and Spain was dubbed the War of Jenkins' Ear (1739–1748).

King George's War (1744–1748), a conflict in which France joined with Spain against Britain and the American colonies, soon overshadowed the War of Jenkins' Ear. The most important military victory from the colonists' point of view occurred at Louisbourg where New England's militias achieved a stunning triumph over the French and seized the mighty fortress on Cape Breton Island that guarded Atlantic access to the Gulf of St. Lawrence and French Canada. Although the fortress was returned to the French as part of the peace treaty ending the conflict, the victory became a source of colonial pride.

The conflict between France and Britain occurred during a period when colonists were particularly eager to settle in the Ohio Valley, a region controlled by the French. The formation of the Ohio Company of Virginia in 1747 facilitated the exploration and settlement of this region, a development that prompted the French to solidify their hold on it by establishing a string of forts (**3.19**). The most important of these was Fort Duquesne, erected at a fork in the Ohio River at what is now Pittsburgh. In 1754, the royal governor of Virginia dispatched militiamen under the command of an ambitious young officer, George Washington, to seize the strategic fort. Overwhelmed by French and Indian warriors, Washington was forced to surrender.

Washington's defeat proved to be only the first skirmish in a protracted battle to control the Ohio territory. In 1755, the British dispatched General Edward Braddock with a larger force, comprising British regular troops and colonial volunteers, again including Washington, to take Fort Duquesne. The French and their Indian allies routed Braddock's forces. Washington escaped, but Braddock was killed, and his troops suffered a 70 percent casualty rate. It was a shocking and ignominious defeat for the British and their colonial allies.

Why did British expansion threaten the middle ground?

View the **Closer Look** *European Claims in North America, 1750 and 1763*

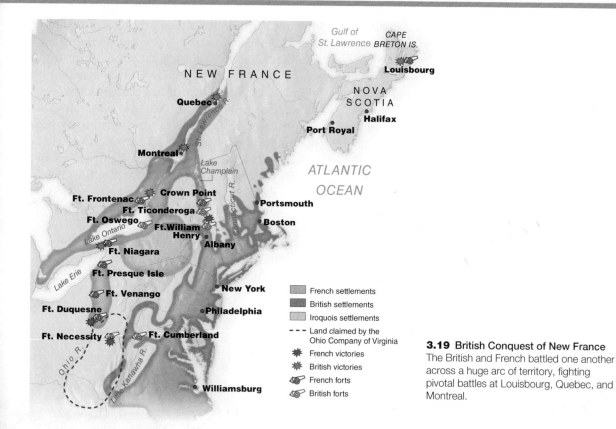

3.19 British Conquest of New France
The British and French battled one another across a huge arc of territory, fighting pivotal battles at Louisbourg, Quebec, and Montreal.

The final phase of the great war for empire, the Seven Years War, what came to be known as the French and Indian War in the American colonies, lasted from 1756 to 1763. In England William Pitt, the ambitious secretary of state appointed by George II to oversee the war effort, believed that the balance of power in Europe hinged on control of America. In 1758, the British embarked on a bold new policy: to root out the French and make a direct assault on the strongholds of Quebec City and Montreal. Pitt promoted young, talented officers including Jeffery Amherst and James Wolfe to lead the campaign against Canada. An army of 10,000 regulars and a sizeable fleet were dispatched to North America. Defeating the French also meant taking on their Indian allies as well, so the conflict was known as the French and Indian War.

The British suffered an early setback when the French General Louis de Montcalm seized Fort William Henry on Lake George in northern New York. Although Montcalm had negotiated a traditional surrender that allowed the British to retreat honorably, his Indian allies refused to accept these terms and sought scalps and other trophies of war. "The Massacre of Fort William Henry" alienated Montcalm from his Indian allies and stiffened the resolve of both the British and the colonists to defeat the French.

British fortunes began to turn when Jeffery Amherst captured Louisbourg again in 1758. A year later British forces captured the city of Quebec. General Wolfe, the British commander, searched for a weakness in the city's formidable defenses and finally settled on a daring attack. Wolfe approached the city from its poorly guarded rear flank. Rather than risk a frontal assault on the heavily fortified city, Wolfe's men scaled the heights behind the city and overpowered the small detachment of troops guarding the cliffs. In the battle that followed, Wolfe and Montcalm were both killed.

Pennsylvania painter Benjamin West commemorated the assault on Quebec in *The Death of General Wolfe* (1771) (**3.20**). West shows the dying general cradled in the arms of one of his officers. Contemporary viewers would have recognized this arrangement from European painting and sculpture: the Pieta, or the image of the dead Jesus sprawled across the Virgin Mary's lap after the crucifixion. To heighten the drama in West's painting, a British soldier runs toward the dying Wolfe with

What was William Pitt's new policy for North America?

the news that the French have been defeated, while an American Indian, a symbol of the noble warrior, looks on respectfully in tribute to the heroism of the general. Next to the Indian warrior, West placed a figure whose clothes include elements of Indian and British dress. The figure, Sir William Johnson, played a vital role helping the British forge and preserve their alliances with Indians in the region. For more on Johnson's role as a cultural and political mediator, see *Competing Visions: Sir William Johnson and the Iroquois: Indian Visions versus British Arms.*

The other important population center in French Canada, Montreal, fell to the British in late 1760, ending French domination in Canada. In 1763, France and Britain signed the Treaty of Paris, permanently altering the map of North America. Quebec remained French culturally, but Britain now controlled Canada. Although the British had defeated the French in Canada, relations with Indians along the frontier, particularly in Ohio, remained tense. In 1762, the Indian revivalist prophet Neolin, developed a pan-Indian movement that rallied the tribes of the Midwest against British colonial expansion. A year later the Ottawa Indian chief, Pontiac, led a pan-Indian force against the British garrison at Fort Detroit. In what the colonists called Pontiac's Rebellion, Indian peoples across the Midwest attacked weakly defended frontier garrisons in what is now Michigan, Indiana, and Ohio and settler communities in western Pennsylvania. Anger over the failure of the colonial

3.20 The Death of General Wolfe
Benjamin West cast the dying Wolfe in the same pose artists used to depict Jesus after the crucifixion. The messenger arriving with the news of victory enters the scene from the light-filled area of the painting, symbolizing the bright future of North America after the British victory.

What role does the Indian figure play in West's painting?

WAR AND THE CONTEST OVER EMPIRE   91

Competing Visions
SIR WILLIAM JOHNSON AND THE IROQUOIS: INDIAN VISIONS VERSUS BRITISH ARMS

In 1762, a delegation of Iroquois leaders met with the British Superintendent for Indian Affairs, Sir William Johnson, at his impressive residence, Johnson Hall, near Saratoga, New York. During the meeting an Onondaga Chief confronted Johnson, revealing a vision that a member of his tribe had received from the "Great Spirit" regarding English expansion into Indian lands. Johnson dismissed Indian visions, and he warned the tribes that Englishmen would not take such claims seriously and that English military power demonstrated that the "Great Spirit" favored the English. What does Johnson's dismissive view of Indian religion reveal about Anglo-Indian relations?

The Onondaga Chief testified to the assembled members of the Iroquois Council and Sir William Johnson about a recent vision to his tribe that revealed the Great Spirit's displeasure with the British displacement of Indian peoples. The revelation contained a thinly veiled threat about the consequences of continuing this policy.

Onondaga Chief:
Brother:

One of our People lately in a vision was told by the Great Spirit above, that when He first made the World. He gave this large Island to the Indians for their Use; at the same time He gave other Parts of the World beyond the great Waters to the rest of his creating, and gave them different languages: That He now saw the white People squabbling, and fighting for these Lands which He gave the Indians; and that in every Assembly, and Company of Governors, and Great Men. He heard nothing scarce spoke, or talk'd of, but claiming, and wanting, large Possessions in our Country. This He said was so contrary to his Intention, and what He expected would be the Consequence at the time when the white People first came, like Children among Us, that He was quite displeas'd and would, altho their Numbers were ever so great, punish them if They did not desist.

Johnson curtly told the members of the Iroquois Council that the British would not pay attention to Indian religious beliefs, which he dismissed as foolish superstitions. In response to the Onondaga's oblique threat, Johnson reminded the Iroquois that British arms were superior to Indian weaponry and that resistance would not be tolerated.

Sir William Johnson
Brethren:

Your romantic Notions, Custom of Dreaming, and Seeing visions, however, usual amongst you, cannot but appear in a very ridiculous Light to White People, who will consider it, only as a Scheme set on foot by some designing Persons to answer their Purposes; and I hope you cannot but be convinced that the Divine Being is satisfied with the Justice of Our Cause, from the great Successes with He has crowned the British Arms—I hope therefore, you will not Suspect us of defrauding you of your Lands.

Sir William Johnson presented this certificate to the Iroquois for their loyalty to "his Britannic Majesty." Diplomacy with Indians included many ceremonial exchanges such as the one depicted in the image at the top of this document.

How did Johnson react to Indian demands that western expansion be halted?

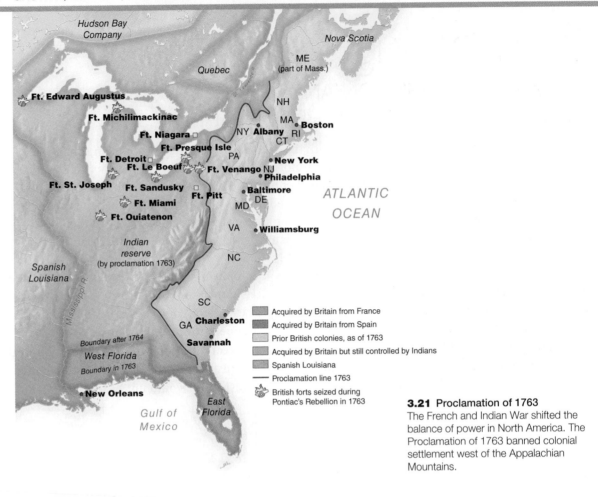

3.21 Proclamation of 1763
The French and Indian War shifted the balance of power in North America. The Proclamation of 1763 banned colonial settlement west of the Appalachian Mountains.

governments to protect them led to protests by western settlers. In Pennsylvania settlers from the frontier settlement of Paxton sought revenge by attacking friendly Indians and marching against the city of Philadelphia demanding the creation of a militia to fight Indians. The march of the "Paxton Boys" might have plunged Pennsylvania into widespread bloodshed, but violence was averted after leading Philadelphia citizens agreed to present the protesters' grievances to the colonial assembly. (See *Choices and Consequences: Quakers, Pacifism, and the Paxton Uprising*, page 93.)

The global struggle between Britain and France, the Seven Years War, not only transformed the political map of North America, it irrevocably altered the history of the region, establishing British supremacy once and for all. Colonists described this conflict as the French and Indian War for good reason. For colonists, British victory meant an end to French

political influence in Canada and a reconfiguration of the balance of power in the vast region of the middle ground that had been a French sphere of influence for generations.

Before the defeat of the French in Canada, western Indians could count on a reliable supply of arms and ammunition from Britain's traditional rival, France. Without this vital support the pan-Indian alliance collapsed. Still Pontiac's Rebellion persuaded the British to be conciliatory toward the more powerful tribes along the frontier. The peace treaty that was signed to end hostilities with Indians not only included favorable terms for trade but also placed severe restrictions on westward expansion by colonists. The Proclamation of 1763 (**3.21**) established a fixed line beyond which colonial expansion westward was prohibited, effectively restricting colonists to territory east of the Appalachian Mountains.

Choices and Consequences
QUAKERS, PACIFISM, AND THE PAXTON UPRISING

Relations between Pennsylvanians and Indians had deteriorated during the eighteenth century as the white population grew. Newcomers, such as the Scots-Irish who dominated the backcountry, began to challenge the Quakers' political power. The violence associated with Pontiac's Rebellion only exacerbated these tensions. Western settlers, including the Paxton Boys, petitioned the Quaker-dominated colonial assembly to pass a mandatory militia law and provide arms for western settlers. Quakers, however, were pacifists who continued to believe that it was possible to maintain peaceful relations with their Indian neighbors. Quakers in the assembly faced a difficult decision.

Choices

1 Support a mandatory militia law and create a well-regulated militia, properly trained and armed.

2 Continue to oppose the creation of a well-regulated militia and seek peaceful non-violent solutions to Indian–settler conflicts.

3 Resign from elected office, so that their pacifism would not prevent the assembly from creating a militia.

Decision

The legislature chose to continue its pacifist policies.

Consequences

Pennsylvania was the only colony without a militia law. This issue continued to spark controversy until the American Revolution. The 1776 Pennsylvania Constitution and Declaration of Rights not only created a militia, but it became the first state to expressly protect a right to bear arms.

Continuing Controversies

Why were Quakers so obstinately against creating a well-regulated militia?
Scholars sympathetic to the plight of the protestors view their challenge to the Quaker government as an expression of the rising tide of democratic sentiment that helped bring about the American Revolution. For those more sympathetic to the Indians, the Quaker government's policies were as exceptional as they were praiseworthy.

Paxton Uprising cartoon

Why did Paxtonians demand that the Quakers create a militia?

1728

Massachusetts battles Crown over salary for the royal governor
Massachusetts House and the royal governor disagree over salary, an important indicator of the growing power of colonial legislatures

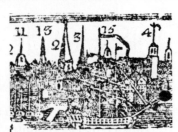

1730

The first synagogue in British North America is built
New York's pluralistic society expands to include Jews as well as Christians

1732

James Oglethorpe founds Georgia
A utopian experiment and a buffer between Carolina and Spanish Florida, Georgia eventually accepted slavery and became a plantation society

Benjamin Franklin founds Library Company
America's first circulating library

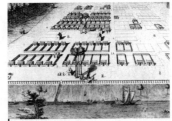

1735

First Moravian community established in America
Moravians, an evangelical Protestant sect from Germany, bring their message to America

Review Questions

1. How did changes in architecture and home furnishing reflect Anglicization and the rise of gentility in colonial America?

2. What were the leading Enlightenment ideals, and what was the significance of America's role in that movement? In what ways did the colony of Georgia strive to embody Enlightenment ideals?

3. How did the experience of slavery differ between the upper South and the lower South?

4. How did the French and Indian War affect colonial–Indian relations? What new problems did the British victory create for the empire?

Key Terms

Enlightenment An international philosophical movement that extolled the virtues of reason and science and applied these new insights to politics and social reform.   **64**

Great Awakening A religious revival movement that emphasized a more emotional style of religious practice.   **64**

Anglicization The colonial American desire to emulate English society, including English taste in foods, customs, and architecture.   **67**

Virtual representation A theory of representation in which legislators do not serve their localities but rather the whole nation.   **71**

Old Lights Opponents of the Great Awakening who favored traditional forms of religious worship.   **75**

New Lights Supporters of the Great Awakening and its more emotional style of worship.   **75**

Middle passage The harrowing voyage across the Atlantic from Africa to the Americas during which slaves endured meager rations and horrendously unsanitary conditions.   **79**

Indentured servants A form of bound labor in which a number of years of service were specified as payment for passage to America.   **83**

Middle ground A cultural and geographical region of the Great Lakes in which Indians and the French negotiated with each other for goods and neither side could impose its will on the other.   **87**

1739

Eliza Pinckney introduces indigo to South Carolina
The sought-after dye produced by indigo became Carolina's second most important export

English preacher George Whitefield arrives in America
The great evangelical preacher creates an inter-colonial sensation and extends the reach of the Great Awakening

1741–1751

Academy of Philadelphia founded
Franklin helps found the University of Pennsylvania

Benjamin Franklin publishes his experiments on electricity
Earns Franklin fame and symbolizes America's contribution to the Enlightenment

1759

Quebec falls
The decisive battle in the French and Indian War signals the defeat of the French in Canada

1763

Proclamation of 1763
To prevent further encroachment on Indian lands and avoid future conflicts, Britain forbids colonial settlement beyond the Appalachian Mountains

Treaty of Paris between Britain and France ends French and Indian War
The formal end of hostilities legally acknowledges British domination in North America

MyHistoryLab Connections

Visit www.myhistorylab.com for a customized Study Plan that will help you build your knowledge of *Growth, Slavery, and Conflict.*

Questions for Analysis

1. In what ways did art and architecture become more English in the early decades of the eighteenth century?

View the Closer Look *Images as History: A Portrait of Colonial Aspiration, p. 67*

2. In what ways did Benjamin Franklin represent the ideals of the Enlightenment?

Read the Document *Profiles: Benjamin Franklin, p. 74*

3. Which regions of the Atlantic world were most heavily involved in the international slave trade?

View the Closer Look *African Slave Trade, 1451–1870, p. 78*

4. How did French and English aims differ and how did these differences impact relations with Indians?

View the Closer Look *European Claims in North America, 1750 and 1763, p. 88*

5. What impact did the French and Indian War have on the colonies?

View the Map *Interactive Map: The Seven Years War, p. 92*

Other Resources from This Chapter

Read the **Document**

- *William Byrd II, Diary: An American Gentleman (1709), p. 68*
- *Benjamin Franklin on George Whitefield, p. 75*
- *Of the Servants and Slaves in Virginia (1705), p. 85*
- *Cadwallader Colden, An Iroquois Chief Argues for his Tribe's Property Rights (1742), p. 87*

View the **Closer Look**

- *Competing Visions: Slavery and Georgia, p. 73*
- *Expanding Settlements c. 1750, p. 86*

View the **Map** *Interactive Map: Colonial Products, p. 83*

Tightening the Reins of Empire p. 98

How did British policy toward the colonies change after the French and Indian War?

Patriots versus Loyalists p. 108

How did revolutionary events in 1775 and 1776 transform the competing visions of Patriots and Loyalists?

America at War p. 113

What were the major battles and turning points in the war from the summer of 1776 to its conclusion?

The Radicalism of the American Revolution p. 117

How did the Revolution's ideals of liberty and equality influence American politics and society?

CHAPTER 4

((•─ Hear the Audio File on myhistorylab.com

◉─ Watch the Video *Critical Visions, Chapter 4*

Revolutionary America

Change and Transformation, 1764–1783

Britain's decisive victory in the French and Indian War in 1763 removed the French threat to its American empire. But the war had been expensive to wage, and the ongoing costs of administering and protecting North America nearly drained the British treasury. To pay these costs, Britain adopted a new set of policies for America, including new taxes, more aggressive ways of collecting them, and more severe methods of enforcing these measures. The colonists viewed these policies as an ominous first step in a plot to deprive them of their liberty.

When King George III (r. 1760–1820) assumed the British throne, monarchism was deeply rooted in American culture, and Americans were proud of their British heritage. Opposition to British policy began with respectful pleas to the king for relief from unjust policies. Gradually, over the next decade, Americans became convinced that it was no longer possible to remain within the British Empire and protect their rights. Resistance to British policies stiffened, and the colonists eventually decided to declare independence from Britain.

Tensions between Britain and the American colonies reached a boiling point with the Tea Act in 1773, the theme of this cartoon, *The Tea-Tax-Tempest.* In the image "Father Time" displays the events of the American Revolution to four figures who symbolize the four continents. The "magic lantern" shows a tea pot boiling over, symbolizing revolution, while British and American military forces stand ready to face one another.

The ideals of liberty and equality that Americans invoked in their struggle against British tyranny changed American society. The claim that "all men are created equal" and that every person enjoyed certain "inalienable rights," as America's Declaration of Independence asserted in 1776, were radical notions for those who had grown up in a society that was ruled by a king and that enthusiastically embraced the idea of aristocracy.

Slavery continued to present a problem for champions of the Revolution. For some slavery was incompatible with the Revolution's ideals, while others sought to reconcile the two. New England effectively eliminated slavery after the Revolution. The new states of the mid-Atlantic adopted a more gradual approach to abolishing slavery. In the South, however, where planters made fortunes from crops produced with slave labor, slavery remained deeply entrenched. Although women were not yet full political participants, revolutionary notions of equality led them to demand that husbands treat wives as partners in their marriage. A new idea of companionate marriage blossomed.

"Yesterday the greatest question was decided . . . and a greater question perhaps never was nor will be decided among men. A resolution was passed without one dissenting colony, that these United Colonies are, and of right ought to be, free and independent states."

JOHN ADAMS, 1776

Tightening the Reins of Empire

The British victory in the French and Indian War in 1763 secured North America against French attack. It also forced the British government to chart a new direction for dealing with America. A cornerstone of the new policy was the Proclamation of 1763, which prohibited settlement in lands west of the Appalachian Mountains (see Chapter 3). Having just fought an expensive war against the French, the British were keen to prevent colonists and Indians from starting a new war. Britain also felt a renewed urgency to raise funds to pay off the war debt and cover the costs of administering the colonies.

Taxation without Representation

In 1763, George Grenville, the new prime minister, ordered a detailed investigation of colonial revenues and was unhappy to discover that American customs' duties produced less than £2,000 a year. The lucrative trade in molasses between British North America and the Caribbean islands alone should have yielded approximately £200,000 a year, apart from all of the other goods traded between North America and Britain, which should also have generated customs duties. To make the colonies pay their share of taxes, Grenville was determined to enforce existing laws and enact new taxes to bring in additional revenue. As the figures in *Envisioning Evidence: A Comparison of Annual Per Capita Tax Rates in Britain and the Colonies in 1765* show, compared to the inhabitants of Britain and Ireland, the tax burden on the American colonists in the 1760s was low. Americans and Britons had come to view taxation differently and these different visions of the morality and legality of Britain's new policies put the two on a collision course.

> ## "The very act of taxing exercised over those who are not represented appears to me to be depriving them of one of their most essential rights as freemen."
>
> JAMES OTIS, *The Rights of the British Colonies Asserted and Proved* (1764)

The first step in Grenville's new program was the Revenue Act (1764), popularly known as the Sugar Act. It lowered the duties colonists had to pay on molasses, but taxed sugar and other goods imported to the colonies and increased penalties for smuggling. It also created new ways for enforcing compliance with these laws. Violators could be prosecuted in British vice-admiralty courts, which operated without jury trials. For some Americans the Sugar Act violated two long-held beliefs: the idea that colonists could not be taxed without their consent and the equally sacred notion that Englishmen were entitled to a trial by a jury of their peers.

The Massachusetts lawyer James Otis attacked the Sugar Act as a violation of the rights of Englishmen. Otis had already achieved notoriety for his opposition to the use of writs of assistance by customs officials. Otis insisted that under British law, a court could issue a search warrant only for a specific place where there was probable cause to suspect illegal activity. Rather than require that officials designate where they intended to search, the new general writs allowed customs officials to search any private property without first demonstrating probable cause or seeking the approval of a magistrate. In his pamphlet attacking the Sugar Act, *The Rights of the British Colonies Asserted and Proved*, Otis denied that the British had the authority to tax the colonists without their consent. But Otis stopped short of recommending active resistance to the Sugar Act. Instead he counseled patience, reminding his readers that we "must and ought to yield obedience to an act of Parliament, though erroneous, till repealed."

Whereas Americans viewed the new tax on sugar and other imports as a burden and a

Envisioning Evidence

A COMPARISON OF ANNUAL PER CAPITA TAX RATES IN BRITAIN AND THE COLONIES IN 1765*

Given the stridency of colonial opposition to British taxation, one might think that Americans were the most heavily taxed people in the British Empire. In fact, however, they were the least heavily taxed part of the empire. Americans were also generally wealthier than their countrymen across the Atlantic. American grievances were less about the levels of taxation than about the constitutional and political issues taxation raised. Policy makers in Britain had trouble understanding this distinction, which had profound consequences for relations with the colonies.

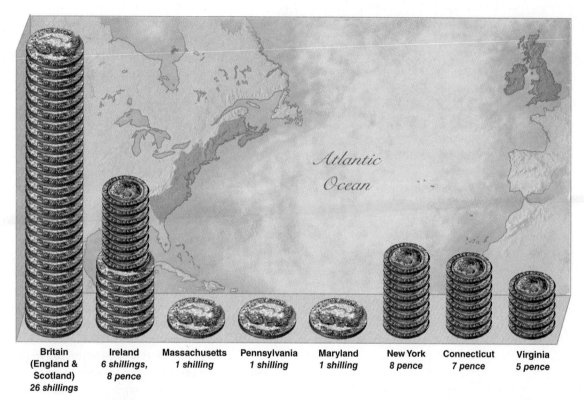

Atlantic Ocean

| Britain (England & Scotland) 26 shillings | Ireland 6 shillings, 8 pence | Massachusetts 1 shilling | Pennsylvania 1 shilling | Maryland 1 shilling | New York 8 pence | Connecticut 7 pence | Virginia 5 pence |

1 shilling = 12 pence

*Until 1970, British currency was denominated in pounds, shillings, and pence: £, s, d. There were 20 shillings to a pound and 12 pence to a shilling. In the 1760s, the daily wage for a skilled worker in London was 2/s 2/d and a beef dinner with a pint of beer cost 1/s. In British North America, wages and prices varied from colony to colony, but free white American males enjoyed a higher standard of living than comparable workers did in Britain. In 1760, a Philadelphia laborer earned just under £60 a year and a merchant £180.

Source: *Adapted from R. R. Palmer,* The Age of Democratic Revolution: A Political History of Europe and America, 1760–1800 *(Princeton, NJ: Princeton University Press, 1959)*

Which parts of the British empire were most heavily taxed?

4.1 The Great Financier
Prime Minister George Grenville holds a balance in which "Debts" far outweigh "Savings." Britannia, symbol of Great Britain, sits off to the right, forlorn. An Indian "princess," symbol of the American colonies, kneels with a yoke around her neck. The writing on the yoke declares "Taxed without representation."

violation of their rights, for the British, the taxes were a modest imposition necessary to pay for the cost of eliminating the French from North America and administering the colonies. This political cartoon (**4.1**), which portrays Grenville holding a balance in which "debts" clearly outweigh "savings," illustrates Britain's financial predicament. The British cartoonist who drew it obviously sympathized with Americans. He shows a Native American "princess," the most common symbol of the colonies in British cartoons, carrying a sack of money and bearing a heavy yoke around her neck. Inscribed on the yoke is the colonists' complaint: "Taxed without representation."

The Stamp Act Crisis

Britain reacted to the colonists' resistance to the Sugar Act by imposing another, harsher tax, the **Stamp Act**, which required colonists to purchase special stamps and place them on everything from newspapers to playing cards. A similar tax existed in Britain, and Parliament believed that requiring colonists to pay such a tax at a lower rate than their brethren in Britain was entirely reasonable. Many colonists, however, rejected this notion. For them, taxation without consent was a violation of their rights.

Opposition was most intense in the seaports; the map (**4.2**) shows how widespread anger against this latest tax was. Stamps had to be affixed to virtually all legal transactions and most printed documents, so the new tax act alienated more Americans than had any previous parliamentary tax. The British could hardly have picked a worse target for their new scheme of taxation. Among those most burdened by the tax were lawyers and printers, two of the most vocal and influential groups in the colonies. Protests against the Stamp Act filled colonial newspapers and produced a spate of pamphlets defending colonial rights. The Massachusetts House of Representatives called on other colonial assemblies to send delegates to New York to frame a response to the Stamp Act crisis. Nine of the thirteen colonies

4.2 Stamp Act Protests
This map shows the scope of opposition to the detested Stamp Act. Protest was most intense in the seaports.

sent a representative to the Stamp Act Congress, and although framed in respectful terms, the "Declaration of the Rights and Grievances of the Colonies" was an important step toward articulating a common response to British policy, forcing representatives from different colonies to work together for a common goal.

Protest against this latest attack on American liberty was not limited to newspapers or legislative chambers. Opposition to the Stamp Act spilled out of doors into the streets of American cities and towns. Angry crowds attacked tax collectors and officials. In a few cases crowds also attacked the homes of British officials, including the home of the lieutenant governor of Massachusetts, Thomas Hutchinson.

George III dismissed George Grenville in 1765, leaving the task of responding to the American crisis to a young English nobleman, Charles Wentworth, Marquess of Rockingham, the new prime minister. Rockingham shepherded two key pieces of legislation through Parliament to deal with the crisis created by the Stamp Act. The Declaratory Act affirmed Parliament's authority to "make laws and statutes" binding on the colonies "in all cases whatsoever." The second piece of legislation repealed the hated Stamp Act. Britain believed that it had reasserted its authority over the colonies, while removing the main cause of colonial protest. British officials misjudged the reaction of colonists opposed to recent policy. For critics of British policy, it appeared that Parliament had embarked on a path that would lead inevitably to the destruction of the colonists' liberty.

Colonial politics had moved from the margins to the center of British politics. The issue of what to do about the colonies would define British politics for the next decade. In the colonies the conflict over British policy also transformed American politics, bringing to the fore a group of Patriots, aggressive supporters of American rights, including the Sons of Liberty, a group devoted to opposing British policy and defending American rights.

An Assault on Liberty

The resolution of the Stamp Act crisis did not eliminate Britain's pressing financial need for colonial revenue, nor did it reduce colonial determination to resist further efforts to tax Americans. What good will the repeal of the Stamp Act generated, Britain quickly squandered as it renewed its efforts to impose new taxes on the colonies. The Townshend Acts (1767), named for Charles Townshend, an ambitious British finance minister, levied new taxes on glass, paint, paper, and tea imported into the colonies. Townshend misinterpreted the Stamp Act protests. He believed that colonists opposed internal taxes targeted at commerce within the colonies, but that Americans would accept external taxes such as customs duties that affected trade between the colonies and other parts of the British Empire. Again, many Americans saw things differently.

The Townshend Acts prompted Americans to clarify their views about taxation. Pennsylvania lawyer John Dickinson's pamphlet *Letters from a Farmer in Pennsylvania* (1767–1768) was an important statement of American views. Dickinson disputed Parliament's right to tax the colonists at all. Parliament could regulate trade among different parts of the empire, he acknowledged, but only the people's representatives could enact taxes designed primarily to raise revenues. Since Americans had no representation in Parliament, that institution could not tax them.

In response to the Townshend Acts, Americans began a **nonimportation movement**, an organized boycott against the purchase of any imported British goods. Women took an active role in the boycott, urging that instead of imported fabrics, Americans wear only clothes made from domestic homespun fabrics. The nonimportation movement offered American women a chance to contribute actively to the defense of American rights. It also raised women's political consciousness. As thirteen-year-old, Anna Green Winslow, wrote in her journal regarding the decision to abandon imported fabrics, "I am (as we say) a daughter of liberty, I chuse to wear as much of our manufactory as possible."

Another import, tea, had become the basis of an important social ritual in colonial society. Amid the growing frustration with British policy, tea drinking took on new political significance. In 1774, Penelope Barker and a group of women in Edenton, North Carolina, organized a tea boycott. Word of the Edenton protest eventually reached England, where a British cartoonist lampooned its support for the American cause (**4.3** on page 102). This satire casts the Edenton women as a motley assortment of hags and harlots, whose unfeminine actions and neglect of their proper duties as women demonstrate their lack of virtue. The tea boycott even inspired nine-year-old Susan Boudinot, the daughter of a wealthy Philadelphia family, to demonstrate her solidarity with the

Read the **Document** *John Dickinson,* Letters from Farmer in Pennsylvania

How did nonimportation transform women's political role in the colonies?

4.3 Patriotic Ladies of Edenton
This sarcastic British cartoon lampoons the efforts of American women to participate in the boycott of British imports. The caricature shows the women as unfeminine and neglectful of their proper subordinate roles as wives and mothers.

"A Lady's Adieu To Her Tea Table,"
No more shall I dish out the once lov'd Liquor,
Though now detestable,
Because I'm taught (and I believe it true)
Its Use will fasten slavish
Chains upon my Country,
And LIBERTY's the
Goddess I would choose
To reign triumphant in
AMERICA.

VIRGINIA GAZETTE, January 20, 1774

colonial cause in her own way. When invited to tea at the home of the royal governor of New Jersey, Susan curtsied respectfully, raised her teacup to her lips, and then tossed the contents out of a window.

The new duties imposed by the British were only one part of a more aggressive policy toward the colonies. Between 1765 and 1768, the British transferred the bulk of their military forces in America from the frontier to the major seaports, sites of the most violent opposition to the Stamp Act. This increased the already tense situation in these localities. In 1768, the simmering tensions between colonists and the British government came to a head when British customs officials in Boston seized merchant John Hancock's ship *Liberty*. Customs officials had long suspected Hancock of smuggling and thought that seizing the *Liberty* would give them the proof to prosecute him. The decision proved to be a serious blunder. The symbolic significance of the British assault on a ship named *Liberty* was not lost on Bostonians, who saw this as an assault on the idea of liberty itself. In response to the seizure of the *Liberty*, Bostonians rioted, driving customs officials from the town. To quell unrest in Boston, the British dispatched additional troops and warships to the area. By 1769, the British had stationed almost 4,000 troops, dubbed redcoats because of their red uniforms, in a city with a population of roughly 15,000.

Relations between Bostonians and the occupying forces were tense. On March 5, 1770, a group of citizens taunted a patrol of soldiers and pelted them with snowballs. In the melee that followed, some of the soldiers fired on the crowd, killing five civilians. The Boston silversmith and engraver Paul Revere published a popular engraving of the Boston Massacre, as the confrontation came to be called, in which he portrayed the British as having deliberately fired on the unarmed crowd (**4.4**). Revere aligns the soldiers in a formal military pose, and portrays the commanders as giving an order to fire. When the soldiers responsible for the shootings were indicted for murder, John Adams, a vocal critic of British policy, volunteered to defend them. Adams sought to demonstrate to the British that the Americans were not a lawless mob, but a law-abiding people. A gifted lawyer, he secured acquittals for all those accused except for two soldiers, who were convicted of the lesser crime of manslaughter. The evidence presented at the trial revealed that Revere's version of the event, while excellent propaganda, was not an accurate rendering of the circumstances.

The new taxes and pressure for compliance had stiffened the colonists' resistance. So although Parliament repealed most of the Townshend Acts in 1770, relations between the colonies and Britain remained strained. Colonists continued to demand the traditional rights of Englishmen, such as trial by jury, but American protests had moved in a new

How does Revere stage the events of the Boston Massacre to evoke sympathy for the colonists' cause?

View the **Closer Look** *Images as History: The Hanging of Absalom*

4.4 Boston Massacre
Paul Revere's influential engraving of the Boston Massacre takes liberties with the facts to portray the British in the worst possible light. The orderly arrangement of the troops and the stance of the officer at their side suggest that they acted under orders. Behind the troops, Revere has renamed the shop "Butcher's Hall."

though it made tea cheaper, and merchants resented the monopoly it gave to the East India Company. Others saw the act as a subtle way of reasserting Britain's right to tax the colonies.

One group of angry colonists in Philadelphia, calling themselves The Tar and Feathering Committee, warned that they would tar and feather any ship's captain who landed with British tea. The British found the colonists' actions thuggish. In this hostile British cartoon, *Bostonians Pay the Excise-Man* (**4.5**), a cruel-looking bunch of colonists force a British customs official, covered in tar and feathers, to drink tea until he becomes sick. A form of public humiliation, tarring and feathering involved pouring hot tar onto the victim's skin and then attaching a coat of feathers. Scraping off the resulting mess was painful and laborious.

4.5 Bostonians Paying the Excise-Man
In this pro-British cartoon, Bostonians are cruel thugs who have tarred and feathered the custom's official and are forcing tea down his throat.

direction, including the view that taxation without representation was a violation of fundamental rights. Resistance to British policy was also becoming more organized. The Sons of Liberty, created during the Stamp Act crisis, continued their criticism and intensified their efforts to coordinate and enforce protests against Parliament's policies.

After the repeal of the Townshend Acts, Americans enjoyed a brief respite from Parliament's attentions, as Britain turned its focus elsewhere in its far-flung empire, especially to India. However, colonists soon faced another effort to tax them.

The Intolerable Acts and the First Continental Congress

In 1773, Parliament decided to help the flagging East India Company increase its tea sales to the colonies. Many members of Parliament had sizable investments in the company. The new law lowered the price of tea to Americans, but kept the tax on tea, and also gave the East India Company a monopoly on the tea trade with the colonies. Again, British authorities miscalculated American reactions. Colonists resented the new law, even

Why did British policy seem to strike at the essence of colonists' liberty?

View the **Closer Look** *The Bloody Massacre*

4.6 *The Able Doctor, or America Swallowing the Bitter Draught*
Paul Revere's engraving presents America as a partially clad Indian princess. Lord Chief Justice Mansfield, a symbol of British law, holds America down. The prime minister, Lord North, shown with a copy of the Boston Port Bill, one of the Intolerable Acts, protruding from his pocket, forces tea down her throat.

The most dramatic response to the tea act occurred in December 1773, when Bostonians, dressed as Indians, boarded a British ship and tossed over 340 chests of tea into the harbor in what came to be known as the Boston Tea Party.

To punish the colonists responsible for this act of what the British considered vandalism, Parliament passed the Coercive Acts, known to colonists as the **Intolerable Acts**. This legislation closed the Port of Boston, annulled the Massachusetts colonial charter, dissolved or severely restricted that colony's political institutions, and allowed the British to quarter (house) troops in private homes. (A generation later Americans adopted the Third Amendment to the Bill of Rights, which forbade quartering troops in civilian homes, a direct response to this detested British practice.) The acts also allowed British officials charged with capital crimes to be tried outside the colonies. Some colonists called the last provision the "Murder Act," since they feared it would allow soldiers charged with murder to avoid prosecution.

Americans were divided over how to respond to the Intolerable Acts. Some saw the Bostonians who dumped tea into the harbor as radicals whose actions besmirched Americans' reputation as law-abiding subjects of the king. Others expressed outrage at the British policy that had forced Bostonians

to resort to such a dramatic protest. This cartoon, *The Able Doctor, Or America Swallowing the Bitter Draught* (**4.6**), gives a different view of Bostonians from the lawless ruffians depicted in *Bostonians Paying the Excise-Man* (4.5). Here the British prime minister, Lord North, brutally accosts America, a half-clad Indian princess, forcing tea down her throat, while Lord Chief Justice Lord Mansfield, the symbol of British law, pins her arms down.

The most important consequence of the Intolerable Acts was the decision by the colonies to convene a Continental Congress in Philadelphia in late 1774. All the colonies except Georgia sent representatives. Among the colonial leaders who attended were Patrick Henry, John Adams, and George Washington. Congress endorsed the Resolves of Suffolk County, Massachusetts, which denounced the Intolerable Acts and asserted the intention of colonists to nullify such a manifest violation of their "rights and liberties." The Congress also recommended that every town, county, and city create a committee to enforce the boycott of British goods. The informal network of committees that had opposed British policy now acquired a quasi-legal status from Congress.

Although many Americans hoped that a peaceful solution to the deepening crisis was possible, in March 1774, the brilliant Virginia orator Patrick Henry urged his fellow delegates in the

What is the symbolic significance Lord Chief Justice Mansfield's actions in this political cartoon?

Read the **Document** *Patrick Henry, "Give me Liberty or Give me Death"*

Virginia legislature to prepare for the inevitable conflict that loomed between the colonies and Britain. Although no contemporaneous copy of his dramatic speech exists, Henry's words were recounted many years later, assuming almost legendary status in American culture. In response to British assaults, Henry declared, "Give me liberty—or give me death!"

Between the passage of the Sugar Act in 1764 and the meeting of the First Continental Congress in 1774, relations between Britain and America had steadily deteriorated. As the chart (**4.7**) shows, Britain had tried various revenue measures to raise funds from the colonies. Americans, however, remained opposed to taxation without representation. Rather than subdue the colonies, British policy only strengthened the resolve of Americans to defend their rights.

Lexington, Concord, and Lord Dunmore's Proclamation

Living on the edge of the British Empire, colonists had come to depend on their own militias as their primary means of public defense. The laws of the individual colonies regulated these organizations of citizen soldiers. During the colonial period the militia was more than just a force available to protect the colonists from hostile Indians or attacks from the French or Spanish. In an era before police forces, the militia also helped enforce public order, putting down riots, rebellions, and other civil disturbances. In January 1775, Virginia's George Mason called on the colonists to put their militia in good order.

4.7 British Policies and their Consequences for Relations with the American Colonies

Date	Act	Policy	Consequences
1763	Proclamation of 1763	Prohibits colonists from moving westward	Intensifies problem of land scarcity in colonies
1764	Sugar Act	Reduces duty on molasses, but provides for more vigorous methods of enforcement	Colonials articulate theory that taxation without representation is a violation of "their most essential rights as freemen"
1765	Stamp Act	Documents and printed materials, including legal documents, newspapers, and playing cards must use special stamped paper	Riots in major urban areas, harassment of revenue officers, colonial representatives meet for Stamp Act Congress
1765	Quartering Act	Colonists must supply British troops with housing and firewood	Colonial Assemblies protest, New York punished for failure to comply with law
1766	Declaratory Act/Repeal of Stamp Act	Britain asserts its right to legislate for colonies in all cases/ Stamp Act repealed	Britain reasserts its authority, while removing the obnoxious provisions of the Stamp Act
1767	Townshend Acts	New duties placed on glass, lead, paper, paint	Non-importation movement gains ground
1773	Tea Act	Parliament gives East India Company monopoly, but provides a subsidy to East India Company that decreases the price of tea for Americans	90,000 pounds of tea tossed into Boston harbor
1774	Coercive Acts (Intolerable Acts)	Port of Boston closed, town meetings restricted	First Continental Congress meets and other colonies express support for Bostonians
1775	Prohibitory Act	Britain declares intention to coerce Americans into submission	Continental Congress adopts a Declaration of Rights asserting American rights

What was the impact of Lord Dunmore's Proclamation on southern colonists?

> "If we view the whole of the conduct of the [British] ministry and parliament, I do not see how any one can doubt but that there is a settled fix'd plan for inslaving the colonies, or bringing them under arbitrary government."
>
> Connecticut Minister, the Reverend
> EBENEZER BALDWIN, 1774

Mason declared that "a well regulated Militia, composed of gentlemen freeholders, and other free-man, is the natural strength and only stable security of a free Government."

The British, too, understood the importance of the militia to colonial resistance. Not only did they pose a military threat, but they were also indispensable to helping mobilize Americans and organizing their opposition to British policy. Disarming the militias became a priority for the British. Their first target was Massachusetts, which had become a hotbed of resistance; the British dispatched troops to Concord in April 1775 to seize gunpowder and other military supplies. Paul Revere, an outspoken member of the Sons of Liberty, was charged with riding from Boston to Lexington and Concord to warn citizens that British troops were on the march. Revere got as far as Lexington before a British patrol captured him. Fortunately for Revere he had already encountered another member of the Sons of Liberty that night, Dr. Samuel Prescott, who was returning from the home of his fiancée. Prescott agreed to carry word that British troops were marching from Boston. The alarm spread throughout the countryside. When the 700 British regulars finally arrived at Lexington's town green, they faced 60–70 militiamen. Although the militia agreed to disperse, someone, it is not clear who, fired a shot, and the two sides exchanged fire. The Battle of Lexington marked the first military conflict between Britain and America, and the colonists had demonstrated their mettle.

The British then marched to Concord, where they confronted a larger and better organized militia detachment at the North Bridge. The militia stood their ground and exchanged fire with the British regulars, who were forced to retreat. While the British retreated back to Boston, colonial reinforcements poured into Concord and the surrounding countryside. The British column was an easy target for militiamen, who took up positions along the roadside and in the adjacent woods. A Rhode Island newspaper captured the views of Patriots when it commented that British aggression marked the start of a "War which shall hereafter fill an important page in history."

Although the British had mounted a direct assault on the Massachusetts militia, they opted for a stealthier plan for disarming the Virginia militia. Under cover of darkness a detachment of Royal Marines entered Virginia's capital of Williamsburg, seized the gun powder, and destroyed the firing mechanisms on the muskets stored in the militia's magazine (storehouse). When citizens of Williamsburg learned of the assault, they marched on the governor's mansion to protest. As word of the British raid spread through the colony, militia led by Patrick Henry planned to march on Williamsburg. Lord Dunmore, the royal governor, warned that if the militia entered Williamsburg he would "declare freedom to slaves and reduce the city of Williamsburg to ashes." At the last moment a compromise was worked out, and the governor made restitution for the stolen powder and damaged guns. Still Dunmore's threat to free Virginia's slaves had shocked the colony.

Two weeks later colonists learned of **Lord Dunmore's Proclamation**. Dunmore offered freedom to any slave who joined the British forces in putting down the American rebellion. Within a month 300 slaves had joined "Dunmore's Ethiopian Regiment," whose ranks would swell to 800 or more. The uniforms of this unit included a sash emblazoned with the motto "Liberty To Slaves." Virginians complained that the British were "using every Art to seduce the Negroes," while others viewed Dunmore's decision as "diabolical." Many Virginians who were wavering on the issue of American independence now concluded that a break with Britain was inevitable, even desirable. Some Virginians recognized that Virginia's slaves were seeking the same liberty that colonists claimed. For example Lund Washington, who managed his cousin George's Mount Vernon estate, including his slaves, observed that "there is not a man of them but would leave us, if they could make their escape."

Why did British regulars choose Concord as their military objective?

Patriots versus Loyalists

 By 1775, the rift between Britain and the colonies had grown precipitously large. Indeed, it was not just colonists who believed that if Britain continued on its present course it would end in disaster. A satirical British cartoon, *The Political Cartoon for the Year 1775* (**4.8**), published in London, vividly captured this view. It depicts King George III riding in a coach heading straight over a cliff. Lord Chief Justice Mansfield holds the reins of the carriage of state, which rides roughshod over the Magna Carta—a legal text closely linked with the Rights of Englishmen—and the British Constitution, another symbol of liberty. The cartoonist's symbolism suggested a view that was becoming increasingly popular in the colonies: Americans could no longer expect the political and legal system of Britain to protect their liberty. Although some Americans were persuaded that Britain was intent on trampling their liberty, other colonists remained loyal to the crown. For Patriots it was becoming increasingly clear that they could no longer count on the legal protections that had safeguarded their liberty for generations. Loyalists, by contrast, disputed this claim. For those loyal to George III, liberty could be maintained only by upholding English law. Loyalists viewed Patriots' actions as lawlessness, not affirmations of liberty.

The Battle of Bunker Hill

Two months after Lexington and Concord, the two sides clashed again in Charlestown, across the Charles River from Boston. American forces had dug in at Bunker Hill and nearby Breed's Hill, prepared to hold off the British in Boston. The main fighting actually took place at Breed's Hill, which was closer to the harbor. The British underestimated the colonists' resolve to hold their ground. Although the British took Bunker and Breed's Hills, they had purchased their victory at a steep cost in dead and wounded. Even more important, Americans had shown the British that

they were not the "untrained rabble" the British had portrayed and that they could become a formidable fighting force. The painter John Trumbull immortalized the battle in his painting *The Death of General Warren at the Battle of Bunker Hill.* For a discussion of this painting and how it reflected the realities of a battle in which neither side won a clear victor, see *Images as History: Trumbull's* The Death of General Warren at the Battle of Bunker Hill (page 108).

Despite the armed confrontations at Lexington, Concord, and Bunker Hill, the Continental Congress had not abandoned hope of reconciliation with King George III. In July 1775, Congress drafted the

4.8 *The Political Cartoon for the Year 1775* George III rides next to Lord Chief Judge Mansfield in a carriage heading toward the edge of a cliff. The carriage crushes the Magna Carta and the British Constitution, symbols of the rule of law, while flames engulf Boston in the background.

What does *The Political Cartoon for the Year 1775* reveal about the nature of relations between the colonies and Britain?

Images as History
TRUMBULL'S *THE DEATH OF GENERAL WARREN AT THE BATTLE OF BUNKER HILL*

American John Trumbull's painting *The Death of General Warren at the Battle of Bunker Hill* (1786), painted eleven years after the battle, captured an important moment in the American war for independence. Like Benjamin West's *The Death of General Wolfe* (see page 90), Trumbull's painting depicts the heroic death of a military figure, but the two paintings differ in a number of fascinating ways. While *The Death of General Wolfe* portrayed a clear victory for the British, *The Death of General Warren* showed a more complex event in which neither side was completely victorious. While the Americans lost the battle, they proved themselves an effective fighting force and exacted a high price from the British for their victory. How did Trumbull's composition reflect the realities of this battle, a struggle in which neither side won a clear victory?

Trumbull's painting *The Death of General Warren* was part of a series of paintings he began to commemorate the "great events of our country's revolution." The artist intended to use his painting as the basis for a set of engravings that he could sell as cheap prints to a popular market on both sides of the Atlantic. With this in mind Trumbull captured the chaotic horror of a battle scene in which both armies displayed heroism and nobility. The American General Warren lies mortally wounded, cradled in the arms of one of his troops, in the same pose in which Benjamin West portrayed British General Wolfe.

One element of the painting meant to appeal to British viewers is the depiction of British Major John Small in the center of the composition near Warren. Small stays the hand of one of his infantryman poised to bayonet the dying Warren. By placing these two noble gestures—Warren's sacrifice and Small's humanitarian intervention—at the center of the painting, Trumbull shifts attention away from the actual outcome of the battle to the idea that virtuous men on both sides performed noble deeds. This decision enhanced the moral complexity of the events while also making it and later engravings based on it attractive to British and American customers—effectively doubling the size of his potential market.

Trumbull's canvas also advanced the democratization of art begun by Benjamin West. In this painting virtue resides neither in one nation nor in any particular class of men. Trumbull portrays a broad range of soldiers heroically—from a gentlemanly British officer to a barefoot colonial soldier. Indeed Abigail Adams, an outspoken supporter of American independence and the wife of the prominent politician John Adams, noted that Trumbull "teaches mankind that it is not rank nor titles, but character alone, which interests posterity."

Trumbull all but ignored African Americans, consigning the two he did include to minor roles in the painting. Trumbull described the African American standing in the lower right corner behind an injured colonial

The Death of General Warren at the Battle of Bunker Hill

How did Trumbull craft his painting so it would appeal to both an American and British audience?

officer as a "faithful negro." At least fourteen African Americans were among the troops defending Breeds Hill and Bunker Hill. The African American Peter Salem played an important role in the actual battle, perhaps firing the shot that killed Major Pitcairn, the British figure collapsing near the center of the painting. The painting's slighting of that role probably reflected Trumbull's own racial ideas and those of his audience, who were not used to seeing African Americans depicted in anything but a subservient role. For the moment the democratization of art was restricted to those of European descent. African Americans' treatment in American art mirrored their marginalization in the larger society.

Rather than portray an African American as heroic, Warren marginalizes this figure, literally placing him in the shadow of a white officer at the end of the canvas.

Trumbull highlights the idea of virtue and honor as universal values by showing a British officer preventing a soldier from bayoneting the dying Warren.

General Warren's pose evokes the image of Jesus being cradled in the arms of Mary.

Major Pitcairn, who led the British assault on Concord, is mortally wounded in this battle.

What does Trumbull's portrayal of African Americans tell us about his views and those of his likely audiences?

"Olive Branch" petition, asking George III to intervene on their behalf. The king rejected the American appeal. With that rejection the time for reconciliation passed, and the supporters of American independence in the Continental Congress gained momentum. The push for independence opened a division within colonial society between colonists who supported independence and those who remained loyal to the British.

Common Sense and the Declaration of Independence

In January 1776, Thomas Paine, a recent immigrant to America from England, wrote a pamphlet that argued forcefully for American independence. In **Common Sense**, Paine not only attacked recent British policy, he framed a stinging indictment of monarchy and defended a democratic theory of representative government. After stating the "simple facts, plain arguments, and common sense" of the matter, Paine concluded that separation from Britain was the only action that made sense for America. Paine's work was printed in a cheap format that allowed artisans, farmers, and others with little money to purchase a copy. He wrote in plain, forceful prose, avoiding literary and classical allusions that would have required knowledge of Latin. The book was a phenomenal publishing success.

Common Sense did more than simply fuel Americans' desire for independence; it helped change the framework in which Americans thought about politics itself. Before Paine's pamphlet most Americans, even those who believed that reconciliation with Britain was impossible, still maintained a respectful attitude toward George III. Most Americans had grown up in a culture that venerated constitutional monarchy, but Paine's savage critique of this institution had a liberating impact. Paine called monarchy "ridiculous." After demonstrating that history proved that monarchy was incompatible with liberty, Paine turned to the current British monarch George III, whom he equated with savagery itself. He denounced the king for his assaults on American liberty, noting that "even brutes do not devour their young." Those who supported reconciliation with Britain found Paine's scathing attacks on George III appalling. Paine also gave a voice to many who wished to radically transform American political life. He was unabashedly democratic at a time when many, including those most eager to separate from Britain, viewed democracy as a danger to be avoided

at all cost. *Common Sense* became a blueprint for those who wished to experiment with democratic government, although not everyone who ardently supported American independence appreciated Paine's ideas.

> "There is something absurd in supposing a Continent to be perpetually governed by an island."
>
> THOMAS PAINE,
> Common Sense *1776*

In July 1775, a month after Congress drafted the "Olive Branch Petition," pleading with George III to abandon the "cruel" policies of his ministers and "such statutes" as "immediately distress" the colonists, the king declared that the American colonists were "in open and avowed rebellion." The Prohibitory Act, which the British Parliament enacted into law in December 1775, banned all trade with the thirteen colonies. Word of the ban arrived in America in February 1776. Coming on the heels of Paine's indictment of British tyranny, the policy further inflamed American resentments against Britain.

After the adoption of the Prohibitory Act, support for independence gained ground. In May Congress instructed the individual colonies "to adopt such Government as shall, in the Opinion of the Representatives of the People, best conduce to the Happiness and Safety of their Constituents." Congress added a preamble five days later that affirmed "the exercise of every kind of authority under the said crown should be totally suppressed." Although Congress had not formally declared independence, it had effectively asserted that the colonies had become independent states no longer under the authority of Parliament or the king.

Richard Henry Lee of Virginia introduced a resolution that "these United Colonies are, and of right ought to be, free and independent states." Congress then debated the Lee resolution and on June 11, 1776, appointed a committee to draft a formal declaration of independence. With John Adams (Massachusetts) as its chair, the committee included Robert Livingston (New York), Thomas Jefferson (Virginia),

---

What arguments did Paine's *Common Sense* present?   ▐▶ **Read** the **Document** *Thomas Paine*, Common Sense

Roger Sherman (Connecticut), and Benjamin Franklin (Pennsylvania). Adams designated Jefferson to take the lead in drafting the formal resolution. On June 28, the committee presented the congressional delegates with the draft. Congress cut about a quarter of the text and made some other revisions to the document. On July 4, 1776, Congress approved the final text of the **Declaration of Independence**, a public defense of America's decision to declare independence from Britain that was to be printed and sent to the individual states. Copies of the declaration were then widely distributed.

Thomas Jefferson admitted that his text reflected the "sentiments of the day, whether expressed in conversation or letters, printed essays." The introductory paragraph explained the reasons for separating from Britain. The second paragraph provided a powerful defense of the liberty and equality and affirmed that "all men are created Equal" and therefore entitled to "life, liberty, and the pursuit of happiness." A long list of grievances against George III took up the bulk of the text. Printed as a single broadside, the indented list of charges against George III was immediately recognizable (**4.9**).

The drafters of the Declaration of Independence aimed it at both a domestic and a foreign audience. It made the case for independence to the American people and announced to the British government the reasons for taking up arms. The declaration also sought to help American diplomacy. If America were to fight the most powerful nation on earth, it would need help from other European powers, such as Holland, Spain, and especially of Britain's long-time rival, France. Because a powerful monarch then ruled France, the declaration refrained from using the inflammatory anti-monarchical rhetoric favored by Thomas Paine in *Common Sense*. George III's misdeeds, not monarchy itself, were to blame for America's demand for independence.

The Plight of the Loyalists

The division between **Patriots**, colonists who supported American independence, and **Loyalists**, those wishing to remain loyal to the king, drove a deep wedge in colonial society. John Adams speculated that Americans were evenly divided among Patriots, Loyalists, and those striving to remain neutral. Although it is difficult to establish hard figures for how colonists divided over

4.9 The Declaration of Independence
The Declaration of Independence was printed as a broadside. This single-sheet format made it easy to post in public places. The layout of the Declaration—the typography and paragraphing—guides the reader through the main parts of its argument.

What audiences did the Declaration of Independence address?

> "We hold these truths to be self-evident, that all men are created equal, that they are endowed by their Creator with certain unalienable Rights, that among these are Life, Liberty, and the pursuit of Happiness."
>
> Declaration of Independence, 1776

4.10 *Magna Britannia Her Colonies Reduced* This image created by Benjamin Franklin plays on the dismemberment of the empire as fatal to both the colonies and the mother country. Franklin used this image early in America's opposition to British policy. Loyalists later used the dismemberment metaphor to persuade Americans to oppose independence.

independence, historians estimate that Patriots constituted about 40 percent of the white population, neutrals another 40 percent, and Loyalists probably about 20 percent.

Many prominent Loyalists had opposed British policy toward the colonies, but refused to accept the decision for independence. Minister Samuel Seabury captured the view of many Loyalists when he wrote: "To talk of a colony independent of the mother-country, is no better sense than to talk of a limb independent of the body to which it belongs." The image of the dismemberment of the empire was a powerful one in the minds of colonials and Britons alike. In the 1760s, supporters of American rights had used such images to persuade Britain to change its policy toward the colonies. At the time Benjamin Franklin was a colonial lobbyist in London, working to repeal British taxes. He designed an engraving, *Magna Britannia Her Colonies Reduced*, to appeal to Parliament, evoking the horror of a possible separation between the colonists and the mother country (**4.10**).

Seabury's reassertion of the horrors that would follow from the dismemberment of the empire tapped into powerful fears and anxieties among Americans unsure about independence.

Loyalists suffered hardships during the struggle for independence. In some places where Patriot feelings were strongest, individuals could be ostracized for refusing to support the Patriot cause. Legal disabilities were also imposed on individuals who refused to take a loyalty oath, including exclusion from service on juries and disarmament. Many states passed laws seizing Loyalist property. A complicated issue arising from these laws was how to deal with women married to Loyalists. Some women brought property from their own family into their marriage. Was this property also liable to confiscation? The story of Grace Growden Galloway illustrates the rapid reversal of fortune that could befall anyone who opposed the Patriots' side in the American Revolution. See *Choices and Consequences: A Loyalist Wife's Dilemma.*

The Loyalist cause appealed to many Americans, not just wealthy men and women like Grace and Joseph Galloway. New York boasted a sizeable Loyalist population, as did parts of the backcountry in the Carolinas. Some religious sects, particularly groups such as the Quakers who were pacifists, opposed the violence of war. Beginning with Lord Dunmore's Proclamation, many slaves had sensed that a British victory, not independence, offered them the best chance for freedom. As many as 100,000 slaves freed themselves by running away during the dislocation created by the war.

How did the metaphor of dismemberment influence Loyalist thought?   🔍 **View** the **Image** *Tory's Day of Judgment*

Choices and Consequences
A LOYALIST WIFE'S DILEMMA

Before the struggle for independence, Grace Growden Galloway stood at the apex of Philadelphia society. Her husband, Joseph Galloway, was wealthy and influential in Pennsylvania politics. Throughout the escalating conflict with Britain, Joseph Galloway supported reconciliation, and when war broke out, he became a Loyalist. Realizing that he could no longer count on the goodwill of his former friends and neighbors to protect him, Galloway and his daughter fled Philadelphia—perhaps the most ardent Patriot city outside New England—for British-controlled New York in 1776. The government of Pennsylvania confiscated Galloway's property, but Grace Galloway was determined to protect the property she had inherited from her own family and had brought into her marriage. She faced a difficult set of choices concerning her property:

Choices

1 Follow her husband and daughter into exile, accepting that neither she nor her husband would probably ever recover their property.

2 Follow her husband and daughter into exile and use every legal means available to prevent the confiscation of her own property and fight an uphill battle to protect it from afar.

3 Stay in Philadelphia and use every legal option to protect the properties that she had brought into her marriage.

Continuing Controversies

What does Grace Growden Galloway's plight reveal about the situation of Loyalists during the American Revolution?

The legal status of the property of a woman married to a Loyalist was complicated. This issue came before American courts in *Martin v. Commonwealth* (1805). Building on a new conception of women as independent political actors, Massachusetts claimed that a woman's choice to stay or flee was hers alone. The Massachusetts high court, however, disagreed with this new view of women's legal autonomy. The court held that the woman's decision to leave the state had been her husband's, not her own, and therefore the state did not have the right to seize her land. Although a defeat for women's rights, the outcome of the case would have certainly pleased Grace Growden Galloway.

Decision

Grace chose to stay and fight. She hoped that by remaining in her home she could avoid eviction. She also concluded that the chances of defending her own property against confiscation would be easier if she stayed in Philadelphia.

Consequences

Grace endured great hardship while defending her rights but was ultimately evicted. Snubbed and shunned by many of her former friends and acquaintances, and driven from her home, she lived in a modest set of rented rooms. In her diary Grace recounts her struggles and the indignities she suffered, including the time she "saw My own Chariot standing at my door for the Use of others while I am forced to Walk." She never rejoined her family and died alone in 1781. Although evicted from her home, she was more successful at protecting the property she had brought into the marriage, which eventually passed on to her descendents.

Eighteenth-century coach

What does *Martin v. Commonwealth* reveal about women's roles in Revolutionary-era America?

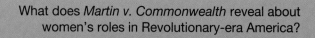

America at War

The British had reason to be confident when they contemplated their military advantages over the colonies at the start of the war. Britain's navy was the most powerful in the world and its army was formidable. The population of the British Isles was more than four times greater than that of the colonies. America began the war with only a citizen's militia. Fighting a powerful army meant that America would have to create a professional force. Congress appointed George Washington the commander of the new Continental Army.

Although Britain's population was much larger than that of the colonies, the relative size of the two armies in the field was not that lopsided. At the start of the conflict British General Howe enjoyed something like a two to one advantage over General Washington. Numbers alone do not tell the whole story. British supply lines were stretched thin and American forces were supplemented by militia forces which not only increased the size of the Patriot forces, but forced the British to deal with fighting both a conventional army and a nonconventional one as well. Even if the British were able to defeat the American armed forces in the field and gain control of America's cities, conquering and pacifying all thirteen colonies would be virtually impossible. The British also never grasped that they were fighting a new type of war: not a struggle against another European power, but a battle against a decentralized independence movement.

The War in the North

Stiff resistance at Breed's Hill and Bunker Hill had convinced the British military that the colonial militias were not an undisciplined rabble that would retreat if confronted by a well-trained professional army. The creation of a Continental Army under the leadership of George Washington underscored this fact and led the British to change their tactics. Rather than employing the army to subdue a rebel population, the British prepared for a sustained military conflict. Realizing that Patriot sympathies in New England were strong, the British retreated to New York, a colony with many Loyalists. New York not only provided a safer base of operations, but the British also believed that if they could hold New York they would cut New England off from the rest of America.

Although determined to defend New York, Washington suffered a major defeat at Brooklyn Heights in August 1776. Washington then retreated to Manhattan, but British Major General Sir William Howe soon drove the Americans from New York. Retreating south through New Jersey, Washington eventually crossed the Delaware River into Pennsylvania. During the winter, however, Washington's ranks dwindled as many militiamen returned home. These citizen soldiers had repulsed the immediate threat. They would also protect the countryside and prevent Loyalist pockets from forming outside of British-controlled territory, but they were ill suited to sustained battle. Washington lamented their unpredictable coming and going: "come in, you cannot tell how" and "go, you cannot tell when, and act you cannot tell where." The militia's lack of discipline

> To place any dependance upon Militia, is, assuredly, resting upon a broken staff . . . . Men accustomed to unbounded freedom, and no controul, cannot brook the Restraint which is indispensably necessary to the good order and Government of an Army; without which, licentiousness, and every kind of disorder triumphantly reign. To bring Men to a proper degree of Subordination, is not the work of a day, a Month or even a year
>
> GEORGE WASHINGTON to the President of Congress, September 24, 1776

Why did Washington have Paine's *The American Crisis* read to the troops before he crossed the Delaware to attack British and German mercenaries?

> "The summer soldier and the sunshine patriot, will in this crisis, shrink from the service of his country; but he that stands it NOW deserves the love and thanks of men and women."
>
> THOMAS PAINE, *The American Crisis* (1776)

and long-term commitment to fight was a constant source of frustration to Washington and American military leaders. Still the militia remained vital, contributing both to the military and political success of the war effort.

Believing that he had decisively defeated Washington, an overconfident Howe established his base camp in New York City and planned to enjoy the winter holidays.

Realizing that America desperately needed a victory, Washington launched a surprise attack on Christmas night 1776. He ordered that Thomas Paine's inspirational essay *The American Crisis* be read to his troops. Paine enjoined Americans not to abandon hope. Leading his soldiers across the partially frozen Delaware River under cover of darkness, Washington overwhelmed an outpost manned by German mercenaries at Trenton. A week later, Washington won another daring victory at Princeton. Howe had squandered his advantage and allowed Washington to regroup and score two important victories. Washington shrewdly abandoned his early strategy of fighting a conventional war. He now realized that his primary goal was to wear down his opponents and avoid a decisive defeat. Such a strategy played to America's natural advantages and would eventually force the British to accept that they could not conquer America. To commemorate Washington's victory at Princeton, the trustees of Princeton College commissioned the eminent American painter Charles Wilson Peale to paint Washington at the Battle of Princeton (**4.11**). The portrait replaced a painting of George III, damaged during the battle when a cannonball removed the king's head.

British strategy shifted in 1777. Howe decided to make more effective use of British naval power.

A key element of this plan was a coordinated effort to capture American cities, including the rebellion's political center, Philadelphia, which fell in September. The British also sought to isolate ardently Patriot New England from the rest of the nation.

4.11 Washington at the Battle of Princeton
In this painting the officer behind Washington is posed in the same position as General Wolfe in Benjamin West's painting, *The Death of General Wolfe.* In this painting, Washington, by contrast, stands firm, a symbol of the virtuous new republic that rises from the noble sacrifice depicted in the background. [*Source:* Princeton University, commissioned by the Trustees. (PP222) photo: Bruce M. White]

View the **Closer Look** *"Washington at the Battle of Princeton"*   How does Peale's painting of Washington differ from Trumbull's *The Death of General Warren?*

4.12 Northern Campaigns
Although the British won important victories around New York City, Washington's triumphs at Trenton and Princeton helped restore American morale. The turning point in the war in the North, however, was the defeat of the British at Saratoga, which helped persuade the French to increase their support for the American cause.

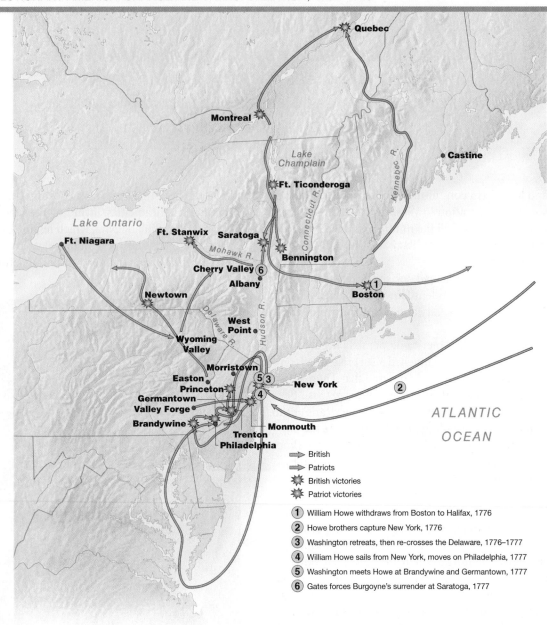

British

Patriots

British victories

Patriot victories

1. William Howe withdraws from Boston to Halifax, 1776
2. Howe brothers capture New York, 1776
3. Washington retreats, then re-crosses the Delaware, 1776–1777
4. William Howe sails from New York, moves on Philadelphia, 1777
5. Washington meets Howe at Brandywine and Germantown, 1777
6. Gates forces Burgoyne's surrender at Saratoga, 1777

A British army under General John Burgoyne marched south from Canada. Burgoyne hoped to join forces with Howe moving up the Hudson River from New York City.

But Howe moved against Philadelphia instead, and an American force under General Horatio Gates defeated Burgoyne at Saratoga, in upstate New York (**4.12**). In addition to providing Americans with an important victory and morale boost, the British defeat at Saratoga persuaded the French to commit troops and naval forces to aid the colonists. Despite this impressive victory, the Americans had failed to retake Philadelphia, and the beleaguered Continental Army took up quarters at Valley Forge, Pennsylvania in the winter of 1777–1778.

The active entry of France in March 1778 changed the dynamics of the conflict. Rather than simply providing money and munitions, France was now at war with Britain and committed to helping America win independence.

In 1778, France and America signed a treaty promising to fight until American independence was secured. Spain soon joined France as an opponent of Britain and attacked British outposts in the Mississippi valley and Florida. Within two years Britain declared war on Holland, which had become an important source of supplies for the American war effort. The great Western European powers were now at war. What had begun as a colonial war for independence fought exclusively in North America had

What role did the French navy play in the victory at Yorktown?

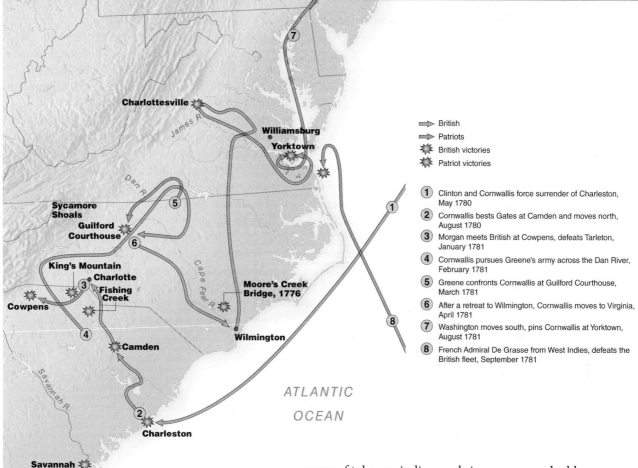

ATLANTIC
OCEAN

British

Patriots

British victories

Patriot victories

1. Clinton and Cornwallis force surrender of Charleston, May 1780
2. Cornwallis bests Gates at Camden and moves north, August 1780
3. Morgan meets British at Cowpens, defeats Tarleton, January 1781
4. Cornwallis pursues Greene's army across the Dan River, February 1781
5. Greene confronts Cornwallis at Guilford Courthouse, March 1781
6. After a retreat to Wilmington, Cornwallis moves to Virginia, April 1781
7. Washington moves south, pins Cornwallis at Yorktown, August 1781
8. French Admiral De Grasse from West Indies, defeats the British fleet, September 1781

4.13 Southern Campaigns
Although the British scored impressive victories in the South in 1780, especially at Charleston and Savannah, American forces recovered and forced Cornwallis to move to Virginia in 1781. This proved to be a strategic error, since it allowed the French fleet to cut off Cornwallis and enabled Washington to trap the British at Yorktown.

mushroomed into a global conflict involving the Mediterranean, Africa, India, and the Caribbean. France attacked Britain's wealthy Caribbean sugar islands and captured some of them. In the Mediterranean a joint French and Spanish force besieged the British fortress of Gibraltar. Britain had to divert resources from North America to protect these possessions. Fighting a war on multiple fronts drained British resources.

The Southern Campaigns and Final Victory at Yorktown

In 1779–1780, the British shifted their attention to the South where there was considerable Loyalist sympathy. They also saw the South, with its cash crops of tobacco, indigo, and rice, as more valuable economically than the North. Initially the British strategy seemed to pay off. In 1780, British troops scored impressive victories at Savannah (Georgia), Charleston (South Carolina), and Camden (South Carolina). But they could not consolidate their power in the region. The colonial militias harassed Loyalists and sustained the Patriot cause. The British were especially vulnerable to hit-and-run operations by commanders such as South Carolina's Francis Marion. Nicknamed the "Swamp Fox," Marion would attack out of nowhere and then disappear into the swamps before the British could retaliate.

The war in the South changed dramatically in 1781 when General Daniel Morgan defeated the British forces at Cowpens (South Carolina). American forces also inflicted heavy losses on the British at Guilford Court House (North Carolina). Although the British still controlled Savannah and Charleston, the British commander, Lord Cornwallis, then moved to Virginia and established a well-fortified base at Yorktown in the winter of 1781 (**4.13**).

Cornwallis's retreat to Yorktown proved to be a strategic blunder for the British that Washington turned to America's advantage. Before Saratoga,

What role did the French navy play in the American victory at Yorktown?

the large French navy had not played a significant part in the war, and America's own small navy was no match for the superior British fleet. With their naval superiority the British were confident that establishing a base at Yorktown made sense. With the guns of the British navy at their disposal, and new supplies coming from New York and London, Yorktown seemed like a strategic location to regroup.

But things went awry for the British when, early in the fall of 1781, the French dispatched a formidable fleet under the command of Admiral Paul de Grasse from the Caribbean to North America. With the arrival of the French navy, the balance of power at sea shifted, giving the Americans a naval advantage. Washington seized the opportunity, asking the large French army in the North under the Comte de Rochambeau to join American troops in an assault on Yorktown. When de Grasse's fleet forced a British squadron that was supposed to help

Cornwallis to withdraw, the Americans and French trapped him in Yorktown. Although French support was indispensable, this fanciful French image of the victory at Yorktown, portrays this historic moment as though the Americans hardly figured in it (**4.14**).

Outnumbered and with his land and sea escapes cut off, Cornwallis surrendered in October 1781. Washington then appointed General Benjamin Lincoln to receive the British surrender, offered by a subordinate of Cornwallis.

The British defeat at Yorktown provided American diplomats with a strong bargaining position in negotiating a peace treaty with Britain. The **Treaty of Paris (1783)** officially ended the war between the newly created United States and Britain. The treaty recognized American independence, acknowledged America's border with Canada, and recognized American fishing rights off Newfoundland.

4.14 Defeat of Cornwallis at Yorktown
A French artist's fanciful depiction of the American and French victory at Yorktown focused entirely on the French navy and army. A medieval-looking walled city in the background also signifies his lack of familiarity with the events.

What was the Treaty of Paris?

The Radicalism of the American Revolution

The American Revolution encompassed two interrelated struggles. The Revolution was both a colonial war for independence and a revolutionary struggle to change American government and society. Thus the war was both a struggle for home rule—the right of Americans to govern themselves— and a war for who should rule at home, a contest to determine the nature of American government and the structure of society. The American Revolution set in motion a social and political transformation that affected nearly every aspect of American society. The Declaration of Independence had articulated the twin ideals of equality and liberty. Some Americans took the Declaration's bold affirmation of liberty and equality to be an endorsement of more than colonial independence. For them these words were revolutionary. The Declaration inspired them to undertake a radical transformation of American politics and society.

The first constitutions drafted by the states in 1776 included language that echoed the Declaration's affirmation of liberty and equality. Few Americans doubted the importance of this affirmation; how far to take it, however, proved controversial. The Pennsylvania Constitution went further than any other state constitution in embracing a democratic conception of equality—at least for white men.

Not every group in America benefited equally from the promise of the Revolution. African slaves, Indians, and women were either excluded from or not included fully in the Revolution's promise of equality and liberty. Although the promise of the Revolution remained unfilled for many in America, oppressed groups throughout American history would use it to seek the full rights of citizenship.

Popular Politics in the Revolutionary Era

British taxation was not the only set of policies that produced violent resistance during the Revolutionary era. Colonists also opposed unfair taxes imposed by their own colonial governments. The colonial elites who dominated government also came under attack. In the Carolinas, a movement sought reform of colonial government. The Regulators, as their name implied, sought to regulate society by eliminating corruption and bringing the rule of law to places that lacked it. The Regulators resented planters and merchants who lived near the coast and were eager to tax western farmers, but were not willing to share political power with them. Thus in backcountry North Carolina, Regulators opposed taxes, including those enacted to pay for a lavish new palace for the royal governor. Some Regulators, such as Herman Husband, combined religious themes with democratic ideas to attack corruption and inequality in North Carolina. Husband fused his religious rhetoric with a class-conscious critique of the eastern elites who dominated state politics. He noted that "obedience to just laws, and subjection to slavery" were not the same. Resistance to unjust authority was legitimate because "God gave all men a knowledge of their privileges, and a true zeal to maintain them." In contrast with Husband's views, the royal governor and his supporters among the clergy asserted that "subjection to lawful authority," not resistance, was the "plain and principal doctrine of Christianity."

In 1770, 1,000 Regulators marched on the courthouse in Hillsborough. The protesters not only shut down the court but also publicly whipped a court official who was notorious for charging excessive fees to process legal documents. The angry crowd also punished lawyers whose high fees angered backcountry residents. Such fees fell heavily on poor folk and blocked their access to the courts. The protests prompted the governor to dispatch the militia, which defeated the Regulators and restored order. Although the Regulators were not victorious, their class-conscious rhetoric and critique of power and corruption resonated in the Carolina backcountry.

Who were the Regulators?

Constitutional Experiments: Testing the Limits of Democracy

When the Continental Congress directed the states to draft new constitutions, they became laboratories for constitutional experimentation. Different visions of constitutional government were set against one another in this vibrant public debate. Virginia broke new ground by framing a detailed Declaration of Rights that became a model for other states. By contrast virtually every other state apart from Vermont rejected Pennsylvania's radical democratic experiment. Massachusetts, like Virginia, also became a model for other states, pioneering constitutional developments that became essential features of American constitutionalism, particularly in the separation of powers and checks and balances between the different branches of government.

In June 1776, the new state of Virginia drafted a Declaration of Rights and a Constitution. The chief architect of the Declaration of Rights was George Mason, an influential Patriot leader. The Declaration asserted that life, liberty, and property were fundamental rights and that "all men are by nature equally free and independent." Some Virginians worried that this language might encourage slaves to revolt. Another delegate calmed these fears by pointing out that the militia would be more than adequate to protect Virginia from its slaves. Indeed, the Declaration of Rights also affirmed "That a well regulated militia, composed of the body of the people, trained to arms, is the proper, natural, and safe defense of a free state; that standing armies, in time of peace, should be avoided as dangerous to liberty; and that, in all cases, the military should be under strict subordination to, and be governed by, the civil power." The Declaration also protected other basic liberties: trial by jury, freedom of the press, and freedom of religion.

Pennsylvania drafted its constitution not long after Virginia's. While members of a slave-owning planter elite drafted Virginia's Declaration of Rights and Constitution, a more democratic coalition that included urban artisans influenced by the ideas of Thomas Paine and backcountry farmers resentful of the old eastern colonial elites, and similar to the Regulators, drafted Pennsylvania's constitution. Echoing Paine's *Common Sense*, the Pennsylvania Constitution created a form of representative government with a single legislature, a system known as unicameralism.

Responding to the frustration of frontier settlers, who had sought the creation of a state militia to protect them from Indian attack, and the necessities of fighting Britain, the Pennsylvania Constitution also created a citizens' militia and became the first state constitution to expressly protect the right of citizens to bear arms "in defense of themselves and the state." In keeping with Paine's democratic ideas, the constitution rejected property requirements for voting. Any male taxpayer who resided in the state for a year could vote. Timothy Matlack, who had helped write this radical constitution, commissioned a portrait that reflected its diverse influences (**4.15**). A powder horn and musket appear in the background. The Pennsylvania Constitution and important British legal texts rest on the table behind him.

The Revolution prompted a public debate over how far to take the idea of democracy. Although Pennsylvania went further than most in implementing these ideas, similar debates occurred in the press in other states. The traditional Whig theory of representation assumed that only property owners could exercise the independent judgment necessary to vote. Individuals without property would be at the mercy of the rich and powerful who could influence their votes on election day. Whig theory also viewed

4.15 Timothy Matlack
To symbolize Matlack's role in drafting the Pennsylvania Constitution of 1776, the painter included several items in the background, including law books, the great seal of Pennsylvania, the Pennsylvania Constitution, and a powder horn and musket.
[*Source:* Gift in memory of Martha Legg McPheeters, and M. Theresa B. Hopkins Fund, Emily L. Ainsley Fund, Juliana Cheney Edwards Collection, and A. Shuman Collection. Photograph ©2010 Musem of Fine Arts, Boston.]

What made Pennsylvania's Constitution so radical for its day?   **Read** the **Document** Pennsylvania Constitution of 1776

the possession of property as an essential way of demonstrating that one had a permanent stake in society. According to the Whigs only men with such an interest could act in the long-term interests of society. The Revolution nurtured a far more democratic vision of government. The anonymous author of the pamphlet *The People the Best Governors* asserted that "the people know best their own wants and necessities, and therefore are best able to rule themselves." According to this view, a propertied elite was not needed to act as a check on the people.

Those who rejected the radical notion of equality implicit in democracy ridiculed the new, more democratic theories. The Reverend Charles Bullman of South Carolina, for example, suggested that if these ideas were not checked, "Every silly clown and illiterate mechanic will take upon him to censure the conduct of his Prince or Governor." Among the Patriot elite no figure expressed greater reservations about the dangers of too much democracy, and of unicameralism, than John Adams who reluctantly conceded that Paine had helped rally Americans to the idea of independence, but also feared that Paine's work had "a better hand at pulling down than building" up governments. Indeed, Adams worried that Paine's "feeble" ideas about government would mislead Americans when the time came to draft new state constitutions. Adams incorporated his own views on the matter into his short, but influential *Thoughts on Government,* which he wrote in response to a request from North Carolina's Provincial Congress, the body responsible for framing its new constitution.

Most states were unwilling to follow Pennsylvania's radical model, opting to retain a property requirement for voting and office holding. In general, however, the new property requirements the states adopted were lower than they had been during the colonial period, so on balance, the pool of eligible voters increased. Although not a resounding victory for those who shared the democratic views of Thomas Paine and the author of *The People the Best Government,* the Revolution clearly led to a greater democratization of politics.

Although not the most democratic experiment in government, the Massachusetts Constitution produced interesting innovations. John Adams played a leading role in helping to draft it. Adopted in 1780, it remains the oldest continuously functioning written constitution in the world. Setting the terms for nearly all subsequent constitution-making in America, Massachusetts took revolutionary-era constitutional ideas in new directions. Massachusetts saw a constitution as the supreme law that had to rest on the express consent of the people. Legislative bodies

had drafted earlier state constitutions, but a special convention drafted the Massachusetts constitution, which it then submitted directly to the people for ratification. Massachusetts also took the unprecedented step of eliminating property requirements for this special ratification process. Thus even those white men who would not meet the property requirements for voting for the legislature under the proposed constitution could vote on the Constitution. The notion that a constitution had to be submitted to the people directly for ratification was a radical innovation that quickly became an accepted feature of American constitutional life.

> ## "Shall We Say, that every Individual of the Community, old and young, male and female, as well as rich and poor, must consent, expressly to every Act of Legislation?"
>
> JOHN ADAMS to James Sullivan, May 1776

The Massachusetts Constitution was also the first to implement an effective system of checks and balances. While all the early state governments supported the principle of separation of powers, making the powers of the legislative, executive, and judicial functions of government distinct, these constitutions had not built in the checks and balances that would make this ideal a practical reality. To make separation of powers effective, the different branches of government had to be able to check one another's power. Massachusetts went further than any other state in achieving this goal. The Massachusetts governor had considerable power, including the right to veto acts of the legislature. This enabled the executive to check the legislature. The legislature could check the governor through its ability to override a veto by a two-thirds vote. Finally, Massachusetts made the governor an office directly elected by the people, not appointed by the legislature as many other states had opted to do.

Another important experiment in constitutional government was the Articles of Confederation, the constitution that Congress framed for the new United States of America. Although Congress drafted the Articles in 1777, the states did not ratify them for another four years. The Articles did not create a national government, but rather "a firm league of friendship" among the sovereign states. Thus Article II affirmed that "Each state retains its sovereignty, freedom, and independence, and every power, jurisdiction, and right, which is not by this Confederation expressly delegated to the United

States, in Congress assembled." Because fighting the British was the top priority, Congress cobbled together the Articles of Confederation without providing many features that the individual states had included in their constitutions. Fear of British-style government also shaped the minds of Congress. Having just cast off a powerful central government with a king, the Articles abandoned the idea of a single unified executive to enforce the law. Nor did Congress have the power to tax, another power that the British had abused. The Articles created a weak government whose ability to raise revenue, engage in military actions, and conduct diplomacy depended entirely on the goodwill of the states.

African Americans Struggle for Freedom

The great English literary figure Dr. Samuel Johnson pointed out the hypocrisy of Americans claiming to be champions of liberty while enslaving Africans. Some slaves invoked the ideas of the Revolution explicitly, whereas others voted with their feet and freed themselves. The dislocations associated with America's war for independence provided opportunities for African Americans to escape bondage. For some, fleeing to the British provided the best chance for freedom. Other slaves seized on the ideas nurtured by the broader revolutionary changes that accompanied the war for independence. The ideas of liberty and equality intensified the burgeoning movement for the abolition of slavery. Although the Revolution did not eradicate slavery, it did put it on the road to extinction in New England and the mid-Atlantic regions.

> ## "How is it that we hear the loudest yelps for liberty among the drivers of negroes?"
> Dr. SAMUEL JOHNSON, 1775

Slaves, eager to cast off their own shackles, appropriated the Revolution's language of liberty. During the Stamp Act protests in South Carolina (1765), slaves staged their own parade chanting "liberty." White South Carolinians viewed such activities as evidence of a plan for rebellion. To thwart the imagined threat, they mobilized the militia, which also served as slave patrols. Blacks in New England fared better when they invoked the Revolution's ideals than did blacks in the South. In 1773, 1774, and 1777, slaves petitioned the government of Massachusetts for their freedom using the language of the Declaration of Independence, including the idea of natural rights and the notion that government rested on the consent of the governed. They asserted: "We have in common with all other men a naturel right to our freedoms without Being depriv'd of them by our fellow men."

Less than a decade later, another slave, Mum Bett, successfully sued for her freedom. A jury in western Massachusetts based its verdict on the language of the state's Declaration of Rights, which stated that "All men are born free and equal, and have certain natural, essential, and unalienable rights; among which may be reckoned the right of enjoying and defending their lives and liberties." Mum Bett changed her name to Elizabeth Freeman, worked as a housekeeper for the lawyer who defended her, and became a respected midwife and nurse. Citing this precedent, the state's highest court abolished slavery in Massachusetts in the 1780s.

New England went further than any other region in its support for the abolition of slavery. Vermont's 1777 Constitution expressly prohibited slavery, the first constitution in the nation to take such a step. In the mid-Atlantic, Pennsylvania and New York adopted gradual emancipation laws.

The American Revolution in Indian Country

The struggle between Britain and the American colonies had enormous consequences for American Indians. Although neutrality appealed to many Indians, avoiding entanglement in the conflict between Britain and America became impossible. Faced with the need to make a choice, many Indian nations sided with Britain, whose colonial policies, including the Proclamation of 1763, had blocked American westward expansion. An American victory would mean more settlers streaming into Indian country and destruction of the habitats that Indians depended on for their survival.

The Declaration of Independence had underscored America's deep-seated fear and hostility toward Indians. Among the complaints Jefferson leveled against the king was: "He has excited domestic insurrections amongst us, and has endeavoured to bring on the inhabitants of our frontiers, the merciless Indian Savages, whose known rule of warfare, is an undistinguished destruction of all ages, sexes and conditions." Jefferson's description of Indians as "savages" engaged in acts of barbarism rallied Americans against the British.

One event that whipped up anti-Indian feelings among Americans was the murder of Jane McCrea in upstate New York by Mohawk Indians. Jane was traveling to meet her fiancé, a British soldier, when pro-British Mohawks attacked her. McCrea's political sympathies did not prevent her from becoming a martyr for the Patriot cause. Colonial newspapers lamented her fate, which was also memorialized in poetry. In 1780, a novel about her demise appeared, and the painter John Trumbull made several sketches of McCrea's murder for a possible painting before moving on to other projects. Joel Barlow, a close friend of Jefferson and important literary figure in early America, memorialized the event in one of his poems, and John Vanderlyn portrayed the event in this dramatic painting (**4.16**), which was displayed in 1804. Vanderlyn's representation of the light-skinned McCrea and the dark-skinned Indians underscores the role of the painting as a morality tale between good and evil. The Indians are depicted as cruel savages about to murder McCrea.

Pro-British tribes scored notable victories on the western frontier during 1782. After these successes, many Indians were stunned to learn that the British had surrendered at Yorktown. Indians were excluded from the negotiations that ended the war. Many viewed the Treaty of Paris (1783), which ceded Indian country between the Appalachians and the Mississippi River to America, as a betrayal.

Liberty's Daughters: Women and the Revolutionary Movement

Women took an active role in the revolutionary cause. One of the most outspoken female Patriots was Mercy Otis Warren, wife of Patriot leader James Warren and sister of James Otis. Warren's gifts as a poet, playwright, and eventually historian allowed her to champion the American cause in literary endeavors. Her satirical plays mocked British policy and leading British politicians and military figures. The fictional names of the characters in her plays communicated Warren's disdain for the British. Her scathing satire mocked the actions of General Hateall, Secretary of State Dupe, and Governor Rapatio. These sinister plotters against American liberty were matched by talented

and virtuous American Patriots, whose names, Brutus and Honestus, signified their commitment to ancient Roman republican virtue.

Women also served in the war effort. When mustered into service, the militia often depended on support from women. An eyewitness to such a mobilization in Cambridge, Massachusetts, in 1774 noted that women "surpassed the Men for Eagerness & Spirit in the Defense of Liberty by Arms." Women not only provided moral support, "animating their Husbands & Sons to fight for their liberties," but also helped "making Cartridges." Some women became "Molly Pitchers," who hauled water and carried supplies to soldiers. Deborah Sampson, disguised herself as a man and served in the Continental Army. A physician discovered Sampson while treating her for fever. The Continental Army also had camp followers—women, including the wives of soldiers, who washed, cooked, nursed, and tended to other needs of soldiers.

The Revolution's emphasis on liberty and equality boosted notions of gender equality. Abigail Adams, wife of John Adams, demanded that her husband "remember the ladies" and work toward greater legal equality for women (see *Competing*

4.16 Death of Jane McCrea John Vanderlyn painted this scene decades after the event occurred. He took liberties with history. McCrea's fiancé, the military figure rushing to rescue her (circled in red), wears the blue uniform of a Continental soldier. In reality McCrea was a Loyalist and her fiancé a British regular.

Why did so many Indians side with the British during the American Revolution?

4.17 *Issac Winslow and His Family* by Joseph Blackburn, 1755
This portrait of the Winslow family done two decades before the American Revolution captures the more patriarchal view of the family. The father stands aloof from his family. [*Source:* Joseph Blackburn, American (born in England), active in North America 1753–1763 *Isaac Winslow and His Family*, 1755 Oil on canvas 138.43 x 201.29 cm (54 1/2 x 79 1/4 in.) Museum of Fine Arts, Boston A. Shuman Collection—Abraham Shuman Fund, 42.684 Photograph ©2011 Museum of Fine Arts, Boston.]

4.18 (right) **Cadwalader Family**
Charles Wilson Peale's portrait of the Cadwalader family evokes the ideal of companionate marriage, in which husbands and wives enjoyed an intimate and egalitarian relationship within marriage.

Visions: Remember the Ladies). A few women even demanded a measure of political equality, at least for women who owned property.

One supporter of this idea was Hannah Corbin, sister of Patriot leader Richard Henry Lee. While Abigail Adams was a model of female propriety, Corbin's unconventional lifestyle made her acutely aware of the inferior legal status of women. After her husband died at age 35, Corbin managed their plantation. Her husband's will stipulated that if she ever remarried, Corbin would lose control of the estate. Corbin was unwilling to accept the choice of remaining a widow or losing control of her property. Rejecting contemporary moral codes, she began a common-law relationship with another man (living together as husband and wife without being legally married). The fact that they were not legally married allowed her to preserve control of her estate. The defiant and independent Corbin later asked her brother why women who owned property were prohibited from voting. Lee could provide no reasonable response. He even conceded that in theory, allowing such women to vote was plausible, but noted that "it has never been the practice either here or in England" and speculated that "Perhaps 'twas thought rather out of character for women to press into those tumultuous assemblages of men."

Every state, except New Jersey, limited suffrage to men. It is not clear if New Jersey's omission was deliberate or accidental. Still New Jersey women who fulfilled the state's property requirements took full advantage of this omission and voted in elections until the state legislature revoked this right in 1807.

Although the Revolution did not usher in the legal or political changes sought by Adams and Corbin, the ideas of equality espoused by the Revolution did influence marriage and family life. Lucy Knox, wife of General Henry Knox, told her husband a year after the Declaration of Independence to "not consider yourself as commander in chief of your own house," but recognize that "there is such a thing as equal command." She viewed marriage as an egalitarian relationship between husband and wife in which the two lived together as companions. Scholars describe this as companionate marriage. The Revolution not only altered ideas about marriage but also changed attitudes about patriarchal authority, a fact reflected in the portraiture of the day. These changes are evident if one compares the pre-revolutionary-era painting of the Winslow Family (**4.17**) and the Revolutionary-era portrait of the Cadwalader Family (**4.18**). In his painting of the Cadwalader family, Charles Wilson Peale gives a model of a companionate marriage. A comparison of the portraits shows how ideas of family relations, including the relationship between husband and wife, and parents and children, had changed. In Peale's painting John and Elizabeth Cadwalader look directly at one another. His hand rests on hers, and their young child reaches for the peach held by her father. The intimacy of the family is evidenced in the physical closeness of its members. By contrast the portrait of the Winslow family reveals little of this closeness. The husband has no physical contact with his wife or his children.

Was Hannah Corbin's argument for women's suffrage consistent with Whig theory?

Read the **Document** *Adams Family Correspondence between Abigail and John (March–April 1776)*

Competing Visions
REMEMBER THE LADIES

A strong supporter of independence, and an articulate and forceful personality, Abigail Adams believed that the American Revolution provided an opportunity for women to gain much-needed legal reform. This was particularly needed in property law, where women were considered legally dead once they married.

In this spirited letter written shortly before Congress declared independence from Britain, Abigail made her displeasure with the inferior legal status of women clear to her husband.

Abigail Adams to John Adams, 31 Mar. 1776

   I desire you would Remember the Ladies, and be more generous and favourable to them than your ancestors. Do not put such unlimited power into the hands of the Husbands. Remember all Men would be tyrants if they could. If particular care and attention is not paid to the Ladies we are determined to foment a Rebellion, and will not hold ourselves bound by any Laws in which we have no voice, or Representation.

In a dismissive reply, Adams nevertheless revealed how the Revolution's ideas about equality permeated American society.

John Adams to Abigail Adams, 14 Apr. 1776

   As to your extraordinary Code of Laws, I cannot but laugh. We have been told that our Struggle has loosened the bands of Government every where. That Children and Apprentices were disobedient—that schools and Colleges were grown turbulent—that Indians slighted their Guardians and Negroes grew insolent to their Masters. But your Letter was the first Intimation that another Tribe more numerous and powerful than all the rest were grown discontented.— This is rather too coarse a Compliment but you are so saucy, I wont blot it out. Depend upon it, We know better than to repeal our Masculine systems.

Abigail Adams

John Adams

Was Abigail Adams's demand for women's rights consistent with the Revolution's ideals?

1764

Sugar Act
British tax molasses, sugar, and other items. Colonies protest being taxed without their consent.

1765

Stamp Act
Colonial protest intensifies against Britain's new policies

1770

Boston Massacre
British troops fire on crowd in Boston

1773–1775

Boston Tea Party
Sons of Liberty toss tea into Boston Harbor

Concord and Lexington
These early battles demonstrated the colonists' capacity to use military force to protect their rights.

Olive Branch Petition
Congress makes final attempt to persuade the king to address American grievances

CHAPTER REVIEW

Review Questions

1. What arguments did colonists use to oppose the Stamp Act?

2. How did Paul Revere's representation of the Boston Massacre in his famous engraving stir up resentment against the British? How did Revere manipulate the events to present them in the worst possible light?

3. How did Jefferson's argument for independence in the Declaration differ from Paine's argument in *Common Sense*?

4. How did the Massachusetts Constitution depart from the earlier models of Virginia and Pennsylvania?

5. Did the Revolution's ideals of liberty and equality significantly affect the lives of blacks, women, and American Indians?

Key Terms

Stamp Act Legislation that required colonists to purchase special stamps and place them on all legal documents. Newspapers and playing cards had to be printed on special stamped paper.   **100**

Nonimportation movement A boycott against the purchase of any imported British goods.   **101**

Intolerable Acts Legislation passed by Parliament to punish Bostonians for the Boston Tea Party. It closed the Port of Boston; annulled the Massachusetts colonial charter and dissolved or severely restricted that colony's political institutions; and allowed British officials charged with capital crimes to be tried outside the colonies.   **104**

Lord Dunmore's Proclamation Official announcement issued by Lord Dunmore, royal governor of Virginia. It offered freedom to any slave who joined the British forces in putting down the American rebellion.   **106**

Common Sense Thomas Paine's influential pamphlet that forcefully argued for American independence, attacked the institution of monarchy, and defended a democratic theory of representative government.   **110**

Declaration of Independence On July 4, 1776, Congress approved the final text of the Declaration of Independence, a public defense of America's decision to declare independence from Britain that was to be printed and sent to the individual states.   **111**

Patriots Colonists who supported American independence.   **111**

Loyalists Colonists who remained loyal to the king and Britain.   **111**

Treaty of Paris (1783) Treaty between the newly created United States of America and Britain that officially ended the war between the two and formally recognized American independence.   **118**

1776

Thomas Paine publishes
Common Sense
Paine states the case for American independence in a pamphlet that becomes an instant best seller

Declaration of Independence
American colonies declare independence

Pennsylvania Declaration of Rights and Constitution
Pennsylvania Constitution adopts simple democratic scheme of government

1777

Jane McCrea murdered by Mohawk Indians
The murder becomes a rallying cry for Americans against British treachery

1780

Massachusetts Constitution
Massachusetts introduces a range of legal innovations including the idea of special ratification conventions to approve its constitution

1781

Defeat of Cornwallis at Yorktown
American and French forces defeat British army at Yorktown, ending the Revolutionary War

MyHistoryLab Connections

Visit **www.myhistorylab.com** for a customized Study Plan that will help you build your knowledge of *Revolutionary America*.

Questions for Analysis

1. **Why did colonists' believe Parliament could regulate trade, but not tax them without representation?**

   Read the **Document** John Dickinson, Letters from a Farmer in Pennsylvania, *p. 101*

2. **What ideas and images helped persuade Americans to support the Patriot cause?**

   View the **Closer Look** The Bloody Massacre, *p. 103*

3. **What military advantages did the Americans possess and how did their strategy shift to take better advantage of these realities?**

   View the **Closer Look** "Washington at the Battle of Princeton," *p. 115*

4. **What impact did the Revolution have on the institution of slavery?**

   Read the **Document** Slave Petition to the Governor of Massachusetts, 1774, *p. 122*

5. **How did the Revolution impact gender roles?**

   Read the **Document** Adams Family Correspondence between Abigail and John (March–April 1776), *p. 124*

Other Resources from This Chapter

Read the **Document**
- *Patrick Henry, "Give me Liberty or Give me Death", p. 104*
- *Thomas Paine, Common Sense, p. 110*
- *Pennsylvania Constitution of 1776, p. 120*

View the **Closer Look**
- *Tea-Tax Tempest, p. 98*
- *Images as History: The Hanging of Absalom, p. 102*

View the **Image**
- *Stamp Act, p. 100*
- *Tory's Day of Judgment, p. 112*

Republicanism and the Politics of Virtue p. 130

What role did the concept of virtue play in American politics after the Revolution?

Life under the Articles of Confederation p. 138

What major problems did America face during the Confederation period?

The Movement for Constitutional Reform p. 143

What were the main differences between the Articles of Confederation and the Constitution?

The Great Debate p. 148

What were the Anti-Federalists' major objections to the Constitution?

CHAPTER 5

((●─Hear the **Audio File** on **myhistorylab.com**

◉─Watch the **Video** *Critical Visions, Chapter 5*

A Virtuous Republic
Creating a Workable Government, 1783–1789

In 1776, Patriot leader John Adams wrote that "public virtue is the only foundation of Republics. There must be a positive passion for the public good, the public interest." Adams echoed many Americans' views when he wrote that republican government depended on the concept of civic virtue, which meant pursuing the public good and placing it ahead of personal interest or local attachments. Men were expected to serve in the militia, sit on juries, and, if they were truly virtuous and wise, take on the burden of public service as elected representatives. Women, too, were expected to play a major role in the political life of the new republic, assuming the role of republican mothers and wives who would instill patriotism and virtue in their children and spouses.

Americans of the revolutionary generation took their cues from the lessons of history, particularly the example of the Roman Republic and its ideal of public virtue. When Dr. Joseph Warren, physician and Patriot leader, addressed Bostonians on the fifth anniversary of the Boston Massacre in 1775, he literally donned a Roman toga, the long flowing gown that symbolized a free, adult Roman man's freedom and citizenship. Warren's dramatic gesture, linking himself with Roman republicanism, was mirrored in the pages of nearly every American newspaper of the day, where letters and essays on political matters were signed with pen names drawn from the history of the Roman Republic, such as the senators Brutus and Cato and the general Cincinnatus.

To mold a new generation of virtuous citizens, Americans looked to education, religion, and even architecture. No American was more enthusiastic about architecture's capacity to instruct than Thomas Jefferson. Public buildings, Jefferson wrote, "should be more than things of beauty and convenience, above all they should state a creed." Rather than emulate contemporary Georgian-style buildings such as the Pennsylvania State House (see Chapter 3), where the Declaration of Independence was drafted, Jefferson argued for a return to the "purity" of Roman architecture. In his design for the Virginia State Capitol (pictured here), Jefferson recreated the simple beauty of Roman architecture. He believed that the Capitol would inspire citizens to emulate the ideals of the ancient Roman Republic, which included an emphasis on civic participation and public virtue.

In the decade following independence, Americans' faith in their ability to create a virtuous republic was challenged. An aborted coup led by disgruntled Continental Army officers, conflicts between debtors and creditors, and an uprising in western Massachusetts drove the nation to a political crisis. The postwar period tested America's faith in republicanism and led some leaders to abandon traditional republican theory, with its emphasis on virtue, and to embrace a new approach to constitutional government that relied on a balance of conflicting interests and a system of checks and balances. The culmination of this struggle between the two competing visions of constitutional government was the U.S. Constitution and the Bill of Rights.

"We may look up to Armies for our Defense,
but Virtue is our best Security. It is not possible that
any State should long remain free,
where Virtue is not supremely honored."
SAMUEL ADAMS, 1775

Republicanism and the Politics of Virtue

 The American Revolution marked a decisive break from ideas and values that had defined British culture for centuries. Monarchy and aristocracy were swept away. America was now a republic. Republicanism placed a premium on the ideal of virtue. As the poet, playwright, and historian Mercy Otis Warren observed, Americans needed "to cherish true, genuine republican virtue." The postwar period would test this commitment in a host of ways.

George Washington: The American Cincinnatus

No individual in America was more closely identified with the ideal of virtue than George Washington. A symbol of the virtuous citizen–soldier, responding to the summons of his nation and retiring to private life once his service was no longer needed—Washington was a model of civic virtue. His reputation for public virtue and ability to command the respect of his troops had helped the beleaguered Continental Army during some of its more dire campaigns. In 1783, Washington faced a different challenge. This time it was not the threat of enemy troops, but the rumors of a military coup by the Continental Army's officers. Washington wielded his personal authority to win over disgruntled members of the corps and made an impassioned appeal to "reason and virtue," crushing the revolt without firing a shot.

Washington had learned of rumors that the army's leadership would no longer tolerate Congress's failure to deal with complaints about their pay and pensions. An anonymous essay had circulated among officers suggesting that the time might soon come to turn their arms against Congress itself. The officers' anger had been simmering for some time. Frustration with the Confederation Congress was widespread; Washington was well aware of the officers' grievances. He had complained about the inefficiency and ineffectiveness of Congress on many occasions. With no power to tax, Congress had to depend on voluntary contributions from the states. Without reliable revenue, it was difficult to wage war or conduct the routine business of governing. Faced with a possible rebellion by his own officers, Washington resolved to address his men in person and persuade them of the folly of their plan.

On a dark wintry day in March 1783, Washington traveled to Newburgh, New York, to address the officer corps. The assembled officers met in a makeshift building that some of them had dubbed the "Temple of Virtue." Washington prepared to read a letter that he hoped would persuade the officers that their demands would be met. Fumbling to find a pair of glasses he had recently acquired, he paused, and then addressed the hushed crowd: "Gentlemen, you must pardon me. I have grown grey in your service, and now find myself growing blind." The impact on his audience was dramatic. "There was something so natural, so unaffected in his appeal," Major Samuel Shaw later wrote, "as rendered it superior to the most studied oratory, and you might see sensibility moisten every eye." Washington's own wartime sacrifices had already provided a powerful role model for the officer corps. Now the figure of their beloved commander growing gray and blind in the service of his country struck a resonant chord. He exhorted his men to give posterity "proof of unexampled patriotism and patient virtue." Civic virtue had triumphed over corruption, and the Newburgh conspiracy was crushed without a shot being fired.

Another event that enhanced Washington's reputation as the embodiment of republican virtue was the public ceremony of turning over his military commission to Congress after the war. In Annapolis, Maryland, where Congress was convened, Washington addressed a room crowded with congressional delegates and a gallery packed with well-wishers. "Having now finished the work assigned me," he informed his audience, many of whom were brought to tears, "I here offer my commission, and take

📖 **Read** the **Document** *George Washington, The Newburgh Address (1783)*

my leave" of "the employments of public life." By abandoning public life and returning to his plow, Washington was seen as placing the good of the nation ahead of personal glory. In the public's view, Washington had transformed himself into the modern Cincinnatus, an allusion to the ancient world's great symbol of public virtue, the Roman general Cincinnatus. After serving the Roman Republic as its supreme commander, Cincinnatus had returned to his farm.

After resigning, Washington went on a triumphal tour of the nation. In Philadelphia, he was saluted by cannons and ringing bells from the city's steeples. He sat for portraits by America's leading painters and enjoyed listening to commemorative verses that compared him to Cincinnatus. Well schooled in the history of the ancient Roman Republic, Americans understood that a popular military leader's decision to emulate Rome's dictatorial general Julius Caesar rather than Cincinnatus would lead to despotism. Years later the Virginia legislature commissioned the French sculptor Jean-Antoine Houdon to create a life-sized statue of Washington as the modern Cincinnatus (**5.1**). Washington stands before a plow, the symbol of the virtuous farmer, the ideal embodied by Cincinnatus.

> "No free Government, or the blessing of liberty, can be preserved to any people but by a firm adherence to justice, moderation, temperance, frugality, and virtue . . ."
>
> Virginia Declaration of Rights, 1776

The Politics of Virtue: Views from the States

The republican emphasis on virtue suffused American culture. The first state constitutions drafted after independence used their declarations of rights to outline the rights of citizens and also instruct citizens in the premises of republican government. In these declarations of rights, the ideal of virtue was literally written into American law. The Virginia Declaration of Rights (1776) asserted that free government could not survive without a virtuous citizenry, a point echoed by the Massachusetts Constitution four years later. Educating citizens in the importance of republican ideals became a priority for the new nation.

Art, architecture, and even fashion were pressed into service to mold the character of a new generation of citizens. Jefferson's design for the new Virginia Capitol was the most ambitious visible symbol of instilling republican values by reforming architecture. (See the chapter opening image, p. 129.) The impact of the Revolution was even seen in home furnishings. Before the Revolution, decorative elements on American furniture copied British fashions, including fanciful designs such as the scrolled pediment with rosettes on this chest of drawers

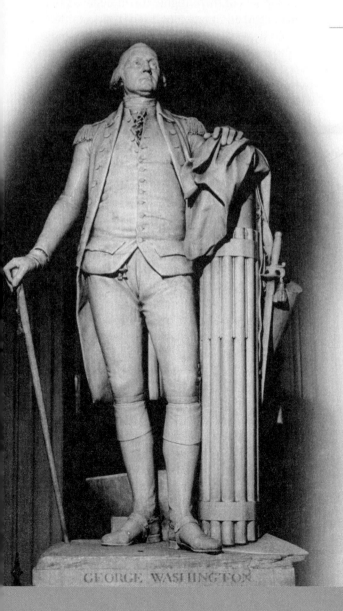

5.1 George Washington as the Modern Cincinnatus George Washington is cast as the modern Cincinnatus in this sculpture. He stands in front of a plow and beside the Roman "fasces," a bundle of rods and an ax that symbolized the legal power of magistrates. His sword rests on the "fasces" a visual reminder that in a republic military power resides with civilian leaders.

GEORGE WASHINGTON

What was the Newburgh Conspiracy?

5.2 Chippendale High Chest
This pre-revolutionary chest reflected British styles, including the floral decorative patterns at the end of the curving swan's neck pediment on top of the chest.

5.3 Samuel McIntire Carving
This piece of furniture made in Salem after the Revolution uses simple classical lines. Symbols of republicanism, such as the goddess of liberty, replaced purely decorative elements.
[*Source:* Samuel McIntire, "Chest-on-chest (detail)"; Mahogany, mahogany veneer, ebony and satinwood inlay, pine; Eighteenth-century American Arts No. 4; the M. and M. Karolik Collection of Eighteenth-Century American Arts, 41.580. Museum of Fine Arts, Boston (41.58). Photograph © 2010 Museum of Fine Arts, Boston]

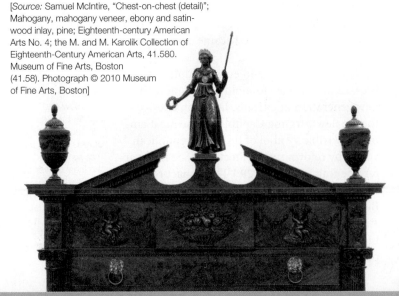

(**5.2**). After the Revolution symbols that represented the republican values of the new nation replaced some of these purely decorative elements. A beautifully crafted example of this adorns a chest of drawers made in Salem, Massachusetts (**5.3**). The broken pediment is a simple classical design. Gone is the fancy carving in the pediment of the late colonial chest (5.2). In its place is the goddess of liberty herself. To reinforce the ideal of Roman republicanism, the chest has two classical columns. These flank another set of carvings that illustrate the prosperity that republicanism will bring to the new nation.

Education was another means of inculcating virtue. The Massachusetts Constitution expressly linked republicanism, virtue, and education. The state achieved this by providing public primary education for boys and girls. Several of the larger towns also provided secondary education for boys. Thomas Jefferson framed the most ambitious proposal to create a public system of education in 1778. In "A Bill for the more General Diffusion of Knowledge," he proposed that Virginia adopt a publicly funded system of education. White children, including boys and girls, would be educated at public expense for three years. The best male students would then be selected for secondary education, and a small select group from among this cohort would later attend the College of William and Mary. Jefferson introduced his bill in the state legislature several times, although it never passed.

Jefferson's faith in education reflected his debt to the ideals of the Enlightenment, the international philosophical movement based on the notion that reason and science would improve humanity. (See Chapter 3.) Following the English philosopher John Locke, Enlightenment thinkers believed that people were born a blank slate upon which society could write its own moral code. Many American Founders, including Jefferson, were also influenced by other Enlightenment ideas. Philosophers of the Enlightenment believed that humans had an innate moral sense, akin to the five physical senses. In the same way that people see different shades of the color spectrum, so the moral sense helped people see the difference between right and wrong. One need only cultivate this inborn sense to produce enlightened citizens. Taken together, Lockean psychology and Enlightenment moral theory led many Americans to put enormous faith in education's ability to shape morality and mold character.

Inspired by Enlightenment ideals about education and the American Revolution's faith in representative government, Americans founded new educational institutions to help create an enlightened citizenry. Ezra Stiles, the president of Yale College, wrote in 1786 that "the spirit for Academy making is vigorous." The charter for one of these new academies in North Carolina declared that "the good education of youth has the most direct tendency to promote the virtue, increase the wealth and extend the fame of any people." North Carolina was one of the states that founded a university. Georgia and Vermont also established public institutions of higher education. Among the new private colleges were Williams (Massachusetts), Transylvania (Kentucky), the College of Charleston (South Carolina), and Bowdoin (Maine).

Educators also published new republican materials to instruct children in reading, writing, and arithmetic. Spellers and readers included patriotic lessons with illustrations that reinforced their republican message. In a book of alphabet rhymes, for example, the bald eagle from the Great Seal of

How did changes in furniture design reflect the influence of republican ideas?

Read the Document *Noah Webster, An American School Teacher Calls for an American Language, 1789*

America, the new nation's official symbol, represented the letter "E" (**5.4**). The design of the great seal had gone through many versions before Congress finally approved one that included an American eagle clutching an olive branch and thirteen arrows, symbolizing the new government's power to make war and negotiate peace. The thirteen states are represented by the same number of stars, stripes, and arrows. Charles Thomson, the secretary of Congress, observed that the eagle bore a shield to symbolize that "the United States ought to rely on their own Virtue."

The expansion of education opened up possibilities for white women. Whereas Jefferson's plan for educational reform called for basic education for women, other reformers recommended more ambitious plans to educate the nation's female population. Jefferson's friend, the eminent Philadelphia physician Benjamin Rush, offered a robust statement of the importance of education in a republic, but also framed a bold call to educate women for their role as republican citizens. Women needed to be familiar with the political ideas of republicanism. As the mothers of future citizens of the republic, women had a special role to play. Rush was not alone in championing female education. The Philadelphia Young Ladies Academy (1787) was typical of the new institutions for educating women. In addition to music, dance, and needlework, these new schools taught girls subjects, such as rhetoric, oratory, and history, once exclusively taught to boys. Martha Ryan, a student at one of the new schools in North Carolina, inscribed the phrase "Liberty or Death" in her cipher book (**5.5**). Although influenced by republican ideas, her book also revealed the continuing importance of traditional ideas about women's roles. Bound into the book were penmanship exercises that intoned such traditional moral injunctions as "Honour Father and Mother." *Images as History: Women's Roles: Tradition and Change* explores the effects of republican ideas on women's roles (page 134).

Supporters of Enlightenment ideas such as Rush and Jefferson believed that education would help nurture the virtue necessary for the survival of republicanism. Other Americans, however, looked to religion to foster virtue. One minister reminded his parishioners that although the "civil authority have no right to establish religion," it was still true that "religion is connected with the morals of the people." Another minister noted that by "instilling good sentiments into the tender minds

5.4 Book of Children's Verses
This book of children's verse uses America's new national symbol, the bald eagle, taken from the Great Seal of the United States. Educational materials such as this one included republican and patriotic themes.

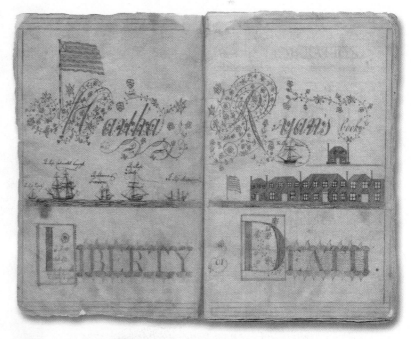

5.5 Martha Ryan's Cipher Book
The cover of Martha Ryan's cipher book proclaims liberty. Yet, the book included penmanship exercises with such traditional precepts as "Honour Father and Mother … A good girl will mind."

Why was education so important to the Founders of the American Republic?

Images as History
WOMEN'S ROLES: TRADITION AND CHANGE

Although republicanism allowed some women to transform the roles assigned to them, it retained the traditional view that a woman's primary duties were to her family. In the engraving *Keep Within the Compass*, the woman who stays within the compass enjoys a life of harmony and prosperity. Stepping outside it carried grave consequences.

Republican ideals of womanhood were stitched into a needlework sampler prepared by a school girl, Nabby Martin of Providence, Rhode Island. Samplers were a standard part of a young woman's education. Nabby included images of young couples, flowers, and domestic animals, common to pre-revolution samplers, but republican themes also show through. The home, the symbol of domesticity, traditionally

the heart and center image of a young girl's sampler, has been replaced by the Rhode Island State House. Politics, not home, is the center of this piece. Nabby also showed her respect for the republican emphasis on education by including the College of Rhode Island (Brown University).

As a female, Nabby Martin was barred from the world of the State House and the College of Rhode Island, but the inclusion of their images in her sampler is significant. Although working with an art form closely tied to women's roles, Martin turned her gaze to the wider world both buildings represented. The republican message of the sampler is clear: Let Virtue be a Guide to Thee. How is virtue represented visually in Martin's needlework?

The text that accompanied this image advised: "Keep within Compass and You shall be sure to avoid many troubles which others endure."

The building pictured is The College of Rhode Island, the forerunner of Brown University.

Keep Within the Compass, 1784
[Courtesy, Winterthur Museum]

When a woman steps outside the compass, she faces arrest and imprisonment.

The message of the sampler is announced in the central text: Let Virtue be a Guide to Thee

Instead of a home, the Rhode Island State House is the central image.

Nabby Martin, Sampler, 1786

How did republican ideas change notions about women's roles?

of children and youth, you will teach them to stand fast in their liberty." Post-revolutionary America remained a predominantly Protestant culture in which religious dissent was tolerated only within limits. Some states continued to bar Catholics and Jews from public office. The assumption behind such laws was that only Protestants could be counted on to have the necessary virtue to seek the public good.

Although excluded from the full benefits of citizenship, religious dissenters were allowed to worship according to the dictates of conscience. Most state bills of rights and constitutions guaranteed the free exercise of religion. Revolutionary ideas of liberty and equality slowly led states to abandon the notion that only Protestants could be trusted to hold public office. Religious tests requiring potential office holders to swear a belief in the divinity of Jesus as a requirement for holding public office were abolished in Virginia (1785), Georgia (1789), Pennsylvania (1790), South Carolina (1790), Delaware (1792), and Vermont (1793).

Before the Revolution, many colonies provided direct government support to religion or followed the English practice of having an official church. Spurred by Revolutionary ideals America moved toward the separation of church and state. The post-revolutionary era witnessed a move to disestablish the Anglican Church in those places where it enjoyed public funding. Two different justifications for the separation of church and state emerged. For champions of the Enlightenment, such as Jefferson, separation of church and state was inspired by the fear that religion might use the power of government to oppress citizens of different religious views or that religion might corrupt government. Dissenting Protestant sects, notably the Baptists and Methodists, opposed state support for religion for a different reason. These groups had long felt oppressed by the state-supported Anglican Church, particularly by taxation to support that church. For Virginia's Baptists, separation of church and state was a means to protect the purity of religion from corruption by government.

Evangelicals and supporters of the Enlightenment came together in Virginia in 1785 when the state legislature considered a bill for non-preferential aid for ministers of the Christian religion. Since the scheme was non-preferential, it would not establish an official state church but rather provide funds to all Protestant churches in a nondiscriminatory fashion. Patrick Henry and Richard Henry Lee, two of the state's leading politicians, campaigned in favor of the bill. James Madison and Thomas Jefferson, champions of Enlightenment values, led the opposition.

Madison and Jefferson outlined their case against state support for religion in *The Memorial and Remonstrance Against Religious Assessments* (1785). This essay not only was instrumental in defeating the bill, it also became a landmark in American church–state relations.

Democracy Triumphant?

According to traditional republican theory, citizens were expected to defer to their betters, who were assumed to be the most virtuous members of society. Before the American Revolution, the state legislatures were dominated by men of wealth. As one legislator noted, "it is right that men of birth and fortune, in every government that is free, should be invested with power, and enjoy higher honours than the people." Virtue, according to this view, required one to have the wealth supposedly necessary to cultivate wisdom and knowledge. One newspaper writer captured this traditional conception of virtue when he wrote that representatives "should be ABLE in ESTATE, ABLE in KNOWLEDGE AND LEARNING."

The Revolution, however, challenged this ideal, substituting a more democratic theory of virtue. A writer calling himself "Democritus" captured the essence of this new theory when he urged that citizens vote only for "a man of middling circumstances" and "common understanding," not members of a wealthy or educated elite. In nearly every state a new type of politician emerged who embodied the more democratic version of republicanism: men such as New York's Abraham Yates, a shoemaker, and Pennsylvania's William Findley, a weaver.

Supporters of the elitist republican view of politics mocked the humble origins of the new politicians and questioned their ability to function as legislators. One contemporary political satirist took aim at Findley's humble origins as a weaver: "It will be more honourable for such men to stay at their looms and knot threads, than to come forward in a legislative capacity."

The post-revolutionary debate over the meaning of virtue and democracy shaped politics. When William Smith, a prosperous Baltimore

Why did many supporters of republicanism fear democracy?

flour merchant, ran for office in 1789, his enemies attacked him by claiming that "Mr. Smith has distilled RICHES from the tears of the POOR; and grown FAT upon their curses." Smith's supporters viewed his independence as one of his main qualifications for office. In their view he was "a Man of great commercial Knowledge, of known integrity, and possessed of a Character and independent Fortune which place him above Temptation." Smith's support for this traditional idea of virtue was reflected in this portrait (**5.6**) painted by Charles Wilson Peale. Rather than include symbols that reflected Smith's life as a prosperous city merchant, Peale depicted Smith as a simply dressed country gentlemen. The books that the artist included, poetical works on rural life, reinforce this notion. Peale also placed Smith in front of a Roman column, another visual cue to symbolize his virtue.

The debate over what made a good representative in part reflected a process of democratization in American culture. The Revolution greatly expanded the number of white male voters eligible to participate in the political process. Most states lowered property requirements for voting, and Pennsylvania abandoned such requirements entirely. Taken together, the expansion of democratic ideas and changes in suffrage requirements changed the character of politics in America. As this graph (**5.7**) reveals, the impact on the composition of state legislatures was profound. After the Revolution the percentage of wealthy citizens elected to the legislature dropped, and the numbers of those of the "middling sort," or middling classes, increased. One Boston newspaper writer complained that "since the war, blustering ignorant men" had unfortunately pushed "themselves into office." Not everyone saw the rise of these new politicians in negative terms. For those who believed in democracy, these trends were a positive development. Now government included "a class of citizens who hither to have thought it more for their interest to be contented with a humbler walk in life."

The new democratic politicians favored policies designed to enable ordinary citizens to

5.6 William Smith and His Grandson
In this portrait of William Smith, the artist conjures up an image of a country gentleman who devoted himself to contemplation. References to Smith's career as a prosperous Baltimore merchant are deliberately excluded.

Why did William Smith's portrait cast him as a country gentleman rather than an urban merchant?

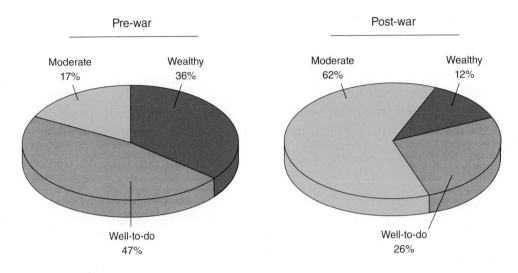

Economic Status of Legislators in New Hampshire, New York, and New Jersey

Pre-war

Moderate 17%
Wealthy 36%
Well-to-do 47%

Post-war

Moderate 62%
Wealthy 12%
Well-to-do 26%

5.7 The Democratization of the State Legislatures The number of wealthy legislators decreased and the number of men of moderate wealth increased. These changes were pronounced in parts of the mid-Atlantic and New England, and are reflected in the data regarding property holdings of legislators elected in New York, New Jersey, and New Hampshire. Adapted from Jackson Turner Main, "Government By the People: The American Revolution and the Democratization of the Legislatures," (*William and Mary Quarterly* 1966)

participate in government. They introduced, for example, higher salaries for elected representatives, encouraging ordinary people to serve in government. They also made efforts to relocate state capitals inland, so that travel to them would be easier for backcountry farmers.

Debtors versus Creditors

Economic issues proved particularly contentious in post-revolutionary America. Spokesmen for these new politicians favored policies to ease the burdens of farmers and artisans. "Stay laws" created generous grace periods for the recovery of debts and protected farmers from having their farms seized for nonpayment of debts. "Tender laws" allowed farmers to pay debts with goods rather than hard currency. Merchants generally opposed these policies.

The lack of specie, silver and gold currency, hindered economic exchange. Spokesmen for debtors argued that government had an obligation to use paper money to ease the shortage of currency. By expanding the money supply and printing more paper currency, the government encouraged inflation. Increasing the amount of money in circulation facilitated commerce. When done cautiously, this type of inflationary policy provided a means of pumping up the economy. As long as the government did not flood the market with paper, driving down its value, debtors and creditors could adjust their behavior to take into account the effects of modest inflation in prices for various commodities. By encouraging economic activity, paper money could provide an important tool for economic growth. Farmers were especially fond of this system because they could repay their debts with depreciated currency— money that was worth less than the amount of the original debt. This system, however, could function only if merchants did not dramatically raise prices to compensate for the declining value of paper money. A rapid rise in prices could lead inflation to spiral out of control. Most merchants, however, viewed paper money as a bad policy that hurt their interests.

No state was more aggressive in using paper money to solve its financial problems than Rhode Island. Unfortunately, however, the decision to print large amounts of paper money never won the support of merchants in Providence and Newport. When presented with paper money, merchants increased prices and eventually refused to accept depreciated paper currency. In response, the state legislature imposed a steep fine on any merchant who refused to accept paper currency. One writer lampooned the situation of "Rogue Island" in verse: "*Hail! realm of rogues, renow'd for fraud and guile All hail, ye knav'ries of yon little isle.*"

How did the composition of the state legislatures change after the American Revolution?

Life under the Articles of Confederation

From the outset, the **Articles of Confederation**, America's first federal constitution, was plagued by problems. Without the power to tax or coerce states to follow the treaties it had negotiated, the Confederation Congress could not resolve the nation's economic problems and diplomatic issues. Leaders also worried that the Confederation lacked the military power to deal with rebellions or foreign foes.

No Taxation with Representation

Americans resented British efforts to tax them prior to the Revolution. Given their fears of strong government and hostility to taxation, the Articles of Confederation, the weak constitution created by the Confederation Congress, did not empower the new central government to tax Americans. Instead, the Articles relied on requisitions made to the states to fund government business. Few states bothered to comply with these requisitions in a timely manner, and the new government of the United States was plagued by shortages of funds.

Although it lacked the power to tax, Congress had to fund the war. To help pay for the war effort, Congress printed almost $250 million in paper currency that was not backed by gold or silver and led to staggering inflation. By 1781, it took more than 150 Continental dollars to purchase what had cost one dollar in 1777. This dramatic drop in the value of Continental currency led to the phrase "As worthless as a Continental" to describe something with no value. As **5.8** illustrates, it would take a pile of Continentals to purchase what a single dollar might have paid for less than five years before.

The Treaty of Paris (1783) formally ended hostilities between Britain and the new United States of America. Peace did not, however, solve the economic problems that the new nation faced. Indeed, the end of the war ushered in new economic

5.8 Continental Paper Currency
The value of Continental paper currency dropped precipitously as Congress printed more money, and faith in the value of the currency dwindled.

problems. Boycotts of British goods and the disruption of trade during wartime meant that consumers had been denied access to luxury items, including china, textiles, and wine. Demand for British goods surged after the war, and the new nation was flooded with imports. British merchants encouraged Americans to buy goods on credit. American merchants by contrast, now faced a host of new obstacles to trade with Britain. In particular, the loss of the lucrative trade with the British West Indies was a severe blow to the American economy. America's trade deficit with Britain drained what little gold and silver reserves were available to the nation. American banks had to curtail loans. When merchants were forced to call in debts to satisfy their British suppliers, they included the debts individuals owed them. This constriction of credit sent the economy into a tailspin. The combination of restricted access to trade with Britain and its empire, falling agricultural prices, and mounting debt produced the new nation's first economic depression.

Diplomacy: Frustration and Stalemate

The new nation also faced military challenges. British troops were still garrisoned in parts of the Ohio Valley. Relations with the Indian tribes along the frontier remained tense. Farther from the nation's borders, Americans faced different problems. Without a powerful navy to protect American commerce, ships were easy prey for pirates. Piracy was particularly rampant in the Mediterranean where the North African states of Morocco, Algiers, Tunis, and Tripoli, known as the Barbary States, sanctioned it. The Barbary pirates extorted money from merchant vessels in exchange for safe passage. Failure to pay resulted in the seizure of ships and imprisonment of sailors. American sailors taken as captives by

Why did the Articles of Confederation fail to give the Confederation Congress power to tax?

Barbary pirates languished in North African prisons or were sold into slavery. In July 1785, when pirates captured two American ships, Algiers demanded nearly $60,000 in ransom to release the vessels and their crews. The American navy was too weak to challenge these pirate fleets. While the loss of trade burdened the nation's fledgling economy, the sad fate of American captives became a source of national humiliation.

Frustration with the inability to defend its interests on the high seas grew, but America faced even more serious problems closer to its borders. Defending the nation's interests in the Mediterranean would have to wait while America dealt with the threats posed by Indians and the British and Spanish in North America. The map (**5.9**) shows the British and Spanish presence along America's borders, a fact that increased American anxiety.

Congress had little power to compel the states to live up to the nation's treaty obligations, including provisions requiring Americans to pay prewar debts and compensate Loyalists for property confiscated during the war. Britain used America's failure to comply with these provisions as a pretext for retaining control of its forts in the **Old Northwest**, the region of the new nation bordering the Great Lakes (5.9). These outposts allowed the British to continue their lucrative fur trade with the Indians.

The war against Britain had strained relations between America and its Indian neighbors. Many Indian peoples, such as the Iroquois in New York and the Creeks in Georgia, had sided with the British.

5.9 Border Disputes in Old Northwest and Southwest
The British refused to abandon their forts in the Old Northwest until Congress complied with all the provisions of the Treaty of Paris. In the Old Southwest, Spain frustrated America's efforts to secure the rights to navigate the Mississippi River.

While British peace negotiators had sought to protect the interests of Loyalists, they did nothing to secure a just peace for their Indian allies. The leader of the Mohawks, another Indian nation that had sided with the British, pointed out that the government of

View the **Map** *Territorial Claims in Eastern America after the Treaty of Paris*

What diplomatic frustrations hampered the new American nation?

George III had "no right whatever to grant away to the States of America their rights or properties without a manifest breach of all justice and equity."

Given the absence of Indian representation in the treaty that ended hostilities between the United States and Britain, it is hardly surprising that the interests of Indian peoples were not reflected in the final terms. The Treaty of Paris ceded the entire Old Northwest territory to the United States. American diplomats were not sympathetic to the claims of Indians. Operating under a theory of conquest in which Indians were "a subdued people," American negotiators assumed that defeated tribes had to relinquish all claims to Western lands. Rejecting this view, Indians organized to resist incursions. Rather than mark the start of an era of peace, the period after the Revolution was one of continued conflict between Indians and Americans. Those tribes that were best organized politically and militarily were better able to defend their interests against American expansionism.

The Indian population east of the Mississippi numbered between 150,000 and 200,000 and was divided into 85 different nations. The white population of the new United States was approximately 2.4 million. Pressure to open up Indian lands for white settlement created conflict. Indians had no illusions about the goal of American policy. The insatiable desire for Indian land led the Creeks to bestow the name "Ecunnaunuxulgee" on Georgians: "people greedily grasping after the lands of red people."

When confronted with the determination of Indians to defend their lands, Americans were forced to negotiate more fairly. American leaders soon realized that missionary work and trade were more likely to secure harmonious relations than conquest and military confrontation. By 1787, Congress had shifted both its tone and strategy for dealing with Indian policy. In place of the theory of conquest, Congress recommended "the utmost good faith" in dealing with the Indians.

The Spanish presence in the Old Southwest was another threat. Navigation of the Mississippi River was crucial for the economic development of this region. Goods traveling down the Mississippi needed to be unloaded at New Orleans and placed on ocean-bound vessels. Spain denied Americans free access to the Mississippi and New Orleans. Congress authorized Secretary of Foreign Affairs John Jay to negotiate with the Spanish. Spain proposed opening its empire to trade with America if the United States renounced its claim to navigate the

Mississippi. The terms would have been a boon to New England merchants, who would have benefited from new trade opportunities with Spanish America, but alienated Southerners, particularly those in the Southwest, who viewed the Mississippi as their pipeline to world markets.

Settling the Old Northwest

The most important achievement of the Confederation period was the plan Congress devised for Western settlement. A committee chaired by Thomas Jefferson devised the initial plan for settling the West (**5.10**). This proposal imagined a rational mathematical scheme for carving out as many as 16 new states from the Northwest Territory. Jefferson's plan combined republican theories of self-government with Enlightenment ideas about geography. Boundaries would be drawn along an orderly grid after being surveyed. Reflecting his debt to classical republicanism, Jefferson's chose names for the new territories such as Polypotamia, "land of many rivers." Republicanism guided this plan in other ways. In his Ordinance of 1784, Jefferson proposed that new territories be incorporated into the union as states on an equal footing with the original thirteen. Jefferson also sought local self-government for settlers almost immediately. When the free population reached 20,000, a constitutional convention would set up a permanent state government. The plan banned slavery after the year 1800 and recommended that land be made available in parcels small enough for average Americans to purchase. Jefferson envisioned the Northwest Territory populated by white yeoman farmers.

The Land Ordinance of 1785 adopted by Congress departed from Jefferson's original proposal. It called for the creation of townships of 36 square miles. Land was to be sold for no less than one dollar an acre in hard currency. Ordinary citizens would have had trouble raising this amount of cash and therefore had little chance to purchase land directly from the government. Jefferson's hope that Western land could be sold directly to citizens and create a republic of small independent farmers was jettisoned in favor of a plan that favored speculators.

The **Northwest Ordinance of 1787** was the final plan for the governance of the new territories. This act was considerably less democratic than Jefferson's original proposal but maintained his orderly model for dividing up the territory. Governors appointed by Congress would rule the Northwest Territories. When the population reached 5,000 adult males, settlers could elect their own territorial legislatures. When the population reached 60,000 free inhabitants, including women, the territories could seek admission to the Confederation. The language of the Northwest Ordinance echoed the republican ideals of the Revolution. Congress proclaimed that "fundamental principles of civil and religious liberty" were the foundation for the new states to be created from the territories. In keeping with the republican ideas about virtue and the need for an educated citizenry, the Ordinance declared: "Religion, morality, and knowledge, being necessary to good government and the happiness of mankind, schools and the means of education shall forever be encouraged." Most important, the Ordinance rejected slavery in the new states to be carved out of the Northwest Territories.

5.10 Jefferson's Plan for the West Jefferson's grid-like map for the settlement of the West was influenced by the ideas of Enlightenment thinkers. The names that Jefferson proposed for these territories were inspired by classical antiquity. Thus, one potential state was named Sylvania, "a forested region."

Shays's Rebellion

The postwar economic downturn hit farmers in Massachusetts particularly hard. As farm foreclosures increased, and families saw their farms seized by their creditors, frustration mounted. Revolutionary War veterans marched on the town of Northampton to shut down the local courts and prevent further foreclosures. The armed crowd prevented the judges, dressed in formal judicial attire, long black robes and gray wigs, from entering the courthouse. The protestors, dubbed Shaysites, after their leader, Daniel Shays, believed they were protecting the "good of the commonwealth" and opposing the "tyrannical government in the Massachusetts State." Governor James Bowdoin condemned the court closings as "fraught with the most fatal and pernicious consequences" that "must tend to subvert all law and government."

Shays's Rebellion had begun. When angry farmers in Great Barrington, another town in western Massachusetts, closed their local court, the governor dispatched the state militia. One member of the crowd sympathetic to the Shaysites

---

"There shall be neither slavery nor involuntary servitude in the said territory, otherwise than in the punishment of crimes whereof the party shall have been duly convicted."

Northwest Ordinance of 1787

View the **Closer Look** *Competing Visions: Reactions to Shays's Rebellion*

What republican features distinguish the Northwest Ordinance?

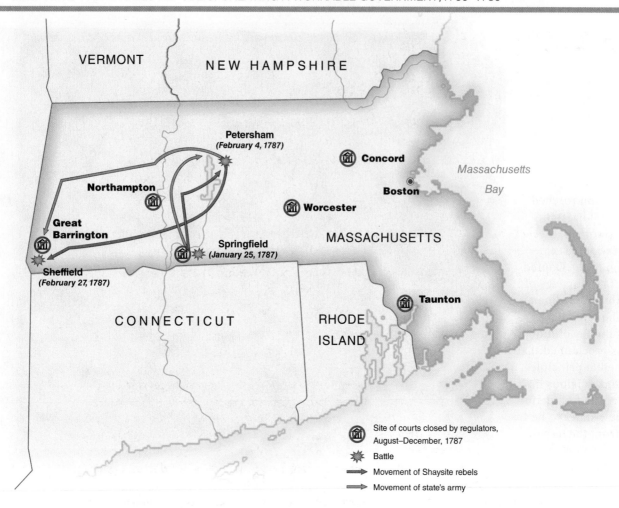

5.11 Court Closings and Major Battles in Shays's Rebellion
Shays and his supporters closed courts in central and western Massachusetts. Forces loyal to the
state routed the Shaysites in a decisive battle at the Springfield state armory.

suggested putting the matter to a vote among
the militiamen: Supporters of opening the court
stood to one side of the road, while those opposed
crossed the highway. Nearly 800 of 1,000 members
of the militia who had been sent to protect the
courts voted with their feet to join the rebels and
keep the courts closed.

The towns affected by the court closing are
shown in the map (**5.11**), which also shows the
location of the armed confrontations between the
Shaysites and government forces. Shays and his followers were defeated in a battle near the state arsenal

in Springfield. The failure of Shays's Rebellion, the
most serious challenge to government authority in
the new nation, gave additional impetus to those
eager to reform the structure of the Articles of
Confederation and create a more powerful central
government. George Washington was among the
most alarmed by events in Massachusetts. The one
figure among the nation's Patriot elite who seemed
relatively unfazed by the rebellion in western Massachusetts was Thomas Jefferson who learned of the
rebellion while living in Paris and serving America
as a diplomat.

The Movement for Constitutional Reform

 The economic, political, and diplomatic problems faced by the Confederation government, including Shays's Rebellion, inspired a small but talented group of politicians to advocate reform of the Articles of Confederation. As nationalists—men who believed in the need for a stronger national government—they regarded constitutional reform as imperative. Rather than continue to put their faith in virtue, nationalists sought to create a powerful central government to protect American interests abroad and deal with internal threats, such as Shays's Rebellion. For the nationalists the postwar era was a time of crisis that demanded decisive action if America were to survive. Nationalists proposed a new model of government to protect individual liberty and promote the common good. The Federal Constitution created by this group relied on a system of checks and balances, not virtue, to protect liberty.

The Road to Philadelphia

Delegates from Maryland and Virginia gathered at George Washington's home in Mount Vernon (1785) to discuss economic matters. A year later in Annapolis, Maryland (1786) delegates from five states discussed the problems of the Confederation. Finally, in 1787, delegates from 12 of the 13 states gathered in Philadelphia to reform the Articles of Confederation. The 55 delegates in Philadelphia included an impressive cast of characters. Virginia sent James Madison and George Mason, two of its most esteemed political figures. Pennsylvania's representatives included the oldest delegate, Benjamin Franklin, then aged 81, and James Wilson, the nation's premier legal mind. New York's delegation boasted the brilliant, but brash, Alexander Hamilton. The delegates chose George Washington to preside over the meeting. Lawyers dominated the convention, and nearly all the delegates were wealthy men.

A strict rule of secrecy was imposed on the proceedings, a decision that facilitated a more frank debate among the delegates, but only intensified rumors about their activities. The rule of secrecy was stringently enforced: The windows of the Pennsylvania State House were nailed shut and a guard posted at the door.

Writing from France, where he was serving as American minister, Jefferson described the assembly as a meeting of "demigods"—men of such impressive accomplishments that they seemed like the mythical heroes of antiquity, part human and part divine. Some contemporaries, however, were suspicious of the convention's secrecy. One Pennsylvania newspaper warned of the "monster" being fashioned behind a "thick veil of secrecy." Later generations of Americans have tended to echo Jefferson's observations: that the convention was composed of extraordinarily talented politicians, a view illustrated by this mid-nineteenth-century painting by Thomas Rossiter (**5.12**) in which the Founders are bathed in light, not shrouded in secrecy.

Large States versus Small States

Instead of arguing over reforming the Articles of Confederation, as originally intended, the Philadelphia Convention took up a bold proposal offered by the Virginia delegation. The **Virginia Plan**, drafted mainly by James Madison, abandoned the federal system created by the Articles, in favor of a new

> "We have probably had too good an opinion of human nature in forming our confederation."
> GEORGE WASHINGTON, 1786

What were the main features of the Virginia Plan?

5.12 Constitutional Convention
Jefferson's observation that the Framers of the Constitution were an "assembly of demigods" is captured in Thomas Rossiter's nineteenth-century painting of the Philadelphia Convention. Rather than appearing in a dark conclave, the members of the convention are bathed in light.

model of government that had both federal and national features. The states would retain power, but the new national government would be supreme in those areas in which it was given authority.

The Virginia Plan created a new government composed of a single executive (the branch of government charged with, among other things, the execution of laws), a two-house legislature (Congress, the lawmaking body), and a separate judiciary (courts). The lower house of Congress would be directly elected by the people, and the upper house would be elected by the lower house from a list provided by the state legislatures. Under the Articles of Confederation, small states such as Maryland had the same vote as large states such as Virginia. Rather than this one-state one-vote principle, each state would have representation in proportion to its population.

The new Congress would have the power "to legislate in all cases to which the separate States are incompetent" or "in which the harmony of the United States may be interrupted by the exercise of individual [state] legislation." Although this did not explicitly address nettlesome issues such as the power to tax, such powers were clearly within the purview of this broad grant of authority. The authors of the Virginia Plan, especially James Madison, thought that a more general grant of authority, rather than a long list of enumerated powers, would be more politically acceptable to the delegates.

Representatives from the small states opposed the Virginia Plan. Two weeks after the Virginia Plan was introduced, William Patterson of New Jersey made a counterproposal, often dubbed the **New Jersey Plan.** It called for a modified federal system based on the existing Articles of Confederation. It proposed a single legislature in which each state would have one vote, which would maintain the parity between small and large states. In contrast to the Articles of Confederation, the new national legislature would be the supreme law of the land and would be binding on the states. The national legislature would have the power to tax and regulate interstate commerce. Although the New Jersey Plan was defeated, it had revealed the difficulty of reaching a consensus without accommodating the concerns of the small states, which feared that the new system would give larger states inordinate influence over the new government.

The figure (**5.13**) shows the differences between the Virginia and New Jersey plans and how each differed from the Articles of Confederation. Although both of these plans would have given the new central government broad new powers, particularly over economic matters, representatives from the large and small states remained divided over how the legislature would be structured. On June 29, 1787, Oliver Ellsworth of Connecticut reintroduced an earlier compromise that he and Roger Sherman (also of Connecticut) had devised. The plan provided for equal representation for large and small states in the upper house and a lower house in which representation would be apportioned on the basis of population. On July 16, 1787, the convention adopted the **Great Compromise** (sometimes known as the Connecticut Compromise because of Ellsworth and Sherman's role in framing it). The Great Compromise solved one of the most difficult issues facing the convention: the struggle over representation based on population versus equal representation among the states.

Conflict over Slavery

Although the Connecticut Compromise solved one of the most difficult problems faced by the convention, it also focused attention on another equally contentious issue: whether to count slaves in the apportionment of the new lower house. The Southern states, seeking sufficient representation in the new legislature to protect slavery, were determined that their slaves be counted. Opponents of slavery, by contrast, wished to see slaves taxed as property but did not wish to count them when calculating representation in the new lower house. The convention settled on a solution in which slaves were counted as three-fifths of a person for purposes of taxation and legislative apportionment. (The three-fifths ratio had been worked out by the Confederation Congress earlier, when it faced another issue pertaining to slavery.)

Conflict flared over the slave trade. One of the most intense attacks on the slave trade was voiced by Virginian George Mason, the largest slave owner in the convention, who warned his fellow delegates of the threat to the republic of the institution of slavery: "Every master of slaves is born a petty tyrant...slavery discourages arts & manufactures." Mason recommended ending the slave trade as a first step toward eliminating slavery. Several delegates viewed Mason's actions cynically. Virginia had an excess of slaves and would profit enormously from an internal slave trade if the external trade with Africa were abolished. South Carolinian

	Articles of Confederation	Virginia Plan	New Jersey Plan
Structure of the Legislature	Single house, one state one vote	Two houses, both determined by population	Single house, one state one vote
Taxation	No power to tax	Power to tax	Power to tax
Judicial Power	No judicial power apart from courts to hear admiralty cases	Federal judiciary	Federal judiciary
Executive Power	No permanent executive, a committee of the states exercises executive functions when Congress is not in session	Single executive chosen by national legislature	Single or plural executive elected by Congress

5.13 Comparison of the Articles of Confederation, Virginia, and New Jersey Plans
Although the Virginia and New Jersey plans differed on representation, each would have given the new government the vital power of taxation.

Watch the **Video** Lecture: Slavery and the Constitution

How did the conflict over slavery shape the debates of the Constitutional Convention?

> "The states were divided into different interests
> not by their difference of size but by other circumstances;
> the most material of which resulted partly from climate,
> but principally from the effects of their having
> or not having slaves."
>
> JAMES MADISON, 1787

Charles Pinckney argued that all the great republics of the ancient world had accepted the necessity of slavery. His cousin, General Charles Cotesworth Pinckney, another delegate from South Carolina, told delegates that his state would never accept the Constitution if the slave trade was banned. Again compromise held the convention together. The new Congress was denied the authority to ban the slave trade until 1808.

Although the word slavery never appears in the Constitution, a number of clauses in the document protected it. Article IV, Section 2, prevented fugitive slaves, defined as any "person held to service or labour in one state," from fleeing to another state to seek asylum and freedom. Article I, Section 8, prohibited the national government from taxing the exports of any state, a provision that prevented the products of slave labor, such as rice, indigo, tobacco, or sugar, from being singled out for sanctions by those hostile to slavery. In James Madison's view, the greatest division in the convention was not the conflict between large states and small states, but slavery.

Filling out the Constitutional Design

After sorting out the structure of the legislative branch of government, the convention struggled over the executive branch. George Mason argued for a three-man executive. A plural executive, he argued, could better represent the different regional interests of the nation. Rejecting this proposal, the convention settled on a unitary executive. There was also disagreement over how to choose the executive. James Wilson wanted to see the executive elected by the people, whereas Mason argued that the people lacked the wisdom to make such a decision. Roger Sherman's plan to have the national legislature pick

the executive was challenged as a threat to the separation of powers.

Eventually the convention settled on an "electoral college" composed of men chosen by each state in a manner to be determined by the individual state legislatures. By giving the states some control over selection of the president, this system provided another way of strengthening the power of the states within the new federal system. The electoral college also reflected the ideals of republicanism held by the delegates. By creating a filtering mechanism for the selection of the president, the electoral college was designed to help ensure that the men chosen were drawn from the ranks of the leading citizens, men renowned for their knowledge and virtue.

Delegates also clashed over the term of office that the executive would serve. Alexander Hamilton proposed that the executive have a life term, but this leaned too close to monarchy for most delegates. Some delegates favored a single term of as much as seven years, while others argued that a shorter term with the possibility of reelection would provide a greater check on the president. The convention ultimately settled on a four-year term with no limits on the number of terms a president might serve. The final structure of the executive branch was detailed in Article II of the Constitution.

Throughout August the convention sketched the barest outline for the third branch of government, the federal judiciary. A new Supreme Court was created, and Congress was authorized to create such inferior courts as it deemed necessary. The Supreme Court's authority extended "in all Cases, in Law and Equity, arising under the Constitution, the Laws of the United States, and Treaties made under their authority." Although a number of delegates assumed that the courts would exercise the power of judicial review, the power to declare acts of Congress

How did the electoral college strengthen the powers of the states and further the ideals of republicanism?

unconstitutional, the Constitution failed to make such power explicit.

Two delegates from New York, Robert Yates and John Lansing, left before the document was completed and therefore did not sign it. Three other delegates—Edmund Randolph, George Mason, and Elbridge Gerry—refused to sign the Constitution because of their reservations about its final draft. Despite these protests, Benjamin Franklin captured the feelings of many delegates when he wrote that despite its faults, it was doubtful "whether any other convention we can obtain may be able to make a better Constitution . . . it therefore astonishes me, Sir, to find this system approaching as near to perfection as it does." After the convention concluded its work and the text of the Constitution was made public, a woman asked Franklin, "'Well Doctor what have we got a republic or a monarchy?' 'A republic,' replied the Doctor, 'if you can keep it.'"

The Constitution reflected the give and take and the spirit of compromise that prevailed at the Convention. The new Constitution was a radical departure from the Articles of Confederation (**5.14**).

The powerful national legislature created by the Constitution was given authority to enact all laws "necessary and proper" to carrying out responsibilities delegated by the Constitution.

The new national legislature had two houses, a House of Representatives and a Senate. Each state had two senators. Representation in the House of Representatives was based on population, with slaves counting as three-fifths of a person. Amendments to the Constitution would require the approval of three-quarters of the states, not the unanimous consent required under the Articles. Although executive power under the Articles of Confederation had been weak, the new president could veto legislation, negotiate treaties, and issue pardons. The ill-defined powers of the new Supreme Court left some wondering if the judiciary would be the weakest of the three branches, not co-equal with the legislature and the executive.

The new federal Constitution also broke with well-established precedents that had shaped the state constitutions drafted after the Revolution. Unlike the typical state constitution, the federal Constitution did not include a declaration of rights stating the basic rights and liberties retained by the people, nor did it reassert the basic republican principles upon which government rested. Most state constitutions created relatively weak executives, another marked contrast with the new Federal Constitution and its strong executive branch.

	Articles of Confederation	Constitution
Structure of the Legislature	Single house, one state one vote	Two houses, one determined by population, upper house equal state representation
Taxation	No power to tax	Power to tax
Judicial Power	No judicial power apart from courts to hear admiralty cases	Federal judiciary
Executive Power	No permanent executive, a committee of the states exercises executive functions when Congress is not in session	Executive chosen by electors chosen by state legislators

5.14 Comparison of the Articles of Confederation and the Constitution
As this chart shows, the new federal government created by the Constitution was far more powerful than the old government under the Articles of Confederation.

What were the most important differences between the federal Constitution and the typical state constitutions of this period?

The Great Debate

 The publication of the Constitution inaugurated one of the most vigorous political campaigns in American history. In taverns and town squares, Americans argued over the new Constitution. As one contemporary remarked, "the plan of a Government proposed to us by the convention—affords matter for conversation to every rank of beings from the Governor to the door keeper." Soon two sides emerged in the debate over ratification.

Federalists versus Anti-Federalists

The supporters of the Constitution described themselves as **Federalists**, thus saddling their opponents with the name **Anti-Federalists**. Never entirely happy with this name, opponents of the Constitution complained that they were the true supporters of federalism and attacked pro-Constitutional forces as "consolidationists" who wished to consolidate the union into a single national government and rob the states of their power. Looking back on the bitter struggle over ratification, one Anti-Federalist quipped that because the issue before the nation was ratification of the Constitution, the two sides were more aptly described as "rats and anti-rats."

Citizens paraded, raised their glasses to toast, or attacked the new government. Some even rioted to express their sentiments. Anti-Federalists in Carlisle, Pennsylvania, burned an effigy of Federalist James Wilson to express their disapproval of the new Constitution. Wilson, a renowned lawyer and a recent immigrant from Scotland, was one of the most important supporters of the Constitution in Pennsylvania. He was also an easy target for ridicule, since he spoke with a thick Scottish accent that his enemies mocked. The supporters of the Constitution also took to the streets to defend it and occasionally to intimidate their opponents. A Federalist crowd wrecked the printing presses of Anti-Federalist publishers in New York City. These disturbances were the exception, however, not the rule.

The debate could be heated, but Americans typically confined their passions to the printed page. Hundreds of columns of newspaper text were devoted to the debate over the merits of the Constitution, and dozens of pamphlets were written for and against it. *The Federalist,* for example, a sophisticated defense of the Constitution written by John Jay, Alexander Hamilton, and James Madison, was first published as newspaper essays in New York. It is now regarded by many scholars as America's most important contribution to Western political philosophy. Writing under the pen name Publius, a hero of the Roman Republic, the authors hoped to cloak themselves in the toga of Roman virtue. This strategy was designed to focus the public's attention on the ideas, not the men responsible for, the essays. *The Federalist* not only responded to Anti-Federalist criticism, it also provided a sophisticated analysis of republican government and a point-by-point discussion of the merits of the Constitution. Although its influence on the outcome of ratification was modest, *The Federalist* soon became the favorite text of judges, legislators, and others interested in interpreting the meaning of the Constitution. It continues to be the text most often cited by the Supreme Court when trying to identify the original understanding of the Constitution.

Anti-Federalists produced no single text comparable to *The Federalist.* However, the writings of Elbridge Gerry and George Mason, prominent Anti-Federalists who had participated in the Philadelphia Convention but had refused to sign the Constitution, were widely reprinted. Authors who adopted the pen names Brutus and Federal Farmer each framed sophisticated critiques of the Constitution. Brutus invoked the same ideal of Roman virtue that Publius had appropriated for the supporters of the Constitution. The name Federal Farmer traded on the association of republican ideals of simplicity associated with the ideal of the yeoman farmer. Both texts developed an alternative vision of republican government. Rather than accept the need for a powerful central government, Anti-Federalists clung to the idea of a system in which the bulk of governmental functions would continue to reside in the states. (See *Competing Visions: Brutus and Publius Debate the Nature of Republicanism.*)

Although the struggle over ratification produced some of the most intellectually sophisticated writings in American history, in other respects it was a textbook example of negative campaigning. If Publius and Brutus provided an example of dispassionate reason, metaphorically invoking Roman ideals of virtue by their pen names, other authors, on both sides, were not above

Why did Federalist and Anti-Federalist authors adopt names such as Publius and Brutus?

Competing Visions
BRUTUS AND PUBLIUS DEBATE THE NATURE OF REPUBLICANISM

One disagreement between Federalists and Anti-Federalists arose from their different views of the nature of republican government. A number of prominent Anti-Federalists clung to the traditional theory that a republican government could only survive if a nation remained small and the people's interests were fairly homogeneous. Federalists, most notably, Publius, argued it would be easier to protect liberty in a large and diverse republic.

The Anti-Federalist author Brutus defended the traditional idea that a free republic could survive only in a small area in which the people shared the same values, culture, and history. When a republic became too large, he argued, it became contentious, and the common good was sacrificed as competing factions vied to promote their own narrow interests. In short, Brutus was confident that history demonstrated the impossibility of a nation the size of the new United States remaining a free republic without a confederation-style government.

If respect is to be paid to the opinion of the greatest and wisest men who have ever thought or wrote on the science of government, we shall be constrained to conclude, that a free republic cannot succeed over a country of such immense extent, . . . as that of the whole United States. . . . History furnishes no example of a free republic, any thing like the extent of the United States. The Grecian republics were of small extent; so also was that of the Romans. . . . in a republic, the manners, sentiments, and interests of the people should be similar. If this be not the case, there will be a constant clashing of opinions; and the representatives of one part will be continually striving, against those of the other. This will retard the operations of government, and prevent such conclusions as will promote the public good. If we apply this remark to the condition of the United States, we shall be convinced that it forbids that we should be one government.

Writing as Publius, in *The Federalist*, James Madison disputed the traditional theory of republicanism advanced by Brutus and other Anti-Federalists. By increasing the number of factions and expanding the size of the republic, Publius argued that it would be less likely for any one faction to further their agenda and dominate politics. According to this new theory, politics would become a kaleidoscope of ever-shifting alliances. Moreover, in a larger republic politics itself would act like a filter and be more likely to select leaders of skill and talents. Finally, Madison noted that the federal system would act like a fire-wall, isolating factions within individual states and preventing them from spreading their wicked agendas to other states.

Men of factious tempers, of local prejudices, or of sinister designs, may, by intrigue, by corruption, or by other means, first obtain the suffrages, and then betray the interests, of the people. The question resulting is, whether small or extensive republics are more favorable to the election of proper guardians of the public . . . . The smaller the society, . . . the fewer the distinct parties and interests, the more frequently will a majority be found of the same party . . . the more easily will they concert and execute their plans of oppression. Extend the sphere, and you take in a greater variety of parties and interests; you make it less probable that a majority of the whole will have a common motive to invade the rights of other citizens; or if such a common motive exists, it will be more difficult for all who feel it to discover their own strength, and to act in unison with each other. . . . The influence of factious leaders may kindle a flame within their particular States, but will be unable to spread a general conflagration through the other States.

In the extent and proper structure of the Union, therefore, we behold a republican remedy for the diseases most incident to republican government.

Why did Brutus and Publius differ about the relationship between size and republicanism?

slinging mud when it served their interests. Federalists, for example, denounced their opponents as Shaysites, a charge repeated in the satirical print, *The Looking Glass for 1787* (**5.15**). In this cartoon, Connecticut appears stuck in the mud, a cart laden with debt is dragged in opposite directions by Federalists and Anti-Federalists. The artist who created this pro-Federalist political cartoon stooped lower than most: One Anti-Federalist character has his trousers pulled down around his ankles and his bottom exposed to his Federalist opponents. Anti-Federalists charged that Federalists were part of an aristocratic elite who wished to dominate common folk. Amos Singletary from Massachusetts warned his fellow citizens that the lawyers and rich merchants who backed the Constitution favored the interests of the aristocratic few over those of the democratic many. In his view, the new Constitution would undo the democratic reforms of the Revolution, returning control to powerful economic groups.

Although Anti-Federalism attracted supporters of democracy such as Singletary, it also appealed to wealthy planters such as Virginia's George Mason, who was less concerned about the Constitution's anti-democratic features and more worried about the centralization of power. Mason feared that liberty would be annihilated if a central government gained too much power. Although Anti-Federalists did not agree about everything, they shared important objections to the Constitution. The essential Anti-Federalist critique emerged early in the debate. At the top was the fear of consolidation, the concern that the federal government would absorb all power into its orbit. Anti-Federalists believed that there would be too few representatives in Congress to represent the diverse interests of the American people. Representatives would also live far from their constituents and lose touch with the concerns of those they served. The extensive powers of the president and the potentially vast jurisdiction of the Supreme Court also worried Anti-Federalists, who feared that the federal government would become tyrannical.

The absence of a bill of rights proved to be one of the Anti-Federalists' most effective criticisms. In their view history demonstrated that once in power even the most virtuous rulers were tempted to increase their powers at the expense of popular liberty. A written declaration stating clearly the rights and powers retained by the people was therefore an essential safeguard for liberty. Rather than accept that the omission of a bill of rights was a serious flaw in the Constitution, Federalists argued that it was unnecessary. James Wilson defended the absence of a bill of rights by noting that the new government was one of delegated power only, and hence all powers not ceded to it were retained by the

people and the states. "It would have been superfluous and absurd," he observed, to stipulate "that we should enjoy those privileges, of which we are not divested either by the intention or the act that brought that body into existence." In *The Federalist,* Publius argued that the inclusion of a bill of rights would be dangerous. By listing exactly which rights were protected, the new government would by implication exclude other rights that it did not explicitly include among those reserved to the people. Since it would be impossible to create a list of all the rights enjoyed by the people, it was better not to list any. For an overview of disagreement between Federalists and Anti-Federalists see **5.16**.

5.15 *The Looking Glass for 1787* This Federalist political cartoon from Connecticut portrays the state as a cart stuck in the mud and weighed down by paper money and debt. While Federalists proclaim "Comply with Congress" and pull the state toward a bright sun, the Anti-Federalists exclaim "Success to Shays" and drag the cart toward a shadowy future symbolized by the dark clouds.

Ratification

Federalists realized that Anti-Federalists would try to block unconditional ratification and seek prior amendments to the Constitution. Early and decisive Federalist successes in Delaware, New Jersey, Pennsylvania, Georgia, and Connecticut established a momentum that Federalists capitalized on to achieve their goal of unconditional ratification. Eventually in Massachusetts Fed-

> "These lawyers, and men of learning, and moneyed men, that talk so finely, and gloss over matters so smoothly, to make us poor illiterate people swallow down the pill, expect to get into Congress themselves . . . and then they will swallow up all us little folks, like the great Leviathan."
>
> AMOS SINGLETARY, 1788

How does *The Looking Glass for 1787* portray the Anti-Federalists?

Read the **Document** *Patrick Henry Speaks Against the Constitution*

5.16 Anti-Federalist versus Federalist Ideas

Anti-Federalists and Federalists each believed in republican government, but they disagreed over how to structure such a government to protect liberty.

James Madison
Federalists

George Mason
Anti-Federalists

Federalists	Anti-Federalists
Support strong central government	Oppose strong central government
Oppose bill of rights as unnecessary and perhaps even harmful to liberty	Favor inclusion of a bill of rights as necessary to protect liberty
Doubt effectiveness of militia and favor federal standing army	Favor militia and oppose federal standing army
Republicanism can survive only in a large and diverse republic	Republicanism can survive only in a small republic
Virtue is a weak foundation for republicanism; a system of checks and balances is better suited to preserving a republican government against corruption	Republicanism depends on a virtuous population to prevent corruption

eralist faced a powerful Anti-Federalist opposition and conceded the need for subsequent amendment once the Constitution was adopted. Federalists' willingness to compromise also won over moderates who might have opposed the Constitution in battleground states

"If men were angels, no government would be necessary. If angels were to govern men, neither external nor internal controls on government would be necessary. In framing a government which is to be administered by men over men, the great difficulty lies in this: you must first enable the government to control the governed; and in the next place oblige it to control itself."

JAMES MADISON, *The Federalist* 1788

such as Massachusetts. Had the Federalists maintained a hard-line, sticking to James Wilson's argument that a bill of rights was unnecessary, the Constitution might never have been ratified. If states with powerful, well-organized Anti-Federalist coalitions, such as Virginia, had held ratification conventions earlier, the Constitution might have been defeated or been radically altered by amendments. New Hampshire's vote to ratify on June 21, 1788 gave Federalists the nine states needed to ratify the Constitution. Although the Constitution was now the new law of the land, it was vital to persuade Anti-Federalists in Virginia and New York to accept it.

Despite opposition from Anti-Federalists like Patrick Henry, Virginia ratified the Constitution on June 25. That left only New York, North Carolina, and Rhode Island outside the new Union. In New York City Federalists staged a "grand federal procession" to show that the Constitution enjoyed broad support, particularly among the city's artisans, who saw a strong government as a way to protect their economic interests from foreign competition. The parade drew members from virtually all of the city's crafts and included dozens of floats. Printers, for example, marched alongside a printing press mounted on a horse-drawn cart which churned out an ode that praised the Constitution. A banner with the name Publius, the author of *The Federalist*, flew proudly above the press, and the printers sported caps with "Liberty of Press" written in large letters. Another group of artisans carried this banner (**5.17**), which celebrated their work with pewter, an alloy of tin and lead that was widely used to make tableware. Their banner carried the following verses:

The Federal Plan Most Solid And Secure
Americans Their Freedom Will Ensure
All Arts Shall Flourish in Columbia's Land
And all Her Sons Join as One Social Band

New York Anti-Federalists had a dilemma: Should they continue to oppose the Constitution or work within the new system of government? To understand how they made their decision, see *Choices and Consequences: To Ratify or Not.*

New York's ratification dashed the last hopes of opponents of the Constitution to secure prior amendments. Federalists had secured unconditional ratification of the new frame of government. Most Americans probably opposed the Constitution when it was first proposed, and the vote on ratification was close in many states. Several factors helped account for the Federalists' victory. Supporters of the Constitution organized themselves around a well-defined goal: ratification. By contrast,

Choices and Consequences

TO RATIFY OR NOT

By the time New York's ratification convention met in Poughkeepsie, nine states had already ratified the Constitution, making it the new law of the land. Could Anti-Federalists continue to oppose the Constitution and thereby place New York outside the new nation? Many Anti-Federalists considered such a prospect unrealistic, so they turned to the question of amending the Constitution. The outcome of the convention depended on the decisions of moderate Anti-Federalists, led by the merchant Melancton Smith. New York Anti-Federalists faced a momentous decision: continue to oppose the Constitution or work within the new system of government.

Choices

1 Support the Constitution with the promise that the First Congress would amend it.	**2** Support the Constitution provisionally until it was amended, but consider seceding from the Union if amendments were not made.

3 Block ratification and continue to oppose the Constitution.

Decision

Smith opted for the first choice, making New York the eleventh state to ratify the Constitution on July 25, 1787. In a powerful speech in the New York convention, he reiterated his hope for future amendments but recognized the need to work through the "mode prescribed by the Constitution."

Consequences

If Smith and other swing Anti-Federalist delegates in the Convention had opposed ratification, New York would have remained outside the Union, and the new nation might have split into separate confederacies. If Smith and other moderates had insisted on amendments before ratification, Federalists would likely have stood their ground and the convention might have failed to ratify the Constitution. As it was, Smith's decision put more pressure on Rhode Island and North Carolina to accept the new Constitution. It also gave impetus to the move to amend the Constitution after ratification. Federalist newspapers seized on the visual image of a Roman-style temple to represent the nation and added a new column for each state that voted to ratify the Constitution. The pillars and temple metaphor, like Jefferson's model for the Virginia State Capitol, evoked Roman ideals of virtue and liberty.

Continuing Controversies

Why did New York Anti-Federalists accept the Constitution and wait for amendments?
Although the Anti-Federalists were defeated in 1788, many of their fears and ideals about government still resonate in American politics. Were the Anti-Federalists backward-looking politicians who failed to grasp the genius of the new Constitution, or visionaries who predicted that the growth and centralization of American government might pose a threat to liberty? Americans still argue over the legacy of Anti-Federalism.

Massachusetts newspaper celebrates New York as "the eleventh pillar."

5.17 Pewterers' Banner
In a New York City parade celebrating the Constitution, Federalist artisans carried a banner that included the U.S. flag and depicted artisans crafting objects of pewter. The verse at the top proclaims the bright future for America under the new Constitution.

Anti-Federalists could not provide a clear alternative. Some favored a new convention to revise the Constitution. Others favored amending the Constitution prior to ratification, and some were content to amend the new document later. Finally, Federalists were more effective at getting their message into print. Many newspaper editors refused to print Anti-Federalist materials.

The dynamics of ratification were complex. No single theory accounts for why individuals and regions supported the Constitution, but the map shows several patterns in voting (**5.18**). Geography, economics, and individual experiences all shaped the vote on the Constitution.

Merchants and artisans in regions tied to commerce, such as seacoasts and inland areas close to navigable rivers, looked to a stronger union to protect their economic interests and became Federalists. Inhabitants of frontier regions that faced Indian threats also supported a stronger central

5.18 Geographical Distribution of the Vote on Ratification
Support for the Constitution was strongest along coastal regions and frontiers exposed to threats from external enemies and among small states such as Delaware, Maryland, and New Jersey. Anti-Federalism was strongest in the backcountry of New England, the mid-Atlantic, and the South.

government because of these security concerns. Except for Rhode Island, small states supported the Constitution. Officers of the Continental Army who had dealt with a weak Congress under the Articles also supported the Constitution.

Anti-Federalists drew together an equally diverse coalition that opposed any effort to centralize authority and lessen the power of the states. Backcountry farmers, particularly those less closely connected to major commercial markets, opposed the Constitution. State politicians, especially the newly empowered men of moderate wealth and more humble origins who dominated politics in states such as Pennsylvania and New York, were strongly Anti-Federalist. Finally, wealthy planters in parts of the South who feared that a distant and powerful government would not represent their interests became Anti-Federalists.

The Creation of a Loyal Opposition

Despite the intensity of the struggle over ratification, Anti-Federalists did not continue their opposition to the Constitution once the nine states needed to ratify adopted it. Indeed, rather than choose to become an anti-Constitutional party, Anti-Federalists accepted having to work within the framework provided by the Constitution. Continued opposition to the Constitution would only have led to anarchy, which most Anti-Federalists wished to avoid as much as did their Federalist opponents. Anti-Federalists turned their attentions to campaigning for election to the First Congress and to securing amendments to the Constitution.

BRITISH CANADA

Lake Superior

Lake Michigan

Lake Huron

Ontario

Lake Erie

Disputed between the United States and Great Britain

VERMONT (disputed between New Hampshire and New York)

St. Lawrence R.

MAINE (to Mass.)

NEW HAMPSHIRE (June 1788)

NEW YORK (July 1788)

MASSACHUSETTS (Feb 1788)

RHODE ISLAND (May 1790)

PENNSYLVANIA (Dec 1787)

CONNECTICUT (Jan 1788)

Ohio R.

NEW JERSEY (Dec 1787)

VIRGINIA (June 1788)

DELAWARE (Dec 1787)

MARYLAND (April 1788)

NORTH CAROLINA (Nov 1789)

SOUTH CAROLINA (May 1788)

GEORGIA (Jan 1788)

ATLANTIC OCEAN

Gulf of Mexico

SPANISH FLORIDA

Federalist majority (for)
Anti-Federalist majority (against)
Evenly divided

View the **Map** Interactive Map: Ratification of the Constitution

Why was there no anti-Constitution movement after ratification?

1782

America adopts a new national symbol
Six years after being proposed, America adopts a new symbol for the nation, The Great Seal of the United States, a design intended to embody the republican ideals of the nation

1783

Newburgh Conspiracy
Washington prevents coup by Continental army officers

Treaty of Paris
Hostilities between United States and Britain conclude and Britain recognizes American Independence

1784

Land Ordinance of 1784
Thomas Jefferson proposes a model for settling the Old Northwest Territory

1785

Thomas Jefferson appointed ambassador to France
Jefferson appointment as French ambassador insulates him from the hysteria surrounding Shays's Rebellion

CHAPTER REVIEW

Review Questions

1. Americans in the post-revolutionary era looked to Rome for inspiration in building a virtuous republic. How were these ideas reflected in American art and architecture in this period?

2. What were the most notable achievements and failures of the Confederation government?

3. What were the most divisive issues the Constitutional Convention faced and what compromises did the delegates reach to solve them?

4. Which groups in society tended to support or oppose the Constitution?

5. Anti-Federalists were alarmed by the power of the federal government. Do you think the Anti-Federalist objections to the Constitution have any validity today?

Key Terms

Articles of Confederation America's first constitutional government in effect from 1781–1788. The articles created a weak decentralized form of government that lacked the power to tax and compel state obedience to treaties it negotiated.   **138**

Old Northwest The region of the new nation bordering on the Great Lakes.   **139**

Northwest Ordinance of 1787 One of several laws adopted by the Confederation Congress designed to provide a plan for the orderly settlement of the Northwest Territory (the area north of the Ohio River and west of Pennsylvania). In addition to providing for a plan for self-governance, the Ordinance also prohibited slavery from the Northwest Territory.   **140**

Shays's Rebellion Uprising in western Massachusetts in which farmers organized themselves as local militia units and closed down courts to prevent their farms from being seized by creditors.   **141**

Virginia Plan A plan framed by James Madison and introduced in the Constitution Convention by Edmund Randolph that called on delegations to abandon the government of the Articles and create a new, strong national government.   **143**

New Jersey Plan Proposal made by William Patterson of New Jersey as an alternative to the more nationalistic Virginia Plan that would have retained the principle of state equality in the legislature embodied in the Articles of Confederation.   **144**

Great Compromise Compromise plan proposed by Roger Sherman and Oliver Ellsworth of Connecticut that called for equal representation of each state in the upper house and a lower house based on population.   **145**

Federalists The name adopted by the supporters of the Constitution who favored a stronger centralized government.   **148**

Anti-Federalists The name applied to opponents of the Constitution who insisted that they, not their opponents, were the true supporters of the ideal of federalism. Anti-Federalists opposed weakening the power of the states and feared that the Constitution yielded too much power to the new central government.   **148**

1786

Virginia Statute for Religious Freedom
Madison and Jefferson win approval of bill promoting religious freedom

Shays's Rebellion begins
Farmers in western Massachusetts close courts

1787

Philadelphia Convention drafts Constitution
Delegates assemble in Philadelphia to revise Articles of Confederation

Hamilton, Madison, and Jay publish the first installment of *The Federalist*
The most sophisticated defense of the Constitution appears in the New York press

1788

New Hampshire becomes ninth state to ratify Constitution
Constitution becomes new law of the land

1789

University of North Carolina chartered
Although the University of Georgia was the first public university chartered in the United States (1785), the University of North Carolina (1789) was the first public institution of higher education to admit students and offer classes

MyHistoryLab Connections

Visit www.myhistorylab.com for a customized Study Plan that will help you build your knowledge of *A Virtuous Republic*.

Questions for Analysis

1. How did George Washington embody the ideas of republicanism?

Read the **Document** *George Washington, The Newburgh Address (1783), p. 130*

2. What impact did republican ideals and nationalism have on American culture after the Revolution?

Read the **Document** *Noah Webster, An American School Teacher Calls for an American Language, 1789, p. 132*

3. What does Shays's Rebellion reveal about the problems of the Confederation government?

View the **Closer Look** *Competing Visions: Reactions to Shays's Rebellion, p. 141*

4. Who were the Anti-Federalists and why did they oppose the Constitution?

Read the **Document** *Patrick Henry Speaks Against the Constitution, p. 150*

5. Did the ideas embodied in the Constitution mark a break with traditional republicanism and Revolutionary-era constitutionalism, or were they a logical outgrowth of them?

Read the **Document** *Federalist No. 10, p. 151*

Other Resources from This Chapter

Read the **Document**

- *Military Reports on Shays's Rebellion, p. 142*
- *Virginia or Randolph Plan, p. 144*

View the **Map**

- *Territorial Claims in Eastern America after the Treaty of Paris, p. 139*
- *Interactive Map: Ratification of the Constitution, p. 153*

Watch the **Video** *Lecture: Slavery and the Constitution, p. 145*

Launching the New Government p. 158

Did the Washington Administration and the first Congress neutralize or exacerbate Anti-Federalist fears?

Hamilton's Ambitious Program p. 160

What were the main features of Hamilton's economic program?

Partisanship without Parties p. 166

How did the press encourage partisanship?

Conflicts at Home and Abroad p. 168

How did the French Revolution influence American politics?

Cultural Politics in a Passionate Age p. 175

Why did reading novels seem so threatening in the 1790s?

The Stormy Presidency of John Adams p. 179

Why did Federalists enact the Sedition Act and was it constitutional?

The New Republic
An Age of Political Passion, 1789–1800

The adoption of the Constitution did little to lessen the divisions in America that had arisen during ratification. The Federalist supporters of the Constitution splintered into two opposing groups. One side rallied around Alexander Hamilton, who became the chief theorist and driving force for an ambitious Federalist agenda. For Hamilton and his allies, the adoption of the Constitution was simply the first step in creating a powerful central government. These Federalists envisioned America as a great commercial empire that would, inspired by Britain's lead, develop a strong military and pursue economic development aggressively.

Opposing this bold agenda was a group that coalesced around Thomas Jefferson, who, with his friend James Madison, a former ally of Hamilton, helped define the core of the Republican opposition. This movement, although lacking the coherence and formal organization of a modern political party, battled its Federalist opponents over political, economic, and constitutional issues. Republicans sought to limit the powers of the new federal government and opposed the creation of a powerful financial and military state.

The radicalism of the French Revolution further polarized American political life, and political passions intensified during the turbulent 1790s. Federalists denounced the excesses of revolutionary France even as Republicans affirmed their support for France.

By the end of the 1790s, the partisan animosities had grown intense, as reflected in this pro-Federalist political cartoon, *The Times, A Political Portrait*. A group of American volunteers rides out to confront an invading French Army. As they march forward, they trample a Republican printer, while a dog urinates on his newspaper. The artist shows Republican James Madison attempting to block the progress of America's troops with a giant pen, while Republicans Albert Gallatin and Thomas Jefferson work from behind to achieve the same goal. The text at the bottom announces the triumph of American government and warns traitors that they will receive their just punishments.

After a decade of Federalist domination, Americans in 1800 turned to Thomas Jefferson, head of the Republican opposition, as their leader. In a close election, power was peacefully transferred from the Federalists to their opponents, and Jefferson became the nation's third president.

"Party spirit is the fashion of the Times . . .
Party spirit makes the worst of everything
that opposes her folly."

Newark Centinel of Freedom, 1799

Stop de wheels et

de gouvernement

Launching the New Government

Although intense partisanship had characterized American politics during the colonial and revolutionary eras, the republican ideas championed during the Revolution stressed the need for a virtuous citizenry. The Constitution created a system designed to check the dangers of factionalism. Leaders were expected to put the good of the nation above any factional interest. Fortunately for America, the nation's first president, George Washington, was such a figure, a leader who tried to remain above partisanship. Appointing Alexander Hamilton and Thomas Jefferson to his cabinet demonstrated his commitment to this ideal. These were men whose views on government were almost at opposite extremes, and from them, Washington sought policy alternatives to deal with the pressing issues facing the new nation.

Choosing the First President

The Constitution had created an **electoral college**, a group of electors appointed by the states who had the responsibility of picking the president. On February 4, 1789, electors from all the states that had ratified the Constitution met in their state capitals and unanimously selected George Washington to be the nation's first president. John Adams, another prominent revolutionary leader, received half that number of votes, becoming the first vice president. The remaining votes were split among ten other candidates.

The nation celebrated Washington's election in a grand style. He traveled from his home at Mount Vernon in Virginia to the site of his inaugural in New York City, feted along the way. Many towns erected triumphal arches, such as this one near Trenton (**6.1**). Although leading men in the community typically greeted Washington, giving him a military salute, in Trenton he met the local women who had erected the arch and who serenaded him. A placard on the arch proudly proclaimed that "The Defender of the Mothers will also Defend the Daughters."

6.1 Triumphal Arch Near Trenton, New Jersey
At Trenton women erected a 20-foot arch made of evergreens and laurels. On the right, Washington rides toward the arch.

The First Federal Elections: Completing the Constitution

Although there had been little doubt that Washington would be America's first president, the divisions between Federalists and Anti-Federalists influenced the first congressional elections. The issue of constitutional amendments was among the most contentious issues debated in the first federal elections.

Federalists were eager to have James Madison run for Congress. Madison agreed to run, but he balked at actively campaigning for a seat, believing that behaving in such a partisan fashion was inconsistent with republican ideals. Fortunately, Madison's supporters persuaded him that if he did not take his case directly to the people, Virginia would send an Anti-Federalist–dominated delegation to Congress. Madison set aside his reluctance to appeal for votes, and won election to Congress. One group critical to Madison's success were the Baptists, who were eager to obtain explicit protection for freedom of religion in the Constitution. The task of shaping a set of amendments thus fell to Federalist James Madison.

Madison recognized that if properly framed, amendments might go a long way to eliminating lingering Anti-Federalist suspicions of the new federal government. Thus, although he had originally opposed Anti-Federalist calls for amendments during the struggle over ratification, Madison now recognized their political necessity. He accepted what he described as "the nauseous project of amendments," knowing that the process would be deeply politicized and that the few ardent Anti-Federalists in Congress would agitate for weakening the federal government. Still, Madison pared down the

Why did Madison shift his views on the need for a Bill of Rights?

View the **Image** George Washington's Arrival in New York City (1789)

dozens of amendments proposed by the state ratification conventions to seventeen. The Senate then whittled these down to twelve provisions and sent them to the states to ratify. The states did not adopt the first two proposed amendments, which dealt with legislative apportionment and congressional salaries. (More than 200 years later, the states finally adopted what became the Twenty-Seventh Amendment, which prohibits raises for Congress from taking effect until a new House of Representatives has taken office, a restraint that makes it more difficult for Congress to vote itself frequent salary increases.)

The first ten of the original twelve amendments to the Constitution, eventually became known as the Bill of Rights, and included protections for both basic individual liberties and for the states. The First Amendment protected freedom of the press and religion. The Second Amendment guaranteed that the people would have a right to keep and bear arms in a well-regulated militia. (This right has since been expanded to include private arms used for individual self-defense within the home.) The Third Amendment forbade the government to quarter troops in the homes of private citizens. Several amendments protected the procedural rights associated with jury trial. The Ninth Amendment declared that enumeration of some rights did not mean the denial of others retained by the people. Finally, lest the new government try to expand its powers by exploiting the vague clauses of the Constitution, the Tenth Amendment stated that those powers not delegated to the federal government were reserved to the states and the people.

These amendments assuaged the concerns of most moderate Anti-Federalists even if they did not placate the most ardent opponents of federal power who wished to restrict the powers of the new central government to those expressly delegated by the text of the new Constitution. Their adoption resolved the most important issue remaining from the struggle between Federalists and Anti-Federalists, clearing the way for new issues to come to the fore.

Filling Out the Branches of Government

The Constitution created a blueprint for the new federal government, but Congress and the president still had to work out important details, including the structure of the executive and the judiciary departments. Congress took almost six months to work out a structure for the new federal courts. Lingering fears about the power of the federal government complicated drafting legislation to set up the federal courts. Senator William Maclay of Pennsylvania warned, for example, that the federal courts would "swallow all the State Constitutions by degree." Eventually Congress created a three-tier system of district courts, circuit courts, and the Supreme Court. Each state would have at least one district court. "Circuit courts" composed of a district court judge and two members of the Supreme Court were supposed to "ride circuit" (travel) to hear appeals from the district courts and to have primary jurisdiction in certain types of cases, such as those between citizens of different states.

For the executive branch, Congress created new cabinet positions for a secretary of state to advise the president on foreign affairs, a secretary of the treasury for economic policy, a secretary of war to oversee the army, and an attorney general to be the chief legal advisor to government.

For his cabinet Washington assembled an impressive group of leaders who had distinguished themselves in American public life. Henry Knox, the secretary of war, was a leading general; Edmund Randolph, the new attorney general, had introduced the Virginia Plan in the constitutional convention; Thomas Jefferson, the secretary of state, had been the primary author of the Declaration of Independence; and the first American minister to France; the first secretary of the treasury, Alexander Hamilton, had been one of the co-authors of *The Federalist* along with John Jay, who became the first chief justice of the Supreme Court. Although none of these men had been Anti-Federalists, Washington's choices cut across a wide section of the political spectrum, with Hamilton representing the extreme nationalist position and Jefferson far more sympathetic to state power.

During ratification Anti-Federalists had expressed fear that the Constitution would create a large, expensive government with a vast bureaucracy. In reality the federal government was far less imposing. Scattered among buildings near New York City's Wall Street, the temporary home of the new government, the government offices bore slight resemblance to the nightmare that Anti-Federalists had predicted. The scale of the new government was modest, and its bureaucracy small, about 350 officers. Jefferson's State Department employed two clerks, two assistants, and a part-time translator. (The modern State Department employs 8,000 people in Washington, D.C., and 11,000 overseas.) The largest department was Hamilton's Treasury. Within a year of its creation, it boasted nearly ten times the number of employees of the Department of State. Its budget was more than triple the combined budgets of the State and War Departments. Apart from his close relationship to Washington, his role as secretary of the Treasury ensured that Hamilton was a figure to be reckoned with in the new government.

Why were some ardent Anti-Federalists not satisfied with the Madison's proposed amendments?

Hamilton's Ambitious Program

 In 1789, Congress requested that Secretary of the Treasury Alexander Hamilton issue a report on the new nation's economy. Between 1790 and 1791, Hamilton responded with a series of reports, each corresponding to a major part of his overall plan to bolster America's economy. These included reports on public credit, a national bank, the establishment of a mint to coin money, and manufactures. Hamilton saw a strong national government as a necessity to promote American prosperity and protect the young nation's economic interests against foreign threats. In his view the Constitution had created a central government with considerable power over the economy. In his reports he urged Congress and the president to use this authority to encourage economic growth. To accomplish this, Hamilton looked to Britain as a model. With a robust manufacturing and financial section, and the powerful Bank of England to energize its economy, Britain had the most diverse and sophisticated economy in Europe.

Hamilton's Vision for the New Republic

Alexander Hamilton envisioned America as a powerful nation with a strong government and a vigorous commercial economy. Before he could implement his ambitious program to realize this vision, however, Hamilton would have to overcome opponents at nearly every turn. Hamilton's bold program not only frightened former Anti-Federalists but also alarmed strong supporters of the Constitution, notably James Madison, who did not wish to see the new government become a powerful state modeled on that of Britain. Hamilton's economic vision also clashed with Thomas Jefferson's vision of a nation of small farmers. The new opposition to Federalist efforts to create a powerful centralized government, who called themselves **Republicans**, united former Anti-Federalists and those Federalists who shared the concerns of Madison and Jefferson. Republicans believed that liberty could flourish only if the states remained powerful enough to protect their citizens from the new federal government.

The leader who conceived this audacious Federalist agenda, a vision that would transform America, was a self-made man who lacked the aristocratic upbringing of his chief opponents, Virginians Jefferson and Madison. Hamilton came from a modest background. Born in the West Indies, the illegitimate son of a Scottish merchant and a planter's daughter, Hamilton was orphaned at an early age but became an apprentice clerk in a merchant firm. At age 14, he wrote "my Ambition is so prevalent that" he loathed the "Grov'ling condition of a Clerk or the like, to which my Fortune etc. condemns me, and would willingly risk my life, tho not my Character, to exalt my station." Hamilton was talented, ambitious, and hard working. The proprietor of the merchant firm recognized his talent and helped him finance his education. Hamilton attended Kings College (now Columbia University) in New York City. During the American Revolution, he rose rapidly through the ranks of the Continental Army to become

> "In place of that noble love of liberty and republican government which carried us triumphantly through the war, [a pro-British] monarchical aristocratical party has sprung up, whose avowed object is to draw over us the substance, as they have already done the forms, of the British government."
>
> THOMAS JEFFERSON, 1796

"In almost all the questions, great and small, which have arisen since the first session of Congress, Mr. Jefferson and Mr. Madison have been found among those who are disposed to narrow the federal authority . . ."

ALEXANDER HAMILTON, 1792

6.2 Alexander Hamilton
New York City's merchants commissioned a portrait of Hamilton in 1792. Hamilton decided against having the painting represent his political career, which was steeped in controversy; he chose instead to have himself painted in a plain brown suit standing beside a table with an inkwell and quill.

Washington's personal aide. Marrying into a prominent New York family, he became an important political figure in that state.

A successful lawyer, he had many friends and allies within New York's merchant community. New York merchants commissioned this portrait (**6.2**) of Alexander Hamilton to honor his contribution to their prosperity. It provides one measure of his power and influence, particularly within the new nation's financial world. Yet the painting is as notable for what the artist omitted as for what he included. Hamilton insisted that no references to his important political accomplishments be included, something that commissioners of the portrait had requested. Realizing that his political life was controversial, Hamilton directed the artist to avoid such references. Rather than depicting the complex, often contentious quality of his life, the painting presents the image of a disinterested republican statesman and writer.

Hamilton was an unabashed American nationalist and an elitist who viewed democracy with suspicion. He believed that there would always be class divisions. To survive and prosper, the new nation had to win the allegiance of the rich and powerful, binding their interests to those of the new federal government.

The Assumption of State Debts

Hamilton's "Report on Public Credit" addressed the war debt of the states and the federal government. The new nation and the states had incurred considerable debt financing the American Revolution. This debt consisted of many different types of paper currency and securities that the Confederation government and the individual states had issued. The new nation owed $75 million, a figure that alarmed some, but not Hamilton, who saw the debt as a means of bringing America into the modern era in which debt was an essential tool of state finance.

Hamilton proposed consolidating the debt of the individual states and the federal government. His scheme called for the **assumption of the state debts**, by which the federal government would fund any outstanding debts that the states owed. Creditors who held state paper would exchange it for a new type of paper that promised to pay interest until the bearer redeemed the original value of the note. Hamilton's "Second Report on Public Credit" focused on financing this scheme and included a plan for taxing whiskey. He envisioned a permanently funded national debt in which income from taxes would service the interest, allowing the federal government to pay its other expenses.

The most controversial feature of Hamilton's plan dealt with the problem posed by speculation in these paper notes. The value of state- and would become a potential source of corruption. Republicans favored paying the full value of the debt to the original holders but not to the speculators. The Republicans would have given speculators a reasonable return on their investment, but not a huge profit. Hamilton argued that this policy would violate the sanctity of contracts and undermine the credit of the new government. Eventually he defeated his opponents, and state debt certificates would be exchanged for federal ones at full face value.

Madison's Opposition

Hamilton was shocked to find his former ally James Madison leading the opposition to his policies. During ratification Madison had sided with Hamilton and together with John Jay wrote

---

"In an agricultural country like this, therefore, to erect and concentrate and perpetuate a large moneyed interest . . . must . . . produce one or other of two evils: the prostration of agriculture at the feet of commerce, or a change in the present form of Federal Government fatal to the existence of American liberty."

Virginia's remonstrance against the assumption of state debts, 16 December 1790

Confederation-issued paper had declined steadily by the 1790s as the hard-pressed states and the fledgling national government simply printed more paper to pay their debts. After the adoption of the Constitution, a few financial speculators had purchased large amounts of this devalued paper, hoping that the new government would redeem it at face value and net them a huge profit. Believing it was vital for the new nation to maintain excellent credit with investors, Hamilton insisted that government had an obligation to honor the debt at full face value.

Republicans feared that Hamilton's funding scheme would give a windfall to speculators. Besides being unjust, they argued, such a plan would create a powerful financial interest that

The Federalist. Madison had also supported Hamilton's efforts to create an effective Treasury Department under the Articles of Confederation. Why did Madison change his position and oppose Hamilton in 1789?

Madison was motivated by his desire to preserve the constitutional system he had labored so hard to create. The speculative frenzy caused by Hamilton's policy of assumption shocked Madison, who came to believe that Hamilton's program would undermine the republican values that the Constitution was designed to protect. Although Hamilton dreamed of a powerful state that might rival Britain, Madison was more interested in preserving his constitutional vision. In Madison's view, Hamilton's system would create vast

Why did Virginians, including Madison and Jefferson, oppose Hamilton's economic program?

inequalities of wealth, encourage corruption, and undermine republican government. Hamilton believed that Madison had been unduly influenced by Jefferson; indeed, Madison had always shared with his fellow Virginian a similar republican vision of an agrarian republic. Hamilton, by contrast, the product of New York's commercial ethos, believed that America's future depended on creating a powerful fiscal-military state.

The split between Hamilton and Madison reflected a profound shift in American political life. A few years before, Madison had decried faction in *Federalist No. 10*. Now faced with the rise of Hamilton's Federalist agenda, Madison revised his thinking about factions and politics. In an essay in the *National Gazette*, "A Candid State of Parties," he conceded that America had become divided into a Republican party and an anti-Republican party (the Federalists).

Opposition to his plan of assumption took a personal toll on Hamilton. Indeed, Jefferson described him as "somb[er], haggard, and dejected beyond comparison." Jefferson invited Hamilton to dinner with Madison, where the three worked out a deal to break the impasse over assumption. In exchange for support for his economic program, Hamilton agreed to move the new capital of the United States from New York City to a site on the Potomac River. Southerners such as Jefferson and Madison feared that keeping the nation's capital in New York City invited domination by commercial and financial interests. Although Hamilton might gain in the short run, Madison and Jefferson believed that the bargain they struck would lessen the influence of financial interests over the government. Meanwhile, the government temporarily relocated to Philadelphia. This cartoon (**6.3**), which shows Congress embarked on the ship *Constitution* as it sails to its eventual home on the Potomac, captures the Republicans' association of urban commercial centers with corruption. The devil lures the ship to its clear doom on the rocky falls leading to Philadelphia.

6.3 Congress Embarked on the Ship *Constitution*
Jefferson and Madison hoped that by relocating the capital to the Potomac, they would reduce the dangers of federal corruption. In this cartoon the devil lures Congress to its temporary home in Philadelphia.

What did Madison and Jefferson gain by moving the location of the new capital to what is now Washington, D.C.?

The Bank, the Mint, and the Report on Manufactures

In his "Report on a National Bank," Hamilton recommended that the federal government charter a national bank. The **Bank of the United States** would serve as a depository for government funds, bolster confidence in government securities, make loans, and provide the nation with a stable national currency. The government would own part of the stock in the new bank, but would allow private investors to buy the majority of stock. At the time of his proposal, there were only three private banks in the United States. A national bank would help stabilize the economy of the new nation and link the interests of the wealthy to the prosperity of the new nation.

Again Madison opposed Hamilton's plan. Much of the debate on this proposal focused on its constitutionality. Madison wanted to see the Constitution interpreted according to the original understanding of the states that ratified it in 1788. Arguing for the narrow interpretation of congressional power, he denied that the Constitution authorized Congress to charter a national bank. Ultimately, however, Hamilton's ideas prevailed, and the Federalist-controlled Congress chartered the Bank of the United States. Republicans then hoped for a presidential veto. Washington sought advice from his cabinet about the constitutionality of the bank. Attorney General Edmund Randolph and Thomas Jefferson both agreed with Madison.

Jefferson took advantage of the occasion to articulate his own views on how to interpret the new Constitution. He acknowledged that the Constitution empowered Congress to enact laws that were "necessary and proper." However, although the creation of a bank was convenient and useful, it was not in his view necessary for Congress to fulfill its obligations to raise revenues. This theory of strict construction approached the text of the Constitution in an almost literal manner. If the Constitution did not grant a power, then, according to the theory of strict construction, the Tenth Amendment reserved that power to the states and the people. Madison and Jefferson designed their slightly different theories of constitutional interpretation to protect the rights of the people and the powers of the states against encroachment by the federal government.

With the weight of Randolph, Madison, and Jefferson's opinions weighing heavily in favor of a veto, Hamilton set out to refute his critics and in the process frame his own alternative theory of how to interpret the Constitution. Hamilton's theory of loose construction interpreted the language of the Constitution broadly. Hamilton believed the federal government enjoyed enormous latitude in determining the appropriate means for accomplishing any legitimate constitutional end. Even if a specific power was not listed, such as the power to charter a bank, Hamilton believed the Constitution implied such a power. Hamilton argued that Jefferson's reasoning would restrict the powers of Congress to enact only those laws that were absolutely "necessary and proper." In response to Madison and Jefferson's suggestion of consulting the original intent of the state ratification conventions, Hamilton argued that "the intention is to be sought in the instrument itself." Interpreters of the Constitution should follow well-established legal rules for understanding statutes and apply them to the Constitution. In other words, the actual text of the Constitution, not the arguments of Federalists, Anti-Federalists, or state ratification conventions, ought to be given primary consideration in constitutional interpretation. The struggle over the proper way of interpreting the Constitution had emerged as a major political battlefield in the new republic. Indeed, the proper interpretation of the Constitution is still controversial and arguments over its original meaning are as contentious today as they were more than 200 years ago.

As he would throughout his first term in office, Washington sided with Hamilton against Madison and Jefferson. The chartering of the Bank of the United States was Hamilton's second major victory in the struggle to define the character of the new republic.

Hamilton's report on the necessity of a federal mint was the one part of his program that Jefferson enthusiastically endorsed. Hamilton proposed a currency that would include a variety of coins in different denominations emblazoned with patriotic symbols. Jefferson not only recognized the need for a federal currency, but as a part-time inventor, he was also fascinated by the mechanics of minting money.

Hamilton's "Report on Manufactures" detailed the remaining part of his plan to reshape the American economy. He called for a comprehensive program to encourage domestic industry by providing incentives for industrial development and tariffs to help American industry compete against imported foreign goods, which were cheaper. Congress refused

How did Hamilton and Jefferson differ in their interpretations of the phrase "necessary and proper?"

6.4 Political Views: Hamilton versus Jefferson

Hamilton	Jefferson
Commercial Republic	Agrarian Republic
Broad Construction	Strict Construction
Standing Army	Militia
Pro-British	Pro-French

to follow Hamilton's recommendation to raise these tariffs sharply. Hamilton's more grandiose scheme to encourage industrial development generated little interest in Congress. Congress did enact new taxes, including one on whiskey. In the struggle to shape the new nation's economy, Hamilton's Federalists had defeated Jefferson, Madison, and the Republican opposition at nearly every turn. Hamilton was largely successful at implementing his visionary economic program.

Jefferson and Hamilton: Contrasting Visions of the Republic

Jefferson and Hamilton were a study in contrasts. Their backgrounds varied greatly: Jefferson was a southern slave owner; Hamilton, a northerner with abolitionist sympathies. Jefferson grew up a Virginia aristocrat, with every advantage; Hamilton was a self-made man who confessed that he was determined to escape his humble origins at almost any cost.

Over several of the most important issues facing the new American nation, the two men found themselves in separate camps, as summarized in the table (**6.4**). In general, Hamilton sought to endow the national government with additional powers;

Jefferson sought to limit the powers of the federal government and protect state authority.

The two men also approached the economy from radically different philosophies. Hamilton's idea of a thriving commercial republic was diametrically opposed to Jefferson's vision of a nation of independent yeoman farmers. "While we have land to labour," Jefferson wrote, "let us never wish to see our citizens occupied at a work bench." Hamilton believed that America needed to emulate the powerful, diversified economy of Britain and foster commerce and manufacture.

A gulf separated the two men over constitutional law as well. Hamilton believed in a broad, or loose, construction of the Constitution: The federal government had to have wide latitude to choose whatever means was best suited to accomplish its legitimate objects. Jefferson, by contrast, believed in a strict construction of the Constitution, so that the powers of the new government would be limited to those clearly established by the Constitution.

In foreign affairs the two men also opposed one another. Hamilton was an Anglophile who believed that Britain's path to economic power ought to guide America. Jefferson savored all things French, from wine to pastry. He thought America's interests were better served by supporting France.

Read the **Document** *Thomas Jefferson*, Notes on Virginia

What were the most important points of disagreement between Hamilton and Jefferson?

Partisanship without Parties

 The idea of political parties was inimical to the republican values of the post-Revolutionary era. In the struggle over ratification in 1788, Madison had written in *Federalist No. 10* that "the public good is disregarded in the conflicts of rival parties." The partisan struggles that dominated American politics after ratification forced Madison to rethink his view of parties. In 1792, Madison conceded that in "every political society, parties are unavoidable." Although Americans increasingly used terms like party to describe the bitter conflicts of the 1790s, the partisan alignments they described had not yet achieved the organized structure of modern political parties. Political conflict in the 1790s was a transitional phase in the evolution of a modern two-party system. Some historians describe this period as that of the first party system, but many characterize it as a proto-party system that set the stage for the later developments of modern parties. Indeed, although Americans were deeply divided politically, neither Federalists nor Republicans functioned as disciplined modern political parties. Neither group organized loyal supporters around well-defined messages at a national level. Nor did either side create permanent political structures that brought local and state politics under the umbrella of a coherent national organization. The partisan conflicts of this era produced two proto-parties, the Federalists and the Republicans.

A New Type of Politician

Although the aristocratic Thomas Jefferson and James Madison dominated the Republican movement, its success owed much to a new type of politician whose expertise lay in mobilizing voters and creating effective political organizations. The most influential of these new politicians was Virginia's John Beckley. In contrast to Jefferson and Madison, who were connected to the gentry elite that dominated political life in Virginia, Beckley rose from the status of an indentured servant to become the clerk of the U.S. House of Representatives. He became indispensable in advancing the Republican cause. Indeed, although aristocratic politicians such as Jefferson and Madison continued to view themselves as members of a virtuous elite who were not motivated by party spite, Beckley and others of this new class of professional politicians immersed themselves in the sometimes sordid task of coordinating campaigns and attacking their opponents.

Beckley and other Republicans who did much of the grassroots organizing were more at home in taverns and coffee houses than they were in the elegant dinner parties that Jefferson and Madison attended. Having worked as a clerk, Beckley felt a kindred spirit with the artisans and merchants of New York City and Philadelphia. He felt a particular kinship with other self-made men, many of whom joined the Republican movement. Beckley's life more closely resembled Hamilton's than Jefferson's. Yet Beckley threw himself into promoting Jefferson's fortunes and attacking Hamilton. Gossip became one means of political warfare that Beckley developed to a fine art. He leaked information about an adulterous affair Hamilton was having with the wife of a shady financier. When the press reported rumors that Hamilton had provided sensitive financial information to his lover's husband, Republican politicians pounced on Hamilton, who was forced to admit the affair but denied any financial improprieties. Beckley's efforts weakened Hamilton but did not destroy the New Yorker's influence among Federalists.

The Growth of the Partisan Press

The expansion of the press facilitated the rise of partisan politics. The number of newspapers increased, from around 100 in 1788 to well over 200 in 1800. While eastern ports still supported the majority of papers, many interior market towns also boasted papers by the 1790s. Many of these papers aligned

What role did the partisan press play in the politics of the 1790s?

themselves with one or the other main political movements in the country. John Fenno's *Gazette of the United States*, which he established "to endear the General Government to the people," articulated the Federalist point of view. To combat Fenno's influence, Jefferson and Madison persuaded the poet Philip Freneau to found the *National Gazette,* which rallied opposition to Hamilton and the Federalists. The resulting battle of words between the two publications intensified the already charged political atmosphere. Federalists and Republicans recognized that political success meant managing public opinion. "All power," Madison noted, "has been traced to public opinion." A free government, therefore, calls for "a circulation of newspapers through the entire body of the people."

Partisan rancor in the press grew during the 1790s. No person was sharper in his attacks than Federalist William Cobbett, who often wrote under the pen name Peter Porcupine, a choice that reflected his prickly personality and barbed writing. Jefferson lamented that "a single sentence got hold of by the 'Porcupines,' will suffice to abuse and persecute me in their papers for months." Cobbett lambasted the Republicans as atheists and radical democrats who sought to destroy government. He compared the leading Republican newspaper, the *Aurora,* to "a lewd and common strumpet" whose illegitimate offspring were falsehood and slander. The Republicans replied with their own stinging attacks. This Republican political cartoon (**6.5**) casts Cobbett, literally represented as Peter Porcupine," doing the devil's work as he is encouraged by Great Britain, represented as a lion.

The Democratic-Republican Societies

The emergence of a new type of political organization helped transform the political life of the new nation. Between 1793 and 1794, 35 **Democratic-Republican Societies** sprouted up across America. Although not official organs of the Republican movement, most of the societies had close ties to local Republican organizations. Their goal was to influence public opinion. The New York Democratic-Republican

Society asserted that public opinion "is the foundation of all our liberties, and constitutes the only solid groundwork for all our Rights." In addition to publishing their sentiments about political issues, the societies staged celebrations, gave festive dinners, and sponsored public orations.

Republicans viewed the societies as a way to improve understanding of political issues and refine public opinion. Federalists denounced these "self-created societies" for sowing the "seeds of jealousy and distrust of the government." For Federalists, the societies not only sapped the people's confidence in their government but also fomented radical ideas. Federalists viewed the role of elected representatives differently from Republicans. Federalists supported a more traditional republican ideal of virtue in which citizens deferred to the wisdom of their leaders once they had been placed in office. Republicans embraced a more democratic ideal in which the voice of the people could be brought to bear on public questions through organizations such as the Democratic-Republican Societies.

6.5 Peter Porcupine
Liberty sits forlorn, while Federalist William Cobbett, "Peter Porcupine," scribbles attacks and insults. The devil and the British lion (wearing a monarch's crown) urge on the Porcupine. A Jay bird, symbolic of Jay's Treaty, perches on the lion.

Why did the Federalists oppose the Democratic-Republican Societies?

Conflicts at Home and Abroad

The French Revolution, the bloody toppling of the monarchy followed by the rise of a radical republican government, shocked Europe and profoundly affected American politics. Republicans supported the Revolution. Federalists quickly came to see it as the embodiment of evil and denounced its excesses. Revolutionary France soon became embroiled in conflict with Britain, and the two nations went to war with one another in 1793. Although Republicans and Federalists continued to support Washington, the contest over the vice presidency in 1792 demonstrated how divided America had become. Federalist John Adams defeated his Republican rival, the former Anti-Federalist George Clinton, but the Republicans carried the entire South.

The line separating foreign affairs and domestic matters in the new Republic was often thin. America still needed to secure its borders against potentially hostile European powers. The British continued to occupy forts in the Old Northwest (the modern states of Ohio, Indiana, and Michigan) and engaged in trade with Indians, including the sale of firearms. The Spanish presence in Florida and Louisiana gave them control of the Mississippi, a vital artery for Western trade. American shipping no longer enjoyed the protection of the British Navy. In the Mediterranean pirates based in North Africa harassed American ships and captured American sailors and cargoes.

Resistance to Hamilton's economic program erupted into violence in western Pennsylvania and Kentucky. Angry over the tax on whiskey, farmers turned to violence to vent their frustration. Washington felt compelled to call out the militia to quell the rebellion. The new federal government had survived its most serious test, but the repression of the rebellion did little to heal the divisions in American political life.

6.6 Revolutionary plate.
This gruesome plate captures the excesses of the French Revolution. The guillotine pictured at the center became a symbol of the violence of the Revolution. The plate also shows the head of King Louis XVI which is proudly displayed by one of his executioners as a trophy.

The French Revolution in America

In 1789, a financial crisis in France precipitated a revolution that transformed a powerful European monarchy into a republic. At first, American support for the French Revolution cut across partisan allegiances. Even the arch-Federalist *Gazette of the United States* described the Revolution as "one of the most glorious objects that can arrest the attention of mankind." Republican James Madison added that events in France were "so glorious to this country, because it has grown as it were out of the American Revolution." Pro-French Republicans began addressing each other as "citizen," a custom borrowed from revolutionary France. Republican women followed suit, some using the term *citizen* and others *citizeness* or *citess* among themselves.

When the French Revolution turned more radical and violent, however, many Americans began to re-examine their support for it. The execution of King Louis XVI and Queen Marie Antoinette in 1793 outraged Federalists. This commemorative plate (**6.6**) showing the execution of the king captures the zeal of the French

Did the French Revolution fullfill or betray the ideals of the American Revolution?

View the **Closer Look** *Competing Visions: Jefferson and Hamilton's Reactions to the French Revolution*

Revolution. The hand-painted plate prominently features the guillotine, a new device for executions developed in revolutionary France that used a heavy blade to decapitate its victims. The executioner proudly displays the king's lifeless head as a trophy, a chilling reminder of the French Revolution's radicalism.

The French Revolution became a symbol for both Republicans and Federalists. The former championed the democratic ideals of the Revolution and excused its violence as a small price to pay for liberty. The latter decried its violence and radicalism. France's new minister to the United States Edmund Genêt arrived two days after word of the execution of Louis XVI reached the U.S. in the spring of 1793. Philadelphia's Republican women turned out in red, white, and blue to welcome him. Although Republican men wore the tricolor red-white-and blue cockade, a small rosette-like decoration, on their hats, women attached tricolor pins to their chests to affirm support for France. One sarcastic Federalist commentator described "these fiery frenchified dames" as "monsters in human shape." (For additional discussion see *Competing Visions: Jefferson's and Hamilton's Reactions to the French Revolution,* page 171.) Federalists not only opposed the French Revolution, but events in France intensified their desire to align America with Britain.

When revolutionary France declared war on Britain in 1793, Americans found themselves reluctantly drawn into European affairs. Attitudes toward France became a political lightning rod, concentrating and focusing political feelings for both Republicans and Federalists. The French Revolution came to symbolize many of the hopes and fears of Americans struggling to come to terms with their own revolutionary heritage. Republicans defined the Revolution by its ideals of liberty, equality, and fraternity; Federalists focused on the Revolution's bloody policies and saw it as confirmation of the danger of taking liberty and equality too far.

Adams versus Clinton: A Contest for Vice President

By 1792, Washington feared that partisan conflict might tear apart the political fabric of the nation. Although Hamilton and Jefferson's mutual antagonism had hardened, both men agreed that Washington was the one figure who could rise above partisan squabbles and unite the nation. Hamilton implored Washington "to make a further sacrifice of your tranquility and happiness to the public good."

Although Republicans did not wish to challenge Washington directly, they decided to run the popular former Anti-Federalist Governor of New York, George Clinton, against John Adams for vice president. Republican newspapers praised Washington but charged that Adams was an avowed supporter of monarchy and aristocracy. Invoking recent events in France, one radical newspaper editor even suggested that the time had arrived in America to "lop off every unfruitful branch, and root out of the soil of freedom all of the noxious weeds of aristocracy." Although Adams defeated Clinton by a comfortable margin, the sectional character of politics was evident in the electoral college. Clinton carried the entire South, the most solidly Republican region.

Diplomatic Controversies and Triumphs

The new American nation had many diplomatic challenges, some arising from the French Revolution, but others stemming from unresolved issues with Britain. American ships no longer enjoyed the protection of the British navy. Closer to home, the British retained control of their forts in the Northwest, defying the Treaty of Paris (1783), which required them to relinquish them. Spain's control of the Mississippi River and New Orleans, both of which were vital to the prosperity of the old Southwest (modern Kentucky, Tennessee, Alabama, and Mississippi), was another concern (**6.7**).

War between France and Britain opened opportunities for American merchants, who traded with both sides. Although Britain remained America's chief trading partner, trade with France was increasingly important.

Britain hoped to use its naval advantage to cut off trade between France and other nations, including America. The British navy impounded more than 250 ships and cargoes of American merchants who violated the British blockade against France. Angry Republicans proposed an embargo on trade with the British. Federalists, however, argued that American economic well-being depended on good relations with Britain, not with France. President Washington appointed

Why did Federalists become such ardent critics of the French Revolution?

6.7 Map of Spanish Interests in the Southwest Spanish control of the Mississippi River and New Orleans was a source of concern to Americans. The Mississippi River was a vital conduit for goods, which were then shipped to New Orleans.

the respected Federalist from New York and chief justice of the Supreme Court, John Jay, as a special envoy to travel to London to negotiate a settlement. In 1783, Jay had helped negotiate the Treaty of Paris, ending conflict between America and Britain. Now in 1794, he negotiated a treaty (called **Jay's Treaty**) by which Britain agreed to compensate America for cargoes seized in 1793–1794 and to vacate forts in the Northwest Territory. However, the British refused to accept the right of neutral nations to trade freely with belligerents.

When the details of Jay's Treaty were leaked to the press, Republicans were outraged, finding the treaty too generous to the British. Across the mid-Atlantic and South where Republican sympathies were strongest, protesters burned effigies of Jay and copies of the treaty. The treaty also provoked a fierce debate in Congress over the role of the House of Representatives in foreign affairs. Republican Congressmen demanded to see Jay's negotiating instructions, believing that Federalists had never intended to exact major concessions from the British. The House

even threatened to withhold funding to implement the treaty until the instructions were published. Federalists denounced this as an unconstitutional intrusion on the treaty-making powers of the president and the senate.

Jay had negotiated with Britain from a position of weakness, but the American envoy charged with obtaining concessions from Spain was in a stronger position. The U.S. minister to Britain, Federalist Thomas Pinckney, traveled to Spain to begin negotiations about American access to the Mississippi and New Orleans. The result was Pinckney's Treaty (1795), which secured America's right to navigate the Mississippi River and use New Orleans. It also settled the boundary between America and Spanish Florida. Spain had feared that America might try to acquire Florida and Louisiana by force, so it was more than willing to cede favorable terms over trade and negotiate the boundary dispute between the two nations.

Violence along the Frontier

Securing the Western frontier—an area that included the Northwest Territory, the Tennessee frontier, and the Mississippi Territory—meant not only negotiating with Britain and Spain but also

Competing Visions
JEFFERSON'S AND HAMILTON'S REACTIONS TO THE FRENCH REVOLUTION

Thomas Jefferson and his Republican allies embraced the cause of the French Revolution. At the outset, even Alexander Hamilton, saw the Revolution as a victory for American ideals of liberty. The radical turn of the Revolution, however, particularly its zealous embrace of violence, caused Hamilton and other Federalists to abandon their support. Despite the increasingly bloody turn of events in France, Jefferson retained his faith in the essential justice of the Revolution's goals. He believed that the Revolution's accomplishments—the destruction of the old regime and of the institutions of aristocracy and monarchy—were worth the cost in blood. Federalists not only denounced France, but they took great pains to contrast Anglo-American concepts of ordered liberty with the licentiousness of the French Revolution.

For Jefferson, the Revolution's contribution to the destruction of tyranny justified whatever means were necessary to accomplish its worthy ends. He compared the innocent victims of "revolutionary justice" to the casualties of war. What does Jefferson's dogged support for the French Revolution reveal about his vision of politics?

Thomas Jefferson to William Short, Philadelphia Jan. 3. 1793

DEAR SIR

The tone of your letters had for some time given me pain, on account of the extreme warmth with which they censured the proceedings of the Jacobins of France.... In the struggle which was necessary, many guilty persons fell without the forms of trial, and with them some innocent. These I deplore as much as any body, and shall deplore some of them to the day of my death. But I deplore them as I should have done had they fallen in battle. It was necessary to use the arm of the people, a machine not quite so blind as balls and bombs, but blind to a certain degree. A few of their cordial friends met at their hands, the fate of enemies. But time and truth will rescue and embalm their memories, while their posterity will be enjoying that very liberty for which they would never have hesitated to offer up their lives. The liberty of the whole earth was depending on the issue of the contest, and was ever such a prize won with so little innocent blood? My own affections have been deeply wounded by some of the martyrs to this cause, but rather than it should have failed, I would have seen half the earth desolated [and].... an Adam and an Eve left in every country, and left free....

Hamilton's revulsion at the excesses of the French Revolution was typical of Federalists. What does Hamilton's view of the French Revolution reveal about his vision of politics?

Alexander Hamilton Unpublished Thoughts on the French Revolution [Philadelphia, 1794]

In the early periods of the French Revolution, a warm zeal for its success was in this Country a sentiment truly universal. The love of Liberty is here the ruling passion of the Citizens of the United States pervading every class animating every bosom. As long therefore as the Revolution of France bore the marks of being the cause of liberty it united all hearts and centered all opinions. But this unanimity of approbation has been for a considerable time decreasing. The excesses which have constantly multiplied, with greater and greater aggravations have successively though slowly detached reflecting men from their partiality for an object which has appeared less and less to merit their regard.

The tricolor French flag was adopted after the French Revolution and became the official flag of the new French republic in 1794.

Why did Republicans oppose Jay's Treaty?

dealing with the Indian nations that occupied much of this land. The government also faced resentments from farmers over federal taxation of locally distilled whiskey.

Settlers streamed into Western territories, invariably resulting in conflicts with the indigenous populations. In the Old Northwest, the Shawnee, Delaware, and Miami confederated to defend their lands against settlers' incursions. In 1790, Little Turtle, a war chief of the Miami, led a pan-Indian force of twelve different tribes that defeated an American army led by General Josiah Harmar in Ohio. A year later Indians in Ohio dealt an even more crushing blow to an army led by General Arthur St. Clair. More than 900 American soldiers were killed or wounded, and St. Clair barely escaped with his life.

These demoralizing defeats prompted a reorganization of the War Department. In 1794, a new, more professional army under General Anthony Wayne decisively defeated Ohio's Indian tribes at the Battle of Fallen Timbers. In 1795, the Treaty of Greenville stipulated that the twelve Ohio tribes relinquish their claims on most of Ohio. In Indian cultures the signing of treaties was a ceremonial occasion in which certain rituals were observed, including the exchange of gifts. Indians gave this wampum belt (**6.8**), an important ceremonial item, to American negotiators at the Treaty of Greenville ceremony. Chippewa Chief Mash-i-pi-nash-i-wish explained the meaning of this gift: "When I show you this belt, I point out to you your children at one end of it, and mine at the other. . . . Remember, we have taken the Great Spirit to witness our present actions; we will make a new world, and leave nothing on it to incommode our children." Wayne and the other American negotiators, however, did not understand the gift of wampum in the same way as the Chippewa did. For Americans, Indians had joined the American family as dependents, not equals.

The most serious test of the new Republic's ability to govern came in 1794, when anger over Hamilton's economic policies turned violent. Resentment against the hated whiskey tax had festered since its enactment in 1791. The **Whiskey Rebellion** erupted when farmers from Pennsylvania and Kentucky took up arms to protest the whiskey excise tax.

Distilling had long been important economically in western Pennsylvania and Kentucky, where farmers distilled grain into whiskey. Farmers could transport the alcohol more cheaply than the bulky and heavy grains from which it was produced. Whiskey also

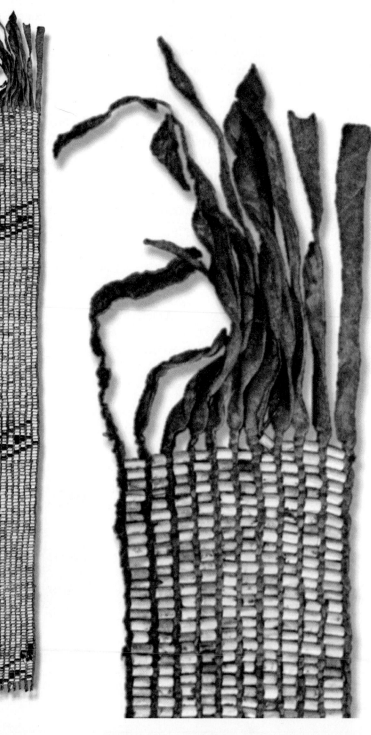

6.8 Wampum Belt

Beads, usually made from seashells, were strung together in a wampum belt. This belt, given during the Treaty of Greenville ceremony, symbolized the Indian belief that they would now join with the United States in one great family. The American negotiators interpreted the gift as a sign of Indian submission.

How did American and Indian views of the Treaty of Greenville differ?

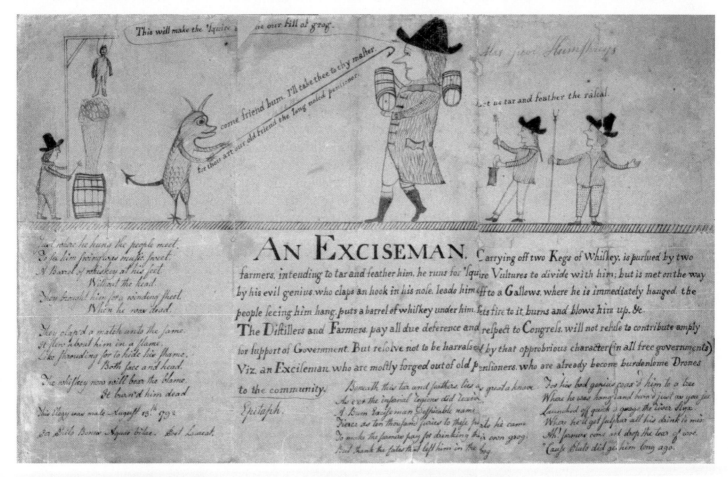

6.9 Political Cartoon, Whiskey Rebellion
In this cartoon, which denounces the hated whiskey tax, two distillers threaten to tar and feather an excise man (tax collector). Meanwhile, a demon hooks the tax collector by the nose and leads him to the gallows.

sold at a higher price than grain, so Western farmers could earn a higher profit on their crops.

Protest against the whiskey tax began peacefully. Opponents of Federalist policy sought repeal of the law, and attacked it in the local press. As anger intensified, angry farmers drew on the rich traditions of protest that Americans had used during the Revolution, such as the one depicted in this contemporary cartoon (**6.9**). The scene shows angry tax protesters who have executed and burned in effigy a local tax collector. By July 1794, frustration turned violent. Five hundred western Pennsylvania farmers, many armed with muskets, marched on the home of a tax collector, John Neville, to intimidate him. Two protestors were killed in the attack and Neville's house was burned to the ground. Two weeks later 6,000 armed men threatened to attack

Pittsburgh if the government did not repeal the tax. Federalists and Republicans differed over the causes of the rebellion and how to respond to it. Federalists blamed the Democratic-Republican Societies for fomenting discord and favored a swift and decisive military response. Republicans faulted Hamilton's economic program and counseled moderation and patience. For an analysis of Washington's decision in dealing with this rebellion, see *Choices and Consequences: Washington's Decision to Crush the Whiskey Rebellion.*

After negotiations failed, Washington dispatched the militia and resistance to government authority crumbled. One hundred and fifty people were arrested, and two obscure figures were convicted of treason. Rather than see them become martyrs, however, Washington pardoned them.

Read the **Document** *Whiskey Rebellion Address, George Washington's 6th Annual Address to Congress*

Why did the Whiskey Rebellion present such a problem for Republicans?

Choices and Consequences
WASHINGTON'S DECISION TO CRUSH THE WHISKEY REBELLION

The armed resistance of Western farmers to the detested whiskey tax posed a serious dilemma for Washington. Should the president negotiate with the rebels or use force to put down the rebellion? Washington's cabinet members differed over the best course of action. The Whiskey Rebellion tested the new government created by the Constitution. The situation was complicated by uncertainty over the militia. Even if Washington wished to use it, it was not clear if the militia would respond. During Shays's Rebellion (Chapter 5), the militia had refused to fire on other citizens and sided with the rebels. Washington had to consider this issue and the larger question of how the new government ought to respond to a direct challenge to its authority. Washington had three choices:

Choices

1 Call up the militia and dispatch them to western Pennsylvania and crush the rebellion swiftly.

2 Adopt a conciliatory posture, make concessions to the rebels, including repealing the tax, and thereby avoid an armed response.

3 Offer the rebels a chance to end their protest; mobilize the militia and have it ready to march if the offer was rejected.

Decision

Republican leaders outside the administration had hoped Washington would adopt a conciliatory posture and recognize that since an unjust tax was the root of the problem, it would make sense to accede to the rebels' demands. Hamilton and other Federalists counseled a decisive show of force. Washington opted instead for the third choice. After efforts to peacefully persuade the rebels to stand down failed, he acted decisively to put down the rebellion. Concerns that the militias of neighboring states might side with the rebels proved unfounded. The rebels were no match for the militia, and the rebellion fizzled once troops marched westward.

Consequences

Washington's decision to put down the rebellion ended it in western Pennsylvania. In other parts of the nation, however, such as Kentucky, where support for tax resistance was more pervasive, resistance proved effective. In Kentucky few citizens were willing to act as tax collectors and juries were unlikely to convict people who refused to pay the taxes. One consequence of the rebellion was the undermining of the authority of the Democratic-Republican Societies, who were blamed for stirring up opposition to the government and fanning the resentments of the Whiskey Rebels.

Continuing Controversies

Why were some Federalists reluctant to use force to put down the Whiskey Rebellion?

Washington's decision to use force has prompted controversy. Supporters of his actions argue that he wisely sought to demonstrate that armed resistance to government authority was not an affirmation of liberty, but threatened to undermine liberty and the rule of law. Detractors of Washington's actions argue that Pennsylvania's own government felt that it was unnecessary to mobilize the militia and that a peaceful resolution to the crisis was possible.

Washington Reviews the Militia

Why did Federalist enforcement of the whiskey tax fail in Kentucky?

Cultural Politics in a Passionate Age

 Politics seeped into every aspect of popular culture after the adoption of the Constitution. Even fashion became a political battleground, so much so that sporting the wrong color badge could lead to violence. The bitter political disputes of the day were also woven into the fabric of a new literary art form, the novel. Novels were particularly important to women, who were among the main readers of novels. In a few exceptional cases women even became successful authors of novels. The way the nation confronted race and slavery were influenced by the political conflicts of the era. The slave uprising in the French Caribbean colony of Saint-Domingue (modern Haiti) focused renewed attention on abolitionism and slavery.

Political Fashions and Fashionable Politics

Nearly every aspect of American culture was swept up in the political passions of the age. In the politically charged 1790s, political debates spilled over into the new nation's streets and town squares. Ordinary citizens read newspapers or attended political meetings to keep abreast of the latest developments. They also used taverns to host political meetings where Federalists and their Republican opponents toasted everything from the militia to the French Revolution. Even the simple act of hoisting a glass of ale could become a political gesture, particularly when the press reported the accompanying toasts. Citizens marched in parades and even rioted to express their frustrations with political developments.

Even fashion was swept up into the political conflicts. Americans signaled their political allegiances and foreign policy preferences by adopting the latest Paris or London styles. Republican supporters of the French Revolution adorned their hats with a tricolor cockade. Federalists favored a black cockade, a decoration soldiers had used during the American Revolution. By the end of the decade, sporting the "wrong" type of ornament on one's hat in the streets of Philadelphia could easily trigger a riot.

Literature, Education, and Gender

By the 1790s, Americans could choose from a staggering range of printed materials. In addition to the expansion of newspapers, books, magazines, broadsides, and pamphlets proliferated. The market for books increased dramatically in the 30 years between the American Revolution and 1800. The number of booksellers in Boston, New York, Philadelphia, and Charleston almost quadrupled in that time. In the 1790s, 266 new lending libraries opened across America. The new libraries were not restricted to prosperous coastal cities, but as one contemporary noted, "in our inland towns of consequence, social libraries have been instituted composed of books designed to amuse rather than to instruct." Although the cost of books may have been beyond those of modest means, a subscription to one of these libraries was often not.

Americans could also turn to magazines for education and amusement. The titles of new magazines suggested an effort to appeal to both men and women. For example, *The Gentlemen and Ladies Town and Country Magazine* began publishing in 1789. *The Lady's Magazine and Repository of Entertaining Knowledge,* founded in 1791 in Philadelphia, targeted the growing audience of female readers.

The rise of a new literary form, the novel, in eighteenth-century England and France helped to spur the enormous expansion in America's publishing industry. Some novelists wove political themes prominently into their tales. Americans eagerly consumed imported novels, and new works written by American authors also appeared. Women became an important audience for the novel; they also wrote many of the most successful early novels. Susanna Rowson's *Charlotte Temple,* first published in England (1791), was reprinted in America in 1794, where the first edition quickly sold out. The story's American setting made it particularly popular in the new republic. The moral of the novel was unmistakable. The heroine, Charlotte Temple, foolishly leaves England for America, where she elopes with a knave who reneges on his promise to marry her.

How did fashion become politicized in the 1790s?

Charlotte is abandoned, suffers physical and mental depredations, and dies soon after giving birth to a child out of wedlock.

Immigrating to America in 1793, Rowson fared much better than Charlotte. After a brief career as an actress, Rowson established the Young Ladies' Academy, in Boston (1797). Her curriculum included reading, writing, arithmetic, and needlework.

Another female author, Judith Sargent Murray, became an outspoken advocate of equality and education for women. Her essay "On the Equality of the Sexes," published in the *Massachusetts Magazine* in 1790 under the pen name "Constantia," argued that women's intellectual abilities were equal to those of men and that if properly educated women could equal men in accomplishment. Murray also used the novel to spread her ideals about the equality of the sexes. Her novel, *The Story of Margaretta* (1798), recast the conventions of sentimental novels such as *Charlotte Temple* to reflect her views of female education. Rather than fall prey to seduction, abandonment, and ruin, a fate typical of many female

6.10 Allegory of Female Education In this needlework, young Maria Crowninshield, a student at the Ladies Academy in Dorchester, Massachusetts, depicts a young student receiving instruction from a female teacher.

characters in popular novels, Margaretta uses her intelligence and superior education to avoid these perils.

Murray helped found the Dorchester Ladies Academy in Massachusetts. A 15-year-old student at the academy, Maria Crowninshield, produced this allegory of female education (**6.10**). Although at one level this fine needlework conformed to the traditional ideas of female education, which included sewing skills, the subject matter signals the artist's commitment to a modern expansive conception of female education. The young girl depicted is reading a copy of English author Hannah Moore's *Strictures on the Modern System of Female Education* (1799). Moore's book, which advocated an expansion of educational opportunities for women, was one of many tracts defending women's education. The most radical voice demanding changes in women's roles was Mary Wollstonecraft, an English writer whose *A Vindication of the Rights of Women* (1792) sparked a lively debate on both sides of the Atlantic in the 1790s about the need for equality of education for men and women.

Federalists, Republicans, and the Politics of Race

The political passions and divisions of the age also extended to the politics of race. This became a major concern as a result of events in the Caribbean, where slaves in Saint-Domingue (modern Haiti) rose up against their French masters and seized control of the colony in 1791. Federalists and Republicans were divided over how to respond to events there.

Toussaint L'Ouverture, a former slave, forged an all-black fighting force that routed the planters. America was forced to decide between supporting this slave revolution and siding with France which sought to repress it. At first the Washington administration supported the ruling white elite, but as L'Ouverture's forces solidified their hold over Saint-Domingue, the American government accepted the need to establish stable relations with the new government. Indeed, as relations with France worsened, many Federalists began to urge Washington to strengthen relations with Saint-Domingue, hoping to renew the lucrative trade with the former French colony. However, whereas Federalists supported recognition of Saint-Domingue, Republicans in Congress opposed it.

How is virtue represented in Maria Crowninshield's allegory of female education?

Read the **Document** *"James Wilson on Woman's Legal Disabilities"* in *James Wilson,* An Introductory Lecture to a Course of Law Lectures *(1791)*

Their opposition was motivated in part by their loyalty to France, which was eager to recapture the colony, but also reflected the party's commitment to protecting slavery. Republicans feared that American slaves might emulate their oppressed brethren in the Caribbean. Saint-Domingue conjured up a nightmare for slave owners, such as the depiction of bloodletting during the revolution produced by a German engraver (**6.11**). Although fears of slave insurrection were most keen in the South, Northern Republicans also voiced concerns.

Congressman Albert Gallatin of Pennsylvania warned that supporters of L'Ouverture's ideas might "spread their views among the Negro people there [in America] and excite dangerous insurrections among them."

Even among those most opposed to slavery, few were willing to support racial equality. Racist attitudes were found among ardent supporters of abolitionism. *Images as History: Liberty Displaying the Arts and Sciences* explores the tensions within early abolitionist thought.

6.11 Saint-Domingue Revolution
For Republicans, particularly in the South, images such as this conjured up their worst nightmare—a bloody slave insurrection.

Why did Republicans oppose normalizing relations with Saint-Domingue?

Images as History
LIBERTY DISPLAYING THE ARTS AND SCIENCES

In the 1790s, the Library Company of Philadelphia, a premier cultural institution founded in 1731 by Benjamin Franklin, commissioned Samuel Jennings's painting *Liberty Displaying the Arts and Sciences.* The painting was to represent the ideals of the new American nation. What symbols does the artist include to show the cultural achievements of the new nation? How does he portray African Americans?

The Library Company directors asked Jennings to include the goddess of liberty along with "Symbols of Painting, Architecture, Mechanics, Astronomy," including a broken chain at the feet of the goddess, a symbol of the painting's abolitionist sentiments. Although Jennings added his own ideas, he followed the directors' suggestions.

The painting reflected the influence of the classical world, including copies of the writings of Homer and Virgil, two of its greatest authors, but

Jennings did not slight the intellectual and cultural achievements of the modern world. He used books by John Milton and Shakespeare to represent modern literary achievements, at least of the English-speaking world. A telescope, symbol of the advancement of science, appears in the lower right-hand corner. Finally, as instructed by his patrons, Jennings included the goddess of liberty with a liberty pole and cap, two symbols linked with the American Revolution.

Jennings included a "Group of Negroes, who are paying Homage to Liberty, for the boundless Blessings they receive through her." Cast in the subservient pose of bowing to liberty, the African Americans do not appear as masters of their own destinies. Nor does Jennings's treatment suggest that African Americans created any of the cultural achievements of the new nation. Although abolitionist in sympathy, the painting does not endorse racial equality.

The goddess of liberty holds a liberty pole topped by a liberty cap.

The broken chains symbolize the abolition of slavery.

A group of African Americans bows before liberty.

The telescope symbolizes the advancements of modern science.

Liberty Displaying the Arts and Sciences [*Source:* The Library Company of Philadelphia]

What symbols does the artist use to represent the achievements of the arts and science in the new American nation?

The Stormy Presidency of John Adams

George Washington did not seek a third term, a decision that set a precedent for subsequent presidents. (The unofficial two-term limit that Washington established bound presidents until 1940 when Franklin Delano Roosevelt won a third term.) In the election of 1796, the Federalist congressional caucus selected John Adams and Thomas Pinckney as candidates, while Republicans put forward Thomas Jefferson and Aaron Burr. Party discipline, however, was lax. When the electoral college met and voted for president and vice president, 52 of the 136 electors voted for men not selected by either the Federalist or Republican congressional caucuses. Adams won the most votes and became president, and Jefferson polled the next most votes and became vice president. Although Adams defeated Jefferson, the bitter electoral contest intensified the partisan divisions within America. Conflict in Europe only exacerbated these tensions. Events in Europe threatened to drag America into war. Fearful that America was threatened from abroad and concerned that domestic radicals were undermining American interests, Federalists passed repressive measures that prompted Republicans to intensify their opposition to Federalist power and rally around their leader, Thomas Jefferson.

In 1800, Jefferson again faced Adams in a presidential election. This time Jefferson won, but the election resulted in a tie between Jefferson and his vice-presidential running mate, Aaron Burr. The Constitution provided that under these circumstances, the House of Representative would determine the outcome. After a flurry of politicking, Federalists agreed to select Jefferson, who became president.

In Richmond, Virginia, the debate over liberty inspired a slave named Gabriel to lead a rebellion to liberate Virginia's slaves. Although the rebellion failed, it highlighted the inescapable conflict between American ideals of liberty and the realities of racial slavery.

Washington's Farewell Address

Washington never wavered in his belief that he acted above party, but by the middle of his second term in office he had adopted most of Hamilton's Federalist agenda, which prompted the most outspoken Republican editors to attack Washington. Rather than respond to these attacks directly, Washington used his Farewell Address, a written statement widely printed in newspapers across the nation in September 1796, to reiterate his political ideals.

In his Farewell Address Washington attacked the growing factionalism, partisanship, and regional tensions in American politics. He warned the nation "in the most solemn manner against the baneful effects of the Spirit of Party, generally." Recognizing that foreign policy disputes had been particularly divisive, he advised that America "steer clear of permanent alliances, with any portion of the foreign world." Washington was not counseling strict isolation, but rather suggesting that America enter only into temporary alliances that served its interests. Above all, he wished to see America pursue a policy free of irrational hatreds or allegiances to foreign nations. The address sought to fuse idealism and realism into a workable approach to foreign policy.

In this famous portrait of Washington done at the end of his presidency (1796), Gilbert Stuart created a painting filled with symbolism that captured the central role of Washington's presidency in launching the new nation (**6.12**). When the painting was first displayed publicly, the announcement noted that Washington was "surrounded with allegorical emblems of his public life in the service of his country,

Read the **Document** *George Washington's Farewell Address*

What advice did Washington offer in his Farewell Address?

"Thomas Jefferson is a firm Republican,
—John Adams is an avowed Monarchist. . . .
Will you, by your votes, contribute to make the
avowed friend of monarchy President?"

Election statement in favor of Jefferson (1796)

which are highly illustrative of the great and tremendous storms which have frequently prevailed" but made clear that "these storms have abated, and the appearance of the rainbow is introduced in the background as a sign" of America's bright future.

Although Stuart's portrait suggested that the nation had weathered its worst storms, the period after Washington's retirement from politics was even more contentious. The election of 1796 was closely fought and bitterly divisive. John Adams defeated Thomas Jefferson by only three electoral votes. Intrigue had marred the election. Alexander Hamilton sought to undermine Adams's candidacy by backing Thomas Pinckney, who was running with Adams. When Adams learned of Hamilton's plan, he arranged to have his supporters in New England divert votes from Pinckney. The Constitution did not anticipate the rise of parties, nor did it envision the idea of presidential tickets with a designated candidate for president and vice president running together. The Founders' system was simpler: The president was the candidate with the most votes, and the vice president was the runner up. In accordance with republican theory, this system would ensure that the executive contained the two men best qualified to lead the nation. When Federalist plots diverted votes from Pinckney, Jefferson received the second most votes and hence became the new vice president. The most obvious pattern in the election

6.12 Portrait of President George Washington
Gilbert Stuart's painting included allegorical elements. The passing storm and the rainbow symbolized the new nation's stormy beginnings and bright future.

How does the artist represent the future of America in this portrait of George Washington?

6.13 Electoral Map 1796
This map of the electoral votes in the presidential election of 1796 shows the regional basis of American politics at that time. The strength of Thomas Jefferson, the Republican candidate, was concentrated in the South and Pennsylvania. John Adams, the Federalist candidate, was strongest in New England, New York, New Jersey, and Delaware.

4 Electoral vote by state	Electoral Vote (%)	Popular Vote
John Adams (Federalist)	71 (51)	Unknown
Thomas Jefferson (Democratic-Republican)	68 (49)	Unknown
Thomas Pinckney (Federalist)	59 (43)	Unknown
Aaron Burr (Democratic-Republican)	30 (22)	Unknown
Maryland (Electors split)	7 for Adams 4 for Jefferson	
Others (Various)	48 (35)	Unknown

was regional. John Adams carried New England and most of the mid-Atlantic. Jefferson took the entire South and Pennsylvania (**6.13**).

The XYZ Affair and Quasi-War with France

Adams, pictured in **6.14**, assumed the presidency just as a crisis with France was coming to a head. In 1796, the French government, still angry over what it viewed as a pro-British tilt in American foreign policy, had recalled its diplomatic envoy. France began seizing American ships trading with Britain. Hoping to avert war, Adams sent three American envoys to France to negotiate a settlement: Charles Cotesworth Pinckney of South Carolina, John Marshall of Virginia, and Elbridge Gerry of Massachusetts. At first, the French Directory, the revolutionary committee that ruled France from 1795 to 1799, snubbed the American delegation. When three French officials, identi-

fied simply as "X," "Y," and "Z," demanded a bribe from America's diplomats as the price of beginning negotiations, public furor erupted over what was dubbed the **XYZ Affair**. These officials sought a bribe of $250,000 for themselves, a loan of over $10 million to France, and an official apology from President Adams for unflattering remarks he had made about the French government. In a contemporary political cartoon (**6.15**) the five-headed "monster" of the French Directory (it had five members) demands a bribe from America's ambassadors.

The XYZ Affair galvanized Americans, who united behind Adams's decision to prepare for war by increasing allocations for the military. "Millions for defense, but not one cent for tribute," became the rallying cry. Hamilton's allies among the Federalists sought a declaration of war against France, but Adams resisted them. Instead an undeclared naval war broke out between France and America. This Quasi-War lasted almost two

6.14 John Adams
John Adams was elected president in 1796 in the first truly partisan presidential campaign in the new nation's brief history.

How did the XYZ Affair affect American politics?

6.15 *The Paris Monster*
This cartoon ridicules French corruption and depravity in the XYZ Affair. The "Many Headed Monster," the symbol of French government, wields a dagger while he solicits a bribe from the American delegation. The American envoys respond, "We will not give you six pence."

years from 1798 to 1800. In addition to creating a new Department of the Navy, Congress tripled the size of the regular army and created a special provisional army numbering 50,000 men. Washington reluctantly agreed to head the provisional army if Hamilton were appointed his second in command, a request that would have given Hamilton authority over many military leaders more experienced than he. Hamilton's bold effort to elevate himself above so many other qualified officers angered many Federalists who aligned themselves with Adams. Federalists were now divided into Adams and Hamilton factions.

The Alien and Sedition Acts

Federalists enacted a broad program to deal with the threats posed by the Quasi-War. To pay for the enormous expansion of the military, the Federalist-controlled Congress passed a new property tax on land, slaves, and buildings. Federalists in Congress then proposed laws, the **Alien and Sedition Acts**, to protect America from foreign and domestic subversion.

The Alien Acts, which included three separate laws, made it more difficult to become a citizen and gave the government far-reaching powers to

Why did the Federalists believe it was vital to American security to restrict immigration?

Read the **Document** *The Alien and Sedition Acts*

deport resident aliens. The Sedition Act made it a crime to "combine or conspire together with the intent to oppose any measure or measures of the government of the United States." The act criminalized any attempt to "write, print, utter, or publish" statements "false, scandalous, or malicious" against "the government of the United States, or either house of Congress of the United States, or the President." Conspicuously absent were penalties for attacking Republican Vice President Thomas Jefferson. The Federalist press was free to hurl whatever invectives it chose at Jefferson with impunity.

Federalists used the Sedition Act to prosecute 25 people, all Republican sympathizers, including printers, outspoken politicians, and other prominent figures. Federalists even prosecuted one drunken Republican for declaring that he did not care if a cannon salute to President Adams "fired thro' his a—." The harshest sentence, a $400 fine and an 18-month prison sentence, went to David Brown, an itinerant preacher and political agitator who had raised a liberty pole in Dedham, Massachusetts, with a placard that read "No Stamp Act, No Sedition, no Alien Bills, no Land Tax: downfall to the Tyrants of America, peace and retirement to the President, long live the Vice-President."

Republicans had tried to use every constitutional means at their disposal to protest the Sedition Act. They first sought to petition Congress to repeal it and then tried to use the courts to challenge its constitutionality. When both of these means failed, Republicans cast about for a new strategy. In 1798, Madison and Jefferson articulated such a strategy in two separate documents, the Virginia Resolution (by Madison) and the Kentucky Resolution (by Jefferson) Both documents defended the rights of the states to judge the constitutionality of federal laws and if necessary to protect their citizens against the federal government. Republicans based this idea on the notion that the Constitution was a compact among the people of the states who not only retained all powers not delegated to the new government but also retained a right to judge when acts of the federal government violated the Constitution. Neither Madison nor Jefferson took the next logical step and asserted a right of the states to actively nullify an unconstitutional act of the federal government. Both men hoped that the states would use persuasion, not force, to challenge an unconstitutional exercise of federal power. In keeping with this notion, Virginia and Kentucky distributed their resolutions to the other state legislatures hoping that other states would also rally against the Sedition Act. However, legislatures in the Federalist-dominated New England states attacked the resolutions as dangerous and unconstitutional assertions of state power. Federalists argued that the final arbiter of the constitutionality of acts of Congress ought to be the federal courts, not the state legislatures.

Angered by the northern Federalist legislatures' reactions, Jefferson authored a second set of Kentucky Resolutions (1799). In these, he introduced the constitutional doctrine of nullification, which asserted that states could nullify unconstitutional laws. Jefferson did not explain how a state would accomplish the goal of constitutional nullification. The Virginia and Kentucky resolutions became the foundation for subsequent arguments about **states' rights**, the theory that the Constitution was a compact among the states and that the individual states retained the right to judge when the federal government's actions were unconstitutional.

The Alien and Sedition crisis also led to the development of a new theory of freedom of the press. This new theory, the basis for modern theories of freedom of the press, argued that political opinions were not subject to government control. Rather than try to limit dissenting ideas, the new view embraced the idea of a marketplace of ideas. More speech, not less, was the antidote to the threat posed by dangerous ideas.

The Disputed Election of 1800

The Quasi-War with France, which was winding down by 1800, had split Federalists into two factions. Although Adams supported a military build up, he never abandoned hope of a negotiated settlement. Hamilton, by contrast, believed that war with France provided an opportunity to crush domestic opposition and forge an alliance with Britain. Adams had little interest in such grandiose schemes, which may have included vague plans for a joint Anglo-American conquest of Spanish America. The president also resented Hamilton's meddling in his administration.

Changes in the French government now made a peaceful solution likely. The radical phase of the French Revolution ended when Napoleon

Bonaparte, an ambitious general, seized control of France in 1799. Eager to gain U.S. support for his military campaigns against Spain and Britain, Napoleon negotiated a treaty with Adams that ended the naval conflict. However, Adams's statesmanlike effort to seek peace angered Hamiltonians. Adams also privately attacked Hamilton's "British faction." In turn, believing that Adams lacked the resolve to deal with France or the Republicans, Hamilton published a pamphlet denouncing the president. The split among Federalists could hardly have come at a worse time: The election of 1800 loomed.

The election of 1800 presented a clear choice between Federalist Adams and Republican Jefferson. Each party indulged in more rancorous campaigning than either side had experienced in previous elections. Federalists attacked Jefferson as an atheist and radical supporter of the French Revolution, themes captured in this political cartoon (**6.16**), which shows Jefferson in league with the devil. One Connecticut minister declared, "I do not believe that the Most High will permit a howling atheist to sit at the head of this nation." Republicans, in turn, prayed for deliverance from "Tories; from Aristocrats."

Despite dire predictions about the dangers of electing Jefferson—some New Englanders hid their family Bibles, fearing that President Jefferson might confiscate them—Republicans garnered enough votes to win. Still, the election was close. As the map (**6.17**) shows, support for Adams was strongest in New England, while Jefferson carried the South and parts of the mid-Atlantic. Only eight votes marked the margin of victory between the two sides.

The Republican victory triggered a constitutional crisis that few would have predicted. The actual vote in the electoral college had produced a tie between Jefferson and the Republican candidate for vice president, Aaron Burr. The Constitution did not direct electors to cast separate ballots for president and vice president. A tie meant that the sitting House of Representatives, dominated by Federalists, would decide the election. The new Republican-dominated House would not take its seats until March 1801. The political situation was tense. Rumors of deals and conspiracies circulated widely. Pennsylvania and Virginia both mobilized their militias, a clear message that they would not sit by while scheming politicians in Congress cast aside the will of the people. The politicians indeed schemed and negotiated, thus making resolution of the deadlock time consuming.

Many Federalists believed that Jefferson was a fanatic, viewing Burr as a safer alternative. Alexander Hamilton, however, who had been Burr's rival in New York politics for more than a decade, disagreed. Rather than see Burr win, Hamilton persuaded Federalists that Jefferson was the lesser of the two evils. Jefferson had also assured Federalists, including Hamilton, that he would not undermine all hard-won Federalist policies of the previous decade. With Hamilton's support and assurances from Jefferson, a deal was finally struck. It took five days and 35 ballots before the House finally elected Jefferson.

Jefferson's victory averted another constitutional crisis. Despite the mobilization of the Virginia and Pennsylvania militias while the House was voting, the election of 1800 peacefully transferred power from Federalists to Republicans, a notable achievement given the tense political atmosphere of the 1790s. To avert future deadlock in presidential elections, the Twelfth Amendment, adopted in 1804, required that electors cast separate ballots for president and vice president.

6.16 Anti-Jefferson Political Cartoon Jefferson's opponents portrayed him as an atheist who drew radical ideas from the French Revolution. In this image the American eagle tries to prevent Jefferson from throwing the Constitution into the flames emanating from the altar of Gallic (French) despotism.

THE PROVIDENTIAL DETECTION

Why did the Federalist political cartoon show Jefferson about to burn the Constitution?

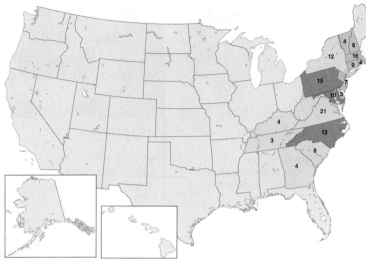

6.17 Electoral Map of 1800
Adams's support in the election of 1800 was concentrated chiefly in New England. Jefferson drew support from the South and the mid-Atlantic.

Electoral vote by state	Electoral Vote (%)	Popular Vote
Thomas Jefferson (Democratic-Republican)	73 (53)	*Unknown*
Aaron Burr (Democratic-Republican)	73 (53)	*Unknown*
John Adams (Federalist) (Incumbent)	65 (47)	*Unknown*
Charles C. Pinckney (Federalist)	64 (46)	*Unknown*
Maryland, North Carolina, Pennsylvania electors split votes for (Federalist) **and** (Democratic-Republican) **candidates**		

Gabriel's Rebellion

The French Revolution and the struggles between Federalists and Republicans leading up to the election of 1800 helped spread ideas about liberty throughout American society, including among slave communities in the South. The most dramatic illustration of this came in Virginia in 1800. **Gabriel's Rebellion**, a slave insurrection, united free blacks and slaves in a plot to liberate Richmond's slaves.

Gabriel, the slave leader of the rebellion, was trained as a blacksmith and enjoyed considerable mobility. His master allowed Gabriel to hire himself out to others and keep part of his earnings for himself. Gabriel used his mobility to make contact with other slaves and free blacks and together with them formulated a bold plan to seize the state arsenal and arm Virginia's slaves. Gabriel not only knew about the slave uprising in Saint-Domingue and the French Revolution but was also keenly aware of the ideas of the American Revolution. He planned to march under a banner emblazoned with the words "death or liberty." Gabriel had taken Patrick Henry's famous words, reversed them, and transformed them into the rallying cry for a slave rebellion. But the state militia easily crushed the rebellion. To deal with the rebels, a special court tried slaves without the benefit of a jury. Twenty-six of those put on trial were convicted and sentenced to death. Although Virginia showed little concern for the rights of the accused slaves, it had to pay close to $9,000 to the owners of the condemned slaves, who were legally entitled to be compensated for the loss of their property.

"Mr. Jefferson, though too revolutionary in his notions, is yet a lover of liberty and will be desirous of something like orderly Government. Mr. Burr loves nothing but himself . . . and will be content with nothing short of permanent power in his own hands."

ALEXANDER HAMILTON, 1800

Read the **Document** *A Virginia Slave Explains Gabriel's Rebellion*

What events in the 1790s helped inspire Gabriel's Rebellion?

1789

Washington inaugurated
Washington becomes America's first president

1790–1791

Hamilton's "Report on Public Credit"
Federalist economic program implemented

Bill of Rights ratified
Constitution amended to protect individual liberty and include additional structural supports for federalism

1793–1794

Whiskey Rebellion
Farmers in western Pennsylvania protest the whiskey excise tax

1795

Jay's Treaty
Senate ratifies Jay's Treaty with Great Britain. Republicans oppose treaty

CHAPTER REVIEW

Review Questions

1. Were Anti-Federalist fears vindicated by the events of the 1790s?

2. How did the French Revolution affect domestic American politics?

3. How did the novel reflect and influence ideas about women's roles in the new republic?

4. Did Republican opposition to the Sedition Act owe more to states' rights or individual rights?

5. How did Federalists view Jefferson in the election of 1800?

Key Terms

Electoral college A group of electors appointed by each state who had the responsibility of picking the president. **158**

Republicans Movement led by Jefferson and Madison that opposed Federalists' efforts to create a more powerful centralized government. **160**

Assumption of the state debts Hamilton's scheme for the federal government to take over any outstanding state debts. **162**

Bank of the United States A bank chartered by the federal government. The bank served as a depository for government funds, helped bolster confidence in government securities, made loans, and provided the nation with a stable national currency. **164**

Democratic-Republican Societies A new type of political organization informally allied with the Republicans whose function was to help collect, channel, and influence public opinion. **167**

Jay's Treaty Diplomatic treaty negotiated by Federalist John Jay in 1794. According to the terms of the treaty, Britain agreed to compensate America for cargoes seized from 1793 to 1794 and promised to vacate forts in the Northwest Territory. However, America failed to win acceptance of the right of neutral nations to trade with belligerents without harassment. **170**

Whiskey Rebellion The armed uprising of western Pennsylvania farmers protesting the whiskey excise in 1794 was the most serious test of the new federal government's authority since ratification of the Constitution. **172**

XYZ Affair The furor created when Americans learned that three French officials, identified in diplomatic correspondence as "X," "Y," and "Z," demanded a bribe from America's diplomats as the price of beginning negotiations. **181**

Alien and Sedition Acts Four laws designed to protect America from the danger of foreign and domestic subversion. The first three, the Alien laws, dealt with immigration and naturalization. The Sedition Act criminalized criticism of the federal government. **182**

States' rights The theory that the Constitution was a compact among the states and that the individual states retained the right to judge when the federal government's actions were unconstitutional. **183**

Gabriel's Rebellion A slave insurrection in Richmond, Virginia, that drew together free blacks and slaves in a plot to seize the Richmond arsenal and foment a slave rebellion. **185**

1796

John Adams elected president
Washington declines to serve a third term and is succeeded by Federalist John Adams

1798

Alien and Sedition Acts
Congress enacts a series of new acts to control aliens and punish attacks on the government

Virginia and Kentucky Resolutions
Madison and Jefferson draft resolutions protesting the Sedition Act and asserting the right of the states to check unconstitutional acts of the federal government

1799

Second Kentucky Resolution
Jefferson introduces concept of nullification in his second Kentucky Resolutions

1800

Jefferson elected president
Peaceful transfer of power from Federalists to Republicans

MyHistoryLab Connections

Visit www.myhistorylab.com for a customized Study Plan that will help you build your knowledge of *The New Republic*.

Questions for Analysis

1. **What was Hamilton's vision for the New Republic?**

   Read the **Document** *Alexander Hamilton, Opposing Visions for the New Nation, p. 160*

2. **What was Jefferson's vision for the New Republic?**

   Read the **Document** *Thomas Jefferson, Notes on Virginia, p. 165*

3. **Did Jefferson's statements about the French Revolution justify Federalist charges that he was a dangerous radical?**

   View the **Closer Look** *Competing Visions: Jefferson and Hamilton's Reactions to the French Revolution, p. 168*

4. **What does the Alien and Sedition Crisis reveal about political tensions in the New Republic?**

   View the **Closer Look** *Competing Visions: Congressional Debates over the Sedition Act, p. 183*

5. **Explain the meaning and significance of Gabriel's Rebellion.**

   Read the **Document** *A Virginia Slave Explains Gabriel's Rebellion, p. 185*

Other Resources from This Chapter

Read the **Document**

- *The Jay Treaty, p. 170*
- *Whiskey Rebellion Address, George Washington's 6th Annual Address to Congress, p. 173*
- *"James Wilson on Woman's Legal Disabilities" in James Wilson,* An Introductory Lecture to a Course of Law Lectures *(1791), p. 176*
- *George Washington's Farewell Address, p. 179*
- *The Alien and Sedition Acts, p. 182*

View the **Image**

- *George Washington's Arrival in New York City (1789), p. 158*
- *Lady's Magazine, p. 175*

Politics in
Jeffersonian
America p. 190

*What was the Jeffersonian
vision of government?*

An Expanding Empire
of Liberty p. 194

*How did Jefferson's policy
toward Indians fit into his
vision of America?*

Dissension at
Home p. 200

*Was Jefferson's response
to the Federalist judiciary
consistent with his political
and constitutional beliefs?*

America Confronts a
World at War p. 201

*What was peaceable coer-
cion and why did it fail to
avert war?*

The Republic Reborn:
Consequences of the
War of 1812 p. 208

*How did the War of 1812
change American society?*

Crises and the
Collapse of the
National Republican
Consensus p. 213

*What did the Missouri Crisis
reveal about the tensions in
American society?*

Jeffersonian America

An Expanding Empire of Liberty,
1800–1824

In 1800, Republican Thomas Jefferson won the presidential election against his Federalist opponent John Adams. After nearly a decade in opposition, Republicans celebrated their presidential triumph with toasts and songs about "Jefferson and Liberty." Federalists, however, feared that the new president—whom they had denounced as an atheist, a tool of the French, and a supporter of Thomas Paine's radical democratic ideas—would undo all their work of the previous decade. In this Federalist political cartoon from 1800, *Mad Tom in a Rage,* Jefferson's ally Thomas Paine and the Devil tear down the federal edifice created by Washington and Adams.

The Federalist fears captured in the cartoon were not only unfounded, but President Jefferson turned out to be a very different person from Vice President Jefferson, the leader of the Republican opposition during the Adams administration. Rather than mount a full-scale attack on Federalist policy, Jefferson adopted a less confrontational approach. In his presidential inaugural, he struck a conciliatory tone and reminded Americans: "We are all republicans—we are all federalists."

Jefferson also promised the nation "a wise and frugal government." Implementing this, however, proved difficult as he took over the reigns of power in his first term. The opportunity to purchase the Louisiana Territory and double the size of the new nation, led him to cast aside constitutional strict construction, which restricted the powers of the federal government to those explicitly delegated by the Constitution. By the end of Jefferson's second term in 1809, some Americans believed that the Jeffersonian Republicans had become indistinguishable from their Federalist opponents. Jefferson's anointed successor, James Madison, made additional compromises that some of his supporters believed betrayed the ideas he had championed as a member of the Republican opposition in the 1790s.

Foreign affairs proved especially vexing for both Jefferson and Madison. Each man had tried to prevent American entanglement in the war between Britain and France. Despite their efforts, however, America was dragged into the European conflict, eventually going to war against Britain in 1812. Although the war was fought against the British, the conspicuous losers in the conflict were the Indian tribes in the Northwest and Southwest, who lost a valuable ally in Britain and suffered defeats by American troops. The demands of fighting the war also forced Republicans to reconsider the necessity of much of Hamiltonian economic policy. By the end of the presidency of James Monroe in 1825, the fourth Virginian to become president, the old political labels of Republican and Federalist had become nearly meaningless, and were soon to be supplanted by two new political parties.

"The revolution of 1800 was as real a revolution in the principles of our government as that of 1776 was in its form; not effected, indeed, by the sword, as that, but by the rational and peaceable instrument of reform, the suffrage of the people."

THOMAS JEFFERSON to Judge Spenser Roane, 1819

Politics in Jeffersonian America

Jefferson's presidential triumph in 1800 ushered in a new era in American political life. After a decade of Federalist rule, and despite the courts remaining bastions of Federalist power, Republicans now controlled the presidency and Congress. Despite Jefferson's efforts to avoid the bitter partisanship that had characterized politics during the previous decade, American politics remained deeply divisive. In an age when gentlemen lived by a code of honor, political insults could easily turn into personal affronts, and might result in tragic results. Before the end of his presidency, Jefferson's vice president, Aaron Burr, would slay Jefferson's longtime opponent, Alexander Hamilton, in a duel, and Burr would become a fugitive from justice. Former president John Adams sarcastically observed that his fellow citizens had made great strides in the "arts of lying and libeling and the other arts which grow out of them, such as wielding the cudgel and pistol."

Liberty and Small Government

Jefferson set out his views of government in his inaugural address on March 4, 1801. Although he invoked shared values, including faith in representative government and the rule of law, Jefferson also made clear how his idea of government differed from that of his opponents. Throughout the 1790s, Federalists had worked to endow the new government of the United States with sufficient power to become a great nation, modeled on Britain's commercial and military might. Following Hamilton's lead, Federalists had increased the size of the central government and military and had also used their expansive view of federal power to crush political opposition. By contrast, Jefferson hoped to reduce the size of the federal government.

Jefferson invoked the ideal of liberty, not power. He described the state governments as the proper defenders of liberty. In contrast to Federalists, who supported a national bank and enacted a host of taxes, including the unpopular whiskey tax, Jefferson sought to reduce the burdens government placed on the people. Rather than favor commerce he emphasized the "encouragement of agriculture" with "commerce as its handmaid." To achieve "economy in public expense," he would scale back the size of government. An alert citizenry, a vigorous militia, and strong state governments were the foundation upon which to build America's future. Finally, opposing laws such as the Sedition Act, Jefferson praised freedom of the press, reminding Americans that political conflict was a testimony to the vitality of American life, not a sign of weakness.

The Jeffersonian Style

Jefferson's inaugural not only set out his philosophical differences with Federalists but also gave him the occasion to dramatize them. Jefferson's vision had always melded democratic ideals to aristocratic tastes. He labored to create a different presidential style from those who came before him. Jefferson loathed the pomp and ceremony that Washington and Adams had used to exalt the presidency. Rather than ride to his inaugural in an elegant coach, Jefferson walked behind a small band of Maryland militia. Instead of delivering his annual address to Congress from a monarch-like throne as his predecessors had done, he had a clerk read them. Jefferson also rejected the elegant balls that Federalists had staged during the Washington and Adams presidencies as smacking too much of European-style monarchy.

Abandoning the pomp and aristocratic style of his predecessors and replacing it with a more democratic style defined the public face of Jefferson's presidency. Yet, Jefferson remained a rich Virginian slaveholder whose tastes were anything but common. Although Jefferson dispensed with much of the formality of his predecessors, his presidency still reflected his aristocratic tastes. Dinner with Jefferson involved an unusual mix of informality and aristocratic style. He dressed informally when he entertained guests, wearing a pair of worn leather slippers, which shocked those used to the formality of Washington and Adams. Yet those invited to Monticello, the home Jefferson designed himself, in the mountains of western Virginia (**7.1**), found themselves in an architectural masterpiece that confidently proclaimed its owner's wealth and exquisite taste. The food and wine served at these dinners were equally impressive. Jefferson regaled his dinner guests with the sensual delights of his table and the dazzling brilliance of his conversation, which ranged over everything from philosophy to agriculture. A connoisseur of fine wines, Jefferson's annual wine bill for his first term in office came to $2,400, almost ten times the yearly income of a typical artisan.

Political Slurs and the Politics of Honor

Literate and urbane, Thomas Jefferson was deeply influenced by the Enlightenment, particularly its emphasis on reason and science. One of his many interests was fossils. Jefferson wrote about mammoths in his book *Notes on Virginia*. Four months after his inauguration, his friend, the artist Charles Wilson Peale, set out to exhume the remains of a mastodon in upstate New York. President Jefferson, enthusiastically supporting Peale, even authorized the use of U.S. military equipment to aid in the dig. The expedition proved to be a monumental undertaking, as reflected in Peale's painting of the event (**7.2**). The disinterment of the giant fossil testified to American ingenuity. To Jefferson, the expedition was a symbol of the new nation's commitment to the values of the Enlightenment.

His interest in fossils and mastodon bones, however, provided an easy target for his enemies, who mocked him as "the mammoth philosopher" or the "mammoth of democracy." In response, his supporters attempted to turn Jefferson's passionate interest in

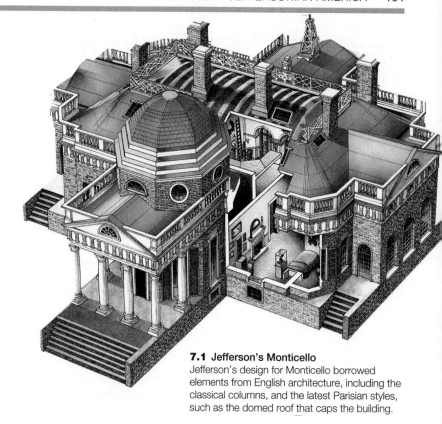

7.1 Jefferson's Monticello
Jefferson's design for Monticello borrowed elements from English architecture, including the classical columns, and the latest Parisian styles, such as the domed roof that caps the building.

mastodons to his advantage. The president was presented with a "mammoth cheese" weighing more than 1,200 pounds. The delivery of the cheese to the president became a sensation and filled newspaper columns for months. Mammoth jokes, however, were among the milder partisan attacks leveled at Jefferson. His lavish home at Monticello also prompted sarcastic comments. Federalists pointed out the obvious contradiction between the president's support for democracy and his own aristocratic tastes in architecture, food, and wine. His enemies also highlighted the contradiction between Jefferson's impassioned defense of liberty and his life as a slaveholder. Monticello was a large working plantation and was therefore home to a sizable African American slave community. Indeed, as the chart and illustration in *Envisioning Evidence: The World of Slavery at Monticello* show, slaves vastly outnumbered Monticello's free white population, which included Jefferson's family and white laborers on the mountaintop.

7.2 *Exhuming the First American Mastodon*
Charles Wilson Peale's painting of the exhumation of the mammoth is a tribute to American ingenuity and the Enlightenment values esteemed by Jefferson. The centerpiece of the painting is not the fossils, but a machine to remove water from the dig, a visual tribute to American science and engineering.

What does Monticello reveal about Thomas Jefferson's ideas and values?

Envisioning Evidence
THE WORLD OF SLAVERY AT MONTICELLO

As the pictogram below illustrates, at Monticello, Thomas Jefferson and his family were surrounded by a large community of African American slaves who worked in the kitchens and gardens, and served as skilled craftsmen. Jefferson owned as many as 150 slaves and he employed them in a variety of occupations at Monticello and on the other lands he owned. Slaves worked the fields, built furniture, manufactured nails, cooked Jefferson's meals, and worked in a variety of other occupations that made it possible for him to maintain his aristocratic lifestyle. Compared to the splendor of the main house at Monticello, the typical dwelling of a slave was extremely humble.

Who Lived at Monticello?

Thomas Jefferson and his family lived at Monticello with enslaved African Americans and free European and American craftsmen. This chart represents the population of this busy plantation in the late 1790s.

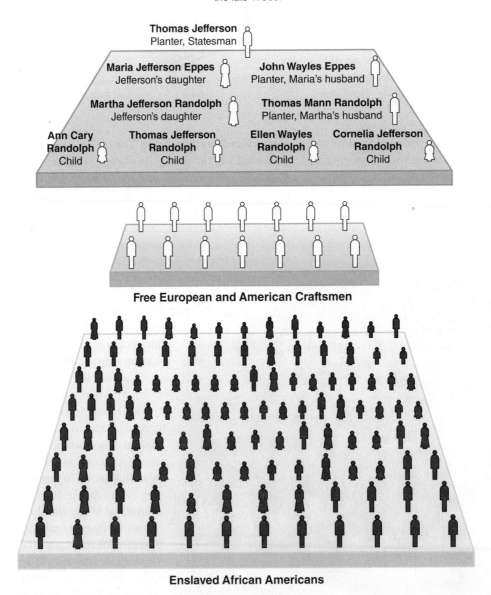

What role did slavery play in life at Monticello?

Jefferson's slaves were housed in cramped and primitive dwellings. The contrast between these humble slave shacks and the mansion inhabited by Jefferson and his family provided a striking visual contrast to anyone who visited Monticello.

Attacks on the president became intensely personal. One of Jefferson's former supporters, the disgruntled newspaper editor James Callender, accused Jefferson of taking Sally Hemings, a Monticello slave, "as his concubine." This political cartoon (**7.3**) portrays Jefferson as a cock courting the hen Sally Hemings. The press charged that the president had a slave mistress, and tales of Jefferson's "Monticellan Sally" appeared in newspapers.

Although Jefferson ignored these accusations, the Sally Hemings scandal persisted long after he left the presidency. Among the descendents of Monticello's slaves, the belief that Jefferson had fathered children with Sally Hemings became part of a family oral tradition that persisted for more than two centuries. Many descendents of Jefferson and modern scholars doubted the truth of these rumors until modern forensic DNA testing provided strong evidence that a male in Jefferson's blood line was the likely father of at least one child by Sally Hemings. Although not everyone has been persuaded, many scholars now believe that Jefferson did have a sexual relationship with Hemings.

Federalist attacks on Jefferson went well beyond slurs on his character. His most vocal critics charged that had white Southerners not been entitled to count three-fifths of their slaves in apportioning electoral votes in 1800, (part of the compromise worked out in the Constitutional Convention, see Chapter 5) Jefferson would have lost to Adams. However, the charge that Jefferson was a "Negro President" was not entirely true, since he won clear majorities in the North and mid-Atlantic and his margin in the Electoral College would have been even greater if presidential electors from those regions had more accurately reflected the popular vote in the states that supported Jefferson.

Jefferson was not the only politician whose reputation was dragged through the mud. Attacks on character were frequent, and in a culture in which honor played a central role, they demanded an appropriate response. If an apology or retraction were not forthcoming, a man might demand satisfaction on the field of honor, resulting in a duel. Leading politicians participated in duels, and gentlemen typically owned dueling pistols. Often, friends intervened and prevented a duel from reaching its deadly conclusion. Efforts to avert tragedy

> ## "Of all the Damsels on the green on mountain or in valley A lass so luscious ne'er was seen As Monticellan Sally"
> *Boston Gazette*, 1802

failed in the most famous duel of the era; no one stopped the face-off between Vice President Aaron Burr and his longtime rival in New York politics, Alexander Hamilton. Burr's candidacy for governor of New York in 1804 was undermined by Hamilton's attacks. A newspaper reported that Hamilton had described the vice president as "a dangerous man and one who ought not be trusted with the reins of government." Hamilton also insulted Burr's personal integrity and honor.

Burr demanded an apology. When Hamilton refused, Burr challenged him to a duel. On July 11, 1804, the two men met across the river from New York City in Weehawken, New Jersey, and Burr fatally shot Hamilton. Authorities in both New York and New Jersey immediately charged Burr with murder, and he fled to Philadelphia, where he remained a fugitive.

News of the duel spread through the country. In Baltimore, angry citizens burned the vice president in effigy. Eventually, the charges against Burr were dropped; although dueling was still illegal in most states, duelers were rarely prosecuted.

7.3 Jefferson and Sally Hemings Jefferson's enemies spread rumors about his illicit sexual relationship with his slave Sally Hemings. This caricature of Jefferson as a cock and Sally Hemings as a hen presents the scandal in comic terms.

📖 **Read** the **Document** Memoirs of a Monticello Slave

What role did honor play in the political culture of Jeffersonian America?

An Expanding Empire of Liberty

Many of Jefferson's supporters hoped that the new president would radically restructure the balance of power between the states and the federal government. They would be disappointed. Rather than a wholesale assault on the Hamiltonian system, Jefferson opted for a more modest, less confrontational approach. The exception was the judiciary. The Federalists had expanded and seeded it with opponents of Jefferson, presenting him with a major challenge. Still Jefferson believed that his election had ushered in a revolutionary change that altered the course of America's future.

Jefferson's vision for the future depended on preserving his ideal of a yeoman republic. Perhaps his greatest challenge was posed by the unexpected opportunity to purchase the entire Louisiana Territory from the French Emperor Napoleon. To justify this purchase, which required an enormous and unprecedented exercise of federal power, Jefferson would need to accept a Hamiltonian view of the Constitution. Jefferson's vision of an expanding "empire of liberty" peopled by independent yeoman farmers came into conflict with his vision of limited government.

Dismantling the Federalist Program

Jefferson's approach to change in government was moderate and conciliatory. Instead of purging all Federalists, he dismissed only those who were corrupt, inept, or who posed serious obstacles to his agenda. Similarly, although Jefferson had contemplated declaring the Sedition Act unconstitutional, he simply refused to bring forward any new indictments, pardoning individuals prosecuted by Federalists and allowing the law to expire.

Jefferson remained committed to the ideal of a republican system in which the states, not the federal government, retained most authority. The powers of the federal government pertained to "the external and mutual relations only of these states." The

> "They have retired into the judiciary as a stronghold. There the remains of federalism are to be preserved and fed from the treasury, and from that battery all the works of republicanism are to be beaten down and erased."
>
> THOMAS JEFFERSON to JOHN DICKINSON, December 19, 1801

states were responsible for the "principal care of our persons, our property." With states' rights in mind, Jefferson reduced the size of the federal government. He directed Secretary of the Treasury Albert Gallatin to eradicate the national debt created by the Federalists. Gallatin severed the connection between the Bank of the United States and the federal government, using the sale of the government's interest in the bank to lower the national debt. To make up for the loss of income from the repeal of unpopular taxes, Jefferson relied on the sale of Western lands and tariffs on imports. Convinced that the militia could protect America's peacetime interests, he slashed the budget of the navy and the army, sharply reducing the size of both. This decision would create problems for Jefferson in his second term. Without a powerful navy to protect American merchant ships, France and Britain could threaten the new nation's commerce.

The Courts: The Last Bastion of Federalist Power

Early in his first term, Jefferson told a supporter that the Federalists "have retired into the judiciary as a stronghold." One of the last acts of John Adams's Federalist administration had been the passage of the Judiciary Act of 1801, which created new circuit and district court judges and other legal offices, such as clerks, federal marshals, justices of the peace, and attorneys. With new appointments, Adams had hoped to solidify the Federalists' control of the judiciary. The Judiciary Act also reduced the number of Supreme Court justices from six to five. (The reduction would take effect upon the death or retirement of one of the sitting justices.) By reducing the number of Supreme Court justices, Federalists hoped to minimize the likelihood that Jefferson would appoint a justice during his tenure. Jefferson instructed Secretary of State James Madison to withhold any of the new appointments that arrived after he was to be sworn in as president. A disappointed office seeker, William Marbury, sued Madison, seeking a court order to compel Jefferson to turn over his commission. In what became a landmark in American constitutional law, *Marbury v. Madison* (1803) strengthened the powers of the federal judiciary, fixing the doctrine of judicial review as a cornerstone of American constitutional law. See *Choices and Consequences: John Marshall's Predicament* on page 196.

The Louisiana Purchase

In his first Inaugural Address, Jefferson described America as a "chosen country, with room enough for our descendants to the thousandth and thousandth generation." To remain a republic of virtuous yeoman farmers and keep alive the ideal of an "empire of liberty," the nation, he argued, would have to expand westward. Jefferson's vision of an expanding empire of liberty, however, had little room for African Americans and demanded that Indians either assimilate or perish. The first test of the limits of the President's vision, especially his concept of liberty, became apparent in his response to news of Gabriel's Rebellion, the slave uprising in Virginia, in 1800 (see Chapter 6). The uprising prompted soul-searching by white Virginians, including a proposal to emancipate slaves and settle them on Western lands. Virginia's Governor James Monroe took this proposal seriously and sought the president's advice. Jefferson opposed the plan, however, because he viewed such lands as vital to America's future. He did not wish to see land that could go to whites and help preserve his vision of a yeoman republic set aside for blacks.

The West was essential to Jefferson's vision of the nation. When he took office, more than 500,000 Americans lived west of the Appalachian Mountains; access to the Mississippi River had become crucial to their prosperity. Agricultural produce destined for New Orleans traveled on large flat boats down the Mississippi. Pinckney's Treaty (1795) with Spain provided navigation rights to this vital economic corridor. When the Spanish ceded Louisiana to France in 1800, they also turned over control of the Mississippi to Napoleon Bonaparte, France's ambitious military ruler. Napoleon's decision to close New Orleans to American shipping alarmed many in Congress. Some Americans advocated seizing the city. Preferring a negotiated settlement, Jefferson sent a delegation to France to purchase the port from Napoleon. When they arrived in Paris, the envoys were astounded to learn that Napoleon was willing to sell all of Louisiana to the United States.

Acquisition of Louisiana would double the size of the United States; but the Constitution did not authorize the president to purchase new territory. To fulfill his dream of securing enough land for the nation to remain a yeoman republic, Jefferson had to abandon his constitutional philosophy of strict construction, which limited the powers of the federal government to those expressly delegated by the Constitution. Although Jefferson contemplated amending the Constitution to enable such a purchase, he feared that Napoleon might withdraw his offer before an amendment could be ratified. So Jefferson abandoned his constitutional ideals to achieve his political objective. With the **Louisiana Purchase**, the United States acquired the Louisiana Territory from France in 1803, thereby securing control of the Mississippi River and virtually doubling the size of the new nation (**7.4** on page 197).

"There is on the globe one single spot, the possessor of which is our natural and habitual enemy. It is New Orleans, through which the produce of three-eighths of our territory must pass to market, and from its fertility it will ere long yield more than half of our whole produce and contain more than half our inhabitants."

THOMAS JEFFERSON, 1802

Read the **Document** *Thomas Jefferson to John C. Breckinridge, "Constitutionality of the Louisiana Purchase" (1803)*

Was the Louisiana Purchase consistent with Jefferson's ideals?

Choices and Consequences

JOHN MARSHALL'S PREDICAMENT

The case of *Marbury v. Madison* pitted President Jefferson against the new Federalist Chief Justice of the Supreme Court, John Marshall. Jefferson, a champion of states' rights, resented the Federalist-controlled judiciary and, in particular, Marshall, an ardent nationalist who supported a strong central government and a powerful judiciary. *Marbury v. Madison* presented Marshall with a tremendous opportunity to enhance the power of the court, but it also set up the possibility of a serious conflict between the court and the executive branch. Could Marshall compel Jefferson to deliver the commission against his will? What if Jefferson refused the court order? Although Marshall sought to strengthen the power of the court, a direct confrontation with Jefferson might have the opposite effect if Marshall ruled against the president and Jefferson ignored the court's ruling. Marshall had three possible options.

Choices

1 Give Marbury his commission.

2 Deny Marbury the commission.

3 Acknowledge the legitimacy of Marbury's claim, while somehow avoiding a showdown between the court and the executive branch.

Continuing Controversies

What role should judicial review play in a democracy?

The power of unelected judges to overturn acts of the legislature struck many Americans in Jefferson's day as undemocratic and inconsistent with representative government. Modern critics still argue that judicial review is undemocratic. Supporters of judicial review argue that the courts serve a necessary *counter-majoritarian* role. By protecting minorities against overbearing majorities, a strong judiciary with the power of judicial review safeguards individual liberty. The controversy that began with *Marbury v. Madison* continues to this day.

Decision

Marshall stated emphatically that Marbury was entitled to the commission. But he asserted just as strongly that he could not order Madison to deliver the commission because the Supreme Court lacked jurisdiction to hear the case. Thus, Marshall used a technical legal issue to avoid a showdown between the executive and the judiciary. To arrive at this result, Marshall declared part of an earlier law, the Judiciary Act of 1789, unconstitutional.

John Marshall

Consequences

Legal scholars usually regard *Marbury v. Madison* as one of the most important and brilliant opinions in Supreme Court history. Marshall gave all the parties in the case a partial victory. By affirming that Marbury was entitled to the commission, Marshall gave him a moral victory, while also handing Jefferson a practical political victory. His ruling strengthened the concept of judicial review, the notion that courts might overturn acts of the legislature when they conflicted with the Constitution, thus giving the biggest victory to the Supreme Court, whose power was enhanced.

How did John Marshall avoid a showdown with Jefferson in *Marbury v. Madison?*

Read the Document *Marbury v. Madison*

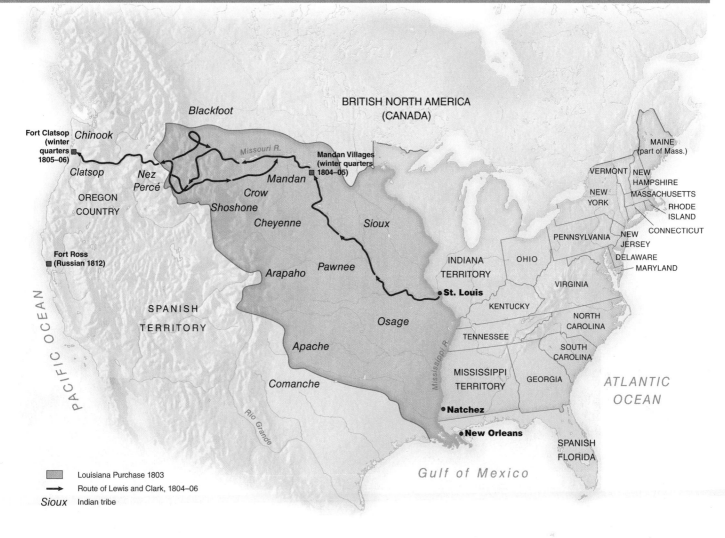

7.4 Louisiana Purchase
Jefferson acquired approximately 827,000 square miles of Western territory, doubling the size of the United States. One of the primary goals of the Lewis and Clark expedition was to map this region.

Lewis and Clark

In January 1803, six months before news of the purchase of Louisiana, Jefferson had requested funds from Congress for an expedition to explore and map the Western parts of the continent. Meriwether Lewis, Jefferson's private secretary, headed the expedition. Lewis invited Captain William Clark, an army officer with experience in mapmaking, to join him in commanding a "Corps of volunteers for North Western Discovery." Beginning their heroic trek westward in the frontier town of St. Louis, the intrepid explorers set out on keelboats, long narrow boats that could carry ten tons of supplies. The expedition traveled up the Missouri River. Progress was slow and the explorers sometimes had to wade along the bank to pull the boats forward by ropes.

Still, if all went well, they could travel 14 miles on a good day.

The purchase of Louisiana added a new element to the mission. In addition to gathering information about native plants, animals, and geography, Lewis was charged with negotiating commercial treaties with Indian tribes and informing the European and American traders inhabiting the Louisiana Territory that they were now subject to the laws of the United States.

The small band of explorers included a French interpreter, Toussaint Charbonneau, and his Shoshone wife, Sacagawea, who served the corps ably as a translator. Her presence also signaled the Indians that Lewis and Clark's intentions were peaceful. An armed group of men might have easily been viewed as a war party. The inclusion of

What role did Sacagawea play in the Lewis and Clark Expedition?

7.5 Jefferson's Indian Hall at Monticello
Jefferson's main entrance hall contained many Indian artifacts, including a Mandan buffalo-hide robe which hung from the balcony (far right). The images painted on these robes often depicted heroic exploits of the warriors who wore them.

Sacagawea and her young child—neither could be perceived as a warrior—helped the Corps of Discovery avoid conflict. Clark stressed the importance of this when he wrote in his journal, "a woman with a party of men is a token of peace." Enduring incredible hardship, including temperatures as low as 45 below zero, the Corps of Discovery traversed almost 4,000 miles. The trek took more than two years. The map (7.4) shows the path of Lewis and Clark. The Corps provided invaluable information about the geography, biology, and peoples of the West.

Jefferson had instructed Lewis and Clark to obtain information about the indigenous cultures they encountered, including their languages, traditions, and occupations. Although gathering intelligence would prove invaluable for future diplomatic negotiations and trade with these peoples, Jefferson's instructions also reflected his lifelong interest in Indian cultures. Many items that Lewis

and Clark collected were displayed in Jefferson's "Indian Hall" at Monticello. Many Indian artifacts were on view in this space, including an impressive Mandan buffalo robe which hangs above the entrance to the room (**7.5**).

Indian Responses to Jeffersonian Expansionism: Assimilation or Revivalism

Jefferson's interest in the Indians was motivated by a paternalistic regard for Indians and Indian cultures. He believed that Indian societies, although inferior to Western culture, had a primitive nobility worthy of respect. In choosing to view Indians this way, Jefferson carried forward a much older notion of noble savagery that had warped European views of Indians since their first encounters more than 300 years earlier.

A student of the Enlightenment, Jefferson also believed that environment shaped culture. Taken together these two beliefs led him to be cautiously optimistic in his view of the future of American-Indian relations, a noticeable contrast with his deeply pessimistic view of future relations between enslaved African Americans and white Americans. Indians simply needed to abandon their traditional ways, and adopt Western agriculture and cultural values. Once they shed their traditions, Indians could then freely intermarry with whites. Assimilation and absorption would solve America's Indian problem. Once Indians were amalgamated into American society, their lands could be made available for settlement, which would help sustain the ideal of a yeoman republic, and thereby ensure the viability of Jefferson's political vision for America.

Jefferson supported trade with Indians, including granting them generous terms of credit which would encourage indebtedness and force Indians to sell their lands to pay off their debts. Jefferson also hoped to teach Indians Western agricultural practices and to promote western-style gender roles in the division of labor. The goal was to have Indian women abandon work in the fields and take up tasks more typical of Western women, including spinning. In 1803, he encouraged Georgia Indian Agent Benjamin Hawkins to help the Creeks pursue "agriculture" and "household manufacture."

Although some tribes followed the path of assimilation, others rejected Western ways entirely. In the 1790s, a cultural revival occurred among the Iroquois in western New York and the Shawnee, Creeks, and Cherokees on the trans-Appalachian frontier. The revival aimed at revitalizing Indian religious beliefs and cultural practices. The revivalists also attacked the European and American practices that had been incorporated into Indian cultures.

One leader in the Indian revival movement was Handsome Lake, who led a revitalization movement among the Seneca of New York beginning in 1799. Among the values he championed was abstinence from alcohol. Traders during the colonial period had introduced alcohol among Indian peoples, creating a serious problem for many indigenous communities. Handsome Lake had himself battled with his own alcohol addiction. A key turning point in his life occurred when he experienced religious visions that led him to revive aspects of the Iroquois Great Law of Peace. This ideal was central to the Great Iroquoian Confederacy and enjoined members of the confederacy to seek diplomatic, not military, solutions to conflicts. In 1801, Handsome Lake traveled to Washington, D.C., to meet with President Jefferson to defend the land claims of his people against encroachment from settlers.

Another effort at religious and cultural revival took place among the Shawnee and other tribes of the Great Lakes region. The leader of this movement, the Prophet Tenskwatawa, also battled with alcohol addiction. His plan for a revival of traditional culture also came to him in religious visions. The Prophet instructed his people to reject Western influences and return to traditional Indian ways. In contrast to Handsome Lake's evocation of peace, Tenskwatawa adopted a more militant stance. He joined his brother, the military leader Tecumseh, in organizing rival Indian nations to work together to resist American expansion into Indian lands. This pan-Indian resistance movement united six tribes to repel white encroachments in Ohio and Indiana. Rather than seek peaceful accommodation with the United States, this movement resolved to defend Indian lands by force.

> "To promote this disposition to exchange lands. . . . we shall push our trading uses, and be glad to see the good and influential individuals among them run in debt, because we observe that when these debts get beyond what the individuals can pay, they becoming willing to lop them off by a cession of lands. . . . In this way our settlements will gradually circumscribe and approach the Indians."
>
> THOMAS JEFFERSON to WILLIAM HENRY HARRISON, 1803

▶◀ **Read** the **Document** *Jefferson's Confidential Message to Congress (1803)*

What were the central beliefs of Handsome Lake's religious revival?

Dissension at Home

In 1804, Jefferson easily defeated his opponent, the Federalist Charles Pinckney, by 162 electoral votes to 14 to start a second term as president. The margin of victory was a tribute to the achievements of his first administration, during which he had overseen a peaceful, relatively smooth transition from Federalist to Republican rule. Jefferson had dismantled parts of the government bureaucracy, overseen a robust economy, and preserved the ideal of a nation of yeoman farmers by acquiring the vast new territory of Louisiana. In contrast to the successes of his first term, however, challenges at home and abroad marred his second four years in office. Divisions within the Republican movement plagued Jefferson's second term. Meanwhile, his effort to avoid entanglement in European conflicts would lead him to institute an embargo against foreign trade that proved extremely unpopular in New England and seaport towns and cities dependent on foreign trade.

Jefferson's Attack on the Federalist Judiciary

The final element in the Republican strategy to rein in the Federalist judiciary involved using the constitutional power of impeachment to remove two of the most controversial Federalist judges. Toward the end of his first term, Jefferson scored a victory by removing Judge John Pickering of New Hampshire, a notorious drunk. Although he had clearly been unqualified to hold office, many of Jefferson's supporters were worried about using impeachment as a partisan tool. Some Republicans doubted that Pickering's deplorable behavior qualified as "high crimes and misdemeanors," the Constitution's criteria for removal from office. Still, Jefferson managed to persuade enough members of the Senate to convict Pickering.

Buoyed by his victory in the election of 1804, Jefferson next turned his attention to Samuel Chase, a federal judge who had used the bench as a pulpit to denounce Jefferson and his ideas by delivering long-winded speeches to juries. Few Republicans would have disputed the charge that Chase was partisan and obnoxious, but neither of these was an impeachable offense if one construed the Constitution according to Jefferson's rule of strict construction. Ardent Republicans argued that impeachment was the only tool to check the excesses of unelected judges. More moderate Republicans and Federalists insisted that an impeachable offense had to be a criminal act; stridency and partisanship were simply not impeachable offenses. The Senate failed to convict Chase, and the episode drove a wedge between the radical and moderate wings of Jefferson's coalition.

The Controversial Mr. Burr

The duel between Hamilton and Burr ended the latter's public political career, but not his political scheming. Burr was soon charged with conspiracy and treason. The exact details of his plot are sketchy, but he appears to have planned to raise a private army to conquer Mexico. The evidence that he intended to invade American territory is less compelling. In any case Burr was certainly one of the more flamboyant personalities of the early Republic, a quality his friend and protégé, painter John Vanderlyn, captured in this portrait (**7.6**).

Jefferson pushed hard to prosecute Burr for treason. Chief Justice John Marshall refused to construe the treason clause in more broad terms, forcing the government to produce two witnesses who could testify that Burr had waged war against the United States. Under this more precise definition of treason, the prosecution was unable to convict Burr. Marshall's decision to read the treason clause in such narrow terms infuriated Jefferson, who on this occasion seemed to embrace a theory of constitutional interpretation at odds with his own preferred theory of strict construction. In essence, when it came to Burr, Jefferson argued that one ought to construe the Constitution's definition of treason in Hamiltonian terms. Having avoided the charge of treason Burr went into exile in Europe after the trial but eventually returned to New York to start a lucrative law practice.

7.6 Portrait of Aaron Burr
Artist John Vanderlyn, a protégé of Burr, painted this striking portrait of the controversial politician during Burr's tenure as vice president.

Why did Jefferson target the federal judiciary and seek to limit its power?

America Confronts a World at War

In 1803, within two weeks of its sale of Louisiana, France was again at war with Britain. Although Napoleon's armies dominated the European continent, Britain's navy commanded the seas and defeated the French fleet at the Battle of Trafalgar in 1805. During the early phases of the European conflict, American merchants reaped enormous profits by trading with both the French and the British. However, both Britain and France, eager to exert economic pressure on their enemies, set out to blockade the ports of their adversaries. The United States argued that neutral nations had a right to carry on nonmilitary trade with both sides in the conflict, but neither Britain nor France honored this idea. The British navy boarded and searched American ships and seized cargoes without providing compensation. Even more galling to Americans was the British practice of impressment, forcing merchant seamen to serve in the British navy. Many American sailors had once served in the British navy but now claimed American citizenship. The British refused to recognize these claims, arguing that the men were deserters still subject to British law. Between 1803 and 1812, the British navy abducted and impressed 6,000 Americans.

The tense environment on the high seas reached a crisis in 1807, when the British warship the *Leopard* fired at an American navy ship, the *Chesapeake*. Three Americans were killed and 18 wounded. The British abducted four American sailors whom they charged were deserters from the Royal Navy. People in America's seaports clamored for revenge for the Chesapeake Affair. Citizens of Norfolk, Virginia, were particularly outraged because the *Chesapeake* had been built in the town's shipyards. Norfolk passed a resolution denouncing this outrageous assault on American liberty and honor. One British diplomat noted that "the lowest order of the Americans are much irritated and inclined for violent measures." Mobs took to the streets to protest in many of the nation's ports. President Jefferson instructed the governors of the states to be prepared to call up 100,000 militia men.

The Failure of Peaceable Coercion

Hoping to avoid war with the British and French, Jefferson proposed a policy of "peaceable coercion." "Our commerce," Jefferson wrote, "is so valuable to them, that they will be glad to purchase it, when the only price we ask is to do us justice." The **Embargo Act of 1807** became the cornerstone of "peaceable coercion." By keeping America's ships out of harm's way and depriving Britain and France of the economic benefits of American trade, Jefferson hoped to pressure both sides to respect the rights of neutrals on the high seas. Smugglers flouted the ban, and it proved unpopular in New England and seaports, where it hit the shipping business hard. American exports fell from $108 million in 1807 to $22 million in 1808. To enforce the embargo along the Canadian border, Jefferson had to send troops, a policy he had decried during the Whiskey Rebellion a decade earlier. Federalists in New England, whose political fortunes had been flagging,

now regained their voice, rallying against Jefferson and his "dambargo." As this cartoon (**7.7**) lampooning Jefferson's efforts to avoid foreign conflict suggests, the embargo did not intimidate Britain or France, but it weakened the American economy.

Madison's Travails: Diplomatic Blunders Abroad and Tensions on the Frontier

The presidential election of 1808 marked the first time that Republicans split over who should lead them. James Madison, who had been Jefferson's closest advisor during the turbulent 1790s, was Jefferson's choice. Quiet, almost scholarly in temperament, Madison had impressive accomplishments. He had been an architect of the Constitution, had drafted the Bill of Rights, and had served as Jefferson's secretary of state. Other choices were former Anti-Federalists George Clinton and James Monroe.

7.7 *Intercourse or Impartial Dealings* Jefferson stands helpless, caught between King George III and Napoleon.

searching and seizing American vessels in neutral waters. However, the British government repudiated the generous terms negotiated by the British ambassador, dashing hopes for peace.

Frustrated by the diplomatic impasse, Congress sought another solution to the problem. A House select committee headed by Nathaniel Macon proposed to provide much-needed customs revenue by allowing British and French goods back into American harbors if they were transported on American ships. Although the measure failed, a second proposal, Macon's Bill No. 2, did pass. The most important provision of Macon's Bill No. 2 stipulated that when either Britain or France repealed its restrictions on neutral trade, America would reinstate sanctions against the other nation. Seizing on this law, Napoleon promised that France would honor the rights of neutrals.

Napoleon, who had little intention of keeping his word, thus used Macon's bill to drive a wedge between the United States and Britain. The British pointed out that Napoleon's promise was hardly sufficient proof to meet the terms set by Macon Bill No. 2 to lift commercial sanctions. Britain complained that America's new posture toward France and continuing hostility to Britain were not justified. Rather than provide a means to normalize relations with both France and Britain, American policy heightened tensions with Britain.

The repeated violation of their neutrality was not the only American grievance against Britain. As American settlers streamed into the new state of Ohio (1803) and the Indiana Territory, many of them blamed the British for instigating Indians to attack them. Britain's lucrative trade with these Indians included the sale of firearms, and these weapons proved especially useful to Tecumseh, whose pan-Indian resistance movement was gathering followers as Indians faced further encroachments on their land. Although Tecumseh's brother, the Prophet, exhorted his followers to reject all aspects of white civilization, European military technology proved too useful to abandon. Tecumseh worked to convince various tribes to unite to oppose further American expansion.

Indigenous peoples' resolve to resist Western expansion intensified after a series of treaties

Clinton's candidacy fizzled, but Monroe gained support. Borrowing from a practice begun in 1800, congressmen met in a caucus to decide on a presidential and vice-presidential candidate. The Republican caucus decided that Madison would carry forward Jefferson's mantle.

Jefferson's Embargo Act not only divided Republicans but also strengthened the fortunes of the Federalists in places such as New England, where the economic impact of the embargo hit hardest. The Federalist candidate, Charles Pinckney, received three times as many votes as he had in 1804, doing particularly well in New England. Despite the strong Federalist showing in New England and New York, Madison defeated Pinckney by 122 to 47 electoral votes to become the fourth president of the United States.

Unfortunately for Madison he had inherited a major foreign policy crisis from Jefferson. The embargo had not forced Britain and France to change their policy. The main casualties from this policy had been Southern agriculture and New England commerce. Madison's faith in a peaceful solution received a boost when Britain's ambassador opened talks about ending the embargo. Britain even accepted Madison's insistence that it pay reparations for the *Chesapeake* incident and offered to stop

signed at Fort Wayne (1809), in which the United States wrested three million acres of land from the Delaware and Potawatomi in Indiana. To squash resistance, William Henry Harrison led a military expedition against Tecumseh and his supporters in 1811. Harrison's expedition burned to the ground the village of Tippecanoe, the center of Tecumseh's pan-Indian movement. After this attack Tecumseh entered into a formal alliance with the British, who supplied further arms to the Indians. Confident that their alliance with the British would help defeat American forces, Tecumseh and his allies stepped up attacks on American settlements along the frontier.

The War of 1812

Frustrated by the inability of peaceable coercion to force Britain to respect American rights on the high seas and angered by British support for Tecumseh, Madison began preparations for war. He called Congress into an early session in fall 1811. Republicans dominated Congress but were divided over war against Britain. Many Republicans from the mid-Atlantic, especially New York, were reluctant to take on the most powerful navy in the world. "Old Republicans," the more radical states' rights wing of the Jeffersonian coalition who were particularly strong in Madison's home state of Virginia, feared that war would lead to the creation of a large military establishment and new taxes. Madison drew his strongest support from a group of War Hawks, young Republican congressmen from the South and West who were intensely nationalistic, resented British attacks on American rights, and favored an aggressive policy of expansion into Indian-occupied territory and the annexation of Canada. The two leading War Hawks were Henry Clay, a first-term congressmen from Kentucky, and John C. Calhoun, an up-country South Carolinian educated at Yale.

The House voted to declare war by 79 to 49. The margin in the Senate was 19 to 13. No single pattern accounts for all the votes, but enthusiasm for the war ran high in many parts of America. Regional, economic, and party identities shaped the final vote. British involvement with western Native American tribes, particularly in the supply of guns, angered Westerners. Northeastern Republicans who favored war were motivated by anger against this latest threat to American freedom from British tyranny. They saw a struggle that had begun during

the Revolution and would not end until America was truly free of British power.

Federalists viewed the vote as another example of the Republicans' distorted vision of the world. For Federalists, France, not Britain, was the true enemy. Federalists were unanimously opposed to the war, a sentiment which intensified when they learned that the British had been prepared to yield on some points of contention. Anger over Federalist opposition to war led to violence. One Baltimore Federalist newspaper editor who criticized the war was targeted by a mob of angry Republicans, who attacked his office and destroyed his printing press. His attempt to resume printing after the incident triggered a full-scale riot that plunged the city into chaos and was put down only when the militia was called out. The resulting destruction of property and loss of life were the worst instance of public unrest in the young nation's short history and earned Baltimore the nickname "Mob Town."

The war pitted the United States against Britain for the second time in less than a half century. As this political cartoon shows (**7.8**), the primary justification for the **War of 1812** was Britain's violation of American neutrality and seizure of American sailors. In the cartoon, Columbia, the symbol of America, reminds France and Britain that they must respect free trade and seamen's rights or face retribution. The other issue, British support for Indian attacks on frontier settlements, also galvanized popular support for the war effort, particularly in the West. For a better understanding of the division over entering the war, see *Competing Visions: War Hawks and Their Critics.*

7.8 *Columbia Teaches John Bull His New Lesson* Columbia, depicted as the goddess of liberty, stands before other symbols of the new American nation, including an eagle and a shield bearing the stars and stripes of the American flag. She warns France's Napoleon and Britain's John Bull to respect American rights.

Competing Visions
WAR HAWKS AND THEIR CRITICS

Americans were deeply divided over the War of 1812. In the Southwest support for the war was motivated by concern over Britain's Indian policy. Representative Felix Grundy, a prominent War Hawk from Tennessee, charged that the British had instigated Indian violence against Americans. Indians killed three of Grundy's brothers in the conflict along the frontier. By contrast, the sharp-tongued, Virginian conservative John Randolph, a prominent "Old Republican" became a vocal critic of the war. Fiercely independent, Randolph dismissed Grundy's suggestion of an Indian–British conspiracy, instead putting the blame for Western conflicts squarely on the settlers who violated Indian land claims. How did Grundy's experiences as a Westerner color his decision to support war? Was Randolph's response likely to attract political support (why or why not)? Why would Randolph opt to frame his opposition in these terms?

In this impassioned speech, Felix Grundy accused the British of arming and inciting American Indians to take up arms against Americans.

"It cannot be believed, by any man who will reflect, that the savage tribes, uninfluenced by other powers, would think of making war on the United States. They understand too well their own weakness and our strength. They have already felt the weight of our arms; they know they hold the very soil on which they live as tenants in sufferance. How, then, sir are we to account for their late conduct? In one way only; some powerful nation must have intrigued with them, and turned their peaceful dispositions towards us into hostilities. Great Britain alone has intercourse with those Northern Tribes."

John Randolph's response to Grundy dismissed the notion of a conspiracy. The source of conflict along America's frontier, Randolph argued, was the greed of Westerners who encroached on Indian lands.

Session after session, their table had been piled up with Indian treaties, for which the appropriations has been voted as a matter of course, without examination. Advantage had been taken of the spirit of the Indians, broken by the war which ended in the treaty of Greenville [1795]. Under the ascendancy then acquired over them, they had been pent up by subsequent treaties into nooks, straightened in their quarters by a blind cupidity seeking to extinguish their title to immense wilderness, for which (possessing, as we do already, more land than we can sell or use) we shall not have occasion for half a century to come. It was our own thirst for territory, our own want of moderation, that had driven these sons of nature to desperation."

A Scene on the Frontiers as Practiced by the "Humane" British and Their "Worthy" Allies

Read the **Document** *Pennsylvania Gazette*, "Indian Hostilities" *(1812)*

Why did Westerners believe that the British were encouraging Indian violence against Americans?

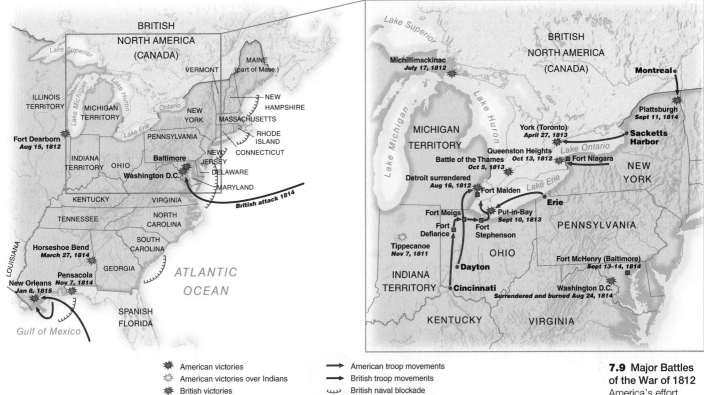

American victories
American victories over Indians
British victories
Forts

American troop movements
British troop movements
British naval blockade

7.9 Major Battles of the War of 1812 America's effort to seize Canada failed, but some of the fiercest fighting occurred along this northern frontier.

Rather than challenge Britain on the high seas, the American war effort concentrated on Canada (**7.9**). Attacking the British in Canada appealed to the War Hawks. Canada was poorly defended, and Americans mistakenly believed that Quebec's large French-speaking population would eagerly join Americans to expel the British from Canada. Seizing Canada would also deprive Tecumseh of his primary source of arms. Given the power of the British Empire, particularly its naval superiority, the focus on conquering Canada, or at least holding it hostage to force Britain to respect neutral rights on the high seas, seemed a promising strategy.

American efforts to wrest Canada from Britain, however, failed miserably as British troops beat back incursions into Canada along the U.S. border. The British also harassed America's coastal settlements and blockaded its ports. In the most audacious move of the war, in August 1814, the British captured Washington, D.C., and burned the capital. The British assault forced President Madison and his wife Dolley to flee. British troops feasted on an elegant dinner that had been set out for the president and his wife and took many items from the executive mansion,

including Madison's medicine chest, which the British government returned 125 years later to President Franklin Roosevelt.

The British next bombarded but failed to take Fort McHenry in Baltimore harbor. An eyewitness to the attack, Francis Scott Key, composed a patriotic poem, "The Star Spangled Banner," that became America's national anthem in the 1930s. Although the American navy was no match for the British Navy in the Atlantic, it did defeat the British on the Great Lakes, at Put-in-Bay and Niagara Falls. While diplomatic efforts to end the war intensified, the British suffered a crushing defeat when they assaulted New Orleans in January 1815. Andrew Jackson, the American commander at New Orleans, led a mixture of regular troops, militia, free blacks, and a few Indians. Jackson even accepted help from French pirates. The victory made him a national hero celebrated in ballads such as the *Hunters of Kentucky*. "Old Hickory" (Jackson's nickname) became a symbol of steadfastness and bravery. Newspapers proclaimed the victory a symbol of the "Rising Glory of the American Republic."

Neither side in this battle knew that the two nations had already signed a peace treaty. It took two weeks for word of peace to reach Louisiana,

> ### "Nothing was adjusted, nothing was settled—nothing in substance but an indefinite suspension of hostilities was agreed to."
>
> JOHN QUINCY ADAMS, describing the Treaty of Ghent (1815)

arriving after the battle was over. The Treaty of Ghent in 1814, named for the Belgian city where the negotiations were conducted, ended the fighting but failed to settle the long-standing issues between the two nations. Indeed, if judged by the terms of the peace treaty, the War of 1812 accomplished little. The issues at stake at the beginning of the war, including the impressment of American sailors and the rights of neutral trade, remained unresolved. In private, some Americans, including John Quincy Adams, who negotiated the treaty, felt it did little more than end hostilities. The American public generally regarded the war as a victory, calling it the Second War for Independence. At least America had defended its honor, forcing the most powerful nation in the world to treat the new republic with respect, a perception reflected in this painting celebrating the treaty (**7.10**); America, represented by Columbia, reaches out the hand of friendship to Britannia.

While the British and Americans had fought to a draw, the most conspicuous losers in the war were the Indians living along the frontier, who lost an important ally when the British withdrew and were forced to make major land concessions to Americans. Pan-Indian nationalists such as Tecumseh suffered a severe setback at the hands of William Henry Harrison and Andrew Jackson, whose military successes secured the trans-Appalachian frontier, the Western territory beyond the Appalachian Mountains, for settlement.

The Hartford Convention

While many Americans celebrated Jackson's victory over the British at New Orleans, Federalists in New England convened at the **Hartford Convention** in Hartford, Connecticut, to protest the War of 1812. Although some Federalists in New England had flirted with secession, the delegates to the Hartford Convention stopped well short of advocating the breakup of the Union. Although New

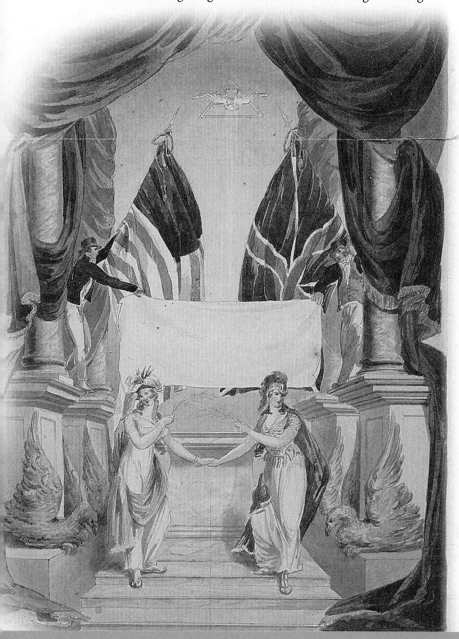

7.10 Treaty of Ghent
In this representation of the peace accord worked out between America and Britain at Ghent, Belgium, Columbia and Britannia hold hands. Two sailors unfurl the flags of their nations, proclaiming a new era of harmony.

What were the main goals of the Hartford Convention?

7.11 The Hartford Convention or Leap, No Leap
In this cartoon George III beckons to Federalists in Massachusetts, Connecticut, and Rhode Island to jump off the cliff and join him, promising them "titles, nobility," and other rewards for abandoning their fellow states.

England Federalists had denounced the radical states' rights ideas that Jeffersonians had espoused in response to the Alien and Sedition Crisis in 1798, they now echoed many of those ideas. The convention delegates proposed constitutional amendments that would strengthen New England's influence in the Union. In particular, they sought to require a two-thirds majority for commercial regulations, declarations of war, and the admission of new states. To weaken the South's influence in Congress, the Hartford Convention also called for a repeal of the three-fifths compromise, which allowed Southerners to count a percentage of their slaves for the purposes of determining a state's representation in the House. The Hartford Convention's proposals were publicized at the same time as news of the Treaty of Ghent and the victory at New Orleans were fueling a new sense of national pride. In this political cartoon ridiculing the Hartford Convention (**7.11**), leading New England Federalists appear ready to leap off a cliff into the welcoming arms of Britain's king. Federalists' narrow sectionalism appeared out of step with the public's new patriotic fervor. Even in their New England stronghold, Federalists saw themselves irreparably damaged as a movement. The War of 1812 facilitated the demise of the Federalists as a viable political organization.

How are the actions of New England states represented in the political cartoon on the Hartford Convention above?

The Republic Reborn: Consequences of the War of 1812

The War of 1812 transformed America, its politics, economy, society, and relations with other nations. The postwar era inaugurated a period of nationalism that was evidenced in diplomacy, economic policy, and law. There was broad popular support for a stronger central government, one capable of dealing with foreign challenges and spurring domestic economic growth. Thus the partisan squabbling of the Jeffersonian era gave way to the necessities of fighting a war. These realities forced leading politicians to unite the best aspects of Jeffersonian politics with Hamiltonian economics. John Quincy Adams, secretary of state under James Monroe, proved to be an effective diplomat, skillfully negotiating important treaties for the United States. The demands of the wartime economy not only spurred economic and technological innovation but also increased demand for manufactured goods, such as firearms and textiles for uniforms. The new nationalist ethos and a more sympathetic attitude toward economic development were evidenced in the decisions of the Supreme Court after the war.

The National Republican Vision of James Monroe

The war radically transformed Republican political and constitutional ideas. In his annual message to Congress in 1815, the first after the Treaty of Ghent, Madison suggested that the nation expand the size of its military and reaffirmed his support for a national bank and for protective tariffs for American industry. Seeking to push beyond this nationalist agenda, Madison floated the idea of chartering a national university and even considered amending the Constitution to give the federal government the power to promote internal improvements such as roads and canals. Madison clung to one traditional republican idea. He believed that to exercise such powers required a constitutional amendment. Although on this one point of constitutional theory Madison reasserted the traditional Republican view of the limited scope of federal

power, as a practical matter he had aligned himself with much of the old Hamiltonian agenda. Indeed, John Quincy Adams, son of the former president and a staunch Federalist, believed that Madison and "the Republicans had out-Federalized Federalism."

The collapse of Federalists after the War of 1812 led to a shift away from the rancor that had characterized politics during the Jeffersonian era. Following Madison as president, James Monroe sought to unite the political ideals of Jeffersonianism with aspects of Hamiltonian economic theory. For a brief period he managed to create an administration free of the partisan divisions that had characterized American politics since Washington's second term. As a gesture toward nonpartisan politics, the Republican Monroe named the brilliant Federalist John Quincy Adams as his secretary of state and appointed men from different regions to heal old sectional tensions. He also took a lesson from Washington, the other president who seemed most successful at rising above party, and embarked on a goodwill tour of the nation. Monroe began his tour in Boston, a city with strong Federalist sympathies. Praising the gesture, a Boston newspaper proclaimed an **Era of Good Feelings** to describe the absence of bitter partisan conflict during Monroe's presidency. Monroe also restored luster to the presidency. He became noted for his stylish entertaining in the executive mansion. To repair the smoke damage to the executive mansion (**7.12**), a result of the British

7.12 *A View of the President's House in the City of Washington after the Conflagration of the 24th of August, 1814* Repairs to the damaged executive mansion included a new coat of white paint. The residence became known as "the White House."

Why was Monroe's presidency described as an "Era of Good Feelings"?

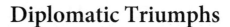

attack on Washington during the War of 1812, Monroe had its exterior painted a brilliant white. The official residence of the President of the United States has been known as the White House ever since.

Monroe not only sought to reconcile Federalist and Jeffersonian ideals. He also served as a bridge between the political cultures of two different centuries, the eighteenth and nineteenth. Monroe was the last president with ties to the generation that fought the Revolution and wrote the Constitution. His roots in the eighteenth century appear in the clothes he wore at his inauguration. Most men had abandoned their wigs and replaced breeches and silk stockings with trousers. But Monroe retained the ideals and dress of eighteenth-century gentility. In this portrait, he wears breeches and silk stockings (**7.13**). If Monroe's personal style and values harked back to the eighteenth century, many of his policies as president reflected newer ideas including the idea that it was vital to encourage the expansion of the nation's "domestic market" encouraging "an active intercourse between the extremes and throughout every portion of our Union." One aging Federalist remarked that "the Party in Power seems disposed to do all that federal men ever wished."

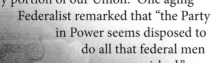

Diplomatic Triumphs

After the war, Secretary of State John Quincy Adams resolved outstanding border disputes with Britain. In the Rush-Bagot Treaty of 1817, the United States and Britain limited naval armaments on the Great Lakes. An accord reached the following year set the new boundary between the Louisiana Territory and Canada at the 49th parallel. The British also recognized American fishing rights off Labrador and Newfoundland, and America and Britain agreed to continue to occupy jointly the Oregon Territory in the Pacific Northwest. These diplomatic successes effectively normalized U.S.-Canadian relations and created a peaceful border between the two countries that has persisted for more than 200 years.

Adams was now free to address the southern boundary disputes with Spain. America had long been eager to wrest Florida from Spain. In March 1818, Andrew Jackson led a raid into Spanish Florida to attack the Seminoles. Under the pretext of protecting American settlements against Indian attack, he captured two Spanish forts, thereby further weakening Spain's bargaining position. Rather than risk war, Spain ceded all claims to Florida and recognized U.S. sovereignty in Louisiana in the Adams-Onis Treaty of 1819.

Spain's empire in the Americas had been crumbling for two decades. In 1811, Paraguay and Venezuela declared independence from Spain. In 1818, Chile declared its independence, and Peru followed suit in 1821. Building on the goodwill generated by the resolution of the northern boundary issue between the United States and Canada, Britain's foreign minister suggested in 1823 that the United States and Britain issue a declaration that neither intended to annex the newly liberated states in Spanish America. Although Monroe was tempted to accept the British offer, Adams advised against it, and Monroe followed his advice. In his annual message to Congress in 1823, he presented a general policy for Spanish America. This statement, the **Monroe Doctrine**, reiterated the policy outlined in Washington's Farewell Address that America would not meddle in European affairs. It also warned European powers that the United States would view intervention in the affairs of the newly independent states of Spanish Americas as a threat to its security.

7.13 Portrait of President James Monroe
This image captures Monroe's role as a transitional figure between the eighteenth-century world of the Founders and a new era in American politics. He appears without the wigs favored by eighteenth-century gentlemen, but his silk stockings and knee breeches reflected the fashions of the founding generation.

Read the **Document** *Monroe Doctrine (1823)*

What were the major ideas associated with the Monroe Doctrine?

Economic and Technological Innovation

The War of 1812 not only led to a renewed political commitment to economic development but also spurred a remarkable period of technological development. America's embargo against foreign goods and the demands of the wartime economy provided incentives for economic innovation. Firearms production was improved, steam engines powered new modes of transportation, and new agricultural technology led to a boom in cotton production. Artist and inventor Samuel Morse captured the age's search for political consensus and fascination with technology in his painting of the House of Representatives. See *Images as History: Samuel Morse's* House of Representatives *and the National Republican Vision*.

Not surprisingly the war spurred innovation in the production of firearms. The federal arsenals at Springfield, Massachusetts, and Harpers Ferry, Virginia, played a pivotal role in advancing these developments. Indeed, by the mid-1820s, Harper's Ferry had pioneered a mass production technique for manufacturing firearms. In place of older artisan methods, in which master craftsmen handcrafted items for production, the system used new power machinery to cut and shape standardized parts. By 1820, John H. Hall had perfected the manufacturing techniques for "fabricating arms exactly alike and with economy by the hands of common workmen." Hall began producing a new breech-loading rifle, an improvement over the traditional muzzle-loading muskets.

A simple, but far-reaching technological improvement in agricultural production transformed the American economy. The **cotton gin**, an invention by Eli Whitney, an industrious Connecticut Yankee working as a tutor on a Southern plantation, easily removed the seeds that adhered tenaciously to short staple cotton, a hearty plant well suited to Southern climate and soil. Whitney's cotton gin revolutionized cotton agriculture. Before his invention, an adult slave needed a whole day to clean a single pound of cotton. Whitney's cotton gin allowed a single slave to clean 50 pounds of cotton a day. In 1790, the South produced 3,000 bales of cotton. By 1810, the cotton gin facilitated the production of 178,000 bales. (Each bale weighed approximately 480 pounds.) Immediately after the War of 1812, cotton production almost doubled again to 334,000 bales. Cotton would provide huge new economic incentives for slave-based agriculture by making it much cheaper to produce cotton for market.

Although cotton exports to Britain consumed much of this new cash crop, some of the cotton was purchased for domestic textile manufacturing. In 1793, Samuel Slater established a mechanized spinning factory in Pawtucket, Rhode Island. His mill was a relatively modest structure whose size and architectural style fit the scale of a small New England village. The first mills depended on water power and took advantage of natural waterfalls to power water wheels (**7.14**). Slater pioneered the mill village model of

7.14 Slater Mill
The earliest factories were not imposing structures belching forth smoke, but small water-powered mills. Slater's first water-powered mill resembled the clapboard wooden structures that had been used to grind grain or saw logs and that easily blended into their rural settings.

View the **Closer Look** *Images as History: Samuel Morse's* House of Representatives *and the National Republican Vision*

What was the economic significance of Whitney's cotton gin?

Images as History
SAMUEL MORSE'S *HOUSE OF REPRESENTATIVES* AND THE NATIONAL REPUBLICAN VISION

In 1819 Samuel Morse began his ambitious painting of the House of Representatives. The painting not only reflected the political ideas of the Era of Good Feelings, it projected a nationalist vision of America's bright future. How did Morse's emphasis on architectural grandeur convey the values of Monroe and Nationalist Republican belief?

Although the crowded chamber bustles with activity, Morse presented a scene of cordiality and harmony. The painting captures the time before formal political business began, a decision that allowed Morse to create a scene free of conflict or tension.

Morse chose a rare evening session of the House to illustrate. This decision allowed him to further shift the focus away from the actions of politicians. Occupying the dramatic center of the painting is the House of Representative's doorkeeper, who is lighting a large chandelier to illuminate the evening's activities. The painting thus pays tribute to America's technological progress. It links America's political institutions symbolically to light and progress.

Benjamin Henry Latrobe, the architect responsible for rebuilding the Capitol after the War of 1812, chose multicolored stones for the columns supporting the roof of the House. This particular architectural element became a visual symbol of the idea of federalism, in which the different states, represented by the stones, blended together in a single harmonious republican structure, a classical column.

A number of distinguished guests are in the House chamber, including the entire Supreme Court, and a number of guests occupy the gallery. The inclusion of the Pawnee chief, Petalesharo, signifies America's inevitable subjection of Indians. Morse's painting idealizes a brief moment in American politics that was already on the wane by the time his painting was displayed. Monroe's vision of a National Republican consensus and the "era of good feelings" was being supplanted by rising sectional tensions over slavery and a new era of partisan conflict.

Morse highlighted the multicolored stone columns, which symbolized the ideal of federalism.

The Indian figure in the gallery symbolized Monroe's diplomatic achievements and the inevitable subjugation of America's indigenous population.

Morse focused on the act of lighting the House's impressive chandelier, a symbol of American progress.

Samuel Morse's
The Old House of Representatives

Why did Morse highlight architecture and minimize the people in his painting?

industrial production. Others later adapted his model by creating entirely new mill villages in which the company owned the adjacent farmland and rented it to men whose families worked in the mills. This Rhode Island or "family" model of the mill village was an important economic development in manufacturing.

> "The present moment is every way favorable to the establishment of a great national policy and of great national institutions, in respect to the army, the navy, the judicial, [and] the commercial … interests of the country."
>
> Justice JOSEPH STORY [1816]

Judicial Nationalism

No figure captured the new nationalist spirit more fully than the young Supreme Court Justice Joseph Story. A brilliant lawyer, Story was only 32 when James Madison appointed him to the Court. Madison hoped that Story, an anti-embargo Republican from Massachusetts, would check the nationalism of Chief Justice John Marshall. Madison would not be the last president to be shocked and disappointed by one of his Supreme Court appointments. Story proved to be as nationalistic as Marshall. Story's decisions on the court supported the power of the federal judiciary and limited that of the states. In landmark decisions, Marshall and Story helped strengthen the federal government and the courts and paved the way for economic growth.

The most famous case dealing with federalism was *McCulloch v. Maryland.* The case arose when the state of Maryland levied a tax on the Baltimore branch of the Second Bank of the United States. Most Republicans had made their peace with the idea of a bank, but some continued to resent this highly visible symbol of Hamiltonian federalism. Marshall declared the Maryland state tax unconstitutional and affirmed an essentially Hamiltonian view of the powers of the federal government. According to Marshall the federal government enjoyed broad powers under the

"necessary and proper" clauses of the Constitution, which allowed it to charter a bank. Marshall further argued that the power to tax was also the power to destroy and allowing the state to tax a federally chartered institution would have allowed Maryland to undermine an act of the federal government. While Marshall conceded that the powers of the federal government were not unlimited, he affirmed that within its sphere of authority it enjoyed enormous latitude to accomplish any legitimate constitutional objective. In contrast to many Republicans who accepted the Jeffersonian idea that individual states could judge the constitutionality of federal acts, the Marshall Court insisted that only the Supreme Court could determine when the federal government had exceeded its authority.

No other decision rendered by the Court generated so much controversy as that of *McCulloch v. Maryland.* For radical opponents of the Marshall Court, *McCulloch* seemed to realize the Anti-Federalists' most dire predictions. Anger over *McCulloch* led many Republicans, particularly in the South, to develop a more aggressive version of states' rights. They challenged the authority of the Supreme Court to decide arguments between the states and the federal government. For nationalists such as Marshall and Story, however, the creation of a more powerful central government was essential to the survival of the United States.

The Marshall Court also decided cases dealing with the law and the economy. One of the most important cases dealing with economic development also expanded the scope of federal power over commerce. In *Gibbons v. Ogden* (1824), a case involving steamboats, the Court grappled with the scope of federal powers over interstate commerce. In that case Marshall construed the word *commerce* broadly to encompass "every species of commercial intercourse." The Court also held that federal power over interstate commerce did not end at the borders of each state, but extended within states when that commerce was intermingled with economic activity that crossed state lines. Although in the nineteenth century the federal government did not exploit its power over interstate commerce to the fullest, the power to regulate interstate commerce is currently one of the most far-reaching possessed by the federal government.

Which Marshall Court decisions best illustrate the Court's nationalism?

Crises and the Collapse of the National Republican Consensus

The patriotic sentiments stirred by the War of 1812 and the emergence of a new consensus around a Hamiltonian economic vision contributed to a period of prosperity and optimism. The new consensus, however, proved fragile, and a severe depression soon followed the postwar economic boom. Slavery also vaulted to national attention when Missouri sought admission to the Union as a slave state. The hope that Monroe's creative synthesis of the Jeffersonian and Hamiltonian visions might usher in a new Era of Good Feelings proved short lived as economic and political crises again divided the nation.

The Panic of 1819

Economic expansion, in part driven by the demand for cotton, led to a growth in the financial sector of the American economy. States chartered new banks, so that the number of banks doubled between 1815 and 1818, from just over 200 to more than 400. In 1816, Congress chartered a Second Bank of the United States, which further fueled economic expansion and land speculation. Between 1815 and 1818, land sales more than tripled.

However, the price of cotton and other agricultural products exported by America dropped in 1819, leading to a severe economic downturn that affected nearly every aspect of the American economy. Since much of the expansion in credit by American banks was tied to agricultural production, the crisis spread to financial institutions. The value of land purchased on credit dropped sharply, and when these loans came due, speculators were unable to repay the banks that had loaned them the money to buy these properties. The American economy, now heavily dependent on cotton, sank into depression. As speculators defaulted on their obligations, banks collapsed. Nearly every region of the country was affected. The **Panic of 1819**, the economic crisis triggered by the drop in agricultural prices and bank failures, produced unprecedented economic hardship. While the sudden downturn in the economy hurt Western land speculators and cotton producers in the Deep South, it also devastated the growing urban centers of the Northeast. In Philadelphia three out of four workers

lost their jobs. In New York the number of people classified as paupers increased from 8,000 to 13,000 in a year.

The Missouri Crisis

The economic downturn was soon overshadowed by another crisis. In 1819, Missouri applied for admission to the Union as a slave state. Congressman John Tallmadge from New York demanded that Missouri ban further imports of slaves and agree to eliminate slavery before joining. Public meetings across the Northeast protested Missouri's proposed admission as a slave state. Slavery now came to the center of American politics.

> "Agricultural languishes—farmers cannot find profit in hiring labourers ... mechanics are in want of employment"
>
> JAMES FLINT, comments on the Panic of 1819 in Letters from America (1822)

The growth of cotton agriculture and the prospect of large swathes of territory in the West entering the Union as slave states prompted a political crisis. Whereas Northern congressmen denounced slavery as a violation of the ideals of the Declaration of Independence and the Constitution, Southerners defended the institution, invoking the

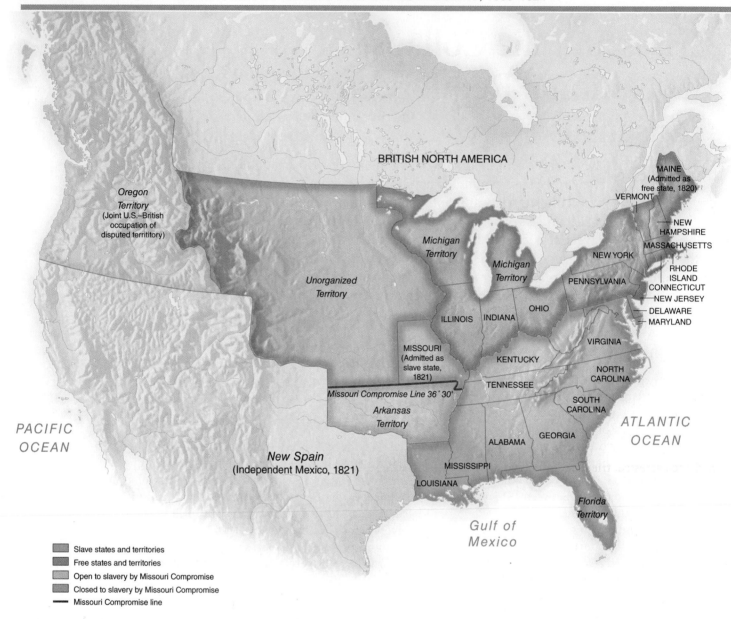

7.15 The Missouri Compromise
The Missouri Compromise established a new policy for dealing with slavery in Western territories. The compromise drew an imaginary line across the map of the United States. Land south of this line acquired during the Louisiana purchase would be open to slavery, whereas territory north of it would be free.

language of the Virginia and Kentucky resolutions to support the right of the states to decide the slavery question. A Georgia congressman warned that Tallmadge had "kindled a fire which all the waters of the ocean cannot put out, which seas of blood can only extinguish." The New Yorker's amendment passed the House, where the Northeast enjoyed a significant majority, but was defeated in the Senate, where the North and South were more closely balanced.

To avert a constitutional crisis, Congress worked out a compromise. Henry Clay, one of the most influential figures in Congress, was a key player in negotiating this solution. The **Missouri Compromise** called for the admission of Missouri as a slave state. Maine, which had been part of Massachusetts but had been seeking independence for some time, entered as a free state, thus preserving the balance between free states and slave states in the Senate. The Missouri

Compromise drew an imaginary line across the territory acquired through the Louisiana Purchase at 36° 30′ latitude (**7.15**). Land below this imaginary dividing line would be slave territory; land above it would be free. Thomas Jefferson wrote to a friend that the crisis struck him as a "fire bell in the night." Being awakened from a sound sleep by a fire alarm, the metaphor chosen by Jefferson, evoked the magnitude of the Missouri crisis. For Jefferson the Missouri crisis had etched the issue of slavery onto the map of the United States and would make any resolution of it in the future impossible. The debate over Missouri prompted John Quincy Adams to write in his diary that "Slavery is the great and foul stain upon the North American Union." For the moment, however, most politicians seemed unwilling to contemplate erasing the great stain.

Denmark Vesey's Rebellion

The problem of slavery resurfaced in summer 1822. Newspapers from Charleston to Boston and as far west as the Illinois Territory carried the sensational story of Denmark Vesey, a free African American artisan from Charleston, South Carolina, who had been arrested, tried, and executed for—so the charges went—leading a slave insurrection.

A talented and charismatic man, Vesey had won a lottery jackpot in 1799 and used his earnings to purchase his freedom and set up a small carpentry shop. A natural leader, he became a prominent member of an African American church that became an important meeting place for free blacks and slaves. Rumors of a slave revolt led authorities to arrest him and charge him with plotting an insurrection, the so-called **Denmark Vesey Uprising**, said to have been aimed to free slaves in Charleston by violence. Modern historians differ over how to interpret the evidence that was used to convict Vesey and his alleged followers. Some historians deny that Vesey was a revolutionary figure bent on leading an uprising and see him instead as an unfortunate victim, a vocal free black leader who became a scapegoat for paranoid Charleston whites ever fearful of slave insurrection. Others believe that there was a plot, although its scope remains uncertain. Whether the proposed insurrection was real or imagined, the evidence gathered to convict Vesey provides a window into the way whites perceived slave culture in the Charleston region.

According to the trial records, urban slaves and free blacks conspired with the many slaves who worked on the plantations surrounding Charleston. The rebels, the records suggest, were poised to take advantage of the mobility enjoyed by African Americans in this region, an area in which travel was less restricted than in other parts of the South. Charleston's slaves were often hired out by their masters and often traveled without direct supervision. The task system employed by Carolina plantation owners also provided slaves with considerable autonomy and mobility. After finishing their day's tasks, slaves could work their own small plots of land, hunt, or fish. Slaves not only used this surplus food to supplement their

"I went up to the Capitol and heard Mr. King in the Senate, upon what is called the Missouri question. . . . He laid down the position of the natural liberty of man, and its incompatibility with slavery in any shape. He also questioned the Constitutional right of the President and Senate to make the Louisiana Treaty . . . .[later] We attended an evening party at Mr. Calhoun's, and heard of nothing but the Missouri question and Mr. King's speeches. The slave-holders cannot hear of them without being seized with cramps. They call them seditious and inflammatory, when their greatest real defect is their timidity."

JOHN QUINCY ADAMS, Reflections on the Missouri Question (1820)

Read the **Document** An Account of the Late Intended Insurrection Among a Portion of the Blacks of this City (*1822*)

How did the Missouri crisis contribute to the climate of fear in Charleston during the Vesey trial?

meager rations but also often sold it in Charleston's markets. The ease of travel facilitated communication between slaves and freedmen. Free black churches provided places for African Americans, both slaves and free blacks, to discuss ideas, including perhaps revolution. The prosecution claimed that Vesey, an active member of Charleston's African Methodist Episcopal Church, had used the church as a place to recruit others to his cause. The alleged insurrection was planned for the summer, when many whites left the city for cooler climates.

If Vesey's plan was real and not invented by his prosecutors, his conception was a bold one. After seizing the city arsenal, Vesey and his followers allegedly planned to burn the city and sail to Haiti. (In 1804, Saint Domingue became the independent country of Haiti.) The Caribbean island's own revolutionary experience might have inspired Vesey, who saw the Haitian uprising as a model for toppling slavery in America. When

South Carolina's governor heard about the plot, he ordered out the militia. The authorities arrested Vesey and others alleged to have been engaged in his conspiracy. The trial record portrays Vesey as an articulate man, well aware of the recent debates over the Missouri Compromise, including the speeches of antislavery congressmen from New England. The rise of abolitionist sentiment in the North was a sign that the time for revolution was ripe. The plot that emerges from the evidence presented at the trial also demonstrates the persistence of African religious and cultural traditions among both free blacks and slaves. One of Vesey's chief co-conspirators, for example, a slave named Gullah Jack, had a reputation as a conjurer who would provide Vesey's followers with magical charms to protect them from harm. There is also evidence that African American culture had developed its own distinctive approach to Christianity. African Christianity highlighted themes taken from the

		(S.)	
		CLASS No. 1.	
	Comprises those prisoners who were found guilty and executed.		
Prisoners' Names.	**Owners' Names.**	**Time of Commit.**	**How disposed of.**
Peter	James Poyas	June 18	Hanged on Tuesday the 2d July, 1822, on Blake's lands near Charleston.
Ned	Gov. T. Bennett	do.	
Rolla	do.	do.	
Batteau	do.	do	
Denmark Vesey	A free black man	22	
Jessy	Thos. Blackwood	23	
John	Elias Horry	July 5	Do. on the Lines near Ch.; Friday, [July 12.
Gullah Jack	Paul Pritchard	do	
Mingo	William Harth	June 21	
Lot	Forrester	27	
Joe	P. L. Jore	July 6	
Julius	Thos. Forrest	8	
Tom	Mrs. Russell	10	
Smart	Robert Anderson	do.	
John	John Robertson	11	
Robert	do.	do.	
Adam	do.	do.	
Polydore	Mrs. Faber	do.	Hanged on the Lines near Charleston, on Friday, 26th July.
Bacchus	Benj. Hammett	do.	
Dick	William Sims	13	
Pharaoh	— Thompson	do.	
Jemmy	Mrs. Clement	18	
Mauidore	Mordecai Cohen	19	
Dean	— Mitchell	do.	
Jack	Mrs. Purcell	12	
Bellisle	Est. of Jos. Yates	18	
Naphur	do.	do.	
Adam	do.	do.	
Jacob	John S. Glen	16	
Charles	John Billings	18	
Jack	N. M'Neill	22	
Cæsar	Miss Smith	do.	Do. Tues. July 30.
Jacob Stagg	Jacob Lankester	23	
Tom	Wm. M. Scott	24	
William	Mrs. Garner	Aug. 2	Do. Friday, Aug. 9.

7.16 List of people executed as listed in published trial record

Why did white residents of Charleston blame northerners for the Vesey insurrection?

View the **Map** *Interactive Map: Missouri Compromise 1820–1821*

plight of the ancient Israelites. Thus Vesey was said to have reminded his followers that God had delivered the children of Israel out of bondage in Egypt and would surely deliver slaves to freedom now.

As this page from the published trial records shows, (**7.16**), Charleston's authorities sent 34 blacks, including Vesey, to the gallows. For the Charleston white elite who prosecuted Vesey, one lesson of the trial was that "the indiscreet zeal in favor of universal liberty, expressed by many of our fellow-citizens in the States north and east of Maryland; aided by the Black population of those States" threatened the institution of slavery. The sectional tensions caused by slavery and the growing animosity between Northern abolitionists, black and white, and Southern defenders of slavery would only turn more bitter.

Jeffersonian America and the Politics of Compromise

Jefferson's election in 1800 ushered in a new era in American politics. Although Jefferson did not usher in a revolution, he did scale back the size of government. By shrinking the government, Jefferson effectively eliminated the threat posed by Hamilton's fiscal and military programs, but without having to repudiate all the accomplishments of the two previous administrations. Indeed, Jefferson discovered that he could put a powerful federal government to good Republican use. The purchase of Louisiana was difficult to reconcile with Jefferson's own theory of strict construction, but Jefferson put his constitutional scruples aside to make the purchase.

By the time James Madison became president, leading Republicans had adopted much of the Hamiltonian economic agenda. America's difficult experiences during the War of 1812 seemed to underscore the wisdom of many of Hamilton's proposals. The next president, James Monroe, took these lessons to heart; his administration sought a nonpartisan synthesis of Jeffersonian and Hamiltonian values. The press hailed Monroe's presidency as an Era of Good Feelings, a time in which partisan rancor gave way to consensus and a new wave of nationalism. This brief respite from partisanship proved short-lived, however. Within a decade, partisan divisions resurfaced and laid the foundation of a new two-party system.

If there were conspicuous losers in the Jeffersonian era it was American Indians and slaves. The former faced a more powerful and well-organized American government eager to expand westward. The War of 1812 had a disastrous impact on Western tribes, who lost an important ally, Britain, in their struggles against the United States. Finally the cotton boom and introduction of land well suited to cotton agriculture meant that the institution of slavery became stronger. The issue of slavery, particularly its expansion, would play an increasingly important role in American public life. The Missouri Compromise demonstrated the potentially divisive nature of the issue of slavery. For the moment, American politics had resolved this crisis, but rather than diffuse this problem, slavery would remain a potentially explosive issue in American politics.

"The cession of that kind of property [slaves] ... would not cost me a second thought; if in that way, a general emancipation and expatriation could be effected.... But, as it is, we have the wolf by the ears, and we can neither hold him, nor safely let him go. Justice is in one scale, and self-preservation is in the other."
THOMAS JEFFERSON to JOHN HOLMES, 1820

What were some of the main political compromises of the Jeffersonian era?

1800–1802

Jefferson elected president
Peaceful transfer of power from
Federalists to Republicans

Sally Hemings scandal
Jefferson is accused of having a
slave mistress

1803

Louisiana Purchase
Jefferson acquires Louisiana
Territory, doubling the size of
the nation

Marbury v. Madison
John Marshall asserts power
of Supreme Court to decide
constitutionality of acts of Congress
(judicial review)

1804

Burr and Hamilton duel
Vice President Burr kills opponent
Alexander Hamilton in a duel

1807

Embargo Act
Jefferson adopts a policy of
peaceful coercion and institutes
an embargo

CHAPTER REVIEW

Review Questions

1. What role did honor play in the political culture of
   the new nation?

2. Why was Jefferson ridiculed as the mammoth of
   democracy?

3. Which features of Jefferson's domestic policy
   agenda were the most successful and why?

4. What were the main causes of the War of
   1812? What were its most important economic
   consequences?

5. What was the "Era of Good Feelings"?

Key Terms

Louisiana Purchase The acquisition by the United States of
the Louisiana Territory from France in 1803, thereby securing
control of the Mississippi River and nearly doubling the size of
the nation.   **195**

Embargo Act of 1807 The cornerstone of Jefferson's plan
of peaceable coercion that attempted to block U.S. trade
with England and France to force them to respect American
neutrality.   **201**

War of 1812 The war fought between Britain and America over
restrictions on American trade. British trade with American
Indians, particularly trade in weapons, was also an issue.   **203**

Hartford Convention A meeting of Federalists in Hartford,
Connecticut, to protest the War of 1812. The convention proposed
several constitutional amendments intended to weaken the powers
of the slave states and protect New England interests.   **206**

Era of Good Feelings A term that the press coined to describe
the absence of bitter partisan conflict during the presidency of
James Monroe.   **208**

Monroe Doctrine A foreign policy statement by President
Monroe declaring that the Americas were no longer open to
colonization and that the United States would view any effort
to reassert colonial control over independent nations in the
Western Hemisphere as a threat to America.   **209**

Cotton gin Eli Whitney's invention for removing seeds from
cotton.   **210**

Panic of 1819 A downturn in the American economy in 1819 that
plunged the nation into depression and economic hardship.   **213**

Missouri Compromise The congressional compromise in
which Missouri entered the Union as a slave state, and Maine
was admitted as a free state to preserve the balance of slave and
free states in Congress. The law also drew an imaginary line at
36° 30′ through the Louisiana Territory. Slavery was prohibited
north of this line.   **214**

Denmark Vesey Uprising An alleged plot led by a free black
man, Denmark Vesey, to free slaves in Charleston and kill their
masters.   **215**

1812

War of 1812
United States and Britain go to war

1814–1815

Treaty of Ghent
Britain and America sign a treaty ending the War of 1812

Battle of New Orleans
Andrew Jackson and his troops defeat the British at Battle of New Orleans

1816

James Monroe elected president
Monroe inaugurates the "Era of Good Feelings"

1819–1822

Missouri Compromise
Settles the issue of slavery in the territories by drawing an imaginary line across the map of the United States and creating a permanent division between slave and free territory

Denmark Vesey charged with plotting an uprising
Slaves and free blacks in Charleston, S.C., are captured, charged with plotting an insurrection, tried, and executed

MyHistoryLab Connections

Visit www.myhistorylab.com for a customized Study Plan that will help you build your knowledge of *Jeffersonian America*.

Questions for Analysis

1. **Was Jefferson successful at implementing his vision of government?**

   Read the **Document** *Jefferson's First Inaugural Address, p. 190*

2. **What role did the Louisana purchase play in Jefferson's vision for the future?**

   Watch the **Video** *Video Lecture: Lewis and Clark: What were they trying to accomplish?, p. 198*

3. **What was the Monroe Doctrine?**

   Read the **Document** *Monroe Doctrine (1823), p. 209*

4. **How did the rise of cotton agriculture help precipitate the Missouri Crisis?**

   View the **Map** *Interactive Map: Missouri Compromise 1820–1821, p. 216*

5. **What does the Denmark Vesey conspiracy trial reveal about the growing tensions over slavery in American politics?**

   Read the **Document** An Account of the Late Intended Insurrection Among a Portion of the Blacks of this City (1822), p. 215

Other Resources from This Chapter

Hear the **Audio File** *Jefferson and Liberty, p. 194*

Read the **Document**

- *Memoirs of a Monticello Slave, p. 193*
- *Thomas Jefferson to John C. Breckinridge, "Constitutionality of the Louisiana Purchase" (1803), p. 195*
- *Marbury v. Madison, p. 196*
- *Jefferson's Confidential Message to Congress (1803), p. 199*
- *Pennsylvania Gazette, "Indian Hostilities" (1812), p. 204*
- *Missouri Act (1820), p. 214*

View the **Closer Look** *Images as History: Samuel Morse's House of Representatives and the National Republican Vision, p. 210*

View the **Image** *British Impressment, p. 202*

View the **Map** *Interactive Map: War of 1812, p. 205*

Democracy in America p. 222

What changes in American society facilitated the rise of democracy?

Andrew Jackson and His Age p. 225

What political and constitutional ideas defined Jackson's presidency?

White Man's Democracy p. 233

How did race shape the nature of democracy in the Jacksonian era?

Democrats, Whigs, and the Second Party System p. 239

Who were the Whigs and what did they believe?

Playing the Democrats' Game: Whigs in the Election of 1840 p. 246

Why did the Whigs win the election of 1840?

Democrats and Whigs
Democracy and American Culture, 1820–1840

George Caleb Bingham's painting, *Stump Speaking or the County Canvass* (1853), captures the drama of a new democratic style of politics that transformed American life starting in the 1820s. The term stump speech referred to politicians' practice in some remote parts of the nation of addressing the electorate by using the nearest tree stump as a rough-hewn platform from which to speak. Bingham, a Whig opponent of the Democratic Party, used the painting to express his reservations about what he considered the dangers posed by too much democracy. Bingham wrote that the politician on the platform in the painting was a "wiry" fellow who had "grown grey in the pursuit of office and the service of his party" and literally bends to the popular will. Across from the speaker, seated amid the crowd, a man in a top hat and light-colored suit listens thoughtfully, refusing to be swayed by the politician's words. Bingham described this figure as an "outstanding citizen" whose noble features not only set him apart from the crowd but also contrast noticeably with the shifty look of the Democratic politician standing at the rostrum. The painting suggests that the "outstanding citizen," a true Whig leader, refuses to pander to the mob.

As this scene reveals, democracy did not yet embrace all Americans; it excluded women, African Americans, and Indians. The crowd Bingham depicts is overwhelmingly male and, apart from a lone African American in the background, all white. Although the white men participate in the political life of the nation, the lone black figure labors on a wagon selling refreshments to the crowd.

No figure better personified this new age than Andrew Jackson, the country's leading Democrat. Jackson's 1828 election changed American politics, forcing his opponents to make more effective use of the tools of democratic politics and the symbols of democracy in their campaigns. Eventually adopting the name, Whig, by 1840 they outdid the Democrats, portraying their candidate William Henry Harrison, as a simple man born in a log cabin who drank hard cider like an ordinary farmer.

Although the Whigs may have learned valuable political lessons from the Democrats about how to campaign, their party steadfastly opposed Jacksonian policies on every major issue of the day. From economic issues to American Indian rights, the two parties offered the American people competing visions and clear choices. Political participation in this period rose as Americans responded to the messages of the two parties and voted in unprecedented numbers.

"American society is essentially and radically a democracy…. In the United States the democratic spirit is infused into all national habits, and all the customs of society."

French traveler MICHAEL CHEVALIER, *Society, Manners, and Politics in the United States* (1839)

Democracy in America

 Between Thomas Jefferson's election in 1800 and Andrew Jackson's victory in his presidential bid in 1828, American culture and politics were transformed. Travelers to America during this period consistently remarked about the democratic character of its society. Democracy appeared to suffuse every aspect of culture and politics. Whereas in 1800 most states had some type of property requirement for voting, within three decades most of these restrictions had been swept aside. Many of the new Western states that entered the Union in the intervening years adopted constitutions with no property requirements. As population shifted westward, the nation's center of political gravity also shifted. Many of the politicians who dominated the national scene came from Western states such as Tennessee and Kentucky, not the older, settled regions such as Virginia and Massachusetts.

Democratic Culture

In 1835, a young French nobleman, Count Alexis de Tocqueville, published an account of his recent trip to America. "No novelty in the United States struck me more vividly during my stay there," he wrote, "than the equality of conditions. It was easy to see the immense influence of this basic fact on the whole course of society." *Democracy in America* (1835), Tocqueville's analysis of the influence of democracy on American life, remains one of the most important books ever written about American society.

The young French aristocrat was hardly the only foreign visitor drawn to America. In the 1820s and 1830s, America attracted the interest of many other foreigners who were impressed by the democratic character of American life. "The term *democrat*, which elsewhere would fill even republicans with terror," Michael Chevalier, another French visitor, noted, "is here greeted with acclamations." Frances Trollope, an English observer, was shocked to see Americans talking to complete strangers "on terms of perfect equality." Democracy nurtured a more egalitarian culture that astonished Europeans. In colonial America a bow or doffed hat and lowered head were all signs of deference to one's social betters. Many of these customs persisted in Europe. Americans, however, had abandoned most of them by the 1830s, preferring to shake hands, a far more egalitarian form of greeting. One English commentator complained that in America he had to "go on shaking hands here, there, and everywhere, and with everybody." Another Englishman confessed his astonishment that travel in America meant mixing with men and women of different classes: "There is but one conveyance, it may be said, for every class of people—the coach, railroad, or steamboat, as well as most of the hotels, being open to all; the consequence is that the society is very much mixed."

A significant political consequence of the growth of democracy was the expansion of suffrage to include virtually all white men. As the maps (**8.1**) show, most of the new Western states that entered the Union after the War of 1812 adopted democratic constitutions that rejected property qualifications for suffrage. Their constitutions generally embraced this ideal from the beginning. When older states such as New York revised their constitutions in the 1820s, the question of suffrage became one of the most contentious. See *Competing Visions: Should White Men Without Property Have the Vote?* on page 224.

Davy Crockett and the Frontier Myth

Tocqueville commented that "in the Western settlements we may behold democracy arrived at its utmost limits." He may well have been thinking of figures like the legendary frontiersman and politician Davy Crockett (1786–1836) when he made that statement. No figure in American public life did more to associate the West with democracy than Davy Crockett. Born in Tennessee, Crockett served under Andrew Jackson during the Creek Wars (1813–1814), where he distinguished himself as a soldier. His home state voters elected him to the Tennessee state legislature and to Congress, where he supported his former commander, Andrew Jackson, another symbol of frontier democracy. Crockett's achievements in the state legislature and Congress paled in significance to the stories about his exploits as a frontiersman and Indian fighter, myths that Crockett helped shape and market to

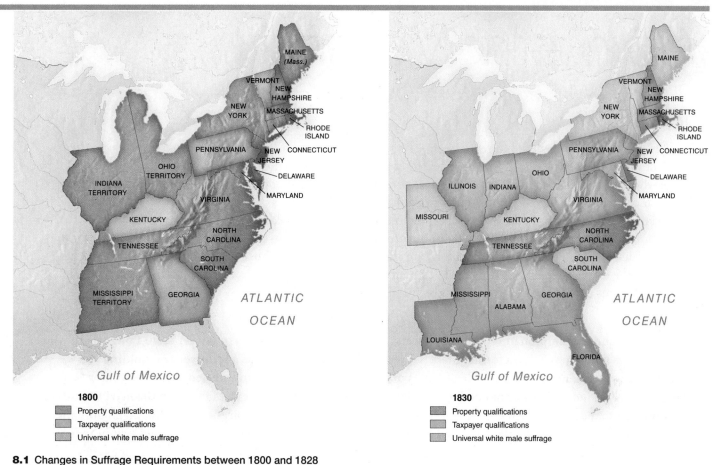

8.1 Changes in Suffrage Requirements between 1800 and 1828
Many of the Western states that entered the Union after 1800 did not impose property requirements for voting. By 1828, most states had eliminated such requirements.

a growing audience of readers eager to learn of his daring exploits. As one contemporary English magazine noted: "Democracy and the far west made Crockett: he is a product of forests, freedom, universal suffrage, and bear hunts."

In his own colorful account, Crockett becomes a politician almost by accident. When coming to town to sell his pelts and furs, he exchanges a few words with local politicians, who immediately recognize him as a natural leader and draft him for the state legislature. Crockett's career in Congress was brief, but his fame grew as literary treatments recounted stories about his exploits. *Crockett's Almanac*, for example, a cheap magazine-like publication, vividly described the frontiersman-politician, whose honesty as a stump speaker and legendary adventures wrestling alligators, hunting bears, and fighting Indians captivated audiences. For Crockett delivering a stump speech meant literally standing on the nearest tree stump, as shown in this illustration from the *A Narrative of the Life of David Crockett* (**8.2**).

Although Crockett was a big hit on the stump and celebrated in popular literature, the most important political figure to make use of the association of the West with democracy was Andrew Jackson. The Tennessee-born Jackson earned a reputation as a fierce Indian fighter during the Creek Wars and distinguished himself as the victor of the Battle of New Orleans. He also served as both a United States representative and senator from Tennessee. A supporter of Jackson described his political style as typical of the Western United States, where democratic values and egalitarian ideals flourished: "In Europe" custom "decreed that kings shall rule and the people submit. In this wilderness, as if by magic, a new and different order of things has appeared." Jackson's effort to link his Western origins with his democratic values became a key component of his political message for the rest of his career in public life.

8.2 Crockett as Politician
Crockett the frontiersman-politician addresses a crowd outside a rural tavern. Crockett reflected and helped shape the myth of frontier democracy in the new Republic.

What aspects of Davy Crockett's life made him a symbol of frontier democracy?

Competing Visions
SHOULD WHITE MEN WITHOUT PROPERTY HAVE THE VOTE?

In 1821, New Yorkers gathered to revise their state's 1777 constitution. The issue of property requirements for elections proved to be one of the most heated in the convention. James Kent, a conservative lawyer and judge who began his career as a Federalist, defended property requirements. His vision of politics was deeply hierarchical, which led him to oppose an expansion of suffrage. Kent was opposed by a group of younger politicians. Nathan Sanford, a man who entered politics fully a decade later than Kent, began his career as a Jeffersonian democrat. Jefferson's election to the presidency in 1800 had not ushered in the reign of terror that his Federalist enemies predicted, and Sanford embraced the growing enthusiasm for democracy that marked politics in the early nineteenth century. Which man has a more optimistic view of human nature? Which theory of politics seems closer in spirit to the ideas behind the Federal Constitution?

The most eloquent champion of retaining property requirements was James Kent, a former State Supreme Court judge and Chancellor of the State of New York (an English-style judicial office that no longer exists). Kent warned that an unchecked democracy in which the property-less and working classes enjoyed the same power as the propertied would threaten political stability and the rights of private property.

The tendency of universal suffrage is to jeopardize the rights of property and the principles of liberty. There is a constant tendency in human society, and the history of every age proves it; there is a tendency in the poor to covet and to share the plunder of the rich; in the debtor to relax or avoid the obligation of contract … there is a tendency in ambitious and wicked men to inflame these combustible materials.

The notion that every man that works a day on the road, or serves an idle hour in the militia, is entitled as of right to an equal participation in the whole power of government is most unreasonable and has no foundation in justice…. Society is an association for the protection of property as well as life, and the individual who contributes only one cent to the common stock ought not to have the same power and influence in directing the property and concerns of the partnership as he who contributes his thousands.

Nathan Sanford was a lawyer from Long Island who entered politics as a Jeffersonian, holding various state offices before being elected as a U.S. senator from New York. Rather than focus on the need to protect property, Sanford argued that those who bore the burdens of government had earned a right to have a say in it.

The question before us is the right of suffrage—who shall, or who shall not, have the right to vote … the principle of the scheme now proposed, is, that those who bear the burthens of the state, [paid taxes, served in the militia, or consented to volunteer to work on public works projects such as roads] should choose those that rule it…. To me, and the majority of the committee, it appeared the only reasonable scheme that those who are to be affected by the acts of the government, should be annually entitled to vote for those who administer it.

Fourth of July in Center Square
by John Lewis Krimmel, 1819

Andrew Jackson and His Age

The new democratic spirit of American politics helped elevate Andrew Jackson's political career, and he in turn did everything in his power to promote his vision of democracy. Jackson's democratic ideas stopped well short of the most radical egalitarian ideas of his day. Indeed, Jackson's vision of democracy had no room for blacks, Indians, or women. Still his invocation of the will of the people marked a turning point in American political development. After Jackson, politicians from across the political spectrum would outdo each other in affirming their commitment to democracy and praising the wisdom of the people.

Jackson's long road to the presidency began with his narrow defeat in 1824, which led to his decisive victory in 1828. Unlike earlier presidents who were drawn from the nation's elite, Jackson was a self-made man. An orphan who became a rich planter and influential political figure in his home state of Tennessee, Jackson became a symbol for American democracy. Indeed, one of his supporters characterized the presidential election of 1828, in which Jackson squared off against John Quincy Adams for the second time, as a struggle in which "the Aristocracy and Democracy of the country are arrayed against each other." Others viewed Jackson's democratic leanings in a less positive light, however, seeing his election as the start of the "reign of King Mob." Jackson's presidency was marred by deep divisions within his own administration and challenges from outside. In particular South Carolina's decision to respond to federal tariff policy by calling a convention to nullify federal law forced a showdown between Jackson and a new radical version of the theory of states' rights.

The Election of 1824 and the "Corrupt Bargain"

James Monroe, the fourth Virginian to occupy the presidency since the adoption of the Constitution (1817–1825), anointed no political figure to be his successor and carry forward his policies and ideas. Following Washington's model Monroe had sought out a talented but diverse collection of men for his cabinet who represented a broad spectrum of political and economic views. Three of these cabinet ministers sought the presidency in 1824: William Crawford, secretary of the treasury; John Quincy Adams, secretary of state; and John C. Calhoun, secretary of war. A fourth candidate was Henry Clay, Speaker of the House of Representatives. Andrew Jackson, hero of the Battle of New Orleans, also joined the race. Jackson had served in Congress, as a judge in Tennessee, and as the appointed governor of the Florida territory.

Crawford, born in Virginia but raised in Georgia, was heir to the old Jeffersonian republican vision of politics with its emphasis on states' rights and strict construction of the Constitution. Crawford opposed Monroe's National Republican synthesis

of Jeffersonian politics with Hamiltonian economics (see Chapter 7). In contrast to the other candidates in the crowded field, Crawford opposed using federal power for economic development. Public expenditures for internal improvements, such as roads and canals, and charters for banks were government functions that the Constitution, Crawford argued, had wisely left to the individual states.

John Quincy Adams, the son of President John Adams, was a New Englander who had been a professor at Harvard and spent considerable time in Europe as a diplomat, serving in Holland, Prussia (part of modern Germany), Great Britain, and Russia. As secretary of state he had not only negotiated the Treaty of Ghent that ended the War of 1812 but also was largely responsible for formulating the Monroe Doctrine (see Chapter 7). A short, balding, intellectual figure, Adams was neither charismatic nor politically astute; he even admitted that he could seem dogmatic and pedantic. Before entering the race for president, his primary experience had been in foreign, not domestic, politics.

John C. Calhoun, the other Southerner in the race, had been a prominent War Hawk during the War of 1812. An astute politician, Calhoun

View the **Image** *1824 Election Cartoon*

What were the strengths of John Quincy Adams as a presidential candidate?

Our Country.....Home Industry.

MANUFACTURERS AND MECHANICS,

Your enemies have rallied under the banner of Gen. Jackson—the same man whom they a few days since declared a tyrant and a murderer. One of their avowed objects is a repeal of all the laws which have been enacted for the encouragement of manufactures.

If the Jackson Party prevail, a majority of the next Congress will be opposed to the tariff, to mechanics, manufacturers, and domestic industry. As proof of this, the Jackson papers, nearly one and all, have published articles recommending the repeal of all laws that have been passed to encourage our mechanics and manufacturers. The consequence will be, that the sound of the shuttle will no more be heard. Our stores will be filled with British and Scotch ginghams, shirtings, checks and bed-ticks; and not a place will be found for a yard of American cloth. British goods, labelled with Jackson's name, and in large quantities, have been sent among us.

The Legislature of Virginia, a majority of whom were Jacksonians, solemnly resolved, that all the laws passed for the protection of mechanics and manufacturers were a violation of the constitution. At a great Jackson meeting, held in South Carolina, a committee, previously appointed to ascertain public opinion, reported that nineteen-twentieths of the southern section of the country were opposed to all laws enacted to encourage manufactures. These are the warm advocates of General Jackson. Will you take away the power from such old tried friends as Henry Clay, who has always been your hearty supporter, and give it to your enemies? If you vote for the Jackson ticket, you will do it. If the Jackson Assembly ticket prevails, they mean to repeal the Electoral law, and appoint Electors that will drive Henry Clay, and all the friends of the American system, from office.

Fellow-citizens, Manufacturers, and Mechanics! be on the look out, or you will be most wofully betrayed. Don't suffer yourselves to be deceived by stories that General Jackson is your friend. He has consented to serve your enemies, and he must be judged by his company. What will his battle of New-Orleans avail you, if you are thrown out of employment and made beggars? Don't fail to go to the polls, and show by your votes that you are not the dupes of such men as Coleman, who has always been your enemy. He tells you to vote for General Jackson; vote directly opposite to his advice, and you will vote for your country. As a proof of this, I ask who has always sided with the British against his country? Will you not answer, Coleman? Who has abused the best patriots America ever produced? Is not Wm. Coleman the man? Who scandalized Henry Clay? Who vilified Jefferson? Who has slandered Madison? Has not Coleman been the man? He now asks you to vote for the party that upheld Jackson, and destroy your best friends; cripple your own occupation; build up England, and ruin the American system. This is the man who exulted when a British fleet lay off the Hook. The Evening Post was received wet from his office on board their ships every day. Nothing but respect for the laws prevented our incensed countrymen from demolishing the press and types that printed the diabolical treason.

Fellow-citizens! Henry Clay was your early friend. He first risked his all to sustain you. His speeches will be read as long as eloquence has admirers. By arguments unanswerable, he brought forward the American system. He has since sustained it; and if he is not sacrificed by those whom he has befriended, he will consummate the system he has begun. If General Jackson's party prevails, a majority of the next Congress will surely turn him, and every friend you have in the Administration, from their places; and the truest, ablest, and best friend you ever had will be destroyed. It is for his friendship to you that Virginia, his native state, has denounced him. It is for this that Georgia and the Carolinas have libelled him. It is for this that the enemies of the American system, the Colemans, Pickerings, and Coopers, whether British by birth or choice, have vilified him, and cruelly endeavoured to blast his character. This is what has made every British agent that lurks in our city the traducer of Henry Clay. The history of depravity affords nothing that exceeds the vileness of their calumny towards him—witness the testimony of their own witness, Buchanan.

Go to the Polls—put down the favorite British candidates—vindicate your friends—and save yourselves and your country.

ON BEHALF OF THE MANUFACTURERS.

8.3 Our Country ... Home Industry
This election broadside links John Quincy Adams with Clay's American System. The images at the top—the loom, ship, and plough—symbolize the way the American system would help manufacturing, commerce, and agriculture.

decided to withdraw from the crowded race and soon emerged as the strongest candidate for vice-president. Calhoun expected to bide his time until the moment was more auspicious to mount another try for the presidency.

Henry Clay, the vivacious speaker of the house from Kentucky, began his career as a War Hawk during the War of 1812. On economic issues Clay had the most clearly developed vision of America's future. Clay built on Monroe's neo-Hamiltonian policies, pushing them in a more nationalistic direction. As a matter of policy, Monroe favored federal support for internal improvements such as roads and canals, but he maintained some of the same constitutional reservations about such policies that his predecessors Jefferson and Madison had articulated. Clay was an unapologetic champion of aggressive federal involvement in economic development. The **American System**, Clay's plan for using the power of the federal government to encourage American industry, included tariffs to

help protect American industry by keeping cheap foreign goods from undermining American producers, continuing support for a national bank, and an ambitious program of federal funding for internal improvements.

Clay's theory sought a harmonious interplay among agriculture, industry, and commerce. Adams endorsed the essence of Clay's American System. This election broadside (**8.3**) reflects his support for Clay's economic policies. The central image of a ship symbolizes commerce, while the two smaller figures depict a farmer at the plow and a worker at a loom. The name of the ship, *John Quincy Adams*, symbolizes Adams's claim to be a proven leader who could pilot the nation to a prosperous future.

Of the major candidates for the presidency in 1824, Andrew Jackson's agenda was the least defined. Clay and Adams sought to portray Jackson as an opponent of the American System, and Jackson tried to finesse the issue by stressing that he wished to support commerce, agriculture, and industry. His campaign focused less on issues and more on character and underlying political values. Jackson fashioned himself as a frontier democrat whose honesty and courage were his primary credentials for the presidency.

In the divided field Jackson won 44 percent of the popular vote and the most electoral votes, but he fell short of the majority in the Electoral College necessary to win the election (**8.4**). Under such circumstances the Constitution directed that the House of Representatives choose from among the top five candidates. Clay had only come in fourth, but as speaker of the house, he was a key player in determining the outcome. Given the choice among Crawford, an old-style Jeffersonian who opposed Clay's vision for America's future; Jackson, whose support for a more nationalist economic program was lukewarm at best; and Adams, who was sympathetic to Clay's American System, the choice was easy for Clay. With Clay's support Adams won.

Having secured the presidency, Adams then chose Clay to be his secretary of state, which in this era functioned as the stepping-stone for aspiring future presidential candidates. (Since World War II, the vice presidency has sometimes served the same function.) Jackson and his supporters charged that Clay had traded his support for the office of secretary of state in a "**corrupt bargain**" that deprived

What role did Clay's American System play in the election of John Quincy Adams?

Read the **Document** Michel Chevalier, *Society Manners and Politics in the U.S.*

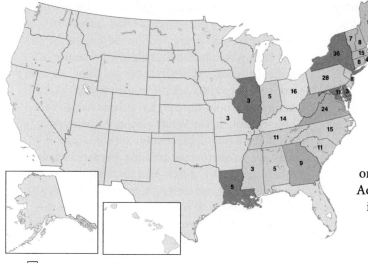

4 Electoral vote by state	Electoral Vote (%)	Popular Vote (%)
John Quincy Adams (Democratic-Republican)	84 (32)	108,740 (31)
Andrew Jackson (Democratic-Republican)	99 (38)	153,544 (44)
William H. Crawford (Democratic-Republican)	41 (16)	40,856 (12)
Henry Clay (Democratic-Republican)	37 (14)	47,531 (14)
States that split electoral votes		

8.4 Electoral and Popular Votes 1824
Although Jackson won the most votes, no candidate gained a majority in the Electoral College. After the House of Representatives decided the outcome, Jackson claimed that Adams and Clay had struck a "corrupt bargain" to deprive him of the presidency.

Jackson of the presidency and gave the election to Adams.

Adams embraced Clay's American System. In addition to supporting Clay's plan for public expenditures on internal improvements, including new roads and canals, Adams hoped to create a national university and an astronomical observatory. Yet while he embraced the forward-looking nationalist vision of economic development associated with Clay's American System, Adams was an eighteenth-century politician when it came to thinking about the role of the president as a virtuous leader who stood above partisan bickering. He believed that Monroe's goal of rising above party was not only laudable but achievable. Rather than use his patronage powers as president to reward his political friends and consolidate his administration's power,

Adams appointed men on the basis of merit, with little concern for their political loyalties or even their commitment to his agenda or to him personally. Adams proudly proclaimed his intention to "discard every element of rancor" and "yield to talents and virtue." One exasperated supporter complained that "the friends of the administration have to contend not only against their enemies," but "against the Administration itself, which leaves its power in the hands of its own enemies." Adams sought to move beyond partisanship at a time when America was becoming more politically polarized.

Adams made another tactical error when he chastised Congress for refusing to embrace his economic agenda. He accused legislators of being hampered "by the will of their constituents." Seen in light of his republican belief in the need for virtuous leadership, Adams was inviting Congress to lead rather than follow the nation. For his opponents, however, the remark smacked of condescension and elitism. His comments were out of step with the rising tide of democratic sentiment that had swept over American society. For those who supported this new, more democratic ethos, Adams had maligned the people. Jackson and his supporters used Adams's gaffe to highlight their own commitment to democracy. Jackson extolled "the voice of the people" and attacked Adams for his apparent haughty contempt for the popular will.

The Election of 1828: "Old Hickory's" Triumph

The election of 1828, which saw Andrew Jackson squaring off with John Quincy Adams for a second try at the presidency, was a pivotal moment in American politics. Jackson trumpeted his humble origins, military career, and support for democratic values. His supporters applauded their candidate's commitment to democracy and lambasted Adams's aristocratic pretensions. Adams's supporters defended his traditional republican ideals and support for the American System and warned voters that Jackson was a demagogue who would undermine America's constitutional system.

Why did Jackson view the election of 1824 as a "corrupt bargain"?

8.5 "Some Account of the Bloody Deeds of General Jackson"

This pro-Adams broadside dubbed the "Coffin Handbill" features the images of coffins prominently. It casts Jackson as a brutal despot whose military record demonstrated that he was unfit to be president. The coffins symbolized militiamen Jackson executed for desertion during the Creek Wars (1813–1814).

At a more fundamental level, Jackson rejected the antiparty sentiments of Monroe and Adams. Jackson set out to win the presidency in 1828, forming an alliance with Crawford and Calhoun to defeat Adams and Clay. New York's Martin Van Buren formulated the strategy for this new alliance. Van Buren was an influential Republican who had served both as a state senator and a U.S. senator. His supporters were nicknamed "Bucktails" because they wore deer tails on their hats instead of feathers. Van Buren embraced the idea of party with a passion. His goal was to re-create the old Jeffersonian coalition, which united "the planters of the South and the plain Republicans of the North."

Jackson felt personally aggrieved by the result of the election of 1824. Charges that Adams had "stolen" that election colored the rhetoric of the 1828 campaign, which marked a new low in the use of personal attacks and negative campaigning. Jackson's campaign portrayed Adams as an aristocrat of dubious morality, pointing out that Adams had installed a billiard table in the White House. Although now considered a popular recreation, originally billiards was an aristocratic pastime. Perhaps the most sensational claim the Jackson campaign made was that during Adams's time as a diplomat in Russia he had "made use of a beautiful girl to seduce the passions of the Emperor." The Jacksonians charged that Adams was a licentious aristocrat with perverse sexual values.

The attack on Adams's character was more than matched by the ferocious assaults on Jackson's morality. The smear campaign also charged Jackson with sexual immorality, challenging the legality of his marriage. Supporters of Adams claimed that Jackson had seduced a married woman and lived with her in "open and notorious lewdness" before she had divorced her first husband. Jackson, they claimed, was a violent, brawling frontiersman who could not be trusted with the nation's highest office. The Adams campaign even attacked Jackson's military record. Philadelphia printer John Binn's "Coffin Handbill" (**8.5**) detailed the "bloody deeds of General Jackson," who had in fact executed six militiamen during the wars against the Creek Indians. Binn warned Americans against putting "at the head of our government, a man who was never known to govern himself."

In Jackson's defense his supporters cast the general as "**Old Hickory**," a rough-and-tumble democrat and latter-day George Washington whose plain frontier code of ethics contrasted with Adams's elitist eastern values. To call attention to Jackson's reputation as the hero of the Battle of New Orleans, his supporters gathered on the anniversary of the victory to plant hickory trees and raise liberty poles made of hickory wood. They ridiculed Adams's bookish temperament, chanting "Adams can write" but "Jackson can fight." Adams's supporters answered the smears by praising "his long and varied public services, his great experience, his talent, his learning."

To get out their message, Jackson's supporters developed a sophisticated campaign apparatus. A central committee in Nashville directed local and state Jackson committees, who in turn worked with

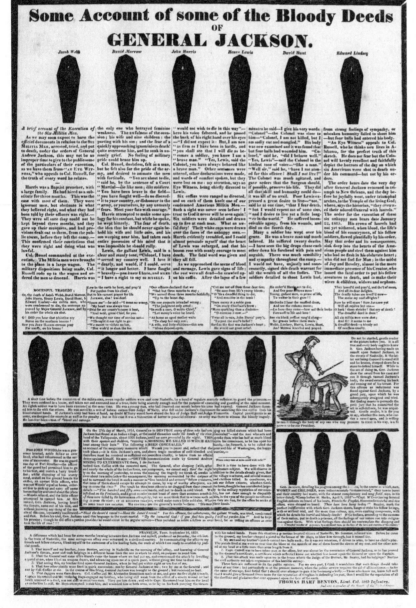

How did the "Coffin Handbill" attempt to discredit Andrew Jackson?

local "Hickory Clubs." In addition to these innovations in campaign organization, Jackson's supporters created a network of pro-Jackson newspapers to get out the word about their candidate. Eighteen new pro-Jackson newspapers sprouted up in Ohio alone. The Jacksonians also pioneered new fundraising tactics to pay for their campaign, including public banquets and other ticketed events in which supporters celebrated the achievements of their candidate. They developed an astonishing range of campaign knick-knacks, and mementos, including badges, plates, sewing boxes, and ceramics. Jacksonians also used rallies and parades to spark enthusiasm for their candidate. The tactics of Jackson and his supporters galvanized the electorate. In 1824, only about one-fourth of the eligible voters had participated; in 1828, more than half of the electorate turned out to vote. In the end Jackson garnered more than twice as many electoral votes as Adams.

The Reign of "King Mob"

Andrew Jackson's inaugural in 1829 captured the new democratic spirit of the age. His supporters poured into Washington for the event, shown in this contemporary print of the crowds who thronged the White House (**8.6**). Margaret Bayard Smith, a Washington socialite, described the scene in detail: "Thousands and thousands of people, without distinction of rank, collected in an immense mass around the Capitol." She was shocked not only by the composition of the crowd but also by its rowdiness. The boisterous attendees, she recounted, broke "glass and bone china to the amount of several thousand dollars." Smith was clearly ambivalent about the inauguration of the "people's president." She was impressed by the "majesty" of the people assembled at the swearing-in ceremony but disturbed by the rude and disorderly behavior of Jackson's supporters at the reception that followed at the White House. This print of the inaugural confirms Smith's impressions that

Jackson's inaugural was a popular affair, drawing a much more diverse crowd than previous inaugurals. Not everyone was as impressed by the people's majesty. Supreme Court Justice Joseph Story complained that Jackson's inaugural had ushered in the "the reign of King Mob."

In contrast to Adams, who refused to use his powers of appointment to reward his political supporters, Jackson was unabashed in appointing his supporters to office. In his first inaugural Jackson defended the need for rotation in government offices. Jackson rejected the traditional republican notion, advanced by John Quincy Adams, that government offices were best reserved for a small elite, typically drawn from the ranks of the wealthy and well educated. "The duties of all public officers," Jackson maintained, were "plain and simple." One Jackson supporter proudly proclaimed that he saw "nothing wrong in the rule that to the victor belong the spoils of the enemy." Opponents mocked Jackson's appointments as "men of narrow minds" who were "hardly gentlemen" and attacked Jackson's system of replacing government officeholders with those loyal to him as the **spoils system**.

8.6 "President's Levee, or all Creation going to the White House"
This image of the boisterous crowd in front of the White House during Jackson's inaugural reception, or levee, captures the fear that his presidency would usher in the "reign of King Mob."

Read the **Document** *John Adams, A Corrupt Bargain or Politics as Usual*

How did the spoils system promote Jackson's democratic agenda?

8.7 Office Seekers
In this attack on the spoils system, a demonic Andrew Jackson dangles the spoils of victory before eager office seekers.

This cartoon (**8.7**) shows Jackson dangling the spoils of victory before eager office seekers. Jackson's practices, however, were less radical than his rhetoric. Only 20 percent of federal officeholders lost their jobs because of his new policy.

Apart from his appointment of Martin Van Buren as secretary of state, Jackson's cabinet comprised undistinguished men selected for their loyalty to him. Shortly after Jackson had assembled his cabinet, a sexual scandal engulfed his administration. The controversy swirled around his new secretary of war, John Eaton, a close friend of the president. Washington society, prone to gossip, began spreading rumors that Eaton's wife, Peggy, the daughter of a Washington tavern keeper, was a promiscuous woman who had engaged in a clandestine affair with Eaton before their marriage. That Peggy's first husband had allegedly committed suicide further besmirched her reputation. Still angry over the attacks on the legitimacy of his own marriage (his wife died before Jackson took office), the president defended Peggy Eaton's reputation and ordered his cabinet members to do likewise. The Eaton scandal, which some contemporaries described as "Eaton Malaria," consumed Jackson's presidency for months, preventing him

from focusing on pressing public matters. Because Floride Calhoun, the wife of the vice president had been one of the most prominent women to snub Peggy Eaton, the Eaton affair also strained the already tense relations between Jackson and Vice President John C. Calhoun. The disruption forced the president to ask most of his cabinet to resign in 1831.

States Rights and the Nullification Crisis

Even if Jackson and Calhoun had not fallen out over the Eaton affair, the two men were on a collision course. The rift between them widened as the politics of states' rights divided the nation. Calhoun's home state of South Carolina became a hotbed of radical states' rights doctrine, and Calhoun had to embrace the doctrine or retire from public life. Choosing to take up the cause, Calhoun became one of its leading spokesmen. The issue that vexed South Carolina was federal tariffs on imported goods. In 1828, Congress enacted high import duties on a variety of goods, including textiles. The South objected to the tariff, believing that Britain would retaliate by raising tariffs on imported cotton, which would hurt Southern agriculture. The objections of the South Carolina legislature were outlined in A *Protest,* and the underlying political and constitutional theory was elaborately described anonymously by Calhoun in his manifesto, the *Exposition.* Calhoun took the theory of states' rights to a new level, defending South Carolina's right to nullify, or make legally void, the 1828 tariff. His manifesto developed ideas first articulated by Jefferson and Madison in the Virginia and Kentucky Resolutions into a radical theory of states' rights (see Chapter 6). According to Calhoun the Union was a sovereign compact among the people of the states. When the states and the national government disagreed over the constitutionality of a federal law, he asserted, the states were entitled to judge the constitutionality of federal laws. This position challenged both the supremacy of the federal government and the power of the federal courts to be the final arbiter on the constitutionality of federal laws. Asserting that a state could call special conventions to nullify federal laws, Calhoun's doctrine of **nullification** went further than either Jefferson or Madison's earlier defenses of states' rights.

The issue of states' rights resurfaced in 1830 when Congress debated a proposal to limit sales of Western lands. Samuel Foot, a senator from Connecticut, proposed to slow Western expansion by cutting back on the public sale of Western lands, a decision that would have also robbed the government of revenues and made it even more dependent on tariffs. Prompting Foot's resolution was a report from the land office that 72 million acres of land already surveyed remained unsold. Senators Thomas Hart Benton of Missouri and Robert Hayne of South Carolina denounced Foot's resolution. Benton and Hayne saw an opportunity to forge a Southern and Western alliance against New England's commercial interests. Benton saw Foot's proposal as a means for New England's industrialists to maintain their supply of cheap labor by making it harder for laborers to settle on Western lands. Hayne took a different tactic; framing the issue in terms of South Carolina's theory of states' rights, he moved beyond the specifics of Foot's proposal to suggest that federal control over Western lands was itself a source of danger since it encouraged the growth of federal power.

Senator Daniel Webster of Massachusetts attacked the South Carolinian's theory of states' rights. The ensuing debate between Hayne and Webster was a brilliant display of oratory. One observer

> "Every seat, every inch of ground, even the steps, were compactly filled, and yet not space enough for the ladies—the Senators were obliged to relinquish their chairs of the State to the fair auditors who literally sat in the Senate."
>
> MARGARET SMITH'S recollections of the Senate Chamber during Webster's reply to Hayne

recalled: "It was a day never to be forgotten by those who witnessed the scene in the Senate Chamber and a day destined to be forever memorable in the Annals of the Senate." In a riveting speech Webster denounced the theory of states' rights and asserted the supremacy of the Union over the individual states: "Liberty and Union, now and forever, one and inseparable." Building on ideas developed by Hamilton and John Marshall (see Chapters 6 and 7), Webster's constitutional nationalism denied that the states could judge the constitutionality of federal laws and rejected the theory of nullification.

Webster's speech was widely reprinted and became an instant classic; schoolchildren would recite it throughout the Northeast for generations. This meticulous historical painting by George Healy (**8.8**) immortalized the debate. Webster,

8.8 Webster's Reply to Hayne George Healy's painting of Webster's famous speech is reminiscent of Bingham's *Stump Speaking*. Calhoun is presented as a wiry character, while Webster stands tall, a model of virtue.

How did Webster's theory of the Union contrast with Calhoun's theory of states' rights?

pausing for a moment's reflection, stands in a hushed Senate chamber. Onlookers crowd the galleries, transfixed by his oratory. Although senators had given up their seats in the chamber to accommodate the many women who attended to hear the speech, Healey placed all the women in the Senate gallery, a decision likely motivated by his belief that viewers would have been shocked to see women on the floor of the Senate.

With the Webster-Hayne debate fresh in everyone's memory, supporters of states' rights gathered in Washington to honor the memory of Thomas Jefferson. Hayne and Calhoun both attended this dinner as did President Jackson. When Hayne concluded a long defense of states' rights, attention turned to Jackson, who was expected to propose a toast to Hayne's pro-states' rights sentiments. Having always been a moderate supporter of states' rights, Jackson would surely support Hayne, the crowd thought. They were shocked, however, when he lifted his glass and proclaimed, "Our Federal Union. It must be preserved." Rather than support Hayne, the president appeared to echo Webster. Vice President Calhoun, who had become an outspoken defender of states' rights, responded with his own toast, "The Union, next to our liberties, the most dear." Realizing that he could not effectively defend South Carolina and promulgate the cause of states' rights from the vice presidency, Calhoun

resigned. South Carolina promptly elected him to the Senate.

The issue of states' rights and nullification moved to the center of American political life as the controversy over tariffs heated up again. Congress intended the Tariff Act of 1832, which President Jackson signed, to be a conciliatory gesture to South Carolina. Although the new act lowered import duties, South Carolinians continued to view tariffs as an effort by one section of the nation to wage economic war against another. South Carolina called a convention and issued a declaration nullifying the tariff. Jackson denounced these actions as "subversive of the Constitution." Privately he warned that if South Carolina spilled a drop of blood in "defiance of the laws of the United States," he would, "hang the first man of them I can get my hands on to the first tree I can find." Missouri Senator Thomas Hart Benton, warned that when President Jackson "begins to talk about hanging, they can begin to look out for ropes." This contemporary cartoon attacking nullification (**8.9**) highlights Jackson's tough stance. The president, restraining one of Calhoun's supporters, declares, "Stop you have gone too far. Or by the Eternal I will hang you all!"

Congress passed a Force Bill that gave the president the power to use military force to collect revenues, including tariffs. While Jackson was adopting a public tough stance, Henry Clay was working behind the scenes to avert a confrontation. On the same day that Congress passed the Force Bill, it also scaled back tariffs. In response to this conciliatory gesture, South Carolina rescinded its act of nullification, but not before nullifying the Force Act. Clay's compromise had narrowly averted a constitutional crisis in which the states and the federal government had nearly come to blows. For the moment the conflict between states' rights and a more nationalist vision of the Constitution had been settled in favor of the latter.

Although Jackson adopted a hard line with South Carolina, he would prove to be far more flexible when federal and state power collided over other issues, notably Indian rights. Jackson's democratic nationalism had little room for anyone but white men. Its narrowness would become increasingly clear during his two terms as president.

8.9 Despotism
In this anti-nullification cartoon Calhoun ascends a platform that leads from nullification to despotism.

How does the political cartoonist represent Calhoun's nullification theory in the cartoon *Despotism*?

Read the **Document** *Andrew Jackson, the Force Bill*

White Man's Democracy

The democratic ideas that swept Andrew Jackson into the presidency were premised on a vision of society that was not truly inclusive: It excluded blacks and Indians, and showed little interest in women's rights. The new state constitutions drafted in the Jacksonian era expanded rights for non-property-owning white men but stripped voting rights from property-owning African Americans. The plight of American Indians also became a major issue during Jackson's presidency. Jackson and his supporters sought to restrict Indians' rights and expropriate their lands.

Although the revised state constitutions systematically stripped away rights from free blacks, African Americans created a network of thriving communities in the free states of the North and the old Northwest (the modern states of Ohio, Indiana, Michigan, and Illinois). However, harassment of African Americans in the nation's cities also increased during the Jacksonian era. Indeed, the struggles of African Americans to achieve economic and social respectability prompted vicious attacks in the popular press and might even lead to violence.

Pressure to find more land for white settlers also intensified, which increased tensions with American Indians who were eager to defend their lands against further encroachments. Jackson and his supporters showed little regard for the rights of Indian peoples. The Cherokee fought a valiant effort to defend their rights within the rules established by the Constitution and learned that the rule of law provided scant protection against racism and a rapacious desire for Indian land.

Race and Politics in the Jacksonian Era

While many states were expanding the suffrage for white men, other states were imposing new restrictions on black men. The 1821 New York state constitutional convention that had abolished property requirements for white men adopted a high property requirement for African Americans that effectively disenfranchised most blacks. Thus, while the state's African-American population numbered some 30,000 in 1825, fewer than 300 black men were eligible to vote. New York's actions were part of a broader pattern of racial exclusion that limited the rights of African Americans throughout the North and West. African Americans lost the right to vote in Rhode Island in 1822 and Pennsylvania in 1838. Most of the new states that entered the Union after 1819 denied suffrage to African Americans.

Many states also regulated the conduct of free African Americans. In 1831, Indiana required that "Negroes and mulattoes emigrating in the state" be required to post a bond (much like prisoners awaiting trial) or be deported. Illinois not only barred blacks from voting but prohibited them from testifying in court or bringing civil suits. Ohio barred African Americans from access to the courts in "any controversy where either party to the sale is a white person" and declared that African Americans "have no constitutional right to present their petitions to the General Assembly for any purpose whatsoever."

Gradual emancipation schemes increased the number of free blacks in the North and West. In part the intensification of racism reflected concern over economic competition from the growing number of free blacks. Yet despite the legal barriers placed in the way of African Americans' economic progress, vibrant communities grew in the North. The most obvious measure of the success of these communities was the rise of a rich array of African American cultural and economic institutions, including churches, fraternal organizations, and benefit societies. African Americans published their first newspaper, *Freedom's Journal,* in New York in 1827.

The efforts of free blacks in the North and West to improve their conditions became a subject of widespread comment in the press. Typically the press lampooned the efforts of African Americans to attain cultural and economic respectability. Exploiting this popular racism, artist Edward William Clay

What types of legal disabilities did free blacks face outside the slave South?

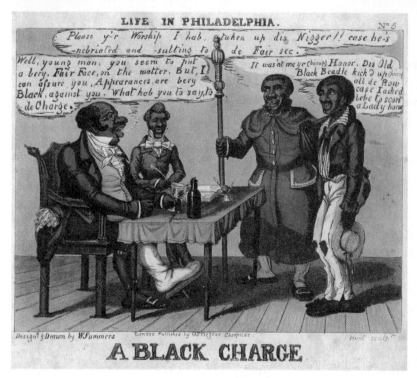

LIFE IN PHILADELPHIA.

A BLACK CHARGE

8.10 *A Black Charge*
From a series of racist caricatures of black life in Philadelphia, this image lampoons African-American aspirations to respectability. A church official disciplines a church member for alleged misconduct.
[*Source:* The Library Company of Philadelphia]

published 14 cartoons ridiculing Philadelphia's African-American community. In *A Black Charge* (**8.10**), Clay mocks a black church official who must attempt to discipline a disorderly member of his community. As was typical in this era, the artist has exaggerated the physical appearances of African Americans and caricatured their speech, suggesting that blacks could only speak a distorted form of English.

Jackson's vision of white man's democracy had tragic consequences for American Indians. His dealings with Indian peoples during his presidency were also consistent with his view that they were culturally inferior to whites, and that their civilization was on the path toward extinction. In Jackson's political calculus white settlers' need for land was paramount and the rights of Indians carried little if any weight. These beliefs shaped his response to the conflict between the state of Georgia and the Cherokees.

The President's views of Indians had been formed during his early military career, in which he was well known as an Indian fighter. At the conclusion of the Creek Wars (1812–1813), he had seized 23 million acres of Creek land, more than half of present-day Alabama and part of Georgia. Jackson treated the Indians as conquered subjects, not as a sovereign people. Rather than continuing to mount violent resistance, a number of Indian tribes adopted American ways. The Cherokee were among the Indian peoples who white Americans described as

the "Five Civilized Tribes:" Cherokees, Choctaws, Seminoles, Creeks, and Chickasaws. These five tribes had to varying degrees chosen the path of cultural assimilation rather than resistance to America's expansionist policies. These tribes together numbered some 75,000 people spread out over the Carolinas, Georgia, Alabama, Mississippi, and Tennessee. Adopting the agricultural practices of their white neighbors and converting to Christianity were two major efforts the tribes made to accommodate to American culture.

No tribe was more committed to accommodation than the Cherokee. They converted to Christianity, established schools, and practiced American-style agriculture; a few prosperous Cherokees even kept slaves to work on their cotton plantations, mimicking their white neighbors in Georgia. They also abandoned their traditional tribal governance, declared themselves an independent republic, and adopted a constitution modeled on the Federal Constitution. As a sovereign nation they claimed to enjoy all the legal privileges that all nations enjoyed and were therefore not subject to the laws of the state of Georgia. However, the Cherokee effort to become an independent nation within the territorial confines of Georgia did not sit well with the government of the state.

When Georgians discovered gold on Cherokee land in 1828, a horde of white prospectors tried to stake out claims on Indian lands, a clear violation of tribal authority and law. Declaring tribal law null and void, Georgia passed a law that stripped the tribe of any legal authority over their lands. Henceforth Georgia law, not Cherokee law, would govern the Cherokee. The state also created a special police force, the Georgia Guard, to patrol Indian territory. The tribe lobbied sympathetic opponents of Jackson and turned to the federal courts for protection, arguing that Georgia's actions violated treaties between the Cherokee and the United States.

While the Cherokee awaited their day in court, Jackson turned up the pressure on them. The president refused the Cherokee's plea for federal troops to protect them. Because Indians could not testify in Georgia courts, the Cherokee were left without any legal means of defending their rights under the laws of Georgia.

Jackson seized the opportunity provided by the crisis to advance a plan to remove the Cherokee from Georgia and relocate them beyond the Mississippi River. He cast himself as benevolent father, intervening to rescue the Cherokee from extinction. His program would not force Indians to leave, but it made it very unattractive for anyone to remain behind. Indians who refused to relocate were relegated to the status of free blacks, who had only minimal legal rights under Georgia law. Jackson presented the Cherokee with two equally disastrous choices: accept the legal destruction of their tribal identity and live as second-class citizens in Georgia, or relocate to a distant territory far from their ancestral homes.

Jackson's opponents in Congress, many of whom had close ties to Protestant churches and missionary societies that had helped convert the Cherokees to Christianity, attacked his proposals. New Jersey's Senator Theodore Frelinghuysen wondered if "it is one of the prerogatives of the white man, that he may disregard the dictates of moral principles, when an Indian shall be concerned." Others attacked the president's proposal as a sham that offered Indians no legal protections if they stayed and allocated few resources to allow them to make a safe journey west. In this cartoon critical of Jackson's Indian policy (**8.11**), the president leads a parade that includes the devil and caged Indians.

The Protestant clergymen who led the opposition to Jackson's policy and who opposed removal were not great champions of Indian culture. Indeed, the religious defense of Indian rights shared many of the racist assumptions about Indians and their cultures that Jackson and others eager to dispossess them espoused. Yet these supporters of

Indians' rights believed that the supposed "inferiority" of Indian culture did not sanction unjust treatment or the violation of Indian rights. Women's reformers also rallied to the cause of Indian rights. Women's groups touted themselves as disinterested guardians of public morality who were not subject to the "blinding influence of party spirit." Jackson's aggressive removal policy threatened the ongoing effort to Christianize and civilize the Indians. Building on a tradition that extended back to the Revolutionary era (see Chapters 4 and 5), women invoked their moral authority as the guardians of the Republic's values, and opposed Jackson's policies as an affront to church, school, and the family. Such appeals were so effective that Martin Van Buren, Jackson's chief lieutenant, was shocked that his own niece opposed Jackson's policy and hoped that the president would lose his bid for reelection in 1832.

The Jacksonians passed their removal bill by a narrow margin. The **Indian Removal Act of 1830** gave President Jackson the authority to exchange Indians lands within the borders of the existing states for land west of the Mississippi. Federal officials put substantial pressure on Indian tribes to accept this offer and stressed that the federal government would not be able to protect Indian rights against state action if Indians did not agree to relocate. In essence, the federal government

8.11 The Grand National Caravan Moving East In this attack on Jackson's Indian policy, the president leads a parade that includes the devil playing a fiddle and caged Indians.

How does the Grand Caravan represent Jackson's Indian policy?

> # "We wish to remain on the land of our fathers. We have a perfect and original right to remain without interruption or molestation."
>
> Address of a council of the Cherokee nation to the people of the United States, written in July of 1830.

informed Indians that if they chose to remain, the government would tacitly allow the states to run roughshod over Indian rights. Although some tribes reluctantly accepted the inevitability of relocation, others resisted. The Cherokee eloquently protested against their forced relocation. Their leaders stated their desire to remain on the land of their ancestors and reminded Americans that their existing treaties with the United States guaranteed them this right. Rather than concede to the unfavorable terms presented by the federal government, or accede to the pressure from state governments, the Cherokee decided to seek a legal remedy in federal court. When Georgia violated Cherokee rights, the tribe sued, and the case ended up in the Supreme Court.

The Cherokee Cases

The struggle between Georgia and the Cherokee raised important constitutional questions. The Cherokee claimed to be a sovereign nation not subject to the laws of the state of Georgia. As was true of any sovereign nation, they claimed the right to govern themselves by rules that their own legislature enacted and to deal with the United States as a sovereign power. Georgia argued that Indians were subjects of the United States and that the idea of an independent Indian state within Georgia was an absurdity. The status of Indian nations in American constitutional law came before the Supreme Court in two separate cases related to the claims of the Cherokee nation.

In the Cherokee Cases, *Cherokee Nation v. Georgia* (1830) and *Worcester v. Georgia* (1832), the Supreme Court determined that Indian tribes retained certain rights traditionally associated with sovereign nations, including the right to govern themselves by their own laws, but lacked other rights, such as the ability to sue the state of Georgia. The latter case came to the Supreme

Court because Georgia had imprisoned two Protestant missionaries, Samuel Worcester and Elizur Butler, charging them with residing on Indian land without obtaining a license from the state. As both men were citizens of the United States, clearly they were entitled to sue in federal courts. Writing for the Court, Chief Justice John Marshall found that the missionaries had been wrongly imprisoned and were entitled to protection by the federal courts. Moreover, Marshall gave the Cherokee an important victory when he held that "the laws of Georgia can have no force" on Cherokee territory. Although the Cherokee did not enjoy all the privileges accorded foreign nations by U.S. law, they did retain the right to make laws within their own lands.

One Cherokee leader, Elias Boudinot, greeted Marshall's ruling in *Worcester* enthusiastically. Andrew Jackson was dismissive and wrote a supporter that the decision was unenforceable. Georgia refused to accept the Court's ruling and did not release the imprisoned missionaries. President Jackson was unwilling to antagonize Georgia, and was ill-disposed to Indians rights, so he refused to enforce Marshall's decision. The case might have precipitated a major constitutional crisis: A president refusing to follow a Court decision would have undermined the legitimacy of the entire federal judiciary. To avoid such a showdown, Jackson persuaded the governor of Georgia to simply pardon Worcester and Butler. Once the men were freed, the legal issue vanished, and Jackson and Marshall were no longer pitted against one another.

Resistance and Removal

The release of the two missionaries eliminated any legal issues and cleared the way for the Jackson administration to pursue its policy of removal. The Cherokee now faced the painful choice of accepting the inevitability of removal or continuing to resist Jackson and the state of Georgia. (See *Choices and Consequences: Acquiesce or Resist? The Cherokee Dilemma.*) In 1835, a minority of the Cherokee leadership signed a treaty agreeing to relocate west of the Mississippi. Many Cherokee denounced the treaty and hoped that their leaders could avert relocation. In 1838, federal troops began rounding up Cherokee and placing them in stockades to await deportation. The squalid conditions in the stockades took a heavy toll, and many of the most outspoken Cherokee

What do the Cherokee cases reveal about the limits of judicial power?

Choices and Consequences
ACQUIESCE OR RESIST? THE CHEROKEE DILEMMA

Should the Cherokee have resisted Jackson's removal policy? The Cherokee nation faced a difficult decision regarding how to deal with the increasing pressure to abandon their land and relocate to what is now Oklahoma. The tribal leadership was divided. Most Cherokee supported Principal Chief John Ross, who believed that there was enough support among Jackson's political opponents to block relocation. A minority within the tribe supported Elias Boudinot, who argued that it was better to relocate than oppose the inevitable.

Choices

1 Agree to the treaty and relocate; seek the best possible terms from the U.S. government to facilitate the removal process.

2 Reject the treaty and resist removal, by force if necessary.

3 Boycott the vote on the treaty and continue to rally support and lobby Congress to protect Indian rights against Georgia.

Decision

A small but vocal minority of the Cherokee, including Elias Boudinot, believed that continued residence in Georgia would only result in further harassment. They reasoned that it would be more prudent to try to obtain the best deal from the United States and relocate west. However, most Cherokee supported John Ross, who believed that it was still possible to rally support among religious groups and other whites sympathetic to Indian rights. Ross also recognized that Senators Daniel Webster and Henry Clay, two of the most powerful figures in the Senate opposed Jackson and were eager to use the plight of Indians to attack him. Most Cherokees refused to participate in the referendum held on the treaty. Supporters of the treaty accepting relocation won, but the treaty was not widely accepted by most Cherokee who had boycotted the vote.

Consequences

Bolstered by popular opposition to the treaty among the Cherokee, John Ross lobbied the Senate hard to reject it and came within one vote of defeating it. Having won a narrow victory, Jackson signed the treaty and the Cherokee were given two years to leave their homes or face military deportation. After relocation, prominent Indian supporters of the treaty, including Elias Boudinot were assassinated.

John Ross

Continuing Controversies

Was it realistic for the Cherokees to think that they might win support for their cause?
Most scholars agree that Jackson's Indian policy was racist and unethical, particularly the violation of existing treaties. There is, however, disagreement over how to make sense of the Cherokee response to the dilemma Jackson's policy created. Supporters of John Ross note that he was a savvy politician whose calculation that opposition to Jackson and sympathy for the plight of Indians made continued resistance a reasonable strategy. Opponents of Ross argue that Boudinot and others who voted in favor of the treaty were more realistic in their assessment of the political situation.

Elias Boudinot

Was resistance to removal a viable strategy for the Cherokee?

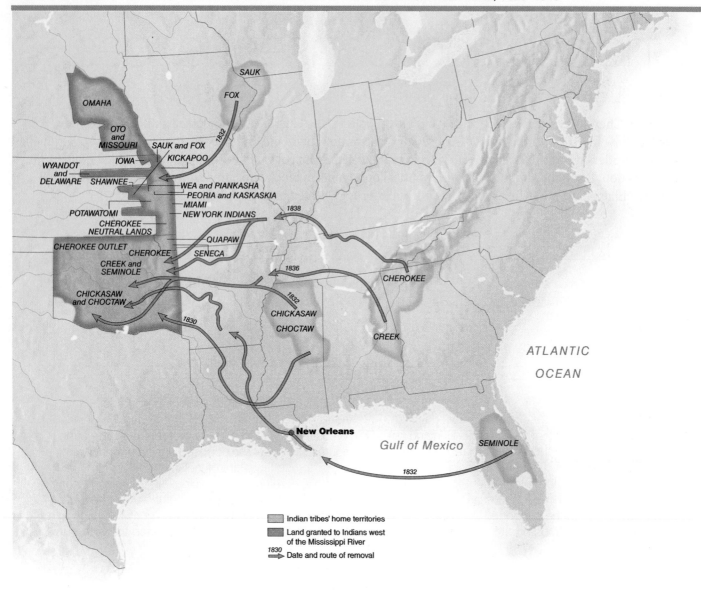

8.12 Indian Removal
This map shows the path taken by Indian tribes who were relocated under Jackson's Indian Removal plan.
Thousands died during the forced migration.

opponents of removal recognized that further re-sistance was futile.

Indian leaders who had continued to protest were joined by a broad coalition that included clergymen, women reformers, and constitutional nationalists such as Henry Clay and Daniel Web-ster, who were horrified at Jackson's behavior toward the Cherokee. The two men were particu-larly outraged by Jackson's disregard for treaty obligations, and his disrespect for the authority of the federal courts. Opposition to Indian removal provided a rallying point for a diverse collection of opponents who believed Jackson had become a tyrant who showed little regard for justice or the rule of law.

During the long and arduous march westward to what is now Oklahoma (**8.12**), thousands of Chero-kee men, women, and children died. Harsh weather, a shortage of supplies, and poor sanitation contrib-uted to a staggering death toll. Estimates vary but as many as 4,000 of the 12,000 Cherokee who were relo-cated perished in the trip. For the Cherokee and their descendants, the move west became known as "the Path Where They Cried," or the "Trail of Tears."

Democrats, Whigs, and the Second Party System

Unlike previous partisan movements Jackson's Democratic Party operated as an efficient and nationally integrated political organization. The new party organization called for a new party name. In the election of 1828, Jackson's supporters had described themselves as Democratic-Republicans, whereas Adams's supporters opted for the name National Republicans. These two labels testify to the transitional nature of the election. Both names harked back to political labels that were associated with the partisan struggles of Jefferson's and Monroe's administrations. By the election of 1832, Jackson supporters were simply calling themselves Democrats.

By contrast Jackson's opposition was still defining itself. A third political party, the Anti-Masonic party, organized in response to the undue influence of the Masonic Order—a fraternal organization whose members included many of the nation's most prominent politicians—capturing the imagination of voters briefly, but then disbanded. During Jackson's second term a new political party, the Whigs, rose out of the ashes of the old National Republicans, stressing the need for a talented, virtuous elite to shape the nation's future. Evoking the name of the seventeenth-century English opponents of absolute monarchy and the Patriot leaders who had opposed George III during the American Revolution, the Whigs saw themselves as defenders of the Constitution against executive despotism. Opposition to Jackson's Indian policy provided a common issue around which many disaffected groups had rallied early in Jackson's presidency. Economic policy, as defined by Clay's American System (which included support for the national bank), and a general opposition to the new vision of executive power personified by Jackson, particularly his Bank Veto, helped define the core issues of the new Whig Party.

Once voters aligned with one of the two main parties, they tended to remain loyal to it during their lifetimes. This intensified the divisions between the two new parties.

Third Party Challenges: Anti-Masonic and Workingmen's Parties

In the election of 1832, Andrew Jackson, aiming at a second term as president, faced Henry Clay, who still saw himself as the heir to James Monroe and John Quincy Adams's National Republicans. Another candidate, William Wirt, a talented lawyer who had argued the Cherokee cases before the Supreme Court, entered the fray as the choice of the Anti-Masonic party. The presence of a third party worked against Clay, splitting the anti-Jackson vote.

The Anti-Masons emerged in New York state as a reaction against the power of the Masonic Order, a secret fraternal organization that included many of the nation's most powerful figures, including Jackson and Clay. Freemasonry had a long history in America. Many members of America's founding generation had been Freemasons, including George Washington and Benjamin Franklin. The Freemasons championed Enlightenment ideals, but they also drew some of their rituals and symbols from mystical traditions. The best-known Masonic symbol, an eye suspended over an unfinished pyramid, appears on the reverse side of the Great Seal of the United States (and also on the modern dollar bill). Several characteristics of the Freemasons made them a target of popular suspicion. Secret handshakes, rituals, passwords, and other Masonic practices aroused unease. That so many prominent politicians were Masons encouraged conspiracy theories about the organization. Freemasonry's support for the Enlightenment also angered religious groups, especially evangelicals, who believed that Masons were anti-Christian.

These suspicions and resentments provided the backdrop to a sensational crime involving the Freemasons. In 1826, a disgruntled ex-Freemason, William Morgan, threatened to expose the order's secret rituals. When Morgan was kidnapped and disappeared, a clamor arose against the order. The Anti-Masonic party capitalized on this sensational crime. Meanwhile, the Freemasons did not remain silent. In this image emblazoned on an apron, the Anti-Masons are cast as the mythical monster the hydra. The image also links Anti-Masons with a host of vices. Freemasons, by contrast, are associated with Enlightenment values, such as science and equality. The apron also makes use of a pyramid, a common Masonic symbol (**8.13**).

The Anti-Masons proved to be innovative politicians, building an effective popular political movement. Although short-lived, their party, the first third-party movement in American history, helped pioneer new political techniques that mainstream parties soon adopted. The Anti-Masonic party used

8.13 Parody of an Anti-Masonic Apron
This parody of the Anti-Masons contrasts their values, "Persecution, Intolerance, Hypocrisy," with the Masons' Enlightenment ideals: universal benevolence, equal rights, tolerance, and scientific inquiry.

> ## "As long as property is unequal: or rather, as long as it is so enormously unequal, as we see it at present… those who possess it, *will* live on the labor of others."
>
> THOMAS SKIDMORE,
> *The Rights of Man to Property!* 1829

a national nominating convention to select a presidential candidate. It was also the first party to adopt an official platform, so that voters could judge the party's position on important questions. This party also energized religious voters who were drawn into public life and politics by the party's efforts.

At the same time that the Anti-Masonic party was organizing, workers in Philadelphia (1828) and New York (1829) formed their own political parties. The Workies, as they were called, won seats in the state legislatures. Among the political reforms they achieved was the abolition of imprisonment for debt. In this pro-Workie cartoon (**8.14**), an honest working man exercises the ballot freely, while a corrupt tool of the moneyed interest serves the devil.

The most radical voice of working class radicalism was that of the artisan Thomas Skidmore, who advocated a comprehensive program to use inheritance taxes to equalize wealth. In his book *The Rights of Man to Property!* (1829), Skidmore tackled the problem of economic inequality head on by proposing that wealth be subject to a huge inheritance tax. Although citizens would be free to accumulate as much wealth as they could during their lifetime, they would not be able to pass it on to their children. The goal was to prevent the creation of a monied aristocracy. Revenue from this inheritance tax would be used by the government to provide each new generation of citizens with a basic economic stake, so that each citizen would start life with the same economic advantages. This radical proposal to redistribute wealth went nowhere.

What lasting contributions did the Anti-Masons make to American politics?

8.14 *No More Grinding the Poor—But Liberty and the Rights of Man* The devil hands money to buy a rich man's vote, telling him to "grind the Workies." A virtuous working man invokes Liberty and the Rights of Man and casts his vote independently, while the goddess of Liberty holds out the ballot box.

But although the Workies were unable to create a national labor party, some of their proposals were popular enough to be picked up by mainstream Democrats. In particular the Workies' attack on banking resonated with Jackson and his followers. The class-conscious rhetoric of the Workies would affect how Democrats framed their message for the American people.

The Bank War and the Rise of the Whigs

Jackson's growing opposition to Clay's American System, including a visceral hatred for the Bank of the United States, emerged as a defining feature of his presidency. The political war that arose over the Bank helped Jackson's opponents to define their identity and create a new political party, the Whigs.

Henry Clay and Daniel Webster, two influential figures within the anti-Jackson National Republican party, believed that the president's hatred for the Bank could be used to defeat him in the election of 1832. Clay reasoned that Jackson's opposition to the Bank would alienate most voters because they would recognize the importance of a national bank. Clay approached Nicholas Biddle, the head of the Bank of the United States, to petition Congress for an early renewal of the Bank's charter in 1832. Clay knew that Jackson was opposed to the Bank and might veto the new charter, which Clay believed would turn the public against the President. Jackson confided to Martin Van Buren his intention to destroy the Bank. "The Bank, Mr. Van Buren, is trying to kill me, but I will kill it!" When Congress renewed the Bank's charter in 1832, Jackson vetoed it, and Clay lacked the votes to override the veto. The Bank then became the central issue of the presidential campaign of 1832.

Although the Bank had many supporters, including some in Jackson's administration, the veto turned out to be popular. Jackson had managed to convert opposition to the Bank into support for democracy itself. In his **Bank Veto Speech**, Jackson not only explained why he opposed re-chartering the Bank of the United States but also laid out his own vision of American democracy and constitutional government. Jackson attacked "the rich and powerful" who "too often bend the acts of government to their selfish purposes." His speech appealed to "the humble members of society—the farmers, mechanics and laborers." Jackson portrayed the Bank as a tool of the rich and powerful, who had obtained a charter by corrupting Congress. Thus, while the Bank Veto Speech sounded

> "The Bank Veto ... falsely and wickedly alleges that the rich and powerful throughout the country are waging a war of oppression against the poor and the weak."
>
> *Boston Daily Atlas*, editorial, 1832

democratic themes, it avoided the most combative class-conscious rhetoric radicals in the Working-men's movement had employed. Jackson did not attack wealth or the wealthy, but only those who used their wealth and influence to gain unfair advantages. Democratic newspapers echoed Jackson's view of the Bank: "The Jackson cause is the cause of democracy and the people against a corrupt and abandoned aristocracy." Jackson also used the Veto Speech to defend his view that federal courts were not the final judges of what the Constitution meant. In his view each branch of the federal government had an obligation to interpret the Constitution for itself.

Opponents attacked the veto as an assault on the Constitution. The press charged that Jackson had become "a DICTATOR." His veto, one newspaper claimed, was the act of a tyrant who had contempt for Congress. Rather than a victory for democracy, Jackson's recklessness was a sign of his corruption. For his opponents Jackson became the embodiment of tyranny.

Jackson's war against the Bank of the United States inspired a rich assortment of political cartoons, both critical and supportive of his policies. Democratic cartoonists cast Jackson as the champion of the common man, while supporters of the bank depicted him as a reckless tyrant. These images are explored in *Images as History: King Andrew and the Downfall of Mother Bank* (see pages 244–245).

Andrew Jackson, the Whigs, and the Bank War

In the election of 1832, Jackson defeated Clay by 200,000 votes and by a roughly 4-to-1 margin in the Electoral College. Clay's strategy of making the Bank the central issue in the campaign had backfired, and Jackson's attack on it had increased his popularity. Still the Bank War helped Jackson's opponents define their political identity and create a new political party, the **Whigs.**

Having defeated its supporters, Jackson might have opted to let the Bank die a natural death by simply allowing its charter to expire. However, fearing that his enemies would try to revive the Bank during the next congressional session and vote it a new charter, he decided to withdraw all federal funds from the Bank, a move that would have made its revival financially impossible. Jackson ordered his secretary of the treasury to remove the government's deposits, but even his own secretary thought such a move rash and damaging to the economy. The president had to fire two men before he could find one willing to become secretary of the treasury and follow his orders. Jackson justified this unusual step by noting that his reelection had given him a popular mandate to destroy the Bank. No previous president had ever cast his election in such terms. Even some congressional Democrats believed that Jackson had risked the economic well-being of the country to satisfy his personal vendetta against the Bank.

Jackson's enemies in Congress condemned his actions as additional proof that he was a tyrant who sought "a total change of the pure republican character of the Government and the concentration of all powers in the hands one man." For the Whigs, Jackson was little better than George III, whom America's own Whig Patriots had opposed more than 50 years before.

Economic Crisis and the Presidency of Martin Van Buren

Jackson's decision to remove funds from the Bank and deposit them in state banks damaged the economy. State banks were far less cautious than the Bank of the United States in loaning money, particularly for speculative land ventures. The resulting expansion of credit led to a speculative frenzy. By 1836, land sales mushroomed, increasing almost tenfold in five years to $25 million. To slow down the overheated economy, Jackson adopted a hard money policy, the Specie Circular, which required that land purchased from the government be paid for with specie—hard currency (before this policy individuals had purchased land with bank notes that were not guaranteed by gold or silver).

Martin Van Buren had become the most influential figure in Jackson's inner circle and was the Democrats' candidate for president in 1836. In most respects Van Buren was nearly the opposite of Andrew Jackson. Political caricaturists made much of the physical and personality differences between the two. Jackson was tall, thin, impulsive, and headstrong, whereas Van Buren was short, stout, cautious, and compromising. The nicknames of the two underscored the differences. Jackson was the "Hero of New Orleans" or "Old Hickory," whereas Van Buren was the "Little Magician" or the "Slippery Elm."

Van Buren won by a narrow margin in 1836, garnering 50.2 percent of the popular vote. He also inherited a weak economy. Within a year of taking office, he was forced to deal with the Panic of 1837, an economic crisis that plunged the nation into economic depression. Unemployment rose dramatically, as did the number of farm foreclosures and business failures. Wages dropped by as much as 50 percent, and a third of the workforce was out of work in hard-hit areas, such as Philadelphia. The cartoon *The Times*

illustrates the hardships associated with the Panic of 1837 and links them with Jackson's economic policies (**8.15**). The images of idle workers staggering drunk, while a respectable-looking woman and child beg for coins, show the plight of the working class. Although Whigs blamed Jackson's war against the Bank, the economic causes of the panic were largely foreign. In 1837, the Bank of England decided to raise its interest rates and restrict the flow of credit to British banks investing in America. This constriction of credit forced American banks to restrict their loans and call in many outstanding debts. Without access to additional credit, many businesses and farms defaulted on their loans. When these loans went bad, many banks, caught short, had to close. These bank failures led to a further constriction of credit, which then triggered another round of foreclosures and business failures. To make matters worse, the price of cotton on the world market plummeted in 1837, leaving many speculators without the funds to cover their loans and causing more bankruptcies. Critics of the president gave him a new nickname—"Martin Van Ruin."

8.15 Panic of 1837
This political cartoon highlights the hardships caused by the Panic of 1837. The spirit of Andrew Jackson, symbolized by his hat, glasses, and clay pipe, hovers over the suffering and despair.

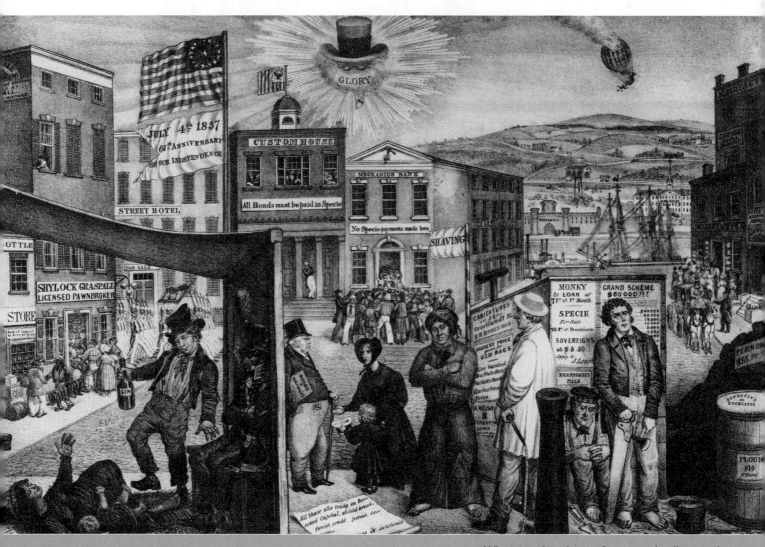

What are the signs of economic distress in this political cartoon on the Panic of 1837?

Images as History
KING ANDREW AND THE DOWNFALL OF MOTHER BANK

Andrew Jackson's war on the Second Bank of the United States provided political cartoonists with an excellent subject for satire. Jackson's enemies seized on his veto of the bill renewing the Bank's charter and his decision to withdraw federal funds from the Bank and deposit them in state banks as proof that the president had become a corrupt tyrant. Reaching back more than a half century to the colonists' struggle against King George III, Jackson's opponents sought to shift attention away from the Bank and focus it on his abuse of executive power. By portraying him as a corrupt monarch,

Jackson wears a royal crown and holds a scepter

The president holds a copy of the Bank Veto in his other hand

Jackson crushes the Constitution beneath his feet.

Why is Jackson portrayed as a monarch in this political cartoon?

who had trampled on the Constitution and recklessly distributed government funds to political cronies, the president's opponents found a potent rhetorical theme that was easily translated into powerful visual images.

The Whig view of Jackson is beautifully illustrated in "King Andrew the First." In this cartoon, he not only sports a crown and scepter, two obvious symbols of monarchy, but is adorned in rich robes fit for a king. Jackson holds a copy of the Bank Veto in one hand and tramples on the Constitution.

Jackson's supporters also found fertile subject for visual treatment. In this cartoon, "the Downfall of Mother Bank," Jackson and a popular cartoon character, Major Jack Downing (a forerunner of the character Uncle Sam) bring down the pillars of the Bank by announcing the withdrawal of Government Funds. The Bank's President, rendered with a demonic head, flees the scene. Jackson's enemies, the Whigs Henry Clay and Daniel Webster also rendered in an unflattering light. Clay begs Webster to save him from the collapse of the Bank's columns.

Nicholas Biddle, the Bank's president, is rendered as a demonic figure and flees the collapse.

Lighting bolts emanating from Jackson's order to withdraw funds from the bank topple its columns.

Henry Clay lies helpless and calls out for fellow Senator Daniel Webster to rescue him.

Playing the Democrats' Game: Whigs in the Election of 1840

 Largely because the Whigs split their vote among different regional candidates in 1836, they lost the election to Van Buren. However, the failure of the Whigs also reflected their problem communicating their message to the American people. Millard Fillmore, a young Whig from upstate New York (who would later become president), lamented the "heterogeneous mass" of the Whig Party, which included "old national republicans, and Jackson men in revolt, Masons and Anti-Masons, Abolitionists, and pro-Slavery men." Fillmore hoped that his party could find some "crucible … to melt them down into one mass of pure Whigs of undoubted good metal." In 1840, the Whigs did unite and learned how to frame their message to appeal to the American people. Drafting a popular military figure, William Henry Harrison, the Whigs reshaped their campaign using the tools and rhetoric that had made the Democrats so successful, especially their direct appeals to the people. In brief they learned to play the Democrats' game. The Whigs also pioneered new techniques for mobilizing voters and made an unprecedented effort to involve women in their cause.

The Log Cabin Campaign

Democrat Martin Van Buren's supporters derided the Whig candidate in 1840, General William Henry Harrison, as "Old Granny" or "Old Tippecanoe." The nicknames alluded to the general's age—he was almost 70—and to his victory over Shawnee Indians at the Battle of Tippecanoe in 1811. One Democratic editor in Baltimore suggested that given his advanced age it might be best to "give him a barrel of hard cider" and let him "sit out the remainder of his days in his log cabin." The effort to ridicule Harrison backfired, however: The Whigs seized on the twin images of hard cider and log cabins as the symbols for their campaign. The new campaign message transformed Harrison's public persona almost overnight: He was no longer the well-educated son of a wealthy Virginia planter (his real background), but was instead a simple farmer born into a log cabin who enjoyed a glass of hard (alcoholic) cider like all common folk. Eager to take advantage of the Democratic mistake, the Whigs plastered log cabins and barrels of hard cider onto an astonishing array of items: badges, banners, buttons, belt bucklers, hair brushes, pewter spoons, lithographed prints, quilts, and song sheets. The Whigs also used miniature wooden log cabins as floats, transforming what had been marches into festive parades.

Whig slogans became two of the most successful campaign slogans in U.S. history: "Tippecanoe and Tyler too" to support Harrison, and "Van, Van is a used up man" to taunt their opponent, Martin Van Buren.

The *Democratic Review,* capturing the irony of the election of 1840, noted that "we have taught them how to conquer us." Whigs not only adapted the Democrat's campaign techniques for mobilizing the popular vote but also developed their own innovative campaign style. With parades and campaign music such as "General Harrison's Log Cabin March & Quick Step," one of several popular campaign songs, the Whigs orchestrated a brilliant campaign and trounced their opponents (**8.16**). One Democratic paper complained: "We could meet the Whigs on the field of argument and beat them." But how were Democrats to respond when the Whigs "lay down the weapons of argument and attack us with musical notes"?

While Whigs cast Harrison and his running mate John Tyler as men of the people, they made Van Buren out to be a dissipated aristocrat who gorged himself on expensive French cuisine and champagne while Americans suffered economic hardship. Although charges of sexual misconduct were not new in American politics—Jefferson had been tarnished by the Sally Hemings scandal

8.16 Harrison Log Cabin and Hard Cider Sheet Music
This piece of sheet music includes the two most common symbols of Harrison's campaign, a log cabin and a barrel of hard cider. To highlight Harrison's military accomplishments, the artist shows him greeting a disabled veteran.

(see Chapter 7)—the smears of the Jacksonian era sunk even lower. Eager to discredit him, the Whigs spread rumors that Van Buren was a sexual pervert who had instructed the groundskeeper at the White House to create a mound in the shape of a breast.

Gender and Social Class: The Whig Appeal

Another innovative aspect of the Whig's electoral strategy was their mobilization of women. Although women could not vote, the Whigs hoped to get them to deliver their husbands' votes. The Whig appeal to women relied on two elements: a defense of morality against corruption and an appeal to economic interest. Whig newspaper editor Horace Greeley's description of the choice Americans faced in the 1840 election captures the appeal of the Whigs to many women. Greeley characterized the Whigs as supporters

of the family and Christian morality and accused the Democrats of being atheists and sexual perverts: "Wherever you find a bitter, blasphemous Atheist and enemy of Marriage, Morality, and Social Order, there you may be certain of one vote for Van Buren." Although such appeals to traditional family values and morality motivated some women to support the Whig cause, other women were inspired by economic arguments that Whigs directed at male voters.

> "The ladies they flock'd to their windows, In numbers, I say not a few, And held out their star-spangled banners All to the honor of Tippecanoe."
> — Harrison campaign lyric, 1840

Why were women drawn to the Whig message?

Democratic policies had left the American economy in shambles, and Whig policies promised to bring back prosperity. Whigs sponsored all-female rallies in support of Harrison, including a meeting in Ohio in which Whig women raised cups of tea in toasts to "Old Tippecanoe." Democrats complained about the Whigs "making politicians of their women," which was "something new under the sun."

Whigs also attacked Democrats for fanning class resentments. Thus one Whig chided the Democrats for their "incessant and unrelenting assaults" that tore "asunder the good feelings which bind men to each other." Rather than highlight the struggle between democracy and aristocracy, a favorite rhetorical theme of Democrats, Whigs stressed the essential harmony of all economic classes. An observer at a Whig rally proudly noted that "all classes" had rediscovered that "their interests were the same." Calvin Colton, a leading Whig, evoked the notion that "This is a country of self-made men." Whig policies would promote prosperity for all hard-working Americans.

The election clearly energized the voters, who turned out in record numbers, nearly four-fifths of eligible voters casting a vote. Harrison defeated Van Buren by 150,000 votes and a 4-to-1 margin in the Electoral College. President Harrison's inaugural speech was the longest in American history, 105 minutes long. His term in office, however, was the shortest. Within a month of becoming president, he contracted pneumonia and died. Vice President John Tyler then became the tenth President of the United States. Some dubbed him "His Accidency" because he inherited his position after Harrison's death.

Democrats and Whigs: Two Visions of Government and Society

The Whigs and Democrats represented opposing political visions. The Whigs favored a strong central government, encouragement for industry, and defense of Indians' rights; in the North and parts of the Midwest, they aligned themselves against slavery. Rejecting the views of old-style conservatives such as Chancellor James Kent, an heir to the Federalist vision of politics, the Whigs adopted the more popular style of politics pioneered by the anti-Masonic party, using it to reach out to voters. Whigs embraced Clay's American System, arguing that would help all Americans so that the rich and poor would each see their fortunes rise. Whigs emphasized the harmonious interaction of different elements of the economy and attacked Democrats for preaching an ideology that fostered class conflict.

The Whig version of democracy was not egalitarian. It recognized the need for a talented and virtuous elite to guide the nation. The Whigs' frank acceptance of inequality allowed them to find a place in their ranks for African Americans, Indians, women, and any other group who needed guidance or protection by an enlightened elite. Although slightly paternalistic in outlook, the Whigs believed they had a duty to protect these groups. Thus Whigs championed the rights of Indians against the efforts of Jackson and other Democrats to forcibly remove them from their lands. Although Southern Whigs supported slavery, Whigs outside the South often supported its abolition. Finally Whigs actively cultivated women's involvement in their campaign efforts.

The Whig Party drew from the Old National Republican Party of John Quincy Adams, adding to their ranks Democrats who opposed Jackson's Bank War. Anti-Masons and the more commercial Southern planters were also drawn to the Whig message. Whiggery also had a significant ethnic and religious basis. Individuals of English origin were also more likely than others to be Whig in sympathy, and mainstream Protestant denominations such as the Congregationalists, Presbyterians, and Episcopalians were more likely to vote Whig.

Democrats' vision of white men's democracy was more egalitarian than that of the Whigs, but it was also more exclusive. Although Democrats often couched their appeals in egalitarian terms, this rhetoric was not inclusive when it came to racial equality. Instead, Democrats reached out to workers, small farmers, and the planter class. Democrats attracted voters who were suspicious of the burgeoning market economy, including those who blamed banks, especially the Bank of the United States, for their economic problems. They asserted their support for the sanctity of private property and for the doctrine of states' rights, meaning that they were the party best suited to protect the interests of Southern slaveholders. Obtaining more land for white farmers, including Southern planters, was the primary goal of Democrats. Promoting this old Jeffersonian ideal of an expanding nation of yeoman farmers meant having to sacrifice the rights of Indians. From Jeffersonianism, Jacksonian Democrats inherited a fear of centralized government and large concentrations of financial power. Thus Democrats opposed Clay's American

What were the most important differences between Whigs and Democrats on economic issues?

View the **Image** *Matty's Dream*

Democrats

Oppose tariffs

Oppose federal support for internal improvements

Oppose Bank of the United States

Favor Indian removal

States' rights

Whigs

Favor tariffs

Favor federal support for internal improvements

Support the Bank of the United States

Oppose Indian removal

Support strong central government

8.17 Democrats and Whigs: Major Beliefs

System and the Whig's emphasis on a powerful federal government involved in economic development. Although not opposed to economic growth, Democrats believed that the individual states, not the federal government, ought to guide economic development.

Rural farmers and urban workers flocked to the ranks of the Democrats. Religious affiliation also dictated Democratic affiliation. Democrats were more popular among the less affluent evangelical Protestant sects such as the Baptists and Methodists, who found Jackson's egalitarian message appealing. Democrats also attracted free thinkers and Catholics who feared that the Whigs were trying to impose Protestant morality on them. For a summary of the ideas of the Democrats and Whigs, see the chart (**8.17**).

Democrats hailed the majesty of the people and attacked aristocracy, particularly artificial privilege and monopolies. Whigs embraced a more measured view of democracy. They warned Americans of the threat posed by demagogues, tyrants who flattered the people but who willingly sacrificed the common good, the rule of law, and the rights of the individual as they pursed their own quest for power and glory.

The expansion of democracy in America was accompanied by profound changes in the economy. The Whigs and the Democrats each grappled with these changes in different ways. Developments in technology, the growth of the factory system, and the burgeoning market would produce changes no less profound than the democratization of politics. Taken together these interrelated changes helped usher in an economic and cultural transformation historians describe as the "market revolution." The Whigs would become the great champions of the market revolution, believing that government, including the national government, could help expand the market economy and promote American prosperity. Democrats accepted the necessity of the market, but were more wary of its changes, and were particularly concerned that government not manipulate the market economy to further the interests of a wealthy elite. They were especially suspicious of the national government, and believed that the states could better promote growth. Whigs and Democrats would also come to view the geographical expansion of the United States in radically different ways. For Democrats, more land meant the fulfillment of the old Jeffersonian dream of creating a nation of independent farmers. Whigs worried about the political side effects of expansion. They sought to improve America, not expand it. Economic development and reform, not geographical expansion, would become the key to the Whigs' very different vision of the American future.

> "The aristocracy of our country ... continually contrive to change their party name. It was first Tory, then Federalist, then no party ... then National Republican, now Whig. ... But by whatever name they reorganize themselves, the true democracy of the country, the producing classes, ought to be able to distinguish the enemy."
>
> FREDERICK ROBINSON, Democrat, 1834

View the **Closer Look** *Images as History: Old Hickory or King Andrew: Popular Images of Andrew Jackson*

What role did ethnic politics play in the contest between Whigs and Democrats?

1824–1826

Tariff of 1824
Congress adopts protective tariff, a key element of Clay's American system

John Quincy Adams elected president
House of Representatives decides presidential election. Jackson charges Adams and Clay with a "corrupt bargain"

1828

Andrew Jackson elected president
In a bitter election campaign, Jackson defeats Adams and claims a broad popular mandate for his democratic agenda

Publication of South Carolina *Exposition and Protest* asserting states rights
South Carolina forcefully states the theory of states' rights and nullification

1829–1830

Thomas Skidmore publishes *Rights of Man to Property!*
Skidmore's book energizes Workingmen's movement

Webster-Hayne Debate
In dramatic speech to a crowded Senate chamber, Daniel Webster defends the Union against supporters of states' rights

1831–1832

Jackson's Bank Veto
Jackson vetoes renewal of Bank of the United States while attacking privileged elites

***Cherokee Nation v. Georgia* decided by Supreme Court**
Supreme Court rules against Cherokees in the first of two cases concerning their status as a sovereign nation

Review Questions

1. What were the main features of Clay's American System?

2. How did states' rights affect Andrew Jackson's presidency?

3. Was Jackson's Indian policy consistent with his democratic ideals? How did Jackson's perception of Indians allow him to reconcile his policy with his ideals?

4. How did Democratic and Whig cartoonists represent Jackson during the Bank War?

5. How did the Whigs out-democrat the Democrats in the election of 1840?

Key Terms

American System Henry Clay's comprehensive national plan for economic growth that included protective tariffs for American industry and government investment in roads and other internal improvements. **226**

"Corrupt bargain" Term presidential candidate Jackson's supporters used to attack the alliance between John Quincy Adams and Henry Clay that deprived him of the presidency. **226**

"Old Hickory" The nickname that General Andrew Jackson earned for seeming as stout as an "Old Hickory tree" in fighting against the British in the War of 1812. **228**

Spoils system The name applied to Jackson's system of replacing government officeholders with those loyal to him. **229**

Nullification A constitutional doctrine advanced by supporters of states' rights that held that individual states could nullify unconstitutional acts of Congress. **231**

Indian Removal Act of 1830 Legislation that facilitated the removal of Indians tribes to lands west of the Mississippi. **235**

Bank Veto Speech Jackson's veto of a bill to re-charter of the Bank of the United States, in which he explained why he opposed the bank and laid out his own vision of American democracy and constitutional government. **241**

Whigs (American, 19th Century) Anti-Jackson political party; the name evoked the seventeenth-century English opponents of absolute monarchy and the Patriot leaders who had opposed the tyranny of George III during the American Revolution. Whigs supported Clay's American System and a stronger central government. **242**

1833

South Carolina nullifies federal tariff
South Carolina becomes the first state to invoke the doctrine of nullification

1836–1837

Martin Van Buren elected president
Democrats retain control of the White House after Jackson's retirement from office

Panic of 1837
Economic downturn is blamed on Jackson's policies

1838

Cherokee Removal (Trail of Tears)
Jackson's policy of pressuring Indians to give up their lands and homes and relocate to Western lands is approved and implemented

1840

William Henry Harrison elected president
Whigs exploit new methods of democratic politics to elect their candidate to the presidency

MyHistoryLab Connections

Visit www.myhistorylab.com for a customized Study Plan that will help you build your knowledge of *Democrats and Whigs*.

Questions for Analysis

1. **Why did so many commentators on American life discuss the democratic character of Jacksonian America?**

   Read the **Document** *Michel Chevalier, Society Manners and Politics in the U.S., p. 226*

2. **Who was Davy Crockett and why did his life become a symbol of America during the Jacksonian period?**

   Read the **Document** *Profile: Davy Crockett, p. 222*

3. **How did images of Jackson represent him and what do they reveal about political life in the 1820s and 1830s?**

   View the **Closer Look** *Images as History: Old Hickory or King Andrew: Popular Images of Andrew Jackson, p. 249*

4. **What role did race play in Jacksonian political rhetoric?**

   View the **Map** *Interactive Map: Native American Removal, p. 235*

5. **Was the Bank Veto an example of radical democracy?**

   Read the **Document** *Andrew Jackson, Veto of the Bank Bill, p. 245*

Other Resources from This Chapter

Hear the **Audio File**

• *Van Buren, p. 241*

Read the **Document**

• *John Adams, A Corrupt Bargain or Politics as Usual, p. 229*
• *South Carolina Refuses the Tariff, p. 230*
• *Andrew Jackson, the Force Bill, p. 232*
• *The Cherokee Treaty of 1817, p. 238*

View the **Closer Look**

• *General Harrison's Log Cabin March—Sheet Music, p.246*

View the **Image**

• *1824 Election Cartoon, p. 225*
• *Matty's Dream, p. 248*

The Market Revolution p. 254

What was the Market Revolution?

The Spread of Industrialization p. 260

How did early industrialization change the nature of work?

The Changing Urban Landscape p. 264

How did the growth of cities affect American society?

Southern Society p. 270

How did race and class shape Southern society?

Life and Labor Under Slavery p. 274

How did African-American culture adapt to the hardships imposed by slavery?

Workers, Farmers, and Slaves

The Transformation of the American Economy, 1815–1848

The United States experienced extraordinary economic growth and change in the first half of the nineteenth century. But the economies of the Northern and Southern regions of the nation evolved along different paths. The North developed a free labor economy marked by industrialization, urbanization, and immigration. Economic growth was spurred by new technologies that made agriculture more productive and factories more efficient, as well as by improvements in transportation and communication that spurred consumer demand for the latest goods. By contrast, while the South experienced some industrialization and urban growth, most of its expansion and development focused on raising cash crops with slave labor. The huge profits generated by cotton cultivation prompted the expansion of plantations into the so-called Black Belt that stretched from Alabama west to east Texas.

By mid-century Northerners and Southerners became increasingly self-conscious about the distinctiveness of the labor system in their own region and more critical of that employed in the other half of the nation. This image, *The Tree of Liberty* (1846), illustrates the radical differences between the vision of liberty defended by Northern proponents of free labor and that of Southern defenders of slavery. On the right side of the tree, a slaveholder reclining in a chair while fanned by a slave announces, "Surrounded by slaves & basking at ease by their labor we can have a clearer conception of the value of liberty." On the other side of the tree, the artist has placed two industrious farmers conversing, and young mill women in front of their factory. A group of gentlemen chat, and one praises the North's expanding population, composed of industrious immigrants from "almost every nation."

Although North and South had developed different labor systems, each was tied to the expanding market economy that Henry Clay praised in 1824. The expansion of the market economy transformed the countryside in both the North and South and fueled urban growth.

> "The greatest want of civilized society is a market for the sale and exchange of the surplus of the produce of the labor of its members.... If we cannot sell, we cannot buy."
>
> HENRY CLAY, 1824

TREE OF LIBERTY.

United States enjoying the refreshing shade of the Tree of Liberty.

The Market Revolution

 In 1800, most rural households produced only a small surplus that was traded locally, often through a system of barter that did not require cash transactions. Most manufactured goods were produced by artisans whose workshops were usually in their homes. During the nineteenth century, the American economy became more commercially oriented. Farmers began producing cash crops for sale in distant markets, and a wider range of consumer goods, many of them made in factories, became available. The **market revolution**, the term used by historians to describe this transformation, encompassed interrelated developments that revolutionized agriculture, industry, technology, transportation, and communications. This market revolution would radically change both North and South in the antebellum period. Improved technology such as iron plows and steam-powered cotton gins enabled farmers to produce more crops, while cheaper, more efficient forms of transportation including the railroad allowed them to deliver these goods to markets. New communication technology, notably the telegraph and steam-powered printing press, increased the speed and volume of news and information available to Americans.

Agricultural Changes and Consequences

Before 1815 most farmers in the South and the North labored to achieve a "competence," which meant enough food to feed their family and a small surplus to trade locally or barter for goods, such as tools, that could not be produced at home. But in the early nineteenth century, American farmers began raising crops for an expanding commercial market to earn profits and accumulate wealth. Periodicals geared to farmers promoted this new emphasis on commercial farming, touted the latest agricultural theories, and advertised the most up-to-date labor-saving devices. Publications such as *The New England Farmer* warned that "the cultivator who does not keep pace with his neighbors as regards agricultural improvements and information will soon find himself the poorer consequence of the prosperity that surrounds him."

In 1819 Jethro Wood introduced one of the earliest and most important of these "improvements"—an iron plow that could double a farmer's efficiency. Within a decade John Deere had improved Wood's design, creating a plow that seemed to move through soil so easily that it was dubbed the "singing plow." In the wheat-growing Midwest, farmers adapted horse-driven machines to tasks such as threshing and raking. Crank-powered churns transformed arduous women's tasks, such as making butter

by hand. The cotton gin (see Chapter 7) transformed Southern agriculture. In 1839, the *Farmer's Almanac* proclaimed that "scarcely a tool…has not been altered for the better in some way or other." The new scientific methods of agriculture helped increase the productivity of the soil.

The creation of a market economy encouraged farmers to concentrate on crops that they could sell for cash in the marketplace, a trend that caused changes in farming patterns that varied by region. The South concentrated on staples for export such as cotton, while farmers in the Midwest produced grain, particularly wheat. Eastern farmers shifted their efforts to livestock production, dairy goods, fruits, and vegetables.

Market-oriented farming, with its emphasis on efficiency and profit, also transformed social values and communal patterns of life. The new, more commercial approach to farming challenged traditional ideas of neighborliness and community that had been central to rural life. Increasingly farmers began to see harvest parties, husking bees (communal celebrations in which corn was husked), dances, and other ritual communal occasions in which work and leisure were combined as inefficient and wasteful. The *Farmer's Almanac* in 1833 advised that "if you love fun, frolic, and waste and slovenliness, more than economy and profit, then make a husking." In this humorous image of a corn husking (**9.1**), a man finds a lucky ear of red corn that entitles him to a kiss, but his advance is met by a girl holding a corn "smut," a weathered ear of corn that gave her the right to refuse her suitor.

Upcountry Southern farmers continued to concentrate on producing food for personal consumption and devoted a relatively small percentage of their land to commercial crops. While other regions of the country sought to improve every parcel of land for commercial agriculture, parts of the South remained committed to practices that encouraged a more self-sufficient style of agriculture, geared to personal use. Unlike in the North, for example, where extensive land was enclosed behind fences, many Southern states enacted laws against fencing in lands not used for agricultural production, so that livestock could roam freely.

A Nation on the Move: Roads, Canals, Steamboats, and Trains

Central to the development of commercial, market-oriented farming were improvements in transportation. These changes allowed those previously unable to deliver farm products to the growing cities of the Northeast and Midwest to enter the market. For those already in the market, the costs of business were dramatically lowered. These changes also spread information, including almanacs, books describing the latest agricultural techniques, and advertisements for the latest goods.

The first major development in transportation was the building of a network of roads and turnpikes that by the 1820s helped knit together the major urban areas along the eastern seaboard. New York state embarked on the most ambitious program of road building, adding 4,000 miles of improved road and turnpikes by 1820. The National Road, the first federally funded road in U.S. history, stretched from Cumberland, Maryland, to Wheeling in what is now West Virginia. By the 1830s, this road would take travelers as far west as Columbus, Ohio. Pennsylvania built the Lancaster turnpike, which eventually was extended to connect Philadelphia and Pittsburgh, making transportation cheaper and more reliable. By the 1820s, 30,000 tons of freight moved by wagon across this route annually.

9.1 Corn Husking Frolic
Alvan Fischer's 1828 painting captures the festive communal atmosphere of a corn husking. [*Source:* William Summers/Alvan Fisher, "Corn Husking Frolic". 1828. Oil on Panel, 70.8 x 62.23 cm Museum of Fine Arts, Boston Assc. #62.27 Photograph © 2010 Museum of Fine Arts, Boston.]

 View the **Closer Look** *Impact of the Transportation Revolution on Traveling Time*

Why did the *Farmers Almanac* frown on huskings and frolics?

The new road network dramatically cut travel times: A coach journey from New York to Boston that had taken four days in 1800 took half that time in 1824. Even more dramatic was the invention of the steamboat. Navigable rivers such as the Mississippi, Ohio, Missouri, and Hudson had long served as vital arteries for moving agricultural products from the interior to market. This water highway system moved almost exclusively in one direction. Traveling upriver from New Orleans to Louisville in Kentucky, for example, was expensive and slow (as long as three to four months). As a result few manufactured goods reached the interior of the nation. The arrival of the steamboat would revolutionize upriver travel, reducing the same New Orleans to Louisville journey to just over a week by 1826. The steamboat proved an economic boon to river cities such as St. Louis, New Orleans, Pittsburgh, Cincinnati, and Louisville. Hannah Stockton Stiles, the daughter of a prosperous merchant, stitched this elaborate needlework quilt, capturing the hustle and bustle of Philadelphia's waterfront. Stiles included a steam boat, with smoke billowing from its smoke stack (**9.2**).

Canals provided another means of moving goods more cheaply and faster than by road. Since the 1780s, private companies had built small canals, usually less than 20 miles long. In 1817, America had about 100 miles of canals, with no single canal longer than 30 miles. In that same year, however, New York's Governor De Witt Clinton persuaded the legislature to fund a canal linking Buffalo on Lake Erie to Albany on the Hudson River. The Erie Canal, as it was called, was over 300 miles long and was an unprecedented undertaking, both in terms of engineering and state investment The New York legislature approved the huge sum of $7 million in bonds to fund the project, roughly a quarter of all the money spent by all the states on internal improvements in the 1820s. Although opponents mocked it as "Clinton's ditch," the Erie Canal was a stupendous success. Before the canal opened, wheat from western New York state took 20 days to reach Albany by wagon and cost almost $100 per ton to transport. After the canal was built, the same ton of wheat could be transported all the way to New York City in ten days at a cost of $5. Much as the steamboat fueled the growth of river towns, the Erie Canal fueled the development of new cities such as Rochester, Buffalo, and Syracuse. The canal's success sparked "canal fever" across the country, and more than 3,300 miles of canals were completed by 1840 at a cost of about $125 million.

In 1825, the same year that the Erie Canal was completed, the first commercial railway began operating in England. In 1830 the Baltimore and Ohio railroad successfully tested a steam-powered train. Americans soon developed their own railroads, and by 1840 railroad mileage surpassed canals. Railroads further increased the speed at which goods and people moved from one part of the country to another. By 1840, the trip between Boston and New York by rail took a mere half-day.

Americans greeted with amazement each innovation of the transportation revolution, but the railroad evoked the most powerful responses. "What an object of wonder!" wrote one American in response to his first sight of a railroad in 1835. Charles Caldwell, the founder of the University of Louisville, praised the railroad as an agent of civilization that would help spread morality and education by linking people together more effectively. Not everyone shared this view of railroads. Critics of the railroad raised concerns about safety, noise, and some expressed fears about the destruction of the landscape. *Images as History: Nature, Technology, and the Railroad: George Inness's Lackawanna Valley (1855)* explores how artists struggled to represent this marvel.

9.2 Trade and Commerce Quilt In this quilt Hannah Stockton Stiles created images of maritime trade on Philadelphia's thriving waterfront.

Images as History

NATURE, TECHNOLOGY, AND THE RAILROAD: GEORGE INNESS'S *THE LACKAWANNA VALLEY* (1855)

The president of the Delaware, Lackawanna, and Western Railroad commissioned George Inness to paint the company's new roundhouse, a facility to house and repair trains. But Inness soon found that his artistic vision conflicted with that of the railroad. For the railroad, artistic considerations were less important than advertising its achievements. The main disagreement between Inness and his patrons was over the representation of the roundhouse. The artist wished to render the facility accurately, which would have diminished its importance in the painting. Ultimately Inness agreed to make the roundhouse appear larger than it would have had he rendered the scene in actual perspective. He sacrificed artistic truth to the necessities of the marketplace.

Inness's painting applies many of the conventions used to represent nature to a scene in which nature and technology coexist in a complex relationship. Thus he includes a reclining youth, a figure often used in landscape paintings. Here, the boy calmly gazes toward the oncoming train. Rather than disrupting the serenity of nature, the train appears to blend harmoniously into it.

Although Inness portrays the railroad in a positive light, he also suggests the cost of technological progress: A field of tree stumps reminds viewers that economic development has taken a toll on the landscape. Which aspects of the painting present a positive view of progress? Which aspects suggest a negative view?

George Inness, *The Lackawanna Valley*

The figure of the boy reclining in the field evokes serenity and harmony with nature.

Although the distant roundhouse should have appeared much smaller, Inness increased its size to please his patrons.

The prominence of so many tree stumps suggests that the artist was aware that technological progress came at a cost: the defilement of nature.

View the **Closer Look** *Images as History: Nature, Technology, and the Railroad*

How did George Inness view technological progress in his painting of the Lackawanna Valley?

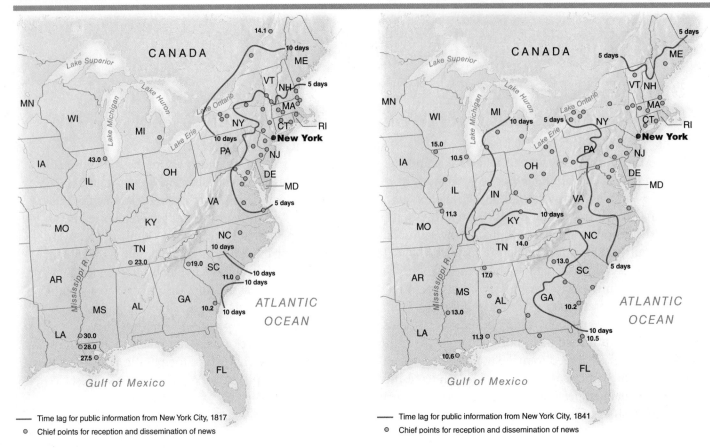

Time lag for public information from New York City, 1817
Chief points for reception and dissemination of news

Time lag for public information from New York City, 1841
Chief points for reception and dissemination of news

9.3 Time Lag for News 1800–1841 Improvements in communication technology and transportation dramatically reduced the time it took for news to travel from the coastal cities to the interior cities.

Spreading the News

Improvements in roads, canals, and railroads facilitated the spread of communication. The near doubling of the number of post offices and miles of improved postal roads between 1810 and 1820 increased the number of letters delivered annually from not quite four million to nearly nine million. It had taken ten days for news to travel from Richmond, Virginia, to New York City in Jefferson's day. By the 1810s, it only took five days. The advent of the railroad, as the figure (**9.3**) shows, accelerated this trend, dramatically cutting the time for news to travel. For example, in 1817, it took 19 days for news to travel from New York to Cincinnati; by 1841, it only took seven days.

The **telegraph**, which used electricity to send coded messages over wires, revolutionized communication. In 1844, Samuel Morse, a painter turned inventor who had patented the device in 1837, transmitted a message taken from a Bible verse—"What hath God Wrought?"—along a telegraph line from Washington, D.C., to Baltimore. The message was in code—the Morse code—that he also developed. Observers predicted correctly that the

nearly instantaneous communication of telegraphy would usher in a new age of communications. By the mid-1850s, companies such the Western Union Telegraph Company had offices across the nation, improving communication between cities as far apart as Boston and New Orleans.

Improvements in print technology sharply reduced the cost of publishing, leading to an enormous increase in the number of newspapers, magazines, and books. In 1801, there were only 200 newspapers in America; by 1835, there were 1,200. The number of magazines also rose dramatically, giving Americans a far greater range of printed materials. While most eighteenth-century magazines and newspapers were directed at the general public, many of these new publications were aimed at specific audiences. The *Farmer's Almanac*, for example, dispensed advice about agriculture, while magazines such as *Godey's Lady's Book* informed a large and growing group of middle-class women readers about the latest ideas in fashion, literature, and family matters. Also on the rise by the 1830s, American book publishing, with an output of at least 1,000 titles a year, nearly rivaled that of Britain. Between 1825 and 1840, the value of the American book business doubled to $5.5 million.

Technological improvements in printing also made better and cheaper images possible. In 1834, Nathaniel Currier began producing colored lithographic images using a new process that was cheaper than traditional engraving techniques. Rather than aspire to provide high art, Currier set out to provide "cheap and popular pictures" of contemporary events, historical figures, and scenes of everyday life. Touted as "Printmakers to the People," his firm, eventually renamed Currier and Ives, produced images costing as little as fifteen cents. These were sold on city street corners, and peddlers carried them to country stores across the nation. Currier and Ives prints often featured patriotic themes, displaying the nation's wealth, ingenuity, and economic achievements. Technological progress was a favorite theme. Consumers could choose from an assortment of steamboats and trains. Although the firm often celebrated technological triumph they also exploited disaster. Currier's first great success was this dramatic print of a fire aboard the steamboat *Lexington* published in 1840 (**9.4**).

Beyond making it easier and faster to send messages and news, the communications revolution also contributed to economic expansion of the market revolution by fueling the desire for new consumer goods and fashions. Newspapers were filled with advertisements for the latest goods. Lavishly illustrated magazines inspired readers to buy the latest fashions.

9.4 Nathaniel Currier's *Conflagration of the Steamboat Lexington* The sensational image of the burning of the steamboat *Lexington* helped launch the career of Nathaniel Currier who later joined with James Ives to form one of the most successful publishing firms of the nineteenth century, Currier and Ives.

Awful Conflagration of the Steam Boat LEXINGTON In Long Island Sound Eve*g.* Jan*y.* 13*th* 1840. by which melancholy occurrence; over 100 PERSONS PERISHED.

Why was the firm of Currier and Ives so successful?

The Spread of Industrialization

In the early nineteenth century, the United States began a transition from a predominantly agricultural economy to an industrial one. This process unfolded unevenly across different sectors of the American economy and followed different models depending on the industry and region. Driven by new manufacturing technology and techniques, industrialization led to a vast increase in the number of goods—everything from clothing and shoes to tools and toys—available to the American consumer. But for many workers, especially skilled artisans, the new industrial economy led to a devaluation of their skills and loss of social status. For less-skilled workers industrialization often meant exploitation, long hours, and low pay. For others, however, the new manufacturing economy opened up opportunities for advancement.

From Artisan to Worker

The group of workers most dramatically affected by the onset of industrialization was artisans, or workers who used specialized skills to produce consumer goods, from shoes to bread to candles. In the colonial period skilled artisans worked in small shops attached to their homes, using hand tools to produce goods for local consumption. They also used an apprenticeship system, training boys in their skills (until about age 20) in exchange for their labor. The relationship between artisan and apprentice was close. Typically an apprentice lived in his master's house, receiving food, clothing, and education.

In the new factory system first pioneered by Samuel Slater in Rhode Island (see Chapter 7), the artisan system of small-scale production was replaced with a new set of roles: owners, managers, and wage workers. The owner provided the money for the enterprise, the manager supervised the workers, and the laborers did the actual work, which was usually less skilled than the traditional crafts practiced by skilled artisans. Some industries, such as textiles, shifted relatively rapidly to the use of power-driven machinery. Shoe production, by contrast, continued to employ many manual laborers into the 1860s. In both cases manufacturers undermined the old craft traditions of artisans by breaking down the productive process into simple steps that could be performed by workers with minimal training.

Factory work forced laborers to give up many aspects of working-class culture. The work rhythm of artisans before the rise of the factory included periods of intense activity followed by slack periods in which artisans might socialize with one another, perhaps meeting in a tavern to drink and discuss politics. Under industrialization the clock ruled. Factory workers were required to follow a strict schedule and perform at a steady pace day in and day out. Beyond the rigid regulations of the workers' day, the factory robbed them of the pride of craft associated with handmade goods. In contrast to **artisan production**, where a skilled craftsman might create one-of-a-kind pieces, factory goods were designed to be identical.

In addition to creating a labor force of less skilled workers, the new system also led to a sharp separation between home and workplace. Before 1800, most artisans in New York had workshops attached to their homes, but by 1840, two-thirds of them lived in one place and worked in another. The factory system separated home and workplace. The apprenticeship system also suffered. By 1827, less than a quarter of apprentices lived with their employers.

If the factory system diminished the control that working people had over their time and work, it increased the goods they could buy. Because factory-made goods cost less to produce, families of modest means could now afford items once available only to the wealthy. Ordinary Americans could now purchase furniture, clocks, dishes, silverware, and the latest fabrics.

Women and Work

The factory system had a tremendous impact on the lifestyle and status of American women. While men's work increasingly shifted to sites outside the home, women's economic activity remained primarily within. Nevertheless, some women participated more directly in the new manufacturing economy through "outwork." In this system skilled processes were broken down into simpler tasks that could be farmed out to women to perform in their homes. Manufacturers provided the materials to women with a specified completion date. They saved money because they did not have to provide a workshop or factory, and they paid women a fraction of the wages a skilled male artisan earned. In New England during the 1830s, 33,000 women took part in outwork production of palm leaf hats. They also produced paper boxes, hoopskirts, artificial flowers, and cloaks. In urban areas many women depended on the meager earnings of outwork for their survival.

In rural areas, such as parts of New England, women might rely on outwork for supplemental income while continuing to do traditional agricultural work, such as producing milk, butter, and cheese. Rural New England women would eventually provide the labor force for one of the most ambitious industrial experiments of the day: the Lowell mills.

The Lowell Experiment

In 1814, a group of Boston merchants decided to expand on Samuel Slater's mill village model (see Chapter 7) and create a large planned industrial town. They built a textile factory in Waltham, Massachusetts, and developed the **Waltham System**, a mill town model that relied on centralized factories, each one of which united all the distinctive steps of cloth production under one roof. The system also came to depend on a large labor force housed in company-owned dormitories.

In 1823, the same group of merchants, led by Francis Lowell, opened an even larger factory on a site in Massachusetts adjacent to the Merrimack River. The Lowell mill consolidated all aspects of cloth production. Cotton from the South arrived at the mills, where it was cleaned, carded, spun, and woven into a finished fabric. Within a decade the new mill town of Lowell boasted 22 mills, and grew to over 50 mills by 1850. Not surprisingly many competing mill towns cropped up all over New England and upstate New York.

The mill owners recruited young, single women from rural New England to work at the factory towns. To accommodate this workforce and appease concerned parents, they built dormitories and libraries and provided boardinghouse matrons to supervise the morality of the workers. Each boardinghouse, with up to ten bedrooms per building, housed between 20 and 40 women. Two women sometimes had to share a single bed. The boardinghouses also contained a kitchen, a dining room, a parlor, and separate quarters for the housekeepers, who were generally older women.

Compared to the remote New England villages from which most of the women came, Lowell offered many amenities. Lowell allowed women to earn significantly more money than did farm labor and domestic service, the two most common occupations for single women. The women operatives in the mills also made friends with their coworkers and enjoyed free time away from the factories to socialize and pursue cultural and educational opportunities not available in their small home towns. As Josephine L. Baker, a mill worker, noted, "there are lectures, evening schools, and libraries, to which all may have access." The mill women even produced their own literary magazine, the *Lowell Offering* (**9.5**). The magazine, nominally independent of the mills, echoed this rosy portrait. Indeed, the cover of this 1845 issue shows a mill girl holding a book and adopting a contemplative pose. She stands in a lush natural setting of flowers, trees, and vines. In its early years the Lowell experiment was touted as an example of American ingenuity, a popular destination for European visitors eager to see the wonders of the new world. British novelist Charles Dickens visited and later wrote with wonder that the mill women were not degraded by factory life, but rather retained "the manners and deportment of young women."

Despite the upbeat image portrayed on the cover of the *Lowell Offering*, life in the mills was hard. The women worked 13-hour days, six days a week. Furthermore, the noise of the machines, the dust and lint generated by the manufacturing processes, and the long hours demanded by the mill owners often

9.5 *Lowell Offering*
The Lowell mill women produced this title page of the final issue of the magazine *Lowell Offering*, presenting an image of industrial harmony. The young mill woman, holding a book, stands amid symbols of natural abundance.

📖 Read the Document *A Second Peep at Factory Life*

What was the Lowell system?

overwhelmed women accustomed to working out of their homes. As one young Vermont mill woman noted in a letter to her family, "It is very hard indeed and sometimes I think I shall not be able to endure it. I never worked so hard in my life."

For a decade the Lowell mill owners enjoyed high profits and peaceful labor relations. But increased competition with other textile producers led them in 1834 to announce a wage cut. Furious, the Lowell mill women went on strike, or "turned out." Critics of the strike saw it as a radical assault on the rights of the mill owners' economic freedom and a display of unseemly behavior for women. The mill women defended their actions as an assertion of their rights as American citizens and an example of the ideals of independence and liberty that had inspired the American Revolution (see *Competing Visions: The Lowell Strike of 1834*). The strike failed to block the wage cut, but it was a milestone in the history of both women's rights and labor organization. In the 1840s, a new organization, the "Lowell Female Labor Reform Association," would join a national struggle for a ten-hour working day for all workers.

Urban Industrialization

Metropolitan industrialization was far more diverse than in industrialization in mill towns. In New York and Philadelphia, factories turned out products by

Average Height of American Men
Serving in the Military, 1800–1860

Year	Inches
1800	68.1
1810	68.1
1820	68.1
1830	68.3
1840	67.8
1850	67.4
1860	67.2

9.6 Average Height of Native-Born American Men by Year of Birth
As the nation's wealth grew during the first half of the nineteenth century, it became more concentrated in fewer hands. The rich controlled an even larger percentage of the nation's wealth by mid-century. [*Source*: Adapted from Steckel, Richard. "A History of the Standard of Living in the United States". EH.Net Encyclopedia, edited by Robert Whaples. http://eh.net/encyclopedia/article/steckel.standard.living.us]

using everything from skilled handwork, similar to artisan production, to steam-powered machinery run by low-skilled factory operatives. The factories produced an enormous range of goods under this system, including chemicals, paints and varnishes, musical instruments, clothing and hats, tools, machines, furniture, and books.

New York emerged as the nation's leading fashion and clothing center during this period. Initially the city led in the production of cheap "Negro cottons," coarse garments assembled for sale in the South to clothe its slaves. By the 1830s, elegant tailoring houses such as the venerable firm of Brooks Brothers were offering well-tailored clothes to the upper classes and the more prosperous members of the middle class, who sought to emulate them.

The industrial economy that emerged in antebellum America created jobs and opportunity for many workers and a vast array of consumer products. But not everyone benefited equally. To protect themselves, skilled workers built a large labor movement; twenty labor newspapers emerged in this period to champion the workers' cause. In 1835, 20,000 Philadelphia workers from a dozen trades walked off their jobs to protest working conditions and demand a ten-hour workday. The strike was the most successful labor action in the nation's short history and made the ten-hour workday the new standard. By 1836, labor councils or federations, a precursor of modern labor unions, had been founded in 13 manufacturing centers across the nation, from Boston to Cincinnati. In the largest cities, such as New York and Philadelphia, more than 50 separate trades joined to form the general councils. The movement collapsed during a severe economic depression that began in 1837. Hard times produced high unemployment and intense competition, undermining labor's ability to bargain for higher pay and better working conditions.

Worker unrest stemmed in part from the awareness that a small group of Americans were benefiting more than others from the new economic order. The distribution of wealth became less equal. Although the wealth of the average citizen grew, the proportion of wealth concentrated in the hands of the nation's wealthiest citizens also increased. One of the most revealing measures of changes in the standard of living of Americans is provided by statistics about the average height of men serving in the military (**9.6**). In the period between 1800 and 1860, the average height of Americans decreased by almost an inch. Given that the overall wealth of the nation increased during this period, this evidence suggests that not all Americans shared in this growing prosperity.

How did urban industrialization differ from other models of industrialization such as the Waltham (Lowell) model?

Competing Visions
THE LOWELL STRIKE OF 1834

In protesting a proposal to cut their wages, the Lowell mill women looked to the language of the American Revolution. They cast the mill owners as tyrants who sought to reduce the workers to economic slavery. For those sympathetic to the mill owners, the strikers were un-American, radical followers of the British feminist thinker Mary Wollstonecraft, the champion of women's equality (see Chapters 5 and 6). Why did the protestors at Lowell seek to wrap their cause in the banner of the American Revolution and its ideals?

The Lowell mill women cast themselves as the heirs to the Patriots who fought the American Revolution. Their appeal for public support focused on issues of rights and independence, themes that echoed the language of the American Revolution.

UNION IS POWER

Our present object is to have union and exertion, and we remain in possession of our unquestionable rights. We circulate this paper wishing to obtain the names of all who imbibe the spirit of our Patriotic Ancestors, who preferred privation [poverty] to bondage, and parted with all that renders life desirable—and even life itself—to procure independence for their children. The oppressing hand of avarice [greed] would enslave us, and to gain their object, they gravely tell us of the pressure of the time, this we are already sensible of, and deplore it. If any are in want of assistance, the Ladies will be compassionate and assist them; but we prefer to have the disposing of our charities in our own hands; and as we are free, we would remain in possession of what kind Providence has bestowed upon us; and remain daughters of freemen still.

"Union Is Power," petition of the striking Lowell women, 1834

In this contemporary report of the Lowell protest, a Boston newspaper highlighted the radical and unladylike behavior of the strikers.

We learn that extraordinary excitement was occasioned at Lowell, last week, by an announcement that the wages paid in some of the departments would be reduced 15 percent on the 1st of March. The reduction principally affected the female operatives, and they held several meetings, or caucuses, at which a young woman presided, who took an active part in persuading her associates to give notice that they should quit the mills…. The number soon increased to nearly 800. A procession was formed, and they marched about the town, to the amusement of a mob of idlers and boys, and we are sorry to add, not altogether to the credit of Yankee girls…. We are told that one of the leaders mounted a stump and made a flaming Mary Wollstonecraft speech on the rights of women and the iniquities of the "monied aristocracy."

Salem Gazette, February 18, 1834

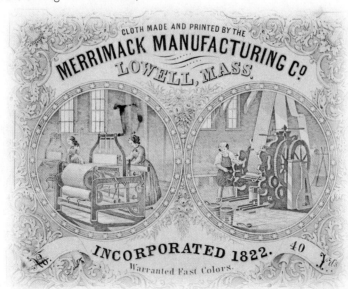

Label showing women at work in the mill
[*Source*: Merrimack Manufacturing Co. 1822 cloth label. American Textile History Museum, Lowell, MA]

View the **Closer Look** *Competing Visions: The Lowell Strike of 1834*

How did ideas about gender shape the response of critics of the Lowell strike?

The Changing Urban Landscape

Industrialization accelerated the growth and changed the nature of American cities. While before 1820 less than ten percent of the nation's population resided in cities (areas of more than 2,500 people), by 1860, that number had grown to 20 percent. Older cities such as New York, Philadelphia, Boston, and Baltimore grew, and new cities in the West such as Pittsburgh, Cincinnati, St. Louis, and Chicago emerged. The population growth in these cities was fueled by migration from the American countryside and foreign immigration, especially from Ireland and Germany. Immigration fostered cultural diversity in cities, but it also led to tensions and violence along ethnic, racial, and religious lines. Hostility between Protestants and Catholics and between whites and blacks increased urban violence. Policing became a far more complex problem in these growing cities.

Old Ports and the New Cities of the Interior

With nineteenth-century industrialization and population growth, major changes occurred in American cities. New kinds of neighborhoods developed that reflected the class and ethnicity of their inhabitants. Distinctive working-class neighborhoods, including the first urban slums, formed. This trend reflected the drop in the number of artisans who owned their homes and the rise of multiple-family dwellings, as well as the number of boardinghouses taking in lodgers.

New York's Five Points neighborhood illustrates the profound changes in the urban landscape caused by rapid economic development. To its working-class inhabitants, Five Points was a poor but thriving multiethnic and racially mixed community. To

9.7 Five Points
This image reflects the elite's view of the Five Points neighborhood. The artist has depicted a robbery in progress in the lower left.

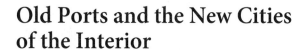

What was the Five Points neighborhood and why did it become so well known?

outsiders, however, its shabby housing and reputation for crime, especially prostitution, made it a symbol of urban decline. Thus while its inhabitants saw the neighborhood as a vibrant and diverse community, New York's elite viewed it as a notorious slum to be avoided. This contemporary image (**9.7**) captures the multiracial character of the neighborhood, but it also reflects the fears of many New Yorkers that Five Points was crime-ridden and dangerous.

Middle- and upper-class families eager to escape contact with working people, immigrants, and free blacks segregated themselves in new, more exclusive neighborhoods. New York's Gramercy Park, for example, was created in 1831 as a private park surrounded by elegant houses. Ringed by a tall gated fence, the park was (and still is) accessible only to the adjacent homeowners who received special keys. This image of a similar exclusive enclave (**9.8**), St. Johns Park in New York, shows a park with a fence that segregates the rich residents from individuals such as the African Americans lampooned in this image for attempting to dress and act above their station in life. The African-American figures are caricatures whose physical features are exaggerated to conform to the racist stereotypes of the day.

In 1800, even America's largest urban centers were "walking cities." A person could easily walk around all of New York, Philadelphia, or Boston in a few hours. By 1820, however, these cities had grown to contain more than half the urban population of the new nation, and by mid-century these once compact walking cities had become sprawling metropolises. Some of this growth came from annexation. Philadelphia in 1854 annexed several of its suburbs, increasing its size from two square miles to 129. Much of the growth was driven by advances in mass transportation that allowed city dwellers to live farther and farther away from where they worked, shopped, and went for entertainment. The first of these modes of transportation, which arrived in 1827, was the "omnibus," an urban stagecoach that carried up to 12 passengers over fixed routes for a flat fee. Expensive, slow, and uncomfortable, it gave way by the 1850s to the horse car, a 20-passenger coach pulled on rails by horses. Faster, cheaper, and more comfortable than the omnibus, horse cars, or street-railway lines, spread to virtually every large city by 1860. Philadelphia alone boasted 155 miles of track. Steam-powered locomotives had also begun to carry commuters—or people who traveled over a significant distance from home to work—to and from outlying areas. Issues of sanitation and the problem of providing fresh drinking water for these expanding cities led cities such as New York and Philadelphia to undertake

9.8 St. Johns Park St. Johns Park, also known as Hudson Square, was one of the gated parks created to separate the poor and working classes from wealthy New Yorkers Access to St. John's Park was limited to residents. [*Source:* The Library Company of Philadelphia]

ambitious construction projects such as Philadelphia's Fairmount Waterworks.

By 1810, New York had surpassed Philadelphia to become the nation's largest city. Central to this development was New York harbor, the largest on the East Coast and one ideally suited to become a major port. The Erie Canal ensured New York's economic supremacy by connecting the city to the Midwest. It increased dramatically the flow of finished goods from Europe and the rest of the United States into the American heartland and the flow of foodstuffs produced by Midwestern farmers into domestic and foreign markets.

Inland cities such as Pittsburgh, Cincinnati, St. Louis, and Chicago were among the fastest-growing urban areas in the nation. Situated on rivers or lakes and soon connected by railroads, inland cities became manufacturing centers and transportation hubs. Between 1800 and 1840, these new cities saw their populations quadruple. If any city in America fit the modern stereotype of a soot-covered industrial town, it was Pittsburgh. The French traveler Michel Chevalier remarked that "a dense black smoke which, bursting forth in volumes from the foundries, forges, glass-houses, and the chimneys of all the factories and houses, falls in flakes of soot upon the dwellings and persons of the inhabitants. It is, therefore, the dirtiest town in the United States." Cincinnati, a small settlement on the Ohio River in 1800, became a major industrial center by 1840, producing a wide range of manufactured products, including furniture, tools, candles,

View the **Closer Look** *Images as History: Fairmont Waterworks Sculptures*

What does the creation of gated parks such as Gramercy Park tell us about urban life in this period?

paper, leather, and soap. The soap industry grew out of the city's many pig-slaughtering houses (Cincinnati's nickname was "Porkopolis") that produced fat renderings that provided an essential ingredient for making soap. The firm of Procter & Gamble was founded in the city in 1837.

Immigrants and the City

The sharp rise in urban populations in the nineteenth century stemmed from two sources: the migration of Americans from rural areas and immigration from Europe. The latter soared from 23,000 in 1830 to 428,000 in 1854. Immigrants left their homelands for the United States for many reasons, including poverty, poor harvests, warfare, and political and religious persecution. The most dramatic exodus in this period was triggered in 1845 when Ireland's potato crop failed. The disaster killed more than one million people and spurred more than a million others, mostly poor peasants, to cross the Atlantic to America. Poor harvests and political turmoil boosted German immigration to the United States. Besides the Irish and Germans, the other large groups of immigrants came from other parts of Britain, notably Scotland and Wales, and from Scandinavia (**9.9**).

The Irish and German immigrants changed America's ethnic composition. For the first time many non-Protestants entered American society. Irish immigrants were almost entirely Catholic, whereas Germans included both Catholics and Protestants. Ethnic enclaves with names like *Kleindeutchland* (Little Germany) and Little Ireland, with their own churches, mutual aid societies, theaters, newspapers, restaurants, and social clubs, developed in many cities.

Irish immigrants generally came from the poorest segments of society; they arrived with

little money and few skills needed in an urban economy. They often ended up in slum neighborhoods like Five Points and came to dominate low-skilled jobs such as laborer and domestic servant. Nonetheless, many Irish immigrants entered the skilled trades and became successful entrepreneurs.

German immigrants were more diverse. As with the Irish, many German immigrants were poor peasants forced off the land, but many others were skilled artisans. Liberal intellectuals also fled Germany after the political upheavals of 1848 that swept over much of continental Europe. Germans were more likely than the Irish to become farmers, shopkeepers, or skilled tradesmen. They also ventured further inland, settling places such as Cincinnati and St. Louis. More skilled on average than their Irish counterparts, Germans transformed a number of fields. Adolph Busch, a skilled brewmaster, brought German-style beer to America, and musical instrument makers helped launch such venerable firms as Steinway and Sons, piano makers.

Free Black Communities in the North

Urban centers in the North and Midwest were home to some of the largest free African-American communities in the nation. Free blacks in enclaves such as Boston's "New Guinea" or Cincinnati's "Little Africa" were probably the most urbanized subgroup in America. Racial segregation was more pronounced in the urban North than in the cities of the South, where urban slaves were likely to live in their masters' homes. Thus an African American in Boston was almost twice as likely to live in a segregated neighborhood as an African American in New Orleans. African-American communities developed thriving institutions, such as churches, schools, and self-help societies.

Still, life for free African Americans was hindered by racial prejudice and discrimination. In the North and parts of the Midwest, exclusion from many of the skilled trades often forced African Americans into the most menial types of labor. This situation worsened in the 1840s and 1850s as immigrants, especially the Irish, took over occupations traditionally dominated by African Americans, such as barbers and cart men. In the cities of the North and West, hostility to African Americans competing for jobs with

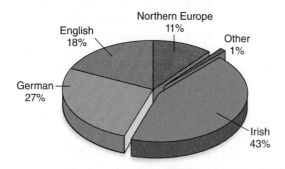

9.9 Sources of European Immigration
Immigrants from Germany and Ireland changed the population mix in much of the nation. The influx of Catholics in particular resulted in tensions with Protestants.

whites intensified. A drawing from the period (**9.10**) exploits white fears of African-American laborers. The racist message of the image is clear: Free blacks will steal the jobs of white workingmen.

Through persistence, talent, and good fortune, some African Americans could still surmount the obstacles they faced in the labor market and achieve financial security or even prosper. Henry Boyd of Cincinnati is an example of one such life. Trained as a carpenter while still a slave, Boyd managed to obtain his freedom and began to ply his trade in Cincinnati. Although Boyd found some work, many employers refused to hire him. Yet in 1836, he accumulated enough money to establish his own furniture-making business, and by 1842, his downtown factory was using the latest steam-powered equipment to make furniture. By the 1850s, Boyd was employing a mixed-race workforce of some 50 people. Nine years later, however, fire destroyed Boyd's factory. Without insurance he could not rebuild his factory, leaving him as he had begun—a struggling artisan.

9.10 *The Results of Abolitionism* This poster warns white laborers that their jobs might be taken by free African Americans. [Courtesy Library Company of Philadelphia]

Riot, Unrest, and Crime

Urbanization in the first half of the nineteenth century was accompanied by a rise in crime and disorder. During the 1830s, there were 115 incidents of mob violence, a steep rise from previous decades. One newspaper reported that "a spirit of riot" had taken over the nation's cities. Violence increased as growing cities became more divided racially, economically, and ethnically. Anti-Catholic sentiment spurred much of the intensified violence. In 1834, a mob attacked and burned a Catholic convent just outside Boston. Ten years later in Philadelphia, the "Bible riots"

left 20 dead and two Catholic churches in ashes. Philadelphia's growing Catholic community opposed the city's policy of using the Protestant version of the Bible for instruction in public schools. After appeals from the city's Catholic community were rejected, protestors took to the streets. Crowds of Catholics and Protestants attacked one another in the streets of the "City of Brotherly Love." The city was plunged in to three days of rioting and mayhem.

Racial animosity also inspired urban unrest. Cincinnati's African-American community faced the ire of white mobs in 1829, 1836, and 1841. A three-day riot in Providence, Rhode Island, in 1831 destroyed most of the African-American part of the city. A riot in New York in 1834 destroyed an African-American church, school, and a dozen houses. Adding to the tensions and occasionally sparking violence were political battles between Democrats and Whigs, antagonisms between supporters and opponents of slavery, and conflicts over regulating or eliminating behaviors such as gambling and drinking.

Contributing to the rise in urban violence was the steady increase in the number of single men living outside traditional family units, a trend that arose from industrialization and immigration. In the 1840s and 1850s, at least 30 percent of male urban dwellers lived outside family units, usually in boardinghouses. Free from the traditional guidance and restraint of adults and relatives, young men developed a masculine subculture in which alcohol and fighting played a central role.

Many young women also streamed into the city looking to improve their economic conditions. The combination of an aggressive masculine sub-culture and a large pool of poor young women led to a significant rise in prostitution, a situation that alarmed many officials. The Reverend Lyman Beecher decried the fact that so many young people were "thrown out upon the open bosom of our city" where they were easily "corrupted by sensuality." Beecher's fears were well founded. At mid-century prostitution ranked as the second biggest industry in New York City! (See *Envisioning Evidence, The Economics and Geography of Vice in Mid-Nineteenth-Century New York.*) Theaters encouraged prostitutes to attend their performances to boost ticket sales, a practice so common that the cheap seats they occupied were dubbed the "guilty third tier."

The expanding news media found salacious tales about the city's seamier side of life a great way to raise circulation. Tales of crime, including the sensational murder of the prostitute Helen Jewett in New York City in 1836, fueled the growth of the press. Rival newspapers competed to be the first to publish the latest revelation about the case, and the story dominated headlines for months. The crime even produced colorful images such as this showing the alleged murderer skulking away (**9.11**). Reflecting the low regard in which prostitutes were held, the lowly clerk accused of killing Jewett was acquitted despite considerable evidence suggesting his guilt.

Most urban crime did not involve sensational tales of murder, but rather petty crimes against property or person. The informal policing mechanisms that cities had relied on in the eighteenth century, including the use of night watchmen and sheriffs who had to rely on community support to quell unrest, proved woefully inadequate to policing a major metropolitan area in the nineteenth century. In 1839, the mayor of New York pushed to create a professional police force, fearing that without strong intervention New York would attain "the character of a riotous city." In 1845, New York created the first modern professional police force in America, modeled on London's Metropolitan Police Force. New York employed 800 men organized in a military structure; they carried clubs (but not firearms) and were deployed to keep the peace and apprehend criminals.

9.11 Murder of Helen Jewett
Currier and Ives's lurid depiction of the murder of the prostitute Helen Jewett was part of the media frenzy surrounding this sensational crime.

What does the murder of Helen Jewett reveal about nineteenth-century city life?

Envisioning Evidence
THE ECONOMICS AND GEOGRAPHY OF VICE IN MID-NINETEENTH CENTURY NEW YORK

The influx of young men and young women into New York City in the early nineteenth century fueled both the supply of and the demand for prostitutes. Indeed, by mid-century, prostitution was the second largest industry in the city, exceeded only by tailoring. If one maps the geography of vice, a fascinating pattern emerges. The greatest concentration of brothels was clustered around New York's Broadway theater district, the notorious Five Points neighborhood (one of the city's poorest), and the docks. "The police do not meddle," an observer of New York life wrote, "unless they [the prostitutes and brothels] are noisy, disturb the peace, or become a public nuisance."

Blocks with prostitution continuously, 1820–1859

COMPARISON OF THE CASH VALUE OF PROSTITUTION AND MANUFACTURED ARTICLES IN NEW YORK CITY, 1855	
Tailor Shops	$7,592,696
Prostitution	$6,350,760*
Silver Wire	$3,809,331
Steam Engine and Boiler Manufacture	$3,292,800
Shipbuilding	$2,593,761
Gristmills	$2,497,719
Chandleries and Soap	$2,230,927
Distilleries	$2,218,200
Furnaces	$2,146,950
Hat and Cap Manufacture	$2,082,502
Gold and Silver Manufacture	$1,966,000
Boot and Shoe Manufacture	$1,839,100
Lard Oil	$1,839,000
Butcher Shops	$1,763,860
Fish and Whale Oil	$1,729,900
Bakeries	$1,727,153
Gas Manufacture	$1,625,500
Printing	$1,545,500
Breweries	$1,377,292
Marble Manufacture	$1,154,500
Sawmills	$1,145,000

* Money spent on prostitution (includes housing and entertainment).

Does the historical evidence support the concerns expressed by moral reformers about the prevalence of commercial sex in New York?

Southern Society

Even as Northern society changed dramatically between 1815 and 1860 due to immigration, urbanization, and industrialization, Southern society remained committed to slavery and a cash crop economy. The rise of cotton cultivation and the expansion of plantations into the band of fertile land from Georgia to Texas transformed slavery. Although most Southerners did not own slaves, slavery suffused Southern culture and society. A few planters dominated the political and economic life of the whole South. One leader reminded a Southern audience in 1850 that slavery was bound up with all of the South's institutions and affected "the personal interests of every white man."

> "I could easily prove that almost all the differences which may be noticed between the characters of the Americans in the Southern and in the Northern states have originated in slavery."
>
> ALEXIS DE TOCQUEVILLE,
> *Democracy in America* (1838)

The Planter Class

Few planters lived in the grand luxury many people today associate with the world of nineteenth-century slavery. For example, at Nottoway, in Louisiana, John Hampden Randolph built a magnificent mansion that contained 64 rooms, 200 windows, and 165 doors. But the typical planter lived far more modestly in a simple two-story wood-framed house. His home, generally described as "the big house" because it was always the largest domestic dwelling on a plantation, was at the center of smaller outbuildings, including a kitchen, well, dairy, ice house, smokehouse, and laundry. More substantial plantations included many other types of buildings, such as barns, stables, sheds, and storehouses. Georgia rice planter Henry McAlpin's Hermitage plantation (**9.12**) resembled a small town, with multiple residences, a hospital, and other buildings. Indeed, the slave quarters constituted an even smaller village within this self-contained community. Most

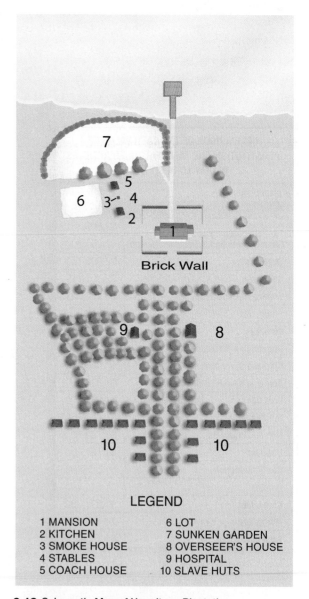

Brick Wall

LEGEND

1 MANSION	6 LOT
2 KITCHEN	7 SUNKEN GARDEN
3 SMOKE HOUSE	8 OVERSEER'S HOUSE
4 STABLES	9 HOSPITAL
5 COACH HOUSE	10 SLAVE HUTS

9.12 Schematic Map of Hermitage Plantation
Large plantations were like small towns. This plantation included a separate overseer's house, hospital, and slave huts.

What do plantation architecture and the arrangement of buildings tell us about slavery?

plantations were far more modest. Most slave owners owned between one and nine slaves. Less than one percent owned 100 or more slaves. The typical slaveholder worked a small family farm of about 100 acres with fewer than ten slaves.

Planters created something akin to English-style landed aristocracy. Thomas Dabney, who had migrated to Mississippi from Virginia in 1835 to establish a large cotton plantation, aspired to this aristocratic lifestyle. He emulated the life of an English country gentleman, taking tea in the afternoon and treating his less affluent neighbors as social inferiors.

While industrialization in the North created a sharp divide between work and home, physically separating the two realms, Southern plantations fused them together. A large body of advice literature geared toward plantation management that appeared in Southern magazines urged planters to act so that "the Negro should feel that his master is his lawgiver and judge; and yet his protector and friend." An 1842 book reminded planters that because slaves were "placed under our control" masters had to care for and instruct them, so that they could "receive moral and religious uplift." In theory masters sought to "govern absolutely." "Plantation government," a Georgia planter wrote, "should be eminently patriarchal." The planter was not only "the head of the family" but also "should, in one sense, be the father of the whole concern, negroes and all."

Planters' wives or widows or the eldest daughters in families without a matriarch often helped manage plantation life. The plantation mistress, as she was called, supervised slaves who might work in the kitchen, nursery, laundry, stable, or garden. Whereas husbands often relied on overseers to assist them and frequently left the plantation to attend to business or public affairs, the planter's wife was often left to her own devices to run a home that was more like a small village. Southern men claimed that slavery had helped elevate the status of the white woman and liberated her from the drudgery of domestic life, making her "no longer the slave, but the equal and idol of man." Hospitality was a central part of Southern plantation culture, and the plantation mistress played a key role in the rituals associated with it. Although lavish entertainment was one part of this reality, the evidence found in the surviving diaries and letters of many mistresses suggest that the typical plantation mistress was more apt to feel isolated than the center of a vivacious social life. Mary Kendall, for example, wrote in her diary about her loneliness: "for about three weeks I did not have the pleasure of seeing one white female face." Kendall's sense of isolation lent her description of plantation life a melancholy quality.

Yeomen and Tenant Farmers

Most Southern whites were not planters but yeoman farmers, independent landowners who worked their own small farms. In 1860, more than three-quarters of Southerners owned no slaves. As a result yeomen farmers depended on neighborliness and communal cooperation to complete tasks such as planting, harvesting, or building. Lacking the urban centers and cheap transportation that allowed many small farmers in the North to enter fully into the market economy, many Southern yeomen did not produce large surpluses for market. Instead they devoted most of their resources to producing food for their own families and generally allocated only a small portion of their lands for cash crops that could be sold to purchase seeds, sugar, and the occasional manufactured good. Since they could not afford the cost of transporting their surpluses to market, yeoman farmers depended on planters to market their small surpluses. They also depended on planters for the use of the plantation mill to grind corn into meal. In much of the South where planters and yeomen resided side by side, a complex web of economic, political, and social ties bound these two classes together. But many yeomen in the upcountry regions of the South were fiercely independent and resented the more affluent planters who dominated their state's militia, legislatures, and courts.

Indeed, most Southern state legislators, judges, and militia officers were drawn from the planter class. But the yeomanry formed the core of the militia system that tried to catch runaway slaves and guard against slave insurrection. In this antislavery woodcut, the slave patrol is terrorizing a slave (**9.13**) traveling without the pass needed to leave the plantation. Passes were written by owners, and traveling slaves had to have them.

Many Southerners owned no land and worked as tenant farmers. In parts of the South, estimates by historians vary, but between 30–50 percent of the white population fell into this category. Although some landless Southerners were young men waiting to inherit land from their fathers, many others rarely entered the ranks of the solid yeomanry. In parts of the Deep South with many African-American slaves, poor whites fraternized with slaves: smuggling liquor into the slave quarters, helping runaways, or forming sexual liaisons and permanent relationships with slaves. More often, however, a white supremacist ideology overcame class solidarity across racial lines.

9.13 *A Slave Caught Without a Pass* In this woodcut from an abolitionist almanac, a slave patrol harasses a slave traveling from one plantation to another.

Free Black Communities

Although most African Americans in the South were enslaved, by 1860, six percent of black Southerners lived as free people of color. Most free blacks resided in the upper South, with large communities in border states such as Delaware and Maryland. A third of the free blacks resided in Southern cities; Baltimore, Richmond, New Orleans, Charleston, Memphis, Mobile, and Natchez had the biggest communities. The South's Slave Codes were even more restrictive than the Black Codes enacted in the North (see Chapter 8). Free Southern blacks had to carry identification to prove that they were not slaves. They could not hold office and in some areas even testify in court against whites.

Although life for free blacks in the South was difficult, the shortage of skilled artisans in many Southern cities enabled them to enter trades such as cabinet making. Southern cities were also less spatially segregated than Northern cities, and Southern African Americans played a prominent role as domestics and in some fields and trades such as tailoring and hair cutting. The free black community in New Orleans was one of the most affluent in the South. It published its own newspapers, and its elite members held lavish balls each year.

Religious institutions were also important for the free African-American community. In addition to tending to the spiritual needs of their congregations, ministers were often community leaders. Southern black churches had much larger memberships than similar institutions in the North. Thus the largest African-American congregation in the North, New York's Abyssinian Baptist Church, had a membership of 440 at mid-century, whereas the First African Church of Richmond, counted 3,160 members.

How did the experience of free blacks in the South compare with those in the North?

View the Image *Free Black Church*

White Southern Culture

Wealthy white Southerners in the antebellum years entertained on a lavish scale, hosting parties, balls, fox hunts, and horse races. Aristocratic affectations even led some to sponsor medieval tournaments that included jousting. Southerners took pride in their resorts along the Gulf Coast, gracious vacation spots characterized by a "quiet ease." New Orleans gradually replaced New York as the horse racing capital of the nation. Blood sports such as cock fighting also remained popular, particularly among less affluent Southerners.

Reputation and honor were central values in the male-oriented Southern culture. An "unsullied reputation," one observer noted, was all that a man required to be "on a social level with his fellows." A Scottish traveler remarked that Southern men "consider themselves men of honor" and "more frequently resent any indignity shown them even at the expense of their life, or that of those who venture to insult them."

When a social inferior insulted a gentleman, the appropriate response was to cane or horsewhip the offender. Dueling was reserved for settling matters of honor among gentlemen. In 1838, John Wilson, a former Governor of South Carolina, published *The Code of Honor; or the Rules for the Government of Principals and Seconds in Duelling*, which explained such things as the role of seconds and the choice of weapons. The centrality of honor to Southern culture was the chief reason dueling endured in this region long after it had been outlawed in the North. Many of the South's leading politicians, including Andrew Jackson and Henry Clay, had fought duels during their careers. This contemporary drawing by a Northern opponent of slavery (**9.14**) portrays the South as a culture dominated by dueling, brawling, and mobbing. For some Northerners, especially those opposed to slavery, the dueling and other violence they associated with the South were a result of the brutality inherent in slavery. The connection between slavery and Southern violence figures prominently in the image, which shows a cruel master whipping a helpless slave child.

9.14 Southern Violence
This Northern drawing links the brawling and dueling of Southerners with the brutal labor regime of slavery. Abolitionist attacks on Southern culture often mentioned the pistol and the lash.

What role did honor play in Southern culture?

Life and Labor Under Slavery

 Slavery was a complex institution that took many forms in the South. Some slaves lived on large plantations and worked in gangs under an overseer, whereas others toiled beside their master on small farms. Still others lived in cities where, if they possessed skills, they were often hired out. But the law treated all slaves as property, leaving them entirely at the mercy of their master who had the power to impose punishment and sell slaves away from their families. To protect themselves, slaves developed various traditions and strategies. Many turned to religion to provide spiritual comfort and cultural resources to resist the domination of their masters. Slaves also developed subtle forms of resistance such as feigned illness, work slow downs, and destruction of tools and other property. Occasionally slaves took more overt measures like running away, either to seek a temporary respite from the harsh labor regime or to escape North to freedom. The most radical and the rarest form of resistance was insurrection, rising up against the established authorities.

Varied Systems of Slave Labor

Slave labor produced a variety of agricultural products—tobacco, hemp, sugar, and rice. But the leading product was cotton, an enterprise in which more than half of all slaves toiled. By 1840, cotton accounted for more than half the nation's exports with most of it heading for European (especially British) textile mills. The remainder was sent north to mills in places like Lowell, Massachusetts.

Yet even in those regions of the South in which cotton was not the primary crop, the cotton economy influenced economic life. Many farmers who did not produce cotton produced foodstuffs and supplies for consumption on cotton plantations. For instance, hemp was turned into rope to bind cotton bales for shipment.

The antebellum South was divided economically into the lower South and the upper South. The warm climate of the lower South was ideal for cotton cultivation, as was the dark rich soil of the region stretching from Alabama to Texas known as the Black Belt. After 1820, cotton cultivation spread rapidly westward, propelled by two factors. First, the great wealth produced by cotton provided huge economic incentives for bringing new lands under cultivation. Second, because cotton exhausted soil of its nutrients, growers constantly sought new lands to bring under cultivation. To grow and harvest this cotton, planters relied on a labor force that was 90 percent enslaved.

The upper South included eight slave states, but it lacked the fertile land and long growing season necessary for cotton agriculture. As a result it embraced agricultural diversification, including grain and livestock. Of the agricultural staples produced in this region, corn, rye, and hemp were particularly important. With each passing decade, slavery became less and less viable in this region, and many masters sold their slaves to the lower South where demand for their labor was high. Although the Constitution had outlawed the international slave trade, a vibrant internal slave trade existed. Sales from the upper South to the lower South were central to this trade.

Most slaves worked as field hands, toiling from sun up to sun down most of the year. On most large plantations slaves worked in the fields in gangs, which gave their masters more control over their labor. Men and women generally worked together, often supervised by a hired white overseer. Masters sometimes employed slaves to act as drivers, or supervisors, a role that required them to discipline other slaves or face punishment themselves. But a clever driver might find a way to protect other slaves from more severe punishment by an overseer. Larger plantations also employed many slave craftsmen as carpenters, blacksmiths, weavers, coopers (people who repaired wooden casks), and other occupations. Household slaves worked as cooks, coachmen, nannies, or maids.

Planters used a system of rewards and punishments to enforce slave discipline. As rewards some planters allowed slaves to maintain a small garden or even sell produce at market. Ultimately, however, labor discipline was enforced by violence. A popular management book that many planters consulted argued that "after reason and persuasion have been exhausted without producing the desired effect, punishment of some sort must be resorted to." As an English observer noted, "Absence from work, or neglect of duty, was punished with stinted allowances, imprisonment, and flogging." Northern abolitionist literature made the image of the whip one of their most prominent metaphors of life in the South as this broadside from an antislavery almanac reveals (**9.15**).

Southern masters also controlled their slaves by threatening to sell them. Slaves in the upper South feared being sold "down river" to a cotton or sugar plantation because it meant separation from family and probably a harsher existence. Sales tore slave families apart. Sales may have dissolved as many as one-third of all slave marriages and separated almost half of the children living in the older parts of the South from a parent. The British artist Eyre Crowe painted a scene in a Richmond slave market, in which men, women, and children wait their turn on the auction block (**9.16**). Scenes such as this were common throughout Virginia and the Carolinas. In 1859, the Georgia

9.15 Broadside with Image of Slave Whipping
To portray the horror of slavery, abolitionists used the image of slave owners whipping their slaves.

planter Pierce Butler sold 450 slaves in a single auction lasting days. A reporter from the *New York Tribune* described the misery of the slaves whose "brothers and sisters" were to be "scattered through the cotton fields of Alabama." The "expressions of heavy grief," the reporter noted, reflected their horror at being "torn from their homes" and separated from their loved ones.

9.16 *The Slave Market, Richmond, Virginia*
An English artist who accompanied the novelist William Makepeace Thackeray on a tour of America captured the dehumanizing realities of a slave auction.

Read the **Document** *A Slave Tells of His Sale at Auction*   What role did violence play in slave society?

Although most of the South's slaves toiled as agricultural laborers, many others worked in some type of industrial enterprise, primarily in the upper South. While the South lagged far behind the North in industrial development, it still exceeded all but the top five or six industrial nations in production of textiles and iron, flour and timber milling, sugar refining, and leather tanning. Most of these upper South industries relied on slave labor, and by 1850, at least five percent of the South's slaves (between 150,000 and 200,000 persons) worked in industry. Employers owned 80 percent of the slaves who worked in industry with the rest hired out on yearly or short-term leases. Enslaved blacks and free whites sometimes worked side by side. Richmond's Tredegar Iron Works employed such a mixed labor force until 1847, when a strike by whites prompted the owners to rely exclusively on enslaved black labor apart from a few white supervisors.

Slaves also worked in nonagricultural enterprises in cities such as Richmond, Mobile, Charleston, and New Orleans. Slaves worked as domestics, artisans, carriage drivers, gardeners, couriers, and nurses. Southern cities also employed slaves for public works projects, including sanitation, road building, and bridge maintenance. Savannah and Charleston even used slaves as firefighters.

Life in the Slave Quarters

Compared to Brazil, where living conditions for slaves were among the worst in the Americas, conditions for American slaves were less harsh. This contributed to a significant natural increase in the slave population in the United States; the population increased nearly fivefold between 1790 and 1850. Still American slave owners often treated their slaves brutally and provided inadequate food, shelter, clothing, and medical care. As a result infant mortality rates for slave children were twice those of white children. Life expectancy for whites in the South was between 40 and 43 years, which was lower than that in other parts of the country, but the average slave lived ten years less even than that.

Fanny Kemble, the wife of planter Pierce Butler, described the slave quarters on her husband's plantation in stark terms: "These cabins consist of one room, about twelve feet by thirteen. Two families (together numbering sometimes eight or ten) reside in one of these huts which are mere wooden frames." Wealthier planters sometimes built sturdier framed houses with wooden floors or even brick houses for their slaves.

The oppressive nature of slavery also shaped family life. Although Southern law did not recognize the legality of slave marriages, many slave men and women sought to form stable family relationships. Slaves developed their own marriage rituals to seal their unions. The most common was "jumping the broom," which derived from traditional African marriage practices. Relatives or close friends of the bride and groom held opposite ends of a broom about a foot off the ground, and the couple would jump together over it as a symbol of their union. Planters encouraged slaves to marry because married slaves were less likely to run away. The offspring of slave marriages also provided planters with additional laborers.

On larger plantations a slave family might reside together. On smaller plantations and farms, husbands and wives might reside on neighboring plantations. Such "abroad" marriages were common. Visiting a spouse under these circumstances required permission, and husbands might see their families only once a week. The slave family included extended kin, such as uncles, aunts, and, most important, grandparents, all of whom helped rear children.

Slave Religion and Music

During the 1830s, Southern churches launched a major effort to convert slaves to Christianity. In proselytizing slaves white ministers stressed the conservative elements of Christian theology, often forbidding slaves from dancing during religious services and reminding them of the passages in the Bible that demanded slaves obey their masters. A popular *Catechism for Colored Persons*, for example, instructed slaves to "count their Masters 'worthy of all honour,' as those whom God has placed over them in the world."

But efforts to use religion to instill docility in slaves largely failed. Rather than accept their masters' vision of Christianity, African Americans recast it to suit their own needs as slaves and articulate their hopes. The biblical story of the Exodus, which told of the flight of the Israelites from slavery in Egypt, was particularly popular. "God was working for their deliverance," a Georgia slave commented, and "would deliver them from bondage as sure as the children of Israel were delivered from Egyptian bondage." African Americans created covert churches called "brush arbors" or "hush arbors" to practice their version of the faith.

Slaves also borrowed elements from African religions, creating a distinctive African-American religious culture. White observers were perplexed by the "ring shout," an ecstatic form of worship that mixed African religious practice with Christian beliefs, describing its chanting as "weird" or "droning" and its dance as "wild" and "barbaric." Yet to the enslaved the ring shout's rhythmic circle dance involving joined hands, counterclockwise movement to a steady beat, hand clapping, and free-form upper-body movements became an important religious ritual.

Funeral practices also reflected this fusion of African and Christian rituals. Slaves often scattered broken ceramics over a grave, a practice carried over from African burial practices. A Maryland observer of a funeral noted that the body was interred with a miniature canoe and paddle. The slaves explained that this would allow the spirit to cross the ocean and return to Africa. Because slaves toiled in the fields during the day, their funerals typically took place at night. Torchlight processions to gravesites, accompanied by drumming and other African-inflected music and chants, unsettled white observers. Still some whites, as this painting of a slave preacher leading a funeral service (**9.17**) shows, overcame their cultural bias and appreciated the beauty of slave burials. Barely discernible between the two trees in the bottom corner of the painting are the plantation master and mistress. They are a visual reminder that slaves were never completely free from the watchful eye of their masters.

Spirituals, a distinctive musical art form created by slaves, drew heavily on biblical themes. The figure of Moses and the plight of the ancient Hebrews who were delivered from slavery were two common themes. Slave spirituals also featured images of crossing over the River Jordan to freedom in this life or redemption in the next.

Music was also important in other aspects of slave culture. Slaves used song to preserve African traditions, help relieve the monotony of work, entertain, or even communicate cryptic messages to other slaves. When slaves "went around singing 'Steal Away to Jesus,'" a former slave recalled, it not only affirmed the hope of redemption but often signaled others that there would "be a religious meeting that night." Virtually every major form of modern popular music: jazz, gospel, blues, rock and roll, and hip-hop derive in part from musical traditions rooted in the experience of American or New World slavery.

Resistance and Revolt

Slaves developed a complex range of behaviors to resist the harsh discipline forced on them. Many used subtle tactics to thwart their owners because they minimized

9.17 *Plantation Burial*
While a slave preacher leads a funeral service, the plantation master and mistress are visible in the woods between the two trees in the lower right corner of the painting.

the chances for punishment. Slaves feigned illness, broke tools, and slowed their pace of work to fight back against their economic exploitation.

Another means of resistance was flight. Typically runaways left only for short periods, seeking a respite from servitude, or to visit kin and spouses on neighboring plantations. Less frequently slaves sought to gain their freedom by fleeing to free territory in the North or in Canada. In the Deep South, some slaves fled to Indian Territory or to swamps to escape detection. In a few celebrated cases, slaves devised daring methods of escape.

The most extreme form of resistance was insurrection. In 1831, Nat Turner led the largest slave uprising in American history. A lay preacher, Turner had a vision of a battle between "white spirits and blacks spirits" that would commence when the "sun was darkened." He believed that the solar eclipse in 1831 was a divine sign that the time for insurrection was ripe. **Nat Turner's Rebellion** lasted two days and attracted between 60 and 80 slaves before authorities subdued the rebels. Before the carnage ended 55 whites were killed and as many African Americans. This woodcut from a contemporary account of the rebellion written by a supporter of slavery depicts the rebels unsympathetically, about to attack defenseless women and children, and the efforts of whites to defend their loved ones as

Why did biblical themes from the story of the Exodus figure so prominently in slave spirituals?

9.18 Woodcut Image of Nat Turner's Rebellion This image reflects the views of Southerners who were horrified by Turner's uprising.

> "Steal away to Jesus! Steal away, steal away home. I ain't got long to stay here. My Lord calls me, He calls me by the thunder; The trumpet sounds within my soul, I ain't got long to stay here."
>
> Spiritual, "Steal Away to Jesus"

heroic (**9.18**). The bottom of the image shows the militia riding to rescue these helpless victims. Many Northerners, however, viewed Nat Turner as a righteous and heroic warrior against the evil of slavery.

After the Rebellion, Southern states enacted more repressive laws to prevent another revolt. These laws prevented African Americans from preaching and limited the access of free blacks to firearms. States also strengthened their militias and made assaults by slaves against whites capital offenses. On the other hand, the Virginia legislature debated abolishing slavery before voting 73 to 58 against a proposal to end it.

Slavery and the Law

Each Southern state passed its own set of laws, or slave codes, governing slavery. These laws described the property rights of masters (slaves were categorized somewhere between property and people), the duties slaves owed to their masters, and the punishments for various crimes. Although laws varied from state to state, slave codes generally accorded slaves minimal rights. These laws curtailed the movements of slaves, forbidding them to travel without written permission from their masters. Laws also proscribed teaching slaves to read or write. Slaves had no right to testify in court, and planters served as both judge and jury on their plantations, meting out punishment. On rare occasions a slave did obtain a day in court, as when a South Carolina court ruled that a slave could not be tried for the same crime twice, an application of the constitutional prohibition on double jeopardy that was a bedrock of American law. Despite such modest protections, however, slaves still enjoyed only the slimmest legal protection and remained at the mercy of their masters (see *Choices and Consequences: Conscience or Duty? Justice Ruffin's Quandary*).

> "No one can read this decision, [*State v. Mann*] so fine and clear in expression, so dignified and solemn in its earnestness, and so dreadful in its results, without feeling at once deep respect for the man and horror for the system."
>
> Abolitionist HARRIET BEECHER STOWE, *The Key to Uncle Tom's Cabin,* (1853)

Who was Nat Turner?

Choices and Consequences

CONSCIENCE OR DUTY? JUSTICE RUFFIN'S QUANDARY

In 1829, Chief Justice Thomas Ruffin of the North Carolina Supreme Court issued his opinion in **State v. Mann**, a case involving an assault on a slave named Lydia by John Mann. Lydia's owner, Elizabeth Jones, instigated the case against Mann (slaves had no legal standing to bring charges) for wounding her slave. Mann had rented Lydia from Jones, and the law recognized that as a temporary owner, he did not have the same long term interests in protecting his property. Thus, although Mann was legally entitled to discipline Lydia, his power over her was more limited than that of her legal owner. When Mann tried to discipline Lydia, she ran off. Mann then shot and wounded her. Rather than try to recover monetary damages in a civil trial, an option precluded because Mann was too poor to pay damages, Lydia's owner pursued criminal charges. A lower court convicted Mann of an assault and battery on Lydia, and Mann then appealed the case to the state Supreme Court. *State v. Mann* explored legal questions at the heart of slavery. In deciding how to handle the case, Justice Ruffin faced difficult choices.

Choices

1. Uphold Mann's conviction and affirm that the doctrine that a temporary master's power to discipline was limited

2. Overrule the lower court and assert that Mann had the same legal authority as Lydia's owner, including the right to punish disobedience, and affirm that a master's power over slaves was unlimited

3. Decide the case on the narrowest grounds possible. Affirm the lower court ruling and avoid sweeping statements about the nature of the master's powers by focusing squarely on the facts: the excessive use of force by a disreputable person with a history of violence.

Decision

Ruffin chose to overrule the lower court. Although tempted to sympathize with the plight of slaves and offer them legal protections, he argued that the law denied them such protections: "The power of the master must be absolute to render the submission of the slave perfect." To bestow on slaves basic rights would undermine slavery itself.

Woodcut image of master shooting slave

Consequences

Within five years, in *State v. Will,* Ruffin's fellow justices partially repudiated his decision. The case did not dispute Ruffin's major premise that a slave must be totally submissive, but it rejected his claim that the only means to accomplish this goal was to give the master total power. The court accepted that the master's power was limited and the use of excessive or lethal force to discipline a slave was not protected by the law of slavery.

Continuing Controversies

What role did ideas of justice play in Justice Ruffin's understanding of the rule of law?

Most modern scholars agree that the decision in *State v. Mann* reflects the fundamental immorality of slavery. But the controversy over the decision focuses on a more basic question about law itself. Does law simply reflect the dominant power relations of society? Or, can the law embody ideals of justice or fairness that are not simply a mask to disguise the naked exercise of power? Ruffin's decision reinforced the power of the planter class, and many view it as vindicating those who believe that the law is a tool that enables the powerful (the masters) to dominate the weak (the slaves). However, Ruffin's anguish and the later ruling in *State v. Will* might be seen as proof that the rule of law does impose constraints on the powerful.

Does the law of slavery support the claim that the law is a tool of the powerful or a constraint on them?

1823–1825

Lowell Mill opens
Waltham System at Lowell, Massachusetts, becomes showcase for the new model of industrial production

Erie Canal opens
One of the great public works projects of the early nineteenth century reduces dramatically the cost of transportation

1829

State v. Mann
Decision affirms the idea that the master's control over the slave is absolute

1830

Steam-powered train makes first trip
First successful steam-powered train tested by the Baltimore and Ohio Railroad

1831

Nat Turner's Rebellion
Virginia slave leads the bloodiest slave uprising in U.S. history

CHAPTER REVIEW

Review Questions

1. What role did technological change play in the market revolution? How did such changes affect values?

2. How did ideas about gender roles change in response to the market revolution?

3. How did slavery shape Southern society and the lives of non-slaveholders?

4. How did slaves modify Christianity to articulate their distinctive religious vision?

5. Why did Judge Ruffin argue masters must have absolute power over slaves?

Key Terms

Market revolution A set of interrelated developments in agriculture, technology, and industry that led to the creation of a more integrated national economy. Impersonal market forces impelled the maximization of production of agricultural products and manufactured goods.   **254**

Telegraph Invention patented by Samuel Morse in 1837 that used electricity to send coded messages over wires, making communication nearly instantaneous.   **258**

Artisan production A system of manufacturing goods, built around apprenticeship that defined the pre-industrial economy. The apprentice learned a trade under the guidance of an artisan who often housed, clothed, and fed the apprentice.   **260**

Waltham System Also known as the mill town model, a system that relied on factories housing all the distinctive steps of cloth production under a single roof.   **261**

Spirituals Religious songs created by slaves. Spirituals' symbolism drew heavily on biblical themes.   **277**

Nat Turner's Rebellion The 1831 Virginia slave uprising led by Nat Turner shocked many in the South and led to a host of new repressive measures against slaves.   **277**

State v. Mann The 1829 North Carolina Supreme Court case that involved a white man's assault on a slave. The case asserted that the domination of the master over the slave was complete.   **279**

1834

First strike at the Lowell Mill

Mill women's strike at Lowell signals the beginning of a new phase of conflict between labor and capital

1836

Helen Jewett murdered

The sensational murder of Helen Jewett shocks the nation and helps spur a huge increase in newspaper circulation

1838

The *Code of Honor* published in South Carolina

Etiquette book describes the rules of dueling

1840

Lexington steam boat disaster

On January 13, 1840, the steamboat Lexington caught fire on route from Boston to New York. The disaster became one of the first great financial successes of printer and publisher Nathaniel Currier and helped launch the company that eventually became the venerable firm of Currier and Ives

MyHistoryLab Connections

Visit www.myhistorylab.com for a customized Study Plan that will help you build your knowledge of *Workers, Farmers, and Slaves.*

Questions for Analysis

1. **How did the Transportation Revolution transform the American economy and society?**

   View the Closer Look *Impact of the Transportation Revolution on Traveling Time, p. 255*

2. **What were some of the negative consequences of rapid economic change for American society?**

   View the Closer Look *Images as History: Nature, Technology, and the Railroad, p. 257*

3. **What does the Lowell Strike reveal about the changing nature of work during the early phase of industrialization?**

   View the Closer Look *Competing Visions: The Lowell Strike of 1834, p. 263*

4. **How did changing patterns of immigration impact American society during the era of the market revolution?**

   Read the Document *Petition of the Catholics of New York (1840), p. 266*

5. **What role did religion play in the lives of slaves?**

   Hear the Audio File *"Go Down Moses", p. 276*

Other Resources from This Chapter

Hear the Audio File *Erie Canal, p. 256*

Read the Document
- *A Second Peep at Factory Life, p. 261*
- *A Slave Tells of His Sale at Auction, p. 275*

View the Closer Look *Images as History: Fairmont Waterworks Sculptures, p. 265*

View the Image *Free Black Church, p. 272*

Watch the Video
- *Coming of Age in 1833, p. 254*
- *Mastering Time and Space, p. 258*

Revivalism and Reform p. 284

How did religion influence reform movements?

Abolitionism and the Proslavery Response p. 290

How did changes in abolitionism affect the pro-slavery argument?

The Cult of True Womanhood, Reform, and Women's Rights p. 295

What values were associated with the new domestic ideal?

Religious and Secular Utopianism p. 298

How did the market revolution influence utopian ideals?

Literature and Popular Culture p. 304

How did literature and popular culture respond to the changes in American society?

Nature's Nation p. 308

How did architecture, parks, and cemeteries reflect the larger changes occurring in American society?

10

Revivalism, Reform, and Artistic Renaissance,

1820–1850

The expansion of democracy and the changes resulting from the market revolution left Americans concerned about their lives and the nation's future. Rising inequality and a bitter debate over slavery intensified anxieties. In this popular lithograph, *The Way of Good and Evil*, the artist portrays the social ills facing America, including alcoholism, prostitution, and crime. A tavern, brothel, and prison represent the path of destruction. Different buildings—a school, home, and church—anchor the center. The path to salvation leads from these institutions through college and eventually up into heaven. In the artist's view Americans faced a clear choice: salvation or eternal damnation.

Americans sought solutions for the nation's social problems and clamored for reforms. Many turned to mainstream religion for guidance or joined religious reform movements. Secular reformers targeted education and prisons or alcohol. Some religious movements viewed the market economy as the root of America's problems and advocated the abandonment of private property. Secular utopian movements came to similar conclusions.

Still other reformers adopted a radically different critique of market society. Champions of Transcendentalism, a literary and philosophical movement, including Ralph Waldo Emerson and Henry David Thoreau, urged Americans to reject the values of the marketplace and turn to nature or their individual consciences for inspiration. The expanding literary marketplace prompted many writers to explore contemporary ills, or use them as a backdrop for stories that probed issues as different as slavery and urbanization. The rise of a more aggressive abolitionist movement and the development of an equally fervid defense of slavery intensified the public debate over this issue. Abolitionism helped radicalize many women and gave them the opportunity to develop organizing skills. Inspired by a more radical theory of equality and equipped with their new skills, women's rights advocates applied their critique of slavery to women's status under American law.

Reform efforts also affected architecture. Many reformers advocated transforming the American landscape itself, including the built environment, to promote social reform and spiritual renewal.

"In the history of the world the doctrine of Reform had never such scope as at the present hour…. We are to revise the whole of our social structure, the state, the school, religion, marriage, trade, science, and explore their foundations in our own nature."

RALPH WALDO EMERSON, *Man the Reformer* (1841)

Revivalism and Reform

The Cane Ridge revival in Kentucky (1801) was the first stirring of the larger revival movement that constituted America's Second Great Awakening. (For a discussion of the First Great Awakening, see Chapter 3.) In the next four decades, this emotional style of evangelical Protestantism attracted many Americans. For those swept up in the revival, the changes transforming American society were seen as a threat to the church and the family. However, the most far-sighted proponents of revival, such as Charles Grandison Finney, realized that the power of the market revolution might be turned to good ends and used to promote religion and reform.

By the 1830s, Americans began to believe that the economic, political, and social changes sweeping over their society were undermining individual morality, the ability of communities to prosper, and the integrity of the family. This belief drove the push for moral reform. In many cases religious impulse inspired reformers. Finney preached that "true saints love reform" and argued that humankind could create a perfect society here on earth if all Americans made "the reformation of the whole world" their priority. Not all reformers were religiously motivated, however. Some reform efforts promoted secular goals and drew on the Enlightenment's ideals of reason, science, and faith in humankind's ability to improve and reshape its surroundings (see Chapters 3 and 4). Secular reform movements led to improvements in schools, care for the mentally ill, and methods of reforming criminals. Whether religious or secular, reform efforts targeted individual behavior such as drunkenness and prostitution.

10.1 *Religious Camp Meeting* A contemporary artist captured the intense emotional experience of a revival meeting.

Revivalism and the Market Revolution

One way of promoting revivalism was the camp meeting, an outdoor religious revival that lasted for days. This painting of *Religious Camp Meeting* (**10.1**) by an English artist captures the emotional intensity of these events, during which grown men and women swooned and collapsed in response to the fiery preaching of ministers. The painting shows overwrought men and women, physically exhausted from the revival, splayed across the ground and on the benches in the foreground. One observer compared the audience's response to the fiery sermons of the camp meeting with the "swelling" of an ocean wave, an awesome spectacle of "fainting, shouting, yelling, crying, sobbing and grieving." The tents in the background of the painting give only a small sense of the scope of these events. Camp meetings could last for a week and attract 3,000 people and 100 preachers.

Revivalists faulted many mainstream ministers for their overly intellectualized preaching. Ministers also blamed America's problems on the materialism associated with the market revolution. One minister feared that the same forces that were "increasing the business and moneyed interests in the Nation" would "by spreading vice and irreligion prove its ruin. Those very things which all regard as improvements will be our destruction." For some, however, the new methods of communication and wealth generated by the market revolution were tools to press into the service of revivalism. No figure proved more adept at turning the tools of the market to religious purposes than Charles Grandison Finney, a lawyer turned preacher who became a leading spokesman for spreading the revivalist message of the Second Great Awakening to towns and cities. His influence was felt particularly strongly in those urban centers most closely associated with the market revolution.

While walking to his law offices one day, Finney experienced a religious conversion. In a lawyerly manner he declared that from that day on he would be on a "retainer from the Lord Jesus Christ to plead his cause." Drawing on his experience as a courtroom lawyer, he fashioned a forceful and direct style of preaching that cajoled, harangued, and pleaded with his audience to embrace salvation. Finney's theology rejected many of the Calvinist assumptions of nonevangelical churches (see Chapter 3). Where Calvinists stressed predestination, the belief that God predetermined our individual destinies, including who will and will not be saved, Finney instead stressed free will, people's ability to seek out salvation through their own efforts. The idea of perfectionism grew out of his emphasis on free will. By aiming for perfection, Finney preached, human beings could usher in the millennium. In contrast to the pessimistic message of Calvinism, which condemned most people to damnation, Finney emphasized sobriety and hard work along with his religious message. His sermons appealed to the expanding middle class and the wealthy.

Finney found an especially eager audience in men and women in the cities and towns along the Erie Canal in upstate New York. A dramatic revival occurred in Rochester, New York, in 1830–1831. Finney adapted many of the new political techniques associated with Jacksonian democracy, designed to get voters involved in politics, to his revivals. Politicians, Finney noted, "get up meetings; circulate handbills and pamphlets; blaze away in the newspapers." The goal of such actions was to stimulate "excitement and bring the people out."

Finney and other evangelicals took advantage of the opportunities provided by the market revolution, particularly the expansion of the publishing industry, to churn out tracts, Bibles, and evangelical periodicals. Organizations such as the American Bible Society and the American Tract Society led the way in marketing evangelical publications, making an effort to use high-quality wood-cut images in many of them to visually reinforce the text.

Temperance

Rising levels of alcohol consumption spurred the growth of **temperance**, the reform movement that advocated abstinence from alcohol. By 1830, consumption of spirits reached an all-time high: almost seven gallons per person of pure alcohol a year (more than twice the amount that the average American drinks today). Alcohol had always been

"We hold these truths to be self-evident; that all men are created temperate; that they are endowed by their Creator with certain natural and innocent desires; that among these are the appetite for cold water and the pursuit of happiness!"
MANIFESTO OF THE WASHINGTON TOTAL ABSTINENCE SOCIETIES, 1841

How did Finney use the tools of the market revolution to further the goals of the Second Great Awakening?

important in America. Every social class imbibed alcohol, and hardly a community function took place without alcohol consumption. Workers on the job often drank alcohol during their midmorning and mid-afternoon breaks. One commentator noted that "a house could not be raised, a field of wheat cut down, nor could there be a log rolling, a husking, a quilting, a wedding, or funeral without the aid of alcohol."

Although Western religions had always frowned on drunkenness, Christians had never deemed the consumption of alcohol a sin. The Great Awakening changed this as spokesmen for the revival fastened on intemperance as an issue. At first proponents of temperance merely sought to promote moderation, but by the mid-1820s, a more radical temperance movement sought complete abstinence from alcohol. The first national temperance organization was founded in 1826, and within three years there were 222 similar organizations. By the mid-1830s, temperance organizations had more than 1.5 million members, and more than two million Americans had taken the movement's pledge of abstinence. Evangelical religious leaders took the lead

"I believe in the existence of a great, immortal, immutable principle of natural law … which proves the absolute right to an education of every human being that comes into the world."

HORACE MANN, 1846

in these organizations, delivering sermons with titles like: "The Nature, Occasions, Signs, Evils, and Remedy of Intemperance." Reformers warned Americans that alcohol threatened their souls as well as their bodies. For Congregational minister Lyman Beecher, a prominent figure in the Second Great Awakening, temperance organizations were "a disciplined moral militia," an ironic metaphor given that the real militia had become another illustration of the problem of intemperance. Although militia musters, the practice sessions of the militia, had always been festive occasions that included drinking, by the mid-nineteenth century, they had become drunken revels, as this depiction of a militia-day muster illustrates (**10.2**). The militiaman in the foreground is so

10.2 A Militia Muster
Although militia musters had always included drinking, the scene depicted here shows a militia man too drunk to stand up. Martial virtue is nowhere to be seen.

What does this painting of a militia muster reveal about alcohol consumption in America?

Watch the **Video** *Video Lecture: Drinking and the Temperance Movement*

inebriated he cannot stand, and the dancing African American suggests that the atmosphere is more carnival-like than military.

Temperance advocates also campaigned for prohibition laws banning the sale of alcohol, and temperance attracted other reformers such as the young Whig politician Abraham Lincoln. The Whigs helped to secure laws to promote sobriety. Maine adopted the most wide-sweeping law in 1851, prohibiting alcohol. By 1855, 13 of the nation's 31 states had passed similar laws. The temperance movement did not banish drinking from American life, but it dramatically reduced alcohol consumption.

Schools, Prisons, and Asylums

Alcohol consumption was hardly the only concern of reformers. They also turned their attention to education, the criminal justice system, and the treatment of the mentally ill. They founded new institutions to deal with these social problems and campaigned to change the way Americans thought about these issues.

Education was central to reform efforts. Lyman Beecher wrote that "we must educate, or we must perish by our own prosperity." Unfettered growth and materialism, according to such leaders as Beecher, would otherwise subvert America's moral foundations. The leading spokesman for educational reform in America was the Whig politician Horace Mann. As a member of the Massachusetts legislature, he worked tirelessly to create a state board of education that would establish a uniform curriculum for Massachusetts and improve teacher training. Mann became the first head of the new state board of education. Massachusetts also became the first state to pass a compulsory school attendance law. For reformers such as Mann, the Common School—universal public education—would cure society's ills. As Mann wrote, "let the Common School be expanded to its capabilities ... and nine tenths of the crimes in the penal code would become obsolete; the long catalogue of human ills would be abridged." Although many types of reform were "curative or remedial," schools, according to Mann, were "preventive." He intended his reforms, like much mainstream educational reform of the day, to

make good citizens and workers. This era saw the development of many features of modern schooling. The assignment of students to grades according to age and ability, the use of standardized procedures for promotion, and the notion of uniform textbooks for instruction all emerged out of the Massachusetts model that Mann helped pioneer.

A new textbook, the popular McGuffey's Reader, appeared in 1836. This text went through multiple editions for the remainder of the nineteenth century. The McGuffey readers carried a clear political message well suited to a society in which wealth was becoming less equally distributed. The readers instructed children not to envy their social betters, but rather to remind them that "it is God who makes some poor, and others rich." A different vision of education shaped the agenda of the Working Men's party, which saw education as an invaluable tool in the ongoing political struggle between the people and the aristocratic few. Although they shared Mann's Whig goal of universal education, they intended education to liberate workers, not make them docile. Thus a Philadelphia Working Men's party committee declared that "despotism" thrived when the "multitude" is consigned to ignorance, and education and knowledge reserved for the "the rich and the rulers."

Although educational reform attracted a wide range of supporters, including religious leaders, Whigs such as Mann, and the Working Men's

> "We find in the United States two distinctly separate systems: the system of Auburn and that of Philadelphia. . . . The two systems opposed to each other on important points, have, however, a common basis, without which no penitentiary system is possible; this basis is the isolation of the prisoners."
> GUSTAVE DE BEAUMONT and ALEXIS DE TOCQUEVILLE (1833)

Read the **Document** *Horace Mann, Report on the Massachusetts Board of Education*

How did Mann's vision of educational reform differ from that of the Working Men's Party?

party, opposition to such reforms could be equally ardent. A variety of groups feared that government involvement in education would endanger individual freedom. Democrats in Massachusetts, for example, viewed Mann's program as a "system of centralization" that would put "power in a few hands" and undermine the "spirit of our democratic institutions." Farmers feared that a longer school year would rob them of a valuable source of labor, and that the increased taxes to fund the new school system would fall heavily on agricultural interests. Finally Catholics feared that the country's Protestant majority had designed the new system to impose its values on non-Protestants. In response to the Common School movement, Catholics began creating their own parochial schools.

Although Mann's utopian vision of education as a cure for society's ills was not realized, the Common School movement did achieve notable successes. By mid-century, over half of the white children in America between ages five and nineteen were enrolled in public schools, the highest percentage in the world. Higher education also expanded dramatically. In 1815 there were 33 colleges in America; by 1835 there were 68, and 113 by 1848. The Great Awakening inspired much of this growth. Almost half these new colleges were affiliated with denominations that took a prominent role in the Awakening: Presbyterians, Methodists, and Baptists. Among the colleges and universities founded in this period were Amherst and Wesleyan in New England, Earlham in the Midwest, and Emory and Duke in the South. Although these schools excluded women, whose educational opportunities lagged behind those for men, some progress occurred in this area. In 1821, Emma Willard founded the Troy Female Seminary in Troy, New York, and in 1837, Mount Holyoke Female Seminary was established in Massachusetts. Oberlin College in Ohio admitted women from its inception in 1833. A hotbed of abolitionist sentiment, Oberlin admitted its first African-American students in 1835. The state universities that date from this period of educational reform include Louisiana, Missouri, Mississippi, and Wisconsin, as do some of the nation's leading Catholic institutions, including Fordham, Holy Cross, Notre Dame, Villanova, and Xavier in Cincinnati.

The new religious emphasis on free will and commitment to moral reform also inspired new approaches to criminal justice. In place of punishment a new reform-based model of incarceration emerged: the "**penitentiary**," where individuals were isolated from one another and given a chance to repent and reform. Earlier approaches to crime had cast behavior in terms of sinfulness and innate depravity and had meted out punishment accordingly.

Two different models for implementing this penitential ideal emerged in prisons. The New York State system employed the first at Ossining, a prison in the Hudson River Valley. Prisoners sent "up the river" from New York City to "Sing Sing" were housed in individual cells at night but were organized in communal work details during the day. Inmates worked ten-hour days in stone quarries; eventually the prisoners manufactured goods, including barrels, boots and shoes, hats, brushes, and mattresses.

Pennsylvania pioneered a different model, which it implemented in Eastern State Penitentiary. Eastern State employed solitary confinement, which isolated prisoners from all contact with other prisoners to force them to reflect on their criminality and seek repentance. The architecture of Eastern State reflected this new approach to penology. Architect John Haviland's vision of the ideal prison combined fashionable Gothic architectural elements with

> "I proceed, gentlemen, briefly to call your attention to the present state of insane persons confined within this Commonwealth, in cages, closets, cellars, stalls, pens! Chained, naked, beaten with rods, and lashed into obedience... "
>
> DOROTHEA DIX, 1843

an Enlightenment emphasis on geometrical forms (**10.3**). Thus although the outside of the prison looked like a medieval fortress, the inside consisted of a series of radiating spokes emanating from a central watch tower. A guard in the central tower could see the prisoners, who themselves were unable to see the guard. Haviland believed his plan would facilitate "watching, convenience, economy and ventilation." This design, which its inventor, British philosopher Jeremy Bentham, dubbed a panopticon, applied the Enlightenment's ideals of reason to prison reform. Prisoners were potentially under surveillance at all times and could never be sure if the eyes of the state were on them. The goal was to impose discipline and have prisoners internalize it as an ideal. This vision of penal reform fit with the Enlightenment's ideals of reason and control.

Life for the mentally ill had always been hard, and people with mental illness were often housed with criminals. In 1841, Dorothea Dix, a schoolteacher, volunteered to provide religious instruction for women in the Massachusetts House of Correction. Shocked by the treatment of the inmates, particularly the mentally ill, who were dressed in rags, confined to one room, and often beaten, Dix sought to change the way mental illness was treated. After visiting jails and poorhouses where the mentally ill were housed, she compiled a report to the Massachusetts legislature detailing the wretched conditions in places such as the House of Correction. Dix recommended that criminals be separated from the mentally ill and argued that the latter would benefit from more humane treatment. Other reformers followed her lead, and by 1860, 28 of 33 states had public asylums for the mentally ill.

10.3 Philadelphia Penitentiary
Architects designed prisons to accommodate the penitential model. Prisoners could be isolated for reflection while still being monitored by prison authorities. The most famous example of this new type of prison was Eastern State Penitentiary in Philadelphia.
[*Source:* The Library Company of Philadelphia]

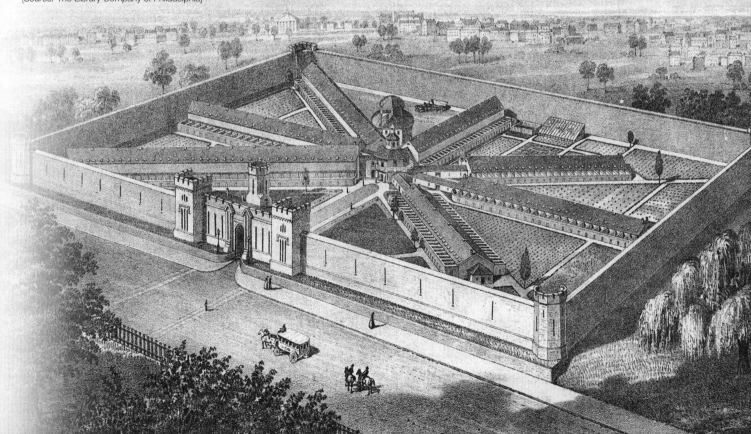

What does prison architecture reveal about reform in this period?

Abolitionism and the Proslavery Response

 The debate over slavery heated up as abolitionists demanded an immediate end to slavery. Like revivalists abolitionists also took advantage of the new tools provided by the market revolution to bombard Southerners with their message, particularly communications technologies such as improvements in printing. The more aggressive style of abolitionism produced a fierce reaction from Southerners, who became increasingly militant in their defense of slavery. Rather than concede that slavery was a necessary evil, as Jefferson and others of the Founding generation had, Southerners now touted slavery as a positive good that reformed and uplifted slaves. The real evils in American society, they argued, were abolitionism and the factory system. By mid-century, the slavery debate created huge divisions within American politics and society.

The Rise of Immediatism

Much of the early opposition to slavery was led by the Quakers. The ideals of the American Revolution also contributed to the rise of abolitionist sentiment, which attracted leading politicians, including prominent Federalists, such as Alexander Hamilton and John Jay. For these abolitionists slavery threatened the republican values of liberty and virtue. Racial equality or justice was not a major concern, the elimination of slavery was necessary to prevent Americans from becoming corrupted by the institution of slavery. James Madison, Henry Clay, and John Marshall championed a plan that included gradually liberating the slaves and returning them to Africa. The American Colonization Society, the organization devoted to implementing this idea, was founded in 1817. It helped to found the West African colony of Liberia and began transporting free blacks there from the United States. Yet by 1830, only 1,400 blacks had been sent to Liberia. Although gradualism and colonization had appealed to many white opponents of slavery, it never attracted much interest among African Americans, who supported a more immediate end to slavery and were committed to remaining in the United States. A convention of free blacks, speaking of the United States, proclaimed in 1831 that "this is our home, and this is our country."

In 1829 abolitionism entered a new era. David Walker, a free black who had grown up in North Carolina and moved to Boston, published an *Appeal*, which he addressed to the "Coloured Citizens of the World, but in Particular, and Very Expressly, to Those of the United States of America." Walker rejected colonization and declared that "America is more our country than it is the whites—we have enriched it with our *blood and tears*." He urged slaves to defend themselves, by force if necessary, against their masters. His call for slave insurrection led Southern states to enact or strengthen laws making it illegal to teach slaves to read. It also marked the end of support among many Southern intellectuals for colonization. Walker's death in 1830 cut short his career as an abolitionist.

Although Walker's radical, insurrectionary appeal had little impact on mainstream abolitionists, his call for immediate abolition resonated with those most eager to abolish slavery. Since the Revolution mainstream abolitionist thought had adopted a gradualist approach, preferring to end

> "I shall strenuously contend for the immediate enfranchisement of our slave population…. I will be as harsh as truth, and as uncompromising as justice. On this subject, I do not wish to think, or speak, or write, with moderation…. I will not equivocate—I will not excuse—I will not retreat a single inch—
> AND I WILL BE HEARD."
> WILLIAM LLOYD GARRISON, *The Liberator*, 1831

Why was David Walker's *Appeal* so radical?   **Read** the **Document** *The American Antislavery Society Declares its Sentiments*

slavery in a piecemeal fashion. Now, abolitionists rejected gradualism in favor of **immediatism**, an immediate end to slavery. The most forceful spokesman for immediatism was William Lloyd Garrison, who founded the newspaper *The Liberator* in 1831. In its first issue, Garrison announced that he had recanted the "popular but pernicious doctrine of gradual abolition."

With other abolitionists, Garrison organized the New England Anti-Slavery Society in 1832. A year later he joined 60 other delegates, including men, women, whites, and free blacks, to create the American Anti-Slavery Society (AASS). By 1840, more than 1,350 antislavery societies had sprung up in the North with combined memberships of 250,000. The success of British abolitionists, who in 1833 had persuaded Parliament to emancipate almost all slaves in the British Empire, inspired American abolitionists.

In 1835, American abolitionists, taking advantage of the new opportunities provided by the market revolution to get their antislavery message across, began to inundate Southerners with antislavery literature. Abolitionists also worked diligently in the North to raise awareness of the evils of slavery. In addition to using traditional print forms such as newspapers and pamphlets, they developed almanacs, songbooks, children's books, and jigsaw puzzles. This children's puzzle (**10.4**) includes scenes typical of abolitionist literature, including images of slaves being whipped and brutalized.

Adept at publicizing their cause, abolitionists seized opportunities provided by dramatic events, such as the escape of Henry "Box" Brown, who had mailed himself from Richmond, Virginia, to Philadelphia in a wooden box (**10.5**). The trip took 26 hours, and Brown arrived in his box in Philadelphia shaken but unscathed. Abolitionists distributed images of his escape, and he later toured the North with a panorama, "The Mirror of Slavery." Panoramas were large pictures mounted on rollers that, when unfurled slowly, gave the viewer the feeling that the picture was moving. Often a narrator accompanied a panorama on tour. Brown's narration complemented the panorama's depiction of the history of slavery in America.

Another event that triggered public interest in slavery was the unveiling of American artist Hiram Powers's sculpture, *The Greek Slave*. Powers's popular work depicted a beautiful Greek woman enslaved by the Ottoman Turks, who were Muslims. The image of a Christian woman

10.4 Abolitionist Puzzle
Abolitionists developed a variety of ways to educate Northern children about the evils of slavery, including jigsaw puzzles.

degraded and held captive by Muslims captivated American audiences. The nude sculpture caused a sensation in the press. Abolitionists used the attention to remind Americans of the evils of slavery. How abolitionists accomplished this—and how Southerners recast its meaning to reflect their views—is the subject of *Images as History: The Greek Slave*.

The antislavery movement attracted a strong following in New England and among transplanted New Englanders in the Midwest, particularly evangelicals. Quakers were active abolitionists, too. A few

10.5 Mailed to Freedom
This image of Henry "Box" Brown who mailed himself to freedom was sold to help finance a speaking tour for Brown, who became a spokesman against slavery.

📖c- **Read** the **Document** *David Walker, A Black Abolitionist Speaks Out*   Who was Henry "Box" Brown?

Images as History
THE GREEK SLAVE

The Vermont artist Hiram Powers's statue, *The Greek Slave* (1844), became one of the most popular sculptures in nineteenth-century America. Powers portrayed the slave stripped naked by her Turkish captors, chained, and placed on the auction block. Religious leaders and even reviewers had denounced earlier artists who, following European conventions, had portrayed women in the nude, but Powers avoided moral censure by explaining to his audience that by depicting the dignity of the slave in the face of such cruel treatment, he had clothed her in an invisible robe of virtue. How would viewers in different parts of the nation have responded to this work of art? How would abolitionists have interpreted its message? How would defenders of slavery?

Cities across America and small towns in New England and Ohio exhibited *The Greek Slave*. The image here shows a crowded gallery of men, women, and children viewing the work in New York. Besides prompting widespread commentary in the press, Powers's work inspired poems. A poet in the *Knickerbocker Magazine* described *The Greek Slave* as "Naked yet clothed with chastity." Public reaction to the sculpture became entwined in the larger debate over slavery. While Southerners praised the work, focusing on the theme of Christian virtue, Northerners compared the slave's suffering to the plight of America's slaves. One New York correspondent wondered how an audience might be driven to tears at the sight of an "insensate piece of marble" and "yet listens unmoved to the awful story of the American slave!" Apologists for slavery mocked such appeals. Noting that many abolitionists had waxed poetic about *The Greek Slave*, one writer wondered why "we have not heard" of a single effort to free her from her chains.

Although a nude figure would have normally been shocking, *The Greek Slave* attracted huge crowds, including women and children. Exhibition guides reminded viewers that the slave was clothed in Christian virtue.

Viewing *The Greek Slave*

The Greek Slave turns away from viewers, a sign of her modesty.

The chains around her wrists signify her status as a slave.

The Greek Slave

prominent Southerners also joined the movement, including Angelina and Sarah Grimké, daughters of a wealthy South Carolina planter, whose conversion to Quakerism facilitated their involvement in abolitionism. The two women left the South to pursue the cause of abolitionism. The antislavery movement galvanized many women, who became the grass-roots activists for abolitionism. By 1840, more than two-thirds of the signers of antislavery petitions submitted to Congress were women.

Anti-Abolitionism and the Abolitionist Response

Proslavery rhetoric intensified as Northern opponents of slavery employed increasingly assertive tactics. Southerners held mass rallies to denounce Northern abolitionists. Garrison's newspaper, *The Liberator,* was especially galling. Within a year of its first issue, the Georgia legislature proposed a $5,000 reward for anyone who would bring Garrison to Georgia for trial. Rewards were posted for bounty hunters to kidnap other prominent abolitionists and bring them to the South for trial. The wealthy New York abolitionist Arthur Tappan had a price of $50,000 on his head at one point. In July 1835, a steamship arrived in Charleston carrying thousands of antislavery tracts and newspapers addressed to Southerners. Angry residents grabbed the mailbags containing the Northern abolitionist literature; the next night 3,000 Charlestonians consigned the letters to a huge bonfire. This antislavery Northern political cartoon ridiculed Southerners'

efforts to prevent the distribution of abolitionist materials (**10.6**).

Southern hostility did not deter abolitionists. They began inundating Congress with petitions calling for an immediate end to slavery. Southerners reacted by passing the "**gag rule**," a procedural motion that required that the House of Representatives automatically table antislavery petitions and not consider them. The gag rule passed with the support of Northern and Southern Democrats. The Senate was unable to pass its own gag rule, but it adopted a practice that produced virtually the same effect. Once the Senate had received slavery petitions, a proslavery senator would simply move to table them. Yet abolitionist petitions continued to pour into Congress, especially from women's groups. In 1836–1837, an all-female petition from Massachusetts gathered 21,000 signatures, a record number. Southern efforts to stymie free speech and the right to petition Congress only underscored abolitionists' belief that slavery was incompatible with liberty. To leading abolitionists interference with the U.S. mail and congressional refusal to deal with petitions made slavery a national, as opposed to a local, issue.

The Proslavery Argument

Leading Southerners of the revolutionary era had attacked slavery even as they continued to profit from it. No member of the Founding generation was more conflicted over slavery than Thomas Jefferson, who told a friend in 1820 that "we have the wolf by the ears, and we can neither hold him, nor safely let him go. Justice is in one scale, and self-preservation in the other." Jefferson hoped that a new generation of statesmen would eliminate slavery. Such hopes diminished, however, as "Alabama fever" swept across the South, and cotton agriculture transformed the American economy. To complicate matters, Nat Turner's insurrection (see Chapter 9) frightened Southerners, who became convinced that Northern abolitionists were stirring up slave insurrections.

10.6 *New Method of Sorting the Mail* The abolitionist mail campaign prompted violent protest in the South. In this drawing Southerners assault the Charleston post office and burn abolitionist mail.

Read the **Document** *Thomas R. Dew's "Defense of Slavery"*

What was the "gag rule"?

In 1832, Thomas R. Dew, a young professor at the College of William and Mary, published his *Review of the Debate in the Virginia Legislature of 1831 and 1832*. In the aftermath of Nat Turner's Rebellion, the legislature had seriously debated ending slavery, but a narrow majority rejected the idea. Dew repudiated the ideas of Jefferson and others who, agonizing over slavery, considered it unjust and recommended its elimination. Dew defended the property rights of slaveholders and dismissed the impracticality of relocating emancipated slaves outside Virginia. He even claimed that slavery was a positive good, sanctioned by ancient philosophers such as Aristotle and justified by the Bible.

In Southern colleges, proslavery spokesmen championed the religious, philosophical, and economic benefits of slavery, and in the South's leading magazines they defended their new proslavery ideology. They even argued that slavery was good not only for masters but for slaves. Southern defenders of slavery cast themselves as benevolent patriarchs; slaves, they argued, were the lucky beneficiaries of this system. This self-serving vision of slavery is reflected in this lithograph appropriately entitled *Slavery As It Exists In America* (**10.7**). The two shocked Northerners depicted express their astonishment that slaves were so well treated and happy. The artist also singles out the evils of British factories for condemnation. Southerners often made similar points about Northern industry, which they argued treated its workers more brutally than Southern plantation owners treated slaves.

One of the most influential apologists for Southern slavery was John C. Calhoun, an eminent South Carolina politician. He argued that the South's "**peculiar institution**," which was the term he coined for Southern slavery, was not "an evil," a cause of shame, but rather "a good—a positive good," to be championed.

10.7 *Slavery As It Exists in America*
This proslavery cartoon portrays slaves as happy and well cared for by masters who are benign patriarchs.

> "The peculiar institution of the South—that, on the maintenance of which the very existence of the slaveholding States depends, is pronounced to be sinful and odious, in the sight of God and man; and this with a systematic design of rendering us hateful in the eyes of the world—with a view to a general crusade against us and our institutions."
>
> JOHN C. CALHOUN, *speech on abolitionist petitions*, 1837

The Cult of True Womanhood, Reform, and Women's Rights

Women took a leading role in reform movements. The most active reformers were members of a growing middle class. Female reformers targeted activities that threatened the family and demeaned women's family role. Prostitution was one prominent target of reformers, but hardly the only social problem that attracted notice from female reformers. They also attacked alcoholism, crime, illiteracy, and even slavery. The social changes brought about by the market revolution, including the rise of the factory system (see Chapter 9), contributed to new ideas about the family and gender roles. A new concept of domesticity and the related notion that men's and women's proper roles lay in separate spheres of activity became the cornerstone of a new middle-class ideal. Society defined the public world of work and politics as male, whereas the private world of home and family became women's domain. Female reformers defended the new ideal and attacked the social evils that threatened it.

The New Domestic Ideal

Horace Bushnell, an influential New England minister, captured the profound change that transformed American economic and social life when he remarked that the "transition from mother-and-daughter power, to water and steam power, is a great one" and had produced a "complete revolution in domestic life." One consequence of the rise of industry was a growing separation between home and workplace. This change facilitated the rise of a new middle-class ideology that defined women's role as a separate sphere of domesticity. A **"cult of true womanhood"** emerged in which female values were defined in opposition to the aggressive and competitive marketplace. Women were identified with piety, motherhood, and sexual passivity.

Although this ideal was largely unattainable for rural farm women, urban working-class women, and free black women—all of whom had to work to maintain even minimal economic subsistence—this middle-class ideal suffused American culture.

Magazines such as *Godey's Lady's Book*, the growing body of middle-class advice literature such as Catherine Beecher's *Treatise on Domestic Economy*, and the ubiquitous prints produced by Currier and Ives all celebrated the new domestic ideal. Lilly Martin Spenser, the most renowned female artist of her day, made the new domestic ideal a central theme in her paintings. Rather than depict her subjects in the formal settings, garbed in rich velvet clothing and seated in poses borrowed from paintings of royalty and aristocracy, characteristic of the family portraits favored by earlier artists, Spencer often chose intimate scenes of domestic life as her settings. In *Domestic Happiness* she depicts a husband and wife standing before their two sleeping children. The mother's hand gently touches her husband, symbolizing the new domestic ideal's emphasis on emotional intimacy between husband and wife (**10.8**). She also appears to be gently

10.8 *Domestic Happiness*
Lily Martin Spencer's painting captures the new ideal of domesticity in which women were assigned the role of instilling the values of piety, family, and sexual passivity.

Read the **Document** *Catherine Beecher, "Treatise on Domestic Economy"*

How does *Domestic Happiness* represent the ideal of the family?

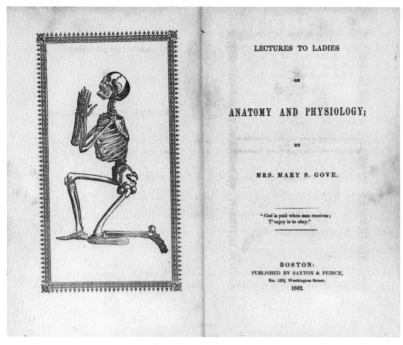

10.9 *Lectures to Ladies on Anatomy and Physiology* The image of a skeleton kneeling in prayer was carefully chosen to avoid offending the reading public. The religious pose and the absence of flesh appealed to the chaste ideals associated with the cult of true womanhood. [*Source*: The Library Company of Philadelphia]

restraining her husband from waking the children, a subtle reminder that in the domestic sphere, women, not men, were in charge.

Controlling Sexuality

The new ideal of domesticity emphasized emotional control, including control of sexuality. In 1834, Lydia Finney, the wife of Charles Finney, established the New York Female Moral Reform Society to champion moral purity. By 1837, the Society had 15,000 members and branches across New England and New York State. It focused on the problem of urban prostitution. Estimates vary but in some urban areas such as New York City, prostitution was the second largest industry in the city, well ahead of publishing, brewing, and baking (see *Envisioning Evidence: The Economics and Geography of Vice in Mid-Nineteenth Century New York,* Chapter 9). The members of the society even visited brothels to urge the "fallen women" to abandon their involvement in commercial sex. Sometimes reformers tried to shame the male clients of the prostitutes by publishing their names in the press. The society also lobbied to criminalize prostitution. Although they could be closed if they created a public nuisance, most brothels easily avoided legal entanglements and plied their trade without fear of prosecution.

The reformer Sylvester Graham formulated a far-reaching critique of sexuality. In his widely reprinted lectures on *Chastity* (1834), Graham advised his

readers to avoid sexual overstimulation, recommending that they "Take more exercise in the open air, and use the cold bath under proper circumstances." He also believed that diet contributed to overstimulation, producing a variety of physical and psychological ailments. His followers abandoned stimulants such as tea, coffee, and alcohol, replacing them with a bland diet built around whole-grain breads and crackers (the forerunner of Graham crackers). Followers of Graham could obtain information about bland diets from the *Graham Journal of Health and Longevity*, or they could attend Graham clubs at college or live in boarding houses committed to Graham's rules.

A follower of Graham's who set off on a different path, Mary Gove became interested in women's reproductive rights and health. She traveled across America lecturing to women about their bodies. Her *Lectures to Ladies on Anatomy and Physiology* (1842) included an image of a female skeleton, kneeling in prayer, on its frontispiece (**10.9**). Gove argued that the idea that women were passionless was a direct result of her "enslaved and unhealthy conditions." She later married the health reformer Thomas Low Nichols, and the two promoted health reform and woman's rights issues. Paulina Wright, another lecturer on women's health, carried around an anatomically correct female mannequin to help demonstrate issues relevant to sexual and reproductive health. Her lectures sometimes proved shocking, causing some to faint or even "run from the room." Interest in sexuality emerged out of a general concern to reform society and behavior. Woman's involvement in antebellum reform led some to examine the values, institutions, and political forces that justified the oppression and exploitation of women.

The Path toward Seneca Falls

Women had already been active in political and moral reform movements, including opposition to President Jackson's policy of Indian removal (see Chapter 8), temperance, and the crusade against prostitution. Participation in these movements had led women to organize themselves, speak out in public, and question the underlying political, legal, and social values that contributed to their oppression. Many women were drawn to the antislavery movement which further radicalized many female reformers.

Of the almost 70,000 signatures on antislavery petitions submitted to Congress in 1837–1838, more than two-thirds were women's. Organizations such as the Philadelphia Female Anti-Slavery Society (1833) provided women with unprecedented opportunities to become actors in one of the most important political dramas of the day. Involvement in the antislavery cause could be a harrowing experience. The virulent hatred abolitionists faced, even in the North, did not make exemptions for gender. In 1838, the Anti-Slavery Convention of American Women refused to exclude black women from its meetings. An antiabolitionist crowd then stormed the building and torched it.

Support for abolitionism also led many women to question their legal status as women. A turning point in the relationship between antislavery and women's rights occurred in 1840 when American reformers Elizabeth Cady Stanton and Lucretia Mott attended an international antislavery conference in London. The female delegates were not allowed to speak at the event and were forced to sit behind an opaque screen out of view of the other delegates. Incensed by their treatment in London, Stanton and Mott saw the oppression of women as an evil requiring the same attention as the oppression of slavery.

Stanton was born into a prosperous family. Her father was a prominent lawyer who became a state Supreme Court judge. She spent hours reading law books in her father's office. What most galled Stanton was the English common law doctrine of coverture, which treated a woman as legally dead once married. American law had inherited this concept, which meant that a husband would control any property a woman might have owned before her marriage and all of the wealth gained during their marriage.

In 1837, Thomas Herttell introduced a bill into the New York legislature to give married women more control over their property. Eleven years later the legislature passed a landmark married women's property act that allowed women to retain control of their inherited property. Stanton helped win approval for this law. The law did not give married women full control of any wealth or property they gathered during marriage, but it was an important step forward.

The year 1848 was a momentous one in the history of women's rights. In the same year that New York adopted the married women's property act, supporters of women's rights gathered in Seneca Falls, New York, not far from Rochester, for a historic meeting. The organizers of the convention were Stanton and Mott, two veterans of moral reform and abolitionism. About 300 men and women, including noted African-American abolitionist Frederick Douglass, assembled in a church for the **Seneca Falls Convention**, during

> ## "The history of mankind is a history of repeated injuries and usurpations on the part of man toward woman…."
>
> "Declaration of Sentiments and Resolutions" of the Seneca Falls, New York, Women's Rights Convention (1848)

which a women's rights manifesto modeled on the Declaration of Independence was drafted. The Declaration of Sentiments and Resolutions declared that "all men and women are created equal." It noted that women were denied economic opportunities, legal rights, and access to education. It also asserted that "it is the duty of women of this country to secure themselves their sacred right to the elective franchise." Seneca Falls prompted more than two dozen other such meetings in the next 12 years.

The ardent abolitionist newspaper founded by Frederick Douglass not only applauded the actions of the convention but also exhorted abolitionists to embrace women's rights alongside their opposition to slavery. The mainstream press, however, was less sympathetic. One newspaper mistakenly concluded that the Declaration of Sentiments was a parody of the Declaration of Independence, not an attempt to appropriate its language for women. Forty percent of American newspapers printed negative accounts of Seneca Falls, but 29 percent were favorable. Although still opposed by most Americans, women's rights had become a topic of national conversation for the first time. The Declaration of Sentiments would become a foundational text for all subsequent efforts to promote equal rights for American women. In Stanton's view the women who gathered in upstate New York in a modest church had instigated "a rebellion such as the world had never seen before."

The women's rights question caused a major schism in the abolitionist movement. In 1840, delegates to the American Anti-Slavery Society (AASS) debated whether women could hold office in the organization. William Lloyd Garrison, a supporter of women's rights, outmaneuvered his opponents and emerged victorious on this question. However, abolitionists opposed to linking the cause with women's rights responded by resigning from the AASS.

◉—[**Watch** the **Video** *Video Lecture: The Women's Rights Movement in Nineteenth Century America*

How did Stanton's upbringing influence her approach to women's rights?

Religious and Secular Utopianism

As many mainstream religious groups preached the necessity of reform and worked to change American society, certain sectarian groups sought a radical transformation of American society. In some cases these groups were attempting to create a heaven on earth, literally preparing the way for Christ's return. The movement for reform also spawned a variety of different secular utopian movements. Both religious and secular groups engaged in bold forms of social experimentation. Many groups abolished private property and embraced some form of socialist or communist ideals, abandoning the idea of private property.

10.10 Millerite
William Miller's prediction that the millennium would arrive in March 1843 prompted this satirical image of one of his followers preparing for the apocalypse by stocking up on cheese and crackers.

Millennialism, Perfectionism, and Religious Utopianism

Millennialism, the belief that the millennium was imminent and that Judgment Day would soon follow, attracted many followers in the mid-nineteenth century. Some believers even named the date of Christ's return to establish the millennium. The followers of William Miller, called Millerites, predicted that Christ would return in March 1843. When that prediction failed to come true, Miller prophesied a new date, October 22, 1844. Again the millennium failed to materialize. The movement collapsed soon after the revised prediction also proved false. Indeed, the failure of the Millerites to predict the true date for the millennium inspired humor. This satirical picture of a Millerite depicts a man prepared to lock himself in a trunk together with crackers, cheese, and plenty to drink, emergency provisions which might come in handy in the chaos that would precede the apocalypse before Judgment Day. The sardonic image captures the popular reaction to Miller's failed predictions (**10.10**). But aspects of Miller's teachings survived and were later incorporated into the Seventh Day Adventists, another nineteenth-century religious sect, one that celebrated Saturday, not Sunday, as their day of worship.

The United Society of Believers in Christ's Second Appearing, or Shakers, created a successful religious utopia, establishing settlements across the nation and attracting

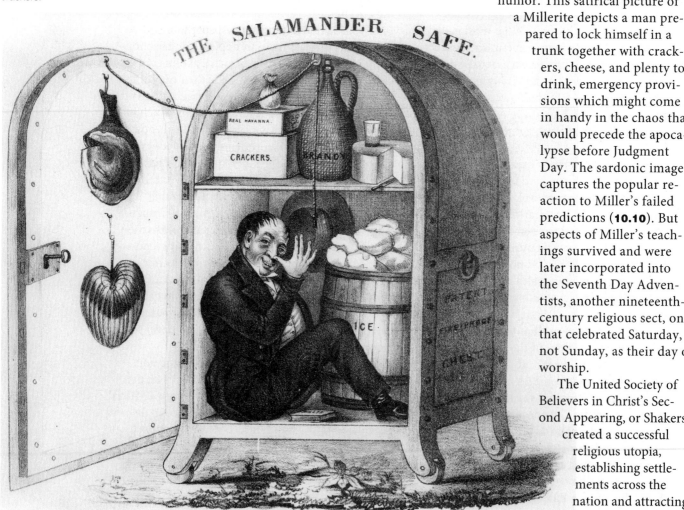

A MILLERITE PREPARING FOR THE 23RD OF APRIL.

How did the Shakers recast the idea of the family?

thousands of followers. The Shaker faith was shaped by the teachings of Mother Ann Lee, an eighteenth-century religious figure who adapted Quaker teachings in light of her own experience and revelations. The wife of an abusive husband whose four children died during infancy, she experienced a revelation that sex itself was the root of human evil. Her followers became known as Shaking Quakers or Shakers because their religious worship involved an ecstatic form of dance that one contemporary described as including "extravagant postures" and "fantastic contortions." The sect also adopted a strict rule of celibacy. Mother Ann's vision of Christianity not only transformed ideas about sexuality but also radically recast gender roles. She preached that God was a combination of the masculine and feminine, a radical teaching given the strongly patriarchal character of most Protestant theology in the nineteenth century. Judged by the standards of the day, the Shakers came closer to the idea of equality of the sexes than almost any other group in America. Within the Shaker community, there were only brothers and sisters—neither husbands and wives nor mothers and fathers. Abandoning procreation, the Shakers grew only by taking in orphans and converting new members. The Shakers radically reconfigured the meaning of the family unit, rejecting the ideal of domesticity and marriage itself. (See *Competing Visions: Reactions to Shaker Gender Roles.*)

Shakers not only rejected the values of domesticity and mainstream attitudes toward family life, but they also developed a complex relationship with the growing market economy around them. Thus while Shakers participated in the expanding market economy, they did not internalize its competitive values. Within the Shaker community, there was no private property. Shaker communities practiced a form of Christian communism. To support the community they sold a variety of goods to outsiders. Shaker craftsmen developed a reputation as skilled furniture makers, and Shakers sold agricultural products, including seeds to eager consumers.

The Shakers were hardly the only radical religious experiment that rejected the values of the market-place and the traditional ideal of the family. One of the most radical utopian leaders was John Humphrey Noyes. A Yale-educated Congregationalist minister, Noyes took the idea of perfectionism, a doctrine that had evolved from Methodism, in a novel direction. Earlier perfectionists had argued that one could attain a perfect state of holiness.

That did not mean that a person was completely free from sin, but rather that one had attained the highest level of spiritual perfection consistent with human nature. In 1840, Noyes created the Putney Association, and by 1844, the small group was practicing a form of Christian communism in which, like the Shakers, all property was commonly owned. The association included 37 people who worshiped together in a small chapel, lived in three houses, farmed, and maintained a store. In 1846, Noyes took his theory of perfectionism in a new direction. If one attained a state of religious perfection and could not sin, then he argued one could be free of many laws enacted to deal with humans' fallen, sinful state. Marriage and monogamy were two such ideals.

Noyes's restructuring of the family and new ideas about sexuality ran afoul of the dominant views of marriage; he was indicted for adultery in Vermont, but fled to upstate New York, to Oneida. There Noyes instituted the practice of "**complex marriage**," in which any man or woman who had experienced saving grace was free to engage in sexual relations with any other person of the opposite sex. Given their commitment to free love, birth control became an important concern of the community. Noyes began to preach the necessity of something he called male continence, a primitive form of natural birth control that required that men engage in sex acts without consummating them. His views mirrored those of other nineteenth-century medical reformers such as Sylvester Graham, who believed that it was important for men to conserve their bodily fluids. Eventually the Oneida community embraced a form of eugenics, a theory that advocated using selective mating to produce superior children and thereby improve humanity. At Oneida only the most spiritually perfect were allowed to consummate their sexual unions and produce children. The interior of the Oneida mansion house was organized to facilitate the idea of complex marriage by weakening notions of privacy. The "tent room" on the third floor replaced private rooms with semiprivate enclosures blocked off by cotton cloth. The "tent room" increased the "sociality" of members and reduced the "cold isolation" of traditional apartments.

Although the practice of complex marriage was radically different from the celibacy practiced by the Shakers, both groups sought to reconfigure the family, sexuality, and their relationship to the market economy. Although each group

Competing Visions
REACTIONS TO SHAKER GENDER ROLES

The unique religious practices of the Shakers drew many comments. For Americans, nothing was more remarkable than the Shakers' reconfiguration of traditional gender roles and the family. Travelers, including the English novelist Charles Dickens, home-grown literary figures such as Nathaniel Hawthorne, and a variety of journalists toured Shaker communities and commented on the sect's unique practices and habitations.

In *The Shaker Bridal*, Nathaniel Hawthorne recounts the plight of two young lovers, Martha and Adam, who give up their chance for earthly love to join the Shakers. Rather than transcend earthly suffering and reach a higher spiritual level, however, her decision to forsake conventional marriage ultimately leaves her despondent and an object of pity.

"I have bidden you to join your hands," said he, "not in earthly affection, for ye have cast off its chains forever; but as brother and sister in spiritual love, and helpers of one another in your allotted task. Teach unto others the faith which ye have received".... The aged Father sank back exhausted, and the surrounding elders deemed, with good reason, that the hour was come when the new heads of the village must enter on their patriarchal duties. In their attention to Father Ephraim, their eyes were turned from Martha Pierson, who grew paler and paler, unnoticed even by Adam Colburn. He, indeed, had withdrawn his hand from hers, and folded his arms with a sense of satisfied ambition. But paler and paler grew Martha by his side, till, like a corpse in its burial clothes, she sank down at the feet of her early lover; for, after many trials firmly borne, her heart could endure the weight of its desolate agony no longer.

The following account of a visit to New York Shakers in 1829 paints a different portrait of life and love among this utopian community. This visitor did not encounter a repressed and puritanical religion, but something close to a religious utopia. The brothers and sisters, in this view, had traded the suffering of the world for their own vision of heaven on earth:

It is impossible to describe the air of tranquility and comfort that diffuses itself over a Shaker settlement. It is no matter what the enemies of such peaceful, unoffending communities may say about them. The acute observer of human manners will testify for them that they do not live after the manner of world.... with the Shakers; the two sexes together bear the burdens, if burden it may be, of celibacy; they enliven its dullness by the amenity of their intercourse with one another.... the union of these people, their uniform kindness to each other, and the singularly benevolent and tender expression of their countenances, speak a stronger language than their profession.

What do reactions to Shaker gender roles reveal about ninteenth-century American values?

approached the family and sex from different perspectives, both groups embraced communal ownership of property, and, although differing in means, they both also attempted to free women from traditional gender roles. See *Choices and Consequences: Mary Cragin's Experiment in Free Love at Oneida.*

Joseph Smith, the founder of the Church of Jesus Christ of the Latter Day Saints, or Mormonism, created another model of a religious utopia. Smith grew up in western New York, where the fires of the Great Awakening burned hot. In this evangelical milieu he had a revelation on which Mormonism was based. According to the Book of Mormon, in 1823, an angel steered him to a set of golden tablets written in an ancient language. With divine help Smith deciphered the tablets, which told of the travails of a lost tribe of Israelites who had settled in America and who Mormons believed were the ancestors of Native Americans. The Book of Mormon was published in Palmyra, New York, in 1830, and this town became the site of one of the earliest Mormon communities. The belief that the Indians were actually descendants of a lost tribe of Hebrews was not unique to the Mormons. The theory attracted attention from several prominent religious authors of the time. Smith's treasure hunting was also not that unusual, spurred on by popular stories about buried treasures gathered by ancient Indian civilizations.

Smith was influenced by the widespread belief that the millennium was at hand, bringing with it an end to debt and the return of Christ and a new era of peace, happiness, and prosperity. The revelations detailed by Smith struck a resonant chord with small farmers, tradesmen, and mechanics whose experience with the expanding market economy had been largely negative. Smith's new revelation attracted thousands of followers. Mormons set up their own community in Kirtland, Ohio, and then a larger community at Nauvoo, Illinois. The Mormons did not go as far as the Shakers or Oneidians in embracing communism, but they had a strong communal economic ethic. Smith's 1831 law of consecration urged Mormons to deed their land to the church, which would distribute it among the faithful and retain any surplus.

Secular Utopias

Secular utopia also attracted individuals frustrated with American society. Hostility to the market revolution provided inspiration for a variety of socialist utopian communities. Robert Owen's New Harmony in Indiana was one such ambitious experiment. A successful textile mill owner who began his career in Scotland, Owen was worried about the impact of industrialization on society and hoped to create an ideal community built on a socialist model. Despite early enthusiasm his community lasted only three years. The French theorist Charles Fourier provided a more popular socialist alternative, including a utopian theory of phalanxes, ideal communities organized around socialist ideals, that gained a considerable following in the 1840s. Indeed, between 1841 and 1846, 25 of these phalanxes popped up across New England, New York, and the Midwest. Rather than accept the values of the marketplace, Fourier championed the ideas of "association" and "cooperation." Individual communities divided the profits produced by agricultural labor or goods manufactured at the phalanx among the members according to a formula that included the amount invested, a person's skills, and the amount of his or her physical labor. Fourier's socialist theories also questioned traditional gender roles. In his view social progress occurred in direct "proportion to the advance of women toward liberty." Women in Fourierist communities enjoyed equal pay and equal opportunities with men and benefited from

"Under our system of isolated and separate households, with separate interests and separate pursuits, instead of association and combination among families, there is the most deplorable waste, which is one of the primary sources of the general poverty that exists; and discord, antagonism, selfishness, and an anti-social spirit are engendered."

ALBERT BRISBANE (American Fourierist), *Concise Exposition of the Doctrine of Association*, 1843

Why did Mormon values appeal to farmers and other small producers in the era of the market revolution?

Choices and Consequences

MARY CRAGIN'S EXPERIMENT IN FREE LOVE AT ONEIDA

Mary Cragin and her husband George were among the many Americans influenced by Charles Grandison Finney's religious leadership in the Second Great Awakening. George worked for a reform paper in New York, the *Advocate of Moral Reform*, as an office manager and accountant. He showed his wife a copy of a letter written by John Humphrey Noyes, which introduced Mary to Noyes's ideas of perfectionism. Mary and her husband were both taken with this doctrine and moved to Vermont. Noyes began his experiment in "communism in love" at Putney. As a member of his first perfectionist community at the Putney, Vermont community, Mary Cragin faced a choice: either leave the community or participate in its bold new experiment in free love.

Choices

| 1 Persuade her husband to leave the community with her. | 2 Leave regardless of her husband's decision. | 3 Stay with her husband and participate in Noyes's system of complex marriage. |

Decision

Mary chose option 3, to stay at Putney with her husband and participate in a complex marriage with Noyes and others.

Mary Cragin

Consequences

Mary eagerly embraced Noyes's theory and eventually traveled with her husband and others to Oneida, becoming founding members of that community. In the published comments in the "First Annual Report of Oneida Community Association" (1849), she declared that her life at Oneida brought her closer to God than anything else she had ever done. She died a year later when the boat she was traveling on capsized.

Continuing Controversies

Why would a nineteenth-century woman be attracted to utopian movements that rejected mainstream views of the family and marriage?

Modern scholars are divided over the impact of "Bible Communism" and "complex marriage" on women's lives. Some argue that compared to the restrictive and oppressive environment most women faced in American society, Oneida provided women with more power, control over their sexual lives, and equality. Although not a feminist utopia, Oneida's system of complex marriage was liberating in many ways for women.

Others view Oneida as just another form of female oppression. The limited choices granted to women did not end male power and authority. At Oneida men continued to dominate women's lives, controlling their sexual and reproductive choices.

Why might a woman like Mary Cragin have been drawn to the Oneida Community?

10.11 Utopian Communities
The heaviest concentration of these religious and social experiments was in New England, western New York, and the Midwest.

> "Although the desire of acquiring the good things of this world is the prevailing passion of the American people … here and there in the midst of American society … sects arise which endeavor to strike out extraordinary paths to eternal happiness."
>
> ALEXIS DE TOCQUEVILLE
> *Democracy in America*, (1835)

an egalitarian attitude toward sex that was unusual for its time.

As the map (**10.11**) shows, utopian experiments, both secular and religious, were scattered across the United States. A host of other smaller utopian experiments were also attempted during this period. At Brook Farm, a community in Massachusetts near Boston, manual labor was supplemented by activities to encourage "intellectual improvement" and "social intercourse, calculated to refine and expand" the mind and soul. Nathaniel Hawthorne used his brief residence in the community as the basis for his novel *The Blithedale Romance*. Like Brook Farm, Bronson Alcott's utopian community Fruitlands emphasized balancing manual and intellectual labor and communal ownership. But in contrast to Brook Farm,

dietary restrictions were an important part of this utopia. Fruitland's members were not only vegetarian but also ate only "aspiring" vegetables—those that grew upward (reaching up for the supreme truths). Potatoes, beets, and carrots, which grew downward, were forbidden.

One utopian community tried to tackle the problem of race directly. Francis Wright, a Scottish abolitionist, founded Nashoba, an interracial cooperative near Memphis, Tennessee, to demonstrate the potential for blacks and whites to live together as equals. At Nashoba slaves were to be given a formal education and allowed to earn enough to purchase their freedom. However, Wright's more radical ideas included the abolition of the nuclear family, religion, and private property. The community lasted only four years.

View the **Map** *Interactive Map: Utopian Communities before the Civil War*

What geographical patterns are evident from this map of utopian communities?

Literature and Popular Culture

The danger posed by the "tyranny of the majority," a subject explored in some detail by Alexis de Tocqueville in *Democracy in America*, attracted the attention of intellectuals and writers such as Ralph Waldo Emerson, a Harvard-trained minister, who rejected orthodox religion in favor of philosophical exploration. Emerson's essays, beginning with his manifesto, "The American Scholar," enjoined Americans to wake up, reject the latest fashions of the marketplace, and discover the deeper philosophical truths to be found in nature and self-reflection. Within two decades of Emerson's address, Nathaniel Hawthorne published *The Scarlet Letter* (1850); Herman Melville, *Moby-Dick* (1851); Henry David Thoreau, *Walden* (1854); and Walt Whitman, *Leaves of Grass* (1855). The vigorous intellectual and poetic activity of these writers and thinkers constituted a veritable American Renaissance. Some of the best-known works of these literary giants explored the problems of American society in a fictional setting.

Although a few literary figures crafted rich and sophisticated works of fiction and poetry, many now forgotten writers marketed their books to the growing mass audience of readers. Many popular works depicted lurid tales of city life, including murder and prostitution. The marketplace also adapted to the intellectual ferment of the era by creating new institutions devoted to presenting to the people lectures by leading intellectuals, including Emerson. In addition to hearing literary figures such as Emerson, one might also learn about the latest intellectual fads, including phrenology, a pseudo-science that purported to enable practitioners to discern a person's character and intellect from the shape of his or her head. Finally, architects explored a variety of different building styles hoping that improvements in the built environment would lead to moral and spiritual uplift. In some cases, architects turned to the lessons of the past, looking to the styles of antiquity: Greek Temples or Egyptian monuments for inspiration. Those seeking a more exalted and spiritual ideal turned to the medieval period for models. These ideas influenced everything from cemetery design to country farm houses.

Literature and Social Criticism

Emerson's *American Scholar* address marked the beginning of one of the greatest periods of American literary achievement. Emerson became the leading exponent of the philosophy of **Transcendentalism**, a loose set of ideas that looked to nature for inspiration and insights. The other leading literary figure associated with this movement was Henry David Thoreau. In his masterpiece *Walden,* Thoreau decried the impact of the market on American society. Ostensibly a tale of his effort to get back to nature, *Walden* asserted that "The mass of men lead lives of quiet desperation…. The greater part of what my neighbors call good I believe in my soul to be bad." Only by rejecting the numbing conformity of American society, the tyranny of the majority, and the worldly values of the marketplace could Americans rekindle the divine spark in each person.

Other American literary figures turned a critical eye to American history and society. Nathaniel Hawthorne parodied the excesses of utopian movements in *The Blithedale Romance* and explored the Shakers' views of the family in the "Shaker Bridal" (see *Competing Visions: Reactions to Shaker Gender Roles*). In *The Celestial Railroad,* he took aim at the connections between revivalism and the market revolution. In this tale, an updating of the Christian story of the religious pilgrim's search for salvation, Hawthorne provided his spiritual seeker with a comfortable seat on a railroad coach. Rather than patiently wait until arriving at the heavenly city, the train's final stop, most of the travelers prefer to exit at "Vanity Fair," a glittering city that was "an epitome of whatever is brilliant, gay, and fascinating." Although they failed to achieve salvation, the residents of Vanity Fair were well supplied with clergy, churches, and lecturers on the latest topics of discussion, and the stores sold the most fashionable goods.

Herman Melville's epic novel *Moby-Dick* told the story of Captain Ahab's pursuit of a great white whale. A rich and complex novel, Ahab's quest provided another metaphor for the search for meaning, spiritual fulfillment, and truth by those working within an economic system that increasingly treated people as commodities. As was true for Hawthorne, Melville's writing grappled with the alienation of Americans resulting from the economic changes wrought by the market revolution. One group Melville discussed was the new expanding middle class of clerks for whom "Ocean reveries" provided an escape from their dreary lives. Melville wrote of these cogs in the great machine of industry, "tied to counters, nailed to benches, clinched to desks." Melville's own experiences at sea not only provided him with details for his tale of the "Great White Whale" but also allowed him to escape the fate of those clerks trapped at their desks that he chronicled in his writing. Indeed, one of Melville's most famous literary creations was a lowly and alienated clerk "Bartleby the Scrivener," a man drained of all creativity and energy who symbolized how commerce could turn individuals into utterly passive victims of larger social and economic forces. Bartleby responds to every request from his employer with the same bored refrain, "I would prefer not to."

Domestic Fiction, Board Games, and Crime Stories

Many popular writers of Hawthorne and Melville's day were women, which prompted Hawthorne to lash out angrily at the "damned mob of scribbling women" whose books often sold in the hundreds of thousands, many more copies than authors of serious fiction such as Hawthorne ever sold. Indeed, women had written the top-five bestsellers by mid-century. Women favored "sentimental writing" and "domestic fiction," which were immensely popular.

Susana Warner's *The Wide, Wide World* (1850) sold more than 40,000 copies in its first year and was reprinted 67 times. This tale of an orphaned but resourceful child who must find her way in the wider world recast the traditional tale of the Christian pilgrim on the road to salvation in terms of the ideals of middle-class domesticity. By discovering her inner strength, the heroine demonstrates her talents and virtues. After proving her determination and character, she finds a virtuous man whom she weds, thus fulfilling the ideal of domesticity. This general plotline carries through most of the era's works of sentimental writing and domestic fiction.

Domestic fiction mirrored the same cultural values that led to the creation of the first popular board game in American history, "The Mansion of Happiness." Ann Abbott, the daughter of a Massachusetts minister, invented the game in 1843. Players traveled along a spiral board that led to the "mansion of happiness" at the center. If they landed on such desirable spaces as "temperance," "piety," and "chastity," they could move forward. Landing on a space such as "idleness" sent the player backward. Rather than use dice, which were associated with the evil of gambling, players used a numbered top to determine how many spaces to move on a turn (**10.12**). The game

10.12 The Mansion of Happiness Modern style board games were invented during the period of the market revolution and moral reform to instill values into children. This popular board game embodied many of the ideals of domestic fiction and prints. The game sets players on a journey along a path toward piety in which they must avoid sin if they hope to finally arrive at the Mansion of Happiness.

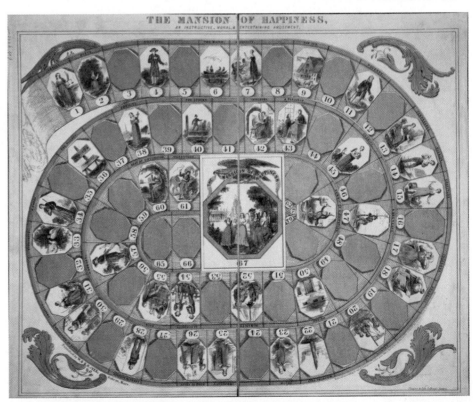

What ideas about the family and religion are reflected in "The Mansion of Happiness"?

shared the ideals of popular prints such as *The Way of Good and Evil*, which also imagined life as a journey along a path between piety and sin (see page 283).

Although domestic fiction and games such as "The Mansion of Happiness" popularized the domestic values esteemed by reformers, there was also a market for stories about the very evils these works advised Americans to avoid lest they wind up in prison or the asylum. The new penny press included a host of papers such as the *National Police Gazette* and the *New York Sun*, whose pages were filled with tales of crime and moral depravity. Literature embraced the sordid as much as the spiritual, and crime fiction was especially popular. George Lippard's *The Quaker City, Or, The Monks of Monk Hall: A Romance of Philadelphia Life, Mystery and Crime* (1845) spun a lurid tale that explored the evils of urban life. In contrast to Susana Warner, Lippard imbued his tale of seduction, murder, and intrigue with a subtle class-conscious critique of the debauched elites who gathered in a dilapidated old mansion, Monk's Hall, filled with secret passages and murder victims. The one writer who managed to transform such gothic tales of crime and horror into high art was Edgar Allan Poe. In stories such as "The Tell-Tale Heart" and the "Black Cat," Poe explored the psychological dimensions of crime.

10.13 First edition of Douglass, *Narrative of the Life of Frederick Douglass, An American Slave* (1845) The eloquence of Douglass led some to suggest that his account of his own escape from slavery could not have been written by an ex-slave. To underscore that the book was genuine, an image of Douglass and a copy of his signature are prominently displayed alongside the title page.

His taut, gripping stories were models of literary craftsmanship. Poe brought the techniques of high literature to bear on topics that were usually the province of popular writers.

Slaves Tell Their Story: Slavery in American Literature

While the writers of the American Renaissance were formulating their critique of American society, other voices were also entering the expanding literary marketplace. Accounts published by runaway slaves described the brutality of slavery.

The most famous and influential slave autobiography was Frederick Douglass's *Narrative of the Life of Frederick Douglass, An American Slave* published in 1845. More than 30,000 copies sold within a decade of its publication. Douglass awakened Americans to the injustice of slavery by exposing "the cruelties of it as I had myself felt them." The accuracy of his account was a key element of its appeal, but critics questioned his book's authenticity. Douglass thus went to great lengths to prove that it was not an abolitionist hoax. Indeed, Douglass worried that his eloquence might itself be used as proof that a former slave could not have written the book. To establish his credibility, Douglass included a daguerreotype image of himself (a forerunner of modern photography), a copy of his signature (a sign of his literacy), and two testimonials swearing that the narrative was indeed authentic (**10.13**).

Harriet Jacobs's *Incidents in the Life of a Slave Girl* was published under the pen name Linda Brent. Jacobs had escaped to freedom in 1842, but it took almost another two decades for her to improve her writing to the point where she could publish an account of her ordeal under slavery. She described her purpose in writing in forceful terms: "I have not written my experiences in order to attract attention to myself, on the contrary,

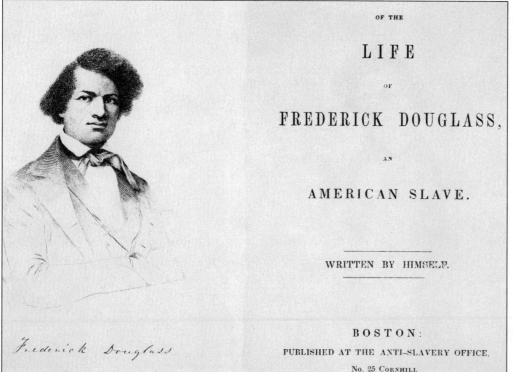

OF THE

LIFE

OF

FREDERICK DOUGLASS,

AN

AMERICAN SLAVE.

WRITTEN BY HIMSELF.

BOSTON:
PUBLISHED AT THE ANTI-SLAVERY OFFICE.
No. 25 CORNHILL.

1845.

Frederick Douglass

Why did Douglass need to prove that he was the author of his autobiography?

it would have been more pleasant to me to have been silent about my own history." Undaunted, she felt compelled to add my testimony to that of abler pens to convince the people of the free states what slavery really is. Jacobs's account of her life, particularly the firsthand accounts of the sexual predations of white Southerners on black women, exposed the plight of female slaves.

Lyceums and Lectures

Josiah Holbrook, a teacher and lecturer, began the Lyceum movement in 1826. Named after the place in ancient Athens where the philosopher Aristotle lectured to his pupils, the Lyceum movement provided a forum for public lectures and debates on intellectual issues. By 1834, more than 3,000 Lyceums appeared in towns and cities across America. As transportation improved with the rise of the railroad, the Lyceum movement created a national market for speakers on topics of general interest.

An especially popular lecture topic was phrenology, a pseudoscience that focused on the relationship between the bumps and shape of the human head and character and personality. Americans could pay to have their heads analyzed by phrenologists at salons in major cities and towns. By the 1850s, the *American Phrenological Journal* had a circulation of more than 50,000. Phrenology became an American obsession in the mid-nineteenth century. Phrenological heads made of plaster or ceramic were commonplace decorations in many American homes, prompting the *Boston Christian Examiner* in 1834 to complain that "heads of chalk, inscribed with mystic numbers, disfigured every mantelpiece." Few of these were as striking as this impressive folk sculpture of a young girl's head with the different zones of the cranium colored according to phrenological theory (**10.14**). Phrenology also attracted the notice of many leading public figures such as Supreme Court Justice Joseph Story, the moral reformer Horace Mann, and the artist Hiram Powers.

Godey's Lady's Book even advised women to use hats and other head coverings to hide or accentuate their phrenological character. Phrenology appealed to Americans at a time when the nation was experiencing rapid change. In particular it spoke to the fears of urban Americans who increasingly lived and worked in a world filled with strangers. The new market economy opened up countless opportunities for swindlers and rogues, prompting a new term, "confidence man," someone who exploited a stranger's trust to fleece him of his property or money. Although one might dress like a member of the respectable middle class, appearances were often deceiving, and the rise of the "confidence man" was symbolic of the danger posed by the anonymous world of the market. Phrenology promised to allow one to see beyond appearances into a person's true character and thus past the masks and disguises of "confidence men."

10.14 Phrenological Head
This colorful folk sculpture of a young girl's head included hand-painted zones that phrenologists believed controlled human emotion and behavior.

Nature's Nation

In honor of the opening of the Erie Canal, a young artist named Thomas Cole staged an exhibition of landscape paintings that became an immediate sensation. Organizers of the show declared that the artist's work "had equaled those works which have been the boast of Europe." Cole's work would "adorn our houses with the American prospects and American skies." While writers such as Emerson and Thoreau extolled nature in prose, painters such as Cole captured its majesty in color on canvas.

The appreciation for nature influenced the design of urban parks and cemeteries. Reform also prompted Americans to embrace architectural styles that would help transform society. Cemetery designers and prison reformers turned to ancient Egypt for inspiration. Architectural reform even influenced phrenologists, who championed the octagon as the perfect housing form.

10.15 *View from Mt. Holyoke*
This dramatic Cole landscape not only captures the wild power of nature, a common theme in Cole's paintings, but it contrasts this untamed natural world with a more placid pastoral world represented by the rich agricultural lands of the Connecticut Valley.

Landscape Painting

The artist Thomas Cole became one of America's most prominent painters. Cole's landscapes became a symbol of America and its uniqueness. For those eager to defend American culture against its European critics, Cole's cause became the cause of America.

An art critic noted that Cole's work proved that American art need not embrace the artificial beauty depicted in so much European art: "Nature needs no fictitious charms, … the eye requires no borrowed assistance from the memory." In 1835, in his "Essay on American Scenery," Cole wrote that "the most distinctive, and perhaps most impressive, characteristic of American scenery is its wilderness."

Many of the themes that would become hallmarks of Cole's work are evident in his dramatic painting, *View from Mt. Holyoke* (**10.15**) Cole contrasts a stormy natural landscape with the more placid panorama of the rich farm lands of the Connecticut River valley. Cole places himself in the midst of the wild mountain landscape nestled between two rock outcroppings to underscore his belief that nature is the true inspiration for artistic creativity.

What does Cole's painting reveal about American views of nature?

> "In this age, when . . . what is sometimes called improvement in its march makes us fear that the bright and tender flowers of the imagination shall all be crushed beneath its iron tramp, it would be well to cultivate the oasis that yet remains to us, and thus preserve the germs of a future and purer system."
>
> THOMAS COLE, *Essay on American Scenary* (1835–1836)

Parks and Cemeteries

When Cole and other landscape painters were celebrating nature, America was undergoing one of its first great waves of urbanization. As agriculture became more efficient, Americans from the countryside streamed into the nation's growing cities. While many urban homes boasted a Currier and Ives print of an idyllic rural setting, a more concrete effort was made to bring nature itself to the city. The creation of urban parks as retreats from the hustle and bustle of city life and a radically new approach to designing cemeteries were two highly visible results of the desire to preserve nature in the midst of rapid urbanization.

New York's Central Park (geographically at the center of Manhattan Island, but originally situated at the edge of the city) was the most ambitious and visible effort to bring the country to the city. Designed by Frederick Law Olmsted and Calvert Vaux in 1857 and officially opened two years later, Central Park sought to bring a varied country landscape, including meadows, rolling hills, lakes, and woodlands, to urban dwellers. To preserve the calming views, the designers sunk roadways beneath the line of sight of most strollers (**10.16**). For many upper- and middle-class Protestant reformers, Central Park was intended to help civilize the city's workers and immigrants. These reformers believed that strolls through the different country

10.16 Central Park
To maintain its country-like setting, the roads running through Central Park were sunk below the line of sight.

What was the rural cemetery movement?

10.17 Mount Auburn
The "rural cemetery movement" aimed to bring the country to the city and honor the dead by creating places of repose and reflection. An Egyptian obelisk sits beside the pond.

settings would spiritually uplift those whose lives were degraded by industrial life and whose private lives were confined to the squalid conditions of areas such as Five Points. Championed by New York's elite and designed with middle-class values in mind, the land for much of the park was acquired by displacing Irish immigrants and destroying one of the city's most long-established African-American communities.

Mount Auburn Cemetery, in Cambridge, Massachusetts, just outside of Boston, reflected the new view of cemeteries. Its opening in 1831 attracted 2,000 people who were treated to orations by leading ministers and Supreme Court

Justice Joseph Story. In contrast to earlier graveyards or burial grounds, designers made the new cemeteries associated with the rural cemetery movement, such as Mount Auburn, places of repose for both the living and the dead. As this painting (**10.17**) of a couple strolling through the landscaped terrain of Mount Auburn suggests, the "repose and sacred loveliness of natural beauty" made the cemetery a destination for nearby city dwellers who wished to experience the ennobling effects of nature. It soon became a major tourist attraction, with as many as 30,000 visitors per year traveling to Boston to see Mount Auburn. Its success led to the creation of other cemeteries designed to provide urban dwellers with places of reflection and repose.

The "rural cemetery movement" inspired an important architectural change. Architects looking for inspiration to represent death found it in ancient Egypt's pyramids, other monumental structures, and its funeral practices. The image of Mount Auburn shown here (10.17) features one of the most common architectural elements borrowed

"Nothing has more to do with the morals, the civilization, and refinement of a nation, than its prevailing architecture."
OLIVER P. SMITH, *The Domestic Architect* (1854)

Why did Egyptian architectural styles inspire Americans in the 1830s?

"1) Fancy articles of any kind, or articles which are superfluously finished, trimmed, or ornamented, are not suitable for Believers, and may not be used or purchased. . . . 5) Believers may not in any case or circumstances, manufacture for sale, any article or articles, which are superfluously wrought, and which may have a tendency to feed the pride and vanity of man . . ."

Shaker MILLENIAL LAWS, 1821

from ancient Egypt, the obelisk. Mount Auburn and other cemeteries also included Egyptian-Revival entrances that borrowed architectural elements from ancient Egyptian temples, including the giant pylons that framed them. The Egyptian Revival also inspired architects working on other public buildings, mainly those with a grim purpose, including Philadelphia's debtor's prison and New Jersey's state prison. New York City's prison, officially named "The Halls of Justice," was nicknamed "the Tombs" because of its forbidding Egyptian-Revival façade.

Revival and Reform in American Architecture

Egypt was not the only ancient culture that inspired American architects and designers in the 1830s. Andrew Jackson's rise to power in 1828 had reflected and facilitated a broad democratization of society (see Chapter 8). The democratization of American life coincided with Greece's war for independence from the Ottoman Empire that began in 1821. The Greek independence movement seemed analogous to America's own struggle against Britain. Not surprisingly American culture developed a fascination with Greece, the birthplace of democracy. As a result Greek Revival was a popular style of architecture, interior design, and dress during the 1820s and 1830s. As a contemporary noted, "a perfect mania for the Grecian orders" pervaded American society and required that "every building from the shop of the tradesmen, to the church and the capitol, must be Grecian." Simple farmhouses were adorned with classical columns and pediments, giving their doorways the appearance of mini-Greek temples.

The rage for all things Greek also shaped the way Americans designed and decorated their homes.

Furniture in this period was fashioned to resemble ancient Greek styles, often including decorative motifs drawn from Greece, such as urns and classical pillars. The obsession with ancient Greece literally transformed the map of the United States. Across America cities and towns sprung up with Greek names; western New York alone, along and near the Erie Canal, saw the appearance of cities named Troy, Ithaca, Utica, and Syracuse. Harriet Martineau, an English novelist who published accounts of her experiences in America, feared that America's youth would grow up thinking that "Utica, Carthage, Athens, Palmyra, and Troy" were simply names of towns in western New York rather than the great cities of antiquity and the cradles of Western civilization. Ohio and Georgia each had its Athens.

Although many Americans embraced Greek Revival, many utopian sects rejected mainstream architectural designs and the furnishings that accompanied them. No group was more self-conscious about the connection between architecture, furnishings, and reform than the Shakers. Shaker buildings were sparsely furnished, and Shaker furniture embodied their ideal of simplicity. The Millennial Law (1823) of the Shakers, a set of rules that governed Shaker communities, prescribed the styles of furniture, including permissible colors, and forbade designs that were "merely for fancy." The Shakers's rejection of the dominant styles of the day is evident if one contrasts the furnishing and design of a typical Shaker sitting room and a Greek Revival parlor in a prosperous home (**10.18** and **10.19** on page 312). The plush cushioned furniture and intricately carved furniture of the Greek-Revival room contrast with the ascetic style of the Shaker room. Shaker furniture was devoid of ornamentation and highly functional, embodying the ideal of simplicity itself.

The power of architecture to transform and uplift individuals inspired reformers to propose using architecture to mold American character and thereby

10.18 and 10.19 Greek Revival Parlor and Shaker Sitting Room
The carpets, elaborate decoration, and elegant furniture in this Greek Revival parlor contrast sharply with the ascetic furnishings of this Shaker sitting room. Shaker furniture was designed to be functional, not fancy.

reform American society. Two of the most influential architectural reformers were Andrew Jackson Downing and Alexander Jackson Davis, who in the 1840s and 1850s helped popularize the Gothic Revival, which looked to medieval Europe for inspiration. Downing authored two popular works on architecture in the early 1840s that went through 20 editions. Downing believed that a properly designed home should serve as a spiritual sanctuary from the commercial world of the market. His Gothic Revival homes, which incorporated medieval architectural elements, such as pointed arches, were meant to uplift those who dwelled in them and inspire those who saw them by literally guiding their gaze toward heaven. The Gothic Revival also drew on renewed interest in nature that had inspired painters such as Thomas Cole and the designers of Mount Auburn Cemetery. Rather than embrace the regularity and balance of Greek classicism, enthusiasts for Gothic Revival championed a more organic and variegated style that mimicked the irregularities of nature.

At one level the Gothic Revival was part of the larger reaction against the excesses of Jacksonian democracy. Its leading champions, such as Downing and Davis, also rejected the democratic values of the Greek Revival, believing that architecture should underscore social position, not seek to erase it. Davis believed that housing ought to announce one's

status: villas for the upper classes, cottages for the middle class, and farmhouses for the working classes. He helped plan the nation's first suburbs, including Llewellyn Park in Orange, New Jersey. Lyndhurst in Tarrytown, New York, was an opulent Gothic Revival villa. Compared to the symmetry of Greek Revival buildings, the irregular roofline and different shaped windows of Lyndhurst evoked the unpredictability of nature (**10.20**).

The popular phrenologist Orson S. Fowler championed octagon-shaped houses as a cure for America's social ills (**10.21**). Building on his phrenological theories, Fowler attacked box-like homes and argued that by more closely approximating a circle, the octagon encouraged harmony. Although most of these houses were built in the Northeast, octagon houses dotted the American landscape from Watertown, Wisconsin, to Natchez, Mississippi. Unlike reformers who feared progress and believed that the expansion of the market threatened American values, Fowler believed that the march of civilization was inevitable. Americans needed to accept acquisitiveness as crucial to the marketplace, while tempering it with insights gained from new areas of knowledge, such as phrenology. The octagon house, he believed, would serve both goals admirably well. The octagon fad dissipated when phrenology's pseudo-scientific doctrines were discredited.

What does Shaker furniture reveal about Shaker values?

View the **Image** *Shaker Village, Maine* (1845)

10.20 Lyndhurst
The Gothic Revival mansion, Lyndhurst, embraced elements of medieval architecture. Gothic Revival architecture's soaring arches focused the viewers' attention on heaven above. The angular lines were intended to mirror and evoke the awesome power of nature.

10.21 Octagon House
Phrenologist Orson S. Fowler believed that a balcony on a house corresponded to the upper portion of the skull and would encourage higher mental functions.

Why did phrenologists favor the octagon as an architectural style?

1826

Foundation of American Society for the Promotion of Temperance
Reformers concerned about the dangers of alcohol organize a national movement to promote sobriety

1829

Eastern State Penitentiary opened
Pennsylvania's new penitentiary becomes a model of the new approach to crime suggested by moral reformers

1830

Charles Grandison Finney leads Rochester revival
The Second Great Awakening targets the towns along the Erie Canal, including the fast-growing town of Rochester

1831

Mount Auburn Cemetery opens near Boston
An expression of the rural cemetery movement's focus on nature, Mount Auburn becomes a major tourist attraction and model for other urban cemeteries

Review Questions

1. What values associated with the Second Great Awakening contributed to the success of the market revolution?

2. What was the cult of true womanhood? How did this ideal fit into the new notion of domesticity?

3. What role did the family play in the utopian worlds created by the Shakers, Oneidians, and Mormons? How were the reform efforts of these movements a response to social and economic conditions?

4. What was phrenology?

5. How did architecture reflect the ideals of social reformers in the mid-nineteenth century?

Key Terms

Temperance A reform movement that developed in response to concern over the rising levels of alcohol consumption in America society. **285**

Penitentiary A new reform-based model of incarceration that isolated individuals from one another and gave them a chance to repent and reform. This method was a radical departure from earlier approaches to crime, which cast behavior in terms of sinfulness, innate depravity, and punishment. **288**

Immediatism Abolitionist doctrine that rejected gradualism and advocated an immediate end to slavery. **291**

Gag rule A procedural motion that required that the House of Representatives automatically table antislavery petitions and not consider them. **293**

"Peculiar institution" A term that John C. Calhoun coined to describe Southern slavery. In Calhoun's view slavery was not "an evil" or a cause of shame but rather "a good—a positive good" to be championed. **294**

"Cult of true womanhood" A set of beliefs in which women's values were defined in opposition to the aggressive and competitive values of the marketplace. **295**

Seneca Falls Convention A convention of women's rights supporters, held in Seneca Falls, New York, whose resolves emphatically declared that "all men and women are created equal." **297**

Complex marriage A system developed by John Humphrey Noyes's followers at Oneida, where any man or women who had experienced saving grace was free to engage in sexual relations with any other person. **299**

Transcendentalism A loose set of philosophical and literary ideas focused on the spiritual power of the individual. Transcendentalists looked to nature for inspiration and philosophical insights. **304**

CHAPTER REVIEW

1836

Thomas Cole publishes his "Essay on American Scenery"
Cole defends the value of nature and helps define an American vision of art

1839–1843

Joseph Smith leads the Mormons to Illinois and founds the Mormon city of Nauvoo
Mormons establish a utopian settlement

Millerite William Miller predicts the end of the world
The Millerites are dispirited and the movement collapses. Elements of their belief are picked up by the Seventh Day Adventists

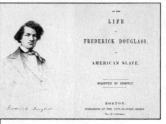

1845–1847

Publication of Frederick Douglass's autobiography
Douglass's popular narrative of his life as a slave expose the evils of slavery

1848

Seneca Falls Convention
Women's rights advocates gather to demand legal equality for women

Oneida Community established in New York
Founding of one of the most radical utopian experiments

MyHistoryLab Connections

Visit www.myhistorylab.com for a customized Study Plan that will help you build your knowledge of *Democrats and Whigs*.

Questions for Analysis

1. What do American concerns about intemperance reveal about cultural anxieties in the era of the market revolution?

👁 **Watch** the **Video** *Video Lecture: Drinking and the Temperance Movement, p. 286*

2. Why did Horace Mann believe education could transform America and eliminate most social ills?

👁 **Watch** the **Video** *Video Lecture: Who was Horace Mann and why were so many schools named after him?, p. 288*

3. What do different responses to the Greek Slave reveal about the problem of slavery in American culture?

🔍 **View** the **Closer Look** *Images as History: The Greek Slave, p. 292*

4. How did woman's rights advocates apply the lessons they learned through their involvement with moral reform?

👁 **Watch** the **Video** *Video Lecture: The Women's Rights Movement in Nineteenth Century America, p. 297*

5. Why did utopian movements appeal to Americans in the era of the market revolution?

🔍 **View** the **Map** *Interactive Map: Utopian Communities before the Civil War, p. 303*

Other Resources from This Chapter

📖 **Read** the **Document**

- *Reverend Peter Cartwright, Cane Ridge and the "New Lights," p. 284*
- *Horace Mann, Report on the Massachusetts Board of Education, p. 287*
- *The American Antislavery Society Declares its Sentiments, p. 290*
- *David Walker, A Black Abolitionist Speaks Out, p. 291*
- *Thomas R. Dew's "Defense of Slavery," p. 293*
- *Catherine Beecher, "Treatise on Domestic Economy," p. 295*
- *Lucretia Mott, "Declaration of Sentiments and Resolutions," Women's Rights Convention, Seneca Falls, New York, p. 296*
- *John Noyes on Free Love at Oneida, p. 299*

🔍 **View** the **Image** *Shaker Village, Maine (1845), p. 311*

Manifest Destiny and Changing Visions of the West p. 318

How did Manifest Destiny influence American ideas about the West?

American Expansionism into the Southwest p. 325

Why did so many Americans oppose Texas annexation?

The Mexican War and Its Consequences p. 330

How did the Mexican War affect American politics?

The Wilmot Proviso and the Realignment of American Politics p. 334

How did President Zachery Taylor appeal to both Northerners and Southerners?

((●—Hear the Audio File on myhistorylab.com

●—Watch the Video *Critical Visions, Chapter 11*

"To Overspread the Continent"

Westward Expansion and Political Conflict, 1840–1848

Richard Caton Woodville's painting, *War News from Mexico* (1848), captures the excitement generated by the Mexican War, the first conflict in which news traveled almost instantaneously by telegraph from the frontlines back to Americans. Woodville's painting shows a group of white men standing on the front porch of the "American Hotel," a symbol of the American nation. The central figure reads the latest headlines from the war front. The expressions on the men's faces range from astonishment to concern, suggesting the diversity of opinions about the war. A white woman looking out from a window is safely inside the "American Hotel," part of the same nation as the white men but not an active participant in their political discussion on the porch. Woodville's painting also shows those excluded from power: A black man sits on the lowest step, and an African-American girl stands outside the building. The war had profound consequences for the issue of slavery. By facilitating westward expansion and bringing new lands into American possession, the Mexican war complicated American politics by making slavery a central issue in national life.

By 1840, all the land east of the Mississippi (except the territories of Florida and Wisconsin) had been organized into new states, but Americans remained hungry for land. Many had come to believe that America was destined to conquer and settle the entire North American continent, from the Atlantic Ocean to the Pacific. As a result tens of thousands of Americans migrated west in search of land and opportunity. Some went along the Overland Trail to the Pacific Northwest; others came with the large Mormon migration to the Great Salt Lake.

The American defeat of Mexico dramatically increased the nation's size. The United States incorporated a huge swath of new territory, from Texas to California. The war also exacerbated the divisions between Democrats and Whigs and intensified the conflict between abolitionists and proslavery forces.

"Our manifest destiny [is] to overspread the continent allotted by Providence for the free development of our yearly multiplying millions."

Newspaper Editor, JOHN L. O'SULLIVAN, 1845

Manifest Destiny and Changing Visions of the West

During the early nineteenth century, American fur traders had engaged in a lucrative trade with Western Indian tribes. The interactions between the traders and Indians created a "middle ground" (see Chapter 3), in which trade and cultural interaction prospered. By the early 1830s, however, this distinctive multiracial society was in decline. The fur trade declined as over-trapping decimated beaver populations and as changing tastes made consumers less eager to purchase furs.

By the mid-1840s, the world of the fur trappers was gone. Americans began viewing the West as a region that had to be incorporated into an expanding democratic nation. Additional land would help preserve the ideal of a yeoman republic of honest and independent farmers that would now stretch from the Atlantic to the Pacific. Americans embraced westward expansion as both their destiny and a practical necessity given the nation's growing population. The rights of the indigenous Indian tribes of these regions mattered little to the champions of westward expansion. Even many sympathetic to Indian civilizations believed they were doomed to extinction. The conquest and settlement of the West became an important theme for artists who helped portray the West for those Americans who did not make the trek westward. Many artists memorialized an ideal version of western expansion, helping to forge important American myths about intrepid pioneers taming a frontier wilderness.

11.1 *The Trapper and His Family*
Artist Charles Deas offers a glimpse into the world of the trapper in this watercolor image. The canoe represents the multicultural world created by trappers in miniature.

The Trapper's World

During the colonial era French and British traders depended on Indians to trap or help them trap fur-bearing animals. American fur traders gradually gained control over this lucrative trade, and by the 1820s, they were the dominant fur traders. The key figures in the trade, the trappers, or "mountain men," played an indispensable role in the early exploration and settlement of the West. Between 1822 and 1840, at least 3,000 white trappers and traders entered this region.

In this painting of a trapper and his family, Charles Deas captures the multicultural world inhabited by the trappers. In the canoe the trapper, his Indian wife, and his mixed-race children work together to navigate the river (**11.1**).

The economic hub of the fur trade was the yearly **rendezvous**, a gathering held in the Rocky Mountains in which Indians and mountain men came to exchange pelts for goods offered by traders. With alcohol pouring freely, gambling aplenty, and a relaxed attitude toward sex among the participants, the rendezvous, which could attract as many as 1,000 participants, was a carnival-like, often riotous affair.

What function did the yearly rendezvous play for fur trappers?

The fur trade yielded huge profits for some men. The most famous trader, John Jacob Astor, was the son of a German butcher who immigrated to America in 1784. Astor became America's first multimillionaire, amassing by the time of his death in 1848 a fortune of $20 million (more than $100 billion in today's terms).

Although such traders prospered, their trade had disastrous ecological consequences for otters and beavers. Once numerous, the sea otters off the California coast were nearly extinct by mid-century. Only a shift in consumer preferences from fur to silk as the fashionable material for hats in the mid-1830s helped stave off extinction for beavers. Relentless trapping and shifting tastes meant that the world of the mountain men was largely gone by the 1840s.

The mountain men and their Native American allies had supplied information as well as furs, which generated interest in the West. More information came from expeditions sponsored by the federal government. Following the tradition established with Lewis and Clark's pioneering expedition from St. Louis to the Pacific Coast in 1804–1806 (see Chapter 7) and Zebulon Pike's expeditions in 1806–1807, the government underwrote an expedition by Stephen Long in 1819 to explore the Great Plains and the Rocky Mountains. His widely reprinted map, first published in an 1822 atlas, erroneously labeled the southern Great Plains (western Kansas, eastern Colorado, and New Mexico) as the "Great American Desert." This misleading label likely deterred many potential settlers from migrating westward in the 1820s and 1830s.

Americans gradually developed a more favorable vision of the West, in part due to the explorations of Lieutenant John C. Fremont of the Army Topographical Corps. Fremont published a popular account (written largely by his wife, Jessie) of his expedition in 1845 that not only dispelled the myth of a "Great American Desert" but also provided to those considering the trek westward many invaluable details. Information about weather, terrain, routes,

and watering holes and grasslands for pasturing animals was essential for those who made the arduous trek. The efforts of these explorers (**11.2**) helped America physically map the West and intellectually comprehend its potential for the first time.

11.2 Western Trails
This map shows the main trails taken by western emigrants to Oregon, California, and Santa Fe.

Manifest Destiny and the Overland Trail

By the early 1840s, information about the West, and its ever more positive impression, sparked a growing interest in migration beyond the Mississippi. Momentum spiked too because of an increasingly popular notion called **Manifest Destiny**. First coined in the summer 1845 issue of the *Democratic Review* by John O'Sullivan, it gave voice to the belief that God had destined America to spread westward to the Pacific. "Our manifest destiny," wrote O'Sullivan,

How did reports of the West both impede and encourage migration?

"[is] to overspread the continent allotted by Providence for the free development of our yearly multiplying millions." Senator Thomas Hart Benton of Missouri echoed O'Sullivan's vision of America's future, explicitly framing it in both racial and religious terms: "The White race alone received the divine command, to subdue and replenish the earth! Civilization or extinction has been the fate of all people who have found themselves in the track of the advancing Whites." Manifest Destiny combined the language of Jacksonian democracy, stressing opportunity for all white Americans, with a Protestant millennial vision that defined the nation's future in terms of the progress of "civilization" and the triumph of Christianity over "savagery." Few believed there was room for Native Americans in this vision of geographical expansion and white man's democracy.

Even before O'Sullivan and Benton voiced the doctrine of Manifest Destiny, word of the lush agricultural lands of Oregon had reached east by the early 1840s. The economic dislocations caused by the Panic of 1837 (see Chapter 8) and the absence of cheap land suitable for agriculture in the East and Midwest also sparked interest in western migration. Propagandists embellished their accounts of the West's riches to help attract potential migrants to the fertile lands of Oregon. Some rhapsodic descriptions of Oregon went beyond mere exaggeration, conjuring up an image of an almost magical place in which "the pigs … [were] already cooked, with knives and forks sticking in them so that you can cut off a slice whenever you are hungry!"

Drawn by these promises many joined an 1843 expedition known as the Great Migration. This 2,000-mile trek along the **Overland Trail** (11.2) consisted of more than 100 wagons and helped pave the way for subsequent waves of migrants. This trail soon became the main route taken by American settlers traveling from the East and Midwest to Oregon, California, and Utah. By 1845, at least 5,000 settlers had made the arduous five- to six-month-long overland journey to Oregon territory.

Migration westward placed an especially heavy burden on women, whose husbands seldom consulted with them before deciding to move. Estimates are that two-thirds of women opposed the idea of relocating to the West. Mary Richardson Walker, the wife of a Protestant missionary who headed to a settlement on the Walla Walla River in what is now Washington, vented her frustration in her diary: "I find it difficult to keep up a usual degree of cheerfulness, If I were to yield to inclination I should cry half my time." Giving up friends and family and dealing not only with their normal responsibilities of cooking, cleaning, and childcare but also the added burdens of a long and perilous journey made the prospect of moving West terrifying.

During the move many women were expected to take on traditional male jobs, such as repairing wagons or helping to construct bridges, while carrying on their traditional roles as mothers and wives. In effect the workload of most women doubled during the move westward.

Few Americans, male or female, were aware of this grim reality. Indeed, their impressions of the West continued to be shaped by writers, speakers, and the many artists who traveled with the migrants and painted scenes that reflected the rosy vision of Manifest Destiny. This mythic image of the West influenced artists working almost a generation later and is beautifully captured by Albert Bierstadt in his 1859 painting, *Emigrants Crossing the Plains* (**11.3**).

11.3 *Emigrants Crossing the Plains* In Bierstadt's painting, a caravan passing through Indian-controlled territory on the western trek to Oregon heads toward the bright sun, symbolic of America's bright future. [*Source:* Albert Bierstadt, "Emigrants Crossing the Plains". 1867. Oil on canvas, 60 × 96 in., A.011.1T, National Cowboy & Western Heritage Museum, Oklahoma City.]

What were the most important ideas associated with Manifest Destiny?

[Read the **Document** *John L O'Sullivan, "The Nation of Great Futurity"*

Bierstadt depicts settlers pausing on their westward journey to allow their livestock to graze and drink. Above them rises a stunning Western landscape; in the foreground Bierstadt places the skeleton of a buffalo. These bones, like the Indian village barely visible in the distance, represent the West's past, whereas the settlers symbolize its future. The sun's location in the Western sky evokes God's blessing and the optimistic vision of Manifest Destiny—a symbol of both the settler's and the nation's bright future.

> "The North Americans will spread out far beyond their present bounds. They will encroach again and again upon their neighbors. New territories will be planted, declare their independence, and be annexed."
>
> DeBow's Commercial Review, 1848

The Native American Encounter with Manifest Destiny

One danger associated with western migration that figured prominently in representations of the West, both in paintings and sensational newspaper accounts, was the threat of attack by hostile Indians. Even though such attacks were relatively rare, these representations of Indians dominated popular culture. Again, American artists helped spread a popular vision of the West. Charles Wimar's 1856 painting, *Attack on Emigrant Train* (**11.4**), casts the Indians as bloodthirsty savages and accentuates the horror of the emigrants trying to fend off the attack. This painting became a model for later images of Indians and was even used a century later by Hollywood directors as a model for Western fight scenes between Indians and settlers. Americans had been prepared for such a view of Indians by a long tradition stretch-ing back to the earliest European representations of the New World (see Chapter 1)and rendered in paintings such as *The Death of Jane McCrea* (see Chapter 4) and in popular literature by *Crockett's Almanac* (see Chapter 8).

Wimar's painting reflected one of two radically different visions of Native Americans that were deeply rooted in American culture. From the beginning of European contact with the Americas, Indians had been depicted as either bloodthirsty savages or noble savages (see Chapter 1). The image of the noble Indian chief had been propagated by artists, such as Benjamin West in *The Death of General Wolfe* (see Chapter 3). Artist George Catlin borrowed from this tradition when he set out to capture the culture of Western Indians. After traveling throughout the West and living among tribes in the 1830s, Catlin organized a popular traveling exhibit of his paintings and the Indian artifacts he had gathered. Acutely aware that American expansion would likely destroy many of the Native American

11.4 *Attack on Emigrant Train* Although Indian attacks on western emigrants were rare, this image was so powerful that it influenced portrayals of Indians in movies made by Hollywood more than a century later.

View the Image *Oregon Trail Marker*

Why were tales of Indian attacks on immigrants so popular in American culture?

societies of the West, Catlin believed that he had a responsibility to preserve a visual record of Indian culture. These themes are discussed in *Images as History: George Catlin and Mah-to-toh-pa: Representing Indians for an American Audience.*

A few Americans rejected both the image of the Native American as a barbaric savage who ought to be exterminated and the noble savage tragically doomed to extinction. Whig and Protestant reformers expressed sympathy for Native Americans and opposed the relocation of Eastern tribes (see Chapter 8). They also opposed the racist and expansionist vision of Manifest Destiny articulated by O'Sullivan and Benton. William Ellery Channing, a Boston minister and reformer, attacked the arrogance and shortsightedness of Manifest Destiny: "We are destined (that is the word) to overspread North America; and, intoxicated with the idea, it matters little to us how we accomplish our fate." For Channing and like-minded reformers, expansion was not an unqualified good to be obtained at any cost, but something that demanded that Americans act honestly and respectfully to Indians and do their utmost to protect them. Yet, despite the qualms of reformers American demand for Western land was insatiable.

The pressure to make more Indian land available for settlement only grew as Americans streamed westward. Following the policy that had been adopted with Eastern tribes, such as the Cherokee (see Chapter 8), the federal government forced Midwestern tribes in Iowa, including the Sauk and Fox, to relocate to the Indian Territory, present-day Oklahoma, Kansas, and Nebraska, after their defeat in the Black Hawk War of 1832. By the early 1840s, the massive relocation of American Indians was nearly complete. One of the few tribes to successfully resist removal, at least temporarily, was the Seminole in Florida. The American army fought a long and costly war to force the tribe to relocate. From 1835–1842, the Seminoles fought off American forces. In the end, the American government spent ten times the amount of money allocated for all of Indian removal to relocate the Seminole.

While Americans in this era generated many descriptions of westward expansion, relatively little material exists written from the Indian perspective. One rare and outstanding exception is the memoir of Sarah Winnemucca, a Paiute Indian from Nevada who became a champion of the rights of indigenous peoples (see **15.16**). Her memoir recounts the full range of experiences with whites, from interactions with "good white people" who traded fairly with her family and her people to traumatic encounters with hostile settlers. In one of the more harrowing episodes, she describes an occasion when a band of white men appeared while the village men were away hunting. Winnemucca's mother and the other women feared that the whites intended to kidnap or sexually assault their children, so she and the other women hid them, burying them in mud and covering their faces with brush. Winnemucca described her anguish— "heart throbbing and not daring to breathe"—as she lay hidden "all day" till the hostile visitors left.

The Mormon Flight to Utah

Most western migrants went in search of economic opportunities. The members of the Church of Jesus Christ of Latter Day Saints were an exception to this rule. Joseph Smith founded this sect, whose members were popularly known as Mormons, in New York in the early 1830s (see Chapter 10). Smith and his followers had been the victims of violent persecution wherever they settled in the East and Midwest, so the West appealed to them as a potential refuge from such hostility. The Mormon trek westward was the largest organized migration in American history.

Prior to their exodus the Mormons endured a long period of internal dissension and harassment by their non-Mormon neighbors. After leaving New York, Joseph Smith established Mormon communities in Ohio and Missouri. In Ohio the Mormons experimented with communal economic arrangements. The Mormon doctrine of "consecration and stewardship" required individuals to deed their property to the church, which then provided an allotment of land whose size was tied to the size of the family unit. Mormons also created cooperative agricultural enterprises, pooling their resources and labor. (For additional discussion of the communal dimensions of Mormonism, see Chapter 10.) Non-Mormons resented the economic advantages such cooperation brought to Mormon farmers and businesses.

As tensions between Mormons and non-Mormons rose, Smith moved most of his followers to Nauvoo, Illinois, on the Mississippi River. The fastest-growing town in the Midwest in the 1840s, surpassing even Chicago, Nauvoo was a boomtown shaped by a distinctive religious vision. By the end of the 1840s, the Mormon population of this booming city had soared to over 10,000. The Mormon system of tithing (required donations to the church) enabled the church to buy land and build a monumental temple

Images as History

GEORGE CATLIN AND MAH-TO-TOH-PA: REPRESENTING INDIANS FOR AN AMERICAN AUDIENCE

Through his paintings of Western Indians, George Catlin sought to preserve a visual record of their culture and accomplishments. He also felt obliged to portray these "doomed" peoples in a noble light. Capturing the nobility of Indians required representing them in a way that would evoke sympathy and respect from his American audience.

One of the many Indians Catlin painted during his years in the West was the Mandan chief Mah-to-toh-pa, also known as "Four Bears." In his diary Catlin noted that the chief wanted to be painted in a manner that reflected the Mandan notions of beauty and masculinity. Both were closely tied to the ideal of the warrior. Accordingly Mah-to-toh-pa dressed for the painting in all the trappings of a warrior chief. Catlin noted in his journal, "His dress … was complete in all its parts, and consisted of a shirt or tunic, leggings, moccasins, head-dress, necklace, shield, bow and quiver, lance, tobacco-sack, and pipe; robe, belt, and knife; medicine-bag, tomahawk, and war-club."

Yet Catlin omitted most of these items, believing that they distracted from the chiefs "grace and simplicity." The notions of beauty that shaped Catlin's artistic decisions stretched back to antiquity and were different from those of the Mandan chief. In essence Catlin painted his subject as if he were a frontier Cincinnatus, an Indian George Washington (see Chapter Five). The resulting painting was an idealized version of how an Indian chief ought to appear to an American audience, not a representation of how a specific Indian chief wished the American people to see him.

How did Catlin represent his Indian subject to his American audience? What does this tell us about American attitudes toward Indians in the early nineteenth century?

Catlin's journal informed his viewers that only a warrior of "extraordinary renown" was allowed to wear horns on his headdress.

By omitting the chief's war club, tomahawk, and other objects associated with his prowess as a warrior, Catlin made him less frightening to an American audience.

Mah-to-toh-pa

To make Mah-to-toh-pa a great figure in the eyes of Americans, Catlin painted him as if he were a Roman general or a modern Cincinnatus like George Washington and poses him accordingly,

Jean Antoine Houdon, *George Washington*

in Nauvoo. As this contemporary image shows, the temple (**11.5**) dominated the landscape around it.

As Smith and his followers faced increasing hostility from their non-Mormon neighbors, the church also encountered internal dissent. When dissident Mormons founded an anti-Smith paper in Nauvoo, Smith, who was also the mayor of Nauvoo, ordered the city marshal and Nauvoo militia to shut down the paper and destroy its printing press. The governor of Illinois then ordered the state militia to seize Smith and bring him to Carthage, Illinois, for trial. While awaiting trial, an angry crowd burst into Smith's jail cell and shot him to death.

Smith's successor, Brigham Young, decided to move the entire Mormon community to the West, beyond the reach of the church's critics. Some 16,000 Mormons eventually migrated to the Salt Lake Valley of what is now Utah. Young's organizational skills and an almost military discipline among his people helped them negotiate the difficult journey. It also helped the Mormons survive and in their new environment. During the first years of settlement, when food rationing became necessary, Young confiscated food surpluses and distributed them to those in need. Mormon communalism again helped the community through a difficult time.

Over time, the Mormons built an economic and religious community that combined communalism and private enterprise. Safely ensconced in the Great Salt Lake Basin, far beyond the control of the federal government, they also began openly to practice polygamy, the practice of men taking more than one wife. Brigham Young himself took over 20 wives. Polygamy shocked Americans, particularly in an era when the dominant culture venerated the conventional nuclear family and the cult of true womanhood (see Chapter 10). In remaking the conventional idea of the family, the Mormons resembled the Shakers and Oneida perfectionists, two other religious movement of the day that experimented with different models of the family and sexual practices (see Chapter 10). Mormon law required men to provide for their wives and children, which meant that most could not afford polygamy. Although the Mormon economic and religious elite practiced it, most Mormons were monogamous.

11.5 The Nauvoo Temple
The Mormon temple at Nauvoo stood on the highest point of land in the new town and towered over the surrounding landscape. Its architecture includes Greek Revival elements, Masonic symbolism, and ideas inspired by Mormon theology.

How did Mormon communalism affect their experiences at Nauvoo?

American Expansionism into the Southwest

 To stabilize and secure its territories that bordered the United States, Mexico adopted policies that transformed its northern provinces in the West and Texas. Changes were made in the way Indians were treated under the old colonial system in California and New Mexico, and Mexico opened Texas to American settlers in the 1820s. But the Americans in Texas became a source of discord for Mexico. Committed to slavery and reluctant to adopt Mexican ways, the Americans fomented an uprising of settlers that created the Republic of Texas. Despite opposition from abolitionists and some Whigs, the United States eventually annexed Texas. Rather than mark the end of expansionist sentiments, the annexation only whetted the appetite of proponents of expansionism. In 1846, the United States declared war on Mexico. The war proved unpopular with some Americans but nonetheless resulted in an American victory and seizure of northern Mexico, vastly increasing the size of the United States.

The Transformation of Northern Mexico

Until 1800, Spain still controlled a huge swath of North America, a holding acquired in the sixteenth and early seventeenth centuries (see Chapter 1) and constituting all of present-day Texas, New Mexico, Arizona, and California and parts of Nevada, Colorado, and Utah. The Spanish had invested most of their resources in mineral-rich areas of Peru and Mexico and the sugar islands of the Caribbean (see Chapter 2), and had neglected this northern region of their colonial empire. But by the mid-eighteenth century, the Spanish had begun to organize California into four coastal presidios (forts) at San Diego, Santa Barbara, Monterey, and San Francisco.

These administrative and military jurisdictions included 21 Catholic missions run by Franciscans and extending as far north as Sonoma, California. Under this mission system thousands of Native Americans were forced to convert to Catholicism and labor for the Spanish. Held in an oppressive condition little better than slavery, they herded livestock, tended crops, and worked as skilled and unskilled laborers. Indeed, the Russian artist and explorer Louis Choris painted this view (**11.6**) of the Presidio of San Francisco in 1816. This image, showing Indian laborers being herded at the point of a lance by a mounted Spaniard, illustrates Choris's belief that the Spanish treated Indians like cattle.

When Mexico declared its independence from Spain in 1821, the economy, politics, and social structure of this region began to change. Apart from achieving internal political stability, one of the new nation's chief concerns was securing its northern border with the United States. Mexico's northern borderlands were underpopulated and controlled by the Comanches and Apaches. The introduction of horses and guns to the region transformed the Comanche and Apache tribes: Both tribes proved extremely adept at the use of both guns and horses and as a result they gained almost complete control of the area between Mexico City and its northern provinces. America's westward expansion also threatened Mexico's control of its distant provinces. Mindful of these threats Mexican officials took steps to gain greater control of the region.

To speed economic development in California, Mexico abolished the mission system and released Indians from their dependent status as bound laborers. To replace the mission system, they adopted the *ranchero* system in California and New Mexico. Huge tracts of former mission-owned land came into the possession of a relatively few families, and poorly paid Indians performed much of the labor. In Texas, to encourage population growth and economic development, the Mexican government in 1824 offered land grants to American settlers who agreed to become Catholics and learn Spanish. By 1830 there were, almost 7,000 American Texans to 4,000 Hispanic Texans, who were known as Tejanos. The

What was the ranchero system?

> "The arrival [of the caravan in Santa Fe] produced a great deal of bustle and excitement among the natives. "Los Americanos!" … "La entrada de la caravana!" [The Americans! The caravan has arrived!]."
>
> JOSIAH GREGG, *Commerce of the Prairies, or the Journal of a Santa Fe Trader* (1844)

11.6 View of the San Francisco Presidio This depiction of the mission system by a Russian artist captures the exploitation of the Indian population.

American settlers were an economic boon to the region. Texans exported an estimated $500,000 worth of goods to New Orleans, mainly cotton and cattle.

Additional trade networks developed elsewhere along the Mexican-American border. In California, New England merchants sought seal and sea otter pelts to sell in China. In 1821, American traders established a trade route from Missouri to Santa Fe. Far safer and less rugged than the nearly 1,700-mile journey to Mexico City, the Santa Fe Trail became a thriving trade route. American traders, whose profits on the sale of goods ranging from cloth to manufactured items such as umbrellas sometimes reached 40 percent, were often paid in hard currency. Indeed, trade with Santa Fe became so crucial that the Mexican silver peso became the unofficial unit of exchange for much of the western United States.

The Clash of Interests in Texas

Although Mexico benefited from the increased trade with the United States, the presence of so many American settlers in Texas worried Mexican officials. Three issues were particularly troubling. First, the Americans flouted the laws requiring they learn Spanish and convert to Catholicism. Second, they brought thousands of slaves into Texas at a time when Mexico was heading toward the abolition of slavery (a goal it achieved in 1829). Third, many American settlers did little to conceal their interest in joining the United States.

A small uprising in 1826 of Americans hoping to secede was easily crushed by the Mexican army. The Mexican government reacted by banning further immigration from the United States. Still Americans came, and Mexico lifted the ban in 1833. Before long there were 30,000 Americans in Texas.

What advantages did Americans have over Mexicans in the lucrative trade with Santa Fe?

View the **Image** *Texas, Home for the Emigrant*

A well-organized effort to separate from Mexico occurred in 1834. This time Americans took advantage of the instability of Mexican politics. In 1834, Mexican General Antonio López de Santa Anna staged a coup and assumed dictatorial powers. When American settlers in Texas revolted, demanding a restoration of the constitution, Santa Anna decided to crush the rebellion. The ensuing war between Santa Anna's forces and the American Texans was brutal. One of the bloodiest battles occurred in early 1836 near San Antonio at the Alamo, an old Spanish mission defended by a small force of Texans, including legendary frontiersman and politician Davy Crockett and Jim Bowie (for whom the Bowie Knife was named). Historians continue to argue over the exact death toll, but few dispute that the fighting was fierce and many died that day. Images such as this woodcut of Crockett's death inspired Americans, whose battle cry for the rest of the war against Mexico became "Remember the Alamo" (**11.7**).

Even as Santa Anna's forces assaulted the Alamo, American Texans declared independence from Mexico (March 2, 1836) and drafted a new constitution.

Meanwhile his victory at the Alamo convinced Santa Anna that the Texas forces were no match for his army. Overconfident he recklessly divided his troops, leading to his defeat and capture at the Battle of San Jacinto by the Texans under Sam Houston.

The Republic of Texas and the Politics of Annexation

The citizens of the now independent Republic of Texas expected the United States to act quickly and annex Texas into the expanding American Republic. They would have to wait nearly a decade, however, as annexation proved to be a divisive issue in American politics. Opponents of slavery feared annexation would upset the delicate balance between free and slave states. Conversely Southerners and others who favored slavery supported Texas annexation. Heated debate in 1836 and 1837 died down as both the Democrats and Whigs sought to avoid the Texas issue. For the moment the economic problems associated with the Panic of 1837 (see Chapter 8) preoccupied Americans.

11.7 *Fall of the Alamo—Death of Crockett* The heroism of the Alamo's defenders is captured in this crude woodcut, which shows Crockett's bravery in the face of battle.

How did Anglo-Texans use their defeat at the Alamo to rally support for their cause?

11.8 Texas Coming In
In this political cartoon Polk welcomes Texas, while Whigs including Henry Clay and Daniel Webster, vainly try to hold back the Lone Star Republic from joining the Union. The Whigs are dragged into the "Salt River" a contemporary political term synonymous with a political dead end, oblivion, or an insurmountable obstacle.

the Union. Texans Stephen Austin (left) and Sam Houston (right) each wave the Lone Star flag of the Texas Republic. Polk's expansionist agenda appealed to Southerners and Northerners who hoped that westward expansion would mean more land for agriculture.

Polk's strong stance on annexation rattled the Whigs, including Clay, who feared the Democratic Party's aggressive stance on Texas was popular enough to give it an electoral victory. Clay equivocated about opposing annexation, and his flip-flop alienated many antislavery Whigs in the North. A small third party, the newly formed **Liberty Party,** adopted a staunchly antislavery, anti-annexation stance and captured 62,000 votes, enough, some scholars argue, to rob Henry Clay of electoral victories in New York and Michigan, thereby handing Polk the presidency in 1844.

Emboldened by Polk's victory, Tyler, the sitting president, secured Texas annexation by a joint resolution of both Houses of Congress, which allowed him to bypass the constitutional requirement that treaties be approved by a two-thirds majority in the Senate; Tyler could have never mustered enough votes to approve a treaty of annexation. This tactic bypassed the constitutional roadblock preventing the acquisition of Texas. Opponents of slavery viewed his actions as yet another example of the unscrupulous nature of proslavery forces. In 1845, Texas entered the Union as a slave state.

Polk's Expansionist Vision

A Tennessee lawyer and a protégé of Andrew Jackson, James K. Polk earned the nickname "Young Hickory," a reference to his mentor Andrew Jackson's reputation as "Old Hickory" (see Chapter 8). Polk shared Jackson's view of the importance of a strong executive and his belief in the necessity and inevitability of western expansion. He also shared Jackson's racial views, which

Texas annexation reemerged as a major political issue in 1844, reviving sectional tensions over slavery and western expansion. It started when President John Tyler, a proslavery Whig, began touting his support for annexation to gain the support of Southern Whigs and secure the party's presidential nomination. His strategy backfired, however, when many Whigs opposed his plans for Texas annexation, viewing it as a thinly veiled effort to expand slavery into the West. Tyler's proslavery stance cost him the nomination when the Whigs, seeking to avoid the controversy, chose Henry Clay, perhaps the best-known Whig politician in America, as their candidate.

The Democrats were also shaken by the annexation and slavery issues. Although Martin Van Buren was the leading figure in the Democratic Party, Southerners opposed him because of his abolitionist leanings. After nine ballots the Democrats finally settled on a proslavery Southerner, James K. Polk, as their candidate. Polk favored annexation of Texas. In this political cartoon from the election of 1844 (**11.8**), the Whigs, led by Henry Clay, attempt to hold back Texas from entering the Union. James K. Polk stands with an American flag, ready to welcome Texas into

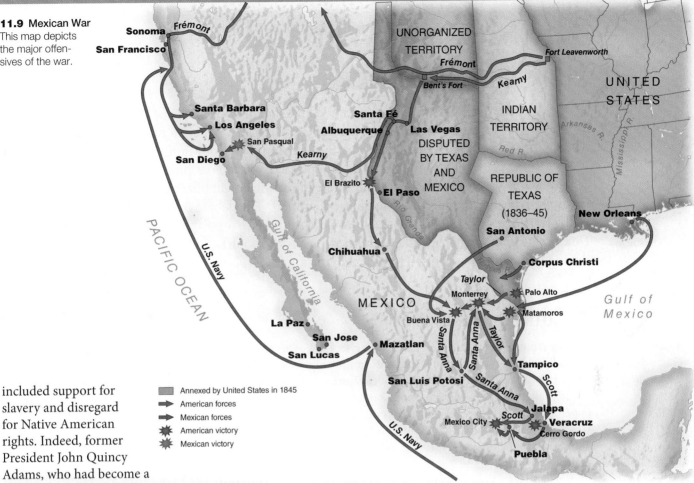

11.9 Mexican War This map depicts the major offensives of the war.

Map labels:
Sonoma — Frémont
San Francisco
Santa Barbara
Los Angeles
San Pasqual
San Diego
Kearny
El Brazito
El Paso
Chihuahua
La Paz
San Jose
San Lucas
Mazatlan
San Luis Potosi
Santa Anna
Buena Vista
Monterrey
Taylor
Palo Alto
Matamoros
Tampico
Jalapa
Scott
Mexico City
Veracruz
Cerro Gordo
Puebla
MEXICO
PACIFIC OCEAN
U.S. Navy
Gulf of California
Gulf of Mexico
New Orleans
Corpus Christi
San Antonio
REPUBLIC OF TEXAS (1836–45)
Rio Grande
DISPUTED BY TEXAS AND MEXICO
Las Vegas
Santa Fé
Albuquerque
Bent's Fort
Frémont
Keamy
Fort Leavenworth
UNORGANIZED TERRITORY
INDIAN TERRITORY
UNITED STATES
Arkansas R.
Red R.
Mississippi R.

Legend:
Annexed by United States in 1845
American forces
Mexican forces
American victory
Mexican victory

included support for slavery and disregard for Native American rights. Indeed, former President John Quincy Adams, who had become a prominent Whig congressman, denounced Polk as a "slave-holding exterminator of Indians." Polk wasted little time in acting on his expansionist vision.

Polk first moved to acquire Oregon, an area that the United States and Britain had been wrangling over for decades. Polk had campaigned on the slogan, "Fifty-four Forty or Fight," a reference to the U.S. demand that the geographical boundary separating Oregon from British Canada be fixed at the latitude 54° 40'. Ultimately Polk agreed to a border further south that extended across the 49th parallel. This shrewd compromise secured the most valuable agricultural lands sought by American settlers. The Oregon settlement in 1846 enabled Polk to focus his attention on Mexico. As the ardently pro-expansion Democratic paper *The New York Herald* noted, "We can now thrash Mexico into decency at our leisure."

The annexation of Texas in 1845 had left open the question of the exact boundary between the United States and Mexico. Polk sent John Slidell, a lawyer and Democratic politician, to Mexico to settle the boundary question and debts that Mexicans owed to Americans. Slidell was also instructed to

inquire about buying California and New Mexico. This aggressive negotiating posture reflected Polk's expansionist desires. He and his advisors feared that Mexico might pay off part of its debts by ceding California to Britain, America's chief commercial rival. By being so belligerent, Polk ensured that the negotiations would fail. Still angry over the loss of Texas, Mexicans were not interested in losing any further land.

The specific issue dividing the United States and Mexico was the exact boundary between Texas and Mexico. The Mexican government claimed the southern boundary of Texas was the Nueces River, not the Rio Grande as the United States maintained (**11.9**). The Rio Grande would give Texas more territory at the expense of Mexico. Polk dispatched American troops under General Zachary Taylor into the disputed zone between the two rivers. When a small group of Mexican forces attacked Taylor's troops on April 25, 1846, Polk informed Congress that "Mexico has passed the boundary of the United States, and shed American blood on American soil." Congress formally declared war on Mexico on May 13.

The Mexican War and Its Consequences

The Mexican-American War lasted only two years and ended in a resounding victory for the United States. America now controlled most of northern Mexico. Although supporters of Manifest Destiny had seen geographic expansion as a panacea for the nation's economic and social problems, few could foresee how the defeat of Mexico and acquisition of new lands would usher in more intense political conflict. The debate over whether to allow slavery in the territories gained from Mexico would strain the two-party system, splitting Whigs and Democrats into Northern and Southern wings. A third party, the Free-Soil Party, emerged during this period committed to blocking the spread of slavery.

A Controversial War

The Mexican War divided Americans along sectional lines and split both the Democratic and Whig parties. Southern Whigs supported Polk's efforts. "Every battle fought in Mexico," one South Carolina paper averred, "insures the acquisition of territory which must widen the field of Southern enterprise and power in the future." Northern Whigs, in contrast, denounced the war as an unjust conflict manufactured by Polk to secure California and New Mexico. "This war is waged against an unoffending people, without just or adequate cause," argued one outraged Whig, "for the purposes of conquest; with the design to extend slavery."

Northern abolitionists denounced "Mr. Polk's War." William Lloyd Garrison went so far as to welcome "the overwhelming defeat of the American troops, and the success of the injured Mexicans." The most profound critique of the war came from the transcendentalist philosopher Henry David Thoreau (see Chapter 10), who defended the ideal of peaceful opposition by citizens to unjust government action. See *Choices and Consequences: Henry David Thoreau and Civil Disobedience.*

The Mexican War was the first conflict America fought primarily on foreign soil. It was also the most logistically complex war in the nation's brief history, involving multiple fronts, long supply lines, and the coordination of ground and amphibious assaults. The Mexican War also produced two of the greatest generals in American history, Zachary Taylor and Winfield Scott. Taylor was the common soldier's general, a man without pretensions whose reputation for bravery earned him the nickname among his troops, "Old Rough and Ready." Scott was in many respects the opposite of Taylor. A brilliant tactician and strategist, "Old Fuss and Feathers" was arrogant and fond of pomp and ceremony. The Mexican War also provided a proving ground for a host of military leaders who later became important generals of the Civil War era, including Ulysses S. Grant, Robert E. Lee, Thomas "Stonewall" Jackson, George McClellan, George G. Meade, and P. G. T. Beauregard.

The United States had clear military superiority over Mexico. American forces under Zachary Taylor scored an early victory in May 1846 at the battle of Palo Alto (11.9). General Stephen Kearny then opened a second front by marching from Fort Leavenworth, Kansas, to Santa Fe and then on to California, where he joined up with an army under Captain John C. Fremont. Fremont had already paved the way for the conquest of California by instigating a rebellion against Mexican authority there known as the "bear-flag revolt" for the grizzly bear emblem that decorated the rebel flag.

Scott's successful amphibious assault at the port of Vera Cruz led to an assault on Mexico City. After five more months of fierce fighting, Scott captured the Mexican capital on May 1, 1847.

The Treaty of Guadalupe Hidalgo ended the war (1848). It settled the border dispute between Texas and Mexico and ceded to the United States a vast swath of new territory in the Southwest—over 500,000 square miles—comprising present-day California, New Mexico, Arizona, and parts of Texas, Utah, Colorado, and Nevada. The United States had seized 55 percent of Mexico's territory.

What were the most important differences between the leadership style of Generals Zachary Taylor and Winfield Scott?

Read the Document *Thomas Corwin " Against the Mexican War"*

Choices and Consequences
HENRY DAVID THOREAU AND CIVIL DISOBEDIENCE

The author Henry David Thoreau was a committed abolitionist. Opposition to the war with Mexico among abolitionists was intense and reflected their view that the war was an effort to expand slavery. In the political cartoon, "Young Texas in Repose," an unsavory Texan sits on a prostrate slave, whose head is rendered as a bale of cotton. Abolitionist protest against the war took a variety of forms, but none have had as profound impact on subsequent history as Thoreau's refusal to pay his poll tax. His actions landed him in jail for a night. In Thoreau's view jail was the only place for a just man in an unjust legal and political system.

Thoreau explored the reasons for his act of defiance two years later. In a lyceum lecture called "The Rights and Duties of the Individual in Relation to Government," he sketched this theory of civil disobedience. A year later a small literary journal published a revised version of this lecture, entitled "Resistance to Civil Government."

Thoreau's essay framed in concise terms the options available to citizens facing government action they believed to be immoral: "Unjust laws exist: shall we be content to obey them, or shall we endeavor to amend them, and obey them until we have succeeded, or shall we transgress them at once?" Here are the options Thoreau envisioned:

Choices

1 Accept the government's decision and not criticize it.	**2** Obey the law but work to change it.	**3** Protest the law by refusing to obey it, and suffer the legal consequences for challenging it.

Decision

Thoreau chose the third option and spent a night in the Concord, Massachusetts, jail.

Consequences

Thoreau's actions had almost no impact at the time, and his essay attracted little attention. However, it became one of the most influential political essays ever written. His theory of civil disobedience influenced the twentieth-century Indian leader Mohandas Gandhi's nonviolent protests against colonial British rule in India and the campaign of Reverend Martin Luther King Jr. against racial discrimination. Protestors around the world continue to use Thoreau's theory to advance human rights.

Young Texas in Repose

Continuing Controversies

Is the notion of a legal right of civil disobedience a contradiction in terms? Philosophers continue to debate the morality of civil disobedience. If one condones civil disobedience, does it invariably lead to anarchy, that is, lawlessness and political disorder, or can one support the rule of law and still accept the moral legitimacy of civil disobedience? Another controversial issue that continues to divide supporters of resistance theory is the role of nonviolence. Must civil disobedience be nonviolent, or can one legitimately use violence to secure justice? Abolitionists debated this latter issue as they pondered what to do about the evil of slavery. The issue continues to divide supporters of the ideal of civil disobedience. Many affirm that the idea can only claim the moral high ground and be effective if it forswears violence.

How significant was Thoreau's essay when it was published?

Divided at the outset of the war, Americans remained divided in its aftermath. The treaty arrived in Washington for ratification just as the city was celebrating the dedication of the cornerstone of the Washington Monument. One orator celebrated the victory over Mexico as the triumph of Manifest Destiny. Comparing American liberty to a "locomotive" that was speeding down the "track of human freedom," he declared that "the whole civilized world resounds with American opinions and American principles." Offsetting this ebullient optimism, however, was a sense of foreboding vividly expressed by Ralph Waldo Emerson: "Mexico will poison us." The controversies created by the acquisition of so much land, particularly the nettlesome question of the future role of slavery in the territories, proved Emerson right.

Images of the Mexican War

The Mexican War was the first conflict in American history that professional journalists covered and reported to the people directly almost daily. The telegraph made such instantaneous communication possible. Competing for readers, newspapers pioneered new techniques for gathering and reporting news, including sending "war correspondents" into battle. This practice freed newspapers from reliance on the military and government, allowing the press to be more independent. To be sure many papers continued to simply echo the official view of the war provided by the government. But many other editors voiced dissent. Abolitionists in particular used their antislavery newspapers to challenge the Polk administration and denounce the war. Indeed, one military officer's complaint about the negative impact of a "thousand prying eyes and brazen tongues" was a direct result of "a free and uncontrolled press."

An equally significant innovation in war coverage involved the use of images by papers like *The New York Herald* to explain important events. The Mexican War was also the first military conflict in America to be captured on film. The daguerreotype, an early form of photography, produced images that are fuzzy by the standards of modern technology but that seemed miraculous in their day. Americans approached the new technology as if it were an actual facsimile of reality and not merely another artistic representation of it. Indeed, the *Herald* proclaimed that it intended its war coverage to be "daguerreotype reports," a term meant to convey unbiased and accurate report of reality in nearly real time. Americans embraced the new pictorial art form enthusiastically. Before shipping off, a soldier might sit for a daguerreotype that he gave to family or loved ones. Soldiers might also carry daguerreotypes of loved ones into battle. Daguerreotypists even followed soldiers into Mexico, setting up temporary studios and recording battle scenes. At least one artist died recording America's war effort. An especially haunting image produced during the war was a daguerreotype of the gravesite of Henry Clay Jr.,

What role did images play in shaping American perceptions of the Mexican War?

son of the noted Whig politician, killed at the Battle of Buena Vista (**11.10**).

The scene is desolate: a cross, an open grave awaiting a coffin, and an adobe vault over Clay's grave, a necessity that protected the burial site from being attacked by wolves or desecrated by grave robbers. Few people were likely to have seen such an image, but for those who did, its emotional impact would have been immense.

This sober image contrasts with a heroic representation of Clay's death in a popular print produced for a mass audience (**11.11**). Rather than capture the desolation of a grave in a distant wilderness, the lithograph shows a fallen leader urging his troops on to victory. The artist focuses on Clay's final dramatic gesture with the pistol given to him by his father. "Take these pistols to my father," he tells a comrade, "and tell him I have done all I can with them, and now return them to him." Heroic images of this sort proved the most popular and influential representations of the war. Nathaniel Currier's firm alone produced at least 85 different images of the war for an American audience eager to purchase them.

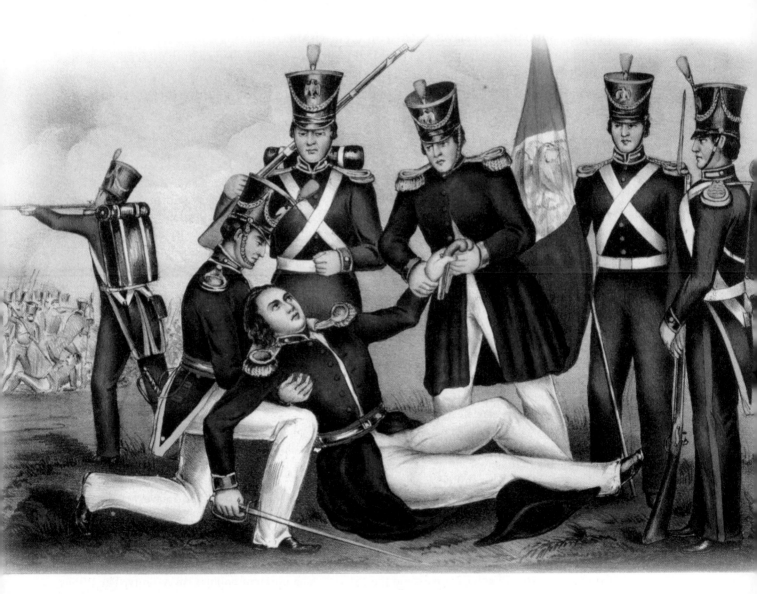

11.10 and **11.11** Clay's Grave and the *Death of Colonel Clay*
These representations of the death of Henry Clay's son capture radically different views of the war. The haunting daguerreotype (left) was a deeply personal artifact, whereas the more widely distributed lithograph was more inspirational than morbid.

Why did the artist pose Henry Clay in the same posture as earlier artists had used for fallen leaders such as General Wolfe?

The Wilmot Proviso and the Realignment of American Politics

 For a young, up-and-coming Whig from Illinois, the War with Mexico was a decisive moment. Abraham Lincoln opposed the war and viewed territorial expansion as a threat to America's future. Whigs argued that economic development, not geographical expansion, was the key to America's prosperity. In what would become a hallmark of his distinctive rhetoric, Lincoln translated this Whig ideal into a folksy idiom. "[Whigs] did not believe in enlarging our field," Lincoln observed in 1848, "but in keeping our fences where they are and cultivating our present possessions, making it a garden, improving the morals and education of the people." Supporters of slavery held a different vision: Acquiring a huge new swath of territory would be a boon for slavery. The problem of how to handle slavery in the territories gained from Mexico would strain America's new two-party system, splitting Whigs and Democrats into Northern and Southern wings and eventually setting the stage for the emergence of a new political party, the Republicans.

The Wilmot Proviso

In response to concerns that land seized from Mexico would lead to the spread of slavery, Congressmen David Wilmot, a Pennsylvania Democrat, introduced a measure, the **Wilmot Proviso,** which would have banned slavery from all territory acquired from Mexico. The bill created a firestorm. The controversy over the Wilmot Proviso heightened sectional tensions and conflict over the future of slavery. Southerners denounced it as a thinly veiled attack on slavery, whereas Northerners insisted that it left slavery untouched where it already existed. The Proviso passed in the House, where Northern representatives outnumbered Southerners, but it was defeated in the Senate, where the balance between slave and free states prevented either side from passing legislation objectionable to the other.

The Wilmot Proviso shifted American political debate to the problem of slavery in the territories, splitting both parties into proslavery and free-soil factions. In response politicians tried to resolve the sectional argument over slavery. President Polk supported a proposal, modeled on the Missouri Compromise (see Chapter 7), to extend the 36° 30′ line across the Louisiana Purchase territories separating free states from slave states to the Pacific coast. Northerners opposed this idea because most of the land gained from Mexico lay below this line and seemed likely to enter the Union ultimately as slave states. Senator Lewis Cass of Michigan suggested another compromise, **popular sovereignty**, which would allow the people in each territory to decide for themselves whether to permit slavery. Hoping to garner both Northern and Southern supporters, he omitted a crucial detail: *when* this decision on slavery would be made. Most Northerners believed this decision would be made when a territorial legislature was established. Southerners, however, accepted John C. Calhoun's interpretation that the decision over slavery would not be made until settlers wrote a state constitution, which opponents of slavery feared would allow slaveholders time to firmly establish slavery in a territory.

Sectionalism and the Election of 1848

The Wilmot Proviso and slavery defined the presidential election of 1848. Both the Democratic and Whig parties tried to downplay the question of slavery to attract voters in the North and South. Democrats nominated moderate Lewis Cass, champion of popular sovereignty. The Whigs had a more difficult time choosing a candidate. Henry Clay had been the clear frontrunner, but his adamant opposition to the seizure of lands from Mexico was a difficult political position to take. Clay had hoped to avoid having to take a stand on

---

Why was the Wilmot Proviso so controversial?

11.12 *The Candidate of Many Parties*
A phrenologist probes General Zachary Taylor's head, looking for some sign of what the presidential candidate thought about key issues. Taylor's campaign tried to avoid taking stands on issues such as the Wilmot Proviso that might alienate voters.

this issue, but the Treaty of Guadalupe Hidalgo undercut him: After the treaty, Clay's policy of non-expansion made no sense. Americans had to decide what to do about slavery in the lands won from Mexico.

Casting Clay aside the Whigs eventually settled on General Zachary Taylor, a Mexican War hero who cast himself as a "no party man" and a unifier above partisanship. Even more useful to the party, because he was a career soldier, Taylor's views on many political issues, including the Wilmot Proviso, were unknown. This humorous political cartoon from the election of 1848 shows a phrenologist (see Chapter 10) probing the general's skull, supposedly to find clues to his political beliefs (**11.12**). The title, *The Candidate of Many Parties*, underscores Taylor's attempt to be all things to all people. Indeed, the Whigs ran two different campaigns in the two regions of the country. To capture Southern voters, they stressed that Taylor owned slaves, asserting that no slaveholder would betray the interests of the South. To appeal to Northerners, the Whigs emphasized Taylor's credentials as a Mexican War hero and his support for a cardinal Whig principle: opposition to a strong executive, including the presidential veto. By stressing his belief that the veto should

be used only in exceptional cases, such as when a law was clearly unconstitutional, Taylor signaled to Northern Whigs that he would not veto a Wilmot Proviso-like law. Embracing this cherished Whig constitutional ideal not only allowed Taylor to underscore his Whig credentials to those who doubted them but also to side-step the slavery issue. Taylor's election strategy enabled him to do the seemingly impossible: campaign as a proslavery candidate in the South and a pro-Wilmot Proviso candidate in the North.

The 1848 election was further complicated by the emergence of a third party—the Free-Soil Party. This party brought together disaffected Democrats who supported the Wilmot Proviso and resented the growing influence of Southerners within their party. Led by former President Martin Van Buren, antislavery Democrats were known as "Barnburners," a nickname that derived from an old Dutch tale about a farmer who burned down his barn to get the rats out. In 1848, the "rats" were proslavery Democrats. A political cartoon shows Van Buren setting fire to a barn. Lewis Cass, viewed as a pro-slavery Democrat by abolitionists, flees along with a bunch of rats (**11.13**). The Free-Soil Party also attracted "Conscience Whigs" who were unwilling to support a slaveholder

View the **Image** *Political Cartoon: Fillmore and Taylor*

Why does this political cartoon show a phrenologist examining Taylor's skull?

as their party's candidate. It also gathered abolitionist supporters of the Liberty Party (the antislavery party founded in 1840). Under the slogan "No more Slave States and no more Slave Territories," the Free-Soil platform took the moderate position of opposing only the extension of slavery into the West.

The Whig, Taylor, won the election handily, but his victory revealed the complexity the slavery issue posed for American politics. See *Competing Visions, Slavery and the Election of 1848.* He won eight of

15 slave states, largely because he was a slave owner. The race was much closer in the North, but Taylor prevailed in the key states of Pennsylvania and New York. He owed his narrow margin of victory in the latter state to the Free-Soil Party, which drew votes away from the Democrats. The Free-Soil Party failed to win a single state, but it polled 300,000 votes (10 percent of the total) and elected two senators and nine representatives to Congress from states in the Northeast and Midwest.

11.13 *Smoking Him Out*
In this political cartoon Martin Van Buren is shown at the side of a burning barn, while proslavery Democrat Lewis Cass, is perched on the roof ready to jump, and rats flee the building. Antislavery Democrats were nicknamed "Barnburners."

> "Let the soil of our extensive domains be kept free for the hardy pioneers of our own land, and the oppressed and banished of other lands, seeking homes of comfort and fields of enterprise in the new world."
>
> Free-Soil Party Platform, 1848

Who were the Barnburners?

Competing Visions
SLAVERY AND THE ELECTION OF 1848

What to do with the vast territory acquired from Mexico became a contentious issue in the election of 1848. The two-party system fractured, producing a new third party, the Free-Soil Party, which opposed the spread of slavery westward. The new party met in Buffalo, New York, as reflected in the cartoon showing Martin Van Buren, its candidate, riding a buffalo. The party platforms of the Democrats and Whig Party each adopted a different approach to slavery.

The Democrat Party Platform reasserted its commitment to states' rights and its corollary: Slavery was an issue that the Constitution had left for the individual states to decide.

The Congress has no power under the Constitution to interfere with or control the domestic institutions of the several states, that such States are the sole and proper judges of everything appertaining to their own affairs, not prohibited by the Constitution; that all efforts of the Abolitionists or others made to induce Congress to interfere with questions of slavery … are calculated to lead to the most alarming and dangerous consequences.

The Whig Platform avoided mentioning slavery. Instead, it focused on the merits of the Whig candidate, Zachary Taylor who was presented as a war hero and a man who put the nation ahead of sectional interests.

That we look on General Taylor's administration of the Government as one conducive to Peace, Prosperity, and Union … we have a candidate whose very position as a Southwestern man, reared on the banks of the great stream whose tributaries, natural and artificial, embrace the whole Union, renders the protection of the interests of the whole country his first trust.

The Buffalo Hunt

What were the most important differences between the strategy of the Whigs and Democrats in the election of 1848?

1804–1819

Federal exploration of the West by Lewis and Clark, Zebulon Pike, and Stephan Long
Americans gain accurate information about the West

1821–1825

Mexico declares independence from Spain
Independence ushers in a period of instability in Mexican politics

First fur rendezvous
Indians, traders, and trappers gather to buy, sell, and promote intercultural exchanges

1835–1837

Texas revolts against Mexico
Texans achieve independence

1839

City of Nauvoo founded
Joseph Smith founds the city of Nauvoo which becomes the fastest growing city in the Midwest

CHAPTER REVIEW

Review Questions

1. What role did ideas of race play in the theory of Manifest Destiny?

2. What symbolic function did Indians play in American artists' representations of the West during the era of expansion?

3. Why did the young Whig Abraham Lincoln oppose the annexation of Texas?

4. Who were the "Conscience Whigs"?

5. How did Zachary Taylor's campaign in 1848 deal with the divisive issue of slavery?

Key Terms

Rendezvous A festive annual gathering held in the Rocky Mountains in which Indians, mountain men, and traders gathered together to exchange pelts for a variety of goods.   318

Manifest Destiny A term coined by editor and columnist John O'Sullivan to describe his belief in America's divine right to expand westward.   319

Overland Trail The 2,000-mile route taken by American settlers traveling to new settlements in Oregon, California, and Utah.   320

Liberty Party The staunchly antislavery, anti-annexation, party was short lived, but captured 62,000 votes, a small number, but enough, some historians argue, to effectively rob Henry Clay of electoral victories in New York and Michigan thereby handing Polk the presidency in 1844.   328

Treaty of Guadalupe Hidalgo This treaty formally ended the war between the United States and Mexico (1848). In addition to settling the border dispute between Texas and Mexico, the United States gained a significant swath of new territory in the Southwest.   330

Wilmot Proviso Bill introduced by Congressman David Wilmot would have banned slavery from the territories acquired from Mexico.   334

Popular sovereignty An approach to the question of slavery in a newly acquired territory that would have allowed the people in each territory to decide for themselves whether to permit slavery.   334

1843

Thousands of pioneers trek west to Oregon
First important wave of overland migration begins

1844–1845

Polk elected president
American government pushes Polk's expansionist agenda

1846

Mexican War begins
Armed conflict with Mexico erupts over border dispute

Wilmot Proviso
Provision to ban slavery from any land gained from Mexico heats up the slavery question in American politics

1848

Taylor elected president
Whigs find a candidate able to unite the party across regional divisions

Treaty of Guadalupe Hidalgo
Mexican War ends

MyHistoryLab Connections

Visit www.myhistorylab.com for a customized Study Plan that will help you build your knowledge of *"To Overspread the Continent": Westward Expansion and Political Conflict, 1840–1848.*

Questions for Analysis

1. How did western expansion transform American life?

○─ View the Map *Atlas Map: National Expansion and Movement West to 1830, p. 319*

2. What was Manifest Destiny?

▭●─ Read the Document John L O'Sullivan, *"The Nation of Great Futurity," p. 320*

3. How did American artists represent the West?

○─ View the Closer Look *Images as History: George Catlin and Mah-To-Toh-Pa, p. 323*

4. Why did Texas annexation arouse such intense feelings?

◉─ Watch the Video *Video Lecture: The Annexation of Texas, p. 328*

5. How did the Wilmot Proviso transform American politics?

○─ View the Image *Political Cartoon: Fillmore and Taylor, p. 335*

Other Resources from This Chapter

▭●─ Read the Document
- *Black Hawk from* Life of Black Hawk, *p. 322*
- *Thomas Corwin "Against the Mexican War," p. 330*

○─ View the Image
- *Oregon Trail Marker, p. 321*
- *Texas, Home for the Emigrant, p. 326*

○─ View the Map *Interactive Map: The Mexican War 1846–1848, p. 329*

The Slavery Question in the Territories p. 342

Why did slavery emerge as a national political issue in the late 1840s?

Political Realignment p. 350

What significant political changes occurred in the mid-1850s?

Two Societies p. 360

What were the major differences between North and South in the 1850s?

A House Divided p. 366

Why did Southerners interpret the election of Abraham Lincoln in 1860 as cause for secession?

Slavery and Sectionalism

The Political Crisis of 1848–1861

The seizure of vast tracts of land from Mexico in 1848 ushered in a period of intense conflict between the North and the South over whether to permit slavery in the territories west of the Mississippi. At the root of these tensions were the starkly different paths of economic and social development being pursued in the two regions. The South prospered in the 1840s and 1850s by expanding its agrarian, slave labor economy; the North, by becoming more urban, industrial, commercial, and multicultural. In the process, the two regions developed divergent visions of the ideal society: The South celebrated the virtues of slavery, states' rights, and white supremacy, while the North touted the benefits of free labor, upward mobility, and equal opportunity.

One of the first and most bitter controversies of the period emerged with the passage of the Fugitive Slave Act in 1850, a law requiring Northerners to assist Southerners in the apprehension of escaped slaves. It produced almost immediately a series of sensational incidents, in which abolitionists tried, with some success, to thwart the law and spirit escaped slaves to freedom.

Drawn by an abolitionist in the midst of this controversy, this image seeks to humanize the plight of escaped slaves while at the same time dramatizing the inhumanity of slave catchers and slaveholders. The quotations from the Bible ('Thou shalt not deliver unto the master his servant which has escaped from his master unto thee …') and the Declaration of Independence ('We hold that all men are created equal …') highlight the fundamental claim of abolitionists that slavery violated both Judeo-Christian morality and republican principles. Southern slaveholders, of course, rejected these claims and asserted their inalienable right to property in all things, including slaves.

This controversy set the tone for a decade that was to be rocked by a series of political, legal, and economic disputes that ultimately led back to the slavery question. By the mid-1850s, each region increasingly came to see the other's system as a threat. Northerners became convinced that Southerners wanted to spread slavery to the West and even to the North, while Southerners believed Northerners sought to destroy slavery and the Southern way of life. When Republican Abraham Lincoln won the presidency in 1860, Southerners declared the Union dissolved, setting in motion events that led to a far more bloody conflict, the Civil War.

Holy Bible

Thou shalt not deliver unto the master h

his master unto thee. He shall dwell

in that place which he shall choose

him best Thou shalt no

"It is an irrepressible conflict between opposing and enduring forces, and it means that the United States must and will, sooner or later, become either entirely a slaveholding nation, or entirely a free-labor nation."

WILLIAM SEWARD, 1858

150 William Str Corner st

hich has escaped from
Even among you
y gates where it liketh
in

Effects of the Fugitive-Slave-Law.

Declaration of independence.
We hold that all men are created equal, that they are ene
their Creator with certain unalienable rights that ame
are life, liberty and the pursuit of happines

341

The Slavery Question in the Territories

 The election of 1848 revealed an emerging sectional divide between the North and South over the issue of slavery. The dispute centered on whether slavery would be allowed in the new territories. Given the small population of white settlers in the West, many politicians hoped that any decision on creating territories and admitting new states would not arise for years. But the discovery of gold in California in 1848 brought tens of thousands of fortune seekers. By late 1849, they constituted a population sufficient to apply for statehood. After much acrimony Congress eventually passed the Compromise of 1850, a set of measures that quieted but did not resolve the fundamental disagreement over the future of slavery in America.

The Gold Rush

Although both Whigs and Democrats in Congress sought to avoid the contentious issue of slavery and the territories, the discovery of gold in California soon forced them to confront it. In December 1848, following four months of rumors, more than 300 ounces of pure gold arrived in Washington, D.C., sent by the new territorial government of California. The news touched off the Gold Rush in 1849, a migration of thousands of gold seekers from farms and workshops in the East to northern California on news of the gold strike near San Francisco. California's population exploded, rising from just 14,000 at the start of 1849 to more than 100,000 by year's end. By 1852, it reached 220,000.

Eighty percent of the new arrivals were American-born (including free African Americans), with the rest coming from Mexico, South America, Europe, and Asia. Most were single white men in their twenties and thirties. They came to California not to settle but to strike it rich and return home.

This fortune-seeking spirit led to the creation of a rough and raucous society. Mining camps and boomtowns sprang up almost overnight only to be abandoned the moment the gold disappeared or word arrived of a fresh strike elsewhere. Most mining towns lacked any formal government, including sheriffs and judges, leading to high rates of crime and violence.

By 1852, most of the gold that could be easily extracted was gone and with it individual earnings as high as $20 per day in 1849 (compared to less than $2 per day back East). With much gold remaining embedded in rock deep beneath the earth's surface, mining shifted from independent miners to corporations possessing the capital to pay for the expensive technology required to extract the hard-to-reach gold. Most of the men who remained in mining after 1852 did so as wage laborers. Among them were thousands of prospectors who had sold their farms and shops in the East in a fruitless quest for easy wealth.

While many panned for gold, thousands of migrants worked in enterprises that supported the mining industry such as hotels, restaurants, banks, saloons, and laundries. They realized that the surest way to riches lay in selling supplies such as pickaxes, shovels, rope, tents, and clothing at outrageous prices to eager miners. Many women earned high wages working in cooking, cleaning, and health care jobs, but many were forced into prostitution to survive, a practice that flourished in the male-dominated society of California. By one estimate, one out of every five women in California in 1850 worked as a prostitute.

Another group that found its dreams of riches thwarted were the Chinese, 45,000 of whom

> "I have no pile yet, but you can bet your life I will never come home until I have something more than when I started."
>
> A Gold Rush migrant on his way to California

arrived in California by 1854. White miners, mo- tivated by racism and greed, used violence and intimidation to confine the Chinese to the least desirable mining areas. The drawing shown here (**12.1**) depicts the segregated world of these Chi- nese miners. No whites appear in the scene, which shows the Chinese engaged in several activities, primarily mining. In 1852, the state legislature imposed a heavy tax on Chinese miners, prompt- ing many to turn from mining to farming, fish- ing, and operating restaurants and laundries. But increased immigration and job competition with whites in the coming decades would lead to es- calating anti-Chinese sentiment and violence in California (see Chapter 16).

Much worse was the fate of the California Indi- ans. The diseases brought by migrants killed tens of thousands, while ruthless bands of miners killed thousands more or drove them off their lands. Of the 150,000 Native Americans who lived in Cali- fornia in 1848, on the eve of the Gold Rush, only 30,000 remained by 1870. Meanwhile, countless *Californios*—Mexicans living in California—lost title to their lands through legal obstacles that the new American government imposed.

The Gold Rush sparked Western development and accelerated the creation of a coast-to-coast American nation. But the immediate con- sequence of the Gold Rush was not eco- nomic or social; it was political. The arrival of tens of thousands of people in 1849 suddenly made California

eligible to organize a territorial government as a pre- lude to statehood. Looming over any discussion of California statehood, however, was the divisive issue of slavery.

Organizing California and New Mexico

Even before the discovery of gold forced national leaders to consider California statehood, the ques- tion of the Western territories and the status of slavery there took center stage in Congress. Tempers flared in the House when Northern representa- tives unsuccessfully attempted to approve a motion upholding the Wilmot Proviso in the Western ter- ritories, draft a bill to organize California as a free territory, and pass a bill ending the slave trade in the District of Columbia.

The tension eventually subsided as congressmen decided to wait for president-elect Zachary Taylor to take office and reveal his opinions on slavery and the Western territories. Within weeks of his inauguration in March 1849, Taylor made it clear that although he was a Southerner who did not oppose slavery, he would put national unity above regional loyalty. Instead of creating territorial governments for California and New Mexico that would leave authority over the slavery issue with Congress, he proposed that they be made states

12.1 Racism in the Gold Fields of California Chinese gold- seekers were often confined to segregated encampments and less desirable mining sites.

View the **Closer Look** *Chinese Gold Mining in California*

How did the Gold Rush affect the Native Americans of California?

immediately and thus have the freedom to decide the slavery question according to popular will. This would remove the contentious issue from Congress where it sparked bitter debate and increasing sectionalism.

> ## "The people of the North need have no apprehension of the further extension of slavery."
>
> President ZACHARY TAYLOR at Mercer, Pennsylvania, July 1849

Residents of New Mexico and California responded enthusiastically to Taylor's invitation. By the fall of 1849, California had approved a state constitution prohibiting slavery and applied to Congress for admission as a free state. They also adopted a seal (**12.2**) to symbolize their vision of the state and its future. In the foreground sits Minerva, the Roman goddess of wisdom, while behind her a miner prospects for gold. (The motto, Eureka, is Greek for "I have found it.") Sheaves of wheat at her feet (symbols of agriculture) and ships (symbolic of commerce) sailing on the nearby waters indicate their

12.2 **The Great Seal of California** The inclusion of 31 stars indicated the hope that California would be admitted as the thirty-first state.

expectations for robust economic growth. In 1850, New Mexico's residents also applied for admission.

Taylor's actions touched off a firestorm of protest in the South. State legislatures forwarded petitions of protest to Washington, while mass meetings across the region denounced Taylor and his Northern supporters. Then in June 1850 hard-line defenders of slavery, often called "fire-eaters," convened a Southern rights convention in Nashville, Tennessee, "to devise and adopt some mode of resistance to Northern aggression."

What angered Southerners most was the threat Taylor's plan posed to the balance of power in Congress. Because of the North's greater population, it sent more representatives to the House. But with slave and free states numbering 15 each, Southerners enjoyed equal representation in the Senate, allowing them to block legislation deemed threatening to slavery or Southern interests (the so-called Southern veto). Admitting California and New Mexico as free states would tip the balance in favor of the North. Under such conditions it would only be a matter of time, warned Southern defenders, before a Congress dominated by Northerners abolished slavery altogether. "For the first time," warned Senator Jefferson Davis of Mississippi, "we are about permanently to destroy the balance of power between the sections."

The Compromise of 1850

As he had done in the Missouri Compromise in 1820 and the Nullification Crisis of 1832–1833, Henry Clay of Kentucky proposed a compromise. His plan admitted California as a free state and organized New Mexico into two territories where the people would eventually vote to decide whether to permit slavery in a process known as popular sovereignty. It also settled the border dispute between New Mexico and Texas, arranged for the federal government to assume Texas's debt, banned the slave trade in Washington, D.C., and established a stronger federal fugitive slave law.

The speeches inspired by the debate over Clay's bill, among the most famous in the history of Congress, revealed an intensifying clash of visions over the future of slavery in America. On March 4 a dying John C. Calhoun of South Carolina had a colleague read his speech expressing the views of proslavery Southern hardliners. He demanded that the Northerners end their attacks on slavery, uphold Southerner's rights in the territories (especially the right to own slaves), and enforce the fugitive slave provisions in the Constitution.

Three days later the renowned Massachusetts Senator Daniel Webster delivered his famous "Seventh of March Address," an impassioned plea for moderation and compromise, warning that both proslavery and antislavery extremism threatened to destroy the Union. William Seward of New York then voiced the views of staunch antislavery Northerners. Rejecting the Southern argument that the Constitution guaranteed the right to extend slavery into the territories, Seward invoked the authority of "a higher law than the Constitution," the law of God under which all people deserved to live in freedom. Congress, he argued, should instead be debating how to eliminate slavery peacefully and gradually.

Debate over Clay's compromise raged for months. The hostility spawned by the differences of opinion over slavery and the Western territories is captured in this 1850 political cartoon, *Scene in Uncle Sam's Senate* (**12.3**). The cartoon is satirical, but it depicts a real incident in which Mississippi Senator Henry S. Foote pulled a pistol on Missouri Senator Thomas Hart Benton (shown holding his coat open and daring his opponent to shoot). The Senate finally voted the compromise down in July.

Then the unexpected occurred. President Taylor died of severe gastroenteritis on July 9, 1850, and

> ## "The South asks for justice, simple justice, and less she ought not to take. . . . Nothing else can, with any certainty, finally and for ever settle the question at issue, terminate agitation, and save the Union."
>
> JOHN C. CALHOUN, March 4, 1850

was succeeded by Vice President Millard Fillmore, a moderate Whig from New York. Compared to Taylor, Fillmore was more sympathetic to the South and eager to reach a compromise. With his support, a young and ambitious senator from Illinois, Stephen A. Douglas, revived the movement for compromise. He broke up Clay's massive bill into separate pieces of legislation and then, without appeals to patriotism or sectionalism, he assembled enough votes to pass each individually.

As the map illustrates (**12.4**), Douglas's bill, or the **Compromise of 1850**, contained five components, some of which appealed to proslavery Southerners and others to antislavery

12.3 Tempers Flare During the Debate over Clay's Omnibus Bill
Reflecting the rising animosity over the status of slavery in the new Western territories, fighting breaks out on the floor of the Senate.

What did Seward mean by a "higher law?"

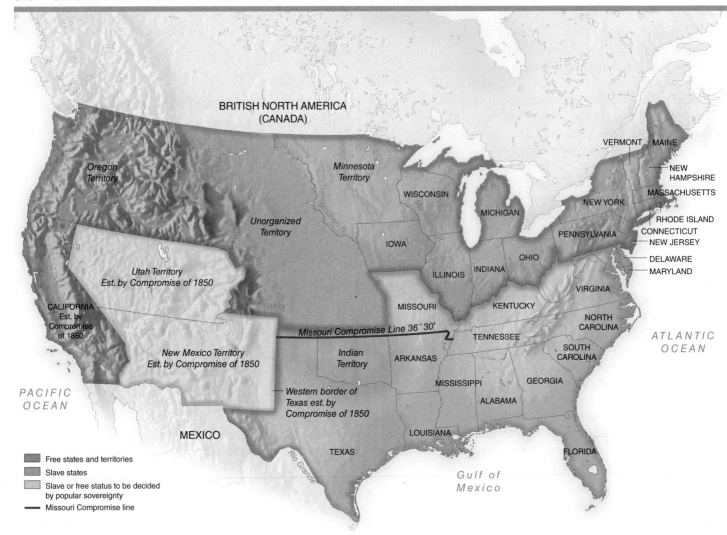

Free states and territories

Slave states

Slave or free status to be decided by popular sovereignty

Missouri Compromise line

12.4 The Compromise of 1850

The Compromise attempted to quell the political storm that arose over the slavery question by making concessions to both sides. Free-Soilers gained the admission of California as a free state, while supporters of slavery won a delay in deciding the slavery question in the New Mexico and Utah territories. The Compromise also settled the dispute regarding the western border of Texas, established a stronger Fugitive Slave Act, and abolished the slave trade in Washington, D.C.

Northerners. First, California entered the Union as a free state. To offset this concession to the opponents of slavery, a second bill created the New Mexico and Utah territories and left the question of slavery to be decided by popular sovereignty when each territory applied for statehood. Left unexplained was the status of slavery in the years leading to statehood. Third, Texas was required to relinquish claims to disputed territory on its western border to New Mexico (pleasing opponents of slavery by reducing the slave state's size) in exchange for the federal government assuming the $10 million debt Texas had incurred as an independent republic (pleasing Southerners who held most of the debt). A fourth provision granted abolitionists a partial victory by banning the slave trade—but not slavery—in Washington, D.C. Finally, a new **Fugitive Slave Act** greatly increased the federal government's commitment to returning escaped slaves to their owners,

something Southern fire-eaters had been demanding for years.

When the bills were all signed by mid-September, joyful crowds gathered in the nation's capital to serenade Congress with song and cheers of "The Union is saved."

But a close examination of the votes on the compromise's bills reveals a weakening of party loyalties and a growing tendency toward voting along sectional lines. Most Northern Whigs, for example, supported the admission of California as a free state and opposed the Fugitive Slave Act. Most Southern Whigs voted in the opposite manner. Only 20 percent of Congress—generally moderate Northern Democrats and Southern Whigs—voted for all five bills. As many anti-slavery Northerners and Southern hardliners correctly predicted, the question of slavery, whether in the territories or elsewhere, would surface again.

How did the Congressional vote on the Compromise of 1850 reveal growing sectionalism?

🔍 **View** the **Closer Look** *The Compromise of 1850*

Sectionalism on the Rise

One element in the Compromise of 1850—the Fugitive Slave Act—sparked a national controversy that intensified the sectionalism, or hostility between North and South over slavery. The act created a force of federal commissioners who possessed broad powers to pursue and return suspected escaped slaves to their owners. It also permitted federal marshals to deputize private citizens to assist in capturing fugitive slaves. Those who refused to help were subject to fines and imprisonment. Once apprehended, an accused fugitive had no right to a jury trial. His or her fate was instead decided by a federal commissioner who stood to earn a fee of $10 if he returned the accused to slavery and only $5 if he released him or her.

Fugitive slaves escaping to the North did not become a major political issue until the 1830s. In that decade the growing abolitionist movement began to encourage and facilitate slave escapes along what came to be known metaphorically as the **Underground Railroad.** It was a network of safe houses and other secret hiding places along a series of routes leading to the North and into Canada where British law prohibited slavery. The existence of such a network is revealed in this page from the 1844 diary of Daniel Osborn, a Quaker living in Alum Creek, Ohio (**12.5**). Between April and September of that year—warm months ideal for travel—Osborn assisted 47 escapees. His home was situated approximately halfway between the borders of northern Kentucky (where all but three of the fugitives came from) and Canada. Many of his Quaker neighbors also harbored fugitives.

Angry slaveholders and eager abolitionists spread fantastic stories of thousands of slaves being spirited north annually, but the Underground Railroad probably brought no more than 5,000 slaves to freedom between 1830 and 1860. Its most famous "conductor" was Harriet Tubman, an escaped slave who made 19 trips to the South to lead scores of slaves, including many of her relatives, to freedom. Osborn's diary occasionally revealed a similar pattern on a smaller scale. In one eight-day period in August 1844, he recorded that an African American man passed through Alum Creek on his way back to Kentucky where he gathered his wife, child, and sister-in-law and returned safely. He was followed by a woman who came from Canada to bring four of her children and one grandchild to freedom. Most

12.5 Abolitionists Assist Escaped Slaves along the Underground Railroad
This page from the diary of Daniel Osborn, a Quaker living in Alum Creek, Ohio, records the assistance he offered escaped slaves heading for Canada in the spring of 1844.

fugitives escaped to the North through less formal arrangements and a combination of perseverance, ingenuity, and luck.

Although the number of escaped slaves remained relatively small, averaging 1,000 per year out of a total slave population that approached four million by 1860, Southern slaveholders grew increasingly angry over the unwillingness of Northerners to assist in the return of their "property." Especially galling were the "personal liberty laws" passed by nine Northern states between 1842 and 1850, which prohibited the use of state officials or facilities like courts and jails for the capture and return of escaped slaves.

With these precedents in mind, Southerners made clear in the weeks following the Compromise of 1850 that they expected Northerners to uphold the Fugitive Slave Act. "It is the deliberate opinion

View the **Map** Interactive Map: The Underground Railroad   Why did Southerners demand a Fugitive Slave Act?

of this Convention," resolved a gathering of Georgia fire-eaters, "that upon the faithful execution of the *Fugitive Slave Law* … depends the preservation of our much beloved Union."

Southern insistence on a new fugitive slave law was full of contradiction. Even though Southern nationalists celebrated the sanctity of states' rights, they condemned Northern states for enacting "personal liberty laws." States' rights doctrine also opposed any increase of federal power, especially when slavery was concerned, yet Southerners made an exception when it came to using federal authority to capture their escaped slaves.

Abolitionists denounced the new fugitive slave law as "a hateful statute of kidnappers." They formed vigilance committees throughout the North and vowed, in the words of one Illinois newspaper, "to trample the law in the dust." Opportunities for resistance soon arose, for unlike the abstract questions raised by the Wilmot Proviso and popular sovereignty, the Fugitive Slave Act created a succession of concrete human dramas in dozens of Northern communities (see *Choices and Consequences: Resisting the Fugitive Slave Act*).

Early and memorable incidents occurred in Boston, the unofficial headquarters of the abolitionist movement. In October 1850, just weeks after the law's enactment, two slave catchers arrived there in pursuit of William and Ellen Craft, who had escaped from Georgia two years earlier. The city's vigilance committee swung into action, hiding the Crafts and posting handbills throughout the city, denouncing the "kidnappers." After five days of sustained harassment and physical threats, the slave catchers left the city. Taking no chances, the Crafts boarded a ship for England.

The controversy over the Fugitive Slave Act played a significant role in popularizing and legitimizing antislavery

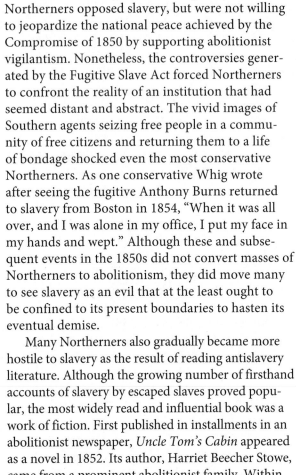

sentiment—though not necessarily abolitionism—in the North. In the early 1850s, few Northerners were abolitionists. Indeed, many were deeply hostile to blacks and rejected racial equality. Other Northerners opposed slavery, but were not willing to jeopardize the national peace achieved by the Compromise of 1850 by supporting abolitionist vigilantism. Nonetheless, the controversies generated by the Fugitive Slave Act forced Northerners to confront the reality of an institution that had seemed distant and abstract. The vivid images of Southern agents seizing free people in a community of free citizens and returning them to a life of bondage shocked even the most conservative Northerners. As one conservative Whig wrote after seeing the fugitive Anthony Burns returned to slavery from Boston in 1854, "When it was all over, and I was alone in my office, I put my face in my hands and wept." Although these and subsequent events in the 1850s did not convert masses of Northerners to abolitionism, they did move many to see slavery as an evil that at the least ought to be confined to its present boundaries to hasten its eventual demise.

Many Northerners also gradually became more hostile to slavery as the result of reading antislavery literature. Although the growing number of firsthand accounts of slavery by escaped slaves proved popular, the most widely read and influential book was a work of fiction. First published in installments in an abolitionist newspaper, *Uncle Tom's Cabin* appeared as a novel in 1852. Its author, Harriet Beecher Stowe, came from a prominent abolitionist family. Within a year her novel sold 300,000 copies, making it the best-selling book of the era. Soon thousands of theatrical versions of the story were being performed in cities across the North. Speeches, diaries, letters, and other evidence indicate that Stowe's account of the brutality of slavery and the humanity of the enslaved moved millions of Northerners to become increasingly hostile to slavery, even if they did not believe in racial equality.

By contrast, Southerners denounced Stowe as a "wretch in petticoats" and banned the book. They also published dozens of proslavery novels with similar titles. This image (**12.6**) from *Aunt Phillis's Cabin or Southern Life as It Is* (1852), portrays slaves dancing, suggesting they enjoy free time and are happy.

12.6 Southerners Refute the Antislavery Claims of Uncle Tom's Cabin
This frontispiece from *Aunt Phillis's Cabin, or Southern Life as It Is* (1852), presents slavery as a happy, carefree existence.

What made *Uncle Tom's Cabin* such an influential piece of antislavery literature?

View the **Closer Look** *The Fugitive Slave Act*
Watch the **Video** *Video Lecture: The Making of Uncle Tom's Cabin*

Choices and Consequences

RESISTING THE FUGITIVE SLAVE ACT

In February 1851, Boston's abolitionists faced a new challenge when federal authorities captured an escaped slave named Shadrach Minkins. As a federal judge ordered a hearing to determine Minkins's status to be held three days later, 200 white and black abolitionists gathered outside the jail where he was held. Intimidating slave catchers and helping the Crafts avoid arrest had constituted *resistance* to the Fugitive Slave Act, but with Minkins in federal custody the question arose of whether abolitionists were willing to *break* the law to uphold their values.

Choices

1 Drawing on the civil disobedience tradition (see Chapter 11), declare the Fugitive Slave Act immoral and organize an extralegal effort to free Minkins.

2 Respect the laws regarding fugitive slaves, but fight through the courts to prevent the extradition of Minkins and other alleged fugitive slaves.

3 Respect the laws regarding fugitive slaves and accept the likely transportation of Minkins back to slavery, but organize a more effective effort to spirit fugitive slaves out of the country (like the Crafts).

Decision

Convinced that the hearing would result in Minkins's return to slavery, 20 African American men opted for Choice 1. They burst into the courtroom, overpowered the guards, and took Minkins to Montreal, Canada. The incident thrilled abolitionists, including Theodore Parker who wrote later,

"I think it is the most noble deed done in Boston since the destruction of the tea in 1773." Southerners and conservative Northerners like President Fillmore denounced the action as lawless.

Consequences

When federal authorities apprehended another escaped slave, Thomas Sims, in Boston two months later, Fillmore sent 250 soldiers to guard the courthouse and escort the captive to a ship bound for Georgia. Nonetheless, similar extralegal incidents by abolitionists occurred elsewhere. In Christiana, Pennsylvania, in October 1851, for example, two dozen armed African American men killed a slaveholder from nearby Maryland who was pursuing two escaped

slaves. These events outraged Southerners, especially pro-secessionist fire-eaters. South Carolina, Mississippi, and Georgia held conventions to denounce abolitionism and consider secession. The furor soon quieted down as the number of slave captures decreased sharply, largely because thousands of free blacks and escaped slaves fled to Canada (Ontario's African American population doubled in the 1850s).

Continuing Controversies

When are acts of civil disobedience and violence to further the cause of justice legitimate?
In the 1850s, abolitionists deemed slavery such an outrageous violation of American freedom that acts of resistance—even violence—were justified. This question would generate heated debate in every subsequent era in American history, including movements for women's suffrage in the 1910s and civil rights in the 1960s.

African Americans drive off the slave catchers in Christiana, Pennsylvania

What caused the furor over the Fugitive Slave Act to eventually subside?

Political Realignment

 Furor over the Fugitive Slave Act subsided after 1851, and American politics experienced a period of relative calm. Some felt a rising optimism over the prospect of territorial expansion into the Caribbean and Latin America. But unprecedented levels of immigration also spawned a powerful antiforeigner political movement that enjoyed widespread support until eclipsed by the reemergence of the slavery issue. Sectional animosity surged in 1854 as Congress debated whether to allow slavery in the Kansas and Nebraska territories. The resulting Kansas-Nebraska Act prompted the collapse of the Whig Party and in 1856–1857, a violent and protracted conflict between pro- and antislavery forces, known as "Bleeding Kansas."

Young America

By late 1852, a prosperous economy and fear of disunion undermined the appeal of extremists in both North and South. Prosperity also helped calm the passions aroused by the Compromise of 1850 and the enforcement of the Fugitive Slave Act. In the presidential election that year, both parties nominated moderate candidates (Democrat Franklin Pierce and Whig General Winfield Scott) and pledged to uphold the Compromise of 1850. Pierce won handily, but the most telling aspect of the election was the woeful performance of the Whig Party in the South (**12.7**) where Scott, allied with the antislavery wing of his party, won only Kentucky and Tennessee. The Whig Party was falling apart and soon would be gone.

Pierce's popularity stemmed from his reputation as a Northerner with Southern sympathies. He was also a member of a brash movement within

> ## "We have a destiny to perform, a 'manifest destiny' over all Mexico, over South America, over the West Indies."
>
> *DeBow's Review*, 1850

the Democratic Party called **Young America**. Enthusiastic about the notion of Manifest Destiny (see Chapter 11), Young America promoted a nationalist vision of territorial expansion, increased international trade, and the spread of American ideals of democracy and free enterprise abroad. America, they argued, possessed the right, even the obligation, to continue its expansion, especially into Latin America and the Caribbean. The Young America program enjoyed broad appeal in both sections of the country and found expression in Democratic newspaper editorials, Fourth of July speeches, advertising imagery, and paintings. Among the paintings, Emanuel Leutze's *Westward the Course of Empire Takes Its Way* depicts pioneers peering out over a vast expanse of Western territory (**12.8**). Native Americans are nowhere to be seen, suggesting that the land is ripe for the taking. By including babies and

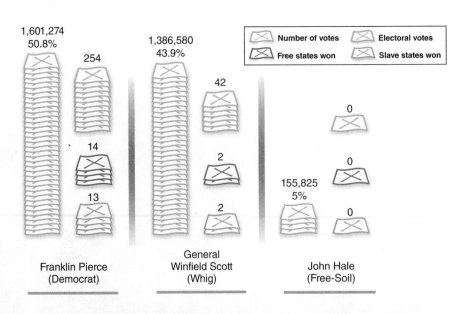

12.7 The Election of 1852 Scott's poor performance in the South (winning only two states) indicated that the Whig Party was fast disintegrating over the slavery issue.

	Number of votes		Electoral votes
	Free states won		Slave states won

Franklin Pierce (Democrat): 1,601,274 — 50.8%; 254; 14; 13

General Winfield Scott (Whig): 1,386,580 — 43.9%; 42; 2; 2

John Hale (Free-Soil): 155,825 — 5%; 0; 0; 0

children, Leutze indicates that generations of future Americans will benefit from the land's bounty. A radiant sunset implies God's blessing on the enterprise.

As president, Pierce proved an ardent proponent of expansion, which he believed would strengthen the Democratic Party and unite the nation. Yet his efforts had nearly the opposite effect. When Pierce entertained proposals to annex Hawaii and purchase Alaska, Southerners in Congress stymied the plans because the treaties would have outlawed slavery. Conversely, Northern representatives denounced his attempt in 1854 to acquire Cuba—with its plantation economy and 300,000 slaves—from Spain. Northerners likewise took a dim view of the invasions of Latin American and Caribbean countries by small armies of expansion-minded adventurers known as "filibusters" (an English corruption of the Dutch word for pirate). These operations delighted Southern slave owners, however, who viewed these lands as ideal, in the words of Mississippi Senator Albert G. Brown, "for the planting and spreading of slavery."

Pierce's support for proslavery expansionism alienated Northern supporters and threatened to upset the sectional peace achieved by the Compromise of 1850. But the controversy over proposed expansion would pale by comparison with that sparked in 1854 over a plan to organize the territories of Kansas and Nebraska.

The Kansas-Nebraska Act

Stephen A. Douglas of Illinois, another leading Young America figure, saw the future development of the United States in the rapid organization of

territories and eventually states in the land west of Iowa and Missouri (essentially the northern half of the Louisiana Purchase). He was not alone. Farmers were eager to settle in the region's fertile Kansas and Platte River Valleys, and promoters of a transcontinental railroad hoped to run a northern route through it. Neither settlement nor railroad construction could occur, however, before the federal government negotiated land treaties with Indians and organized the area as a territory.

Douglas faced strong opposition from Southern congressmen who feared the new territories would eventually become two free states. They also had their sights set on a *southern* route for the transcontinental railroad, from New Orleans through the New Mexico territory to San Francisco. They told Douglas they would support his plan only if it included a repeal of the ban on slavery north of 36° 30' that had been a part of the Missouri Compromise in 1820. Promises of popular sovereignty, they warned, would not be enough.

Fully aware that it would "raise a hell of a storm," but hopeful it would boost his presidential ambitions for 1856, Douglas introduced his **Kansas-Nebraska Act** as a solution to the issues arising over these Western territories. In addition to repealing the ban on slavery north of 36° 30', the act

12.8 An Enthusiastic Vision of Westward Expansion This 1861 painting, *Westward the Course of Empire Takes Its Way*, by Emmanuel Leutze, vividly expresses the expansionist spirit of the Young America movement.

Why did many Southerners support efforts to annex Cuba and seize other Caribbean and Latin American countries?

called for splitting the area into two separate territories, Kansas west of Missouri and Nebraska west of Iowa (**12.9**). He intended this last provision to placate both North and South by allowing the eventual establishment of Kansas as a slave state (since its soil and climate were similar to neighboring Missouri) and Nebraska as a free state.

The Kansas-Nebraska Act touched off a national debate more intense than that of 1850. Most Northerners, both Whigs and Democrats, considered the 36° 30' line an untouchable agreement that had ensured national peace for more than 30 years. Although some moderates had been willing in 1850 to allow slavery (via popular sovereignty) into Western territory lying south of the line, they now balked at doing so in land north of it.

Free-Soilers and abolitionists denounced the bill as conclusive evidence that the South, now increasingly referred to as the "Slave Power," was bent on spreading the curse of slavery wherever possible. They organized hundreds of "anti-Nebraska" rallies across the North and forwarded petitions to Congress. "Despite corruption, bribery, and treachery," asserted one typical resolution, "Nebraska, the heart of our continent, shall forever remain free."

Undeterred, Douglas prevailed, and his bill passed in May 1854. But it was a costly victory that seriously weakened his Democratic Party and hampered his presidential ambitions by associating him with controversy. The impact on the Whigs was even worse, shattering the party along sectional

12.9 The Kansas-Nebraska Act
The goal of Stephen A. Douglas in gaining passage of the Kansas-Nebraska Act was to open the Great Plains to settlement and facilitate the construction of a transcontinental railroad (ideally running through his home state of Illinois). His repeal of the Missouri Compromise Line and the ensuing vigilante conflict in Kansas reignited the slavery controversy.

Free states and territories

Slave states

Indian Territory (unorganized)

Slave or free to be decided by popular sovereignty, Kansas–Nebraska Act

Slave or free to be decided by popular sovereignty, Compromise of 1850

Why did most Northerners oppose the repeal of the Missouri Compromise line of 36° 30'?

View the Map *Interactive Map: The Compromise of 1850 and the Kansas-Nebraska Act*

lines. Every Northern Whig in the House and Senate voted against the measure, whereas most Southern Whigs joined the Democrats in support. More seriously, the death of the Whig Party in the South indicated that the bitter fight over Nebraska had permanently ended the long-standing spirit of accommodation between the North and South. Many Northerners resolved to make no more concessions to the Slave Power, whereas a growing number of Southerners resolved to preserve their rights from attacks by abolitionists.

This intensifying polarization between North and South is revealed in these two sculptures of "Freedom" by Thomas Crawford (**12.10**). Crawford was commissioned in 1854 to create a statue of a monumental figure representing liberty to top the Capitol building in Washington, D.C. One year later he submitted a proposed model for the sculpture to Secretary of War Jefferson Davis, who was overseeing the renovation of the Capitol. Davis approved of the overall scheme—a large classically robed woman holding a sword and shield—but one detail infuriated the vociferous defender of slavery from Mississippi. Crawford had given "Freedom" a cap worn by freed slaves in ancient Rome. Sensing an abolitionist plot (Crawford was a friend of leading abolitionist Senator Charles Sumner), Davis threatened to cancel the commission. Crawford quickly replaced the cap with a helmet surrounded by stars and a bald eagle.

Republicans and Know-Nothings

The political impact of the Kansas-Nebraska controversy became clear in the 1854 Congressional elections. Free-Soilers, ex-Whigs, and antislavery Democrats in the North formed dozens of local parties under names like the Anti-Nebraska or the People's Party. The most popular name, and the one under which they would eventually unite, was Republican. Despite their varied names, the parties shared an overriding commitment to opposing further concessions to Southern slave interests.

As this loose collection of antislavery groups coalesced into the Republican Party, the Democratic Party was transformed. In the midterm elections of 1854, Northern Democrats lost control of the House of Representatives and all but two free-state legislatures. Many of the defeated Democrats lost because they had voted for the Kansas-Nebraska Act. But in the South the Democratic Party grew stronger

with the addition of proslavery Whigs. From that point the party came under growing Southern, proslavery control.

The nascent Republican Party was not the only movement seeking to succeed the defunct Whig Party. Although many Northerners harbored growing concern about the Slave Power, others perceived a greater threat to their way of life: mass immigration. The flow of immigrants into the United States, rising steadily since the 1820s, became a tidal wave in the mid-1840s. Industrialization, population growth, and crop failure in Europe led hundreds of thousands of Irish, German, and other Western Europeans to seek new lives in America, where industrial jobs and cheap land abounded. Between 1845 and 1855, three million immigrants arrived, with most settling in Northern cities.

12.10 Slavery and the Republican Image
Crawford's design for a sculpture to top the Capitol's dome included a hat worn by freed slaves in ancient Rome (above left). Bowing to proslavery objections, Crawford redesigned "Freedom's" hat as a helmet surrounded by stars and topped by a bald eagle.

What events led to the formation of the Republican Party?

This surge in immigration caused anti-immigrant sentiment, or nativism—native-born Americans' belief in their superiority to the foreign born—to rise sharply. As *Images as History: The "Foreign Menace"* shows, Americans were upset not merely by the number of immigrants arriving, but also by their perceived character. Although most immigrants in previous decades had been Protestants from Britain—many of them with money and skills—a large majority of immigrants in the 1840s and 1850s were poor unskilled Catholics from Germany and Ireland. Anti-Catholicism, with roots in American history going back to the nation's earliest European founders, surged into near hysteria. Some of the best-selling books in the antebellum period charged that Catholicism, with its emphasis on clerical authority and loyalty to the Pope in Rome, was incompatible with democracy. Nativists—those born in the United States—also feared that immigrants took American jobs, drank too much alcohol, refused to assimilate, and increased poverty, disease, and crime.

> ## "The ill-clad and destitute Irishman is repulsive to our habits and our tastes."
>
> *The Christian Examiner* (N.Y.), 1848

Anti-immigrant sentiment reached a fever pitch in 1854 with the emergence of the American Party. Its core constituents were members of secret anti-immigrant societies founded in cities in the late 1840s. Because secrecy required them to answer "I know nothing" when asked about their organization, they earned the name "**Know-Nothings**." Their political platform condemned both political parties as hopelessly corrupt and called for legislation restricting office to native-born citizens, barring public funds for parochial schools, and raising the period of naturalization for citizenship from five to 21 years.

With the Whig Party in decline and the Democrats closely associated with the immigrant vote, Know-Nothings achieved stunning success in 1854, winning control of the state governments in Delaware, Pennsylvania, and Massachusetts. About 75 Know-Nothing congressmen were sent to Washington. Elections one year later in 1855 saw the party win Maryland and Kentucky, elect scores of nativists in New York and California, and post impressive tallies across the South.

After the elections of 1854, the big question was which of these two new political forces—antislavery Republicans or anti-immigrant Know Nothings—would replace the defunct Whig Party. But the American Party disintegrated almost as quickly as it arose, splitting like the Whig Party along sectional lines over slavery. Most of its members eventually joined the Republican Party. Although many former members retained their dislike of foreigners, they perceived the growing aggression of the Slave Power as a greater threat to the nation's well-being. This threat seemed most menacing in the newly created territory of Kansas.

Ballots and Blood

Even as opponents denounced Douglas's plan to allow popular sovereignty to decide the status of slavery in the territories, they devised a plan to ensure the results went their way. "We will engage in competition for the virgin soil of Kansas," William Seward warned his Southern colleagues in Congress just before passage of the Kansas-Nebraska Act, "and God give victory to the side which is stronger in numbers as in right." Wealthy New England abolitionists established the Emigrant Aid Company and financed the migration of more than 2,000 antislavery settlers to Kansas. Thousands more went on their own.

Proslavery interests, however, proved equal to the task of opposing them. To offset the soaring numbers of Northern settlers in Kansas, they organized bands of proslavery "border ruffians" to cross into Kansas from Missouri. Although some came as settlers, most were illegal voters determined to see Kansas enter the Union as a slave state. In spring 1855 men from Missouri cast nearly 5,000 illegal votes helping elect a proslavery territorial government that gathered in the town of Lecompton and legalized slavery.

Antislavery settlers rejected the legitimacy of this "bogus legislature." In fall 1855, they drew up a free-state constitution, held elections that resulted in an antislavery legislature and governor located in the town of Lawrence, and asked Congress to admit the territory as a free state. Kansas now had two governments, bitterly opposed to each other.

Kansas quickly became a divisive issue in Congress. Although the Senate (controlled by

Images as History
THE "FOREIGN MENACE"

From the colonial period up to the present, Americans have held conflicted visions about immigration. On the one hand, Americans proudly view their country as a "nation of immigrants" that has incorporated millions of newcomers while fashioning an ethos of tolerance. On the other, periods of virulent anti-immigrant sentiment have punctuated American history. In the 1840s and 1850s, nativists—native-born Americans who believed themselves superior to the foreign born— mobilized to oppose immigration. Although they failed to stop the mass influx of foreigners, their movement revealed a vision of immigration as a serious threat to the well-being of the republic.

The cartoon below reflects the belief that immigrants represented a threat to American democracy. The drawing beneath it expresses the fear that Catholic immigrants were part of a conspiracy to claim America for the Pope. What attitudes and actions might these kinds of images have inspired among native-born Americans?

By clothing the Irishman and German in whiskey and beer barrels, the artist reflects the widely held view that immigrants drank too much alcohol.

The brawl at the polling site suggests that immigrants threaten democracy because they use violence rather than persuasion to win elections.

The theft of the ballot box reveals the nativist fear of the rising political power of immigrants in the 1850s.

Immigrants as a Threat to Democracy, c. 1850.

Borrowed from the Great Seal of the United States, this eagle emphasizes the importance of public schools to American democracy.

Placing the Bible under the Pope's foot played on the belief that Catholic priests and bishops prohibited people from reading the Bible on their own, something Protestants believed essential to Salvation.

Declaring Catholicism un-American, the artist presents the Pope as the antithesis of republican authority, a royal figure seated on a throne.

Alleging a papal plot to overthrow America, the Pope points to the public school while a priest in the schoolyard organizes an attack.

Popery Undermining Free Schools, and Other American Institutions, 1855

Watch the Video *Video Lecture: Burn Down the Convent*   Why did anti-immigrant sentiment rise in the 1850s?

Democrats) voted to recognize the proslavery government of Lecompton, the House (controlled by Republicans) recognized the free-state government in Lawrence. On May 20, 1856, Senator Charles Sumner of Massachusetts, a rising figure in the abolitionist movement, delivered a speech titled the "Crime Against Kansas," a harsh denunciation of Southern efforts to force slavery into the territory. Days later, South Carolina Congressman Preston Brooks attacked Sumner with a cane in the Senate chamber for his affront to Southern honor. Sumner nearly died from his injuries and never fully recovered his health.

As the image suggests (**12.11**), antislavery Northerners hailed Sumner as a near martyr. The artist's emphasis on Brooks's brutality and Sumner's vulnerability (he is armed with only a pen) popularized the abolitionist vision of slavery as an inherently barbarous institution and its supporters, both in Congress and on the plains of Kansas, as violent criminals who did not respect democracy or free speech. In contrast Brooks became a hero in the South for defending Southern rights and dignity. Hundreds mailed him notes of congratulations, and a few even sent canes as a symbol of their support, inscribed with phrases like "Hit Him Again."

Only days after Sumner's speech, heavily armed proslavery vigilantes attacked Lawrence, Kansas, home to the antislavery territorial government.

The posse sacked the town, setting fire to the main hotel and destroying its two newspaper presses. Antislavery settlers arrived too late to prevent the devastation. Among them was John Brown, a zealous abolitionist who believed himself God's chosen instrument for eradicating slavery. Three days later he led abolitionist avengers in a counterassault at Pottawatomie Creek, Kansas. Falling upon a settlement of proslavery families, the abolitionists pulled five men from their beds and murdered them with swords.

The violence touched off a wave of vigilante reprisals and counter-reprisals by proslavery and antislavery forces. Newspapers began referring to **"Bleeding Kansas"** to describe the quasi-civil war taking place there. The antislavery press in the North, as exemplified by this political cartoon from 1856 (**12.12**), inflamed abolitionist passions. Note how the artist depicts key Democratic politicians as "border ruffians," the pejorative name used by opponents of slavery to describe proslavery vigilantes. In the center kneels Liberty, begging for mercy ("O spare me gentlemen, spare me!") while President Pierce (to her left) and Democratic Senator Lewis Cass of Michigan (right) stand on the American flag and taunt her. In the right-hand corner, Senator Stephen A. Douglas scalps a Free-Soil settler. In the background border ruffians burn a house and club a

12.11 The Slavery Controversy Sparks Violence in Congress This lithograph depicting Representative Preston Brooks about to beat Senator Charles Sumner with a cane was circulated throughout the North, where it stoked hostility toward the South and defenders of slavery.

How did events in Kansas expose the flaw in the policy of popular sovereignty?

Read the **Document**   *John Gihon, Kansas Begins to Bleed (1856)*

LIBERTY, THE FAIR MAID OF KANSAS_IN THE HANDS OF THE "BORDER RUFFIA

man to death. Images like this, along with editorials, sermons, and speeches, inspired Northerners to send money and guns to aid the Free-Soil cause, or to join Free-Soil settlers heading for Kansas to thwart proslavery efforts. By the time President Pierce sent a new governor and 1,300 troops to Kansas in 1856, 200 people lay dead, including one of John Brown's sons. The decades-long bitter debate over the status of slavery had erupted into armed conflict.

The highly charged events of 1854–1856 benefited the young Republican Party. Thousands of Free-Soil, Whig, and Democratic voters joined its ranks, making it the largest party in the North. Yet it was also a purely sectional party with no support in the South. Democrats had the advantage of being the only true national party, with strength in both sections.

For the presidential election of 1856, Republicans nominated the famed Western explorer John C. Frémont and waged a campaign likened to an evangelical crusade. Groups calling themselves "Wide Awakes" staged torchlight processions across the North, touting "Free Soil, Free Speech, Free Men, Frémont!" Democrats chose James Buchanan of Pennsylvania, who, like Winfield Scott and Lewis Cass, presidential candidates in elections before him, was a Northerner with pro-Southern credentials. The centerpiece of Buchanan's campaign was to play on the racism of many Northern voters by branding his opponents "Black Republicans," a racist pejorative that suggested that Republicans who opposed the extension of slavery into the Western territories were dangerous radicals who favored abolition and racial equality. The fast-fading American Party nominated ex-Whig and former president Millard Fillmore.

12.12 Bleeding Kansas
With this 1856 political cartoon, *Liberty, The Fair Maid of Kansas—in the hands of the "Border Ruffians,"* opponents of slavery sought to dramatize the atrocities committed by proslavery "border ruffians" in Kansas. By portraying prominent Democratic politicians as "border ruffians," the artist placed the blame for the bloodshed at the feet of the Democratic Party.

How did events in Kansas benefit the Republican Party?

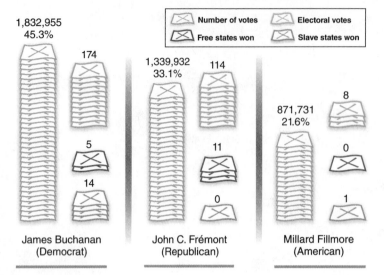

	Number of votes		Electoral votes
	Free states won		Slave states won

12.13 The Election of 1856 The Republican Party, founded only two years earlier, earned the second-highest vote tally, but its support came almost exclusively from the North.

James Buchanan (Democrat)
1,832,955
45.3%
174
5
14

John C. Frémont (Republican)
1,339,932
33.1%
114
11
0

Millard Fillmore (American)
871,731
21.6%
8
0
1

The three-way contest played out as two distinct sectional elections. As shown in the chart (**12.13**), Buchanan won easily in the South, though Fillmore polled 44 percent of the vote there. In the North Frémont outpolled Buchanan, but the latter's national total won him the overall election.

Deepening Controversy

Buchanan barely had time to settle into the White House in March 1857 when the slavery issue again seized center stage with a controversial Supreme Court decision. Dred Scott had spent years living in different parts of the country as the slave of army surgeon John Emerson. When he returned to the slave state of Missouri, Scott sued for his freedom, arguing that his years in the free state of Illinois and the Wisconsin Territory (where the Missouri Compromise barred slavery) had made him a free man. The state supreme court in Missouri rejected his suit, but Scott enlisted the help of abolitionist lawyers and appealed to the Supreme Court.

Dominated by proslavery Southerners, including Chief Justice Roger B. Taney, the court ruled in ***Dred Scott v. Sandford*** that African Americans, both free and enslaved, could never become citizens, and thus had no right to sue. Recognizing an opportunity to defend Southern rights and undermine the efforts of abolitionists, the justices also declared that Congress lacked the right to regulate slavery in the territories. In other words, the Court established as the law of the land the extreme Southern position that the right to property in slaves was inviolable and untouchable by any level of American government.

Opponents of slavery denounced the Court's decision as "a wicked and false judgment" and a "willful perversion" of the law. They seized on the decision as an example of the corruption of government by a slave power intent on spreading slavery into every corner of the nation, including free states. Already in control of the White House and disproportionately influential in Congress, they argued, slaveholders now controlled the judiciary. Heightening their sympathy for Scott were antislavery publications, such as the widely-read *Frank Leslie's Illustrated Weekly,* which showed him as a dignified man with a loving family (**12.14**). Some abolitionists declared the ruling "not binding in law and conscience," but most seemed to recognize that the only way to reverse the decision was by naming new justices to the Court. That would happen only if the Republicans could win the White House in 1860.

As both North and South considered the meaning of the *Dred Scott* decision, Kansas again became the focus of growing sectional animosity. The introduction of federal troops in 1856 had temporarily ended the spiral of vigilante violence. But tensions reached the breaking point in June

"They [African Americans] had no rights which the white man was bound to respect."

Chief Justice of the U.S. Supreme Court, ROGER B. TANEY, majority of the opinion in the *Dred Scott* case

id the Supreme Court use the Dred Scott case pand and protect the rights of slaveholders?

Read the **Document** *A Slave Sues for Freedom in 1857*

1857 when proslavery Kansans (who controlled the territorial legislature) held a convention in Lecompton and drafted a proslavery state constitution as a preliminary step to applying to Congress for statehood. When these proslavery men put the Lecompton Constitution before the people of Kansas in a referendum, antislavery residents, deeming both the legislature and the convention illegitimate, boycotted it. As a result, the constitution won approval easily and was forwarded to Congress. To complicate matters, however, in the fall the antislavery party won control of the territorial legislature and immediately authorized a second referendum on the proslavery constitution. This time proslavery residents boycotted, and the constitution was rejected by more than two-thirds of the voters, who were overwhelmingly antislavery.

The scene then shifted to Washington. President Buchanan gave in under intense pressure from Southerners in his cabinet and in Congress, who threatened secession if the proslavery Lecompton Constitution was not accepted and Kansas admitted as a slave state. Douglas came out against Lecompton because it was unpopular in his home state of Illinois, and it mocked his vaunted principle of popular sovereignty (even as it exposed its weakness). Months of rancorous debate ensued. A brawl broke out in the House, and some members of Congress began to come to the chamber armed. The Senate approved the Lecompton Constitution, but the House narrowly rejected it. Kansas would remain a territory indefinitely.

12.14 A Sympathetic Portrayal of Dred Scott and His Family
Frank Leslie's Illustrated, a widely read weekly sympathetic to abolitionism, presented Dred Scott and his family on its cover to emphasize his humanity after a Supreme Court decision declared him nothing more than property.

▸▶ **Watch** the **Video** *Video Lecture: Dred Scott and the Crises that Led to the Civil War*   Why did Congress reject the Lecompton Constitution?

Two Societies

From an economic standpoint the 1850s brought stronger bonds of interdependence between North and South. Northern textile manufacturers depended on a steady supply of Southern cotton, whereas Southerners relied on Northern manufactured goods, credit, and shipping. Yet overshadowing the increased economic integration of North and South was their splitting into two distinct societies. Northeastern and Midwestern states industrialized at a stunning pace, symbolized by the spread in these regions of the railroad and factory. In much of the South, by contrast, economic growth arose from an ever-expanding system of staple crop production, notably cotton that depended on the labor of four million slaves. Along with these divergent economies, North and South developed distinct philosophies that defined their vision of the proper social order.

The Industrial North

12.15 The Crystal Palace, 1853 Hundreds of thousands of visitors flocked to New York City in 1853 to view the "Exhibition of the Industry of the World" in the Crystal Palace. The main building itself, made of cast-iron and glass, was an expression of the latest industrial materials and design.

The industrial revolution that began in places like Lowell, Massachusetts in the early 1800s, and then staggered after the Panic of 1837, reached new heights after the economic recovery in the early 1840s. Centered almost entirely in the North, this boom was triggered by three main developments. First, starting in the firearms industry and spreading into clocks, sewing machines, and farming equipment, Americans pioneered in the creation of machines made of interchangeable parts, thus facilitating the rapid manufacture of inexpensive goods. Second, manufacturers began to power their machines with steam, an energy source that was more powerful, reliable,

and flexible than water power provided by rivers. Finally, manufacturers benefited from the huge pool of cheap labor provided by a steady influx of immigrants. Manufacturing output soared, and by 1860 the total value of all goods produced in the North reached $1.5 billion (compared to $483 million for the entire nation in 1840).

The dynamic and innovative character of the Northern industrial economy was displayed for all the world to see in 1853 at the Crystal Palace Exhibition in New York City. Modeled on a similar exhibition in London in 1851, the "Exhibition of the Industry of the World," as it was officially known, featured more than 4,000 exhibits, most of them American. Even the building itself (**12.15**), a monumental cast-iron

What developments helped spur industrialization in the North?

and glass structure, reflected the latest trends in architecture, design, and construction materials. More than one million people came to see the latest in modern technology, including Cyrus McCormick's mechanical reaper, Richard M. Hoe's rotary printing press, and Elisha Otis's elevator. The only Southern exhibitions of new technology were improved versions of the cotton gin.

The same spirit of enthusiasm and confidence that inspired the Crystal Palace Exhibition is also captured in this advertisement for the Colt Patent Fire Arms Manufacty in 1862 (12.16). Samuel Colt from Connecticut patented a design for a revolver in 1837 and then established an enormously successful firearms manufacturing business in Hartford. The image that dominates the advertisement conveys two main ideas. First, it shows a huge manufacturing establishment, the very size of which is intended to suggest strength and power. Second, the image shows the modern factory nestled neatly within a small New England town, suggesting that industry poses no threat to small-town American values. Colt's was one of many arms-manufacturing businesses that flourished in the 1840s and 1850s. Nearly all of them were located in the North, accounting for 90 percent of national output.

Equally important to the emerging industrial economy was the building of a massive railroad network. Trackage soared from more than 9,000 miles in 1850 to over 30,000 in 1860. Because most of this track lay west of Pennsylvania, it bound the states of the Northeast more closely with those in the Midwest, such as Illinois. Trade increasingly moved east to west along railroads and canals rather than north to south along rivers as in earlier decades, accentuating the growing sectional divide.

The growth of the railroads, along with two additional technological innovations—the reaper and the cast steel plow—revolutionized Northern and Western agriculture, which was still the foundation of the national economy. Cyrus McCormick's

mechanical reaper was a piece of equipment on small wheels pulled by a horse. As it passed through a field, sharp blades moved back and forth severing stalks of wheat. The harvested grain was then collected in a cradle. The reaper allowed for a much faster harvest—often crucial in times of bad weather—and eliminated the need to hire expensive farm labor. John Deere's cast steel plow sliced smoothly through the toughest soil, making farming much easier and more efficient. Both inventions allowed farmers to expand the size of their farms, knowing they could handle the additional plowing and harvesting. The railroad also allowed farmers to sell their produce in markets hundreds of miles away and to turn from raising a mixture of animal, fruit, vegetable, and grain products to specializing in single crops such as wheat, corn, or oats. Rising prices and growing demand from abroad for American grain augmented this trend.

Industrialization brought rising wages and opportunity to most Northerners, but also new levels of poverty—especially among unskilled and immigrant workers who formed a growing class of urban poor. Wages in many industrializing sectors, such as shoe making and textiles, were too low for one earner to support a family. To increase their family's income, growing numbers of women and children worked in factories or performed "outwork" in their homes, often for 60 or 70 hours per week. Many workers became unemployed for

12.16 Celebrating Northern Industry This 1862 advertisement for Colt's Patent Fire Arms Manufacty celebrated the power of American industry. The image of the factory situated neatly within a New England town also suggested that modern industry posed no threat to American values and lifestyles.

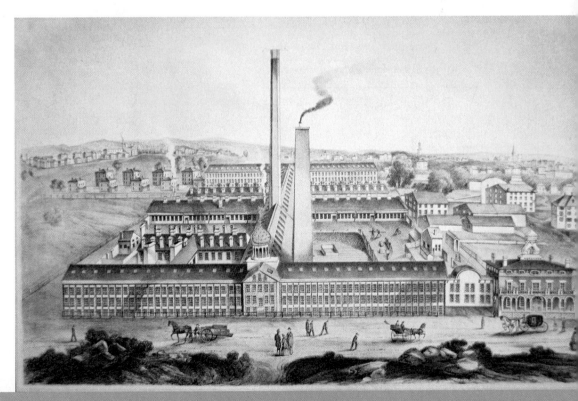

How did new technology transform American agriculture?

Envisioning Evidence
THE RISE OF KING COTTON

Many Americans associate cotton cultivation with slavery, but the relationship really only took form in the last half century of slavery's existence in the United States (roughly between 1810 and 1860). The growth of textile manufacturing in Britain and the Northern United States in the early 1800s created a booming demand for cotton. At the same time, the expulsion of Native Americans from the fertile lands of Georgia, Alabama, Mississippi, Louisiana, Arkansas, Texas, Florida, and North and South Carolina opened the way for cotton cultivation on a mass scale. Between 1815 and 1860 millions of white settlers moved into these lands. They brought with them millions of slaves who they put to work raising cotton. By 1830 cotton had become the South's most profitable product and slavery the single most important source of capital investment. Cotton's value only increased over the next three decades, leading many Southerners to conclude that if the rising controversy over slavery led to secession, the South was strong enough to flourish on its own. "Cotton was King," went a popular slogan in the late 1850s.

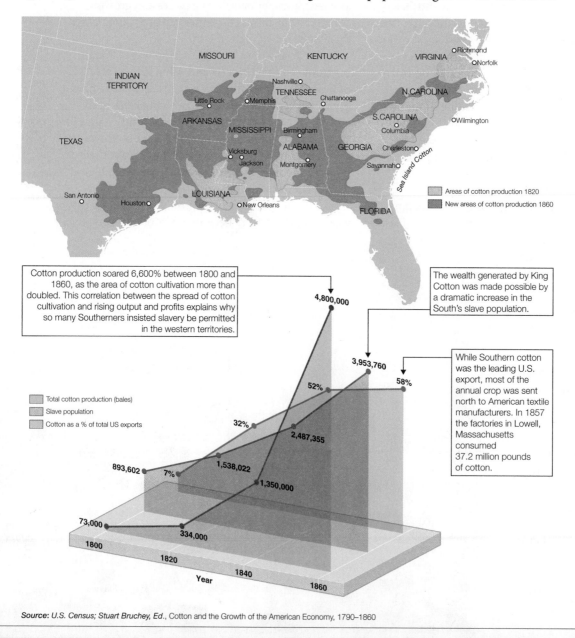

Cotton production soared 6,600% between 1800 and 1860, as the area of cotton cultivation more than doubled. This correlation between the spread of cotton cultivation and rising output and profits explains why so many Southerners insisted slavery be permitted in the western territories.

The wealth generated by King Cotton was made possible by a dramatic increase in the South's slave population.

While Southern cotton was the leading U.S. export, most of the annual crop was sent north to American textile manufacturers. In 1857 the factories in Lowell, Massachusetts consumed 37.2 million pounds of cotton.

Areas of cotton production 1820
New areas of cotton production 1860

Total cotton production (bales)
Slave population
Cotton as a % of total US exports

Source: U.S. Census; Stuart Bruchey, Ed., Cotton and the Growth of the American Economy, 1790–1860

What made cotton production so profitable between 1830 and 1860?

long stretches, especially in winter, and the number of poor families living in the squalid tenement districts of cities like New York and Boston rose.

Cotton Is Supreme

Industry also flourished in the upper South, especially in Maryland, Delaware, Kentucky, Tennessee, and Missouri. But it paled in comparison to industrialization in the North and constituted only a fraction of the overall Southern economy. Production of cash crops such as tobacco, sugar, and rice soared, as did prices. Nothing, however, outperformed the South's main staple crop, cotton. Production jumped from 1.35 million bales in 1840 to 4.8 million bales by 1860. (Each bale weighed approximately 480 pounds.) Southern cotton by this time accounted for three-fifths of American exports and three-quarters of the world supply. As one Southern nationalist put it, "Cotton is King."

What made cotton king in this period was the labor of slaves—nearly four million by 1860. As a social and economic institution, slavery was pervasive throughout the South, but the details of slave ownership reveal the region's highly stratified class structure. Only one-quarter of Southerners owned slaves, and about 70 percent of them owned fewer than ten. The center of economic, social, and political power in the South was found among a small planter elite—about 10,000 wealthy families who owned more than 50 slaves.

> "There is no such thing as a freeman being fixed for life in the condition of a hired laborer. The *free* labor system opens the way for all."
>
> ABRAHAM LINCOLN, 1860

Most of the Southern cotton this system produced was shipped to Northern factories, indicating a growing economic integration between the two regional economies. But the relationship was by no means equal, and Southerners increasingly resented their economic dependence on the North. "We purchase all our luxuries and necessities from the North," lamented a Southern newspaper editor in 1851. "Our slaves are clothed with Northern manufactured goods and work with Northern hoes, ploughs, and other implements. . . . The slaveholder dresses in Northern goods. . . . In Northern vessels his products are carried to market . . . and on Northern-made paper, with a Northern pen, with Northern ink, he

resolves and re-resolves in regard to his rights." A vociferous advocate of Southern economic diversification, James D. B. DeBow, started a magazine with the motto "Commerce is King" and held commercial conventions throughout the South.

By 1860, DeBow and other proponents of greater Southern economic independence could point to substantial progress. Southern railroad mileage had increased fourfold to 9,000 miles, and there were 18,000 factories, most in the upper South. But the economy of the North grew even faster. Even as the South increased its textile manufacture by 44 percent in the 1850s, its share of manufacturing nationwide declined by two percent. Indeed, in 1860, the city of Lowell, Massachusetts, operated more textile spindles than all the Southern states combined. The South remained an agricultural society. So long as staple crops brought high prices, only a handful of Southerners seemed willing to pursue industrialization.

The Other South

As important as slavery was to the Southern economy, politics, and culture, fully three-quarters of Southerners owned no slaves at all, and as the price of slaves rose in the 1850s, the number of slaveholding families decreased. Most white Southerners were modest yeomen farmers who worked small patches of rough backcountry land, often barely at subsistence levels. Because Southern states invested relatively little money (compared to the North) in roads, canals, and railroads, most backcountry farmers had only limited access to markets where they might sell their crops or livestock. They also possessed limited political power even though they comprised a sizeable majority of the population. With limited access to capital and few educational opportunities (20 percent of Southern whites were illiterate), few small farmers could expect to enter the planter class.

Why then did poor Southern whites support a slave society in which they had so little influence and apparently so little stake? Some did so because members of their extended family owned slaves or because they themselves aspired to own slaves, a sign of wealth and status. Others embraced a long-standing Southern doctrine that white freedom depended on slavery. Because slaves performed hard, menial labor, slavery established a floor in the Southern economy, below which even the poorest whites could not descend. "Break down slavery," argued one Virginian, "and you would with the same blow destroy the great Democratic principle of equality among men"—by which he meant, white men. Above all, poor Southerners supported slavery because they accepted the essential tenets of white supremacy, in particular the notion that blacks were inferior to whites and destined to live under their dominance. "Now suppose they was free," said a white Alabama farmer about slaves to a Northerner touring the South in the 1850s, "they'd all think themselves just as good as we.... how would you like to hev a nigger feelin' just as good as a white man?"

Divergent Visions

Southern society not only preached the superiority of whites over blacks, but also the superiority of slave labor over Northern wage labor. The most prominent defender of slavery was George Fitzhugh. In books and pamphlets published in the 1850s, he argued that all great societies in history practiced slavery and that the Southern version was remarkably humane because masters felt obliged to feed, clothe, and shelter their slaves. "The negro slaves of the South," he wrote, "are the happiest, and, in some sense, the freest people in the world." Moreover, argued Fitzhugh and others, such as the artist who drew this image that idealized slavery (**12.17**), slavery rescued Africans from the so-called barbarism of Africa and exposed them to "civilization" and Christianity. Pointing to the North's urban slums swelled with poor industrial workers, Fitzhugh ridiculed the Northern contention that wage labor was morally superior to slavery. Northern factory workers, he asserted, were little more than "wage slaves." Their condition was worse than that of the black slave because factory owners owed them nothing but the lowest possible wage. "Capital exercises a more perfect compulsion over free laborers than human masters over slaves," wrote Fitzhugh, "for free laborers must at all times work or starve, and slaves are supported whether they work or not." Northern society with its "hireling labor," claimed an official in Charleston, was characterized by "pauperism, rowdyism, mobism and anti-rentism."

Republicans had an answer for the likes of Fitzhugh: a free labor philosophy that celebrated the virtues of individualism, independence, entrepreneurship, and upward mobility. As Fitzhugh did for the slave South, they offered an idealized vision of the industrial North that conveniently ignored the hopeless plight of many poverty-stricken city dwellers. "In the constitution of human nature," wrote *New York Tribune* editor Horace Greeley, "the desire of bettering one's condition is the mainspring of effort." In contrast to the South, which reserved hard labor for slaves, argued Greeley, in the North all work was noble and moral, no matter how menial. Better still, for the ambitious, wage labor need only be temporary. If a man labored hard, saved his money, avoided drink, and sought opportunity, went the free labor philosophy, he would soon possess his own farm or small business. Nothing—not lack of money, family ties, formal education, or American birth—stood in the way of success.

A slave-based society, then, for these Republicans, was the antithesis of this dynamic society of democratic opportunity. "Enslave a man," wrote Greeley, "and you destroy his ambition, his enterprise, his capacity." To Northern abolitionists, slavery also stifled the capacity of most poor and middling whites, protecting the privileges of the aristocratic few and leaving the rest with little opportunity for success. Even worse, slavery led to a culture that celebrated laziness, luxury, and decadence as opposed to the capitalist virtues of hard work, thrift, and self-restraint. Northern writers like Frederick Law Olmsted, who traveled the South in the 1850s, frequently commented on the backwardness of Southern life, its lack of public education, railroads, factories, and substantial cities as well as a general tone of despair and fatalism among poor whites. This ideological war of words intensified when a financial panic on Wall Street sent the economy plunging into a deep recession in late 1857, bringing unemployment and hard times to the industrial Northeast and agrarian West. But because the Southern economy was so geared toward the export of cotton, it experienced little of the Panic of 1857. Southern nationalists pointed to this as evidence that "cotton is supreme" in comparison to Northern industry. Southerners also argued that it proved the South could prosper on its own should the Union ever dissolve.

The development of these divergent philosophies in the 1850s played a major role in creating a climate of extreme mistrust between North and South. Given the moral and social dimension of

ATTENTION PAID A POOR SICK WHITE MAN.

ATTENTION PAID A POOR SICK NEGRO.

12.17 Proslavery Propaganda: Slavery and Free Labor Contrasted
This 1852 woodcut captures the argument of George Fitzhugh and other proslavery propagandists, claiming that masters care for their slaves even when sick and unable to work, whereas cold-hearted Northern factory owners simply dump their sick or injured workers at the poor house.

the proslavery argument, Southerners perceived Northern criticism of slavery and attempts to prevent its spread as attacks on their "way of life." Likewise, Southern celebration of slavery and criticism of capitalist free labor convinced many Northerners that the slave power intended to spread slavery everywhere, including into the industrial North. The successful efforts by Southerners in Congress to defeat proposals for higher tariffs to protect Northern industry, land grants to promote a transcontinental railroad, and a homestead act to give 160 acres of public land to Western settlers accentuated hard feelings in the North. In 1858, a leading ideologue of the Republican Party, William Seward, predicted "an irrepressible conflict" between the two societies.

How did the Panic of 1857 strengthen the Southern argument for secession?

A House Divided

By the late 1850s, slavery dominated national politics. Nowhere was this more apparent than in the congressional elections of 1858, especially in Illinois where Senator Stephen A. Douglas engaged in a series of famous debates, mostly on the slavery issue, with a little-known Republican challenger named Abraham Lincoln. Increasingly, Southerners became convinced that Northerners wanted not simply to exclude slavery from the Western territories but to destroy it. John Brown's abolitionist raid on Harpers Ferry, Virginia in late 1859 only added to this perception. The subsequent election the following year of Abraham Lincoln, whose Republican Party Southern hardliners believed was committed to abolition, sparked a secession movement that soon brought the nation to the brink of civil war.

The Lincoln-Douglas Debates

In 1858, national attention turned to Illinois, where Stephen A. Douglas, a leading Democrat and certain 1860 presidential candidate, was running for reelection to the Senate. Many Americans were eager to see which direction he would take on the slavery issue. Opposing him was Abraham Lincoln, a former Illinois state representative and congressman. No abolitionist, Lincoln nevertheless believed slavery was immoral and hoped to prevent its spread to the Western territories. "A house divided against itself cannot stand," warned Lincoln in his speech accepting the Republican nomination to run for senator. "I believe this Government cannot endure permanently half-*slave* and half-*free*."

The overwhelming underdog in the contest, Lincoln boldly challenged Douglas to a series of seven debates across Illinois. The ensuing **Lincoln-Douglas debates** focused on the fate of slavery, the legal and social status of African Americans, and the viability of popular sovereignty in the wake of the *Dred Scott* decision. Douglas portrayed Lincoln as a radical abolitionist and "Black Republican" whose policies would destroy the Union, elevate blacks to social and legal equality with whites, and promote interracial marriage. Lincoln denied these charges but made clear that a black man was "entitled to all the natural rights enumerated in the Declaration of Independence, the right to life, liberty, and the pursuit of happiness." In this "he is my equal and the equal of Judge Douglas, and the equal of every living man." Lincoln also castigated Douglas for his professed moral indifference toward slavery. "If slavery is not wrong," Lincoln asserted, "nothing is wrong."

Douglas won reelection to the Senate, but Lincoln had forced him to make statements that appeared both indifferent to slavery and willing to let residents in the Western territories ban it, thereby antagonizing both Southern fire-eaters and Northern free soilers. His opponents would use these words against him in the presidential campaign in 1860. More important, the debates made Lincoln a national figure and a rising star within the Republican Party.

John Brown's Raid

In 1857, just months after staging the Pottawatomie Creek massacre in Kansas, abolitionist John Brown began plotting an invasion of the South that he hoped would lead to a widespread slave revolt and the end of slavery. A deeply religious man raised from an early age to hate slavery, Brown believed God had called upon him to destroy slavery.

His sense of mission is revealed in this 1847 daguerreotype (**12.18**). In it Brown reenacts a scene from a decade earlier when he stood up in a crowded church, raised his right hand, and pledged to commit his life to abolition. Brown's passion for the cause inspired many supporters and by the summer of 1859, with secret assistance from a number of prominent abolitionists, he had gathered 17 whites (including three of his sons) and five blacks and moved to a farm in Maryland.

John Brown's raid began at eight o'clock on the evening of October 16. Leading his raiders across the Potomac River to Harpers Ferry, Virginia, Brown quickly took control of the town and seized its federal arsenal full of guns and ammunition. They planned to fan out across the South, arming slaves and touching off a wave of rebellion. But they were quickly cornered, and on October 18 U.S. Marines under Colonel Robert E. Lee stormed their stronghold. The soldiers killed ten of Brown's men, including two of his sons, and took Brown and six others prisoner.

How did the Lincoln-Douglas debates harm Douglas's presidential ambitions?

⬛ **Read** the **Document** *The Lincoln-Douglas Debates of 1858*

12.18 John Brown Vows to Destroy Slavery
In 1847, John Brown stood for this daguerreotype taken by African-American photographer Augustus Washington, reenacting a pledge he made to destroy slavery ten years earlier at an abolitionist meeting.

Six weeks later a Virginia jury found Brown and his men guilty of treason and sentenced them to hang. When given the opportunity to speak, Brown declared that he had acted in accordance with the Bible's call to fight for justice, a cause for which he was prepared to die. On the day of his execution, Brown wrote one last note that proved eerily prophetic of the coming Civil War. "I, John Brown, am now quite certain that the crimes of this guilty land will never be purged away but with blood."

If in life Brown had failed to overthrow slavery, in death he furthered the abolitionist cause by becoming an instant martyr to many in the North. On the day of his execution, bells tolled in hundreds of towns from Boston to Chicago. At rallies and church services, Brown was lionized as a righteous instrument of God. Ralph Waldo Emerson wrote of Brown as a Christ-like figure who had made "the gallows as glorious as the cross." Abolitionist William Lloyd Garrison, a life-long pacifist, told an audience in Boston, "I am prepared to say 'success to every slave insurrection at the South and in every slave country.'"

Not all Northerners were so enthusiastic, however; opponents of slavery like Lincoln and Greeley criticized Brown's use of violence. Still there was no denying, observed one Northerner, that the "death of no man in America has ever produced so profound a sensation."

Sensation also struck in the South, but it was one of fear and outrage. Brown's audacious act rekindled among Southerners what Frederick Douglass called the ever-present "dread and terror" of slave insurrection. Brown's glorification by Northern editorialists, politicians, and ministers convinced many Southerners that Northern abolitionists would continue to conspire to instigate future slave uprisings to destroy Southern society. "Mr. Seward and his followers," charged a Mississippi legislator saying that the North's leading abolitionists, "have declared war upon us." Increasingly, Southerners talked of dissolving their union with the North to protect their property and way of life. Robert Toombs of Georgia voiced the most pressing concern of Southerners: "Never permit this Federal government to pass into the traitorous hands of the black Republican party."

The Election of 1860

Throughout the 1850s, the Democratic Party had managed to withstand the strains of sectional discord that demolished the Whigs and created a Republican Party with virtually no support in the South. But when the Democrats met in April 1860 in Charleston, South Carolina, to nominate a presidential candidate, disagreements between Northern and Southern delegates caused the convention to disband, unable to agree on a nominee. The sectional split became official when a Baltimore convention of mostly Northern Democrats nominated Stephen A. Douglas, a man Southerners had become convinced would not protect slavery. A week later a convention of Southern Democrats also met in Baltimore and nominated John C. Breckinridge, Buchanan's vice president and a staunch proslavery man from Kentucky. To complicate matters, former Southern Whigs and Know-Nothings formed the Constitutional Union Party and nominated John Bell of Tennessee, a pro-Union slaveholder of moderate views.

The split among the Democrats and the emergence of the Constitutional Union Party enhanced Republican chances for victory. Deeming Seward too controversial on the slavery issue, Republicans

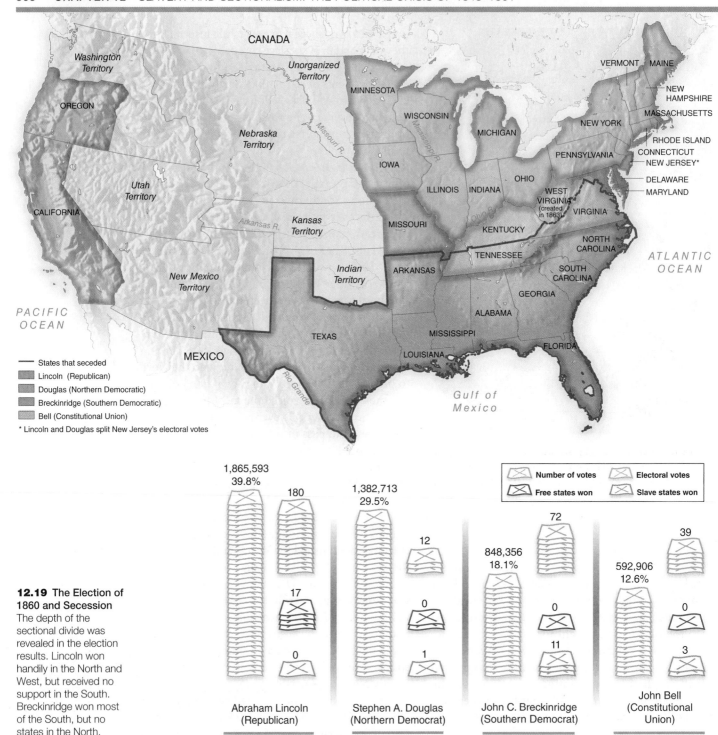

12.19 The Election of 1860 and Secession
The depth of the sectional divide was revealed in the election results. Lincoln won handily in the North and West, but received no support in the South. Breckinridge won most of the South, but no states in the North.

Legend:
- States that seceded
- Lincoln (Republican)
- Douglas (Northern Democratic)
- Breckinridge (Southern Democratic)
- Bell (Constitutional Union)

* Lincoln and Douglas split New Jersey's electoral votes

Key:
- Number of votes
- Electoral votes
- Free states won
- Slave states won

Abraham Lincoln (Republican): 1,865,593 — 39.8% — 180 — 17 — 0

Stephen A. Douglas (Northern Democrat): 1,382,713 — 29.5% — 12 — 0 — 1

John C. Breckinridge (Southern Democrat): 848,356 — 18.1% — 72 — 0 — 11

John Bell (Constitutional Union): 592,906 — 12.6% — 39 — 0 — 3

selected Abraham Lincoln, a man with few political enemies and an established reputation as a moderate. The party then adopted a platform touting Republican ideals of free labor, support for a homestead act, and a moderate approach to the slavery question that merely opposed its extension westward.

The national mood grew apprehensive as Election Day approached. The candidates appealed to specific sections rather than to the national electorate. The result of the sectionalism, many feared, would be the very thing political leaders had struggled to prevent during the 1850s: disunion.

Lincoln won the four-way election with just under 40 percent of the popular vote. He swept all the states in the North except New Jersey, plus California and Oregon, while Douglas, who won only Missouri and some electoral votes from New Jersey, finished second with 29 percent of the popular vote (**12.19**).

What was unique about Lincoln's victory in the election of 1860?   **View** the **Closer Look** *1860 Election Cartoon*

Breckinridge won all the Deep South states but polled just 18 percent of the popular vote. Bell of the Constitutional Union Party finished fourth taking three states of the upper South and 13 percent of the popular vote. For the first time in the nation's history, a purely regional party, the Republicans, had won the White House. It was precisely the scenario Southern extremists had threatened would lead to dissolution of the Union.

Secession

Southern fire-eaters, having warned Southerners that the election of a "Black Republican" would lead to the end of slavery and the destruction of their society, wasted no time in calling for secession. Secessionist rallies broke out across the South. Nowhere was secession sentiment stronger than in the epicenter of Southern nationalism, South Carolina. Brushing aside the pleas of moderates to wait until the slave states could agree on a united course of action, South Carolina legislators called a convention to consider secession from the union. On December 20, 1860, this convention unanimously resolved that the "union now subsisting between South Carolina and the other States … is hereby dissolved." In less than two months, six more states—Mississippi, Florida, Alabama, Georgia, Louisiana, and Texas—also seceded (12.19). One by one their representatives in Washington delivered speeches, resigned, and headed home.

Six of the seceded states sent delegates to Montgomery, Alabama, in early February where they organized a government similar to the one they had just left. The major exception, of course, was that its constitution declared slavery legal and protected everywhere in the new nation. They called their new nation the Confederate States of America and elected Jefferson Davis of Mississippi as its first president and Alexander Stephens of Georgia as vice president. They also created a Confederate Seal (**12.20**) that featured George Washington—not only the foremost Founding Father, but a Virginian and a slave owner—at the center and established his birthday, February 22, as the official birth of the Confederacy. These choices reflected the Confederates' goal to legitimize secession by comparing it to the thirteen colonies breaking away from Britain during the American Revolution.

Even as the new Confederate government took shape, President James Buchanan, a weak and timid leader with Southern sympathies, did little to avert the crisis, claiming that he lacked constitutional

> "That the South can afford to live under a Government, the majority of whose citizens … regard John Brown as a martyr and a Christian hero, rather than a murderer … is a preposterous idea."
>
> *Baltimore Sun*, November 28, 1859

authority to do anything. Moderates mobilized to see if they could, as in previous sectional crises in 1820, 1833, 1850, and 1854, devise a compromise acceptable to both sections. Senator John J. Crittenden of Kentucky put forth the leading proposal. The **Crittenden Compromise** proposed constitutional amendments to protect slavery, including one extending the old Missouri Compromise line of 36° 30' to the Pacific, permitting slavery south of it, prohibiting it to the north. But while president-elect Lincoln expressed a willingness to compromise—including supporting a constitutional amendment protecting slavery where it existed in the South—he would not support the Crittenden Compromise. "On the territorial question," he said in reference to the Republican opposition to extending slavery into the West, "I am inflexible." With that the proposal died.

Confederate President Jefferson Davis likewise professed an aversion to conflict, but rejected compromise. For the Confederate States of America, the decision to secede was permanent. The citizens of the Confederacy, he argued, asked simply to be left alone.

The impasse left moderates in despair, but Lincoln placed his faith in pro-Union sentiment in the South. He believed that for all

12.20 The Confederate Seal: Linking Secession with the Spirit of 1776 By placing George Washington at the center of the Confederate Seal, Southerners sought to legitimize secession by comparing it to the decision of the thirteen colonies to break away from Britain in 1776.

View the **Map** *Atlas Map: Secession*

What prevented a compromise in the spring of 1861?

"The tea has been thrown overboard; the revolution of 1860 has been initiated."

Charleston (S.C.) *Mercury*, reacting to Lincoln's election

their bluster, Southern fire-eaters would eventually pull back from the brink of disunion and civil war as they had so many times before. After all, eight slave states in the upper South still remained within the Union. His inaugural address (see *Competing Visions: Secession or Union?*) emphasized reconciliation while also declaring the Union indivisible and secession illegal.

Lincoln also asserted his intent to "hold, occupy, and possess" all federal property in the seceded states. Although the seceding states had seized nearly all federal property within their borders, two harbor forts remained in federal control, Fort Pickens in Pensacola, Florida, and Fort Sumter in Charleston, South Carolina.

With food and other necessities running low at Fort Sumter, Lincoln informed the South Carolina government of his intention to send a ship with non-military supplies to resupply the garrison. For Confederate leaders the moment of truth had arrived. If they submitted to federal authority, secession would appear hollow. If they fired on the ship, they would be branded as the aggressors in the coming struggle. Confederate officials decided to force the issue before the ship arrived and ordered Major Robert Anderson, in command of the fort, to surrender. When Anderson refused, Confederate General P. G. T. Beauregard began an artillery assault on the morning of April 12, and by afternoon the next day, the Union garrison surrendered. Southerners exulted in their quick victory, and immediately raised the Confederate flag over the ruins as a symbol of their triumph and sovereignty as an independent nation (**12.21**). On April 15, Lincoln declared the lower South to be in a state of "insurrection" and called for 75,000 men to enlist to put down the rebellion. The Civil War had begun.

12.21 **The Confederate Flag Flying in Triumph over Fort Sumter**
Taken the morning following the fort's surrender, this photograph of Fort Sumter with a Confederate flag snapping defiantly in the breeze captured the exuberance of the Southern victory and grim reality of the Union defeat.

Why did Lincoln attempt to resupply Fort Sumter?

Competing Visions
SECESSION OR UNION?

Mississippi's declaration of secession and Abraham Lincoln's inaugural address from March 1861 present opposing views on secession. Note how both parties invoke the Constitution and other American traditions to justify their positions. How do the secessionists support their claim that the mere election of Lincoln justified secession? How does Lincoln reject the idea of secession and seek to place the responsibility for hostilities on the seceded states?

Patterned on the Declaration of Independence, Mississippi's declaration of secession sets forth a list of alleged attacks on slavery and states rights by the North.

Our position is thoroughly identified with… slavery—the greatest material interest of the world. Its labor supplies the product which constitutes… the largest and most important portions of commerce of the earth…. These products have become necessities of the world, and a blow at slavery is a blow at commerce and civilization….

The hostility to this institution commenced before the adoption of the Constitution….

It has grown until it denies the right of property in slaves, and refuses protection to that right on the high seas, in the Territories, and wherever the government of the United States had jurisdiction.

It refuses the admission of new slave States into the Union, and seeks to extinguish it by confining it within its present limits, denying the power of expansion….

It has nullified the Fugitive Slave Law in almost every free State in the Union…

It advocates negro equality, socially and politically, and promotes insurrection and incendiarism in our midst.

It has enlisted its press, its pulpit and its schools against us, until the whole popular mind of the North is excited and inflamed with prejudice….

It has recently obtained control of the Government, by the prosecution of its… schemes, and destroyed the last expectation of living together in friendship….

Utter subjugation awaits us in the Union, if we should consent longer to remain in it. It is not a matter of choice, but of necessity. We must either submit to degradation, and to the loss of property worth four billions of money, or we must secede from the Union framed by our fathers, to secure this as well as every other species of property. For far less cause than this, our fathers separated from the Crown of England.

Our decision is made. We follow their footsteps. We embrace the alternative of separation…

The flag of Mississippi, adopted after the state's secession in January 1861.

Lincoln used his inaugural address in March 1861 to respond directly to the assertions contained in the declarations of Mississippi and other seceded states. He attempted to reassure Southerners that his administration was not hostile to their interests, while rejecting their justification for secession.

Fellow citizens of the United States:

… I hold that, in contemplation of universal law and of the Constitution, the Union of these States is perpetual. Perpetuity is implied, if not expressed, in the fundamental law of all national governments. It is safe to assert that no government proper ever had a provision in its organic law for its own termination….

It follows from these views that no State upon its own mere motion can lawfully get out of the Union; that Resolves and Ordinances to that effect are legally void; and that acts of violence, within any State or States, against the authority of the United States, are insurrectionary or revolutionary, according to circumstances.

I therefore consider that, in view of the Constitution and the laws, the Union is unbroken; and to the extent of my ability I shall take care, as the Constitution itself expressly enjoins upon me, that the laws of the Union be faithfully executed in all the States….

In doing this there needs to be no bloodshed or violence; and there shall be none, unless it be forced upon the national authority.

In YOUR hands, my dissatisfied fellow-countrymen, and not in MINE, is the momentous issue of civil war. The government will not assail YOU. You can have no conflict without being yourselves the aggressors. YOU have no oath registered in heaven to destroy the government, while I shall have the most solemn one to "preserve, protect, and defend it."

I am loathe to close. We are not enemies, but friends. We must not be enemies….

The flag of the United States, updated in January 1861 to include a thirty-fourth star for the new state of Kansas.

How did the slavery issue factor into Mississippi's decision to secede?

1848

Gold discovered in California.
Population boom leads California to apply for statehood, renewing debate over whether slavery would be permitted in the Western territories.

1850–1852

Congress passes the Compromise of 1850.
Offers concessions to both supporters and opponents of slavery, temporarily calming sectional tensions. But subsequent fugitive slave incidents stoke abolitionist sentiment in the North and anger among Southerners.

Harriet Beecher Stowe publishes *Uncle Tom's Cabin*.
Best-selling antislavery novel convinces many Northerners that slavery is wrong.

1854

Congress passes the Kansas-Nebraska Act.
Allows Kansas and Nebraska to decide the slavery question by popular sovereignty.

Whig Party collapses.
Replaced by the Republican Party.

Know-Nothing movement reaches high point.
Nativist candidates elected throughout Northeast and Midwest, but movement soon fades.

1855–1856

Armed conflict between proslavery and antislavery forces in the Kansas territory.
The bloodshed lasts into 1857 and discredits the principle of popular sovereignty.

Senator Sumner assaulted for his "Crimes Against Kansas" speech.
Increases sectional animosity as Southerners hail Brooks as a hero and Northerners denounce him as a violent villain.

CHAPTER REVIEW

Review Questions

1. Why did slavery emerge as a national political issue in the late 1840s?

2. What led to the rise of the Republican Party? How did the party define its position on slavery?

3. What were the sources of nativism that led to the rise of the Know-Nothings?

4. Why did many Northerners believe that Southern slaveholding interests had gained control of the national government?

5. What role did economic development play in the rise of sectional tension?

Key Terms

Compromise of 1850   An attempt by Congress to resolve the slavery question by making concessions to both the North and South, including admission of California and a new Fugitive Slave Act.   **345**

Fugitive Slave Act   A component of the Compromise of 1850 that increased the federal government's obligation to capture and return escaped slaves to their owners.   **346**

Underground Railroad   A network of safe houses and secret hiding places along routes leading to the North and into Canada (where slavery was prohibited) that helped several thousand slaves gain their freedom between 1830 and 1860.   **347**

Young America   The movement within the Democratic Party that embraced Manifest Destiny and promoted territorial expansion, increased international trade, and the spread of American ideals of democracy and free enterprise abroad.   **350**

Kansas-Nebraska Act   An 1854 act designed to resolve the controversy over whether slavery would be permitted in the Western territories. It repealed the ban on slavery north of 36° 30' (the Missouri Compromise) and created two separate territories, Kansas west of Missouri and Nebraska west of Iowa.   **351**

Know-Nothings   The nickname for the constituents of the nativist, or anti-immigrant, American Party, who called for

legislation restricting office holding to native-born citizens and raising the period of naturalization for citizenship from five to twenty-one years.   **354**

Bleeding Kansas   A phrase used to describe the wave of vigilante reprisals and counterreprisals by proslavery and antislavery forces in Kansas in 1856.   **356**

Dred Scott v. Sandford   The highly controversial 1857 Supreme Court decision that rejected the claim of the slave Dred Scott, who argued that time spent with his owner in regions that barred slavery had made him a free man. It also declared that Congress lacked the right to regulate slavery in the territories.   **358**

Lincoln-Douglas debates   A series of high-profile debates in Illinois in 1858 between Senate candidates Stephen A. Douglas and Abraham Lincoln that focused primarily on the slavery controversy.   **366**

John Brown's raid   A failed assault led by the radical abolitionist on the federal arsenal at Harpers Ferry, Virginia, on October 16, 1859, intending to seize the guns and ammunition and then touch off a wave of slave rebellions.   **366**

Crittenden Compromise   An unsuccessful proposal by Kentucky senator John J. Crittenden to resolve the secession crisis in the spring of 1861 with constitutional amendments to protect slavery.   **369**

1857–1858

The U.S. Supreme Court decides the *Dred Scott* case.
Court rules that slaves are property, not people or citizens, and that the Missouri Compromise prohibition on slavery above 36° 30' is unconstitutional.

Lincoln and Douglas Debate
A relatively unknown Abraham Lincoln earns national attention as he forces Stephen A. Douglas to make controversial statements about slavery.

1859

John Brown's failed raid on Harper's Ferry, Virginia.
The South vilifies Brown as an abolitionist fanatic; the North hails him as a martyr.

1860

Abraham Lincoln is elected president.
Lincoln wins despite receiving no support in the South, revealing the deepening sectional rift over slavery.

South Carolina secedes from the Union.
Six more slave states follow suit and unite as the Confederate States of America.

1861

South Carolinians fire upon the Union-held Fort Sumter.
First shots of the Civil War prompt the Lincoln administration to issue a call for 75,000 military volunteers. Four more Southern states secede.

MyHistoryLab Connections

Visit www.myhistorylab.com for a customized Study Plan that will help you build your knowledge of *Workers, Farmers, and Slaves.*

Questions for Analysis

1. What did Calhoun argue constituted the primary threat to the Union?

📖 **Read** the **Document** *John C. Calhoun, Proposal to Preserve the Union (1850), p. 344*

2. How did abolitionists try to characterize the Fugitive Slave Act as a violation of American ideals?

🔍 **View** the **Closer Look** *The Fugitive Slave Act, p. 346*

3. Why did many Americans come to see immigrants as a danger to the republic?

👁 **Watch** the **Video** *Video Lecture: Burn Down the Convent, p. 355*

4. How was Christianity cited as a source to defend as well as condemn slavery?

🔍 **View** the **Closer Look** *Competing Visions: Slavery and Christianity, p. 364*

5. Which Southern states had the most counties opposed to secession?

🔍 **View** the **Map** *Atlas Map: Secession, p. 369*

Other Resources from This Chapter

🔊 **Hear** the **Audio** *John Brown: An Address by Frederick Douglass, pamphlet excerpt, p. 367*

📖 **Read** the **Document**

- *John L. O'Sullivan, "The Great Nation of Futurity" (1845), p. 350*
- *John Gihon, Kansas Begins to Bleed (1856), p. 356*
- *A Slave Sues for Freedom in 1857, p. 358*
- *The Lincoln-Douglas Debates of 1858, p. 366*

🔍 **View** the **Closer Look**

- *Chinese Gold Mining in California, p. 343*
- *The Compromise of 1850, p. 346*
- *1860 Election Cartoon, p. 368*

🔍 **View** the **Image** *Gold Mines of California Lecture Announcement, p. 342*

🔍 **View** the **Map**

- *Interactive Map: The Underground Railroad, p. 347*
- *Interactive Map: The Compromise of 1850 and the Kansas-Nebraska Act, p. 352*
- *Interactive Map: Slavery in the South, p. 363*

👁 **Watch** the **Video**

- *Video Lecture: The Making of Uncle Tom's Cabin, p. 348*
- *Video Lecture: Dred Scott and the Crises that Led to the Civil War, p. 359*

Mobilization, Strategy, and Diplomacy p. 376

What advantages and disadvantages did the North and South possess at the outbreak of the war?

The Early Campaigns, 1861–1863 p. 381

Why did Lincoln expand the goal of war from preserving the Union to including emancipation?

Behind the Lines p. 387

How did the demands of war lead to changes in government policy and lifestyle on the home front?

Toward Union Victory p. 392

What decisions by the Lincoln administration and Union army commanders led to the defeat of the Confederacy?

((•─[**Hear** the **Audio File** on **myhistorylab.com**

◉─[**Watch** the **Video** *Critical Visions, Chapter 13*

A Nation Torn Apart
The Civil War, 1861–1865

The Civil War began in 1861 as a conflict over whether Southern states possessed the right to secede from the Union. But when Lincoln's Emancipation Proclamation took effect on January 1, 1863, it became a war against slavery. The soldiers depicted in this joyous scene were among the nearly 200,000 African American soldiers who contributed to the Union army's successful campaign to defeat the Confederacy. In February 1865, a few weeks after the second anniversary of the Emancipation Proclamation, the popular magazine, *Harper's Weekly*, published this drawing, "Entrance of the Fifty-Fifth Massachusetts (colored) Regiment into Charleston Feb 21, 1865." The image reflected not merely a growing acceptance of slavery's demise among Northerners, but also the celebration of emancipation as a noble cause, along with restoration of the Union, that helped the North justify the terrible human cost of the war.

Emancipation was but one of the many extraordinary aspects of the Civil War that make it the most written-about event in American history. The war pitted American against American, in some cases brother against brother. Senator John J. Crittenden of Kentucky, for example, saw two sons become generals, one Confederate and the other Union. Mary Todd Lincoln, the president's wife, lost three brothers who fought for the Confederacy. The Civil War was also an unusually bloody war. The 618,000 Americans who died in the four years of conflict far outnumber the 117,000 lost in World War I and the 417,000 in World War II. The war also brought to the fore larger-than-life personalities such as Generals William Tecumseh Sherman, Ulysses S. Grant, Robert E. Lee, and Thomas "Stonewall" Jackson, and it produced moments of heroism that would become the stuff of legend.

If these aspects of the war explain its popularity as a historical subject, they also indicate why the Civil War has generated such heated debate. For generations Americans have argued over the true cause of the war and why the North won (or as some like to put it, why the South lost). They have debated the significance and wisdom of crucial decisions such as Lee's move to attack the North in 1863 or Union General George Meade's failure to pursue the weakened Confederates after Gettysburg.

Yet for all this debate, few commentators dispute this fact: The Civil War brought profound social, political, and economic change to the United States. Most also agree that although the war ended the contentious question of slavery, it immediately raised equally challenging questions about racial equality.

"War for the destruction of liberty
must be met by war for the
destruction of slavery."
African American leader FREDERICK DOUGLASS

Mobilization, Strategy, and Diplomacy

 Neither the North nor South envisioned the character and course of the war that began with the South's firing on Fort Sumter in April 1861. Both sides had to hastily mobilize, recruit, train, and outfit modern armies. The North possessed overwhelming advantages in population and industry, but the South enjoyed superior military leadership, a white population largely united against invading Union armies, and a hope that France or Britain would intervene in the conflict on their behalf.

Comparative Advantages and Disadvantages

As North and South prepared for war, both sides believed they would win decisively. Journalist Horace Greeley spoke for many Northerners when he boasted of the president of the Confederate States of America and his administration that "Jeff Davis and Co. will be swinging from the battlements at Washington at least by the 4th of July." On paper this confidence seemed justified. As the table (**13.1**) illustrates, the Northern states possessed more than twice the population of the Confederacy, giving the North an enormous advantage in soldiers, farmers, and industrial workers. The North also possessed a vast industrial system, nine times greater than that of the Confederacy. Producing 97 percent of the nation's firearms, 94 percent of its cloth, and 90 percent of its shoes and boots, this system could

provide the Union armies with unlimited supplies. The North also had a modern railroad system twice the size of the Confederacy's, and it was far more integrated.

A final advantage was the firm belief among many Northern soldiers that they were fighting to uphold the Constitution, and the Union. This sentiment was stoked by a profusion of speeches, songs, and printed matter like the poster *The Eagle's Nest* (**13.2**), extolling the Union cause. Demonizing secession as treason by invoking the famous 1830 declaration of President Andrew Jackson, a Southerner and slave owner, "The Union! It must and shall be preserved," it also draws on familiar images of patriotism such as the bald eagle and the American flag. Many Northerners believed they were indebted to the Founding Fathers, whose sacrifices won American independence and established a republic where all possessed equal opportunity to succeed.

Southerners likewise sought to boost their wartime morale. As the song sheet "Secession Quick Step" (**13.3**) shows, they often drew on the same patriotic images and themes as Northerners. This song and the accompanying image seek to connect the colonists' break from Britain during the American Revolution with the South's quest for Confederate independence. Note the reference to "Minute Men" the "Don't Tread on Me" snake, a popular image of colonial resistance to British authority in the 1770s (see Chapter 4).

Southerners also matched Northerners in their confidence about achieving a quick victory. "Just throw three or four shells among those blue-bellied Yankees," boasted one North Carolinian, "and they'll scatter like sheep." Confederates were keenly aware that although they lacked population, industry, and infrastructure, they possessed certain advantages. To begin with, they

	Union	Confederacy
Population	22,000,000	5,500,000 white 3,500,000 enslaved
Industrial Workers	1,300,000	110,000
Factories	110,000	18,000
Value Goods Manufactured	$1.5 billion	$155 million
Railroad Mileage	22,000	9,000
Weapons Manufacturing (Percent U.S. total)	97%	3%
Banking Capital	$330,000,000	$27,000,000

13.1 Union Advantages on the Eve of War, 1861
The enormous disparities between North and South suggested to many a quick Union victory. But many factors beyond these statistics, notably superior Confederate military leadership, would make for a long and bloody war.

What significant advantages did the North hold over the South on the eve of war?

((•─ Hear the Audio *Battle Hymn of the Republic*

13.2 The Eagle's Nest
Northerners promoted patriotic sentiment in speeches, songs, and printed matter. This poster, "The Eagle's Nest," linked the Union cause to familiar images such as the bald eagle and the flag.

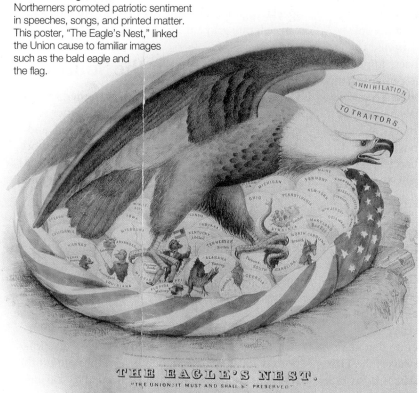

THE EAGLE'S NEST.
"THE UNION: IT MUST AND SHALL b PRESERVED"

were fighting a war for independence that carried with it a sense of destiny that would sustain them through the difficult times ahead—just as it had sustained, they reminded themselves, the overmatched colonists in their fight for independence from a superior Great Britain nearly a century earlier.

The South also enjoyed an important geographic advantage: To deny Confederate independence, the North had to conquer the South, an area as large as Western Europe. Furthermore, this monumental invasion and occupation would likely unify the South, including poor whites who might otherwise view the conflict as a war to protect the interests of slaveholders. The South could thus fight a defensive war until the North grew tired of the conflict and withdrew, or until a European power, most likely Britain, which depended heavily on Southern cotton, intervened militarily and forced the North to let the states secede.

Finally, whether they knew it or not, in April 1861 Southerners had the upper hand in military leadership. For the first half of the war, generals such as Robert E. Lee and Thomas "Stonewall" Jackson would stymie much larger and better-equipped Northern armies led by inept generals.

Mobilization in the North

Mobilization of the Union Army began days after the firing at Fort Sumter with Lincoln's call for 75,000 volunteers for 90 days' service and the imposition of a naval blockade along the Southern coast. Eager volunteers jammed recruiting stations, convinced the Union would win quickly and with little loss of life. Among those who clamored to join the Army were thousands of free African Americans anxious to defeat the slaveholding South. Yet they were turned away because of an overabundance of white volunteers and Lincoln's desire to sidestep issues of slavery and race to avoid provoking the slaveholding states that remained in the Union—Kentucky, Maryland, Delaware, and Missouri—from seceding.

13.3 Connecting to the Colonial Cause
As in the North, Southerners fostered unity, emphasizing the connection between the colonists' revolt against British rule during the American Revolution and the Confederate bid for Southern independence.

Why did Southerners seek to link secession to the American Revolution?

Unfortunately for Lincoln, the Union Army's enthusiasm was no substitute for experience. In 1861, there were only 16,000 professional soldiers in the Army, most of them stationed in the West. One-third of the Army's officers joined the Confederacy. Of those officers who remained, few possessed any real combat experience. To make matters worse, because state officials named the officers to command the new regiments of volunteers, they invariably chose men whose chief qualifications were their political connections and fondness for parading. One regiment, the 11th New York Volunteer Infantry, was perhaps the most vivid example of this phenomenon. As this print (**13.4**) shows, these volunteers donned flashy uniforms patterned after the Zouaves, France's famous regiments in Algeria, replete with red silk pantaloons and green jackets. The New York Zouaves enjoyed great celebrity at the war's outset, and one of them, Colonel Elmer Ephraim Ellsworth (at right), became the Union's first martyr when he was killed pulling down a Confederate flag in Virginia. Despite their stylishness, however, the 11th New York Zouaves performed disastrously at Bull Run. As the war progressed both armies replaced special regimental uniforms with Union blue and Confederate gray.

13.4 The Zouaves of the 11th New York
Many regiments raised to fight for the Union and the Confederacy included inexperienced men whose romantic visions of warfare were expressed in their fanciful uniforms.

Mobilization in the South

Unlike the North, the Confederacy needed to create an Army from scratch. Immediately after seceding, Southern states revived, reorganized, and expanded their militias, many of which were more like social clubs than military units. In March 1861, the Confederate Congress established an army of 100,000 volunteers for one-year terms of service, leading to the merging of most state militia companies into the Confederate Army. To thwart the Union's intended blockade of the Southern coastline, the Confederacy commenced creating a navy and authorizing privateers to seize Union ships.

Equipping their soldiers and sailors proved a far greater challenge. Lacking the industrial base of the North, the South built arms factories that eventually turned out some 350,000 rifles. They also imported 700,000 more. Nonetheless, throughout the war Confederate soldiers often needed to scavenge battlefields to find weapons and ammunition. The Confederate effort to thwart the Union blockade was similarly hampered by a lack of shipyards.

The Davis administration also had to pay for the war. Possessing few banks and limited reserves of gold and silver, the government tried several schemes, including requiring individual states to pay for the war and imposing an income tax. When none of these policies worked, the Confederate government simply printed paper money. With more than $1 billion in circulation by 1864 (twice the amount issued in the North), the citizens of the Confederacy faced punishing inflation, which reached 9,000 percent by 1865 (as compared with 80 percent in the Union).

Another obstacle to Confederate victory was the South's popular doctrine of states' rights. It envisioned the ideal national government as one that left most power and authority to the states. Even though the Confederacy ultimately managed to overcome states' rights opposition and create a centralized national government and military, its efforts were hindered by vociferous critics. Governors Zebulon B. Vance of North Carolina and Joseph E. Brown of Georgia, for example, opposed the incorporation of their state militias into the Confederate Army. Later when the Confederacy enacted a military draft, they raised a loud protest and created hundreds of exemptions for friends and state officials.

How did the doctrine of states' rights hinder the Southern war effort?

The Struggle for the Border States

While both sides readied for war, they also struggled for the loyalty of the **Border States**: Missouri, Kentucky, Delaware, and Maryland, the slave states along the border of the Confederacy that had not seceded (**13.5**). These held enormous strategic value for both sides. Missouri and Kentucky bordered the vital Mississippi River. Kentucky also controlled key sections of the Ohio and Kentucky Rivers. A seceded Delaware could cut off water access to Philadelphia. Worst of all, if Maryland seceded it would leave Washington, D.C. surrounded by Confederate territory, and cost the Union its main railroad route west.

The Davis administration had strong incentive to lure the Border States into joining the Confederacy. These four states contained nearly half the South's white male population and 80 percent of its industry. Given the South's disadvantages in manpower and manufacturing, the loss of these states would seriously weaken the Confederate war effort.

Ultimately, the Union managed to hold all four states. Delaware, where less than two percent of the white population owned slaves, proved relatively easy to hold. Kentucky remained divided between Union and Confederate sympathies. But Lincoln's subtle approach, along with the arrival of federal troops, secured the state for the Union.

Maryland, where pro-Confederate sentiment ran high, presented a far greater challenge. On April 19, 1861, a pro-Confederate mob attacked the 6th Massachusetts Regiment as it passed through Baltimore on its way to Washington. The inexperienced soldiers panicked and opened fire, killing 12. The mob then destroyed tracks, bridges, and telegraph lines, prompting Lincoln to declare martial law, arrest dozens of Confederate sympathizers,

Border states (did not secede)
Confederacy
Union

Note: The western counties of Virginia remained loyal to the Union and were admitted as the state of West Virginia in 1863.

13.5 The Vital Border States
The Border States (Missouri, Kentucky, Maryland, and Delaware) held enormous strategic, military, economic, and symbolic value for both sides. In the end, the Lincoln administration succeeded in keeping them in the Union.

and suspend habeas corpus—the right of a person to petition a judge for release from unlawful imprisonment.

Securing Union control of Missouri also required a heavy hand. The situation there resembled that of "Bleeding Kansas" in 1857 (see Chapter 12), with pro-Confederate and pro-Union forces fighting for control of the state. But Union forces under General Nathaniel Lyon thwarted the efforts of state officials to steer Missouri into the Confederacy.

The Union's success in preventing the secession of the Border States weakened the Confederate cause in two ways. First, it deprived the Confederacy of soldiers and factories. Second, the retention of four slave states in the Union undermined a primary Confederate justification for secession, namely, that it was necessary to protect slavery.

What made the Border States so economically and militarily valuable to the Confederacy?

Wartime Diplomacy

Davis hoped to gain from Britain and France diplomatic recognition for the Confederacy and perhaps even military intervention. He knew the leaders and aristocracy of both countries sympathized with the Confederate cause and that their economies depended heavily on Southern cotton. Accordingly, Davis sent emissaries to Britain and France to lobby for recognition.

To increase the chances of foreign intervention, the Confederacy in 1861 also established a **cotton embargo**, a ban on the export of cotton, the South's most valuable commodity. Because the Confederacy wanted to avoid any appearance of blackmailing cotton-importing nations like Britain and France, the embargo was voluntary and unofficial. Although the embargo damaged the Southern economy, Confederates believed it a worthwhile risk if it caused enough economic pain in Britain and France to, in the words of one Charleston newspaper editor, bring about either "the bankruptcy of every cotton factory in Great Britain or France or the acknowledgement of our independence."

Keenly aware that foreign intervention would likely demolish his goal of restoring the Union, Lincoln dispatched his own emissaries to Britain and France. Shortly after Fort Sumter both nations, seeking to avoid war, declared their neutrality and agreed to honor the Union blockade. This was crucial to the North because had Britain or France insisted on their right as neutrals to trade with the South, Lincoln would have been forced either to stop their ships—a policy certain to draw them into the war—or allow them to pass and thereby provide the Confederacy with badly needed supplies.

Despite diplomatic efforts, conflict with Britain soon erupted, threatening British neutrality. In November 1861, a U.S. warship stopped the British ship *Trent* and removed two Confederates heading for Europe to press for foreign recognition. As indicated in this cartoon (**13.6**) from the British magazine *Punch*, Britain reacted with outrage to the **Trent Affair**, putting its military forces on alert. "You do what is right," Britannia warns a bellicose but smaller America, "or I'll blow you out of the water." Lincoln, determined to avoid war, released the two Confederates, claiming that the captain had acted without authority. The roles were reversed in 1863 when the British government, faced with a Union threat of war, prevented delivery to the Confederacy of two ironclad warships built in a British shipyard.

LOOK OUT FOR SQUALLS.

JACK BULL.—"YOU DO WHAT'S RIGHT, MY SON, OR I'LL BLOW YOU OUT OF THE WATER."

13.6 A Diplomatic Dust-Up
Jack Bull (Great Britain) threatens Uncle Sam in the wake of the Trent Affair, an incident that nearly prompted the British to intervene in the war.

Why did Lincoln decide to back down and release the Confederates in the Trent Affair?

The Early Campaigns, 1861–1863

 Beginning with Bull Run in July 1861, the Confederacy won repeated victories in Virginia, thwarting Union attempts to seize Richmond, the Confederate capital. The Union found success in the West and moved closer to securing control of the Mississippi River. By 1862, new technologies in communications, transportation, and armaments made warfare more complex, protracted, and deadly. The war also assumed a revolutionary character, as slaves flocked to invading Union armies, eventually convincing the Lincoln administration to embrace emancipation as a goal of the war.

No Short and Bloodless War

In the weeks following Fort Sumter, pressure mounted in both the North and South for a decisive victory, despite the disorganized state of their armies. Although some argued that given the South's limited resources, its best chance of victory lay with a defensive military posture, most Southerners wanted their army to take the offensive, believing that one or two early victories would bring foreign intervention or prompt Lincoln to abandon efforts to restore the Union by force. Northern leaders faced similar demands. General Winfield Scott had devised a grand strategy called the Anaconda Plan to slowly envelop and strangle the South, but popular sentiment demanded an immediate strike to crush the rebellion.

The anticipated first clash, the first Battle of Bull Run, came in mid-July 1861. General Irwin McDowell led 30,000 Union soldiers of the Army of the Potomac south toward the town of Manassas, Virginia, site of an important railroad junction and a small Confederate force commanded by General P. G. T. Beauregard. Hundreds of curious and confident spectators from Washington, D.C., followed the army, many with picnic baskets in hand, hoping to witness some of the excitement.

Beauregard positioned his army above Manassas on the south side of a small stream named Bull Run. On July 21 McDowell attacked and nearly drove the Confederates from the field. Beauregard, however, stabilized his troops, and with reinforcements staged a counterassault. Lines of exhausted and undisciplined Union soldiers soon disintegrated into a chaotic, humiliating retreat to Washington.

Victory boosted Confederate spirits and confirmed their belief that one Southerner could whip ten Yankees. For the North the stunning humiliation demolished the notion of a short and bloodless war.

Within a week of the debacle, Lincoln authorized the enlistment of one million volunteers for three-year terms of service.

To rebuild the demoralized Army of the Potomac, Lincoln turned to General George B. McClellan. Dubbed the "Young Napoleon" by the press, McClellan was an impressive but arrogant man who treated Lincoln with barely disguised contempt. Lincoln tolerated this disrespect because McClellan inspired professionalism among his troops and by the spring of 1862, had transformed a mass of inexperienced volunteers into a well-trained army numbering some 150,000.

> "I seem to have become the power of the land. I almost think that were I to win some small success now I could become Dictator or anything else that might please me."
> GEN. GEORGE B. McCLELLAN to his wife, 1861

As the Army of the Potomac regrouped, Union forces in the West gained two desperately needed victories. As indicated in the map (**13.7** on page 382), in February 1862, Union forces led by a virtual unknown named Ulysses S. Grant seized Forts Henry and Donelson.

The twin victories gave the Union control of vital communication and transportation routes on the Tennessee and Cumberland Rivers and drove the Confederates out of Kentucky and most of Tennessee. They also created an early hero—Ulysses S. Grant—whose initials, the press suggested, stood for "Unconditional Surrender."

Grant continued south along the Tennessee River to seize more railroad lines as part of the

13.7 Major Battles in the West, 1862–1863
Grant's army and Farragut's naval force moved swiftly in 1862 to seize control of the Mississippi to cut the Confederacy in half.

larger Union strategy of taking control of the Mississippi to divide the Confederacy and open the Deep South to invasion. While Grant was encamped near Shiloh Church, Tennessee, Confederates under Albert Sidney Johnston and Beauregard surprised his army on April 6, nearly destroying it. But reinforcements allowed Grant to hold his position. He counterattacked the next day and drove the Confederates off. Grant's victory secured Union control of the Mississippi River south to Vicksburg, Mississippi by June 1862 (see 13.7).

The Confederacy suffered another setback that same month when David G. Farragut's Union

fleet captured New Orleans. This loss deprived the Confederacy of its largest city and chief source of credit and closed virtually the entire Mississippi to Confederate shipping.

The Peninsular Campaign

Lincoln welcomed the successes in the West, but recognized that defeat of the Confederacy required victory over its armies in Northern Virginia. Accordingly, he pressed McClellan to begin an offensive early in 1862. Despite his gallant martial image, however, McClellan seemed unwilling to fight, claiming his troops were not yet prepared. Only after weeks of goading did he agree to begin an offensive.

The **Peninsular Campaign**, as his plan was known, reflected McClellan's flamboyant style. Rather than a direct overland march on Richmond, he designed a complex plan whereby 400 ships deposited 120,000 soldiers on a long peninsula just east of Richmond at Fortress Monroe, between the James and York Rivers (**13.8**). To Lincoln's frustration it took three weeks for the soldiers to get in place. Then McClellan continued to delay.

The Confederates exploited McClellan's delays by sending 17,000 men under General Thomas "Stonewall" Jackson into the Shenandoah Valley. There between early May and June, he defeated larger Union forces, raising fears that he would capture Washington. Concerned for the capital's security, Lincoln withheld a large force of 30,000 that was scheduled to join McClellan.

When McClellan finally began to inch his army toward Richmond in late May, he confronted Confederate General Joseph E. Johnston in the Battle of Fair Oaks from May 31 to June 1, 1862. Although technically a Union victory since Johnston failed to dislodge McClellan's army, the battle proved inconclusive. Yet it was a turning point in the war because Johnston, severely injured, was replaced by General Robert E. Lee.

Lee proved a brilliant commander and strategist who made the most of the Confederacy's limited resources to bedevil and defeat much larger Union forces. Often this meant taking the offensive as in the Seven Days Battle (June 25–July 1, 1862). Lee attacked with 85,000 troops against McClellan's 110,000 and forced the Union commander to retreat to a secure location on the James River.

The week-long clash produced staggering carnage, but McClellan lost proportionately fewer men than Lee, and his army lay just 25 miles from Richmond. He refused, however, to move on Lee's

View the **Map** Interactive Map: The Civil War Part I 1861–1862

and, lacking any alternative, placed McClellan in command of all Union armies in northern Virginia. Vainglorious and ineffective as he was, McClellan still commanded the loyalty of his soldiers.

A New Kind of War

By this time Confederate and Union soldiers had grown accustomed to the rigors of army life. Most of the more than three million who served in the two armies were young men from small farms and towns. One of their first challenges was learning to accept the discipline and authority of military life. They also had to set aside their romantic visions of glory and get used to spending most of their time attending to routine duties, drilling, and enduring long periods of inactivity. Soldiers also suffered from bad food and from disease that raged in the camps and claimed three lives for every one lost in actual combat.

Boredom, disease, and hardship, although difficult to endure, were not new to military life. But certain aspects of the Civil War set it apart from previous wars in ways that have led many historians to declare it the first modern war. Although traditional warfare used relatively small armies and emphasized seizing and holding territory, modern warfare employed enormous armies that utilized the emerging technologies of the Industrial Revolution. The telegraph allowed for instant communication across vast territory between armies and civilian leaders. Railroads made it possible to shift thousands of reinforcements hundreds of miles in less than a day. Ironclad ships revolutionized naval strategy.

Yet what made this war truly modern was the carnage caused by advances in weaponry. Artillery became more accurate and deadly, while both armies used improved rifled muskets capable of

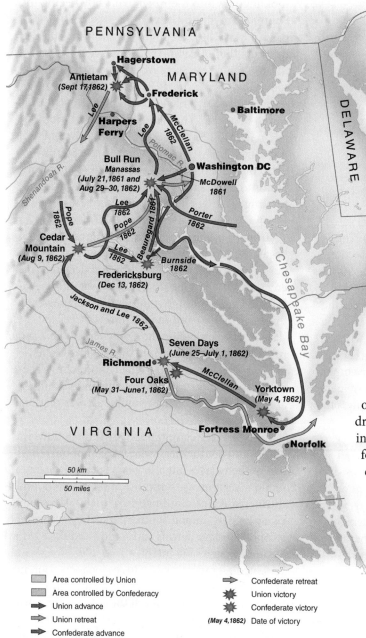

13.8 Major Battles in the East, 1861–1862
McClellan devised an elaborate plan to land his army on the Virginia peninsula below Richmond. But his slowness in moving the army and hesitancy in attacking handed the initiative to the Confederates and led to defeat.

weakened army, claiming inadequate intelligence, supplies, and men. Thoroughly frustrated, Lincoln ordered McClellan to abandon the Peninsular Campaign, remove his forces to northern Virginia, and unite with General John Pope's army for an overland assault on Richmond. But before slow-moving McClellan reached him, Lee defeated Pope in the Second Battle of Bull Run (August 29–30, 1862). Lincoln reassigned Pope to an army in Minnesota

Why is the Civil War considered the first modern war?

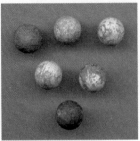

13.9 The Minie Ball
The conical-shaped minie ball (left) replaced round musket balls (right) and increased the accuracy of rifle fire. Its adoption during the Civil War contributed to the high death toll in combat.

killing a man from a distance of 400 to 500 yards (versus 100 yards for traditional muskets). The key technological breakthrough for the rifle was the minie ball, invented in France in the 1840s. As these photographs (**13.9**) show, the conical-shaped minie ball (left) replaced round musket balls (right) and were the forerunners of the bullet. The grooves inside the rifle barrel caused the minie ball, when fired, to spiral much like a football, increasing its accuracy. Other aspects of modern war included the emphasis on destroying the enemy's army rather than merely seizing and holding territory and a willingness to inflict suffering on the civilian population.

Military commanders on both sides, however, were slow to adjust to these changes. Schooled in traditional warfare at military academies such as West Point, most were reluctant to abandon the strategy of attacking entrenched enemy positions with massed infantry. When defenders of these positions turned their modern weaponry on charging soldiers, the results were horrific.

Toward Emancipation

Along with modern technology, slavery also shaped the Civil War. At the outset of the conflict, moderates like Lincoln insisted the goal of the war was to preserve the Union, not to abolish slavery. They realized that while many Northerners opposed slavery, they also rejected the idea of racial equality. They also feared that talk of emancipation would cause the Border States to secede and alienate pro-Union residents of the South, who Lincoln hoped would overthrow Confederate rule and return their states to the Union. Abolitionists, however, argued that because the Southern states seceded to protect slavery, reunion could occur only after it was destroyed.

But while white Northerners debated emancipation, enslaved African Americans in the South took matters into their own hands by fleeing to Union Army lines. Only weeks after the war began, in May 1861, an angry Virginia slaveholder demanded the Union Army observe the terms of the 1850 Fugitive Slave Act and return his three escaped slaves. General Benjamin Butler refused, declaring fugitive slaves contraband of war, or seized property. The Lincoln administration endorsed the contraband policy as a shrewd war tactic likely to cause havoc in the South. Self-emancipating slaves continued to arrive at Union Army camps in ever-growing numbers, totaling close to one million by the war's end (see *Images as History: Who Freed the Slaves?*).

In response to these events, Congress slowly began the process of dismantling slavery. In August 1861, the First Confiscation Act declared free any slaves used in the Confederate war effort. A Second Confiscation Act in July 1862 empowered the army to seize and render "forever free" the slaves of anyone aiding the Confederacy. That same month Congress authorized the president to let African Americans fight in the Union Army. These measures demonstrated a growing understanding among Northerners that winning the war required the abolition of slavery.

The threat to slavery posed by these actions was not lost on Southerners, who feared not only the loss of their slaves but also a large-scale slave insurrection. Slave escapes, rumors of slave revolts, and the increased insubordination of many slaves led to rising anxiety among Southerners. They accordingly stepped up slave patrols and scrutinized slave behavior for any sign of ill intent.

Lincoln gradually came to see emancipation not merely as inevitable but as essential for Union victory, since it would "strike at the heart of the rebellion" and prevent British intervention. On July 22, 1862, he informed the cabinet of his intent to issue a decree of emancipation. But to avoid the appearance of acting in desperation, Lincoln waited for a Union victory before issuing this decree.

The Union victory came two months later in mid-September at the Battle of Antietam, in Maryland. Lee, choosing to wage a bold offensive, led his army north into Maryland. McClellan, even after acquiring a copy of the Confederate battle plan, reacted slowly, allowing Lee to consolidate his troops. Finally, on September 17, 1862, McClellan attacked Lee's army. After squandering several chances to defeat Lee, McClellan's forces were eventually stymied by the last-minute arrival of Confederate reinforcements. The next day,

How did Lincoln expect the Emancipation Proclamation to benefit the Union war effort?

View the **Closer Look** *Lincoln visits McClellan*

Images as History
WHO FREED THE SLAVES?

Why did Abraham Lincoln decide to issue the Emancipation Proclamation in 1862, after stating many, many times that he had no intention of abolishing slavery? There were several reasons, not the least of which was that one year into the war the Confederacy seemed as strong as ever. Lincoln decided that attacking slavery would hasten the end of the war. But there is another, often overlooked reason for Lincoln to change and decide to embrace abolition: From the moment the war began, thousands of slaves began to flee to freedom, often to the camps of Union soldiers. This wave of self-emancipation, vividly captured in this 1867 painting by Theodor Kaufmann, "*On to Liberty*," forced the Lincoln administration to formulate wartime policies regarding slavery, a process that ultimately led to emancipation.

But even as Kaufmann and others celebrated African Americans' role in their own liberation, white Americans after the war began to present a different—and inaccurate—version of the story (see Chapter 14). Former slaves raised most of the money to pay for the Freedmen's Memorial that was unveiled in 1876 in Washington, D.C. But they were excluded from the committee in charge of the monument's design. As a result, the monument celebrated President Lincoln as the sole individual responsible for emancipation while depicting African Americans as passive figures who played no role at all in gaining their freedom.

Unlike most images of African Americans in this period, Kaufmann portrays these women as dignified and courageous agents pursuing freedom for their families.

Kaufmann contrasts the darkness of slavery, which the escapees are fleeing, with the bright light of freedom they are moving toward.

This smoke is emanating from a battle between Union and Confederate armies. Long before the Emancipation Proclamation, slaves came to believe that the Union Army somehow represented their liberation. So they headed to Union lines, despite the danger.

By presenting Lincoln as standing over the kneeling slave, the sculptor emphasizes his—and by extension all white people's—superiority over African Americans. Note how there are no white people in Kaufmann's scene of liberation.

These two children are reluctant to keep moving ahead, probably because of the gunfire from the battle in the distance.

The chained slave kneels in a submissive, passive position that suggests that African Americans were merely *receiving* freedom, rather than playing a key role in *seizing* it by self-emancipating on a mass scale as depicted in Kaufmann's painting.

Holding the Emancipation Proclamation in his right hand, while outstretching his left, Lincoln appears like a biblical prophet, or even like Christ, bestowing a blessing upon a sinner.

How did the actions of slaves push Lincoln toward emancipation?

McClellan chose not to attack, despite superior numbers and the shattered condition of Lee's army. The following day Lee led his army back into Virginia, handing McClellan a technical victory (a frustrated Lincoln, however, soon removed him from command). The battle, as indicated by the grim scene (**13.10**) of its aftermath captured by photographer Alexander Gardner, claimed 6,000 lives and left 17,000 wounded, making it the deadliest single day of the war.

Shortly after Antietam in September 1862, Lincoln issued his preliminary **Emancipation Proclamation**. Unless the seceded states and parts thereof that were not under Union Army control returned to the Union by January 1, 1863, the decree warned, their slaves "shall be then, thenceforward, and forever free." Even though the decree left slavery intact in the Border States and areas held by the Union Army, Lincoln knew conservatives, Northern Democrats, and Border State Unionists would react negatively and that Republicans might suffer at the polls that November. Still, he reasoned, the benefits of emancipation far outweighed the risks as it would cause chaos by encouraging slaves to flee their masters and make it highly unlikely that Britain, where anti-slavery sentiment was strong, would intervene in the conflict.

Though some radicals and abolitionists expressed dismay because the proclamation freed slaves only in the seceded states, they recognized that Lincoln's simple, terse statement of military policy had transformed the meaning of the conflict. If Northerners by late 1862 realized the war was no mere "insurrection," they also understood that its goal was something greater than simply a restored Union. It was now a war of subjugation. Reunion would occur only after the fabric of Southern society was destroyed.

Slaughter and Stalemate

Restoring the Union and abolishing slavery, of course, depended entirely on victory in the field. But the Army of the Potomac, now commanded by General Ambrose E. Burnside, suffered a devastating defeat at the Battle of Fredericksburg on December 13, 1862. Burnside tried one more offensive on January 22, 1863, a disastrous mid-winter effort that became mired in muddy, impassible roads. A despondent Lincoln replaced Burnside with General Joseph Hooker.

Not all the news from the Union battlefields in late 1862 was negative. On December 31 Union troops under General William S. Rosecrans turned back an attempt by Confederate General Braxton Bragg to regain western Tennessee and Kentucky in the Battle of Murfreesboro. Bragg's retreat left the West firmly in the hands of the Union Army for the rest of the war.

Lee and his Army of Northern Virginia, however, continued to thwart the Union effort to take Richmond. In the Battle of Chancellorsville, April 30–May 6, 1863, despite commanding a force half the size of Hooker's, Lee scored a smashing victory. But it came at a price: Stonewall Jackson, the man Lee had come to count on most, was killed accidentally by his own men.

13.10 Dead Soldiers along the Sunken Road, Antietam (1862) The Civil War was the first military conflict in American history captured by the relatively new medium of photography. Photographs such as this one taken by Alexander Gardner after the Battle of Antietam, brought home to millions of Americans the brutality of modern war.

Why did photography have a more powerful impact on the public than artists' depictions of battles?

View the **Closer Look** *Images as History: Photography and the Visualization of Modern War*

Behind the Lines

The war brought challenges and hardships to the Union and Confederate home fronts. Civilians faced shortages of goods, soaring inflation, and conscription. These conditions were more severe in the South where many civilians also came under Union military rule. These problems, coupled with mounting death tolls, led to sagging morale and rising criticism of political leaders in both regions. Occasionally discontent exploded into violent riots. The war placed an especially great demand on women, who assumed new occupational and civic roles.

Meeting the Demands of Modern War

While war raged in the East and West, Republicans took advantage of their dominant position in Congress to enact legislation long opposed by Southerners. Most were policies to promote industrialization (a high tariff) and westward settlement (the Homestead and Pacific Railway Acts). Several laws, however, were part of an unprecedented effort to outfit and finance a modern army. The National Bank Acts of 1863 and 1864 established a national banking system whereby member banks could issue treasury notes, or "greenbacks," as currency. The nation's first income tax, the sale of $400 million in bonds to the public, and the borrowing of $2.6 billion from banks helped pay for the war. The cost of the war increased the federal budget twenty-fold during the war, from $63 million in 1861 to $1.3 billion in 1865. All told, the war effort greatly expanded the size and scope of the federal government.

In contrast to the Union's ability to sustain the war effort, Davis and other Confederate leaders soon discovered that there were limits to Southerners' willingness to adapt to the demands of modern warfare. In response to the need for more soldiers and revenue, the Confederate Congress established a military draft and an income tax in April 1862. Officials across the Confederacy denounced the measures as gross violations of states' rights. Among the loudest protestors was Alexander Stephens, Davis's own vice president. Southerners evaded both the draft and income tax to such an extent that neither measure produced the needed men or money. Draft and tax evasion also occurred on a large scale in the North, to be sure, but greater supplies of men and money diminished their impact.

These limits were compounded by President Davis. Despite his extensive political and military experience, he proved an ineffective leader for a time of crisis. Unlike Lincoln, he selected a weak cabinet to prevent challenges to his authority and bristled at the slightest disagreement. He also micromanaged the War Department, firing or driving to resignation five secretaries of war in four years. The Confederate Army's success in the war's first two years obscured Davis's flaws, but as the Army's fortunes declined after 1862, the president's leadership style sparked rancor and disunity.

Hardships on the Home Front

While soldiers fought in the field, civilians in the North and South faced a number of hardships. In the North the arms, metalworking, boot making, and shipbuilding industries boomed, but the scarcity of cotton caused widespread layoffs and closures in the textile industry. Workers' wages rose by 40 percent, but prices rose even faster as inflation averaged 15 percent annually. In response many workers formed and joined craft unions, but appeals to patriotism and the use of strikebreakers discouraged strikes.

Southerners faced far worse economic problems. The Southern economy was hard-hit by the cessation of trade with the North and Europe due to the Union blockade. Southern industry and agriculture were hindered by chronic labor shortages due to military service and by the flight of slaves, and the destruction or seizure of farms and factories by Union armies. As a result, the production of goods and agricultural produce in the South decreased by 30 percent during the war. By contrast Northern output increased significantly. These conditions led to shortages of nearly everything in the South,

How did the Union fund the war?

including food, and the emergence of a thriving black market. The cartoon (**13.11**) from a Richmond newspaper captured the anger among Southerners directed at speculators and black marketers. A cold-hearted speculator counts his profits as a hungry mother and child look through his window. "Anathema on him who screws and hoards / who robs the poor of wheat, potatoes, and bread," read the first two lines of the accompanying poem.

New Roles for Women

The war changed the lives of millions of women who remained behind the lines in both the North and South. With hundreds of thousands of men gone to war, women assumed new roles running farms and shops and working in factories and offices. Many did so out of a sense of duty to the war effort, whereas others worked to earn badly needed income, as military pay was low and inflation pushed up the cost of living.

The war also enabled women to enter previously male-dominated professions such as teaching, civil service, and nursing. In nursing, the shortage of men and the recruitment efforts by women like Dorothea Dix, head of the U.S. Sanitary Commission, led to thousands of women volunteering to serve as nurses in field hospitals despite opposition from male doctors and others who disapproved of women working in such indelicate situations. Supporters argued that women brought to the profession nurturing and domestic skills. As Clara Barton, Civil War nurse and future founder of the American Red Cross, put it, at the end of the war, the American woman "was at least fifty years in advance of the normal position which continued peace would have assigned her." Over the next 30 years women took over almost completely the profession of nursing. Many women also joined organizations that actively supported the Union cause, such as the Women's Central Association of Relief, whose 7,000 chapters across the North raised money and sent supplies to the soldiers in the field.

Southern women experienced similar changes during the war. They took on new responsibilities such as running farms and plantations, managing stores, working in government, and serving as nurses. Many worked in factories, including more than 500 employed by the Confederate Ordnance Department to fill cartridges, dangerous work that killed dozens in explosions. Their jobs grew more demanding as the war demolished the Southern economy and sent food prices soaring. The Union Army's sweep across the South in late 1864 and early 1865 left many Southern women and their children destitute and hungry.

13.11 Anger on the Home Front Runaway inflation and scarcity of necessities sparked angry accusations that speculators were hoarding supplies and selling them at extortionate prices. Here a speculator counts his profits while a starving mother and child look on.

What new opportunities did the war open up for women?

View the **Closer Look** *Nurse Ann Bell Tending to Wounded…*
Read the **Document** *Memoirs of Clara Barton*

> "You have given your boys to die for their country, now you can give your girls to nurse them."
>
> MARY STINEBAUGH-BRADFORD, convincing her father to let her care for Union soldiers

Many Southern women also faced the challenge of maintaining the slave labor system, an increasingly difficult task as thousands of slaves fled to Union lines, leaving farms and plantations with inadequate labor. Many slaves who did not flee took advantage of a planter's absence and challenged the authority of women unaccustomed to the role of master. As one exasperated wife wrote to her husband, "The Negroes are all expecting to be set free very soon and it causes them to be very troublesome."

Copperheads

One group that benefitted from the hard times in the North was the Democratic Party. Even though many Northerners associated it with secession and the Confederacy, it remained a viable political power in the North during the war. After all, it had received 44 percent of the popular vote there in 1860. Many Democrats supported the war against secession, but **Copperheads** (or "peace Democrats") argued for a cease-fire, followed by a negotiated peace settlement even if it resulted in an independent Confederacy. A few Copperheads even expressed support for the Confederacy.

Lincoln viewed the opposition of Copperheads to the Union war effort as seditious, if not treasonous, and took steps early to squelch it. After the pro-Confederate rioting in Baltimore in 1861, he suspended habeas corpus, citing the section of the Constitution providing "the privilege of the writ of habeas corpus shall not be suspended, unless when, in cases of rebellion or invasion, the public safety may require it." In so doing, Lincoln established a principle he followed for the rest of the war. To save the Union and the Constitution, he would not hesitate to suppress Constitutional guarantees of free speech and the right to a speedy trial. Over the next few years, thousands of Copperheads were jailed for lengthy periods without trial. Copperheads initially attracted few followers, but dissatisfaction with the war rose in the winter of 1862–1863 after repeated Union Army failures and the enactment of the controversial Emancipation Proclamation and military draft. Led by former Ohio Congressman Clement Vallandigham, Copperheads denounced Lincoln as a tyrant who abused his power and suppressed free speech by shutting down opposition newspapers and arresting people who voiced hostility toward the Union war effort or sympathy for the Confederacy. Copperheads gained support among farmers in the West by claiming the new Republican tariff hurt them economically and among urban workers and immigrants by stoking racial fears that emancipation would lead to social chaos and job competition.

To counter rising Copperhead sentiment, pro-Union speakers, editors, and cartoonists vilified Copperheads as dangerous, disloyal men who threatened the Union. In February 1863, *Harper's Weekly* printed the cartoon shown in *Competing Visions: Civil Liberties in a Civil War* (see page 390). The cartoonist shows the goddess Liberty, who is bearing a shield labeled "Constitution" and a drawn sword, being prevented from engaging in battle against the Confederacy by three peace Democrats depicted as copperhead snakes. To squelch Copperhead activism, the Lincoln administration stepped up arrests. On May 5, 1863, a Union Army commander in Ohio arrested Vallandigham after he delivered a speech denouncing the war and the draft.

Conscription and Civil Unrest

Despite the Lincoln administration's crackdown on Copperhead dissent, opposition to the war among Northerners increased in 1863, especially among those expected to fight. The poor performance of the Union Army in the field, coupled with staggering numbers of killed and wounded, extinguished much of the early enthusiasm for war. Despite offers of cash bonuses and time off in exchange for reenlistment, Union soldiers were heading home as their enlistment terms expired, and recruitment offices now went begging for new recruits.

To solve the manpower problem, in March 1863, Congress passed the **Conscription Act**, which declared all male citizens (and immigrants who had applied for citizenship) aged 20–45 eligible for draft into the army. Each state was assigned a quota of men. If drafted a man could avoid service. He could buy his way out by paying a "commutation fee" of

Competing Visions
CIVIL LIBERTIES IN A CIVIL WAR

The following opinions present opposing views on the constitutionality of Lincoln's policy toward Copperheads. One is a series of resolutions adopted and sent to Lincoln by Democrats. The other is Lincoln's formal response. Note what the parties define as the greatest threat to civil liberties and the Constitution. Were Lincoln's actions justified? Are principles such as civil liberties subject to different treatment during a national crisis such as war?

On May 19, 1863, a meeting of Democrats, including former Congressman Erastus Corning, in Albany, New York, passed and delivered to Lincoln a series of resolutions accusing the administration of having acted unconstitutionally in placing military authority over civil authority.

… Resolved, … we denounce the recent assumption of a military commander to seize and try a citizen of Ohio, Clement L. Vallandigham, for no other reason than words addressed to a public meeting, in criticism of the course of the administration, and in condemnation of the military orders of that general.

Resolved, That this assumption of power by a military tribunal, if successfully asserted, not only abrogates the right of the people to assemble and discuss the affairs of government, the liberty of speech and of the press, the right of trial by jury, the law of evidence, and the privilege of habeas corpus, but it strikes a fatal blow at the supremacy of law, and the authority of the State and federal constitutions.

Resolved, … That, regarding the blow struck at a citizen of Ohio as aimed at the rights of every citizen of the north, we denounce it as against the spirit of our laws and Constitution, and most earnestly call upon the President of the United States to reverse the action of the military tribunal which has passed a "cruel and unusual punishment" upon the party arrested, prohibited in terms by the Constitution, and to restore him to the liberty of which he has been deprived.

On June 12, 1863, Lincoln defended his actions as both constitutional and necessary for the preservation of the Union.

GENTLEMEN: …Ours is a clear, flagrant, and gigantic case of rebellion; and the provision of the Constitution that "the privilege of the writ of habeas corpus shall not be suspended, unless when, in cases of rebellion or invasion, the public safety may require it," is the provision which specially applies to our present case….

… Mr. Vallandigham avows his hostility to the war on the part of the Union; and his arrest was made because he was laboring, with some effect, to prevent the raising of troops; to encourage desertions from the army; and to leave the rebellion without an adequate military force to suppress it. He was not arrested because he was damaging the political prospects of the administration, or the personal interests of the commanding general, but because he was damaging the army, upon the existence and vigor of which the life of the nation depends. He was warring upon the military, and this gave the military constitutional jurisdiction to lay hands upon him.

Long experience has shown that armies cannot be maintained unless desertion shall be punished by the severe penalty of death…. Must I shoot a simple-minded soldier boy who deserts, while I must not touch a hair of a wily agitator who induces him to desert? … I think that in such a case, to silence the agitator and save the boy is not only constitutional, but withal a great mercy.

I … [am un]able to appreciate the danger apprehended by the meeting [in Albany] that the American people will, by means of military arrests during the rebellion, lose the right of public discussion, the liberty of speech and the press, the law of evidence, trial by jury, and habeas corpus, throughout the indefinite peaceful future, … any more than I am able to believe that a man could contract so strong an appetite for emetics during temporary illness as to persist in feeding upon them during the remainder of his healthful life.

Northern Unionists depicted Copperheads as traitors who threatened the Republic. Here Liberty defends herself from the Copperheads with the shield of Union.

How did Lincoln justify the suspension of habeas corpus?

$300 to the government or hire a substitute to serve in his place. Men lacking such substantial sums of money ($300 was equivalent to a year's pay for a common laborer) could simply disappear—which more than 20 percent of draftees did.

The draft began in early July and touched off widespread protest. Disturbances broke out in Boston; Troy, New York; Wooster, Ohio; Portsmouth, New Hampshire; and other cities. Opposition to the draft was greatest in New York City, where on July 13, 1863, it erupted in unprecedented violence known as the **Draft Riots**. For four days mobs of mostly poor, immigrant, and working-class rioters attacked draft offices, Union Army recruiting stations, institutions associated with the Republican Party or abolition, and symbols of wealth and privilege, reflecting animosity toward the inequity that allowed the rich to pay a $300 fee to avoid the draft. Rioters also attacked African Americans. As the image (**13.12**) illustrates, they lynched at least eighteen. Rioters blamed blacks as the cause of the war and feared them as potential labor competition.

The riots resulted in at least 119 deaths and $5 million in property damage. Officials eventually defused opposition to the draft by raising money to pay the $300 commutation fee or hire substitutes for draftees not willing to join the army and allowing

easy exemptions for reasons of health or family considerations.

Discontent and unrest also rocked the Confederate home front. In October 1862, the Confederate Congress passed what came to be known as the "Twenty Negro Law." It exempted from the draft one white man per plantation that held 20 or more slaves. Supporters argued that the measure was vital to maintaining order and productivity on plantations, but to poor white Southerners it engendered levels of anger and protest similar to those evoked by the commutation provisions in the North. Many cited the law as the reason they deserted from the Confederate Army.

Another source of discontent was the shortage of food brought about by drought, the blockade, and Union conquest of Southern territory. When shortages and high prices reached critical proportions in 1863, Southern women led food riots in several towns and cities, including most dramatically in Richmond. "Bread! Bread!" they cried, "Our children are starving while the rich roll in wealth!" The reference to the rich reflected the widespread belief that Confederate leaders and merchants were profiting from the war.

13.12 Opposition to the Draft Turns Violent Poor New Yorkers rioted against the draft in July 1863, venting their anger on army recruiting stations and against African Americans, whom they blamed for the war.

Read the **Document** *Testimony from Victims of New York's Draft Riots, July 1863*

Why did New Yorkers riot against the draft?

Toward Union Victory

Despite many setbacks, by mid-1863, the North's superior industrial strength, large population, and improved military leadership gave the Union the advantage. So, too, did the decision to allow African Americans to serve in the army, for they provided the Union with badly needed manpower when enlistments were declining. Victories at Gettysburg, Vicksburg, and Atlanta boosted morale in the North and led to Lincoln's reelection in 1864. Relentless military offensives by Grant in Virginia and William T. Sherman in Georgia led to the Confederate surrender in April 1865. The assassination of President Lincoln, however, dampened the North's joy.

Turning Point: 1863

Although the destruction and antiwar sentiment in New York City shocked Lincoln, events elsewhere in 1863 gave him hope. Back in May, Lee had convinced Davis to approve another invasion of the North. It was risky, but they believed it might force Lincoln to pull troops out of the western theater where Grant was threatening to seize the entire lower Mississippi. A victory on Northern soil would also demoralize the Lincoln administration and strengthen the Copperheads and Peace Democrats who were calling for a negotiated settlement. It might even convince France or Britain to intervene.

In June, Lee headed north through Virginia's Shenandoah Valley into Maryland and Pennsylvania. Although slow to react, the Army of the Potomac, now under General George G. Meade, eventually caught up with Lee in central Pennsylvania. On July 1, the two armies collided at Gettysburg, a small town at the junction of several major roads. Although outnumbered 90,000 to 75,000, the Confederates made significant advances that day. The following day the battle's momentum swung back and forth before Union forces pushed the Confederates back to the previous day's position. On the third and decisive day, Lee recklessly ordered an all-out assault on the fortified Union center. "Pickett's Charge," as it became known, proved gallant, but suicidal. Union forces devastated General George Pickett's 12,000 men as they tried to cross a mile of open field and ascend Cemetery Ridge. "Picket's division just seemed to melt away," recalled one witness. "Nothing but stragglers came back." With 23,000 Union and 28,000 Confederate soldiers killed and wounded, Gettysburg was by far the bloodiest battle of the war.

The next day, July 4, having lost one-third of his men, Lee retreated back toward Virginia. Although frustrated that Meade failed to pursue, Lincoln nonetheless recognized that the Union had won a major victory. Gettysburg marked the last time the Confederate Army invaded the North.

That same day Lincoln received news of a vital victory in the West. In May Grant had begun a siege of Vicksburg, the Confederacy's last stronghold on the Mississippi River. It fell on July 4, severing the Confederacy in two and giving the Union control over the entire Mississippi.

African Americans under Arms

But the Union Army was still far from ultimate victory. One of the most formidable challenges it faced was finding new recruits. Declining enlistments of whites, and lobbying by black leaders and abolitionists eventually convinced Union officials to form African American regiments. Thousands of free African American men already toiled for the Union Army, moving supplies and building fortifications; now they would have the chance to fight to defeat the Confederacy and end slavery.

One of the first and the most famous of all the African American regiments was the 54th Massachusetts, organized in 1863 by leading black abolitionists. "I urge you to fly to arms and smite with death the power that would bury the government and your liberty in the same hopeless grave," read a recruitment pamphlet written by Frederick Douglass. Among the regiment's members were two of Douglass's sons, Lewis and Charles, and the grandson of Sojourner Truth, James Caldwell. Colonel Robert Gould Shaw, son of a leading white Massachusetts abolitionist family, commanded the regiment.

Why did Lee decide to invade the North a second time?   **Read** the **Document** *Abraham Lincoln, "Gettysburg Address" (1863)*

African American soldiers experienced many forms of racism within the Union Army. They served in strictly segregated units under white officers and, as this drawing (**13.13**) indicates, initially served mainly in noncombat duty as guards and laborers. Many also charged that they received substandard medical care compared to white soldiers. Most galling, as seen in *Choices and Consequences: Equal Peril, Unequal Pay* (page 394), was that African American soldiers received lower pay than white soldiers.

African American soldiers also faced brutal treatment at the hands of Confederates when captured. The Davis administration announced that African American soldiers taken prisoner would be subject to execution as rebellious slaves. Lincoln's threat of retaliation prevented the Confederacy from carrying out this policy on a wide scale, but African Americans were murdered, tortured, and mutilated. In the most egregious incident (**13.14** on page 395), the Fort Pillow Massacre in Tennessee, Confederate troops murdered dozens of captured black soldiers

in April 1864. This image, which ran in a popular Northern magazine, depicted Confederates as brutal and inhumane. Southern publications ran similar images that alleged Northern atrocities.

The creation of all-black units in the Union Army raised another critical issue beyond the question of equality of pay or the assignment of white officers to lead them. Would these units be sent into actual combat? Racist notions led whites to question whether African Americans possessed the courage to fight. Others cautioned that if black

13.13 Held Back by Racism
Believing African Americans lacked the courage to fight under fire, Union commanders initially relegated them to noncombat roles. Eventually, however, blacks fought in 449 battles, including the Battle of Milliken's Bend on June 7, 1863 (center).

"We … have dyed the ground with blood, in defense of the Union, and Democracy. … We have done a Soldier's Duty. Why can't we have a Soldier's pay?"

Letter of CORPORAL JAMES HENRY GOODING of 54th Massachusetts to President Lincoln, September 1863

How were African American soldiers treated in the Union Army?

Choices and Consequences

EQUAL PERIL, UNEQUAL PAY

At first, the War Department planned to pay African American soldiers the same $13 per month (plus $3.50 for clothes) as white soldiers. Indeed, as the recruitment poster below shows, many early black recruits received equal pay. But in June 1863, the Lincoln administration, fearing a backlash among white soldiers who did not see African Americans as their equals, adopted a two-tier wage scale that paid black soldiers just $7 per month (plus $3 for clothes). Outraged, African American officers and enlisted men of the 54th and 55th Massachusetts (Colored) Infantry pondered their options.

Choices

1 Quietly accept the lower wages as a regrettable but unavoidable trade-off that allowed them to enlist in the Union Army and fight to end slavery.

2 Accept the unequal wages as better than nothing and necessary to maintain their families, while protesting the injustice and lobbying for equal pay.

3 Reject the lower wages on principle, despite the financial hardship on their families, while fulfilling their duties as soldiers, protesting the injustice, and lobbying for equal pay.

4 Lay down their arms and refuse to obey orders until they received equal pay.

Decision

The men chose the third option, rejecting the lower wages on principle, despite the financial hardship on their families. They even rejected an offer by the governor of Massachusetts to pay the $6 per month difference out of the state treasury, citing the principle of equality that was at stake. Meanwhile they fulfilled their duties as soldiers, protested the injustice, and lobbied the Lincoln administration for equal pay.

Consequences

The soldiers and their families hung on for more than a year until Congress in June 1864 authorized an equal pay scale for all soldiers regardless of race. By then, given the well-documented professionalism and courage exhibited by black soldiers on the battlefield, the distinction in pay had become an embarrassment to Lincoln's administration. Not all black regiments, however, made the same decision as the Massachusetts 54th and 55th, and the consequences of their actions were starkly different. Sergeant William Walker of the 21st U.S. Colored Infantry had his men lay down their arms in protest over unequal pay. He was convicted of mutiny and executed.

Continuing Controversies

How were African Americans in the military treated after the Civil War?
The U.S. army eradicated the two-tier pay scale, but not racial segregation. African American leaders protested segregation, but for all subsequent wars through World War II, black soldiers and sailors served in segregated units under mostly white officers. President Harry Truman ordered the military desegregated in 1948.

What role did African American soldiers play in the Union war effort?

Read the **Document** *James Henry Gooding, "Letter to President Lincoln" (1863)*

regiments were not used judiciously, critics would accuse the army of racism, asserting it carelessly sent them into harm's way.

The first well-publicized test of African American soldiers came on July 18, 1863, when the 54th Massachusetts led a nighttime assault on Fort Wagner, a key Confederate outpost that guarded Charleston harbor. The Confederates repulsed their attack. But the courage exhibited by the soldiers—the unit lost 100 dead and 146 were wounded—won them universal praise and undermined the racist belief that blacks would not fight.

All told 198,000 blacks, including 144,000 former slaves, served in the Union Army and Navy. This number amounted to 10 percent of the total enlisted men even though African Americans comprised only 1 percent of the Northern population. African American soldiers participated in over 449 separate engagements against Confederate troops and 38,000 died during the war. Sixteen black soldiers and four black sailors received the Medal of Honor. "The colored soldiers in this four years' struggle," wrote one African American soldier, "have proven themselves in every respect to be men." Their contribution to the Union war effort proved vital to winning the war.

Most significant, African American service in the war empowered them to claim full citizenship after the war. "Once let the black man get upon his person the brass letters, U.S., let him get an eagle on his button and a musket on his shoulder and bullets in his pocket," said Frederick Douglass, "there is no power on earth that can deny that he has earned the right to citizenship."

The Confederacy Begins to Crumble

News of the losses at Gettysburg and Vicksburg caused dismay across the South. Moreover, Davis and the Confederate leadership had other reasons to worry. The immediate problem was a lack of men. A draft instituted in April 1862 failed to attract enough recruits. Protests by poor whites forced the revision in 1863 of a provision in the draft law that exempted wealthy whites who held 20 or more slaves, but still new recruits fell short of the number needed. The continued loss of territory to the Union Army exacerbated this trend, as did a sharp rise in desertions, which topped 100,000 by late 1864. (See *Envisioning Evidence: Human Resources in the Armies of the Civil War.*)

13.14 The Massacre at Fort Pillow In April 1864, Confederate soldiers slaughtered dozens of captured African American soldiers at Fort Pillow in Tennessee.

Why did Lincoln initially agree to pay African American soldiers less than white soldiers?

Envisioning Evidence
HUMAN RESOURCES IN THE ARMIES OF THE CIVIL WAR

At the outset of the Civil War the Union possessed roughly two and a half times the population of the Confederacy (23 million vs. 9 million). This advantage translated into an immediate and lasting military advantage, as it allowed the Union to field a much larger army and navy throughout the course of the war. Indeed, as the data below shows, this manpower advantage increased over the course of the four-year conflict, in part because of the Lincoln administration's decision to allow African Americans to serve in the military (and the Confederacy's resistance to this idea until the last weeks of the war). The Union also enjoyed a much larger and steadily increasing population of immigrants from which to draw fresh recruits. Had the war lasted two or three years, these differences in manpower might not have had played such an important role in determining its outcome. But it lasted four years and it was in the last one that the manpower disparity became most pronounced and significant in determining the final outcome.

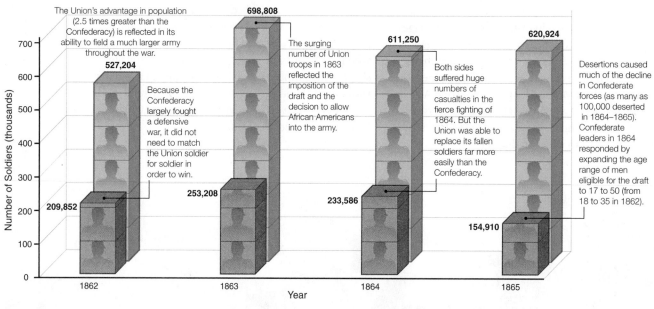

Relative Military Strength, 1862–1865

The Union's advantage in population (2.5 times greater than the Confederacy) is reflected in its ability to field a much larger army throughout the war.

Because the Confederacy largely fought a defensive war, it did not need to match the Union soldier for soldier in order to win.

The surging number of Union troops in 1863 reflected the imposition of the draft and the decision to allow African Americans into the army.

Both sides suffered huge numbers of casualties in the fierce fighting of 1864. But the Union was able to replace its fallen soldiers far more easily than the Confederacy.

Desertions caused much of the decline in Confederate forces (as many as 100,000 deserted in 1864–1865). Confederate leaders in 1864 responded by expanding the age range of men eligible for the draft to 17 to 50 (from 18 to 35 in 1862).

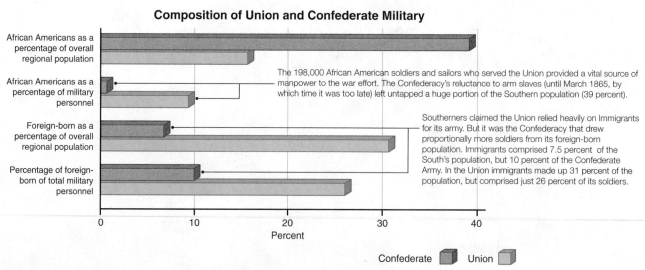

Composition of Union and Confederate Military

The 198,000 African American soldiers and sailors who served the Union provided a vital source of manpower to the war effort. The Confederacy's reluctance to arm slaves (until March 1865, by which time it was too late) left untapped a huge portion of the Southern population (39 percent).

Southerners claimed the Union relied heavily on immigrants for its army. But it was the Confederacy that drew proportionally more soldiers from its foreign-born population. Immigrants comprised 7.5 percent of the South's population, but 10 percent of the Confederate Army. In the Union immigrants made up 31 percent of the population, but comprised just 26 percent of its soldiers.

Sources: James McPherson, Ordeal by Fire *(New York: Knopf, 1982)*; James McPherson, Battle Cry of Freedom *(New York: Oxford University Press, 1988)*; U.S. Census, Historical Statistics.

How did the Union's 2:1 advantage over the Confederacy in overall population play a role in winning the war?

By mid-1863, the inherent weaknesses of the Confederate economy began to show. The Union blockade, which had stopped only one in eight Confederate ships in 1862, grew increasingly effective. By 1864, it stopped one out of every three Confederate blockade-runners and half of them by 1865. The impact on the import-dependent Southern economy was devastating. Civilians and soldiers alike suffered shortages of food, clothing, and equipment.

The growing success of the Union blockade also exposed a critical miscalculation made by the Davis administration in 1861. The embargo on cotton exports failed because Britain possessed a surplus of cotton in 1861 and later found alternative sources in Egypt and India. Moreover, English workers, including an estimated half million who lost their jobs due to cotton shortages, expressed strong sympathy for the Union and thereby made British intervention on behalf of the Confederacy politically controversial. When the South finally lifted the embargo in 1862, the Union blockade was much stronger.

The Confederacy's economic dilemma posed a serious threat to its chances for success. It desperately needed hard currency to buy ships, weapons, ammunition, and other supplies for the war. But the main product it had to sell—cotton—was bottled up in Southern ports, unable to reach markets in Europe. This conundrum is captured in the image (**13.15**) that adorned "cotton bonds" authorized for sale by the Confederacy in Europe. A Southern version of "Columbia" holds the Confederate flag and leans on cotton bales while looking out to sea at a patrolling Union ship. In exchange for cash (usually 90 percent of face value), investors were promised payment in Southern cotton with interest. The plan brought in

> **"The state of despondency that now prevails among our people is producing a bad effect upon the troops. Desertions are becoming very frequent."**
>
> ROBERT E. LEE, February 24, 1865

only $7 million to the Confederate treasury, far less than needed. The Emancipation Proclamation also shook Southern society, as Lincoln had hoped it would. Inspired by word that freedom was at hand, thousands of slaves left their places of bondage and headed for the Union Army or to the Northern states, exacerbating the Confederacy's labor shortage and further weakening Southern agriculture.

Despite these hardships, the Confederacy remained undefeated and the longer Confederates defended their independence, the greater their chances of success. For even as the Union won major victories at Gettysburg and Vicksburg, discontent and war weariness among Northerners grew. If Lincoln hoped to preserve the Union, he needed more military victories—and soon.

Victory in Battle and at the Polls

The key to winning the war, Lincoln realized, was effective military leadership. After suffering many disappointments and near disasters with a succession of poor generals, Lincoln finally found his man

13.15 Cotton for Sale?
A Confederate version of "Columbia" (a precursor to Lady Liberty) leans on cotton bales that cannot reach European markets due to the Union blockade represented by the ship passing on the horizon. This image was featured on "cotton bonds" sold in Europe to raise cash for the Confederacy.

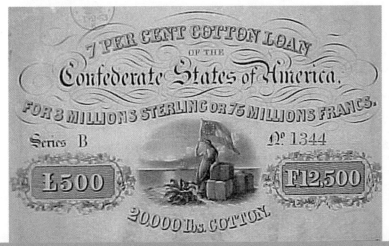

Read the **Document** *The Working Men of Manchester, England Write to President Lincoln on the Question of Slavery in 1862*

How did the Union blockade affect the Confederate war effort?

in Ulysses S. Grant who at the end of 1863 delivered yet another badly needed victory for the Union at the Battle of Chattanooga.

On November 23, Grant and the general he increasingly counted on, William T. Sherman, drove Braxton Bragg's army from Tennessee into Georgia, putting most of eastern Tennessee and the vital Tennessee River under Union control. Already cut in two after the fall of Vicksburg, the Confederates now faced being sliced into thirds. Their main hope was that Northerner dissatisfaction with the war might lead to Lincoln's defeat in the election of 1864, or at least force him to accept peace negotiations.

In early 1864, Lincoln named Grant commander of all the Union armies. Many in the War Department objected, arguing that the rough-hewn soldier who had left the Army in disgrace in 1854 for heavy drinking was an alcoholic who could not be entrusted with a major assignment. But Lincoln had had enough of generals with impressive résumés and martial airs. He saw in Grant a commander who understood the key to victory in modern warfare—seek out and destroy the enemy's army and sources of supplies.

Pursuing this policy with single-minded determination, Grant in 1864 devised a two-pronged attack to finish off the Confederacy. As shown in the map (**13.16**), he sent the Army of the Potomac, now swollen to nearly 120,000, south to destroy Lee's army of 66,000 and take Richmond. In the West Grant sent General William T. Sherman, a man who shared his understanding of modern warfare, and an army of 90,000 east from Tennessee to destroy General Joseph E. Johnston's force of 60,000 and seize Atlanta (**13.17**).

The first clash of this campaign, the Battle of the Wilderness, began with Lee attacking Grant on May 5. Over the next two days, aided by the rough, wooded terrain and sluggish Union leadership, the Confederates survived the clash despite Grant's vastly superior numbers. The inconclusive battle

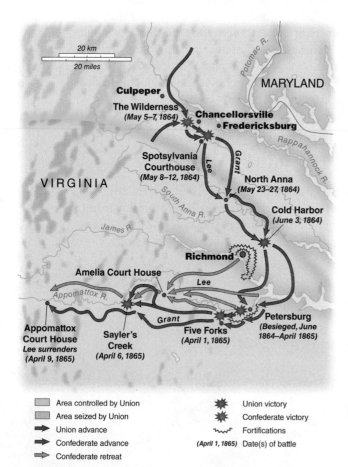

▨	Area controlled by Union	✹	Union victory
▨	Area seized by Union	✹	Confederate victory
➡	Union advance	∿	Fortifications
➡	Confederate advance	(April 1, 1865)	Date(s) of battle
➡	Confederate retreat		

13.16 The Final Battles in the Virginia Campaign, 1864–1865
Grant's strategy for defeating Lee was to combine superior strength and a relentless offensive. It resulted in high casualties, but eventually cornered Lee at Petersburg. Lee surrendered at nearby Appomattox Courthouse on April 9, 1865.

▨	Area controlled by Union	➡	Confederate retreat
▨	Area seized by Union	✹	Union victory
▨	Area controlled by Confederacy	(Dec 22, 1864)	Date(s) of battle
➡	Union advance		

13.17 Sherman's March to the Sea, 1864–1865
Sherman dealt a decisive blow to the Confederate cause by waging a scorched-earth campaign across Georgia, destroying vital supplies and weakening Southern morale.

What distinguished Grant's approach to war from his predecessors'?

View the **Map** Interactive Map: The Civil War Part II 1863–1865

left 18,000 federals and 10,000 Confederates killed, wounded, or missing. Normally after so great an engagement, Union commanders spent weeks, if not months, repairing their armies. But the next day Grant ordered his army to move against Lee. Possessing total confidence in his strategy, he also knew that, unlike Lee, he could replace his fallen soldiers. On May 8, the two armies clashed again, ten miles closer to Richmond in the Battle of Spotsylvania Court House, an epic struggle that left another 30,000 casualties between the two armies.

Still Grant remained resolute, driving the Union Army southward, trying to draw Lee out for a final, decisive battle. Lee maneuvered his army between Grant and Richmond, playing for time and avoiding total defeat. On June 3 at Cold Harbor, Grant again ordered a massive assault against Lee's smaller but heavily entrenched force. The result was the greatest loss of life since Fredericksburg. Many Northerners, appalled at the 55,000 Union casualties (to 30,000 Confederate) in a single month, questioned Grant's competence; others simply called him a butcher. Peace Democrats renewed their calls for an end to the conflict.

Altering his strategy, Grant marched his army south to seize the vital railroad junction at Petersburg and cut Richmond off from the rest of the Confederacy. But Lee managed to dig in around Petersburg just before Grant arrived. By now Grant recognized the futility of staging frontal assaults against entrenched troops and settled down for a siege. It was not the aggressive form of warfare he preferred, but the fall of Petersburg and Richmond seemed only a matter of time.

Rising popular dissatisfaction with the seemingly endless bloodshed in summer 1864, however, imperiled Lincoln's chances for reelection (Davis, was serving a six-year term). Democrats tried to capitalize on the dour mood by nominating former Union General George B. McClellan for president and calling for a cease-fire and peace conference. They also hoped McClellan's outspoken criticism of emancipation would draw votes from racist Northerners.

The Republican Party recognized its vulnerability (it had lost many seats in the 1862 congressional elections) and tried to broaden its appeal heading into the 1864 election. First, Republicans adopted the name Union

Party to attract pro-war Democrats. Second, they replaced Lincoln's vice president with Andrew Johnson of Tennessee, a pro-Union Democrat and the only Southern senator not to resign during the secession winter of 1861. Finally, as this campaign broadside (**13.18**) illustrates, Lincoln's campaign argued that a vote for McClellan was a vote for slavery and military defeat. While Lincoln shakes hands with an artisan (representing the "free labor" North), McClellan shakes hands with Jefferson Davis who stands beneath the flag of an independent Confederate nation with a slave auction taking place in the background. Behind Lincoln white and black children enjoy the benefits of freedom and education. As late as August 1864, however, Lincoln and many of his supporters expected to lose.

In September 1864, however, Lincoln received news that Sherman had captured Atlanta. This crushing blow all but doomed the Confederacy to collapse. It also boosted morale across the North and weakened the Democrats' peace strategy. Two months later Lincoln soundly defeated McClellan, winning every state except for Kentucky, New Jersey, and Delaware to garner 55 percent of the popular vote. Still his margin of victory—just ten percent—demonstrated just how essential military success was to political victory.

War Is Hell

Six weeks after Lincoln won reelection, Sherman began to march his army across Georgia (see 13.17) to deprive the Confederate Army of

13.18 Lincoln Promises Victory and Union Lincoln's 1864 presidential campaign suggested that while he stood for liberty, his opponent, Democrat George B. McClellan, would make peace with the Confederates and preserve slavery.

What steps did the Republican Party take to improve Lincoln's chances for victory in 1864?

badly needed supplies and to demoralize the Southern people. Simultaneously, General George H. Thomas all but destroyed the Confederate army under General John B. Hood at the Battle of Nashville (December 15–16, 1864). One week later, Sherman's army captured Savannah.

Known as **Sherman's March to the Sea**, the "scorched earth" campaign traversed 285 miles of Georgia. Sherman's soldiers lived off the land, taking what agricultural produce and livestock they needed and destroying the rest. They also destroyed Southern infrastructure, tearing up railroad tracks, burning bridges, and pulling down telegraph wires to impair the Confederacy's ability to move goods, soldiers, and information. Sherman's army also enticed thousands of slaves to flock to its camps. By the time it reached the coast, Sherman's campaign of destruction left the Confederate army bereft of a major source of supplies. More important, the campaign demonstrated the effectiveness of a tactic that would become central to modern warfare in the twentieth century: bringing the conflict to the civilian population to undermine its willingness to support the war. "We are not only fighting hostile armies," Sherman told his men, "but a hostile people, and we must make old and young,

13.19 Total War and Vengeance Fires set by retreating Confederates, freed slaves, and undisciplined members of Sherman's army left half of Columbia, South Carolina, in ruins.

rich and poor, feel the hand of war, as well as their organized armies."

Sherman compounded the horror felt by Georgians with his policy toward the state's freed slaves. After meeting with Secretary of War Edwin Stanton and 20 African American ministers to discuss the fate of the freed slaves, Sherman issued **Special Field Order No. 15**. This directive set aside more than 400,000 acres of seized Confederate land for distribution to former slaves in 40-acre plots. Congress soon followed with the Thirteenth Amendment, which abolished slavery everywhere in the United States (it would be ratified 11 months later).

With Georgia in ashes, the stage was set for the final phase of Grant's plan—crushing Lee's army between his and Sherman's forces. On February 1, Sherman left Savannah and headed north into South Carolina. He faced almost no opposition, a sign Southern resistance was disintegrating. As this photograph (**13.19**) indicates, fire destroyed more than half of Columbia, the capital of South Carolina. Evacuating Confederates and liberated slaves set some of the fires, but some were also started by Union soldiers motivated by vengeance against the state that for decades leading up to the war represented Southern nationalism and ultimately,

Why did Sherman destroy so much property in Georgia?

secession. Sherman's men kept moving north into North Carolina where the meager opposition provided by General Joseph E. Johnston's force slowed him only slightly.

As the situation grew critical for the Confederacy, its leaders tried desperate measures. Among them were secret peace negotiations held in February 1865 at Hampton Roads, Virginia, which failed: Union representatives insisted on unconditional surrender (with the suggested possibility of compensated emancipation), while their Southern counterparts demanded recognition of Confederate independence. Confederate officials also began drafting soldiers as young as 17 and as old as 50. The depth of Confederate desperation was revealed in March 1865 when the Confederate Congress authorized a draft of up to 300,000 slaves to serve as soldiers (only two regiments were raised and neither saw combat).

> "If slaves make good soldiers our whole theory of slavery is wrong."
>
> CONFEDERATE MAJOR GENERAL HOWELL COBB, Georgia

By now Grant's nearly nine-month-long siege of Lee's army at Petersburg began to take its toll. Cut off from supplies, Lee's men were starving. Thousands had deserted. On April 1 in the Battle of Five Forks, General Philip Sheridan's cavalry and a large force of infantry cut the only remaining railroad line into Petersburg. When Grant attacked all along the Confederate line the next day, he forced Lee to retreat from both Richmond and Petersburg. Lee's remaining hope was to slip his ragged army west and south to join forces with Johnston in North Carolina. To prevent this, Sheridan's cavalry headed them off at a small town named Appomattox Courthouse, Virginia. On April 8, Lee made one last attempt to break out, but failed. "There is nothing left for me to do," he sadly informed his officers, "and I would rather die a thousand deaths." The next day, April 9, 1865, Lee surrendered.

Lincoln had set a tone of reconciliation in his second inaugural address a month earlier, when he spoke "With malice toward none, with charity for all," of the need "to bind up the nation's wounds, to care for him who shall have borne the battle and for his widow and his orphan, to do all which may achieve and cherish a just and lasting peace among ourselves and with all nations." Accordingly, Grant gave generous terms. The 30,000 men in Lee's army were permitted to go home, providing they swore never again to take up arms against the federal government. Grant also ordered they be given three days' rations of food and stopped his men from firing their weapons in victory celebration.

Celebrations broke out across the North as people, weary of four years of war, reveled in both the victory and the peace. The exultation quickly changed to despair. On the night of April 14, just five days after Lee's surrender, Confederate sympathizer John Wilkes Booth shot Lincoln at close range as he watched a play at Ford's Theatre in Washington. Lincoln died early the following day. The tragedy elicited an outpouring of grief for the martyred president among Northerners and freed slaves in the South. After a somber funeral procession in Washington, a train carried Lincoln's body back to Springfield, Illinois, past some seven million people who lined the tracks.

Lincoln's counterpart Jefferson Davis, who had fled hoping to establish a new Confederate government in Texas, was captured on May 10 and cast in prison. As this image (13.20) shows, the popular anger over the war and Lincoln's assassination focused on Davis, with many Northerners demanding his execution for treason. Passions cooled, however, and Davis was released after two years without being tried.

After Lee's surrender, the war came to a rapid conclusion. On April 26, Sherman accepted Johnston's surrender in North Carolina. Others followed suit, with the last Confederate units laying down their arms on June 23. With that, the bloodiest war in American history, one that cost 618,000 lives, was over.

13.20 A Thirst for Vengeance After the war many Northerners called for Jefferson Davis and other high-ranking Confederates to be hanged as traitors.

Watch the **Video** *Video Lecture: The Meaning of the Civil War for Americans*

What conciliatory measures toward the Confederates did Grant adopt at Lee's surrender?

1861

First battle of Bull Run
Confederacy wins in a clash of inexperienced armies

Confederate diplomats removed from the British ship *Trent*
Nearly causes a war between the Union and Great Britain

1862

Gen. Grant captures Forts Henry and Donelson in Tennessee
Boosts Union morale and brings attention to Grant's military skill

Lee repulses McClellan's Peninsular Campaign
Exposes again the poor military leadership in the Union Army

1862

McClellan defeats Lee at Battle of Antietam
Victory allows Lincoln to issue the Emancipation Proclamation

Lee defeats Burnside at Battle of Fredericksburg
Northern morale, boosted after Antietam, sags once again

1863

Lee defeats Hooker at the Battle of Chancellorsville
Confederate victory is offset by death of Gen. Thomas "Stonewall" Jackson

Meade defeats Lee at Battle of Gettysburg
Turning point in the war, ends the Confederate gamble of invading the North

Clement Vallandigham arrested
Prompts outrage from Copperheads but Lincoln defends action as necessary to win the war

Review Questions

1. What advantages allowed the Confederacy to enjoy military success in the early years of the war?

2. Why did both North and South consider the Border States vital?

3. How did African Americans contribute to emancipation?

4. How did the war change Northern society and the federal government?

5. What approach to warfare set Generals Ulysses S. Grant and William T. Sherman apart from less successful Union military leaders?

6. How did social, economic, and class differences in Southern society contribute to the Confederacy's defeat?

Key Terms

Border States The four slave states, Missouri, Kentucky, Maryland, and Delaware that bordered the Confederacy. The Lincoln administration succeeded in keeping them in the Union. **379**

Cotton embargo A ban imposed by Confederates in 1861 on the export of cotton, the South's most valuable commodity, to prompt cotton-importing nations like England and France to intervene to secure Confederate independence. **380**

Trent Affair A diplomatic incident in November 1861 when a U.S. Navy vessel stopped the British ship *Trent* and removed two Confederates heading for Europe to press for British and French intervention. **380**

Peninsular Campaign The complex plan developed by General George B. McClellan to capture the Confederate capital, whereby 400 ships deposited 120,000 soldiers just east of Richmond at Fortress Monroe between the James and York Rivers. **382**

Emancipation Proclamation The decree announced by Lincoln in September 1862 and taking effect on January 1, 1863, declaring slaves in the seceded states not under Union army control "forever free." **386**

Copperheads Northern Democrats (sometimes called "Peace Democrats") who opposed the war and the Lincoln

administration and favored a negotiated settlement with the Confederacy. **389**

Conscription Act A law passed by Congress in March 1863 to offset declining volunteers to the Union Army. It declared all male citizens (and immigrants who had applied for citizenship) aged twenty to forty-five eligible to be drafted into the Union Army. The rich could pay a $300 fee to avoid the draft. **389**

Draft Riots Four days of rioting in New York City in July 1863 by mostly poor, immigrant, and working-class men who opposed the draft. **391**

Sherman's March to the Sea The 285-mile "scorched earth" campaign of General William T. Sherman across Georgia in late 1864 and early 1865. Sherman's soldiers seized or destroyed $100 million in goods, hurting Southern morale and depriving the Confederate army of supplies. **400**

Special Field Order No. 15 The directive announced by General Sherman in January 1865 during his March to the Sea that set aside more than 400,000 acres of seized Confederate land for distribution to former slaves in 40-acre plots. **400**

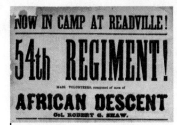

1863

Grant seizes Vicksburg
Entire length of Mississippi River under Union control, severing the Confederacy in two

Bread riots break out in Confederacy. Draft Riots erupt in New York City
Reveal growing discontent over the cost and duration of the war

The 54th Massachusetts participates in attack on Fortress Wagner
Their courage undermines the belief that African Americans will make poor soldiers

1864

Lincoln names Grant Commander of all Union Armies
Unlike the inept generals before him, Grant understands the nature of modern warfare

Grant defeats Lee in the Battles of the Wilderness, Spotsylvania, and Cold Harbor
Lee's army digs in at Petersburg near Richmond; Grant begins siege

1864

Union General William T. Sherman captures Atlanta
Sherman begins his "March to the Sea," destroying Georgian agriculture and infrastructure

Lincoln wins reelection
Ensures the Union war effort will continue

1865

Thirteenth Amendment passed
Abolishes slavery (ratified late 1865)

Grant captures Petersburg and Richmond
Lee surrenders, ending the war

Lincoln assassinated by John Wilkes Booth
Lincoln becomes a martyr figure

MyHistoryLab Connections

Visit www.myhistorylab.com for a customized Study Plan that will help you build your knowledge of *A Nation Torn Apart*.

Questions for Analysis

1. **How did both the Union and Confederacy use religious and patriotic ideals to bolster support for the war?**

   Hear the **Audio** *Battle Hymn of the Republic*, p. 376

2. **Why did the Union army have so much difficulty in defeating the Confederacy?**

   View the **Closer Look** *Lincoln visits McClellan*, p. 384

3. **How did the war create new opportunities for women?**

   View the **Closer Look** *Nurse Ann Bell Tending to Wounded...*, p. 388

4. **What did African Americans hope to achieve by serving in the Union army?**

   Read the **Document** *Letter from a Free Black Volunteer to the Christian Recorder*, p. 395

5. **How did abolitionist sentiment in Britain benefit the Union war effort?**

   Read the **Document** *The Working Men of Manchester, England Write to President Lincoln on the Question of Slavery in 1862*, p. 397

Other Resources from This Chapter

Hear the **Audio** *When This Cruel War Is Over*, p. 399

Read the **Document**

- *Joseph E. Johnston, A Confederate General Assesses First Bull Run (1861)*, p. 381
- *Memoirs of Clara Barton*, p. 388
- *Letter from J. R. Underwood to Wm. H. Seward (October 24, 1863)*, p. 389
- *Testimony from Victims of New York's Draft Riots, July 1863*, p. 391
- *Abraham Lincoln, "Gettysburg Address" (1863)*, p. 392
- *James Henry Gooding, "Letter to President Lincoln" (1863)*, p. 394

View the **Closer Look** *Images as History: Photography and the Visualization of Modern War*, p. 386

View the **Map**

- *Interactive Map: The Civil War Part I 1861–1862*, p. 382
- *Interactive Map: The Civil War Part II 1863–1865*, p. 398

Watch the **Video** *Video Lecture: The Meaning of the Civil War for Americans*, p. 401

Preparing for Reconstruction p. 406

How did Reconstruction efforts during the war reveal conflicting visions over the kind of freedoms former slaves would be granted?

The Fruits of Freedom p. 409

How did freedmen envision and act on their freedom after the war?

The Struggle to Define Reconstruction p. 412

Why did Northern Republicans reject President Johnson's Reconstruction plan?

Implementing Reconstruction p. 418

What policies did the Republican Party in the South pursue?

Reconstruction Abandoned p. 423

How did changing Northern attitudes affect the end of Reconstruction?

The New South p. 428

What were the key economic developments in the South after 1877?

Now That We Are Free

Reconstruction and the New South, 1863–1890

The Civil War ended in April 1865, concluding the bloodiest and most divisive conflict in American history. The period that followed came to be known as Reconstruction for several reasons. Most obviously, the name called to mind the need to rebuild the war-torn South. It also referred to the effort to reestablish the Union torn apart by secession. Finally, it indicated the need to remake Southern society in the wake of slavery's destruction.

The complexities and challenges of this last goal are evident in Winslow Homer's 1876 painting, *A Visit from the Old Mistress*, which depicts ex-slaves being visited by their former owner. The elegant clothing worn by the "Old Mistress" suggests she has money, but clearly the relationship between the women has changed significantly in the wake of emancipation. To begin with, the mistress has come to visit the former slaves in their home, suggesting a diminishing of her status and power relative to them. The scene also lacks any sense of the affection that plantation owners always assured themselves existed between slaves and masters. Indeed, the three African American women eye the mistress warily. One of them even chooses to remain seated in what surely would have been considered a show of contempt. The old order was gone, but what would replace it remained unclear in the aftermath of the war.

Americans entered the Reconstruction period facing the profound questions raised by war and emancipation. Could whites and former slaves live together in peace and mutual respect? What rights were the freedmen entitled to, and who would guarantee these rights? The different answers articulated by freedmen and white Southerners revealed sharply divergent visions of the future and led to a bitter struggle to define the meaning of freedom. "Verily," observed ex-slave Frederick Douglass, "the work does not end with the abolition of slavery, but only begins."

"Never before had I a word of impudence from any of our black folk, but they are not ours any longer."

SUSAN BRADFORD, observing the defiant attitude among former slaves on her Florida plantation, 1865

Preparing for Reconstruction

Long before the Emancipation Proclamation took effect on January 1, 1863 countless thousands of enslaved Africans took advantage of the chaos produced by the war to liberate themselves. Their actions raised a host of questions about what rights the freedmen would be entitled to, including land ownership and voting. Lincoln and his advisers preferred to wait until the war was won before addressing these questions, but actions taken by the freedmen to assert their rights and secure their liberty forced the Lincoln administration to develop policies during the war that ultimately shaped postwar Reconstruction.

Emancipation Test Cases

Even before the Emancipation Proclamation took effect, the federal government realized that it needed to enact policies regarding the growing numbers of freedmen in areas of the South occupied by the Union army. These policies varied by region and were shaped by local customs and the attitudes of freedmen and white officials. As such, they amounted to test cases for the coming debate over Reconstruction. Three of these test cases revealed both the promise and the conflict surrounding emancipation.

The first test case began when federal forces seized the Sea Islands off the coast of South Carolina in November 1861. They found a vast system of cotton plantations, but no planters. The latter had fled, leaving behind 10,000 slaves, who moved quickly to establish new lives based on their understanding of freedom. While clearly posed, "Planting Sweet Potatoes" (**14.1**), shot by a New Hampshire photographer visiting a regiment from his state stationed on one of the islands, captured one fundamental way in which ex-slaves expressed their freedom. Rejecting cotton, a crop they associated with slavery, they planted crops of their own choosing, such as sweet potatoes and corn for local consumption. Freedom for the African Americans of the Sea Islands

meant a future as independent farmers living free of white control.

Many Northern whites who arrived after the military takeover, however, brought with them a different vision of the future for the Sea Islands. Convinced that Sea Island blacks should resume their labors on cotton plantations—not as slaves but as paid wage earners—federal officials chose not to grant land to the freedmen. This decision was driven in part by the sincere belief that subsistence farming on small tracts of land was backward, harmful to the long-term

14.1 Freedmen in the Sea Islands Cultivating Sweet Potatoes, 1862
Most freedmen refused to grow cotton, considering it a symbol of slavery. They grew sweet potatoes and other crops, such as corn, primarily for their own consumption.

How did freedmen define freedom in the Sea Islands?   **Read** the **Document** *Charlotte Forten, "Life on the Sea Islands"*

interests of the freedmen and also by the racist notion that African Americans could not handle freedom responsibly without the guidance of white employers. Consequently, they auctioned the land off to the highest bidder. Northern investors bought most of the land, hired freedmen as wage laborers, and resumed cotton cultivation.

A second test case unfolded on Davis Bend, the Mississippi plantations owned by Confederate President Jefferson Davis and his brother Joseph. Before the Civil War, they had tried to make Davis Bend a model slave-labor community, where slaves received better food and were granted considerable autonomy. The Davis brothers hoped other planters would follow their example and thus refute the abolitionist argument that slavery was inhumane. Instead, Davis Bend became a model of a very different sort of ideal, one that vividly demonstrated what freedmen could achieve if granted land and autonomy. When General Ulysses S. Grant arrived and found the former slaves running the plantations, he ordered federal officials to lease land to the freedmen. Unlike the freedmen of the Sea Islands, the African American residents of Davis Bend did not have to contend with Northerners seeking to reassert white control over the land and impose a wage labor system. As a consequence, by 1865 Davis Bend residents had established their own local government and cleared a profit of $160,000 in cotton sales.

A third and far larger test case for emancipation policy began in Louisiana and was eventually extended up the Mississippi Valley affecting some 700,000 former slaves. Soon after Union forces seized New Orleans in April 1862, army officers established a policy to guide the transition from slavery to emancipation. As in the Sea Islands, the policy reflected the racist belief among Northern whites that African Americans could not responsibly handle their freedom and therefore needed strict rules of conduct and work. Blacks were required to remain on their plantations, working as wage laborers bound by one-year contracts. Those wishing to travel, even for short distances, required a pass from the plantation owner. Runaways and resisters, as depicted in this 1864 drawing (**14.2**), would be forcibly returned to their plantations. Offsetting these harsh provisions was a ban on corporal punishment for plantation labor. Freedmen bitterly opposed the new system, arguing that it rendered them nearly

14.2 **Freedmen Forcibly Returned to Their Plantations, 1864** Violators of the Reconstruction plan were deemed "vagrants" and forcibly returned to their plantations.

Why did Union officials define freedom for former slaves so narrowly in Louisiana?

powerless under the authority of their former masters. In New Orleans, home to the South's largest free black population before the war, African Americans began to demand equal rights for all freedmen, including the right to vote and hold office. Although their efforts failed, they sparked a national debate over freedmen's rights that would dominate Reconstruction.

The experiences in the Sea Islands, Davis Bend, Louisiana, and elsewhere during the war created conflicting visions regarding the rights of freedmen, land redistribution, and the authority of ex-slave owners. Yet emancipation also revealed the optimism of the freedmen and their commitment to defend their newly won freedom and make the most of it.

Lincoln's Ten Percent Plan

Even as the Civil War raged, President Lincoln had begun to formulate an official Reconstruction policy. In keeping with his moderate political views before the war, Lincoln proposed a moderate Reconstruction policy. As he suggested so eloquently in his second inaugural address, he intended to deal with the defeated South "with malice toward none" and "charity for all" to "achieve and cherish a just and lasting peace among ourselves…." He believed that extending lenient terms to the South would convince Confederates to surrender sooner and speed the healing process necessary for the good of the Union. Vengeance, he held, would only delay Reconstruction. It might even inspire defeated Confederate soldiers to form renegade bands of insurgents to wage a war of terrorism for years to come.

> ## "A more studied outrage on the legislative authority of the people has never been perpetuated."
>
> Wade-Davis Manifesto denouncing Lincoln's veto of the Wade-Davis Bill

In December 1863, Lincoln issued his Proclamation of Amnesty and Reconstruction, also known as the **Ten Percent Plan**. Intended to establish Southern state governments, the plan pardoned all Southerners (except high-ranking military officers and Confederate officials) who took an oath pledging loyalty to the Union and support for emancipation. As soon as 10 percent of a state's voters took this oath, they could call a convention, establish a new state government, and apply for federal recognition.

Radical Republicans Offer a Different Vision

Lincoln's lenient plan enraged many Radical Republicans. In July 1864, Radical Republican leaders Senator Benjamin Wade of Ohio and Congressman Henry W. Davis of Maryland cosponsored the Wade-Davis Bill, a Reconstruction program designed to punish Confederate leaders and destroy the South's slave society. Southerners could reestablish new state governments only after a majority of a state's voters signed an "ironclad" oath declaring they never aided the Confederate army or government. Southerners who served as high-ranking army officers or government officials would be stripped of their citizenship, including the right to vote and hold office. The former Confederate states would be readmitted only after a long period of punishment and a clear demonstration of their commitment to the Union, emancipation, and freedmen's rights.

Lincoln quietly pocket vetoed the bill. Furious, Radicals sought to replace him as the Republican Party presidential nominee in 1864. Although the effort failed, it exposed the deeply divided opinions regarding Reconstruction.

Lincoln and his fellow Republicans did manage to find common ground on two issues. In late January 1865, at the urging of Lincoln's administration, Congress passed the Thirteenth Amendment, abolishing slavery. The measure ended any ambiguity over the Emancipation Proclamation, abolishing slavery everywhere in the United States and offering no compensation to former slaveholders. By year's end 27 states, including eight former Confederate states, would ratify the amendment.

In March 1865, Congress established the Bureau of Refugees, Freedmen, and Abandoned Lands. Known simply as the **Freedmen's Bureau**, it became an all-purpose relief agency in the war-ravaged South, distributing food, providing emergency services, building schools, and managing confiscated lands. It represented the first attempt by the federal government to provide social welfare services and quickly became the bedrock institution for implementing Reconstruction policy.

What advantages did Lincoln see in a moderate Reconstruction policy?

Read the **Document** Carl Schurz, "Report on the Condition of the South" (1865)

The Fruits of Freedom

Many Southerners were stunned by the response of their slaves to freedom. Clinging to self-serving paternalistic notions of the plantation as one big family under the benign authority of the master and planter, they were taken aback when their slaves refused to obey their orders or exhibited anger or disrespect toward them. Susan Bradford, a young woman living on a Florida plantation, wrote in her diary that she was "hurt and dazed" when one of her former slaves refused to prepare a dinner for her mother. "Tell her if she want any dinner," sneered the free woman, "she kin cook it herself." "I believed that these people were content, happy, and attached to their masters," wrote one South Carolina planter in 1865, unable to comprehend why slaves abandoned their masters "in [their] moment of need." It would be the first of many such shocking experiences for whites, who never imagined that slavery might one day be abolished.

> **INFORMATION WANTED**
> OF A MAN BY THE NAME OF ELIAS LOWERY McDERMIT, who used to belong to Thomas Lyons, of Knoxville, East Tennessee. He was sold to a man by the name of Sherman about ten years ago, and I learned some six years ago that he was on a steamboat running between Memphis and New Orleans, and more recently I heard that he was somewhere on the Cumberland river, in the Federal army. Any information concerning him will be thankfully received. Address Colored Tennessean, Nashville, Tenn. From his sister who is now living in Knoxville, East Tennessee.
> je24-1m]   MARTHA McDERMIT.

> SAML. DOVE wishes to know of the whereabouts of his mother, Areno, his sisters Maria, Neziah, and Peggy, and his brother Edmond, who were owned by Geo. Dove, of Rockingham county, Shenandoah Valley, Va. Sold in Richmond, after which Saml. and Edmond were taken to Nashville, Tenn., by Joe Mick; Areno was left at the Eagle Tavern, Richmond
> Respectfully yours,
> SAML. DOVE.
> Utica, New York, Aug. 5, 1865-3m
> U. S. CHRISTIAN COMMISSION,
> NASHVILLE, TENN., July 19, 1865.

Freedom of Movement

Even before the guns of the Civil War went silent, African Americans had begun to explore the meaning of their freedom and formulate their own vision of a reconstructed postwar South, both of which included unrestricted mobility. Under slavery, movement was sharply limited, and few slaves ventured far from their plantations. In the chaos of war, however, and later with official emancipation, African Americans hit the road. Many did so to escape the plantations that were home to their former masters and countless bitter memories. Others simply reveled in free and unfettered movement. They wandered for the pleasure of it with no particular destination in mind. As these advertisements (**14.3**) from the *Colored Tennessean*, Tennessee's only African American–owned newspaper, indicate, many freedmen also journeyed in search of loved ones sold away years before.

African American mobility led to a sharp rise in the black population of Southern cities. In contrast to rural life, black settlements in cities offered more varied job opportunities, albeit nearly always menial, difficult, and low paid. Urban life also provided freedmen access to strong black institutions such as churches, charities, and newspapers.

Southern whites reacted to black mobility with both alarm and disdain. Just as former slaves equated freedom with mobility, their former masters saw in it a shocking reminder that the old order was gone. As a consequence, in one of the first expressions of resistance to black freedom, white Southerners passed vagrancy laws intended to restrict African American mobility.

Forty Acres and a Mule

Many freedmen also tried to become landowners. If travel was a symbolic expression of their new freedom, land was freedom in concrete form. Land, the freedmen believed, would give their freedom meaning by providing an independent living, free of planter control.

The idea that freedmen would receive land in addition to their freedom originated during the war. As Southerners abandoned their plantations before the advancing Union army, ex-slaves often took control, partitioned land, and planted crops. Freedmen defended these extralegal actions as simple justice, citing the generations of unpaid labor that they and their ancestors had performed on farms and plantations. "The property which they [former slaveholders] hold," asserted a group of freedmen, "was nearly all earned by the sweat of our brows."

14.3 Freedmen Searching for Loved Ones Sold Away during Slavery
These classified advertisements in the August 12, 1865 *Colored Tennessean* were just two of thousands published in mainly black-owned newspapers during Reconstruction. They vividly highlight the efforts of freed-men to overcome one of slavery's harshest legacies.
[*Source:* (t) ICHi-36218; Information Wanted: Of a man by the name of Elias Lowery McDermit; Nashville, Tennessee; 1865; Creator - "The Colored Tennessean"; (b) ICHi-36219. Saml Dove wishes to know of the whereabouts of his mother; Utica, NY. Aug 5 1865. Looking for his mother, Areno and his sisters and brother.]

> "Give us our own land and we take care of ourselves; but without land, the old masters can hire or starve us, as they please."
>
> A South Carolina freedman speaking to a Northern journalist, 1865

To bring order to these unofficial acts of confiscation, General William T. Sherman issued in early

Read the **Document** James C. Beecher, "Report on Land Reform" (1865, 1866)

Why did freedmen believe they were owed land?

1865 Special Field Order No. 15. It announced that 400,000 acres of abandoned land from northern Florida to the South Carolina Sea Islands would be distributed to freedman in 40-acre plots. Weeks later Congress established the Freedmen's Bureau, authorizing it to rent to freedmen 40-acre plots of confiscated and abandoned land, along with a mule. By June some 40,000 freedmen lived on land distributed by Sherman, while thousands more rented plots under control of the Freedmen's Bureau.

Whether they owned land or worked as farm laborers for wages, African Americans used their freedom to change the way they worked. They often refused to work in gangs under overseers because it reminded them of slavery. Instead they preferred working independently, under the direction of elder family members. Many African American women left the field to work in their homes and care for children.

African Americans and Radical Republicans wanted land redistribution programs, popularly known as "forty acres and a mule," enacted across the South. Before long, however, their optimism would give way to bitter disappointment as nearly all the land was returned to its original white owners.

Uplift through Education

Along with land, freedmen sought education as an essential element of their freedom. Laws prohibiting the education of slaves had left most freedmen illiterate. But if they learned to read and write, they could conduct their own legal and business affairs, acquire better-paying jobs, read newspapers, and participate more fully in politics.

General O. O. Howard, the first head of the Freedmen's Bureau, also viewed education as an essential goal of Reconstruction. Working with charitable societies and African American leaders, the Freedmen's Bureau helped build 3,000 schools across the South that by 1870 served 150,000 students of all ages. By 1875, literacy among freedmen jumped from 10 percent to 30 percent (and 52 percent by 1900).

In the early years of Reconstruction, educated single white women from the North like the Cooke sisters (**14.4**) made up the majority of the teachers in these schools. Often sponsored by Northern charitable societies, they saw themselves as missionaries dedicated to the uplift of the freedmen. The journal that published this image in 1866, *Frank Leslie's Illustrated Weekly,* shared this vision. Note how the artist depicted the children in spotless attire with all of them focused on their studies.

That the vision of these teachers and their sponsors went beyond merely teaching ex-slaves to read is shown in this image (**14.5**) of a brief biography of African American poet Phillis Wheatley. Published in 1866 by a Boston Christian organization, it demonstrates an effort to inspire ex-slaves' quest for education and independence by instilling pride in African American achievement.

Educating freedmen, however, proved no easy job. Southern whites often put up fierce resistance

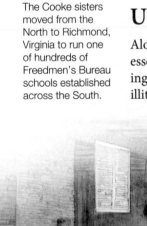

14.4 The Misses Cooke's School Room, Freedman's Bureau, 1866
The Cooke sisters moved from the North to Richmond, Virginia to run one of hundreds of Freedmen's Bureau schools established across the South.

14.5 Education and Inspiration
Some Northern charitable societies, like the Boston Tract Society, published and distributed books to both teach reading and inspire African Americans.

to African American education, especially in more remote areas. One report in 1865 described the hardships teachers faced: "Compelled to live on the coarsest diet ... subjected to the jeers and hatred of her neighbors ... swamped in mud—the school shed a drip, and her quarters little better; raided occasionally by rebels, her school broken up and herself insulted, banished, or run off."

The Freedmen's Bureau and Northern aid societies also established more than a dozen black colleges, including Howard in Washington, D.C., and Hampton in Virginia. One of their most immediate goals was to train black teachers. By 1870, African American teachers outnumbered white teachers in freedmen's schools. Many freedmen teachers became community leaders and ran for political office. At least 70 former teachers won seats in Southern state legislatures during Reconstruction.

The Black Church

The vast network of black churches established during Reconstruction provided an even greater source of community leadership. Black churches had existed in the South before the Civil War, but most were part of larger white congregations and subject to strict white control. Southern whites usually insisted that white ministers lead black congregations to ensure that preaching never challenged slavery and white domination.

When the war ended, countless African American congregations of Methodists, Baptists, Presbyterians, and other sects separated from white ones. They resented their inferior status in white-controlled churches and longed to practice a more emotional, expressive worship style disdained by whites. Most important, they wanted black clergymen who could address their spiritual and social needs.

Often churches assumed a central place in the lives of freedmen. Religious services provided spiritual and psychological support for blacks' daily struggles. Churches also ran schools and provided charitable services to the community. As this illustration (**14.6**) of a freedmen community at Trent River, North Carolina, demonstrates, African Americans built a church in the center that doubled as a schoolhouse and meeting place. Churches also offered African Americans a degree of self-government, electing members to serve as trustees and on committees overseeing parish life and budget management. African American women, in particular, filled numerous roles, planning events, raising money, and running programs such as temperance societies. Like their white counterparts, African American churches also sponsored countless initiatives, such as burial societies, fraternal organizations, and youth groups.

With the church taking so prominent a place in African American life, black ministers, like black teachers, assumed major leadership roles. White hostility convinced most ministers to concentrate on building up their communities from within. Still, many ministers entered politics to advance the cause of black equality, including more than 100 elected to Southern state legislatures during Reconstruction. Reverend Richard H. Cain, for example, went to Charleston, South Carolina, in 1865, where he assisted at a black church. Two years later he served as a delegate to the state constitutional convention, followed by terms in the state senate and U.S. House of Representatives.

African Americans' response to emancipation showed that they understood freedom as more than simply an end to slavery. Freedom included the right to free movement and travel, to labor for themselves under conditions of their own choosing, on land granted to them by the government. It meant self-improvement through education and self-help organizations. It meant establishing their own institutions and building their own communities. It also meant full civil and social equality with whites, including the right to vote and hold office.

14.6 The Black Church Anchors Freedmen Communities
African Americans organized thousands of churches across the South to address both their spiritual and social needs. In the freedmen settlement of Trent River, North Carolina, a simple structure served as a church, school, and meetinghouse (from *Harper's Weekly*, June 9, 1866).

How did the black church become such a vital institution in freedmen communities?

The Struggle to Define Reconstruction

 As freedmen in the South worked to define, protect, and extend their freedoms, political leaders in Washington, D.C., debated how to reconstruct the South. The debate revealed sharply divergent visions of the postwar South's social, political, and economic order. Radical Republicans wanted to replace the old slavocracy with an interracial democracy protected by federal authority. Conservatives sought to limit Reconstruction to granting ex-slaves freedom and opposed proposals to distribute land and grant full equality to ex-slaves. Moderates held the balance of power in deciding most of these questions, but they lacked a clear vision of the postwar South and made their decisions in response to events as they unfolded.

The Conservative Vision of Freedom: Presidential Reconstruction

Andrew Johnson, who became president after Lincoln's assassination in April 1865, was a complicated man. Although he once owned slaves, like many other poor whites from the backcountry of eastern Tennessee, he grew up deeply suspicious of the planter aristocracy. As a politician, he gained a wide following among poor farmers for his populist criticism of planter power. He opposed secession and was the only senator from a seceding state who did not withdraw from the Senate in early 1861. Lincoln appointed Johnson governor of Tennessee after the state came under Union occupation. In 1864, Republicans sought to appeal to Southern unionism and picked Johnson as Lincoln's vice presidential running mate.

Initially Johnson indicated he intended to deal harshly with the South. He spoke of punishing ex-Confederates for their "treason." He also talked of the need to assist former slaves in their transition to freedom. Radical Republicans, who shared these views, were thrilled.

But their joy was soon replaced by anger. First, despite his harsh anti-planter rhetoric, Johnson

was a bitter racist who abhorred the notion of black equality. Committed to maintaining white supremacy, Johnson outlined in May 1865 a lenient policy toward the South designed to rapidly re-establish Southern state governments and restore the Union. It offered pardons, amnesty, and the return of all confiscated property to Southerners who took an oath of allegiance to the Union. Former Confederate leaders and planters possessing more than $20,000 in personal wealth, however, would have to apply to him personally for a pardon.

> "We have turned loose … four million slaves without a hut to shelter them or a cent in their pockets.… This Congress is bound to provide for them until they can take care of themselves."
>
> Congressman THADDEUS STEVENS, December 18, 1865

Second, Johnson set out the terms for readmitting ex-Confederate states to the Union. As soon as Johnson appointed a temporary governor, a state could then convene a constitutional convention of elected delegates (chosen only by those citizens granted amnesty or pardons). If the convention ratified the Thirteenth Amendment, renounced secession, repudiated all Confederate debts, and held elections for state office and Congress, Johnson would recognize the state as a fully reconstructed member of the Union.

With Congress out of session, Johnson's plan faced little formal opposition. By the fall of 1865, all but a few planters and high-ranking ex-Confederates had been pardoned and had

What was Andrew Johnson's primary motivation in devising his lenient Reconstruction policy?

View the **Closer Look** *Competing Visions: Federal Authority and Equal Rights*

restored to them virtually all their lands, including the vast tracts of land that had been set aside in 40-acre plots for freedmen. In December, with all 11 former Confederate states having established new governments under his terms, Johnson announced the Union was restored, and Reconstruction was over.

Johnson's actions outraged Northern Republicans, including moderates. This political cartoon (**14.7**) shows Johnson accepting bags of cash from a former Confederate (depicted as the devil) in exchange for a pardon, while a "Pardoned Reconstruction Rebel" in the lower left kills "Union men and freedmen." Three developments in the supposedly "reconstructed" South stoked Republican discontent. First, many of the state constitutional conventions had failed explicitly to ratify the Thirteenth Amendment; some even demanded financial compensation for the loss of their slaves. Second, and even more galling, in the state elections in November 1865, Southern voters elected dozens of ex-Confederate

officials and army officers. Among them was Alexander Stephens, former vice president of the Confederacy, chosen to represent Georgia in the Senate. Third, new Southern state governments, beginning in late 1865 with Mississippi and South Carolina, passed laws known as **Black Codes** to limit the civil and economic rights of freedmen and create an exploitable workforce. Observing these developments less than a year after the end of the Civil War, many Northerners wondered if the great conflict had been fought in vain. Had hundreds of thousands died to defeat the Confederacy only to see its leaders quickly resume power? Had slavery been abolished only to be replaced with a similar system of unfree labor?

One of the most common Black Codes (first established in Mississippi in 1865 and then replicated across the South) established the vague charge of "vagrancy"—having no regular home or employment—as a pretext for controlling freedmen. (See *Competing Visions: Demanding Rights, Protecting Privilege.*) Any freedman who

14.7 Johnson's Leniency Angers the North
Johnson's pledge to punish the South ("Treason must be made odious") is ridiculed in this 1866 political cartoon. His sweeping pardons of ex-Confederate leaders and planters and easy terms for readmission of Southern states provoked anger in the North.

What events in the South in 1865–1866 angered Northern Republicans?

Competing Visions
DEMANDING RIGHTS, PROTECTING PRIVILEGE

In the aftermath of the Civil War, one question dominated the minds of Americans North and South: Now that slavery was abolished, what would be the status of the freedmen? While newspaper editors, clergymen, and members of Congress debated the issue, white and black Southerners set out to answer the question themselves. As you read the following documents, one from a convention of freedmen and the other from the state legislature of Mississippi, consider the starkly contrasted visions for the future of Southern society. Why do the freedmen feel compelled to say they bear no ill will toward their "former oppressors?" Why do Mississippi legislators define vagrancy in such vague terms?

"Address to the Loyal Citizens and Congress of the United States of America," Proceedings of the Convention of the Colored People of Virginia, Held in the City of Alexandria, August 2, 3, 4, 5, 1865.

We, the delegates of the colored people of the State of Virginia … solemnly declaring that we desire to live upon the most friendly and agreeable terms with all men; we feel no ill-will or prejudice toward our former oppressors; are willing and desire to forgive and forget the past, and so shape our future conduct as shall promote our happiness and the interest of the community in which we live …

We must, on the other hand, be allowed to aver and assert that we believe that we have among the white people of this State many who are our most inveterate enemies; who hate us as a class, who feel no sympathy with or for us; who despise us simply because we are black, and more especially, because we have been made free by the power of the United States Government …

We claim, then, as citizens of this State, the laws of the Commonwealth [of Virginia] shall give to all men equal protection; that each and every man may appeal to the law for his equal rights without regard to the color of his skin; and we believe this can only be done by extending the franchise, which we believe to be our inalienable right as freemen, and which the Declaration of Independence guarantees to all free citizens of this Government and which is the privilege of this nation. We claim the right of suffrage:

1st. Because we can see no other safeguard for our protection.

2nd. Because we are citizens of the country and natives of this State.

3rd. Because we are as well qualified to vote who shall be our rulers as many who do vote for that purpose who have no interest in us, and do not know our wants.

Mississippi legislators in December 1865 enacted the first "Black Codes" to limit the freedoms of African Americans. Defining vagrancy in such vague terms allowed white Southerners to arrest freedmen at will and to curtail their freedom of movement. These measures were quickly copied in the remaining ex-Confederate states.

Section 1. All rogues and vagabonds, idle and dissipated persons, … persons who neglect their calling or employment, misspend what they earn, or do not provide for the support of themselves or their families, or dependents shall be deemed and considered vagrants, … and upon conviction thereof shall be fined not exceeding one hundred dollars, with all accruing costs, and be imprisoned … not exceeding ten days.…

Section 5.… In case of any freedman, free negro or mulatto shall fail for five days after the imposition of any or forfeiture upon him or her for violation of any of the provisions of this act to pay the same, that it shall be, and is hereby, made the duty of the sheriff of the proper county to hire out said freedman, free negro or mulatto, to any person who will, for the shortest period of service, pay said fine and forfeiture and all costs …

Colored Men's Convention 1869.

What is significant about the freedmen's use of the term citizen?

Read the **Document** *"Address of the Colored State Convention to the People of the State of South Carolina" (1865)*

hit the road seeking new opportunities could be arrested as a vagrant and fined. If a freedman could not pay his fine, he could be hired out for a time to a local plantation owner willing to pay his fine. As this drawing (**14.8**) dramatically shows, in some cases the contracts for such labor were auctioned off to local planters. The artist intended to conjure in the minds of Northerners a grim scene reminiscent of a slave auction, suggesting that one of the war's chief accomplishments, emancipation, was being undermined. Some Black Codes required that the children of "vagrant" freedmen be forced to accept apprenticeships that bound them to an employer until age 21. Others coerced blacks to sign long-term work contracts as proof of employment, a practice that left them at the mercy of employers who were not required to pay them for work performed if they quit before the contract expired. Other laws restricted freedmen to renting land only in rural areas (to keep them on plantations), prohibited ministers from preaching without a license,

outlawed interracial marriages, and barred blacks from serving on juries.

Congressional Reconstruction and the Fourteenth Amendment

Republicans in Congress vowed to block Johnson's rapid and lenient Reconstruction program for both idealistic and practical reasons. Excepting emancipation, none of the Republicans' goals for changing Southern society had been accomplished, and the former slavocracy appeared poised to resume power—a result certain to revive the Democratic Party. A slower process of Reconstruction would allow the Republican Party to take root in the South, especially if African Americans were granted the right to vote, as many Radicals like Congressman Thaddeus Stevens of Pennsylvania demanded.

The confrontation began in January 1866 when Congress reconvened. Republicans first refused

14.8 The Black Codes in Action Unable to pay his fine for "vagrancy" as defined in the Black Codes of Florida, a freedman is auctioned off. The high bidder won the right to a freedman's labor for months or years.

Read the **Document** *Affidavit of Former Slave Enoch Braston (1866)*

How did Black Codes calling for freedmen to sign labor contracts curtail their freedom?

14.9 *Race Riot in Memphis*
White mobs, unrestrained by police, killed 46 blacks in Memphis, Tennessee on May 1–2, 1866. News of the atrocities, conveyed in images such as this one, stoked Northern opinion against Johnson's lenient Reconstruction policies.

to admit the senators and representatives from the former Confederate states Johnson had declared reconstructed. Next, they established the Joint Committee on Reconstruction, a body that gathered evidence and testimony from hundreds of witnesses detailing widespread lawlessness and violence against freedmen and their white allies in the South.

To counteract Southern resistance and the oppression of freedmen, Congress passed two bills. The first expanded the powers of the Freedmen's Bureau and authorized it to continue operations for two more years. The second, the Civil Rights Act, declared African Americans and all persons born in the United States (except Native Americans) citizens. It also defined the rights of all citizens regardless of race—for example, the right to sue and to make contracts. Taking direct aim at the Black Codes, the law prohibited state

governments from depriving any citizen of these "fundamental rights." Johnson, infuriated at Congress's rejection of his Reconstruction program and determined to thwart efforts to establish racial equality, vetoed both bills.

Congress overrode the vetoes and the bills became law, but by June 1866, Republicans decided bolder action was necessary. Johnson remained opposed to freedmen's rights, and violence against blacks was on the rise in the South. The worst incident (**14.9**), was a race riot in Memphis, Tennessee, on May 1–2 that left 46 blacks, many of them Union army veterans, and two whites dead. This drawing from *Harper's Weekly*, a widely read publication that favored freedmen's rights, was intended to arouse anger in the North over Southern intransigence and support for congressional action. The Civil Rights Act was an unprecedented piece of legislation,

How did the Civil Rights Act promote equal rights for all Americans, regardless of race?

Read the **Document** *Charles F. Johnson and T. W. Gilbreth, The Memphis Riot (1866)*

but its supporters knew that it could easily be overturned by a future Congress. An amendment, on the other hand, became a permanent part of the Constitution.

On June 13, 1866, Republicans passed the **Fourteenth Amendment** to the Constitution. Its five main provisions radically redefined the role of the federal government as the guarantor of individual civil rights. First, it declared all persons born or naturalized in the United States as citizens, a definition that necessarily included all freedmen. Second, all citizens were entitled to "equal protection of the laws" of the states where they lived. Third, states that denied adult male citizens, including African Americans, the right to vote would have their representation in Congress reduced. Fourth, all high-ranking former Confederates were prohibited from holding public office, unless pardoned by act of Congress. Fifth, it repudiated the Confederate debt (thus punishing those who lent money to the Confederacy) and prohibited financial compensation for ex–slave owners.

Johnson greeted the unprecedented amendment with an unprecedented response: He went on the campaign trail to urge its defeat. Hoping to make the midterm state and congressional elections in November 1866 a referendum on the amendment, Johnson and his allies played on white racism, conjuring up images of racial equality and racial intermarriage to alarm Northern whites. Republicans responded in kind, portraying Johnson and the Democrats as traitors who waged war on the Union. Republicans won a sweeping victory in November. Northern voters, although still leery of racial equality, rejected Johnson's lenient form of Reconstruction because it required too little of Southerners and restored planter rule.

Republicans Take Control

Emboldened by their legislative and electoral success, congressional Republicans moved to take complete control of Reconstruction policy. In March 1867, Congress passed the first of four Reconstruction Acts. They divided the South (except Tennessee) into five military districts, each governed by a military commander empowered to restore peace and protect individuals, especially freedmen. As soon as order was established, the ex-Confederate states could begin a new, stricter readmission process. The act called for elections to select delegates to state constitutional conventions—elections that permitted African American men to

vote, but barred Southerners who had served in the Confederate government and army. The new state constitutions drawn up by these conventions had to allow universal male suffrage, regardless of race. As soon as a state's voters approved the new constitution, the state could hold elections to fill government offices. Finally, if Congress approved the state's constitution and the state legislature ratified the Fourteenth Amendment, the state would be readmitted to the Union.

Two years after the end of the Civil War, the federal government had finally adopted a clear Reconstruction plan. The delay was understandable, given Lincoln's assassination and the lack of precedent. Yet delay granted Southerners time to recover from the war and mount an effective resistance to federal intervention.

> "The President has no power to control or influence anybody and legislation will be carried on entirely regardless of his opinion or wishes."
>
> Republican Senator JAMES W. GRIMES, Iowa, January 1867

President Johnson promptly vetoed the Reconstruction Acts, but the Republican Congress passed them again over his veto. Some of the more radical Republicans grew so embittered by the president's actions and words that they attempted to remove him from office. When Johnson dismissed Secretary of War Edwin Stanton in August 1867, Republicans charged him with violating the Tenure of Office Act, a constitutionally dubious measure they had passed in March. It required the president to seek congressional approval before removing a cabinet official. The House voted to impeach the president, charging him with 11 offenses. The trial began in March 1868 and after two months of heated debate and accusation, the Senate failed—by one vote—to convict Johnson and remove him from office.

Johnson was saved by some moderate Republicans who feared setting a bad precedent if a politically motivated campaign succeeded in removing a president from office. Many moderate Republicans also considered Johnson's likely replacement, Senator Benjamin Wade, far too radical. They also knew Johnson had less than a year left in office.

View the **Map** *Interactive Map: Congressional Reconstruction*

Why did moderate Republicans decide not to remove Johnson from office?

Implementing Reconstruction

As Congress engaged in its impeachment struggle with President Johnson in 1867–1868, the Reconstruction Acts took effect. A coalition of African Americans, poor up-country whites, and economically ambitious merchants (many originally from the North) and white planters formed the Republican Party in the South. They seized the opportunity presented by the congressional Reconstruction program and dominated the process of electing state governments and gaining readmission to the Union. The task would not be easy, especially as their different goals conflicted with each other and with those of most white Southerners, who would clearly oppose—politically, economically, and violently—any attempt to establish what they called "Negro rule."

14.10 The Hated Scalawag
Scalawags became despised figures in the popular Southern mind. Here a scalawag is depicted as an opportunist seeking political power by manipulating the black vote.

The Republican Party in the South

The process of remaking state governments under the Reconstruction Acts fell to the Republican Party in the South, an organization comprising three distinct and in some cases antagonistic groups: Northerners who settled in the South, white Southerners, and former slaves. Northerners who moved south after the war were derided as **carpetbaggers** by white Southerners. The term suggested they were poor opportunists who carried to the South only a cheap suitcase, or carpetbag, which they intended to fill with plunder garnered from Southerners still reeling from the war. In reality most were middle class, often former Union soldiers or merchants, ministers, artisans, and professionals who viewed the South as a region of opportunity where they planned to settle permanently. Others came as idealistic relief workers, sent by Northern charitable and religious societies, intent upon aiding ex-slaves in their transition to freedom.

The Republican Party in the South also contained many white Southerners. Most white Southerners referred to them derisively as **scalawags** and considered them traitors to their region and race, men eager to accrue riches and power by manipulating black voters (**14.10**). Most scalawags came from the less developed backcountry regions of the South, especially eastern Tennessee and Kentucky, northern Alabama and Georgia, and western North Carolina. Like carpetbaggers, they believed that the Republican Party offered them and their region the best chance for economic betterment. Most did not, however, embrace on the idea of racial equality.

Former slaves made up the largest (about 80 percent), most significant segment of the South's Republican Party. Empowered with the vote by the Civil Rights Act of 1866 and Reconstruction Act of 1867, African Americans turned out in huge numbers in late 1867 to vote in elections held to select delegates to state constitutional conventions. For supporters of black suffrage, this extraordinary moment—persons only recently considered property now exercising for the first time the right to vote—was captured in

Why did many Northerners move south after the Civil War?

"But be sure to vote for no Southern men that was a rebel or secessionist; for, if you do, you are pulling them hemp to hang yourself with."

R. I. CROMWELL, advising his fellow freedmen, *New Orleans Tribune*, April 25, 1867

this *Harper's Weekly* drawing (**14.11**). The dignified scene depicts three voters who symbolically represent a spectrum of blacks that includes common laborers, educated blacks who were free before the war, and Union army veterans. Most African American Republican leaders came from the second group. They tended to come from the North and possessed more wealth and education than the average freedman.

The three factions of the Republican Party—carpetbaggers, scalawags, and freedmen—formed an uneasy alliance as they came together to reestablish Southern state governments. Nonetheless, their combined votes in the 1867 elections for delegates to state constitutional conventions led to a sweeping Republican victory. White Republicans, even though they comprised only 20 percent of party membership, won most of the seats. But freedmen won 265 seats overall and a majority of seats in South Carolina and Louisiana.

Creating Reconstruction Governments in the South

Republican delegates soon drafted new constitutions for former Confederate states according to the guidelines established by the Reconstruction Acts. In a few states, notably Virginia and Texas, conservatives delayed the process for more than a year. But by the end of 1868, seven Southern states had ratified new constitutions, created new governments, and been readmitted to the Union.

These Republican governments achieved remarkable results. To begin with, they represented a revolutionary advance in the status of the freedmen. Held as slaves and denied citizenship only a few years before, African Americans now enjoyed

14.11 Casting Their First Votes
For supporters of racial equality like the Northern publication *Harper's Weekly*, whose cover featured this drawing, the large turnout of black voters in the 1867 elections was exhilarating.

the right to vote and hold office. Between 1869 and 1901, 22 African Americans would serve in Congress (20 representatives and 2 senators). More than 600 would win seats in state legislatures and to other state offices.

While embittered white Southerners decried what they termed "Negro rule," statistics show that white Republicans held a far greater share of offices than blacks. No African American was elected governor, and no state legislature ever had a black majority (the South Carolina lower house briefly had a black majority). What white Southerners really objected to was Republican rule

View the **Closer Look** *First Vote*

How did African American voting affect the political situation in the South in 1867–1868?

and what it stood for: African American equality and empowerment.

Republican-controlled Southern state governments also achieved several significant reforms. In contrast to the tightfisted governments of the antebellum era, they funded public works projects, built hospitals and orphanages, and founded public school systems. They also enacted more equitable tax codes and passed laws to help indebted farmers keep their land. Opponents of Republican rule denounced these initiatives (and the higher taxes needed to fund them) as wasteful and poorly managed. Fundamentally, they objected to their social and racial implications, since many of the projects were designed to aid the poor and freedmen.

But the charges of corruption, mismanagement, and debt lodged by the opponents of Reconstruction governments were not entirely groundless. The rapid expansion of government services and expenditures caused many states to run up large deficits. It also created opportunities for graft and bribery which some Reconstruction legislators took advantage of.

Democratic opponents railed against these abuses as alleged evidence that blacks were incapable of holding office and that their white allies were interested only in plunder. In reality the corruption in Southern state governments paled in comparison to that found in the North. New York's Tammany Hall political machine, for example, under William "Boss" Tweed, stole more than $20 million from 1869 to 1871. Moreover, the spending by Southern state governments on social programs looked large only compared to the paltry expenditures on education, health care, and public works before the war. Nonetheless, charges of corruption and excessive spending, coupled with increased taxes, diminished support for the Southern Republican governments and created an unfavorable impression in the North.

> ## "We cannot vote without all sorts of threats and intimidations. Freedmen are shot with impunity."
> Report of a Republican official, 1868

The Election of 1868

By summer 1868, there was little doubt whom the Republican Party would nominate for president. General Ulysses S. Grant enjoyed widespread popularity across the North and among Southern Republicans for defeating Robert E. Lee and ending the Civil War. Grant conveyed a tone of moderation in a time of partisan and sectional acrimony. "Let us have peace," became his campaign slogan.

Democrats, still weak in the aftermath of the war and the disenfranchisement of many ex-Confederates, faced an uphill battle against Grant. Note how this political cartoon (**14.12**) "'Tis But A Change of Banners" from a pro-Republican journal sought to link the Democratic nominees for president Governor Horatio Seymour of New York and for vice president Francis Blair of Maryland with both secession and postwar racial violence. But as this racist Democratic campaign song makes clear (**14.13**), Seymour ran an aggressive campaign designed to arouse fears that the Republican Party and black suffrage threatened the rights of white Americans. Republicans, his campaign claimed, must be prevented from spreading the disastrous experiment in black political empowerment to the North.

Running on a message of political moderation, fiscal responsibility, and an even-handed approach

14.12 Linking the Democrats to Secession and Civil War This political cartoon from a pro-Republican periodical sought to demonize Democrats Horatio Seymour and Francis Blair by reminding voters that their Democratic Party was the party of Southern secessionists.

14.13 The Politics of Racism
The campaign of Democratic Party nominees Horatio Seymour and Francis Blair appealed to white voters' racism though the nominees' speeches, campaign literature, and songs such as this one, "The White Man's Banner."

on the rise, many Republicans argued that another amendment was necessary to guarantee unequivocally the right of African Americans to vote.

Women's rights activists agreed, but many also argued for universal suffrage—the vote for all adult citizens regardless of race or gender. Bitterly disappointed over the reference to only "male citizens" in the Fourteenth Amendment, feminists, such as Elizabeth Cady Stanton and Susan B. Anthony, demanded that any subsequent amendment include women.

This demand was opposed by former abolitionists and Radical Republicans, including fellow feminists like Lucy Stone and Frances Harper, who argued that gaining the vote for African American men was a higher priority. Including women, they argued, would doom the amendment because the nation was not ready for such radical change. The cause of women's suffrage could be taken up immediately after black suffrage was secured. Stanton and Anthony rejected this reasoning, leading to a twenty-year split in the women's rights movement. Most Republicans in Congress, however, agreed with Frederick Douglass's assertion that this was the "Negro's Hour," and they drafted the **Fifteenth Amendment** to read succinctly: "The right of citizens of the United States shall not be denied or abridged by the United States or by any state on account of race, color, or previous condition of servitude."

Passed by Congress in late 1869 and ratified in 1870, the Fifteenth Amendment presented a striking contradiction. It established a revolutionary experiment in interracial democracy, something no other slave society, such as those in the Caribbean or

to Reconstruction, Grant won 214 electoral votes to Seymour's 80. The popular vote, however, was much closer: 53 percent for Grant, 47 percent for Seymour (**14.14**). This outcome reflected three things. First, it indicated the wide appeal of Seymour's blatantly racist message to conservative whites in both North and South. Second, it showed how vital the freedman vote was for the Republican Party. Grant received nearly 500,000 African American votes, but won by only 300,000 votes. Third, it revealed the effectiveness of violence as a weapon in electoral politics. A reign of terror unleashed by violent whites before the election, especially in Georgia and Louisiana, kept thousands of black voters away from the polls.

The Fifteenth Amendment

After the 1868 election, congressional Republicans decided that black suffrage required an explicit constitutional guarantee. Black male suffrage was implied in the Fourteenth Amendment's phrase, "all male citizens," but with Southern resistance

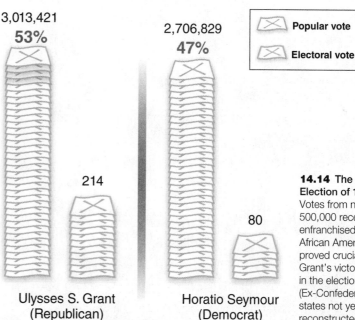

3,013,421
53%

2,706,829
47%

☒ Popular vote

☒ Electoral vote

214

80

Ulysses S. Grant
(Republican)

Horatio Seymour
(Democrat)

14.14 The Election of 1868
Votes from nearly 500,000 recently enfranchised African Americans proved crucial to Grant's victory in the election. (Ex-Confederate states not yet reconstructed did not participate.)

Why did some women's rights activists oppose ratification of the Fifteenth Amendment?

Latin America, did so soon and so completely after emancipation. Yet its spare wording left wide open the possibility that states could devise clever ways to deny blacks the right to vote that did not directly invoke "race, color, or previous condition of servitude."

The Rise of White Resistance

The secret white terrorist organizations that first arose in 1866 and that wrought havoc in parts of the South during the 1868 election grew bolder and more violent by 1870–1871, especially during election season. Known by various names, including the White Brotherhood, Knights of the White Camelia, and especially the Ku Klux Klan, they functioned in much the same manner. As illustrated in a popular Northern newspaper (**14.15**), Klansmen often operated at night, wearing hoods, robes, and other regalia to hide their identities and terrify their victims. Blacks (and occasionally carpetbaggers and scalawags) targeted for "punishment" were beaten and frequently killed. Some had their crops or homes burned or their mules killed. Klansmen also targeted symbols of black self-improvement and independence, such as black churches, businesses, and schools.

14.15 *Another Victim of the Klan* Terrorist violence by white vigilante groups soared in the early 1870s. In this scene from Moore County, North Carolina, a freedman pleads for his life, surrounded by Klansmen in full regalia.

Klan terrorism served many purposes. For the poor whites who made up the bulk of Klansmen, the violent suppression of African Americans provided the psychological reassurance that they were not at the bottom of the social order. For white elites who approved of and often assisted the violence, it prevented a political alliance between poor whites and blacks. It also maintained a large, exploitable workforce for plantations and industry by keeping African Americans powerless and poor. Klan violence also discouraged African American voting and thus threatened the Republican Party in the South.

In response to surging violence in the South, Republicans in Congress, with strong support from the Grant administration, passed several Enforcement Acts in 1870 and 1871, outlawing "armed combinations" that deprived anyone of their civil or political rights. The Justice Department vigorously enforced these laws across the South, arresting and prosecuting thousands and weakening significantly the Klan and similar organizations by 1872. Although the Enforcement Acts demonstrated that federal authority could effectively protect the rights of freedmen, they also revealed the vulnerability of freedmen should the federal commitment to Reconstruction ever wane.

Why did groups like the Klan indulge in anti-black violence?

Read the **Document** *Hannah Irwin Describes Ku Klux Klan Ride (Late 1860s)*

Reconstruction Abandoned

 By the end of Grant's first term in office in 1873, supporters of Reconstruction and freedmen's rights could look with satisfaction at the many extraordinary changes that had taken place in the South. Yet ominous signs suggested Reconstruction was in trouble. Despite the crackdown on the Klan, white Southerners increasingly demonstrated their commitment to seizing power and imposing a new form of servitude on African Americans. Northerners, by contrast, seemed less and less willing to support a vigorous Reconstruction policy. Slowly, from 1872 to 1877, the extraordinary experiment in interracial democracy and progressive government in the South was dismantled in favor of oligarchy and white supremacy.

Corruption and Scandal

A major factor in the pullback from Reconstruction was a series of corruption scandals that plagued the Grant administration. Grant himself was honest, but also politically naive and given to a hands-off style of leadership that gave officials in his administration unusual independence. Many of them took advantage of Grant's trust to enrich themselves through illegal schemes.

For example, in the 1869 "Black Friday" scandal, Wall Street titans Jay Gould and Jim Fisk conspired with Grant's brother-in-law to corner the gold market. The plan failed but not before hundreds of innocent investors were ruined. In the Credit Mobilier scandal, Grant's vice president and several high-ranking members of Congress took bribes from the company involved in the completion of the government-subsidized Union Pacific Railroad. In the so-called "Whiskey Ring" scandal, Treasury Secretary Orville E. Babcock made a fortune by illegally allowing whiskey distillers to avoid paying excise taxes. In yet another scandal, Secretary of War William W. Belknap accepted bribes from companies engaged in corrupt activities on Indian reservations.

With so much negative publicity stirred up by corruption scandals, Grant's administration took steps to minimize political controversies. To secure his reelection and keep the Republican Party in power, Grant adopted a more conservative approach to Reconstruction, by now a frequent source of rancor in Washington.

In summer 1872, for example, Grant lobbied Congress for and then signed into law the Amnesty Act, granting a general pardon to all but a few hundred former Confederate leaders. Now eligible to vote and hold office, these planters and ex-Confederate army officers and officials wasted little time in reasserting their authority.

Republican Disunity

The retreat from Reconstruction in the 1870s was also hastened by growing dissention within the Republican Party. Many Republicans, including some former Radicals, began to question the wisdom of maintaining a strong federal role in the affairs of Southern states. Some argued the fundamental goals of Reconstruction—citizenship, civil rights, and suffrage for the freedmen—had been accomplished. There was, they believed, a constitutional and moral limit to what the federal government could do for the freedmen. Now was the time for freedmen to use their new rights to elevate themselves economically, socially, and politically.

Other Republicans argued for an end to Reconstruction for less idealistic reasons. Even though some of them had been abolitionists before the war and advocates of freedmen's rights in the first years that followed, they now considered Reconstruction a failure. These Liberal Republicans, as they came to be called, had grown tired of the political strife produced by debates over freedmen's rights.

> "It seems to me that we are drifting, drifting back under the leadership of the slaveholders. Our former masters are fast taking the reins of government."
>
> GEORGE M. ARNOLD, African American Republican

Read the **Document** *Credit Mobilier/Union Pacific Railroad Scandal Testimony of C.P. Huntington (1873)*

How did the scandals of the Grant administration undermine Reconstruction?

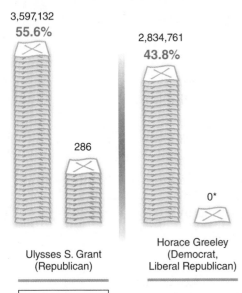

3,597,132
55.6%

286

Ulysses S. Grant
(Republican)

2,834,761
43.8%

0*

Horace Greeley
(Democrat,
Liberal Republican)

| | Popular vote |
| | Electoral vote |

* Greeley died before the electoral college met and therefore received no votes

14.16 The Election of 1872 Ulysses Grant easily won reelection when opposed by a weak candidate, Democrat Horace Greeley. Scandals and economic turmoil soon undermined his popularity and power.

They also worried about the growing power of the federal government.

Liberal Republicans also expressed disgust over the corruption and mismanagement of Southern Reconstruction governments. They accepted the argument of Southerners that freedmen and their white allies were incapable of honest and effective government. No one embodied this dramatic change of heart more than Horace Greeley, the progressive editor of the *New York Tribune*. Once the outspoken champion of abolition and freedmen's rights, by the early 1870s, he advocated returning the South to white rule. Blacks, he wrote in 1870, were a "worthless race," who would rather accept charity than help themselves. Their Reconstruction governments were based on "ignorance and degradation." A similar transformation from a progressive to a reactionary view of Reconstruction was revealed in the political cartoons of Thomas Nast (see *Images as History: Political Cartoons Reflect the Shift in Public Opinion*).

The Election of 1872

The dissatisfaction of Liberal Republicans reached full bloom in summer 1872. Disturbed by the prospect of Grant being renominated for a second term, they broke with the Republican Party and held their own convention in Cincinnati where they nominated Greeley for president. A divided Democratic Party also endorsed Greeley.

But the election of 1872 proved disastrous for Greeley and his backers. The public viewed Greeley as an eccentric who during his long career in public life had supported many fringe causes such as vegetarianism, spiritualism, and utopianism. Greeley's call for an end to Reconstruction and reconciliation between North and South also repelled many Northern voters who still associated Southerners and the Democratic Party with secession and civil war.

In Grant's sweeping victory over Greeley (**14.16**), Republicans had good reason to cheer. The Democrats' and Liberal Republicans' call for

ending Reconstruction and returning the South to white rule had been rejected. Moreover, the Grant administration's crackdown on the Klan had allowed African Americans unprecedented freedom to vote. Still, Northerners and Republicans in Congress were not prepared to support federal intervention in the South indefinitely. As new pressing issues emerged after 1872, support for Reconstruction rapidly eroded.

Hard Times

The American economy had boomed after the Civil War. Hundreds of thousands of new businesses were established. These included massive factories that employed hundreds, in some cases thousands, of workers. Aiding this economic growth was the dramatic expansion of the railroad and telegraph systems and increased availability of capital through banks and stock sales.

The booming economy encouraged businesses to expand and investors to take bigger risks. When these trends reached a critical point in late1873, a panic on Wall Street ensued. Some of the nation's most prominent financial houses and banks went bankrupt. As credit became scarce, businesses began to fail. Hundreds of thousands of workers lost their jobs. By early 1874, the nation's economy had plunged into a deep depression that lasted until 1877.

The Panic of 1873 directly affected Reconstruction. As hard times set in, the fate of the freedmen became less of a concern to Northerners. Economic issues like currency reform and the tariff took precedence over civil rights and white vigilante violence against freedmen. The public, declared one Republican, is tired of hearing about Southern violence against the freedmen: "Hard times and heavy taxes make them wish the 'everlasting nigger' were in hell or Africa." The public expressed its discontent in the congressional elections of 1874 by voting in a Democratic majority in the House for the first time since the war.

The Return of Terrorism

Reconstruction was also undone by a resumption of violence waged by white terrorist groups like the Klan. As the Grant administration bowed to political pressure to reduce federal intervention in Southern affairs, advocates of white supremacy seized the opportunity. In one notorious incident in 1873, a large band of heavily armed whites overran

Images as History
POLITICAL CARTOONS REFLECT THE SHIFT IN PUBLIC OPINION

One of the nation's most skilled and popular political cartoonists in the Reconstruction era was Thomas Nast. An immigrant from Germany, he landed a job in 1861 at *Harper's Weekly,* the nation's leading journal of politics and society. Nast's artistic talent, combined with *Harper's* vast circulation, soon turned him into one of the most influential illustrators of his day. As a staunch Republican and Unionist, his drawings during the Civil War were as intensely patriotic and pro-Lincoln as they were anti-Confederate.

After the war, Nast's widely distributed cartoons continued to shape Northern opinion about Reconstruction and freedmen's rights. Cartoons like *And Not This Man?* (August 5, 1865) proclaimed the dignity and humanity of the freedmen and their moral right to full citizenship and suffrage. In *This is a White Man's Government* (September 5, 1868), he stressed the violent intent of white Southerners to reclaim power and the necessity of federal authority in carrying out the goals of Reconstruction.

Nevertheless, Nast's cartoons eventually reflected the growing disillusionment of Northern Republicans regarding Reconstruction. While he rejected the Liberal Republican call to end Reconstruction, Nast nonetheless expressed the fear that African Americans were incapable of responsible government. Note the contrast between his earlier depictions of freedmen and that in *Colored Rule in a Reconstructed (?) State (March 14, 1874).*

"Columbia," an early symbol of America and democracy, advocates black suffrage. The globe is actually a nineteenth-century ballot box.

By showing African Americans in Union Army uniforms, Nast sought to remind Americans that blacks had earned the right to full citizenship through their service and sacrifice (note the missing leg) in the war.

And Not This Man?

A freedman wearing a Union Army uniform is crushed beneath an Irish immigrant (left), a white supremacist ex-Confederate (center), and a Northern capitalist (right). Nast saw these three groups as members of an opportunistic alliance.

A ballot box, representing the freedman's claim on citizenship and voting rights, has been kicked aside.

This is a White Man's Government

Reflecting Nast's disillusionment, "Columbia" chastises African American political leaders.

In 1874, frustrated with what he saw as inept and selfish African American political leadership in the South, Nash changed his depiction of blacks from noble individuals worthy of citizenship to racist caricatures.

Colored Rule in a Reconstructed (?) State

Why are political cartoons so popular and effective?

Colfax, Louisiana and slaughtered over 100 African Americans.

Just as in the late 1860s, white vigilante violence had two goals: to strip away the freedmen's hard-won rights and prevent them from voting and holding office. This effort peaked in Mississippi in 1875 when armed groups of whites closely allied with the Democratic Party waged a campaign of terror that came to be known as the **Mississippi Plan**. Through threats, beatings, and killings, they delivered an unambiguous message: blacks and their white allies who dared vote Republican risked their lives. But the Grant administration rejected Governor Adelbert Ames's request to send troops to keep the peace and protect the polls.

Not surprisingly, more than 60,000 Mississippi voters—nearly all black and Republican—stayed away from the polls on Election Day. Democrats swept to victory and took control of the state legislature for the first time since the Civil War. Immediately they threatened Governor Ames with impeachment and forced him to resign. The success of the Mississippi Plan in intimidating black voters and demolishing the Republican Party is indicated in this 1876 image, *Of Course He Wants to Vote the Democratic Ticket* (**14.17**). The artist shows the ruthless character of the white supremacy movement and the vulnerability of freedmen left without federal protection.

Other Southern states soon employed their own version of the Mississippi Plan. One by one the remaining Reconstruction governments

14.17 The Mississippi Plan in Action In much of the South, violence kept most freedmen away from the polls. Here a freedman is threatened with death unless he votes for the Democratic Party.

fell to a new class of political leaders known as **Redeemers**. As the name suggests, they cast themselves in almost biblical terms as saviors of Southern society. By 1876, only South Carolina, Louisiana, and Florida remained under Republican control—largely because of the presence of federal troops. The removal of these troops in 1877 opened the way for the complete "redemption" of the former Confederacy and the restoration of white supremacy.

Defenders of Reconstruction and the rights of freedmen in Congress were appalled at the rising tide of Redeemer oppression. In response they managed one final measure to bolster the rights of freedmen, the **Civil Rights Act of 1875**. It required that state governments provide equal access in public facilities such as schools and allow African Americans to serve on juries. The law was largely ignored, and in 1883 the Supreme Court ruled it unconstitutional.

The End of Reconstruction

The final blow to Reconstruction occurred as the result of the presidential election of 1876. With the Democratic Party reinvigorated by gaining a majority in the House in 1874 and control of most Southern state governments by 1876, a close election was expected. The Democrats nominated Samuel J. Tilden, governor of New York and a well-known reformer. Republicans nominated Ohio governor and Civil War veteran Rutherford B. Hayes. The issues centered on political corruption, the failed economy, and of course, Reconstruction.

On Election Day Tilden received 250,000 more popular votes than Hayes (**14.18**). But the electoral vote—which actually determines the victor—was unclear. Voting irregularities in South Carolina, Louisiana, and Florida left both sides claiming victory—and the 19 electoral votes at stake in those states (one electoral vote was also in dispute in Oregon). Tilden needed to be declared the winner in only one of these four states to win a majority of electoral votes and thus the presidency. Hayes needed to win all three Southern states plus the Oregon vote to put him one electoral vote ahead of Tilden and into the White House.

Both sides refused to budge, and a constitutional crisis loomed. Eventually they agreed

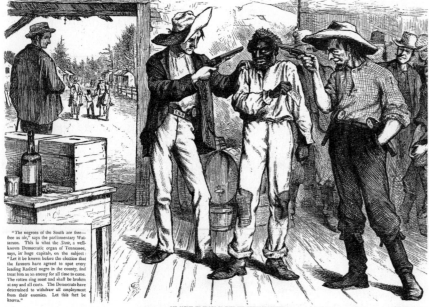

"The negroes of the South are free—free as air," says the parliamentary Watterson. This is what the *State*, a well-known Democratic organ of Tennessee, says, in huge capitals, on the subject: "Let it be known before the election that the farmers have agreed to spot every leading Radical negro in the county, and treat him as an enemy for all time to come. The rotten ring must and shall be broken at any and all costs. The Democrats have determined to withdraw all employment from their enemies. Let this fact be known."

"OF COURSE HE WANTS TO VOTE THE DEMOCRATIC TICKET."
DEMOCRATIC "REFORMER." "You're as free as air, ain't you? Say you are, or I'll blow yer black head off!"

Read the **Document** *Blanche K. Bruce, Speech in the Senate (1876)*

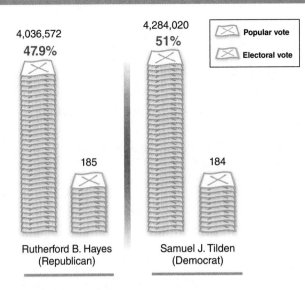

4,036,572
47.9%

4,284,020
51%

Popular vote

Electoral vote

185

184

Rutherford B. Hayes
(Republican)

Samuel J. Tilden
(Democrat)

14.18 The Election of 1876
In one of the most controversial presidential elections in U.S. history, Samuel B. Tilden won the popular vote (4,284,020 to 4,036,572), but lost the electoral vote to Rutherford B. Hayes, 185 to 184.

March 2, 1877, the commission issued its decision, known as the **Compromise of 1877**. By a vote of eight to seven, the 15-member commission awarded all 20 disputed electoral votes to Hayes, giving him a 185 to 184 electoral vote victory over Tilden.

Democrats denounced the "stolen election." Yet the result proved beneficial to the party. Hayes's presidency was weakened by the aura of illegitimacy (detractors referred to him as "his fraudulency"). More important, as part of a behind-the-scenes deal, he oversaw the final steps in the dismantling of Reconstruction. By the end of 1877, the last federal troops were removed from the South, and as the map (**14.19**) indicates, the last Reconstruction governments fell to Democratic Redeemers.

14.19 The Readmission of Southern States and Return of White Rule
Most former Confederate states were readmitted to the Union under the direction of Republican-controlled state governments. But as the dates in parentheses indicate, in most cases, conservative white Democratic governments soon seized control.

to abide by the decision of a bipartisan commission. The commission authorized an investigation and heard testimony. Behind the scenes members of Congress and party leaders conducted intense negotiations. On

Military Districts established under Reconstruction Act of 1867

1870   Date of readmission to the Union

(1871)   Date of reestablishment of conservative white government

Why is the eventual result of the election of 1876 considered the end of Reconstruction?

The New South

The optimism with which white Southerners greeted the end of Reconstruction gave rise to the term **New South**. It reflected the South's development of a new system of race relations based on segregation and white supremacy. Even more so, the New South pointed to a profound economic transformation that swept across the region, bringing with it a boom in manufacturing, railroad construction, and urbanization.

Redeemer Rule

The Redeemer governments that took control of Southern states by 1877 represented a new ruling oligarchy. Before the war a small and powerful class of planters dominated Southern politics. Now, in the aftermath of Reconstruction, a new elite took control. Although some were planters and former planters, most were men who drew their wealth and power from a new Southern economy based on industry, finance, commerce, and railroad construction.

As men of business their politics reflected the dominant conservative economic theory of the era, which argued that the best form of government was small, frugal, and pro-business. Accordingly, Redeemer governments slashed taxes and spending on social programs and public education created during Reconstruction.

Redeemer politics also championed a return to white supremacy. The return of one-party (Democratic) rule in most Southern states resulted in a steady decline in office holding by African Americans and Republicans. Intimidation and violence also led to a marked decrease in black voting across the South. Despite these setbacks, however, African Americans in many Southern states managed to vote and hold office in appreciable numbers into the 1880s and 1890s.

Redeemer rule did not go unchallenged. In several states anger among poor farmers coalesced into full-fledged political challenges to oligarchic rule, inequitable taxation, and cuts to social programs. These insurgents denounced the new elite as "Bourbons" (the name of the former French royal family), a derogatory term that implied aristocratic ambitions. In Virginia, for example, a coalition of Republicans and disaffected Democrats called Readjusters turned out the Redeemer government in 1879. All of these challenges to Redeemer rule, however, ultimately failed.

The Lost Cause

Southerners after 1877 embraced not only Redeemer rule, but also an image of the prewar South as an ideal society and the Confederate bid for independence a valiant Lost Cause. Southerners clung to this image because it provided them with a psychologically soothing explanation for why they lost the war. According to the Lost Cause idea, Confederate society was more virtuous than the North and its soldiers braver, but the South lost because the Yankees possessed overwhelming advantages in population, industry, arms, and ruthlessness. Defeat, while bitter and painful, was also a glorious martyrdom for a people and a way of life.

Southerners expressed this interpretation of the war as a glorious, yet ill-fated campaign in poems, plays, songs, speeches, sermons, and books. One of the most popular Lost Cause poets was Rev. Abram Ryan, a Catholic priest from Norfolk, Virginia. Many of his poems, such as "The Conquered Banner," became required recitations among white Southern schoolchildren for decades. These works by Ryan and others stressed courage, glory, duty, sacrifice, and the need for true Southerners to honor their Confederate heroes forever. As Ryan put it in one of his poems:

> But their memories e'er shall remain for us,
> And their names, bright names, without stain for us;
> The glory they won shall not wane for us,
> In legend and lay
> Our heroes in Gray
> Shall forever live over again for us.

The Lost Cause carried with it an obligation to keep alive the memory of Confederate glory. Southerners built elegant battlefield cemeteries to inter the war dead and monuments to celebrate Confederate victories. White Southern women, many widowed by the war, played a major role in these efforts,

What groups constituted the political leadership of the New South?

Read the **Document** *R. B. Buckley, Confederate Song, "I'm a Good Old Rebel" (1866)*

founding organizations such as the Ladies Memorial Association (1867) and the United Daughters of the Confederacy (1894). Southerners also erected thousands of statues honoring Confederate soldiers, including legends like Generals Robert E. Lee, Stonewall Jackson, and Nathan Bedford Forrest. The photograph (**14.20**) demonstrates how enthusiasm for the Lost Cause only grew the further the Civil War receded into history. Lee had discouraged efforts to raise monuments to the Confederate cause, but soon after he died in 1870, they sprang up across the South, including this monumental rendering unveiled in Richmond in 1890. Thousands turned out for the dedication of the heroic statue by French sculptor Antonin Mercie and to hear Colonel Archer Anderson laud Lee for his "courage, will, energy …

fortitude, hopefulness, joy in battle … [and] unconquerable soul." Nothing that day, certainly not the speeches or Lee's triumphant pose, recalled the fact that Lee had lost the war.

But the Lost Cause legend served a second purpose beyond helping Southerners cope with their defeat in the war. It celebrated a nostalgic vision of the prewar South that supported their arguments for a resumption of white rule and African American subservience. Through literature, art, and music, Southerners (and some Northerners) fashioned romantic depictions of the "Old South" as a harmonious paradise where benevolent masters treated loyal, contented slaves with kindness, where chivalrous Southern gentlemen protected delicate, charming women, and where everyone revered tradition, family, and the Bible. Yet even as they glorified slavery, the proponents of the Lost Cause downplayed its importance as a cause of secession. The real issue, they insisted, was "states' rights" and attempts by Northerners to run roughshod over them in the 1850s.

The Lost Cause thus presented Southerners as victims of misguided and unjustified Yankee aggression who, in the wake of devastating war and humiliating Reconstruction, ought to be left alone to run their own affairs. The overt racism and self-serving depictions of slavery in Lost Cause rhetoric and imagery served to justify a resumption of white rule and the return of African Americans to the status of powerless, exploitable laborers.

The New South Economy

Even as Southerners revered the Lost Cause and Old South, their new leadership steered the region's economy into an industrial future. In the 1870s and 1880s, they joined with Northern entrepreneurs who settled in the South during Reconstruction to develop a modern, market-oriented, and diversified economy. This effort entailed not simply the establishment of banks, textile mills, and railroads, but also the celebration and spreading of capitalist values, such as hard work, risk taking, thrift, and the profit motive.

14.20 Celebrating the Lost Cause As the commemorative ribbon indicates, this monument to Robert E. Lee was erected in the former Confederate capital of Richmond, Virginia in 1890. It was one of thousands of monuments to the Confederacy erected across the South.

View the Image *Cotton plantation, United States of America*   How was the Lost Cause a useful myth for Southerners?

14.21 Celebrating the New South
The Atlanta Exposition of 1895 offered a great opportunity for boosters of the New South to showcase the region's newly diversified economy.

The leading figure in this movement to establish a New South economy was Henry Grady, editor of the *Atlanta Constitution*. Beginning in the mid-1870s, in editorials and speeches, he proclaimed industrialization as the solution to the South's devastated postwar economy. His message inspired many Southerners, especially those who had never been part of the planter elite, to start businesses, invest, and support pro-business policies. Grady also convinced many Northerners, to invest in New South enterprises.

The vast expansion of manufacturing represented the most stunning change in the New South. Drawn by low taxes, cheap labor, ample water power, proximity to cotton supplies, and the absence of unions, textile manufacturers moved their operations from New England to the South,

especially the Carolinas. By 1900, the South had become the nation's leading producer of textiles. A similar transformation occurred in the tobacco industry, as the South went from merely producing raw tobacco to become the nation's leading producer of finished tobacco products like cigarettes.

Another significant aspect of the New South economy was the lumber and furniture industry. New South entrepreneurs took advantage of the region's tremendous forest reserves and new technologies, such as rotary saws and dry kilns, and an expanded railroad system, and soon made the South the leading producer of lumber. In Mississippi alone the number of lumber mills jumped from 295 in 1880 to 608 in 1899. The furniture industry likewise boomed in the New South, especially in places like High Point, North Carolina, where a single factory opened in 1889, followed by 30 more over the next decade.

Industry also flourished in the lower South. Birmingham, Alabama had only a few hundred residents when founded in 1871, but its position at the junction of two major railroads and nearby deposits of coal, iron, and limestone soon attracted iron and steel factories and the nickname, "Pittsburgh of the South." By 1890, the South produced 20 percent of U.S. iron and steel. As this promotional poster (**14.21**) makes clear, the booming and increasingly diverse economy of the New South was the central theme of the 1895 Atlanta Exposition. Here "Liberty" carries in her left arm a cornucopia filled with symbols of traditional Southern products like cotton and sugar, but also steel and iron. Note the imagery at the bottom that suggests the Civil War–and all its destruction and lingering controversies—is long gone.

As in the North the expansion of industry in the South relied on the existence of a large pool of cheap labor. But unlike the North, where millions of immigrants made up much of the workforce, the South relied on a rising population of poor white farming families pushed off the land by indebtedness, falling crop prices, and crop failure. In the rare

> "The growth of the iron interests of the South during the last few years has been the marvel of the age, attracting the attention of the entire business world."
>
> New South booster, M. B. HILLYARD, 1887

What weaknesses limited the success of the New South economy?

instances where African Americans secured industrial employment, it was usually in the most menial, dangerous, and poorly paid jobs.

Southern workers earned wages 50 percent lower than their Northern counterparts, revealing the limited success of the New South economy in overcoming the region's poverty and social problems. Despite decades of impressive growth in industry, mining, and railroads, the South in 1900 lagged far behind the North in virtually every category of economic and social progress. Most Southern industry, for example, was small scale and focused on low-skilled labor, including growing numbers of child laborers. Per capita incomes in the South remained stagnant from 1880 to 1900.

Other indications of backwardness and under-development abounded. The infant mortality rate far exceeded the national average. And because Redeemer governments had slashed per pupil spending in public education to half the average in the North, the South led the nation in illiteracy; its high school graduation rate was one-third that in the Midwest.

14.22 Poverty and Independence
Sharecropping condemned most African Americans to poverty, but it also helped to free them of immediate white control. No longer confined to slave cabins, they also worked on their own, free of white oversight and coercion.

The Rise of Sharecropping

The limitations of the New South economy was most vividly revealed in the preponderance of Southerners engaged in agriculture. The region's economy remained fundamentally tied to the production of cash crops, particularly tobacco, sugar, rice, and of course, cotton. Only 6 percent of the Southern workforce in 1900 was employed in manufacturing.

The condition of Southern farmers, both white and black, deteriorated sharply between 1875 and 1900. While cotton production soared, the price plummeted, from 18 cents per pound in the early 1870s to 5 cents per pound in 1894. Shrinking profits forced many Southern farmers to forfeit title to their land and became tenant farmers. Some rented land for a set fee which left them free to grow whatever crops they desired. But most tenant farmers resorted to the sharecropping system, whereby they received the right to farm a plot of land in exchange for rent paid in the form of a share (generally one-third to one-half) of the harvest. By 1900, more than 70 percent of the South's farmers (white and black) earned their living in this manner.

Sharecropping granted African Americans a measure of independence. White landlords generally allowed their tenants to control their own time and to set their own work routines. The people in this photograph (**14.22**) are poor and live in a ramshackle house, but like most sharecroppers they work as families free of direct white supervision. Freedmen cherished this independence, given their experience in slavery of gang labor under the brutal control of overseers. And yet, as a closer look at this image shows, a well-dressed white man is in the background—probably the landlord who arranged for the photograph to be taken. Sharecroppers were not slaves, but as this photograph makes clear, they lived under the control of their white landlords.

Read the Document *James T. Rapier, Testimony before U.S. Senate Regarding the Agricultural Labor Force in the South (1880)*

How did sharecropping provide limited independence to freedmen?

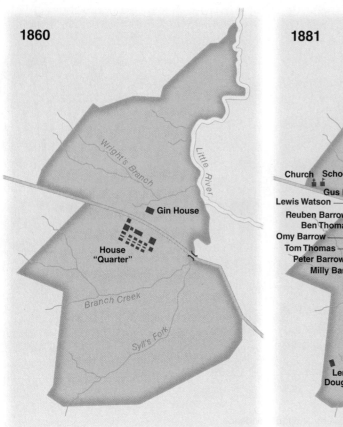

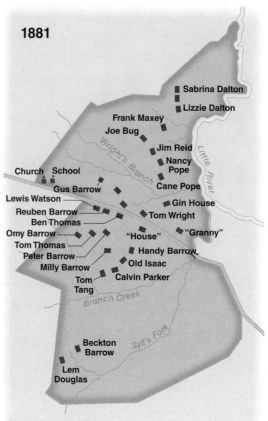

14.23 Moving from Slavery to Freedom: The Barrow Plantation, Oglethorpe County, Georgia, 1860 and 1881 Under slavery the Barrows confined their slaves' housing to a narrow section of the plantation. Sixteen years after emancipation, African Americans on the plantation, living beyond the immediate oversight of the Barrows, established a church and school.

The transformation from the tightly controlled plantation system to the relative independence of sharecropping can be seen in this map (**14.23**) of a Georgia plantation. The 1860 map shows the Barrow Family Plantation before the abolition of slavery. Note the layout of the slave quarters—in tight rows clustered within sight and earshot of the master. Seeking maximum control over their enslaved laborers, the Barrows kept them close at hand.

Twenty-one years later, many of the Barrow's former slaves and their descendents still lived on the plantation. But as the 1881 map indicates (see 14.23), the relationship between the Barrows and their workers had changed considerably, reflecting a sharp conflict in visions regarding the social order in the postwar South. Initially the Barrows had tried, like so many other former slave owners, to limit the freedom of their former slaves, hiring them as wage workers bound by annual labor contracts and trying to coerce them into accepting gang labor under an overseer. The freedmen, however, resisted and eventually negotiated to work as tenant farmers. By 1881, most ex-slaves lived in separate households scattered on the former plantation, working as sharecroppers

on 25- to 30-acre farms. The 1881 map also indicates the presence of two key institutions of African American freedom—a church and a school. Within the narrow limits allowed by hostile whites, freedmen enjoyed privileges they had been deprived of under slavery.

Nonetheless, tenancy exploited the freedmen. Landlords demanded they grow cash crops like tobacco, wheat, and especially cotton. Because they often needed to buy seed, tools, and animals on credit (usually on unfavorable terms) from their landlords or local suppliers, most tenants found themselves in a condition of ever-mounting debt which prevented them from moving to better land or to a landlord offering better terms. It also exposed freedmen to economic reprisals should they try to vote or stand up for their rights.

Jim Crow

Although life in the New South for most African Americans meant poverty and exploitation as sharecroppers, some managed to achieve a measure of economic success. Despite racism, poverty, and a hostile white business community, they bought property and started small businesses. Some of these endeavors blossomed into large, prosperous enterprises. For example, in 1898 two African American men in Durham founded the North Carolina Mutual and Provident Insurance Company. By 1907, the company boasted more than 100,000 policy holders. Other African Americans took advantage of the many black schools and colleges established during Reconstruction to enter the professions as teachers, professors, lawyers, doctors, nurses, and ministers. These members of a black middle class worked almost exclusively in segregated settings providing services to their fellow African Americans.

How did the poverty and indebtedness associated with sharecropping curtail the freedom of African Americans?

View the **Map** *Atlas Map: The Rise of Tenancy in the South (1880)*

These educated and relatively affluent African Americans provided leadership and direction for their communities, building social networks of churches, fraternal societies, and self-help organizations. The directors of the aforementioned North Carolina Mutual and Provident Insurance Company, for example, used their financial resources to support schools and establish a hospital, bank, and library to serve the black community of Durham. As *Heroes of the Colored Race* (**14.24**) suggests, middle-class blacks also cultivated pride in the accomplishments of African Americans after emancipation. This lithograph was published in 1881 for sale to African Americans. Note its emphasis on education and the role of African Americans in the Civil War and later as members of Congress.

14.24 *Heroes of the Colored Race* African Americans kept alive their hopes for a better future by cultivating an appreciation for their history.

But in the late 1870s and early 1880s, Southern political leaders began to create a social and legal system of segregation and disenfranchisement that came to be called Jim Crow (named for a derogatory black character in a popular minstrel show). They understood that as long as some African Americans possessed civil, economic, and political rights, especially the right to vote, white supremacy was called into question. Redeemer politicians also recognized that stoking racial animosity protected their privileged status as a ruling elite by deflecting the frustration and anger of poor Southern whites away from them and onto African Americans.

The Jim Crow system consisted of three main elements: segregation, disenfranchisement, and violence. The goal of segregation was to foment racial divisions by separating African Americans from as many aspects of everyday life as possible. Initial efforts focused on barring African Americans from hotels, restaurants, and railroad cars. Blacks denounced these violations of their constitutional rights-especially the Fourteenth Amendment-and challenged them in court.

But a conservative Supreme Court sharply restricted the authority of the Fourteenth Amendment and its guarantee of equal protection. In *Hall v. DeCuir* (1878), for example, the Court

declared unconstitutional a Louisiana law prohibiting racial discrimination on steamboats because the vessel was engaged in interstate commerce (running routes between Louisiana and Mississippi), which only Congress could regulate. Five years later, in the Civil Rights Cases, the Court declared the 1875 Civil Rights Act unconstitutional, asserting that the Fourteenth Amendment did not empower Congress to outlaw racial discrimination by private individuals and organizations. The ruling cleared the way for private individuals such as hotel owners and institutions such as men's clubs to bar African Americans, but left standing the right of Congress to prohibit discrimination by state government institutions. As explained in *Choices and Consequences: Sanctioning Separation* (page 434), this issue came before the Court in an 1896 case, *Plessy v. Ferguson*.

Hand-in-hand with segregation came the effort to eradicate black political power by circumventing the Fifteenth Amendment. Violence and intimidation in the 1870s had reduced black voting and office holding significantly, but not completely. In Mississippi, for example, black voter turnout averaged 39 percent in the 1880s. But rising fears over the voting power of both blacks and disgruntled poor whites led Redeemer

((•─ **Hear** the **Audio** *The Black Laws by Bishop B.W. Arnett, pamphlet excerpt*

What role did the black middle class play in the Jim Crow South?

Choices and Consequences
SANCTIONING SEPARATION

In 1890, Louisiana required separate cars for black and white passengers on all railroads in the state. To challenge the law, an African American carpenter named Homer A. Plessy bought a first-class ticket on the East Louisiana Railroad and sat in the whites-only first-class car. As expected he was arrested. Plessy argued before a local judge named John H. Ferguson that the law violated the Thirteenth Amendment's prohibition of slavery and the Fourteenth Amendment's equal protection clause. Ferguson ruled in favor of the railroad, stating that separation did not violate Plessy's rights, a decision upheld by the state's Supreme Court. When Plessy appealed to the U.S. Supreme Court, the justices considered three major options:

Choices

1 Refuse to hear the case and thus not render a judgment on the constitutionality of segregation, letting stand the Louisiana State Supreme Court decision.

2 Rule in favor of Plessy and declare Louisiana's segregation law unconstitutional.

3 Reject Plessy's appeal and uphold Louisiana's segregation law as constitutional.

Continuing Controversies

How should African Americans respond to the imposition of Jim Crow laws?

Black leaders in the 1890s were divided over the best strategy to oppose segregation. Booker T. Washington, the nation's most prominent African American leader, argued that efforts to overturn segregation were doomed to failure due to black Americans' lack of political and economic power (see Chapter 18). Instead he recommended blacks focus their energy and resources on self-improvement, especially in education, a strategy that would one day empower them to challenge segregation. Founding member of the National Association for the Advancement of Colored People (NAACP), W. E. B. Dubois, rejected this policy and insisted that African Americans keep up a sustained legal and political effort to end segregation. Ultimately it was Dubois's vision and NAACP attorneys that ended legalized segregation. In *Brown v. Board of Education of Topeka* in 1954, the Supreme Court overturned *Plessy* and rejected the concept of "separate but equal."

JIM CROW LAW.

UPHELD BY THE UNITED STATES SUPREME COURT.

Statute Within the Competency of the Louisiana Legislature and Railroads—Must Furnish Separate Cars for Whites and Blacks.

Washington, May 18.—The Supreme Court today in an opinion read by Justice Brown, sustained the constitutionality of the law in Louisiana requiring the railroads of that State to provide separate cars for white and colored passengers. There was no inter-

Decision

On May 18, 1896, the Supreme Court by a vote of 7 to 1 chose the third option and rejected Plessy's claim that the law violated his constitutional rights. The Thirteenth and Fourteenth Amendments, argued the majority, were never intended to establish full social equality of the races. Furthermore, legal separation of the races, a doctrine subsequently known as "separate but equal," was constitutional so long as states provided equal facilities. The lone dissenting justice, John Marshall Harlan, blasted the majority opinion, declaring the law a racist violation of the nation's "color-blind" Constitution.

Consequences

In sharply limiting the Fourteenth Amendment's equal protection provisions, the court allowed state governments to establish separate schools, hospitals, parks, theaters, restaurants, and public transportation across the South. The decision also opened the way for segregation laws aimed at Mexicans in the Southwest and Asians in California. In practice "separate but equal" proved only half accurate as segregated facilities were indeed separate, but never equal in terms of funding, staffing, and supplies.

How did the Supreme Court play a role in the imposition of segregation?

politicians to commence a program of disenfranchisement.

Given the sparse and direct language of the Fifteenth Amendment, the proponents of disenfranchisement needed to devise laws that deprived African Americans of the right to vote without making specific mention of "race, color, or previous condition of servitude." In 1889, Tennessee became the first of many Southern states to enact a poll tax, an annual tax imposed on all adult citizens in the state. Those who failed to pay it could not vote. As the image (**14.25**) of a Florida poll tax receipt for 1900 shows, the tax of $1 was low enough so that most white voters like Henry R. Nicks could pay it, but high enough to disenfranchise thousands of impoverished African Americans. Most states also required that all unpaid poll taxes from previous years be paid off before a citizen could vote, meaning that a black man who had fallen behind in his taxes for five years would need to pay $5 before entering a polling place.

In 1890, Mississippi enacted a poll tax and an additional measure to facilitate disenfranchisement: the literacy test. It allowed state and local officials to bar from voting anyone who failed a literacy test. It usually required a potential voter to read a complicated section of the state constitution and explain its meaning—a provision aimed at excluding African Americans given their low levels of education. Most Southern states soon adopted similar tests.

In the mid-1890s, Southern states added a third disenfranchisement policy, the so-called grandfather clause. It guaranteed the vote to anyone, even if they could not pass a literacy test, if their grandfather had been eligible to vote before 1867. Since no African Americans could vote before 1867, they were the only ones subject to literacy tests.

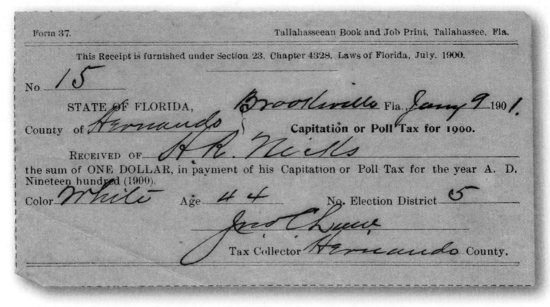

14.25 Disenfranchisement through the Poll Tax
Because H. R. Nicks, a white man in Hernando County, Florida, in 1900, could pay his poll tax of $1, he was eligible to vote. Mired in poverty, many African Americans could not afford the fee and lost their right to vote.

Adding to the effectiveness of the segregation and disenfranchisement movements was a stepped-up campaign of violence against African Americans. Vigilante groups across the South composed largely of poor whites, but often aided by local law officers and prominent citizens, launched an unprecedented wave of beatings, humiliations, and murders intended to intimidate blacks and "put them in their place." Often an unsubstantiated accusation of rape or murder brought out a community's lynch mob, but many killings were prompted by minor incidents of alleged disrespect such as arguing with a white man. Lynchings in the 1890s soared to an average of 187 per year, or roughly one killing every two days.

By 1900, these disenfranchisement policies had reduced overall black voting in the South by 62 percent. In some states black voting was effectively eliminated. In Louisiana, for example, the number of black voters dropped from 130,334 in 1896 to 1,342 in 1904—a reduction of 99 percent. Thousands of poor whites were also disenfranchised, reducing the total white vote by 27 percent by 1900. White supremacy had triumphed.

1863–1865

The Ten Percent Plan
Lincoln proposes moderate terms for readmission of Southern states

Thirteenth Amendment (Ratified 1865)
Abolishes slavery in every state

1866

Ku Klux Klan founded
Groups of armed white vigilantes wage campaign of violence to suppress freedmen's rights

Fourteenth Amendment (ratified 1868)
Defines citizenship to include African Americans and guarantees equal protection before the law

1867–1868

The Reconstruction Acts
South placed under military rule and freedmen guaranteed voting rights

Progressive state governments take power in South
Freedmen wield their newly won right to vote and hold office

Republicans impeach Johnson
Reflects the divisive politics of Reconstruction

1869–1871

Fifteenth Amendment (ratified 1870)
Establishes the right to vote for all male citizens regardless of "race, color, or previous condition of servitude"

Enforcement Acts passed
Empowers Grant administration to weaken Ku Klux Klan and like groups

North Carolina elects first Redeemer government
Signals a return to white supremacy in the South; other Southern states soon follow

Review Questions

1. Why did African Americans want land? How did they justify their claims to plantation lands?

2. Why did Reconstruction become violent? How did Congress and the Grant administration try to curb the violence?

3. How did feminists react to the Fifteenth Amendment? How did this affect the women's rights movement?

5. Why did Reconstruction end?

6. What was the Lost Cause? What purposes did it serve in the post-Reconstruction South?

7. Who were the "Bourbons" and what was their vision for the New South?

Key Terms

Ten Percent Plan Pardoned all Southerners (except high-ranking military officers and Confederate officials) who took an oath pledging loyalty to the Union and support for emancipation. As soon as 10 percent of a state's voters took this oath, they could call a convention, establish a new state government, and apply for congressional recognition.   **408**

Freedmen's Bureau Relief agency for the war-ravaged South created by Congress in March 1865. It provided emergency services, built schools, and managed confiscated lands.   **408**

Black Codes Laws designed by the ex-Confederate states to sharply limit the civil and economic rights of freedmen and create an exploitable workforce.   **413**

Fourteenth Amendment Drafted by Congress in June 1866, it defined citizenship to include African Americans, guaranteed equal protection before the law, and established the federal government as the guarantor of individual civil rights.   **417**

Carpetbagger White Southerners' derogatory term for Northerners who came south after the war to settle, work, or aid the ex-slaves. It falsely suggested they were penniless adventurers who came south merely to get rich.   **418**

Scalawag White Southerners' derogatory term for fellow whites considered traitors to their region and race for joining the Republican Party and cooperating with Reconstruction policy.   **418**

Fifteenth Amendment Constitutional amendment passed by Congress in 1869 providing an explicit constitutional guarantee for black suffrage.   **421**

Mississippi Plan Campaign of violence and intimidation waged by armed groups of whites closely allied with the Democratic Party that drove Republicans from power in the Mississippi state elections of 1874. Copied by other Southern states.   **426**

Redeemers Name for white Southern political leaders who successfully returned their states to white Democratic rule in the mid-1870s. The name was intended to depict these leaders as saviors of Southern society from rule by freedmen, scalawags, and carpetbaggers.   **426**

Civil Rights Act of 1875 Passed by Congress in 1875, it required state governments to provide equal access in public facilities such as schools and to allow African Americans to serve on juries. In 1883 the U.S. Supreme Court ruled it unconstitutional.   **426**

Compromise of 1877 Resolution of the disputed presidential election of 1876 that handed victory to Republican Rutherford B. Hayes over Democrat Samuel J. Tilden. Democrats agreed to the deal in exchange for patronage and the continued removal of federal troops from the South.   **427**

New South Optimistic phrase white Southerners used to describe the post-Reconstruction South, reflecting the South's development of a new system of race relations based on segregation and white supremacy and pointing to a profound economic transformation that swept across the region.   **428**

CHAPTER REVIEW

1872–1873

Amnesty Act
Pardons and restores full political rights to most ex-Confederates

Panic of 1873
Begins four years of severe economic depression that weakens Northern support for Reconstruction

1874–1875

The Mississippi Plan
Violence by white terrorist groups keeps thousands of blacks from voting. Restores the Democratic Party to power

Second Civil Rights Act passed
Guarantees equal access to public facilities and affirms the right of blacks to serve on juries

1876–1877

Compromise of 1877
Republican Rutherford B. Hayes becomes president; Republicans promise to remove federal troops from the South. End of Reconstruction

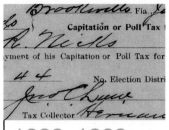

1883–1889

Civil Rights Act of 1875 Declared Unconstitutional
Clears the way for adoption of Jim Crow policies across the South

Tennessee enacts first poll tax
Sharply reduces black voting; adopted by other Southern states. Followed by literacy test and grandfather clause

MyHistoryLab Connections

Visit www.myhistorylab.com for a customized Study Plan that will help you build your knowledge of *Now That We Are Free*.

Questions for Analysis

1. How did former slaves make use of their new freedoms?

📖 **Read** the **Document** Charlotte Forten, "Life on the Sea Islands", p. 406

2. Why did some Americans believe the federal government was obligated to assist the freedmen?

🔍 **View** the **Closer Look** Competing Visions: Federal Authority and Equal Rights, p. 412

3. What changes did Republican governments bring to Southern society?

🔍 **View** the **Closer Look** First Vote, p. 419

4. How did the system of sharecropping sharply limit the freedom of African Americans?

📖 **Read** the **Document** James T. Rapier, Testimony before U.S. Senate Regarding the Agricultural Labor Force in the South (1880), p. 431

5. What role did violence play in establishing white supremacy in the New South?

🔊 **Hear** the **Audio File** A Georgia Lynch Law, p. 435

Other Resources from This Chapter

🔊 **Hear** the **Audio File** The Black Laws by Bishop B.W. Arnett, pamphlet excerpt, p. 433

📖 **Read** the **Document**

- Carl Schurz, "Report on the Condition of the South" (1865), p. 408
- James C. Beecher, "Report on Land Reform" (1865, 1866), p. 409
- "Address of the Colored State Convention to the People of the State of South Carolina" (1865), p. 414
- Affidavit of Former Slave Enoch Braston (1866), p. 415
- Charles F. Johnson and T. W. Gilbreth, The Memphis Riot (1866), p. 416
- Hannah Irwin Describes Ku Klux Klan Ride (Late 1860s), p. 422
- Credit Mobilier/Union Pacific Railroad Scandal Testimony of C.P. Huntington (1873), p. 423
- Blanche K. Bruce, Speech in the Senate (1876), p. 426
- R. B. Buckley, Confederate Song, "I'm a Good Old Rebel" (1866), p. 428

🔍 **View** the **Image** Cotton plantation, United States of America, p. 429

🔍 **View** the **Map**

- Interactive Map: Congressional Reconstruction, p. 417
- Atlas Map: The Rise of Tenancy in the South (1880), p. 432

👁 **Watch** the **Video** Video Lectures: The Schools that the Civil War and Reconstruction Created, p. 410

Appendix

- **The Declaration of Independence**

- **The Articles of Confederation**

- **The Constitution of the United States of America**

- **Amendments to the Constitution**

- **Presidential Elections**

- **Presidents and Vice Presidents**

For additional reference material, go to
www.pearsonamericanhistory.com
For the on-line appendix, click on Pearson American History Study Site.
The on-line appendix includes the following:

- The Declaration of Independence
- The Articles of Confederation
- The Constitution of the United States of America
- Amendments to the Constitution
- Presidential Elections
- Vice Presidents and Cabinet Members by Administration
- Supreme Court Justices
- Presidents, Congresses, and Chief Justices, 1789–2001
- Territorial Expansion of the United States (map)
- Admission of States of the Union
- U.S. Population, 1790–2000

- Ten Largest Cities by Population, 1700–1900
- Birthrate, 1820–2000 (chart)
- Death Rate, 1900–2000 (chart)
- Life Expectancy, 1900–2000 (chart)
- Urban/Rural Population, 1750–1900 (chart)
- Women in the Labor Force, 1890–1990
- United States Physical Features (map)
- United States Native Vegetation (map)
- Ancient Native American Communities (map)
- Native American Peoples, c. 1500 (map)
- Present-Day United States (map)

The Declaration of Independence

In Congress, July 4, 1776

The Unanimous Declaration of the Thirteen United States of America

When, in the course of human events, it becomes necessary for one people to dissolve the political bonds which have connected them with another, and to assume, among the powers of the earth, the separate and equal station to which the laws of nature and of nature's God entitle them, a decent respect to the opinions of mankind requires that they should declare the causes which impel them to the separation.

We hold these truths to be self-evident: That all men are created equal; that they are endowed by their Creator with certain unalienable rights; that among these are life, liberty, and the pursuit of happiness; that, to secure these rights, governments are instituted among men, deriving their just powers from the consent of the governed; that whenever any form of government becomes destructive of these ends, it is the right of the people to alter or to abolish it, and to institute new government, laying its foundation on such principles, and organizing its powers in such form, as to them shall seem most likely to effect their safety and happiness. Prudence, indeed, will dictate that governments long established should not be changed for light and transient causes; and accordingly all experience hath shown that mankind are more disposed to suffer, while evils are sufferable, than to right themselves by abolishing the forms to which they are accustomed. But when a long train of abuses and usurpations, pursuing invariably the same object, evinces a design to reduce them under absolute despotism, it is their right, it is their duty, to throw off such government, and to provide new guards for their future security. Such has been the patient sufferance of these colonies; and such is now the necessity which constrains them to alter their former systems of government. The history of the present King of Great Britain is a history of repeated injuries and usurpations, all having in direct object the establishment of an absolute tyranny over these states. To prove this, let facts be submitted to a candid world.

He has refused his assent to laws, the most wholesome and necessary for the public good.

He has forbidden his governors to pass laws of immediate and pressing importance, unless suspended in their operation till his assent should be obtained; and, when so suspended, he has utterly neglected to attend to them.

He has refused to pass other laws for the accommodation of large districts of people, unless those people would relinquish the right of representation in the legislature, a right inestimable to them, and formidable to tyrants only.

He has called together legislative bodies at places unusual, uncomfortable, and distant from the depository of their public records, for the sole purpose of fatiguing them into compliance with his measures.

He has dissolved representative houses repeatedly, for opposing, with manly firmness, his invasions on the rights of the people.

He has refused for a long time, after such dissolutions, to cause others to be elected; whereby the legislative powers, incapable of annihilation, have returned to the people at large for their exercise; the state remaining, in the mean time, exposed to all the dangers of invasions from without and convulsions within.

He has endeavored to prevent the population of these states; for that purpose obstructing the laws for naturalization of foreigners; refusing to pass others to encourage their migration hither, and raising the conditions of new appropriations of lands.

He has obstructed the administration of justice, by refusing his assent to laws for establishing judiciary powers.

He has made judges dependent on his will alone, for the tenure of their offices, and the amount and payment of their salaries.

He has erected a multitude of new offices, and sent hither swarms of officers to harass our people and eat out their substance.

He has kept among us, in times of peace, standing armies, without the consent of our legislatures.

He has affected to render the military independent of, and superior to, the civil power.

He has combined with others to subject us to a jurisdiction foreign to our constitution, and unacknowledged by our laws, giving his assent to their acts of pretended legislation:

For quartering large bodies of armed troops among us;

For protecting them, by a mock trial, from punishment for any murder which they should commit on the inhabitants of these states;

For cutting off our trade with all parts of the world;

For imposing taxes on us without our consent;

For depriving us, in many cases, of the benefits of trial by jury;

For transporting us beyond seas, to be tried for pretended offenses;

For abolishing the free system of English laws in a neighboring province, establishing therein an arbitrary government, and enlarging its boundaries, so as to render it at once an example and fit instrument for introducing the same absolute rule into these colonies.

For taking away our charters, abolishing our most valuable laws, and altering fundamentally the forms of our governments;

For suspending our own legislatures, and declaring themselves invested with power to legislate for us in all cases whatsoever.

He has abdicated government here, by declaring us out of his protection and waging war against us.

He has plundered our seas, ravaged our coasts, burned our towns, and destroyed the lives of our people.

He is at this time transporting large armies of foreign mercenaries to complete the works of death, desolation, and tyranny already begun with circumstances of cruelty and perfidy scarcely paralleled in the most barbarous ages, and totally unworthy the head of a civilized nation.

He has constrained our fellow-citizens, taken captive on the high seas, to bear arms against their country, to become the executioners of their friends and brethren, or to fall themselves by their hands.

He has excited domestic insurrection among us, and has endeavored to bring on the inhabitants of our frontiers the merciless Indian savages, whose known rule of warfare is an undistinguished destruction of all ages, sexes, and conditions.

In every stage of these oppressions we have petitioned for redress in the most humble terms; our repeated petitions have been answered only by repeated injury. A prince, whose character is thus marked by every act which may define a tyrant, is unfit to be the ruler of a free people.

Nor have we been wanting in our attentions to our British brethren. We have warned them, from time to time, of attempts by their legislature to extend an unwarrantable jurisdiction over us. We have reminded them of the circumstances of our emigration and settlement here. We have appealed to their native justice and magnanimity; and we have conjured them, by the ties of our common kindred, to disavow these usurpations, which would inevitably interrupt our connections and correspondence. They, too, have been deaf to the voice of justice and of consanguinity. We must, therefore, acquiesce in the necessity which denounces our separation, and hold them, as we hold the rest of mankind, enemies in war, in peace friends.

We, therefore, the representatives of the United States of America, in General Congress assembled, appealing to the Supreme Judge of the world for the rectitude of our intentions, do, in the name and by the authority of the good people of these colonies, solemnly publish and declare, that these United Colonies are, and of right ought to be, FREE AND INDEPENDENT STATES; that they are absolved from all allegiance to the British crown, and that all political connection between them and the state of Great Britain is, and ought to be, totally dissolved; and that, as free and independent states, they have full power to levy war, conclude peace, contract alliances, establish commerce, and do all other acts and things which independent states may of right do. And for the support of this declaration, with a firm reliance on the protection of Divine Providence, we mutually pledge to each other our lives, our fortunes, and our sacred honor.

John Hancock

Button Gwinnett	Francis Lightfoot Lee	Jno. Witherspoon
Lyman Hall	Carter Braxton	Fras. Hopkinson
Geo. Walton	Robt. Morris	John Hart
Wm. Hooper	Benjamin Rush	Abra. Clark
Joseph Hewes	Benja. Franklin	Josiah Bartlett
John Penn	John Morton	Wm. Whipple
Edward Rutledge	Geo. Clymer	Saml. Adams
Thos. Heyward, Junr.	Jas. Smith	John Adams
Thomas Lynch, Junr.	Geo. Taylor	Robt. Treat Paine
Arthur Middleton	James Wilson	Elbridge Gerry
Samuel Chase	Geo. Ross	Step. Hopkins
Wm. Paca	Caesar Rodney	William Ellery
Thos. Stone	Geo. Read	Roger Sherman
Charles Carroll of Carrollton	Tho. M'kean	Sam'el Huntington
George Wythe	Wm. Floyd	Wm. Williams
Richard Henry Lee	Phil. Livingston	Oliver Wolcott
Th. Jefferson	Frans. Lewis	Matthew Thornton
Benj. Harrison	Lewis Morris	
Thos. Nelson, Jr.	Richd. Stockton	

The Articles of Confederation

Between the States of New Hampshire, Massachusetts Bay, Rhode Island and Providence Plantations, Connecticut, New York, New Jersey, Pennsylvania, Delaware, Maryland, Virginia, North Carolina, South Carolina, Georgia

ARTICLE 1

The stile of this confederacy shall be "The United States of America."

ARTICLE 2

Each State retains its sovereignty, freedom and independence, and every power, jurisdiction, and right, which is not by this confederation expressly delegated to the United States, in Congress assembled.

ARTICLE 3

The said states hereby severally enter into a firm league of friendship with each other for their common defence, the security of their liberties and their mutual and general welfare; binding themselves to assist each other against all force offered to, or attacks made upon them, or any of them, on account of religion, sovereignty, trade, or any other pretence whatever.

ARTICLE 4

The better to secure and perpetuate mutual friendship and intercourse among the people of the different states in this union, the free inhabitants of each of these states, paupers, vagabonds, and fugitives from justice excepted, shall be entitled to all privileges and immunities of free citizens in the several states; and the people of each State shall have free ingress and regress to and from any other State, and shall enjoy therein all the privileges of trade and commerce, subject to the same duties, impositions, and restrictions, as the inhabitants thereof respectively; provided, that such restrictions shall not extend so far as to prevent the removal of property, imported into any State, to any other State of which the owner is an inhabitant; provided also, that no imposition, duties, or restriction, shall be laid by any State on the property of the United States, or either of them.

If any person guilty of, or charged with treason, felony, or other high misdemeanor in any State, shall flee from justice and be found in any of the United States, he shall, upon demand of the governor or executive power of the State from which he fled, be delivered up and removed to the State having jurisdiction of his offence.

Full faith and credit shall be given in each of these states to the records, acts, and judicial proceedings of the courts and magistrates of every other State.

ARTICLE 5

For the more convenient management of the general interests of the United States, delegates shall be annually appointed, in such manner as the legislature of each State shall direct, to meet in Congress, on the 1st Monday in November in every year, with a power reserved to each State to recall its delegates, or any of them, at any time within the year, and to send others in their stead for the remainder of the year.

No State shall be represented in Congress by less than two, nor by more than seven members; and no person shall be capable of being a delegate for more than three years in any term of six years; nor shall any person, being a delegate, be capable of holding any office under the United States, for which he, or any other for his benefit, receives any salary, fees, or emolument of any kind.

Each State shall maintain its own delegates in a meeting of the states, and while they act as members of the committee of the states.

In determining questions in the United States, in Congress assembled, each State shall have one vote.

Freedom of speech and debate in Congress shall not be impeached or questioned in any court or place out of Congress: and the members of Congress shall be protected in their persons from arrests and imprisonments, during the time of their going to and from, and attendance on Congress, except for treason, felony, or breach of the peace.

ARTICLE 6

No State, without the consent of the United States, in Congress assembled, shall send any embassy to, or receive any embassy from, or enter into any conference, agreement, alliance, or treaty with any king, prince, or state; nor shall any person, holding any office of profit or trust under the United States, or any of them, accept of any present, emolument, office or title, of any kind whatever, from any king, prince, or foreign state; nor shall the United States, in Congress assembled, or any of them, grant any title of nobility.

No two or more states shall enter into any treaty, confederation, or alliance, whatever, between them, without the consent of the United States, in Congress assembled, specifying accurately the purposes for which the same is to be entered into, and how long it shall continue.

No State shall lay any imposts or duties which may interfere with any stipulations in treaties entered into by the United States, in Congress assembled, with any king, prince, or state, in pursuance of any treaties already proposed by Congress to the courts of France and Spain.

No vessels of war shall be kept up in time of peace by any State, except such number only as shall be deemed necessary by the United States, in Congress assembled, for the defence of such State or its trade; nor shall any body of forces be kept up by any State, in time of peace, except such number only as, in the judgment of the United States, in Congress assembled, shall be deemed requisite to garrison the forts necessary for the defence of such State; but every State shall always keep up a well regulated and disciplined militia, sufficiently armed and accoutred, and shall provide, and constantly have ready for use, in public stores, a due number, of field pieces and tents, and a proper quantity of arms, ammunition and camp equipage.

No State shall engage in any war without the consent of the United States, in Congress assembled, unless such State be actually invaded by enemies, or shall have received certain advice of a resolution being formed by some nation of Indians to invade such State, and the danger is so imminent as not to admit of a delay till the United States, in Congress assembled, can be consulted; nor shall any State grant commissions to any ships or vessels of war, nor letters of marque or reprisal, except it be after a declaration of war by the United States, in Congress assembled, and then only against the kingdom or state, and the subjects thereof, against which war has been so declared, and under such regulations as shall be established by the United States, in Congress assembled, unless such States be infested by pirates, in which case vessels of war may be fitted out for that occasion, and kept so long as the danger shall continue, or until the United States, in Congress assembled, shall determine otherwise.

ARTICLE 7

When land forces are raised by any State for the common defence, all officers of or under the rank of colonel, shall be appointed by the legislature of each State respectively, by whom such forces shall be raised, or in such manner as such State shall direct; and all vacancies shall be filled up by the State which first made the appointment.

ARTICLE 8

All charges of war and all other expences, that shall be incurred for the common defence or general welfare, and allowed by the United States, in Congress assembled, shall be defrayed out of a common treasury, which shall be supplied by the several states, in proportion to the value of all land within each State, granted to or surveyed for any person, as such land and the buildings and improvements thereon shall be estimated according to such mode as the United States, in Congress assembled, shall, from time to time, direct and appoint.

The taxes for paying that proportion shall be laid and levied by the authority and direction of the legislatures of the several states, within the time agreed upon by the United States, in Congress assembled.

ARTICLE 9

The United States, in Congress assembled, shall have the sole and exclusive right and power of determining on peace and war, except in the cases mentioned in the 6th article; of sending and receiving ambassadors; entering into treaties and alliances, provided that no treaty of commerce shall be made, whereby the legislative power of the respective states shall be restrained from imposing such imposts and duties on foreigners as their own people are subjected to, or from prohibiting the exportation or importation of any species of goods or commodities whatsoever; of establishing rules for deciding, in all cases, what captures on land or water shall be legal, and in what manner prizes, taken by land or naval forces in the service of the United States, shall be divided or appropriated; of granting letters of marque and reprisal in times of peace; appointing courts for the trial of piracies and felonies committed on the high seas, and establishing courts for receiving and determining, finally, appeals in all cases of captures; provided, that no member of Congress shall be appointed a judge of any of the said courts.

The United States, in Congress assembled, shall also be the last resort on appeal in all disputes and differences now subsisting, or that hereafter may arise between two or more states concerning boundary, jurisdiction or any other cause whatever; which authority shall always be exercised in the manner following: whenever the legislative or executive authority, or lawful agent of any State, in controversy with another, shall present a petition to Congress, stating the matter in question, and praying for a hearing, notice thereof shall be given, by order of Congress, to the legislative or executive authority of the other State in controversy, and a day assigned for the appearance of the parties by their lawful agents, who shall then be directed to appoint, by joint consent, commissioners or judges to constitute a court for hearing and determining the matter in question; but, if they cannot agree, Congress shall name three persons out of each of the United States, and from the list of such persons each party shall alternately strike out one, in the petitioners beginning, until the number shall be reduced to thirteen; and from that number not less than seven, nor more than nine names, as Congress shall direct, shall, in the presence of Congress, be drawn out by lot; and the persons whose names shall be drawn, or any five of them, shall be commissioners or judges to hear and finally determine the controversy, so always as a major part of the judges who shall hear the cause shall agree in the determination; and if either party shall neglect to attend at the day appointed, without shewing reasons which Congress shall judge sufficient, or, being present, shall refuse to strike, the Congress shall proceed to nominate three persons out of each State, and the secretary of Congress shall strike in behalf of such party absent or refusing; and the judgment and sentence of the court to be appointed, in the manner before prescribed, shall be final and conclusive; and if any of the parties shall refuse to submit to the authority of such court, or to appear or defend their claim or cause, the court shall nevertheless proceed to pronounce sentence or judgment, which shall, in like manner, be final and decisive, the judgment or sentence and other proceedings being, in either case, transmitted to Congress, and lodged among the acts of Congress for the security of the parties concerned: provided, that every commissioner, before he sits in judgment, shall take an oath, to be administered by one of the judges of the supreme or superior court of the State where the cause shall be tried, "well and truly to hear and determine the matter in question, according to the best of his judgment, without favor, affection, or hope of reward": provided, also, that no State shall be deprived of territory for the benefit of the United States.

All controversies concerning the private right of soil, claimed under different grants of two or more states, whose jurisdictions, as they may respect such lands and the states which passed such grants, are adjusted, the said grants, or either of them, being at the same time claimed to have originated antecedent to such settlement of jurisdiction, shall, on the petition of either party to the Congress of the United States, be finally determined, as near as may be, in the same manner as is before prescribed for deciding disputes respecting territorial jurisdiction between different states.

The United States, in Congress assembled, shall also have the sole and exclusive right and power of regulating the alloy and value of coin struck by their own authority, or by that of the respective states; fixing the standard of weights and measures throughout the United States; regulating the trade and managing all affairs with the Indians not members of any of the states; provided that the legislative right of any State within its own limits be not infringed or violated; establishing and regulating post offices from one State to another throughout all the United States, and exacting such postage on the papers passing through the same as may be requisite to defray the expences of the said office; appointing all officers of the land forces in the service of the United States, excepting regimental officers; appointing all the officers of the naval forces, and commissioning all officers whatever in the service of the United States; making rules for the government and regulation of the said land and naval forces, and directing their operations.

The United States, in Congress assembled, shall have authority to appoint a committee to sit in the recess of Congress, to be denominated "a Committee of the States," and to consist of one delegate from each State, and to appoint such other committees and civil officers as may be necessary for managing the general affairs of the United States, under their direction; to appoint one of their number to preside; provided that no person be allowed to serve in the office of president more than one year in any term of three years; to ascertain the necessary sums of money to be raised for the service of the United States, and to appropriate and apply the same for defraying the public expences; to borrow money or emit bills on the credit of the United States, transmitting, every half year, to the respective states, an account of the sums of money so borrowed or emitted; to build and equip a navy; to agree upon the number of land forces, and to make requisitions from each State for its quota, in proportion to the number of white inhabitants in such State; which requisitions shall be binding; and, thereupon, the legislature of each State shall appoint the regimental officers, raise the men, and cloathe, arm, and equip them in a soldier-like manner, at the expence of the United States; and the officers and men so cloathed, armed, and equipped, shall march to the place appointed and within the time agreed on by the United States, in Congress assembled; but if the United States, in Congress assembled, shall, on consideration of circumstances, judge proper that any State should not raise men, or should raise a smaller number than its quota, and that any other State should raise a greater number of men than the quota thereof, such extra number shall be raised, officered, cloathed, armed, and equipped in the same manner as the quota of such State, unless the legislature of such State shall judge that such extra number cannot be safely spared out of the same, in which case they shall raise, officer, cloathe, arm, and equip as many of such extra number as they judge can be safely spared. And the officers and men so cloathed, armed, and equipped, shall march to the place appointed and within the time agreed on by the United States, in Congress assembled.

The United States, in Congress assembled, shall never engage in a war, nor grant letters of marque and reprisal in time of peace, nor enter into any treaties or alliances, nor coin money, nor regulate the value thereof, nor ascertain the sums and expences necessary for the defence and welfare of the United States, or any of them: nor emit bills, nor borrow money on the credit of the United States, nor appropriate money, nor agree upon the number of vessels of war to be built or purchased, or the number of land or sea forces to be raised, nor appoint a commander in chief of the army or navy, unless nine states assent to the same; nor shall a question on any other point, except for adjourning from day to day, be determined, unless by the votes of a majority of the United States, in Congress assembled.

The Congress of the United States shall have power to adjourn to any time within the year, and to any place within the United States, so that no period of adjournment be for a longer duration than the space of six months, and shall publish the journal of their proceedings monthly, except such parts thereof, relating to treaties, alliances or military operations, as, in their judgment, require secrecy; and the yeas and nays of the delegates of each State on any question shall be entered on the journal, when it is desired by any delegate; and the delegates of a State, or any of them, at his, or their request, shall be furnished with a transcript of the said journal, except such parts as are above excepted, to lay before the legislatures of the several states.

ARTICLE 10

The committee of the states, or any nine of them, shall be authorized to execute, in the recess of Congress, such of the powers of Congress as the United States, in Congress assembled, by the consent of nine states, shall, from time to time, think expedient to vest them with; provided, that no power be delegated to the said committee for the exercise of which by the articles of confederation, the voice of nine states, in the Congress of the United States assembled, is requisite.

ARTICLE 11

Canada acceding to this confederation, and joining in the measures of the United States, shall be admitted into and entitled to all the advantages of this union; but no other colony shall be admitted into the same, unless such admission be agreed to by nine states.

ARTICLE 12

All bills of credit emitted, monies borrowed and debts contracted by, or under the authority of Congress before the assembling of the United States, in pursuance of the present confederation, shall be deemed and considered as a charge against the United States, for payment and satisfaction whereof the said United States and the public faith are hereby solemnly pledged.

ARTICLE 13

Every State shall abide by the determinations of the United States, in Congress assembled, on all questions which, by this confederation, are submitted to them. And the articles of this confederation shall be inviolably observed by every State, and the union shall be perpetual; nor shall any alteration at any time hereafter be made in any of them, unless such alteration be agreed to in a Congress of the United States, and be afterwards confirmed by the legislatures of every State.

These articles shall be proposed to the legislatures of all the United States, to be considered, and if approved of by them, they are advised to authorize their delegates to ratify the same in the Congress of the United States; which being done, the same shall become conclusive.

The Constitution of the United States of America Preamble

PREAMBLE

We the People of the United States, in Order to form a more perfect Union, establish Justice, insure domestic Tranquility, provide for the common defence, promote the general Welfare, and secure the Blessings of Liberty to ourselves and our Posterity, do ordain and establish this Constitution for the United States of America.

ARTICLE 1

Section 1

All legislative Powers herein granted shall be vested in a Congress of the United States, which shall consist of a Senate and House of Representatives.

Section 2

The House of Representatives shall be composed of Members chosen every second Year by the People of the several States, and the Electors in each State shall have the Qualifications requisite for Electors of the most numerous Branch of the State Legislature.

No Person shall be a Representative who shall not have attained to the Age of twenty five Years, and been seven Years a Citizen of the United States, and who shall not, when elected, be an inhabitant of that State in which he shall be chosen.

Representatives and direct Taxes shall be apportioned among the several States which may be included within this Union, according to their respective Numbers, *which shall be determined by adding to the whole Number of free Persons, including those bound to Service for a Term of Years, and excluding Indians not taxed, three fifths of all other Persons.** The actual Enumeration shall be made within three Years after the first Meeting of the Congress of the United States, and within every subsequent Term of ten Years, in such Manner as they shall by Law direct. The Number of Representatives shall not exceed one for every thirty Thousand, but each State shall have at Least one Representative; *and until such enumeration shall be made, the State of New Hampshire shall be entitled to chuse three, Massachusetts eight, Rhode-Island and Providence Plantations one, Connecticut five, New York six, New Jersey four, Pennsylvania eight, Delaware one, Maryland six, Virginia ten, North Carolina five, South Carolina five, and Georgia three.*

When vacancies happen in the Representation from any State, the Executive Authority thereof shall issue Writs of Election to fill such Vacancies.

The House of Representatives shall chuse their Speaker and other Officers; and shall have the sole Power of Impeachment.

Section 3

The Senate of the United States shall be composed of two Senators from each State, chosen by the Legislature thereof, for six Years; and each Senator shall have one Vote.

Immediately after they shall be assembled in Consequence of the first Election, they shall be divided as equally as may be into three Classes. The Seats of the Senators of the first Class shall be vacated at the Expiration of the second Year, of the second Class at the Expiration of the fourth Year, and of the third Class at the Expiration of the sixth Year so that one third may be chosen every second Year; and if Vacancies happen by Resignation, or otherwise, during the Recess of the Legislature of any state, the Executive thereof may make temporary Appointments until the next Meeting of the Legislature, which shall then fill such Vacancies.

No Person shall be a Senator who shall not have attained to the Age of thirty Years, and been nine Years a Citizen of the United States, and who shall not, when elected, be an Inhabitant of that State for which he shall be chosen.

The Vice President of the United States shall be President of the Senate, but shall have no Vote, unless they be equally divided.

The Senate shall chuse their other Officers, and also a President pro tempore, in the Absence of the Vice President, or when he shall exercise the Office of President of the United States.

The Senate shall have the sole Power to try all Impeachments. When sitting for that Purpose, they shall be on Oath or Affirmation. When the President of the United States is tried the Chief Justice shall preside: And no Person shall be convicted without the Concurrence of two thirds of the Members present.

Judgment in Cases of Impeachment shall not extend further than to removal from Office, and disqualification to hold and enjoy any Office of honor, Trust or Profit under the United States: but the Party convicted shall nevertheless be liable and subject to Indictment, Trial, Judgment and Punishment, according to Law.

---

*Passages no longer in effect are printed in italic type.

Section 4

The Times, Places and Manner of holding Elections for Senators and Representatives, shall be prescribed in each State by the Legislature thereof; but the Congress may at any time by Law make or alter such Regulations, except as to the Places of chusing Senators.

The Congress shall assemble at least once in every Year, *and such Meeting shall be on the first Monday in December, unless they shall by Law appoint a different Day.*

Section 5

Each House shall be the Judge of the Elections, Returns and Qualifications of its own Members, and a Majority of each shall constitute a Quorum to do Business; but a smaller Number may adjourn from day to day, and may be authorized to compel the Attendance of absent Members, in such Manner, and under such Penalties as each House may provide.

Each House may determine the Rules of its Proceedings, punish its Members for disorderly Behaviour, and, with the Concurrence of two thirds, expel a Member.

Each House shall keep a Journal of its Proceedings, and from time to time publish the same, excepting such Parts as may in their Judgment require Secrecy; and the Yeas and Nays of the Members of either House on any question shall, at the Desire of one fifth of those Present, be entered on the Journal.

Neither House, during the Session of Congress, shall, without the Consent of the other, adjourn for more than three days, nor to any other Place than that in which the two Houses shall be sitting.

Section 6

The Senators and Representatives shall receive a Compensation for their Services, to be ascertained by Law, and paid out of the Treasury of the United States. They shall in all Cases, except Treason, Felony and Breach of the Peace, be privileged from Arrest during their Attendance at the Session of their respective Houses, and in going to and returning from the same; and for any Speech or Debate in either House, they shall not be questioned in any other Place.

No Senator or Representative shall, during the Time for which he was elected, be appointed to any civil Office under the Authority of the United States, which shall have been created, or the Emoluments whereof shall have been encreased during such time, and no Person holding any Office under the United States, shall be a Member of either House during his Continuance in Office.

Section 7

All Bills for raising Revenue shall orginate in the House of Representatives; but the Senate may propose or concur with Amendments as on other Bills.

Every Bill which shall have passed the House of Representatives and the Senate, shall, before it become a Law, be presented to the President of the United States; If he approve he shall sign it, but if not he shall return it, with his Objections to the House in which it shall have originated, who shall enter the Objections at large on their Journal, and proceed to reconsider it. If after such Reconsideration two thirds of that House shall agree to pass the Bill, it shall be sent, together with the Objections, to the other House, by which it shall likewise be reconsidered, and if approved by two thirds of that House, it shall become a Law. But in all such Cases the Votes of both Houses shall be determined by yeas and Nays, and the Names of the Persons voting for and against the Bill shall be entered on the Journal of each House respectively. If any Bill shall not be returned by the President within ten Days (Sundays excepted) after it shall have been presented to him, the Same shall be a Law, in like Manner as if he had signed it, unless the Congress by their Adjournment prevent its Return, in which Case it shall not be a Law.

Every Order, Resolution, or Vote to which the Concurrence of the Senate and House of Representatives may be necessary (except on a question of Adjournment) shall be presented to the President of the United States; and before the Same shall take Effect, shall be approved by him, or being disapproved by him, shall be repassed by two thirds of the Senate and House of Representatives, according to the Rules and Limitations prescribed in the Case of a Bill.

Section 8

The Congress shall have Power To lay and collect Taxes, Duties, Imposts and Excises, to pay the Debts and provide for the common Defence and general Welfare of the United States; but all Duties, Imposts and Excises shall be uniform throughout the United States;

To borrow Money on the credit of the United States;

To regulate Commerce with foreign Nations, and among the several States, and with the Indian Tribes;

To establish an uniform Rule of Naturalization, and uniform Laws on the subject of Bankruptcies throughout the United States;

To coin Money, regulate the Value thereof, and of foreign Coin, and fix the Standard of Weights and Measures;

To provide for the Punishment of counterfeiting the Securities and current Coin of the United States;

To establish Post Offices and post Roads;

To promote the Progress of Science and useful Arts, by securing for limited Times to Authors and Inventors the exclusive Right to their respective Writings and Discoveries;

To constitute Tribunals inferior to the supreme Court;

To define and punish Piracies and Felonies committed on the high Seas, and Offences against the Law of Nations;

To declare War, grant Letters of Marque and Reprisal, and make Rules concerning Captures on Land and Water;

To raise and support Armies, but no Appropriation of Money to that Use shall be for a longer Term than two Years;

To provide and maintain a Navy;

To make Rules for the Government and Regulation of the land and naval Forces;

To provide for calling forth the Militia to execute the Laws of the Union, suppress Insurrections and repel Invasions;

To provide for organizing, arming, and disciplining, the Militia, and for governing such Part of them as may be employed in the Service of the United States, reserving to the States respectively, the Appointment of the Officers, and the Authority of training the Militia according to the discipline prescribed by Congress;

To exercise exclusive Legislation in all Cases whatsoever, over such District (not exceeding ten Miles square) as may, by Cession of particular States, and the Acceptance of Congress, become the Seat of the Government of the United States, and to exercise like Authority over all Places purchased by the Consent of the Legislature of the State in which the Same shall be, for the Erection of Forts, Magazines, Arsenals, dock-Yards, and other needful Buildings;—And

To make all Laws which shall be necessary and proper for carrying into Execution the foregoing Powers, and all other Powers vested by this Constitution in the Government of the United States, or in any Department of Officer thereof.

Section 9

The Migration or Importation of such Persons as any of the States now existing shall think proper to admit, shall not be prohibited by the Congress prior to the Year one thousand eight hundred and eight, but a Tax or duty may be imposed on such Importation, not exceeding ten dollars for each Person.

The Privilege of the Writ of Habeas Corpus shall not be suspended, unless when in Cases of Rebellion or Invasion the public Safety may require it.

No Bill of Attainder or ex post facto Law shall be passed.

No Capitation, or other direct, Tax shall be laid, unless in Proportion to the Census or Enumeration herein before directed to be taken.

No Tax or Duty shall be laid on Articles exported from any State.

No Preference shall be given by any Regulation of Commerce or Revenue to the Ports of one State over those of another: nor shall Vessels bound to, or from, one State, be obliged to enter, clear, or pay Duties in another.

No Money shall be drawn from the Treasury, but in Consequence of Appropriations made by Law; and a regular Statement and Account of the Receipts and Expenditures of all public Money shall be published from time to time.

No Title of Nobility shall be granted by the United States: And no Person holding any Office of Profit or Trust under them, shall, without the Consent of the Congress, accept of any present, Emolument, Office, or Title, of any kind whatever, from any King, Prince, or foreign State.

Section 10

No State shall enter into any Treaty, Alliance, or Confederation; grant Letters of Marque and Reprisal; coin Money; emit Bills of Credit; make any Thing but gold and silver Coin a Tender in Payment of Debts; pass any Bill of Attainder, ex post facto Law, or Law impairing the obligation of Contracts, or grant any Title of Nobility.

No State shall, without the Consent of the Congress, lay any Imposts or Duties on Imports or Exports, except what may be absolutely necessary for executing its inspection Laws: and the net Produce of all Duties and Imposts, laid by any State on Imports or Exports, shall be for the Use of the Treasury of the United States; and all such Laws shall be subject to the Revision and Controul of the Congress.

No State shall, without the Consent of Congress, lay any Duty of Tonnage, keep Troops, or Ships of War in time of Peace, enter into any Agreement or Compact with another State, or with a foreign Power, or engage in War, unless actually invaded, or in such imminent Danger as will not admit of delay.

ARTICLE II
Section 1

The executive Power shall be vested in a President of the United States of America. He shall hold his Office during the Term of four Years, and, together with the Vice President, chosen for the same Term, be elected, as follows:

Each State shall appoint, in such Manner as the Legislature thereof may direct, a Number of Electors, equal to the whole Number of Senators and Representatives to which the State may be entitled in the Congress: but no Senator or Representative, or Person holding an Office of Trust or Profit under the United States, shall be appointed an Elector.

The Electors shall meet in their respective States, and vote by Ballot for two Persons, of whom one at least shall not be an Inhabitant of the same State with themselves. And they shall make a List of all the Persons voted for, and of the Number of Votes for each; which List they shall sign and certify, and transmit sealed to the Seat of the Government of the United States, directed to the President of the Senate. The President of the Senate shall, in the Presence of the Senate and House of Representatives, open all the Certificates, and the Votes shall then be counted. The Person having the greatest Number of Votes shall be the President, if such Number be a Majority of the whole number of Electors appointed; and if there be more than one who have such Majority, and have an equal Number of Votes, then the House of Representatives shall immediately chuse by Ballot one of them for President; and if no Person have a Majority, then from the five highest on the List the said House shall in like Manner chuse the President. But in chusing the President, the Votes shall be taken by States, the Representation from each State having one Vote; A quorum for this Purpose shall consist of a Member or Members from two thirds of the States, and a Majority of all the States shall be necessary to a Choice. In every Case, after the Choice of the President, the Person having the greatest Number of Votes of the Electors shall be the Vice President. But if there should remain two or more who have equal Votes, the Senate shall chuse from them by Ballot the Vice President.

The Congress may determine the time of chusing the Electors, and the Day on which they shall give their Votes; which Day shall be the same throughout the United States.

No person except a natural born Citizen, *or a Citizen of the United States, at the time of the Adoption of this Constitution*, shall be eligible to the Office of President; neither shall any Person be eligible to that Office who shall not have attained to the Age of thirty five Years, and been fourteen Years a Resident within the United States.

In Case of the Removal of the President from Office, or of his Death, Resignation, or Inability to discharge the Powers and Duties of the said Office, the Same shall devolve on the Vice President, and the Congress may by Law provide for the Case of Removal, Death, Resignation or Inability, both of the President and Vice President, declaring what Officer shall then act as President, and such Officer shall act accordingly, until the Disability be removed, or a President shall be elected.

The President shall, at stated Times, receive for his Services, a Compensation, which shall neither be encreased nor diminished during the Period for which he shall have been elected, and he shall not receive within that period any other Emolument from the United States, or any of them.

Before he enter on the Execution of his Office, he shall take the following Oath or Affirmation:—"I do solemnly swear (or affirm) that I will faithfully execute the Office of President of the United States, and will to the best of my Ability, preserve, protect and defend the Constitution of the United States."

Section 2

The President shall be Commander in Chief of the Army and Navy of the United States, and of the Militia of the several States, when called into the actual Service of the United States; he may require the Opinion, in writing, of the principal Officer in each of the executive Departments, upon any Subject relating to the Duties of their respective Offices, and he shall have Power to grant Reprieves and Pardons for Offences against the United States, except in Cases of Impeachment.

He shall have Power, by and with the Advice and Consent of the Senate, to make Treaties, provided two thirds of the Senators present concur; and he shall nominate, and by and with the Advice and Consent of the Senate, shall appoint Ambassadors, other public Ministers and Consuls, Judges of the supreme Court, and all other Officers of the United States, whose Appointments are not herein otherwise provided for, and which shall be established by Law: but the Congress may by Law vest the Appointment of such inferior Officers, as they think proper in the President alone, in the Courts of Law, or in the Heads of Departments.

The President shall have Power to fill up all Vacancies that may happen during the Recess of the Senate, by granting Commissions which shall expire at the End of their next Session.

Section 3

He shall from time to time give to the Congress Information of the State of the Union, and recommend to their Consideration such Measures as he shall judge necessary and expedient; he may, on extraordinary Occasions, convene both Houses, or either of them, and in Case of disagreement between them, with Respect to the Time of Adjournment, he may adjourn them to such Time as he shall think proper; he shall receive Ambassadors and other public Ministers; he shall take Care that the Laws be faithfully executed, and shall Commission all the officers of the United States.

Section 4

The President, Vice President and all civil Officers of the United States, shall be removed from Office on Impeachment for, and Conviction of, Treason, Bribery or other high Crimes and Misdemeanors.

ARTICLE III
Section 1

The judicial Power of the United States, shall be vested in one supreme Court, and in such inferior Courts as the Congress may from time to time ordain and establish. The Judges, both of the supreme and inferior Courts, shall hold their offices during good Behaviour, and shall, at stated Times, receive for their Services, a Compensation, which shall not be diminished during their Continuance in Office.

Section 2

The judicial Power shall extend to all Cases, in Law and Equity, arising under this Constitution, the Laws of the United States, and Treaties made, or which shall be made, under their Authority;—to all Cases affecting Ambassadors, other public Ministers and Consuls;—to all Cases of admiralty and maritime Jurisdiction;—to Controversies to which the United States shall be a Party;—to Controversies between two or more States;—between a State and Citizens of another State;—between Citizens of different States;—between Citizens of the same State claiming Lands under Grants of different States, and between a State, or the Citizens thereof, and foreign States, Citizens or Subjects.

In all Cases affecting Ambassadors, other public Ministers and Consuls, and those in which a State shall be Party, the supreme Court shall have original Jurisdiction. In all the other Cases before mentioned, the supreme Court shall have appellate Jurisdiction, both as to Law and Fact, with such Exceptions, and under such Regulations as the Congress shall make.

The Trial of all Crimes, except in Cases of Impeachment, shall be by Jury; and such Trial shall be held in the State where the said Crimes shall have been committed, but when not committed within any State, the Trial shall be at such Place or Places as the Congress may by Law have directed.

Section 3

Treason against the United States, shall consist only in levying War against them, or in adhering to their Enemies, giving them Aid and Comfort. No person shall be convicted of Treason unless on the Testimony of two Witnesses to the same overt Act, or on Confession in open Court.

The Congress shall have Power to declare the Punishment of Treason, but no Attainder of Treason shall work Corruption of Blood, or Forfeiture except during the Life of the Person attainted.

ARTICLE IV
Section 1

Full Faith and Credit shall be given in each State to the public Acts, Records, and judicial Proceedings of every other State. And the Congress may by general Laws prescribe the Manner in which such Acts, Records and Proceedings shall be proved, and the Effect thereof.

Section 2

The Citizens of each State shall be entitled to all Privileges and Immunities of Citizens in the several States.

A Person charged in any State with Treason, Felony, or other Crime, who shall flee from Justice, and be found in another State, shall on Demand of the executive Authority of the State from which he fled, be delivered up, to be removed to the State having Jurisdiction of the Crime.

No Person held to Service or Labour in one State, under the Laws thereof, escaping into another, shall, in Consequence of any Law or Regulation therein, be discharged from such Service or Labour, but shall be delivered up on Claim of the Party to whom such Service or Labour may be due.

Section 3

New States may be admitted by the Congress into this Union; but no new State shall be formed or erected within the Jurisdiction of any other State; nor any State be formed by the Junction of two or more States, or Parts of States, without the Consent of the Legislatures of the States concerned as well as of the Congress.

The Congress shall have Power to dispose of and make all needful Rules and Regulations respecting the Territory or other Property belonging to the United States; and nothing in this Constitution shall be so construed as to Prejudice any Claims of the United States, or of any particular States.

Section 4

The United States shall guarantee to every State in this Union a Republican Form of Government, and shall protect each of them against Invasion; and on Application of the Legislature, or of the Executive (when the Legislature cannot be convened) against domestic violence.

ARTICLE V

The Congress, whenever two thirds of both Houses shall deem it necessary, shall propose Amendments to this Constitution, or, on the Application of the Legislatures of two thirds of the several States, shall call a Convention for proposing Amendments, which, in either Case, shall be valid to all Intents and Purposes, as Part of this Constitution, when ratified by the Legislatures of three fourths of the several States, or by Conventions in three fourths thereof, as the one or the other Mode of Ratification may be proposed by the Congress; Provided that *no Amendment which may be made prior to the Year One thousand eight hundred and eight shall in any Manner affect the first and fourth Clauses in the Ninth Section of the first Article; and that no State, without its Consent, shall be deprived of its equal Suffrage in the Senate.*

ARTICLE VI

All Debts contracted and Engagements entered into, before the Adoption of this Constitution, shall be as valid against the United States under this Constitution, as under the Confederation.

This Constitution, and Laws of the United States which shall be made in Pursuance thereof; and all Treaties made, or which shall be made, under the Authority of the United States, shall be the supreme Law of the Land; and the Judges in every State shall be bound thereby, any Thing in the Constitution or Laws of any State to the Contrary notwithstanding.

The Senators and Representatives before mentioned, and the Members of the several State Legislatures, and all executive and Judicial Officers, both of the United States and of the several States, shall be bound by Oath or Affirmation, to support this Constitution; but no religious Test shall ever be required as a Qualification to any Office of public Trust under the United States.

ARTICLE VII

The Ratification of the Conventions of nine States, shall be sufficient for the Establishment of this Constitution between the States so ratifying the Same.

Done in Convention by the Unanimous Consent of the States present the Seventeenth Day of September in the Year of our Lord one thousand seven hundred and Eighty seven and of the Independence of the United States of America the Twelfth*
IN WITNESS whereof We have hereunto subscribed our Names,

---

*The Constitution was submitted on September 17, 1787, by the Constitutional Convention, was ratified by the Convention of several states at various dates up to May 29, 1790, and became effective on March 4, 1789.

George Washington
President and Deputy from Virginia

Delaware
George Read
Gunning Bedford, Jr.
John Dickinson
Richard Bassett
Jacob Broom

Maryland
James McHenry
Daniel of St. Thomas Jenifer
Daniel Carroll

Virginia
John Blair
James Madison, Jr

North Carolina
William Blount
Richard Dobbs Spraight
Hugh Williamson

South Carolina
John Rutledge
Charles Cotesworth
     Pinckney
Charles Pinckney
Pierce Butler

Georgia
William Few
Abraham Baldwin

New Hampshire
John Langdon
Nicholas Gilman

Massachusetts
Nathaniel Gorham
Rufus King

Connecticut
William Samuel Johnson
Roger Sherman

New York
Alexander Hamilton

New Jersey
William Livingston
David Brearley
William Paterson
Jonathan Dayton

Pennsylvania
Benjamin Franklin
Thomas Mifflin
Robert Morris
George Clymer
Thomas FitzSimons
Jared Ingersoll
James Wilson
Gouverneur Morris

Amendments to the Constitution

AMENDMENT I

Congress shall make no law respecting an establishment of religion, or prohibiting the free exercise thereof; or abridging the freedom of speech, or of the press; or the right of the people peaceably to assemble, and to petition the Government for a redress of grievances.

AMENDMENT II

A well regulated Militia being necessary to the security of a free State, the right of the people to keep and bear Arms, shall not be infringed.

AMENDMENT III

No Soldier shall, in time of peace be quartered in any house, without the consent of the Owner, nor in time of war, but in a manner to be prescribed by law.

AMENDMENT IV

The right of the people to be secure in their persons, houses, papers, and effects, against unreasonable searches and seizures, shall not be violated, and no Warrants shall issue, but upon probable cause, supported by Oath or affirmation, and particularly describing the place to be searched, and the persons or things to be seized.

AMENDMENT V

No person shall be held to answer for a capital, or otherwise infamous crime, unless on a presentment or indictment of a Grand Jury, except in cases arising in the land or naval forces, or in the Militia, when in actual service in time of War or public danger; nor shall any person be subject for the same offense to be twice put in jeopardy of life or limb; nor shall be compelled in any criminal case to be a witness against himself, nor be deprived of life, liberty, or property, without due process of law; nor shall private property be taken for public use, without just compensation.

AMENDMENT VI

In all criminal prosecutions, the accused shall enjoy the right to a speedy and public trial, by an impartial jury of the State and district wherein the crime shall have been committed, which district shall have been previously ascertained by law, and to be informed of the nature and cause of the accusation; to be confronted with the witnesses against him; to have compulsory process for obtaining witnesses in his favor, and to have the Assistance of Counsel for his defence.

AMENDMENT VII

In Suits at common law, where the value in controversy shall exceed twenty dollars, the right of trial by jury shall be preserved, and no fact tried by a jury, shall be otherwise reexamined in any Court of the United States, than according to the rules of the common law.

AMENDMENT VIII

Excessive bail shall not be required, nor excessive fines imposed, nor cruel and unusual punishments inflicted.

AMENDMENT IX

The enumeration in the Constitution, of certain rights, shall not be construed to deny or disparage others retained by the people.

AMENDMENT X*

The powers not delegated to the United States by the Constitution, nor prohibited by it to the States, are reserved to the States respectively, or to the people.

AMENDMENT XI
[ADOPTED 1798]

The Judicial power of the United States shall not be construed to extend to any suit in law or equity, commenced or prosecuted against one of the United States by Citizens of another State, or by Citizens or Subjects of any Foreign State.

AMENDMENT XII
[ADOPTED 1804]

The Electors shall meet in their respective states, and vote by ballot for President and Vice President, one of whom, at least, shall not be an inhabitant of the same state with themselves; they shall name in their ballots the person voted for as President, and in distinct ballots the person voted for as Vice President, and they shall make distinct lists of all persons voted for as President, and of all persons voted for as Vice President, and of the number of votes for each, which lists they shall sign and certify, and transmit sealed to the seat of the government of the United States, directed to the President of the Senate;—The President of the Senate shall, in the presence of the Senate and House of Representatives, open all the certificates and the votes shall then be counted;—The person having the greatest number of votes for President, shall be the President, if such number be a majority of the whole number of Electors appointed; and if no person have such majority, then

---

*The first ten amendments (the Bill of Rights) were ratified and their adoption was certified on December 15, 1791.

from the persons having the highest numbers not exceeding three on the list of those voted for as President, the House of Representatives shall choose immediately, by ballot, the President. But in choosing the President, the votes shall be taken by states, the representation from each state having one vote; a quorum for this purpose shall consist of a member or members from two-thirds of the states, and a majority of all the states shall be necessary to a choice. And if the House of Representatives shall not choose a President whenever the right of choice shall devolve upon them, before the fourth day of March next following, then the Vice President shall act as President, as in the case of the death or other constitutional disability of the President.—The person having the greatest number of votes as Vice President, shall be the Vice President, if such number be a majority of the whole number of Electors appointed, and if no person have a majority, then from the two highest numbers on the list, the Senate shall choose the Vice President; a quorum for the purpose shall consist of two-thirds of the whole number of Senators, and a majority of the whole number shall be necessary to a choice. But no person constitutionally ineligible to the office of President shall be eligible to that of Vice President of the United States.

AMENDMENT XIII
[ADOPTED 1865]

Section 1

Neither slavery nor involuntary servitude, except as a punishment for crime whereof the party shall have been duly convicted, shall exist within the United States, or any place subject to their jurisdiction.

Section 2

Congress shall have power to enforce this article by appropriate legislation.

AMENDMENT XIV
[ADOPTED 1868]

Section 1

All persons born or naturalized in the United States, and subject to the jurisdiction thereof, are citizens of the United States and of the State wherein they reside. No State shall make or enforce any law which shall abridge the privileges or immunities of citizens of the United States; nor shall any State deprive any person of life, liberty, or property, without due process of law; nor deny to any person within its jurisdiction the equal protection of the laws.

Section 2

Representatives shall be apportioned among the several States according to their respective numbers, counting the whole number of persons in each State, excluding Indians not taxed.

But when the right to vote at any election for the choice of electors for President and Vice President of the United States, Representatives in Congress, the Executive and Judicial officers of a State, or the members of the Legislature thereof, is denied to any of the male inhabitants of such State, being twenty-one years of age, and citizens of the United States, or in any way abridged, except for participation in rebellion, or other crime, the basis of representation therein shall be reduced in the proportion which the number of such male citizens shall bear to the whole number of male citizens twenty-one years of age in such State.

Section 3

No person shall be a Senator or Representative in Congress, or elector of President and Vice President, or hold any office, civil or military, under the United States, or under any State, who, having previously taken an oath, as a member of Congress, or as an officer of the United States, or as a member of any State legislature, or as an executive or judicial officer of any State, to support the Constitution of the United States, shall have engaged in insurrection or rebellion against the same, or given aid or comfort to the enemies thereof. But Congress may by a vote of two-thirds of each House, remove such disability.

Section 4

The validity of the public debt of the United States, authorized by law, including debts incurred for payment of pensions and bounties for services in suppressing insurrection or rebellion, shall not be questioned. But neither the United States nor any State shall assume or pay any debt or obligation incurred in aid of insurrection or rebellion against the United States, or any claim for the loss or emancipation of any slave; but all such debts, obligations and claims shall be held illegal and void.

Section 5

The Congress shall have power to enforce, by appropriate legislation, the provisions of this article.

AMENDMENT XV
[ADOPTED 1870]

Section 1

The right of citizens of the United States to vote shall not be denied or abridged by the United States or by any State on account of race, color, or previous condition of servitude.

Section 2

The Congress shall have power to enforce this article by appropriate legislation.

AMENDMENT XVI

[ADOPTED 1913]

The Congress shall have power to lay and collect taxes on incomes, from whatever source derived, without apportionment among the several States, and without regard to any census or enumeration.

AMENDMENT XVII

[ADOPTED 1913]

The Senate of the United States shall be composed of two Senators from each State, elected by the people thereof, for six years; and each Senator shall have one vote. The electors in each State shall have the qualifications requisite for electors of the most numerous branch of the State legislatures.

When vacancies happen in the representation of any State in the Senate, the executive authority of such State shall issue writs of election to fill such vacancies: Provided, That the legislature of any State may empower the executive thereof to make temporary appointments until the people fill the vacancies by election as the legislature may direct.

This amendment shall not be so construed as to affect the election or term of any Senator chosen before it becomes valid as part of the Constitution.

AMENDMENT XVIII

[ADOPTED 1919, REPEALED 1933]

Section 1

After one year from the ratification of this article the manufacture, sale, or transportation of intoxicating liquors within, the importation thereof into, or the exportation thereof from the United States and all territory subject to the jurisdiction thereof for beverage purposes is hereby prohibited.

Section 2

The Congress and the several States shall have concurrent power to enforce this article by appropriate legislation.

Section 3

This article shall be inoperative unless it shall have been ratified as an amendment to the Constitution by the legislatures of the several States, as provided in the Constitution, within seven years from the date of the submission hereof to the States by the Congress.

AMENDMENT XIX

[ADOPTED 1920]

The right of citizens of the United States to vote shall not be denied or abridged by the United States or by any State on account of sex.

Congress shall have power to enforce this article by appropriate legislation.

AMENDMENT XX

[ADOPTED 1933]

Section 1

The terms of the President and Vice President shall end at noon on the 20th day of January, and the terms of Senators and Representatives at noon on the 3d day of January, of the years in which such terms would have ended if this article had not been ratified and the terms of their successors shall then begin.

Section 2

The Congress shall assemble at least once in every year, and such meeting shall begin at noon on the 3d day of January, unless they shall by law appoint a different day.

Section 3

If, at the time fixed for the beginning of the term of the President, the President elect shall have died, the Vice President elect shall become President. If a President shall not have been chosen before the time fixed for the beginning of his term, or if the President elect shall have failed to qualify, then the Vice President elect shall act as President until a President shall have qualified; and the Congress may by law provide for the case wherein neither a President elect nor a Vice President elect shall have qualified, declaring who shall then act as President, or the manner in which one who is to act shall be selected, and such person shall act accordingly until a President or Vice President shall have qualified.

Section 4

The Congress may by law provide for the case of the death of any of the persons from whom the House of Representatives may choose a President whenever the right of choice shall have devolved upon them, and for the case of the death of any of the persons from whom the Senate may choose a Vice President whenever the right of choice shall have devolved upon them.

Section 5

Sections 1 and 2 shall take effect on the 15th day of October following the ratification of this article.

Section 6

This article shall be inoperative unless it shall have been ratified as an amendment to the Constitution by the legislatures of three fourths of the several States within seven years from the date of its submission.

AMENDMENT XXI

[ADOPTED 1933]

Section 1

The eighteenth article of amendment to the Constitution of the United States is hereby repealed.

Section 2

The transportation or importation into any State, Territory, or possession of the United States for delivery or use therein of intoxicating liquors in violation of the laws thereof, is hereby prohibited.

Section 3

This article shall be inoperative unless it shall have been ratified as an amendment to the Constitution by conventions in the several States, as provided in the Constitution, within seven years from the date of the submission hereof to the States by the Congress.

AMENDMENT XXII

[ADOPTED 1951]

Section 1

No person shall be elected to the office of the President more than twice, and no person who has held the office of President, or acted as President, for more than two years of a term to which some other person was elected President shall be elected to the office of the President more than once. But this Article shall not apply to any person holding the office of President when this Article was proposed by the Congress, and shall not prevent any person who may be holding the office of President, or acting as President, during the term within which this Article becomes operative from holding the office of President or acting as President during the remainder of such term.

Section 2

This article shall be inoperative unless it shall have been ratified as an amendment to the Constitution by the legislatures of three-fourths of the several States within seven years from the date of its submission to the States by the Congress.

AMENDMENT XXIII

[ADOPTED 1961]

Section 1

The District constituting the seat of Government of the United States shall appoint in such manner as the Congress shall direct:

A number of electors of President and Vice President equal to the whole number of Senators and Representatives in Congress to which the District would be entitled if it were a State, but in no event more than the least populous State; they shall be in addition to those appointed by the States, but they shall be considered, for the purposes of the election of President and Vice President, to be electors appointed by a State; and they shall meet in the District and perform such duties as provided by the twelfth article of amendment.

Section 2

The Congress shall have power to enforce this article by appropriate legislation.

AMENDMENT XXIV

[ADOPTED 1964]

Section 1

The right of citizens of the United States to vote in any primary or other election for President or Vice President, for electors for President or Vice President, or for Senator or Representative in Congress, shall not be denied or abridged by the United States or any state by reason of failure to pay any poll tax or other tax.

Section 2

The Congress shall have the power to enforce this article by appropriate legislation.

AMENDMENT XXV

[ADOPTED 1967]

Section 1

In case of the removal of the President from office or his death or resignation, the Vice President shall become President.

Section 2

Whenever there is a vacancy in the office of the Vice President, the President shall nominate a Vice President who shall take the office upon confirmation by a majority vote of both houses of Congress.

Section 3

Whenever the President transmits to the President pro tempore of the Senate and the Speaker of the House of Representatives his written declaration that he is unable to discharge the powers and duties of his office, and until he transmits to them a written declaration to the contrary, such powers and duties shall be discharged by the Vice President as Acting President.

Section 4

Whenever the Vice President and a majority of either the principal officers of the executive departments or of such other body as Congress may by law provide, transmit to the President pro tempore of the Senate and the Speaker of the House of Representatives their written declaration that the President is unable to discharge the powers and duties of his office, the Vice President shall immediately assume the powers and duties of the office as Acting President.

Thereafter, when the President transmits to the President pro tempore of the Senate and the Speaker of the House of Representatives his written declaration that no inability exists, he shall resume the powers and duties of his office unless the Vice President and a majority of either the principal officers of the executive department or of such other body as Congress may by law provide, transmit within four days to the President pro tempore of the Senate and the Speaker of the House of Representatives their written declaration that the President is unable to discharge the powers and duties of his office. Thereupon Congress shall decide the issue, assembling within 48 hours for that purpose if not in session. If the Congress, within 21 days after receipt of the latter written declaration, or, if Congress is not in session, within 21 days after Congress is required to assemble, determines by two-thirds vote of both houses that the President is unable to discharge the powers and duties of his office, the Vice President shall continue to discharge the same as Acting President; otherwise, the President shall resume the powers and duties of his office.

AMENDMENT XXVI
[ADOPTED 1971]

Section 1

The right of citizens of the United States, who are 18 years of age or older, to vote shall not be denied or abridged by the United States or any state on account of age.

Section 2

The Congress shall have the power to enforce this article by appropriate legislation.

AMENDMENT XXVII
[ADOPTED 1992]

No law, varying the compensation for the services of the Senators and Representatives shall take effect, until an election of Representatives shall have intervened.

Presidential Elections

Year	Candidates	Parties	Popular Vote	Electoral Vote	Voter Participation
1789	**George Washington**		*	69	
	John Adams			34	
	Others			35	
1792	**George Washington**		*	132	
	John Adams			77	
	George Clinton			50	
	Others			5	
1796	**John Adams**	**Federalist**	*	71	
	Thomas Jefferson	Democratic-Republican		68	
	Thomas Pinckney	Federalist		59	
	Aaron Burr	Dem.-Rep.		30	
	Others			48	
1800	**Thomas Jefferson**	**Dem.-Rep.**	*	73	
	Aaron Burr	Dem.-Rep.		73	
	John Adams	Federalist		65	
	C. C. Pinckney	Federalist		64	
	John Jay	Federalist		1	
1804	**Thomas Jefferson**	**Dem.-Rep.**	*	162	
	C. C. Pinckney	Federalist		14	
1808	**James Madison**	**Dem.-Rep.**	*	122	
	C. C. Pinckney	Federalist		47	
	George Clinton	Dem.-Rep.		6	
1812	**James Madison**	**Dem.-Rep.**	*	128	
	De Witt Clinton	Federalist		89	
1816	**James Monroe**	**Dem.-Rep.**	*	183	
	Rufus King	Federalist		34	
1820	**James Monroe**	**Dem.-Rep.**	*	231	
	John Quincy Adams	Dem.-Rep.		1	
1824	**John Quincy Adams**	**Dem.-Rep.**	108,740 (31%)	84	26.9%
	Andrew Jackson	Dem.-Rep.	153,544 (44%)	99	
	William H. Crawford	Dem.-Rep.	40,856 (12%)	41	
	Henry Clay	Dem.-Rep.	47,531 (14%)	37	
1828	**Andrew Jackson**	**Democratic**	647,286 (56.0%)	178	57.6%
	John Quincy Adams	National Republican	508,064 (44.0%)	83	
1832	**Andrew Jackson**	**Democratic**	688,242 (54.2%)	219	55.4%
	Henry Clay	National Republican	473,462 (37.4%)	49	
	John Floyd	Independent		11	
	William Wirt	Anti-Mason	101,051 (7.8%)	7	

Year	Candidates	Parties	Popular Vote	Electoral Vote	Voter Participation
1836	**Martin Van Buren**	**Democratic**	**762,198 (50.8%)**	**170**	57.8%
	William Henry Harrison	Whig	549,508 (36.6%)	73	
	Hugh L. White	Whig	145,342 (9.7%)	26	
	Daniel Webster	Whig	41,287 (2.7%)	14	
	W. P. Magnum	Independent		11	
1840	**William Henry Harrison**	**Whig**	**1,274,624 (53.1%)**	**234**	80.2%
	Martin Van Buren	Democratic	1,127,781 (46.9%)	60	
	J. G. Birney	Liberty	7069	—	
1844	**James K. Polk**	**Democratic**	**1,338,464 (49.6%)**	**170**	78.9%
	Henry Clay	Whig	1,300,097 (48.1%)	105	
	J. G. Birney	Liberty	62,300 (2.3%)	—	
1848	**Zachary Taylor**	**Whig**	**1,360,967 (47.4%)**	**163**	72.7%
	Lewis Cass	Democratic	1,222,342 (42.5%)	127	
	Martin Van Buren	Free-Soil	291,263 (10.1%)	—	
1852	**Franklin Pierce**	**Democratic**	**1,601,274 (50.8%)**	**254**	69.6%
	Winfield Scott	Whig	1,386,580 (43.9%)	42	
	John P. Hale	Free-Soil	155,825 (5.0%)	—	
1856	**James Buchanan**	**Democratic**	**1,832,955 (45.3%)**	**174**	78.9%
	John C. Frémont	Republican	1,339,932 (33.1%)	114	
	Millard Fillmore	American	871,731 (21.6%)	8	
1860	**Abraham Lincoln**	**Republican**	**1,865,593 (39.8%)**	**180**	81.2%
	Stephen A. Douglas	Democratic	1,382,713 (29.5%)	12	
	John C. Breckinridge	Democratic	848,356 (18.1%)	72	
	John Bell	Union	592,906 (12.6%)	39	
1864	**Abraham Lincoln**	**Republican**	**2,213,655 (55.0%)**	**212**[†]	73.8%
	George B. McClellan	Democratic	1,805,237 (45.0%)	21	
1868	**Ulysses S. Grant**	**Republican**	**3,013,421 (53%)**	**214**	78.1%
	Horatio Seymour	Democratic	2,706,829 (47%)	80	
1872	**Ulysses S. Grant**	**Republican**	**3,597,132 (55.6%)**	**286**	71.3%
	Horace Greeley	Dem.; Liberal Republican	2,834,761 (43.8%)	66[‡]	
1876	**Rutherford B. Hayes**[§]	**Republican**	**4,036,572 (48.0%)**	**185**	81.8%
	Samuel J. Tilden	Democratic	4,284,020 (51.0%)	184	
1880	**James A. Garfield**	**Republican**	**4,454,416 (48.5%)**	**214**	79.4%
	Winfield S. Hancock	Democratic	4,444,952 (48.1%)	155	
1884	**Grover Cleveland**	**Democratic**	**4,874,986 (48.5%)**	**219**	77.5%
	James G. Blaine	Republican	4,851,981 (48.2%)	182	
1888	**Benjamin Harrison**	**Republican**	**5,439,853 (47.9%)**	**233**	79.3%
	Grover Cleveland	Democratic	5,540,309 (48.6%)	168	

Year	Candidates	Parties	Popular Vote	Electoral Vote	Voter Participation
1892	**Grover Cleveland**	**Democratic**	5,556,918 (46.1%)	277	74.7%
	Benjamin Harrison	Republican	5,176,108 (43.0%)	145	
	James B. Weaver	People's	1,041,028 (9%)	22	
1896	**William McKinley**	**Republican**	7,104,779 (51.1%)	271	79.3%
	William Jennings Bryan	Democratic People's	6,502,925 (47.7%)	176	
1900	**William McKinley**	**Republican**	7,207,923 (51.7%)	292	73.2%
	William Jennings Bryan	Dem.-Populist	6,358,133 (45.5%)	155	
1904	**Theodore Roosevelt**	**Republican**	7,623,486 (57.9%)	336	65.2%
	Alton B. Parker	Democratic	5,077,911 (37.6%)	140	
	Eugene V. Debs	Socialist	402,400 (3.0%)	—	
1908	**William H. Taft**	**Republican**	7,678,908 (51.6%)	321	65.4%
	William Jennings Bryan	Democratic	6,409,104 (43.1%)	162	
	Eugene V. Debs	Socialist	402,820 (2.8%)	—	
1912	**Woodrow Wilson**	**Democratic**	6,296,547 (41.9%)	435	58.8%
	Theodore Roosevelt	Progressive	4,118,571 (27.4%)	88	
	William H. Taft	Republican	3,486,720 (23.2%)	8	
	Eugene V. Debs	Socialist	900,672 (6.0%)	—	
1916	**Woodrow Wilson**	**Democratic**	9,129,606 (49.4%)	277	61.6%
	Charles E. Hughes	Republican	8,538,221 (46.2%)	254	
	A. L. Benson	Socialist	585,113 (3.2%)	—	
1920	**Warren G. Harding**	**Republican**	16,152,200 (60.4%)	404	49.2%
	James M. Cox	Democratic	9,147,353 (34.2%)	127	
	Eugene V. Debs	Socialist	917,799 (3.4%)	—	
1924	**Calvin Coolidge**	**Republican**	15,725,016 (54.0%)	382	48.9%
	John W. Davis	Democratic	8,386,503 (28.8%)	136	
	Robert M. La Follette	Progressive	4,822,856 (16.6%)	13	
1928	**Herbert Hoover**	**Republican**	21,391,381 (58.2%)	444	56.9%
	Alfred E. Smith	Democratic	15,016,443 (40.9%)	87	
	Norman Thomas	Socialist	267,835 (0.7%)	—	
1932	**Franklin D. Roosevelt**	**Democratic**	22,821,857 (57.4%)	472	56.9%
	Herbert Hoover	Republican	15,761,841 (39.7%)	59	
	Norman Thomas	Socialist	884,781 (2.2%)	—	
1936	**Franklin D. Roosevelt**	**Democratic**	27,751,597 (60.8%)	523	61.0%
	Alfred M. Landon	Republican	16,679,583 (36.5%)	8	
	William Lemke	Union	882,479 (1.9%)	—	
1940	**Franklin D. Roosevelt**	**Democratic**	27,244,160 (54.8%)	449	62.5%
	Wendell L. Willkie	Republican	22,305,198 (44.8%)	82	
1944	**Franklin D. Roosevelt**	**Democratic**	25,602,504 (53.5%)	432	55.9%
	Thomas E. Dewey	Republican	22,006,285 (46.0%)	99	

Year	Candidates	Parties	Popular Vote	Electoral Vote	Voter Participation
1948	**Harry S Truman**	Democratic	**24,105,695 (49.5%)**	304	53.0%
	Thomas E. Dewey	Republican	21,969,170 (45.1%)	189	
	J. Strom Thurmond	State-Rights Democratic	1,169,021 (2.4%)	38	
	Henry A. Wallace	Progressive	1,157,326 (2.4%)	—	
1952	**Dwight D. Eisenhower**	Republican	**33,778,963 (55.1%)**	442	63.3%
	Adlai E. Stevenson	Democratic	27,314,992 (44.4%)	89	
1956	**Dwight D. Eisenhower**	Republican	**35,575,420 (57.6%)**	457	60.6%
	Adlai E. Stevenson	Democratic	26,033,066 (42.1%)	73	
	Other	—	—	1	
1960	**John F. Kennedy**	Democratic	**34,227,096 (49.9%)**	303	64%
	Richard M. Nixon	Republican	34,108,546 (49.6%)	219	
	Other	—	—	15	
1964	**Lyndon B. Johnson**	Democratic	**43,126,506 (61.1%)**	486	61.7%
	Barry M. Goldwater	Republican	27,176,799 (38.5%)	52	
1968	**Richard M. Nixon**	Republican	**31,785,480 (44%)**	301	60.6%
	Hubert H. Humphrey	Democratic	31,275,166 (42%)	191	
	George Wallace	American Indep.	9,906,473 (14%)	46	
1972	**Richard M. Nixon**	Republican	**46,740,323 (60.7%)**	520	55.2%
	George S. McGovern	Democratic	28,901,598 (37.5%)	17	
	Other	—	—	1	
1976	**Jimmy Carter**	Democratic	**40,828,587 (50.0%)**	297	53.5%
	Gerald R. Ford	Republican	39,147,613 (47.9%)	241	
	Other	—	1,575,459 (2.1%)	—	
1980	**Ronald Reagan**	Republican	**43,901,812 (50.7%)**	489	52.6%
	Jimmy Carter	Democratic	35,483,820 (41.0%)	49	
	John B. Anderson	Independent	5,719,437 (6.6%)	—	
	Ed Clark	Libertarian	921,188 (1.1%)	—	
1984	**Ronald Reagan**	Republican	**54,455,075 (59.0%)**	525	53.3%
	Walter Mondale	Democratic	37,577,185 (41.0%)	13	
1988	**George H. W. Bush**	Republican	**48,886,097 (53.4%)**	426	50.3%
	Michael S. Dukakis	Democratic	41,809,074 (45.6%)	111	
1992	**William J. Clinton**	Democratic	**44,908,254 (43%)**	370	55.1%
	George H. W. Bush	Republican	39,102,343 (37.5%)	168	
	Ross Perot	Independent	19,741,065 (18.9%)	—	
1996	**William J. Clinton**	Democratic	**45,590,703 (50%)**	379	49%
	Robert Dole	Republican	37,816,307 (41%)	159	
	Ross Perot	Reform	7,866,284 (8%)	—	
2000	**George W. Bush**	Republican	**50,456,062 (47.88%)**	271	49.3%
	Al Gore	Democratic	50,996,582 (48.39%)	266‖	
	Ralph Nader	Green	82,955 (2.72%)	—	
	Other		834,774 (less than 1%)	—	

Year	Candidates	Parties	Popular Vote	Electoral Vote	Voter Participation
2004	**George W. Bush**	**Republican**	**60,934,251 (51.0%)**	**286**	**55.6%**
	John F. Kerry	Democratic	57,765,291 (48.0%)	252	
	Ralph Nader	Independent	405,933 (less than 1%)	—	
2008	**Barack H. Obama**	**Democratic**	**69,456,897**	**365**	**56.8%**
	John McCain	Republican	59,934,814	173	
	Ralph Nader	Independent	738,475	0	

*Electors selected by state legislatures.

†Eleven secessionist states did not participate.

‡Greeley died before the electoral college met. His electoral votes were divided among the four minor candidates.

§Contested result settled by special election.

‖One District of Columbia Gore elector abstained.

Presidents and Vice Presidents

	President	Vice President	Term
1.	George Washington	John Adams	1789–1793
	George Washington	John Adams	1793–1797
2.	John Adams	Thomas Jefferson	1797–1801
3.	Thomas Jefferson	Aaron Burr	1801–1805
	Thomas Jefferson	George Clinton	1805–1809
4.	James Madison	George Clinton (d. 1812)	1809–1813
	James Madison	Elbridge Gerry (d. 1814)	1813–1817
5.	James Monroe	Daniel Tompkins	1817–1821
	James Monroe	Daniel Tompkins	1821–1825
6.	John Quincy Adams	John C. Calhoun	1825–1829
7.	Andrew Jackson	John C. Calhoun	1829–1833
	Andrew Jackson	Martin Van Buren	1833–1837
8.	Martin Van Buren	Richard M. Johnson	1837–1841
9.	William H. Harrison (d. 1841)	John Tyler	1841
10.	John Tyler	—	1841–1845
11.	James K. Polk	George M. Dallas	1845–1849
12.	Zachary Taylor (d. 1850)	Millard Fillmore	1849–1850
13.	Millard Fillmore	—	1850–1853
14.	Franklin Pierce	William R. King (d. 1853)	1853–1857
15.	James Buchanan	John C. Breckinridge	1857–1861
16.	Abraham Lincoln	Hannibal Hamlin	1861–1865
	Abraham Lincoln (d. 1865)	Andrew Johnson	1865
17.	Andrew Johnson	—	1865–1869
18.	Ulysses S. Grant	Schuyler Colfax	1869–1873
	Ulysses S. Grant	Henry Wilson (d. 1875)	1873–1877
19.	Rutherford B. Hayes	William A. Wheeler	1877–1881
20.	James A. Garfield (d. 1881)	Chester A. Arthur	1881
21.	Chester A. Arthur	—	1881–1885
22.	Grover Cleveland	Thomas A. Hendricks (d. 1885)	1885–1889
23.	Benjamin Harrison	Levi P. Morton	1889–1893
24.	Grover Cleveland	Adlai E. Stevenson	1893–1897
25.	William McKinley	Garret A. Hobart (d. 1899)	1897–1901
	William McKinley (d. 1901)	Theodore Roosevelt	1901
26.	Theodore Roosevelt	—	1901–1905
	Theodore Roosevelt	Charles Fairbanks	1905–1909
27.	William H. Taft	James S. Sherman (d. 1912)	1909–1913
28.	Woodrow Wilson	Thomas R. Marshall	1913–1917
	Woodrow Wilson	Thomas R. Marshall	1917–1921
29.	Warren G. Harding (d. 1923)	Calvin Coolidge	1921–1923
30.	Calvin Coolidge	—	1923–1925

	President	Vice President	Term
	Calvin Coolidge	Charles G. Dawes	1925–1929
31.	Herbert Hoover	Charles Curtis	1929–1933
32.	Franklin D. Roosevelt	John N. Garner	1933–1937
	Franklin D. Roosevelt	John N. Garner	1937–1941
	Franklin D. Roosevelt	Henry A. Wallace	1941–1945
	Franklin D. Roosevelt (d. 1945)	Harry S Truman	1945
33.	Harry S Truman	—	1945–1949
	Harry S Truman	Alben W. Barkley	1949–1953
34.	Dwight D. Eisenhower	Richard M. Nixon	1953–1957
	Dwight D. Eisenhower	Richard M. Nixon	1957–1961
35.	John F. Kennedy (d. 1963)	Lyndon B. Johnson	1961–1963
36.	Lyndon B. Johnson	—	1963–1965
	Lyndon B. Johnson	Hubert H. Humphrey	1965–1969
37.	Richard M. Nixon	Spiro T. Agnew	1969–1973
	Richard M. Nixon (resigned 1974)	Gerald R. Ford	1973–1974
38.	Gerald R. Ford	Nelson A. Rockefeller	1974–1977
39.	Jimmy Carter	Walter F. Mondale	1977–1981
40.	Ronald Reagan	George H. W. Bush	1981–1985
	Ronald Reagan	George H. W. Bush	1985–1989
41.	George H. W. Bush	J. Danforth Quayle	1989–1993
42.	William J. Clinton	Albert Gore, Jr.	1993–1997
	William J. Clinton	Albert Gore, Jr.	1997–2001
43.	George W. Bush	Richard Cheney	2001–2005
	George W. Bush	Richard Cheney	2005–2009
44.	Barack H. Obama	Joseph R. Biden, Jr.	2009–

Glossary

Alien and Sedition Acts (p. 183) Four laws designed to protect America from the danger of foreign and domestic subversion. The first three, the Alien laws, dealt with immigration and naturalization. The Sedition Act criminalized criticism of the federal government.

American System (p. 226) Henry Clay's comprehensive national plan for economic growth that included protective tariffs for American industry and government investment in roads and other internal improvements.

Anglicization (p. 67) The colonial American desire to emulate English society, including English taste in foods, customs, and architecture.

Anti-Federalists (p. 148) The name applied to opponents of the Constitution who insisted that they, not their opponents, were the true supporters of the ideal of federalism. Anti-Federalists opposed weakening the power of the states and feared that the Constitution yielded too much power to the new central government.

Archaic Era (p. 5) Period beginning approximately 9,000 years ago lasting an estimated 6,000 years. It was marked by more intensive efforts by ancient societies to shape the environment to enhance food production.

Articles of Confederation (p. 138) America's first constitutional government in effect from 1781–1788. The articles created a weak decentralized form of government that lacked the power to tax and compel state obedience to treaties it negotiated.

artisan production (p. 260) A system of manufacturing goods, built around apprenticeship that defined the pre-industrial economy. The apprentice learned a trade under the guidance of an artisan who often housed, clothed, and fed the apprentice.

assumption of the state debts (p. 162) Hamilton's scheme for the federal government to take over any outstanding state debts.

Aztec (p. 6) Led by the Mexica tribe, the Aztec created a powerful empire whose capital, the great city of Tenochtitlán, was built on an island in Lake Texcoco in 1325 CE.

Bacon's Rebellion (p. 55) A popular uprising in Virginia in 1676 named after its leader, Nathaniel Bacon.

Bank of the United States (p. 164) A bank chartered by the federal government. The bank served as a depository for government funds, helped bolster confidence in government securities, made loans, and provided the nation with a stable national currency.

Bank Veto Speech (p. 241) Jackson's veto of a bill to re-charter of the Bank of the United States, in which he explained why he opposed the bank and laid out his own vision of American democracy and constitutional government.

Bill of Rights (p. 159) The first ten of the original twelve amendments to the Constitution, which included protections for basic individual liberties and protections for the states.

Black Belt (p. 274) A swath of dark rich soil well suited to cotton agriculture that stretched from Alabama westward, and eventually reached the easternmost part of Texas.

Black Codes (p. 413) Laws designed by the ex-Confederate states to sharply limit the civil and economic rights of freedmen and create an exploitable workforce.

Black Republican (p. 357) A racist pejorative that Democrats used to suggest that Republicans were dangerous radicals who favored abolition and racial equality.

Bleeding Kansas (p. 356) A phrase used to describe the wave of vigilante reprisals and counterreprisals by proslavery and antislavery forces in Kansas in 1856.

Border States (p. 379) The four slave states, Missouri, Kentucky, Maryland, and Delaware that bordered the Confederacy. The Lincoln administration succeeded in keeping them in the Union.

Boston Massacre (p. 102) A confrontation between a group of Bostonians and British troops on March 5, 1770, during which the troops opened fire on the citizens, killing five.

capitalism (p. 11) An economic system in which the market economy determines the prices of goods and services.

Carpetbagger (p. 418) White Southerners' derogatory term for Northerners who came south after the war to settle, work, or aid the ex-slaves. It falsely suggested they were penniless adventurers who came south merely to get rich.

Cherokee Cases (p. 236) *Cherokee Nation v. Georgia* (1830) and *Worcester v. Georgia*, the two cases in which the Supreme Court of the United States determined that Indian nations retained certain rights of sovereign nations, but did not enjoy the full powers of a sovereign nation.

Chesapeake Affair (p. 202) An incident in 1807 when the British ship the Leopard fired at an American navy ship, the Chesapeake. The British abducted four American sailors, whom they charged were deserters from the Royal Navy.

Civil Rights Act of 1875 (p. 426) Passed by Congress in 1875, it required state governments to provide equal access in public facilities such as schools and to allow African Americans to serve on juries. In 1883 the U.S. Supreme Court ruled it unconstitutional.

Columbian Exchange (p. 16) The term used by modern scholars to describe the biological encounter between the two sides of the Atlantic, including the movement of plants, animals, and diseases.

Common Sense (p. 110) Thomas Paine's influential pamphlet that forcefully argued for American independence, attacked the institution of monarchy, and defended a democratic theory of representative government.

companionate marriage (p. 124) A term used by scholars to describe a more egalitarian relationship between husband and wife in which the two act as companions.

Complex marriage (p. 299) A system developed by John Humphrey Noyes's followers at Oneida, where any man or women who had experienced saving grace was free to engage in sexual relations with any other person.

Compromise of 1850 (p. 345) An attempt by Congress to resolve the slavery question by making concessions to both the North and South, including admission of California and a new Fugitive Slave Act.

Compromise of 1877 (p. 427) Resolution of the disputed presidential election of 1876 that handed victory to Republican Rutherford B. Hayes over Democrat Samuel J. Tilden. Democrats agreed to the deal in exchange for patronage and the continued removal of federal troops from the South.

Conscription Act (p. 389) A law passed by Congress in March 1863 to offset declining volunteers to the Union Army. It declared all male citizens (and immigrants who had applied for citizenship) aged twenty to forty-five eligible to be drafted into the Union Army. The rich could pay a $300 fee to avoid the draft.

contraband of war (p. 384) The term introduced by General Benjamin Butler to justify his refusal to return fugitive slaves to their owners because they were seized property.

Copperheads (p. 389) Northern Democrats (sometimes called "Peace Democrats") who opposed the war and the Lincoln administration and favored a negotiated settlement with the Confederacy.

"corrupt bargain" (p. 226) Term presidential candidate Jackson's supporters used to attack the alliance between John Quincy Adams and Henry Clay that deprived him of the presidency.

cotton embargo (p. 380) A ban imposed by Confederates in 1861 on the export of cotton, the South's most valuable commodity, to prompt cotton-importing nations like England and France to intervene to secure Confederate independence.

cotton gin (p. 211) Eli Whitney's invention for removing seeds from cotton.

Crittenden Compromise (p. 369) An unsuccessful proposal by Kentucky senator John J. Crittenden to resolve the secession crisis in the spring of 1861 with constitutional amendments to protect slavery.

"cult of true womanhood" (p. 295) A set of beliefs in which women's values were defined in opposition to the aggressive and competitive values of the marketplace.

Declaration of Independence (p. 111) On July 4, 1776, Congress approved the final text of the Declaration of Independence, a public defense of America's decision to declare independence from Britain that was to be printed and sent to the individual states.

Democratic-Republican Societies (p. 167) A new type of political organization informally allied with the Republicans whose function was to help collect, channel, and influence public opinion.

Denmark Vesey Uprising (p. 215) An alleged plot led by a free black man, Denmark Vesey, to free slaves in Charleston and kill their masters.

Draft Riots (p. 391) Four days of rioting in New York City in July 1863 by mostly poor, immigrant, and working-class men who opposed the draft.

Dred Scott v. Sandford (p. 358) The highly controversial 1857 Supreme Court decision that rejected the claim of the slave Dred Scott, who argued that time spent with his owner in regions that barred slavery had made him a free man. It also declared that Congress lacked the right to regulate slavery in the territories.

electoral college (p. 158) A group of electors appointed by each state who had the responsibility of picking the president.

Emancipation Proclamation (p. 386) The decree announced by Lincoln in September 1862 and taking effect on January 1, 1863, declaring slaves in the seceded states not under Union army control "forever free."

Embargo Act of 1807 (p. 202) The cornerstone of Jefferson's plan of peaceable coercion that attempted to block U.S. trade with England and France to force them to respect American neutrality.

Enlightenment (p. 64) An international philosophical movement that extolled the virtues of reason and science and applied these new insights to politics and social reform.

Era of Good Feelings (p. 209) A term that the press coined to describe the absence of bitter partisan conflict during the presidency of James Monroe.

Federalists (p. 148) The name adopted by the supporters of the Constitution who favored a stronger centralized government.

Fifteenth Amendment (p. 421) Constitutional amendment passed by Congress in 1869 providing an explicit constitutional guarantee for black suffrage.

Force Bill (p. 232) A bill enacted by Congress that gave President Jackson the power to use military force to collect revenue, including tariffs.

Fourteenth Amendment (p. 417) Drafted by Congress in June 1866, it defined citizenship to include African Americans, guaranteed equal protection before the law, and established the federal government as the guarantor of individual civil rights.

free labor (p. 364) A procapitalist Northern philosophy that presented an idealized vision of the industrial North, celebrating the virtues of individualism, independence, entrepreneurship, and upward mobility.

Freedmen's Bureau (p. 408) Relief agency for the war-ravaged South created by Congress in March 1865. It provided emergency services, built schools, and managed confiscated lands.

Fugitive Slave Act (p. 346) A component of the Compromise of 1850 that increased the federal government's obligation to capture and return escaped slaves to their owners.

Gabriel's Rebellion (p. 186) A slave insurrection in Richmond, Virginia, that drew together free blacks and slaves in a plot to seize the Richmond arsenal and foment a slave rebellion.

gag rule (p. 293) A procedural motion that required that the House of Representatives automatically table antislavery petitions and not consider them.

Glorious Revolution (p. 57) The relatively bloodless revolution that led to the ascension of William and Mary, which was widely seen as a vindication for English liberty.

Great Awakening (p. 64) A religious revival movement that emphasized a more emotional style of religious practice.

Great Compromise (p. 145) Compromise plan proposed by Roger Sherman and Oliver Ellsworth of Connecticut that called for equal representation of each state in the upper house and a lower house based on population.

Hartford Convention (p. 207) A meeting of Federalists in Hartford, Connecticut, to protest the War of 1812. The convention proposed several constitutional amendments intended to weaken the powers of the slave states and protect New England interests.

headright (p. 40) An incentive system to encourage additional immigrants by giving 50 acres to any man who would pay his own fare to Virginia and 50 additional acres for each person brought with him.

humanists (p. 13) Individuals who advocated a revival of ancient learning, particularly ancient Greek and Roman thought, and encouraged greater attention to secular topics including a new emphasis on the study of humanity.

immediatism (p. 291) Abolitionist doctrine that rejected gradualism and advocated an immediate end to slavery.

impressment (p. 201) The practice of forcing merchant seamen to serve in the British navy.

indentured servants (p. 83) A form of bound labor in which a number of years of service were specified as payment for passage to America.

Indian Removal Act of 1830 (p. 235) Legislation that facilitated the removal of Indians tribes to lands west of the Mississippi.

Intolerable Acts (p. 104) Legislation passed by Parliament to punish Bostonians for the Boston Tea Party. It closed the Port of Boston; annulled the Massachusetts colonial charter and dissolved or severely restricted that colony's political institutions; and allowed British officials charged with capital crimes to be tried outside the colonies.

Islam (p. 10) Monotheistic faith that emerged in the seventh century, whose teachings followed the word of the prophet Muhammad, and whose followers controlled most of the overland trade routes to the Far East.

Jay's Treaty (p. 172) Diplomatic treaty negotiated by Federalist John Jay in 1794. According to the terms of the treaty, Britain agreed to compensate America for cargoes seized from 1793 to 1794 and promised to vacate forts in the Northwest Territory. However, America failed to win acceptance of the right of neutral nations to trade with belligerents without harassment.

John Brown's raid (p. 366) A failed assault led by the radical abolitionist on the federal arsenal at Harpers Ferry, Virginia, on October 16, 1859, intending to seize the guns and ammunition and then touch off a wave of slave rebellions.

Kansas-Nebraska Act (p. 351) An 1854 act designed to resolve the controversy over whether slavery would be permitted in the Western territories. It repealed the ban on slavery north of 36° 30' (the Missouri Compromise) and created two separate territories, Kansas west of Missouri and Nebraska west of Iowa.

Know-Nothings (p. 354) The nickname for the constituents of the nativist, or anti-immigrant, American Party, who called for legislation restricting office holding to native-born citizens and raising the period of naturalization for citizenship from five to twenty-one years.

Ku Klux Klan (p. 422) The best-known of the many secret white terrorist organizations. It arose in the South in 1866 and targeted freedmen and symbols of black self improvement and independence and played a key role in reestablishing white supremacy by the late 1870s.

Liberty Party (p. 328) The staunchly antislavery, anti-annexation, party was short lived, but captured 62,000 votes, a small number, but enough some historians argue, to effectively rob Henry Clay of electoral victories in New York and Michigan thereby handing Polk the presidency in 1844.

Lincoln-Douglas debates (p. 366) A series of high-profile debates in Illinois in 1858 between Senate candidates Stephen A. Douglas and Abraham Lincoln that focused primarily on the slavery controversy.

Lord Dunmore's Proclamation (p. 106) Official announcement issued by Lord Dunmore, royal governor of Virginia. It offered freedom to any slave who joined the British forces in putting down the American rebellion.

Louisiana Purchase (p. 195) The acquisition by the United States of the Louisiana Territory from France in 1803, thereby securing control of the Mississippi River and nearly doubling the size of the nation.

Loyalists (p. 111) Colonists who remained loyal to the king and Britain.

Manifest Destiny (p. 319) A term coined by editor and columnist John O'Sullivan to describe his belief in America's divine right to expand westward.

market revolution (p. 254) A set of interrelated developments in agriculture, technology, and industry that led to the creation of a more integrated national economy. Impersonal market forces impelled the maximization of production of agricultural products and manufactured goods.

mercantilism (p. 61) Theory of empire that advocated strict regulation of trade between colonies and the mother country to benefit the latter.

middle ground (p. 87) A cultural and geographical region of the Great Lakes in which Indians and the French negotiated with each other for goods and neither side could impose its will on the other.

middle passage (p. 79) The harrowing voyage across the Atlantic from Africa to the Americas during which slaves endured meager rations and horrendously unsanitary conditions.

militia (p. 105) An organization of citizen soldiers regulated by the laws of the individual colonies that provided the primary means of public defense in the colonial period.

mission system (p. 325) The colonial system devised by the Spanish to control the Indian population, forcing them to convert to Catholicism and work the land.

Mississippi Plan (p. 426) Campaign of violence and intimidation waged by armed groups of whites closely allied with the Democratic Party that drove Republicans from power in the Mississippi state elections of 1874. Copied by other Southern states.

Missouri Compromise (p. 214) The congressional compromise in which Missouri entered the Union as a slave state, and Maine was admitted as a free state to preserve the balance of slave and free states in Congress. The law also drew an imaginary line at 36° 30′ through the Louisiana Territory. Slavery was prohibited north of this line.

modern warfare (p. 383) Military conflict involving enormous armies that utilize the technologies of the Industrial Revolution in the areas of communications, transportation, and firearms. Victory is secured by destroying the enemy's army and inflicting suffering on civilian populations.

Monroe Doctrine (p. 210) A foreign policy statement by President Monroe declaring that the Americas were no longer open to colonization and that the United States would view any effort to reassert colonial control over independent nations in the Western Hemisphere as a threat to America.

Nat Turner's Rebellion (p. 277) The 1831 Virginia slave uprising led by Nat Turner shocked many in the South and led to a host of new repressive measures against slaves.

New Jersey Plan (p. 144) Proposal made by William Patterson of New Jersey as an alternative to the more nationalistic Virginia Plan that would have retained the principle of state equality in the legislature embodied in the Articles of Confederation.

New Lights (p. 75) Supporters of the Great Awakening and its more emotional style of worship.

New South (p. 428) Optimistic phrase white Southerners used to describe the post-Reconstruction South, reflecting the South's development of a new system of race relations based on segregation and white supremacy and pointing to a profound economic transformation that swept across the region.

nonimportation movement (p. 101) A boycott against the purchase of any imported British goods.

Northwest Ordinance of 1787 (p. 140) One of several laws adopted by the Confederation Congress designed to provide a plan for the orderly settlement of the Northwest Territory (the area north of the Ohio River and west of Pennsylvania). In addition to providing for a plan for self-governance, the Ordinance also prohibited slavery from the Northwest Territory.

nullification (p. 231) A constitutional doctrine advanced by supporters of states' rights that held that individual states could nullify unconstitutional acts of Congress.

"Old Hickory" (p. 228) The nickname that General Andrew Jackson earned for seeming as stout as an "Old Hickory tree" in fighting against the British in the War of 1812.

Old Lights (p. 75) Opponents of the Great Awakening who favored traditional forms of religious worship.

Old Northwest (p. 139) The region of the new nation bordering on the Great Lakes.

Overland Trail (p. 320) The 2,000-mile route taken by American settlers traveling to new settlements in Oregon, California, and Utah.

Paleo-Indians (p. 4) The name given by scientists to the first inhabitants of the Americas, an Ice Age people who survived largely by hunting big game, and to a lesser extent by fishing and collecting edible plants.

Panic of 1819 (p. 213) A downturn in the American economy in 1819 that plunged the nation into depression and economic hardship.

Panic of 1873 (p. 424) A financial panic on Wall Street that touched off a national economic recession causing financial houses, banks, and businesses to fail. Hundreds of thousands of workers lost their jobs.

pan-Indian resistance movement (p. 199) Shawnee leaders Tenskwatawa and Tecumseh's plan to unite Indian tribes to repel white encroachments in Ohio and Indiana, thus defending indigenous lands and reasserting the traditional values of Indian culture.

Patriots (p. 111) Colonists who supported American independence.

"peculiar institution" (p. 294) A term that John C. Calhoun coined to describe Southern slavery. In Calhoun's view slavery was not "an evil" or a cause of shame but rather "a good—a positive good" to be championed.

Peninsular Campaign (p. 382) The complex plan developed by General George B. McClellan to capture the Confederate capital, whereby 400 ships deposited 120,000 soldiers just east of Richmond at Fortress Monroe between the James and York Rivers.

penitentiary (p. 288) A new reform-based model of incarceration that isolated individuals from one another and gave them a chance to repent and reform. This method was a radical departure from earlier approaches to crime, which cast behavior in terms of sinfulness, innate depravity, and punishment.

plantation (p. 28) An English settlement or fortified outpost in a foreign land dedicated to producing agricultural products for export. (Later the term would become synonymous with a distinctive slave-based labor system used in much of the Atlantic world.)

popular sovereignty (p. 334) An approach to the question of slavery in a newly acquired territory that would have allowed the people in each territory to decide for themselves whether to permit slavery.

privateer (p. 29) A form of state-sponsored piracy, usually directed against Spanish treasure fleets returning from the Americas.

proprietor (p. 40) This English legal title carried with it enormous political power, giving its possessor almost king-like authority over his domains. Colonial proprietors carried similar powers.

Quakers (p. 48) The Society of Friends, who believed each individual possessed a divine spark of grace, an inner light that could lead to salvation.

Redeemers (p. 426) Name for white Southern political leaders who successfully returned their states to white Democratic rule in the mid-1870s. The name was intended to depict these leaders as saviors of Southern society from rule by freedmen, scalawags, and carpetbaggers.

Reformation (p. 13) The movement for religious reform started by Martin Luther.

Rendezvous (p. 318) A festive annual gathering held in the Rocky Mountains in which Indians, mountain men, and traders gathered together to exchange pelts for a variety of goods.

Republicans (p. 160) Movement led by Jefferson and Madison that opposed Federalists' efforts to create a more powerful centralized government.

Restoration (p. 52) In 1660 Charles II became king of England, restoring the monarchy to power after the Civil War and Cromwellian rule.

Scalawag (p. 418) White Southerners' derogatory term for fellow whites considered traitors to their region and race for joining the Republican Party and cooperating with Reconstruction policy.

Seneca Falls Convention (p. 297) A convention of women's rights supporters, held in Seneca Falls, New York, whose resolves emphatically declared that "all men and women are created equal."

Separatism (p. 42) This strain of English Protestantism argued for a total separation from the established Church of England.

Shays's Rebellion (p. 141) Uprising in western Massachusetts in which farmers organized themselves as local militia units and closed down courts to prevent their farms from being seized by creditors.

Sherman's March to the Sea (p. 400) The 285-mile "scorched earth" campaign of General William T. Sherman across Georgia in late 1864 and early 1865. Sherman's soldiers seized or destroyed $100 million in goods, hurting Southern morale and depriving the Confederate army of supplies.

Spanish Inquisition (p. 15) A tribunal devoted to finding and punishing heresy and rooting out Spain's Jews and Muslims.

Special Field Order No. 15 (p. 400) The directive announced by General Sherman in January 1865 during his March to the Sea that set aside more than 400,000 acres of seized Confederate land for distribution to former slaves in 40-acre plots.

spirituals (p. 277) Religious songs created by slaves. Spirituals' symbolism drew heavily on biblical themes.

spoils system (p. 229) The name applied to Jackson's system of replacing government officeholders with those loyal to him.

Stamp Act (p. 100) Legislation that required colonists to purchase special stamps and place them on all legal documents. Newspapers and playing cards had to be printed on special stamped paper.

State v. Mann **(p. 279)** The 1829 North Carolina Supreme Court case that involved a white man's assault on a slave. The case asserted that the domination of the master over the slave was complete.

States' rights (p. 184) The theory that the Constitution was a compact among the states and that the individual states retained the right to judge when the federal government's actions were unconstitutional.

Sugar Act (p. 98) British tax aimed at sugar, molasses, and other goods imported into the colonies; it also created a new mechanism for enforcing compliance with custom's duties.

telegraph (p. 258) Invention patented by Samuel Morse in 1837 that used electricity to send coded messages over wires, making communication nearly instantaneous.

temperance (p. 285) A reform movement that developed in response to concern over the rising levels of alcohol consumption in America society.

Ten Percent Plan (p. 408) Pardoned all Southerners (except highranking military officers and Confederate officials) who took an oath pledging loyalty to the Union and support for emancipation. As soon as 10 percent of a state's voters took this oath, they could call a convention, establish a new state government, and apply for congressional recognition.

Transcendentalism (p. 304) A loose set of philosophical and literary ideas focused on the spiritual power of the individual. Transcendentalists looked to nature for inspiration and philosophical insights.

Treaty of Guadalupe Hidalgo (p. 330) This treaty formally ended the war between the United States and Mexico (1848). In addition to settling the border dispute between Texas and Mexico, the United States gained a significant swath of new territory in the Southwest.

Treaty of Paris (1783) (p. 118) Treaty between the newly created United States of America and Britain that officially ended the war between the two and formally recognized American independence.

Trent Affair (p. 380) A diplomatic incident in November 1861 when a U.S. Navy vessel stopped the British ship Trent and removed two Confederates heading for Europe to press for British and French intervention.

Underground Railroad (p. 347) A network of safe houses and secret hiding places along routes leading to the North and into Canada (where slavery was prohibited) that helped several thousand slaves gain their freedom between 1830 and 1860.

unicameralism (p. 120) A form of representative government with only one legislature. Pennsylvania's 1776 constitution created a unicameral system.

Virginia Plan (p. 143) A plan framed by James Madison and introduced in the Constitution Convention by Edmund Randolph that called on delegations to abandon the government of the Articles and create a new, strong national government.

virtual representation (p. 71) A theory of representation in which legislators do not serve their localities but rather the whole nation.

Wade-Davis Bill (p. 408) A Reconstruction program designed to punish Confederate leaders and permanently destroy the South's slave society.

Waltham System (p. 261) Also known as the mill town model, a system that relied on factories housing all the distinctive steps of cloth production under a single roof.

War Hawks (p. 203) Young Republican congressmen from the South and Western regions of the country who favored Western expansion and war with Britain in 1812.

War of 1812 (p. 204) The war fought between Britain and America over restrictions on American trade. British trade with American Indians, particularly trade in weapons, was also an issue.

Whigs (American, 19th Century) (p. 242) Anti-Jackson political party; the name evoked the seventeenth-century English opponents of absolute monarchy and the Patriot leaders who had opposed the tyranny of George III during the American Revolution. Whigs supported Clay's American System and a stronger central government.

Whigs (English, 17th Century) (p. 60) The group that supported parliamentary power after the Glorious Revolution.

Whiskey Rebellion (p. 173) The armed uprising of western Pennsylvania farmers protesting the Whiskey excise in 1794 was the most serious test of the new federal government's authority since ratification of the Constitution.

Wilmot Proviso (p. 334) Bill introduced by Congressman David Wilmot would have banned slavery from the territories acquired from Mexico.

XYZ Affair (p. 182) The furor created when Americans learned that three French officials, identified in diplomatic correspondence as "X," "Y," and "Z," demanded a bribe from America's diplomats as the price of beginning negotiations.

Young America (p. 350) The movement within the Democratic Party that embraced Manifest Destiny and promoted territorial expansion, increased international trade, and the spread of American ideals of democracy and free enterprise abroad.

Credits

Warner House; **p. 66:** (top left) Archive Photos/Getty Images; (bottom right) The Metropolitan Museum of Art/Art Resource, NY; **p. 67:** (bottom left) Art Resource, NY; (bottom center) Art Resource, NY; **p. 68:** (top left) Smithsonian Institution/Office of Imaging, Printing, and Photographic Services; (bottom left) Williams Owens/Alamy; (bottom center) Courtesy, The Winterthur Ligrary: Printed Book and Periodical Collection; **p. 69:** Maryland Historical Society; **p. 70:** Archive Photos/Getty Images; **p. 72:** (bottom center) National Portrait Gallery, London; (top left) The Philadelphia Museum of Art/Art Resource, NY; **p. 73:** Georgia Historical Society; **p. 74:** The Philadelphia Museum of Art/Art Resource, NY; **p. 76:** Moravian Historical Society; **p. 77:** Abby Aldrich Rockefeller Folk Art Museum, The Colonial Williamsburg Foundation, Williamsburg, Va; **p. 79:** © North Wind Picture Archives/Alamy; **p. 80:** View of Mulberry, House and Street. 1805, by Thomas Coram (1756–1811) Oil on paper. © Image courtesy of The Gibbes Museum of Art/Carolina Art Association, 1968.018.001; **p. 82:** Abby Aldrich Rockefeller Folk Art Museum, The Colonial Williamsburg Foundation, Williamsburg, Va; **p. 83:** (top left) Collection of The New-York Historical Society; **p. 85:** Collection of The New-York Historical Society; **p. 87:** National Gallery of Canada; **p. 90:** National Gallery of Canada; **p. 91:** "Indian Testimonial given to N.Y. State Indians by Sir William Johnson in the 18th century, engraved April 1770 by Henry Dawkins; see negative #2611. Collection of the New York Historical Society."; **p. 93:** The Historical Society of Pennsylvania; **p. 94:** (top left) Getty Images; (top left center) Collection of The New York Historical Society; (top right center) Courtesy of the Georgia Historical Society; (top right) From the Collection of the Moravian Historical Society, Nazareth, PA; **p. 95:** (top left) The Philadelphia Museum of Art/Art Resource, NY; (top left center) The Philadelphia Museum of Art/Art Resource, NY; (top right center) National Gallery of Canada.

CHAPTER 4

p. 96: (top left) Library of Congress Prints and Photographs Division [LC-USZ62-45399]; (upper center left) Susan Van Etten/PhotoEdit; (center left) Princeton University, commissioned by the Trustees. (PP222) photo: Bruce M. White; (bottom left) The Granger Collection, NYC—All rights reserved; **pp. 96–97:** W. Humphreys/Lilly Library; **p. 98:** Library of Congress Prints and Photographs Division[LC-USZ62-45399]; **p. 100:** (top left) Library of Congress Prints and Photographs Division [LC-USZ62-45399]; **p. 102:** (1775) Stock Sales WGBH/Scala/Art Resource, NY; **p. 103:** (top left) Bettmann/CORBIS; (bottom left) The Granger Collection, NYC—All rights reserved; **p. 104:** Library of Congress Prints and Photographs Division[LC-USZC4-5289]; **p. 107:** (top left) Susan Van Etten/PhotoEdit; (bottom center) Library of Congress Prints and Photographs Division[LC-USZC4-5292]; **pp. 108–109:** Yale University Art Gallery/Art Resource, NY; **p. 111:** Susan Van Etten/PhotoEdit; **p. 112:** Library of Congress Prints and Photographs Division[LC-USZ62-34866]; **p. 113:** The Granger Collection, NYC—All rights reserved; **p. 114:** Princeton University, commissioned by the Trustees. (PP222) photo: Bruce M. White; **p. 115:** Princeton University, commissioned by the Trustees. (PP222) photo: Bruce M. White; **p. 118:** Library of Congress Prints and Photographs Division; **p. 119:** The Granger Collection, NYC—All rights reserved; **p. 120:** Gift in memory of Martha Legg McPheeters, and M. Theresa B. Hopkins Fund, Emily L. Ainsley Fund, Juliana Cheney Edwards Collection, and A. Shuman Collection. Photograph © 2010 Musem of Fine Arts, Boston; **p.123:** Wadsworth Atheneum Museum of Art/Art Resource, NY; **p. 124:** (bottom left) Joseph Blackburn, American (born in England), active in North America 1753–1763 Isaac Winslow and His Family, 1755 Oil on canvas 138.43 × 201.29 cm (54 1/2 × 79 1/4 in.) Museum of Fine Arts, Boston A. Shuman Collection—Abraham Shuman Fund, 42.684 Photograph © 2011 Museum of Fine Arts, Boston; (bottom

right) The Philadelphia Museum of Art/Art Resource, NY; **p. 125:** (bottom left) The Granger Collection, NYC—All rights reserved; (bottom right) John Trumbull/"White House Historical Association (White House Collection)" (25); **p.126:** (top left) Library of Congress Prints and Photographs Division[LC-USZ62-45399]; (top center) The Granger Collection, NYC—All rights reserved; (top right) Bettmann/CORBIS; **p.127:** (top left) Susan Van Etten/PhotoEdit; (top left center) Wadsworth Atheneum Museum of Art/Art Resource, NY; (top right center) John Trumbull/"White House Historical Association (White House Collection)" (25); (top right) Library of Congress Prints and Photographs Division.

CHAPTER 5

p. 128: (top left) Time & Life Pictures/Getty Images; (center left) Thomas Prichard Rossiter/Independence Historical National Park; (bottom left) Library of Congress Prints and Photograph Division[LC-USZC4-1722]; **pp. 128–129:** Library of Congress Prints and Photograph Division; **p. 130:** Time & Life Pictures/Getty Images; **p. 131:** Time & Life Pictures/ Getty Images; **p. 132:** (top left) Courtesy, Winterthur Museum; (bottom left) Samuel McIntire, "Chest-on-chest (detail)"; Mahogany, mahogany veneer, ebony and satinwood inlay, pine; Eighteenth-century American Arts No. 4; the M. and M. Karolik Collection of Eighteenth-Century American Arts, 41.580. Museum of Fine Arts, Boston (41.58). Photograph © 2010 Museum of Fine Arts, Boston; **p. 133:** (top right) American Antiquarian Society; (bottom right) University of North Carolina/ Wilson Library; **p. 134:** (bottom left) Henry Francis Dupont/Courtesy, Winterthur Museum; (bottom right) © 2007 Museum of Art, RISD. All Rights Reserved; **p.136:** Virginia Museum of Fine Arts, Richmond. Purchase, Robert G. Cabell III and Maude Morgan Cabell Foundation and Arthur and Margaret Glasgow Fund Photo: Katherine Wetzel © Virginia Museum of Fine Arts; **p. 141:** William Clements Library, University of Michigan; **p. 143:** Thomas Prichard Rossiter/Independence Historical National Park; **p. 144:** Thomas Prichard Rossiter/Independence Historical National Park; **p. 148:** Library of Congress Prints and Photographs Division[LC-USZC4-1722]; **p.149:** National Archives and Records Administration; **p. 150:** Library of Congress Prints and Photographs Division[LC-USZC4-1722]; **p. 151:** (top left) Bettmann/CORBIS; (top center) The Granger Collection, NYC—All rights reserved; **p. 152:** Library of Congress Prints and Photographs Division[LC-USZ62-45589]; **p. 153:** (top right) Collection of The New-York Historical Society, [1903.12] **p. 154:** (top left) American Antiquarian Society; (top left center) Time & Life Pictures/Getty Images; (top right center) William Clements Library, University of Michigan; (top right); The Granger Collection, NYC— All rights reserved. **p. 155:** (top left center) Library of Congress Prints and Photographs Division[LC-DIG-ppmsca-17522]; (top right center) Library of Congress Prints and Photographs Division[LC-USZ62-45589]; (top right) © 2007 Museum of Art, RISD. All Rights Reserved.

CHAPTER 6

p. 156: (top left) Library of Congress Prints and Photographs Division[LC-USZ62-338]; (upper center left) Niday Picture Library/ Alamy; (center left) The Granger Collection, NYC—All rights reserved; (lower center left) Courtesy of the Atwater Kent Museum of Philadelphia; (upper bottom left) Courtesy of the Peabody Essex Museum, Salem, Massachusetts; (bottom left) Reproduced by permission of The Huntington Library, San Marino, California; **pp. 156–157:** Collection of The New-York Historical Society, PR010, #1795-1; Neg. #2737; **p. 158:** (top left and bottom) Library of Congress Prints and Photographs Division [LC-USZ62-338]; **p. 160:** Niday Picture Library/Alamy; **p. 161:** Niday Picture Library/Alamy; **p. 163:** Library of Congress Prints and Photographs Division[LC-USZCN4-216]; **p. 165:** (top left) National Portrait

Gallery, Smithsonian Institution/Art Resource, NY; (top right) The Granger Collection, NYC—All rights reserved; **p. 166:** The Granger Collection, NYC—All rights reserved.; **p. 167:** The Granger Collection, NYC—All rights reserved.; **p. 168:** (top left) Courtesy of the Atwater Kent Museum of Philadelphia; (bottom) The Bowes Museum, The Barnard Castle, County Durham, England; **p. 171:** Shutterstock; **p. 172:** The Ohio Historical Society; **p. 173:** Courtesy of the Atwater Kent Museum of Philadelphia; **p. 174:** The Granger Collection, NYC—All rights reserved.; **p. 175:** Courtesy of the Peabody Essex Museum, Salem, Massachusetts; **p. 176:** Courtesy of the Peabody Essex Museum, Salem, Massachusetts; **p. 177:** The Granger Collection, NYC—All rights reserved.; **p. 178:** Library Company of Philadelphia.; **p. 179:** Reproduced by permission of The Huntington Library, San Marino, California.; **p. 180:** National Portrait Gallery, Smithsonian Institution/Art Resource, NY; **p. 181:** (bottom) Library of Congress; **p. 182:** Reproduced by permission of The Huntington Library, San Marino, California.; **p. 184:** The Granger Collection, NYC—All rights reserved.; **p. 186:** (top left) National Portrait Gallery, Smithsonian Institution/Art Resource, NY; (top center left) Niday Picture Library/Alamy; (top center right) Courtesy of the Atwater Kent Museum of Philadelphia; (top right) The Granger Collection, NYC—All rights reserved.; **p. 187:** (top left) Library of Congress; (top center left): Reproduced by permission of The Huntington Library, San Marino, California.; (top center right): The Granger Collection, NYC—All rights reserved.; (top right): The Granger Collection, NYC—All rights reserved.

CHAPTER 7

p. 188: (top left) American Antiquarian Society; (upper center left) Collection of The New-York Historical Society, Acc. #1931.58; (center left) Library of Congress Prints and Photographs Division[LC-USZC4-5643]; (lower center left) Rhode Island Historical Society Library and Museum; (bottom left): The University of North Carolina at Chapel Hill; **pp.188–189:** The Granger Collection, NYC—All rights reserved; **p. 190:** American Antiquarian Society; **p. 191:** (bottom left) MA5911, Courtesy of the Maryland Historical Society; (top right) Richard Draper/DK Images; **p. 193:** American Antiquarian Society; **p. 196:** The Granger Collection, NYC—All rights reserved; **p. 198:** Thomas Jefferson Foundation, Inc. at Monticello, photograph by Charles Shoffner; **p. 200:** (top and bottom) Collection of The New-York Historical Society, Acc. #1931.58; **p. 201:** Library of Congress Prints and Photographs Division[LC-USZC4-5643]; **p. 202:** The Granger Collection, NYC—All rights reserved; **p. 203:** Library of Congress Prints and Photographs Division[LC-USZC4-5643]; **p. 204:** Library of Congress Prints and Photographs Division[LC-USZC4-4820]; **p. 206:** Library of Congress Prints and Photographs Division[LC-USZC4-3657]; **p. 207:** Library of Congress Prints and Photographs Division[LC-USZC4-12748]; **p. 208:** (top left) Rhode Island Historical Society Library and Museum; (bottom right) Library of Congress Prints and Photographs Division; **p. 209:** Bettmann/CORBIS; **p. 210:** Rhode Island Historical Society Library and Museum; **p. 211:** The Granger Collection; **p. 213:** The University of North Carolina at Chapel Hill; **p. 216:** The University of North Carolina at Chapel Hill; **p. 218:** (top left) American Antiquarian Society; (top right center) Collection of The New-York Historical Society, Acc. #1931.58; (top right) The Granger Collection, NYC—All rights reserved; **p. 219:** (top left) Library of Congress Prints and Photographs Division[LC-USZC4-4820]; (top center left) Library of Congress Prints and Photographs Division[LC-USZC4-3675]; (top center right): Bettmann/CORBIS; (top right): The University of North Carolina at Chapel Hill.

CHAPTER 8

p. 220: (top left) The Granger Collection, NYC—All rights reserved; (upper center left) The Granger Collection, NYC—All rights reserved; (center left) Library of Congress Prints and Photographs Division [LC-USZ62-9646]; (lower center left) North Wind/North Wind Picture Archives; (bottom left) Library of Congress Prints and Photographs Division[LC-USZC4-4551]; **pp. 220–221:** Art Resource, NY; **p. 222:** The Granger Collection, NYC—All rights reserved; **p. 223:** The Granger Collection, NYC—All rights reserved; **p. 224:** The Historical Society of Pennsylvania (SHP), John Lewis Krimmel; **p. 225:** The Granger Collection, NYC—All rights reserved; **p. 226:** Library of Congress Prints and Photographs Division[LC-USZ62-32512]; **p. 228:** Collection of The New-York Historical Society, New York City; **p. 229:** Ron Sachs/CNP/Sygma/CORBIS; **p. 230:** The Granger Collection, NYC—All rights reserved; **p. 231:** George P.A. Healy/Courtesy of the Boston Art Commission 2009; **p. 232:** Bettmann/CORBIS; **p. 233:** Library of Congress Prints and Photographs Division[LC-USZ62-9646]; **p. 234:** William Summers/The Library Company of Philadelphia; **p. 235:** Library of Congress Prints and Photographs Division[LC-USZ62-9646]; **p. 237:** (bottom left) MPI/Getty Images; (bottom right) Courtesy of Oklahoma Historical Society; Dr. Joseph Thoburn Collection; **p. 239:** North Wind/North Wind Picture Archives; **p. 240:** Library of Congress Prints and Photographs Division[LC-USZC4-8077]; **p. 241:** The Granger Collection, NYC—All rights reserved; **p. 243:** Collection of The New-York Historical Society, New York City; **p. 244:** North Wind/North Wind Picture Archives; **p. 245:** Library of Congress Prints and Photographs Division; **p. 246:** Library of Congress Prints and Photographs Division[LC-USZC4-4551]; **p. 247:** Library of Congress Prints and Photographs Division[LC-USZC4-4551]; **p. 249:** (left and right) Art Resource, NY; **p. 250:** (top left) Library of Congress Prints and Photographs Division[LC-USZ62-32512]; (top left center) Ron Sachs/CNP/Sygma/CORBIS; (top right center) George P.A. Healy/Courtesy of the Boston Art Commission 2009; (top right) North Wind/North Wind Picture Archives; **p. 251:** (top left) Bettmann/CORBIS; (top left center) Collection of The New York Historical Society, New York City; (top right center) Library of Congress Prints and Photographs Division [LC-USZ62-9646].; (top right): Library of Congress Prints and Photographs Division[LC-USZC4-4551].

CHAPTER 9

p. 252: (top left) Hannah Stockton Stiles/Fenimore Art Museum, Cooperstown, New York. Photo by Richard Walker. New York State Historical Association; (upper center left) Library of Congress Prints and Photographs Division; (center left) The Granger Collection, NYC—All rights reserved; (lower center left) The Granger Collection, NYC—All rights reserved.; (bottom left) Jan White Brantley/The Historic New Orleans Collection. accession no. 1960.46; **pp. 252–253:** Library of Congress Prints and Photographs Division[LC-USZ62-89561]; **p. 254:** Hannah Stockton Stiles/Fenimore Art Museum, Cooperstown, New York. Photo by Richard Walker. New York State Historical Association; **p. 255:** William Summers/Alan Fisher, "Corn Husking Frolic". 1828. Oil on Panel, 70.8 × 62.23 cm Museum of Fine Arts, Boston Assc. #62.27 Photograph © 2010 Museum of Fine Arts, Boston; **p. 256:** Hannah Stockton Stiles/Fenimore Art Museum, Cooperstown, New York. Photo by Richard Walker. New York State Historical Association; **p. 257:** George Inness, "The Lackawanna Valley". 1856. Oil on Canvas, 33 7/8" × 50 3/16". Image © 2010 Board of Trustees, National Gallery of Art, Washington, D.C.; **p. 259:** Library of Congress Prints and Photographs Division[LC-USZC4-3102]; **p. 260:** Library of Congress Prints and Photographs Division; **p. 261:** Library of Congress Prints and Photographs Division; **p. 263:** Museum of American Textile History; **p. 264:** (top and bottom): The Granger Collection, NYC—All rights reserved; **p. 265:** The Library Company of Philadelphia; **p. 267:** The Library Company of Philadelphia; **p. 268:** Richard P. Robinson/Collection of The New-York Historical Society, Neg.

#40696; **p. 269:** The New-York Historical Society; **p. 270:** The Granger Collection, NYC—All rights reserved; **p. 272:** Manuscripts, Archives and Rare Books Division, Schomburg Center for Research in Black Culture, The New York Public Library, Astor, Lenox and Tilden Foundations; **p. 273:** The Granger Collection, NYC—All rights reserved; **p. 274:** Library of Congress Prints and Photographs Division[LC-USZ62-38902]; **p. 275:** (top right) The Granger Collection, NYC—All rights reserved; (bottom): Francis G. Mayer/CORBIS; **p. 277:** Jan White Brantley/The Historic New Orleans Collection. accession no. 1960.46.; **p. 278:** Library of Congress Prints and Photographs Division[LC-USZ62-38902]; **p. 279:** Manuscripts, Archives and Rare Books Division, Schomburg Center for Research in Black Culture, The New York Public Library, Astor, Lenox and Tilden Foundations; **p. 280:** (top left) Courtesy of the Library of Congress; (top left center): Manuscripts, Archives and Rare Books Division, Schomburg Center for Research in Black Culture, The New York Public Library, Astor, Lenox and Tilden Foundations; (top right center): George Inness, "The Lackawanna Valley". 1856. Oil on Canvas, 33 7/8" × 50 3/16". Image © 2010 Board of Trustees, National Gallery of Art, Washington, D.C.; (top right): Library of Congress Prints and Photographs Division[LC-USZ62-38902]; **p. 281:** (top left): Museum of American Textile History; (top left center): Richard P. Robinson/Collection of The New-York Historical Society, Neg. #40696; (top right center): The Granger Collection, NYC—All rights reserved; (top right): Library of Congress Prints and Photographs Division[LC-USZC4-3102].

CHAPTER 10

p. 282: (top left) J. Maze Burbank/Old Dartmouth Historical Society/New Bedford Whaling Museum; (upper center left) Division of Rare and Manuscript Collections, Cornell University Library; (center left) Domestic Happiness, 1849 (oil on canvas), Spencer, Lilly Martin (1827–1902)/Detroit Institute of Arts, USA/Gift of Dr and Mrs James Cleland Jr./The Bridgeman Art Library International; (lower center left) Library of Congress Prints and Photographs Division[LC-USZ62-23784] (upper bottom left) © Aurora Photos/Alamy; (bottom left) Thomas Abad/Alamy; **pp. 282–283:** Library of Congress Prints and Photographs Division [LC-USZC4-2671]; **p. 284:** J. Maze Burbank/Old Dartmouth Historical Society/New Bedford Whaling Museum; **p. 286:** Courtesy of the Pennsylvania Academy of the Fine Arts, Philadelphia. Bequest of Henry C. Carey (The Carey Collection); (top left center); **p. 289:** The Library Company of Philadelphia; **p. 290:** Division of Rare and Manuscript Collections, Cornell University Library; **p. 291:** (top center) Division of Rare and Manuscript Collections, Cornell University Library; (bottom right) Library of Congress Prints and Photographs Division[LC-USZC4-4659]; **p. 292:** (bottom left) Yale University Art Gallery/Art Resource, NY; (bottom right) Library of Congress Prints and Photographs Division [LC-USZ62-50519]; **p. 293:** Library of Congress Prints and Photographs Division[LC-USZ62-92283]; **p. 294:** The Granger Collection, NYC—All rights reserved; **p. 295:** Domestic Happiness, 1849 (oil on canvas), Spencer, Lilly Martin (1827–1902)/Detroit Institute of Arts, USA/Gift of Dr and Mrs James Cleland Jr./The Bridgeman Art Library International; **p. 296:** Mary Sargeant Grove/The Library Company of Philadelphia; **p. 298:** Library of Congress Prints and Photographs Division[LC-USZ62-23784]; **p. 300:** The Granger Collection, NYC—All rights reserved; **p. 302:** Oneida Community Mansion House; **p. 304:** © Aurora Photos/Alamy; **p. 305:** Library of Congress Prints and Photographs Division[LC-USZC4-5133]; **p. 306:** © Aurora Photos/Alamy; **p. 307:** Asa Ames (1824–1851), "Phrenological Head". Evans, New York. c. 1850, paint on wood. American Folk Art Museum; **p. 308:** Tomas Abad/Alamy; **p. 309:** Central Park Conservancy; **p. 310:** Thomas Chambers, "Mount Auburn Cemetery". Mid-19th C. Oil on Canvas, 14" × 18 1/8". Image

© 2010 Board of Trustees, National Gallery of Art, Washington, D.C. Gift of Edgar William and Bernice Chrysler Garbisch; **p. 312:** (top left) Lizzie Himmel/Courtesy, Winterthur Museum; (top right) Pat & Chuck Blackley/Alamy; **p. 313:** (top) Lee Snider/Photo Images/CORBIS; (bottom) Andre Jenny/Alamy; **p. 314:** (top left) Courtesy of the Pennsylvania Academy of the Fine Arts, Philadelphia. Bequest of Henry C. Carey (The Carey Collection); (top left center) The Library Company of Philadelphia Arts, Philadelphia. Bequest of Henry C. Carey (The Carey Collection); (top right center) Old Dartmouth Historical Society Whaling Museum; (top right) The National Gallery of Art, Washington, DC; **p. 315:** (top left) Thomas Abad/Alamy; (top left center) Library of Congress Prints and Photographs Division[LC-USZ62-23784]; (top right center) © Aurora Photos/Alamy; (top right) From the Collection of the Oneida Community Mansion House, Oneida, NY.

CHAPTER 11

p. 316: (top left) The Granger Collection, NYC—All rights reserved; (upper center left) Library of Congress Prints and Photographs Division [LC-USZ62-10802]; (lower center left) Beinecke Rare Book and Manuscript Library, Yale University; (bottom left) Library of Congress Prints and Photographs Division[LC-USZ62-10355]; **pp. 316–317:** Bettmann/CORBIS; **p. 318:** The Granger Collection, NYC—All rights reserved; **p. 320:** Albert Bierstadt, "Emigrants Crossing the Plains". 1867. Oil on canvas, 60 × 96 in., A.011.1T, National Cowboy & Western Heritage Museum, Oklahoma City; **p. 321:** Bequest of Henry C. Lewis/University of Michigan Museum of Art; **p. 323:** (bottom left) Smithsonian American Art Museum, Washington, DC/Art Resource, NY; (bottom right) Time & Life Pictures/Getty Images; **p. 324:** Minnesota Historical Society; **p. 325:** Library of Congress Prints and Photographs Division[LC-USZ62-10802]; **p. 326:** The Bancroft Library; **p. 327:** The Granger Collection, NYC—All rights reserved; **p. 328:** Library of Congress Prints and Photographs Division[LC-USZ62-10802]; **p. 330:** Beinecke Rare Book and Manuscript Library, Yale University; **p. 331:** Beinecke Rare Book and Manuscript Library, Yale University; **p. 332:** Unknown photographer. Burial Place of Son of Henry Clay in Mexico. Daguerreotype, 1847, 2 3/8 × 2 15/16 inches. Amon Carter Museum of American Art, Fort Worth, Texas, P1981.65.40; **p. 333:** Library of Congress Prints and Photographs Division[LC-USZC4-6197]; **p. 334:** Library of Congress Prints and Photographs Division[LC-USZ62-10355]; **p. 335:** Library of Congress Prints and Photographs Division[LC-USZ62-19668]; **p. 336:** Library of Congress Prints and Photographs Division[LC-USZ62-40071]; **p. 337:** Library of Congress Prints and Photographs Division[LC-USZ62-10355]; **p. 338:** (top right) The Granger Collection, NYC—All rights reserved; **p. 339:** (top left) Albert Bierstadt, "Emigrants Crossing the Plains". 1867. Oil on canvas, 60 × 96 in., A.011.1T, National Cowboy & Western Heritage Museum, Oklahoma City; (top left center) Library of Congress Prints and Photographs Division[LC-USZ62-10802]; (top right) Library of Congress Prints and Photographs Division[LC-USZ62-19668].

CHAPTER 12

p. 340: (top left) Eon Images; (upper center left) Library of Congress Prints and Photographs Division[LC-USZC4-12985]; (lower center left) Library of Congress Prints and Photographs Division[LC-USZC4-2341]; (bottom left) National Archives and Records Administration; **pp. 341–342:** The Granger Collection, NYC—All rights reserved; **p. 342:** Eon Images; **p. 343:** The Granger Collection, NYC—All rights reserved; **p. 344:** California State Archives; **p. 345:** Eon Images; **p. 347:** The Granger Collection, NYC—All rights reserved; **p. 348:** Indiana State Library; **p. 349:** Library of Congress Prints and Photographs Division[LC-USZ62-75974]; **p. 350:** (top left) Library of Congress Prints and

Index

A

Abbott, Ann, 305
The Able Doctor, Or America Swallowing the Bitter Draught (Revere), 104
Abolitionism, 282, 348
Abolitionists, 340, 367
  attitudes of racism and, 177
  denunciation of Kansas-Nebraska Act by, 352
Academy of Philadelphia, 95
Act of Union (1707), 61
Adam and Eve (Cranach), 12
Adams, Abigal, 108, 123–124, 125
Adams, John, 97, 102, 104, 110, 111, 121, 125, 128, 168, 225
  as first vice president, 158
  presidency of, 179–185
  tribute to Benjamin Franklin, 74
Adams, John Quincy, 209, 215, 225, 226–227, 248, 329
  attacks on character of, 228
Africa
  Portuguese connection with, 21–22
  slavery in, 21–22
  societies, Islam and trade in early, 20
African Americans. *See also* Free blacks; Freedmen
  barriers for, 233
  during Civil War, 392–393
  in colonial era, 77–80
  communities, 266–267
  first newspaper published by, 233
  freedom of movement for, 409
  pay of, during Civil War, 394
  racial prejudice and discrimination against, 266–267
  struggle for freedom, 122
Agriculture, 252
  before 1815, 254
  changes to, 254–255
  of Eastern Woodlands Indians, 8
  migration, settlement, and rise of, 5–6
  sugar, 50
  tobacco and political reorganization, 37–40
Alabama feveer, 293

Alien and Sedition Acts, 182–183, 186, 206–207
America. *See also* United States
  accounts of early, 2
  conflict with Indians in, 140
  debtors *versus* creditors, 137
  diplomatic controversies and triumphs in, 169–170
  French Revolution in, 168–169
  growth of partisan press in, 168–169
  Hamilton's vision of, 160–161
  map of Spanish interests in, *170*
  migration from Asia to, 4
  new type of politician in, 166
  politics in Jeffersonian, 190–193
  refinement in, 66–68
  as republic, 128
  scarcity of land in rural, 86
American Anti-Slavery Society (AASS), 291, 297
American colonies. *See also specific colonies*
  back country of, 85–86
  immigration to, 83
  regional economies of, 83
  strong assemblies and weak governors in, 70–71
American Colonization Society, 290
The American Crisis (Paine), 115
American Party, 357
American Philosophical Society, 72, 74
American Red Cross, 388
American Revolution. *See also* Revolutionary War
  in Indian country, 122–123
  literature, education, and gender after, 175–176
  radicalism of, 119–127
American System, 226, 227, 250
  economic policy, as defined by, 239
  Jackson's opposition to, 241
Amerigo Vespucci Awakens a Sleeping America, 2
Amherst, Jeffrey, 89
Amnesty Act, 423
Amsterdam, 10
Anderson, Archer, 429
Anderson, Robert, 370

Anglicization, 67, 70, 94
  architecture and, 68–70
Animism, 8, 20
Anne (queen of England), 64, 68
Anti-Catholicism, 354
Antietam, battle of, 384
Anti-Federalists, 148–150, 154, 158
  vs. Federalists, 148–150
  as loyal opposition, 153
Anti-Masonic party, 239–241
Antinomians, 47–48, 49
Anti-Slavery Convention of American Women, 297
Antwerp, 10
Archaic Era, 5, 32
Argall, Samuel, 37
Army of the Potomac, 381, 386, 398
Articles of Confederation, 121–122, 154, 162
  Constitution and, *147*
  convention to reform, 143
  life under, 138–142
  revisions to, 144
Artisan production, 260, 280
Asia
  effect of contact with, 10
  migration from, to America, 4
  search for route to, 16
Assumption of the state debts, 162, 186
Astor, John Jacob, 319
Asylums, public, 289
Atlantic slave trade, 77–79
Atlantic world, 24–30
Aztecs, 6–7, 9, 32
  conquest of, 17–19

B

Babcock, Orville E., 423
Back country, 85–86
Bacon, Nathaniel, 56
Bacon's Rebellion, 34, 55, 62
Baker, Josephine L., 261
Baldwin, Ebenezer, 106
Bank of the United States
  Jackson and, 241
  Jefferson and, 194
Bank of the United States, chartering, 164–165, 186

Bank Veto Speech, 241–242, 250
Bank War, 242
Barbados, 54
   slavery in, 50–51
Barbary States, 138–139
Barker, Penelope, 101
Barnburners, 335–336
Barton, Clara, 388
Beaumont, Gustave de, 287
Beauregard, P. G. T., 330, 370, 381
Beaver wars, 87
Beckley, John, 166
Beecher, Catherine, 295
Beecher, Lyman, 268, 286, 287
Belknap, William W., 423
Bell, John, 367
Benin, 22
   Portugal and international slave
      trade, 23
Bentham, Jeremy, 288
Benton, Thomas Hart, 231, 232, 320,
      322
Berkeley, Sir William, 55
Bett, Mum, 122
Bible riots, 267
Biddle, Nicholas, 241
Bierstadt, Albert, 320–321
Bill of Rights, 159
Bingham, George Caleb, 220, 231
Black Belt, 252, 274
Black Codes, 272, 413–415, 415, 436
Black Death, 10
"Black Friday" scandal, 423
Black Haw War of 1832, 822
Black Legend, 24
Black Republicans, 357, 366, 369
Blair, Francis, 420
Bleeding Kansas, 356, 357, 372
Blue jeans, 19
Board games, 305–306
Board of Trade, 61
Border ruffians, 356, 357
Border States, 379, 402
   free black communities in, 272
Bostonians Paying the Excise-Man, 103,
      104
Boston Massacre, 103, 126
Boston Tea Party, 126
Boudinot, Elias, 437
Boudinot, Susan, 101
Bowdoin, James, 141
Boycotts, 138
Boyd, Henry, 267

Braddock, Edward, 88
Bradford, Susan, 409
Bradford, William, 42, 44
Bragg, Braxton, 386, 392, 398
Breckinridge, John C., 367
Brisbane, Albert, 301
Britain
   emissaries to, during Civil War, 380
   reestablishing Protestant monarchy
      in, 57
   as sovereign nation-state, 14–15
Brook Farm (Massachusetts), 303
Brooks, Preston, 356
Brown, Henry "Box," 291
Brown, John
   at Harper's Ferry, Virginia, 366–367
Brown, Joseph E., 378
Brutus, 148, 149
Buchanan, James, 357, 358, 367, 369
Buena Vista, battle of, 333
Bullman, Rev. Charles, 121
Bunker Hill, battle of, 107–110
Bureau of Refugees, Freedman, and
      Abandoned Lands. See Freedmen's
      Bureau
Burgoyne, John, 116
Burns, Anthony, 348
Burnside, Ambrose E., 386
Burr, Aaron, 184
   duel between Hamilton and, 193
   Jefferson and, 200
Burroughs, George, 58
Busch, Adloph, 266
Butler, Benjamin, 384
Butler, Pierce, 275, 276
Byrd, William, 68

C

Cadwalader, Elizabeth, 124, 124
Cadwalader, John, 124, 124
Cahokia, 7
Cain, Richard H., 411
Caldwell, Charles, 256
Caldwell, James, 392
Calhoun, Floride, 230
Calhoun, John C., 203, 225–226, 230,
      344, 345
   as apologist for Southern
      slavery, 294
   union, according to, 231
California
   discovery of gold in, 342–343

Great Seal of, 344, 344
Native Americans in, before Gold
      Rush, 343
organizing, 343–344
Callender, James, 193
Calvert, George (second Lord Balti-
      more), 40–41, 52
Calvinists, 13–14, 42, 285
Calvin, John, 13
Camp meetings, 284
Canada, early migration to, 4
Canals, 256
Canary Islands, 21
The Candidate of Many Parties, 335
Cane Ridge rival, 284
Capitalism, 32
   defined, 11
   European, 12
Caravels, 17
Cárdenas, Juan de, 19
Caribbean colonies, 50, 50–51
Carpetbaggers, 418–419, 436
Cartier, Jacques, 27
Cass, Lewis, 334, 335, 355, 357
Catherine of Aragon (queen of Eng-
      land), 14
Catholicism, forced conversion to, 25
Catholics
   negative feelings toward, 354
   parochial schools and, 288
Catlin, George, 323
Cemeteries, 310–311
Central Park (New York City), 309,
      309–310
Channing, William Ellery, 322
Charbonneau, Toussaint, 197
Charles I (king of England), 40, 42, 44,
      48
Charles II (king of England), 53
Charlotte Temple (Rowson), 175–176
Cherokee Cases, 236
Cherokee Nation v. Georgia, 236
Chesapeake (American navy ship), 201,
      202
Chesapeake colonies, 36–41
Chevalier, Michael, 221
Chevalier, Michel, 265
Chicago, 265
The Chickahominy Become "New Eng-
      lishmen"
   (de Bry), 34
China, 17
Chinese, Gold Rush and, 342–343

Christianity, 20
Church of Jesus Christ of Latter Day
    Saints. *See* Mormons
Cincinnati, 265–266
Cincinnatus, 130
Cities
    free black communities in Northern,
        266–267
    growth and Inequality in, 86
    immigration and, 266
    industrialization in, 262
    old ports and new, of the interior,
        264–266
    riot, unrest and crime in, 267–268
    "walking," 265
Civil disobedience, 331
Civilization(s)
    early American, 56
    in sixteenth-century Africa, 20
Civil Rights Act of 1875, 426, 436
Civil Rights Bill (1866), 416–417
Civil War
    African Americans under arms,
        392–393
    civil liberties during, 390
    comparison of North and South
        before, 376–377
    Confederacy begins to crumble,
        389–391
    conscription and civil unrest during,
        389–391
    Copperheads, 389
    diplomacy during, 380
    early campaigns (1861–1863),
        381–386
    final battles in Virginia campaign,
        392
    hardships on home front during,
        387–388
    human resources in armies of, 396
    major battles in East, *383*
    major battles in West, *382*
    meeting demands of modern
        war, 387
    mobilization of North, 377–378
    mobilization of South, 378
    as new kind of War, 383–384
    pay of African Americans in, 394
    Penninsular Campaign, 382–383
    roles for Women in, 388–389
    Sherman's March to the Sea, *293*
    start of, 370
    struggle for Border States during, 379

turning point: 1863, 392
    unrealistic notions of, 381–382
Clark, William, 197
Clay, Edward William, 233–234
Clay, Henry, 203, 225, 228, 232, 241,
    245, 252, 253, 273, 328, 334, 344
    American System of, 226, 227, 239,
        241
    policies favored by, 226
Clay, Henry, Jr., 332–333
    daguerreotype of gravesite of, *333*
Clinton, De Witt, 256
Clinton, George, 168, 169, 201–202
Clovis points, 4–5
Cobbett, 167
Cobb, Howell, 401
The Code of Honor (Wilson), 273
Cole, Thomas, 308, 309, 312
Colleges, creation of for African Ameri-
    cans, 411. *See also* Education
Colonies. *See also* American colonies;
        specific colonies
    Caribbean, *50,* 50–51
    Chesapeake, 36–41
    seventeenth-century English main-
        land, *52*
Colonization
    British, 28
    English experiments in, 34
    European, of Atlantic world, 24–30
    exploitation and, 2
Colt, Samuel, 361
Columbian Exchange, 16–17, 32
Columbus, Christopher, 16, 50
Common Sense, 110–111, 126, 127
Communication, 258–259
    time lag for news (1800-1841), *258*
Companionate marriage, 96
Complex marriage, 299, 314
Compromise of 1850, 344–346, *346,*
    372
Compromise of 1870, 427, 436
Compromise of 1877, 427
Concord, Battle of, 106, 126
Confederacy, begins to crumble,
    395–397. *See also* South
Confederate Army, 378, 387
    desertion from, 391
Confederate States of America,
    369, 378
Confidence men, 307
Conflagration of the Steamboat Lexington
    (Currier), *259*

Congress
    approval of Declaration of
        Independence by, 111
    gag rule of, 293
    use of paper money by, 138
Connecticut Compromise. *See* Great
    Compromise
Conquistadores, 17, 18
Conscription Act, 389–391, 402
Constantia. *See* Murray, Judith Sargent
Constitutional Convention. *See* Phila-
    delphia Convention
Constitutional Union Party, 367
Constitution of the United States
    adoption of, 158
    amendments to, 158–159
    Articles of Confederation and, *147*
    bill of rights and, 150
    checks and balances created by, 150
    designing, 146–147
    filling out branches of government,
        159
    ratification of, 150–153
Continental Army, 114–117, 123
Continental Congress. *See* Congress
Contraband of war, 384
Coode, John, 58
Cooper, Mary, 75
Copperheads, 389, 402
Corbin, Hannah, 124
Corn Husking Frolic (Fischer), 255
Corning, Erastus, 390
Cornwallis, Charles, 117–118
Coronado, Francisco Vasquez de, 25
Corps of Discovery, 197–198
Corrupt bargain, 226–227, 250
Cortés, Hernán, 18–19, 32
Cotesworth, Charles, 146
Cotton
    embargo, 380, 402
    slave labor and, 274
    supremacy of, in South, 362–363
Cotton gin, 210, 218
Cotton, John, 47
Coureurs des bois (runners of the
    woods), 87
Couverture, doctrine of, 297
Craft, Ellen, 348
Craft, William, 348
Cragin, George, 302
Cragin, Mary, 302
Cranach, Lucas, 12
Crawford, Thomas, 353

Crawford, William, 225
Credit Mobilier scandal, 423
Creek Wars, 222, 234
Crittenden Compromise, 369, 372
Crittenden, John J., 369, 374
Crockett, Davy, 222–223, *223*
    at Alamo, *328*
    death of, *328*
Crockett's Almanac, 223
Cromwell, Oliver, 48
Cromwell, R. I., 419
Crowe, Eyre, 275
Crusades, 10
Crystal Palace Exhibition, 360–361
Cult of true womanhood, 295, 314
Culture
    colonial, 66–68
    democratic, 222
    in eighteenth-century America, 64
    French, 87
    white Southern, 273
Currier and Ives, 259, 309
Currier, Nathaniel, 259
    lithograph, *259*

D

Dabney, Thomas, 271
Daguerreotype, 332
Darnall, Henry, III, 68, 69, *69*
Davenport, James, 76
Davenport, Rev. John, 48
Davis, Alexander Jackson, 312
Davis, Henry W., 408
Davis, Jefferson, 344, 353, 369, 387, 407
    challenges facing, 378
Davis, Joseph, 407
The Death of General Warren at the Battle of Bunker Hill (Trumbull), 107, 108–109
DeBow, James D. B., 363
De Bry, Theodore, 30, 31, 34, 40
Declaration of Independence, 111, 126, 127
    ideals of, 119
Declaration of Sentiments and Resolutions, 297
Declaratory Act, 101
Deere, John, 254, 361
Democracy in America (Toqueville), 222, 304
Democracy, symbols of frontier, 222–223

Democratic Party
    during Civil War, 389
    election of 1848 and, 337
Democratic-Republican Societies, 167, 186
Democratic Review, 246
Democrats, 220
    Texas issue and, 327–328
    weakening of, 353
    and Whigs: two visions of government and society, 248–249
Denmark Vesy Uprising, 215–217, 219
Dew, Thomas R., 294
Dickens, Charles, 261
Dickinson, John, 101
Diplomacy
    frustration and stalemate, 138–140
    Louisiana Purchase, 195, *197*
    XYZ Affair, 181–182
Diseases, brought to New World, 17
Dix, Dorothea, 288, 289, 388
Domestic fiction, 305
Domesticity, new ideal of, 295–296
Dominican Republic, 18
Douglass, Frederick, 297, 367, 375
    autobiography written by, 306
Douglas, Stephen A., 345, 351–352, 356, 366
Downing, Andrew Jackson, 312
Draft Riots, 391, 402
Dred Scott v. Sandford, 358–359, 366, 372
Dueling, 193, 200, 273
Duquesne, Fort, 88

E

Eastern State Penitentiary, 288–289, *289,* 314
Eastern Woodlands Indians, 8–9, 12
East India Company, 103
Eaton, John, 230
Eaton, Peggy, 230
Ecology, Columbian Exchange and, 16–17
Economy. *See also* Industrialization
    Aztec, 7
    crisis regarding, and Van Buren's presidency, 242–245
    Embargo Act of 18071 and, 201
    following Civil War, 424
    Indians and trans-Atlantic, 87
    industrial, 262

market, 252
    New South, 429–431
    of North, 252
    in post-revolutionary America, 137
    of South, 252
Education. *See also* Colleges
    expansion of, 132–133
    reform efforts and, 287–288, *288*
    republicanism and, 132
Edwards, Jonathan, 75, 81
Edward VI (king of England), 15, 28
Elbridge, 147
Elections
    of 1824, 225–227
    of 1828, 227–229
    of 1832, 241
    of 1854, 353–354
    of 1856, 358
    of 1860, 367–369
    of 1868, 420–421
    of 1872, 423, 424, *424*
    of 1876, 426–427
Electoral College, 186
    choosing national leader through, 147
    creation of, 158
Elizabeth I (queen of England), 28, 29, *29,* 42
Ellsworth, Elmer Ephraim, 378
Ellsworth, Oliver, 145
Emancipation, 374
    African Americans' response to, 411
    Lincoln's view of, 384
    test cases, 406–408
Emancipation Proclamation, 374, 386, 402
Embargo Act of 1807, 201, 218, 304
Emerson, Ralph Waldo, 282, 283, 332, 367
Emigrant Aid Company, 354
Emigrants Crossing the Plains (Bierstadt), *320*
Encomienda, 26
Enforcement Acts, 422
English Bill of Rights, 58, 60
Enlightenment, 64, 72, 94
    American champions of, 73–74
    in colony of Georgia, 73
    effects on Jefferson, 132, 191
    Freemasonry and, 239–240
    ideas, supporters of, 133–135
Equiano, Olaudah, 77
Era of Good Feelings, 208, 218

Erie Canal, 256, 265
Eugenics, 299
Europe
    American societies on eve of contact
        with, 9
    Black Death in, 10
    effect of capitalism on rural, 11
    holy wars waged by, 10
    new monarchs and rise of nation-
        states in, 14–15
    slave trade and, 22
    trade between China and, 17
    turmoil of civilization in, 10–15
Expansion. *See* Westward expansion
Expansionism philosophy, of Young
    America, 350–351
Exploration, 2
    of African coast, 21–22
    of Atlantic, major European, *24*
    England's entry into, 28–29

F

Factory system, 210–211
    women and, 260–261
Fallen Timbers, Battle of, 172
Farmer's Almanac, 254, 258
Farmers, effect of capitalism on, 11. *See
    also* Agriculture
The Federalist, 148, 155
Federalist No. 10, 163
Federalists, 148–150, 154
    vs. Anti-Federalists, 148–150
    anti-Jefferson cartoon of, *189*
    dismantling program o, 194
    Hartford Convention and, 206–207
    Republicans, and politics of race,
        176–177
Female Anti-Slavery Society, 296
Female Moral Reform Society, 296
Ferdinand of Aragon (king of Spain), 15
Fifteenth Amendment, 421, 433, 436
54th Massachusetts, 389, 395
Fillmore, Millard, 246, 345, 357
Finney, Charles Grandison, 284, 285,
    296, 302, 314
Finney, Lydia, 296
Firearms, production of, 210
First Amendment, 159
First Battle of Bull Run, 381
First Confiscation Act, 384
First Continental Congress, 104
Fischer, Alvan, 255

Fisk, Jim, 423
Fitzhugh, George, 364
Five Civilized Tribes, 234
Florence, 10
Foot, Samuel, 231
Force Bill, 232
Forrest, Nathan Bedford, 429
Fort Pillow Massacre, *389*, 393
Fourier, Charles, 301
Fourteenth Amendment, 417,
    433, 436
Fowler, Orson S., 312, *313*
Fox, George, 48
France
    American Revolutionary War and,
        116–117
    emissaries to, during Civil War, 380
    Indians and, 27, 87
    North Atlantic empire of, 26–28
    at war, 87
    XYZ Affair, 181–182
Frank Leslie's Illustrated Weekly, 358
Franklin, Benjamin, 72, 74, 95, 111,
    112, 147, 178, 239
Fredericksburg, battle of, 386
Free blacks, 233
    lower South communities of, 272
    Northern communities of,
        266–267
Freedmen
    cultivating sweet potatoes, *406*
    education for, 410–411
    forcibly returned to
        plantations, *407*
    forty acres and a mule for, 409–410
Freedmen's Bureau, 408, 410, 436
    schools built by, 410
Freedom's Journal, 233
Freeman, Elizabeth, 122
Freemasonry, 239–240
Free-Soil Party, 335–336, 336
Free will, 285
Fremont, John C., 319, 330
Frémont, John C., 357
French and Indian War, 64
    expense of, 96
French Revolution, 168–169
    Jefferson's and Hamilton's reactions
        to, 171
    radicalism of, 158
Frontier
    democracy, symbols of, 222–223
Fruitlands, 303

Fugitive Slave Act, 340, 346, 347–348,
    372, 384
    effects of, *340–341*
Fur trade, 27

G

Gabriel's Rebellion, 185, 186, 195
Gag rule, 293, 314
Gallatin, Albert, 158, 177, 194
Galloway, Grace Growden, 112–113
Galloway, Joseph, 113
Gama, Vasco da, 20–21
The Gaols Committee of the House of
    Commons (Hogarth), 72
Gardner, Alexander, 386, *386*
Garrison, William Lloyd, 290, 291, 293,
    297, 330, 367
Gates, Horatio, 116
Gender, in post-Revolutionary era,
    175–176. *See also* Women
Genêtm Edmund, 169
George I (king of England), 70
George II (king of England), 73
George III (king of England), 96, 101,
    107–110
Georgia, founding of, 73
Gerry, Elbridge, 147, 148, 181
Gettysburg, battle of, 392
Ghent, Treaty of (1814), 206, 219
Gibbons v. Ogden, 212
Glorious Revolution, 34, 57–58, 60, 62,
    63, 70
Godey's Lady's Book, 258, 295, 307
Gooding, James Henry, 393
Gothic Revival, 312
Gould, Jay, 423
Gove, Mary, 296
Government
    in colonies, 70–71
    competing visions of constitutional,
        128
    components of republican, 128
    launching new American, 158–159
    toward more democratic, 135–137
Grady, Henry, 430
Graham, Sylvester, 296, 299
Grant, Ulysses S., 330, 374, 381–382,
    392–393, 398, 420–421, *421*
Grasse, Paul de, 118
Great American Desert, 319
Great Awakening, 64, 72, 74–76, 94
    spread of Christianity to slaves by, 81

Great Compromise, 145, 154
Great Migration (1630–1642), 45
Great Seal of America, 132–133, 154
  Masonic symbol on, 239
Greece, obsession with ancient, 311
Greek Revival, 311–312
The Greek Slave (Powers), 291, 292
Greeley, Horace, 247, 364, 367, 376, 424
Greenville, Treaty of, 172
Gregg, Josiah, 326
Grenville, George, 98, 101
Grimes, James W., 417
Grimké, Angelina, 292
Grimké, Sarah, 292
Grundy, Felix, 204
Guadalupe Hildago, Treaty of (1848),
  330, 335, 338

H

Haidt, John Valentine, 76
Haiti, 18
Hall, John H., 210
Hall v. DeCuir, 433
Hamilton, Alexander, 143, 146, 148,
  158, 159, 231
  abolitionist sentiment and, 290
  Bank of the United States, the Mint
    and Report on Manufacturers,
    164–165
  duel between Burr and, 193, 200
  Jefferson and, 165
  Madison's opposition to, 162–163
  reaction to French Revolution, 171
  vision of America held by, 160–161
Hancock, John, 102
Handsome Lake, 19
Hariot, Thomas, 30
Harmar, Josiah, 172
Harper's Weekly, 374
  Nast cartoons from, 425
Harrington, James, 54
Harrison, William Henry, 199, 203, 220,
  246
  log cabin campaign of, 246–247
Hartford Convention, 206–207, 218
Hart Room, Metropolitan Museum of
  Art, 66
Harvard University, 84
Haviland, John, 288–289
Hawkins, Benjamin, 200
Hawkins, John, 29
Hawthorne, Nathaniel, 300, 303, 304

Hayne, Robert, 231–232
Headright, 62
Healy, George, *231*
Height, of native-born American men
  by year, *262*
Hemings, Sally, 193, 218, 246
Henry VII (king of England), 14
Henry VIII (king of England), 14–15,
  28, 32
Henry, Patrick, 104–105, 106, 135, 151
Heretics, 15
  Antinomians, 47–48, 49
Hermitage plantation, 270, *270*
Herttell, Thomas, 297
Hetem, 40
Hickory Clubs, 228–229
Hillyard, M. B., 430
Hispaniola, 18
Hoe, Richard M., 361
Hogarth, William, 72, 73
Holbrook, Josiah, 307
Holland. *See* Netherlands, the
Homer, Winslow, 04
Hooker, Joseph, 386
Hooker, Thomas, 48
Houdon, Jean-Antoine, 131, 323
House of Burgesses, 39
House of Correction (Massachusetts),
  289
House of Tudor, 14
Houston, Sam, 328
Howard, O. O., 410
Howe, Sir William, 114, 116
Humanists, 13, 32
Husband, Herman, 119
Hutchinson, Anne, 47–48, 62

I

Ice Age, 4, 5
Igbos, 20
Immediatism, 314
  defined, 291
  rise of, 290–291
Immigrants, in Virginia, 40
Immigration, 355. *See also* Migration
  to American colonies, 83
  cities and, 266
  perceived threat of mass, 355–356
  sources of European, 266
Incas, conquest of, 17–19
Incidents in the Life of a Slave Girl
  (Jacobs), 306–307

Indentured servants, 79, 94
Independence Hall, 70
Indian Removal Act of 1830, 235, 250
Indians. *See also* Native Americans
  American Revolution and, 122–123
  Archaic Era, 5
  Britain's trade with, 139
  Catlin's representation of, 323
  Cherokee resistance and removal,
    236–238
  conflict between Americans and, 140
  Eastern Woodlands, 8–9
  English and Virginia, 34
  epidemics devastating, 343
  epidemics devastating to, 17
  fate of California, 343
  French and, 27
  Jackson's views of, 234–f235
  New England conflicts with, 48
  religious conversion of, 25
  religious renewal movement among,
    76
  responses to Jeffersonian expan-
    sion by, 198–199
  threats posed by, 139
  violence along frontiers, 171–172
Indians Fishing (White), 12
Indigo, 19, 68
Industrialization
  from artisan to worker, 260
  changing urban landscape due to,
    264–268
  Lowell experiment, 261–262
  urban, 262
Industrial Revolution, Civil War and,
  383–384
Inflation
  in post-revolutionary America, 138
  during 1790s, 162
Inness, George, 257
Intolerable Acts, 103–105, 126
Iroquois Great Law Peace, 199
Iroquois League of Five Nations, 9
Isabella of Castile (king of Spain), 15,
  16
Islam, 10

J

Jackson, Andrew, 205–206, 220, 273
  appointments to office of, 229
  attacks on morality of, 228
  background of, 223

Cherokee Cases, 236
Cherokee resistance and removal, 236
Creek Wars and, 222
election of 1828, 227–229
hard money policy of, 242
inauguration of, 229
as "Old Hickory," 228
popular images of, *244–245*
race and politics during era of, 233–236
reign of "King Mob," 229–230
states' rights and nullification crisis, 230–232
views of Indians, 234–235
war on Second Bank of the United States, 244
Jackson, Thomas "Stonewall," 330, 374, 386, 429
Jacobs, Harriet, 306–307
James, duke of York. *See* James II (king of England)
James I (king of England), 36, 40
James II (king of England), 53, 57
Jamestown, 62
founding of, 36–37
James VI (king of Scotland). *See* James I (king of England)
Jay, John, 140, 159, 162, 170
abolitionist sentiment and, 290
Jay's Treaty, 170, 186
Jefferson, Thomas, 70, 110, 111, 122, 142, 143, 154, 158, 159, 180, 184, 199, 246
attack on Federalist judiciary, 200
Enlightenment and, 132
faith in education, 132
government of, 188
Hamilton and, 165
importance of architecture to, 128
interests in Indians of, 198–199
issue of slavery and, 293
plan for settling of West, 140
reaction to French Revolution, 171
scandal surrounding, 193
Jennings, Samuel, 178
Jerusalem, 10
Jesuit missionaries, 12, 27
Jewett, Helen, 268
murder of, *268*
Jews
in New Amsterdam, 50
Spanish Inquisition and, 15

Jim Crow, 432–435
John Brown's raid, 366–367, 372. *See also* Brown, John
Johnson, Andrew
conflict between congressional Republicans and, 417
leniency of, angers North, *413*
opposition to rights of freedmen and, 417
Johnson, Anthony, 56
Johnson, Sir William, 91
Johnston, Joseph E., 392
Jones, Elizabeth, 279
Judicial nationalism, 212
Judiciary Act of 1801, 194

K

Kansas
two governments in, 356
violence in, 356–357
Kansas-Nebraska Act, 351–353, 372
Kaufmann, Theodor, 385
Kearny, Stephen, 330
Kemble, Fanny, 276
Kendall, Mary, 271
Kent, James, 224
Key, Francis Scott, 20
King George's War, 88
King Philip's War, 55, *56*, 58
King Philip (Wampanoag leader), 55
Kingsley, Bathsheba, 75
Knights of the White Camelia, 422
Know-Nothings, 354, 372
Knox, Henry, 124, 159
Kühn, Justus Engelhart, 69, *69*
Ku Klux Klan, 422, 424–426

L

Labor demand, in Americas, 22
The Lackawanna Valley (Inness), 257
Ladies Memorial Association, 429
Land, of scarcity, 86
Land Ordinance of 1784, 154
Landscape painting, 308
Lansing, John, 147
Las Casas, Bartholemé, 24–25
Leaves of Grass (Whitman), 304
Lee, Mother Ann, 299
Lee, Richard Henry, 110, 124, 135
Lee, Robert E., 330, 366, 386, 392, 397, 429
surrender of, 420, *429*

Leopard (British ship), 201
Letters from a Farmer in Pennsylvania (Dickinson), 101
Leutze, Emanuel, 350–351, *351*
Lewis and Clark expedition, 197–198
Lewis, Meriwether, 197
Lexington, Battle of, 106, 126
Liberal Republicans, 424
The Liberator, 293
Liberia, 290
Liberty Displaying the Arts and Sciences (Jennings), 178
Liberty Party, 328, 338
Liberty, seizure of, 102
Library Company, 74, 178
Lincoln, Abraham, 340, 363, 366, 367
debate between Douglas and, 366
declares lower South to be in state of insurrection, 370
election of 1860 and, 368–369
emissaries dispatched by, 380
handling of dissent during Civil War by, 389–391
issuance of Emancipation Proclamation, 385
Ten Percent Plan, 408
view of emancipation of, 384
Lincoln, Benjamin, 118
Lincoln-Douglas debates, 366, 372
Lincoln, Mary Todd, 374
Lippard, George, 306
Literature
popular culture and, 305–306
slavery in American, 306–307
social criticism and, 304–305
Little Turtle, 172
Livingston, Robert, 110
Locke, John, 68, 132
London, 11
Long, Stephen, 319
The Looking Glass of 1787, 150
L'Oouverture, Toussaint, 176–177
Lord Dunmore's Proclamation, 105–106, 126
Lord Proprietors, 54
Lost Cause, 428–429
Louisiana Purchase, 194, 195, *197,* 218
Louis XVI (king of France), 168
Lowell Female Labor Reform Association, 262
Lowell, Francis, 261
Lowell mill, 261–262
strike at, 262, 263

Lower South, 85, 274. *See also* South
Loyalists, 126
   division between Patriots and, 111
   plight of, 111–113
Luther, Martin, 13
Lyceum movement, 307
Lynchings, 435
Lyndhurst, 312, *313*

M

Macon, Nathaniel, 202
Macon's Bill No. 2, 202
Macpheadris, Archibald, 64
Madison, Dolly, 205
Madison, James, 135, 143, 144, 146,
     148, 149, 158, 168, 201–292, 205
   opposition to Hamilton of, 162–163
   slavery and, 290
Mah-to-toh-pa (Mandan chief), 323
Manifest Destiny, 338, 350
   Native Americans encounter with,
     321–322
   origin of term, 319–320
   "triumph of," 332
Mann, Horace, 286, 287–288, 307
Mann, John, 279
Marbury v. Madison, 195, 196, 218
Marbury, William, 195
Marie Antoinette (queen of France),
    168
Marion, Francis "Swamp Fox," 117
Market economy
   economy expansion of, 259
   expanding, 252
Market revolution, 280
   agricultural changes and conse-
     quences, 254–255
   defined, 254
   revivalism and, 284–285
   roads, canals, steamboats, and trains,
     255–256
Marshall, John, 181, 196, 201, 212, 231
   slavery and, 290
Martin, Nabby, 134
Mary I (queen of England), 28
Maryland, 40–41, 61
Mason, George, 105, 120, 143, 145, 147,
    148
Massachusetts Bay Colony
   Hutchinson banished from, 48
Massachusetts Constitution, 121, 127,
    132
Mather, Increase, 55

Matlack, Timothy, 120, *120*
Maya, 5
Mayflower Compact, 44, 61
Mayflower (ship), 44
McAlpin, Henry, 270
McClellan, George, 330, 384–385, 399
McClellan, George B., 381, 382–383
McCormick, Cyrus, 361
McCrea, Jane, 122–123, 127
McCulloch v. Maryland, 212
McDowell, Irwin, 381
McGuffy reader, 287
Meade, George G., 330, 392
Melville, Herman, 304, 305
Memphis, race riot in, 416, *416*
Mercantilism, 61, 62
Mercie, Antonin, 429
Mesoamerica, 5
Metacom (Wampanoag leader), 55
Métis, 87
Mexican War
   controversy surrounding, 330–332
   images of, 332–333
   map of major offensives, *329*
Mexico
   agricultural settlements in early, 5
   central plaza in Mexico City, *26*
   clash of interests in Texas, 326–327
   declares independence from Spain,
     325–326
   land ceded after, 330
Mid-Atlantic region, 84
Middle ground, 87, 94
Middle passage, 78, 79, 94
Migration. *See also* Migration
   from Asia to America, 4
   in Europe, 111
   Mormon flight to Utah, 322–324
   to New England, 42
   settlement, and rise of agriculture,
     5–6
   Western, 320
Militia, Southern, 271
Millennialism, 298
Millennial Law (1823), 311
Millerites, 298
Miller, William, 298
Mills, 210–211
Mill villages, 212, 261
Mining, gold, 342
Minkins, Shadrach, 349
Minnie ball, invention of, 384
Missionaries, 27
Mississippi Plan, 426, 436

Mississippi River, 140, 195
   Spain's control of, 170
Missouri Compromise, 214–215, 219,
    344
Missouri Crisis, 213–215
Moby-Dick (Melville), 304, 305
Modern warfare, 383–384
   photography and visualization,
    386
Monotheism, 20
Monroe Doctrine, 209, 218
Monroe, James, 201, 225
   national Republican vision of,
    208–209
Montcalm, Louis de (French general),
    89
Monticello, 190–191, *191, 198*
   residents of, *192*
Moore, Hannah, 176
Moravians, 76, 81, 94
Morgan, Daniel, 117
Morgan, William, 240
Mormons, 301
   flight to Utah, 322–324
Morse, Samuel, 258
Morton, Thomas, 9
Mott, Lucretia, 297
Mound Builders, 7
Mountain men, 319
Mount Auburn Cemetery, *310,*
    310–311, 314
Mourning wars, 87
Muhammad, 10, 20
Murfreesboro, battle of, 386
Murray, Judith Sargent, 176
Muslims, 10
   slave trade of, 22
   Spanish Inquisition and, 15

N

Napoleon Bonaparte, 183–184, 195, 202
*A Narrative of the Life of David
    Crockett,* 223
Nashoba, 303
Nast, Thomas, 425
National Bank Acts, 387
Nationalism, judicial, 212
National Republicans, 241
National Road, 255
Native Americans. *See also* Indians
   before California Gold Rush, 343
   encounter Manifest Destiny,
    321–322

forced conversion of, 325
French encounter with, 27
mountain men and, 319
Nativism, 354
Nativists, 354, 355
Nat Turner's Rebellion, 277–278, 280, 294
woodcut image of, *278*
Nauvoo, Illinois, 301, 822–824
Neolin (Delaware Indian prophet), 76, 90
Netherlands, the, 42, 52–53
New Amsterdam, 53
Newburg conspiracy, 130, 154
New England, 84
expansion of, 48
King Philip's War, 55, *56*
town structure in, *46*
witchcraft hysteria in, 58–59, 63
New England Anti-Slavery Society, 291
New England Farmer, 254
New France, 27, 87
British conquest of, *89*
New Jersey Plan, 144–145, 154
New Lights, 75, 94
New Mexico
organizing, 343–344
New Netherlands, 53
New Orleans, 140
Battle of, 206, 219, 228
Spain's control of, 170
Union capture of, 382
New South, 436
defined, 428
economy, 429–431
New Spain, 24–25
Newspapers, 332
New World, 2
diseases brought to, 17
theories on early travel to, 4
New York City
economics and geography of vice in mid-nineteenth century, 269
Five Points Neighborhood, *264,* 264–265
Nichols, Thomas Low, 296
Ninth Amendment, 159
Nonimportation movement, 101, 126
North
advantages and disadvantages of, 376–377
economy, 252
economy of, 340

free black communities in, 266–267
industrial, 360–363
mobilization of, 377–378
personal liberty laws, 347–348
and South, divergent philosophies of, 364–365
North America, 30
balance of power in, 64
British and Spanish in, 139, *139*
control of, 88–91
lack of large domesticated animals in, 9
migration to, 4
Spanish exploration of, 24–25
Spanish holdings in, 325
North Carolina, 29, 54
North Carolina Mutual and Provident Insurance Company, 432
Northwest Ordinance of 1787, 140–141, 154
Notes on Virginia (Jefferson), 191
Noyes, John Humphrey, 299
Nullifcation Crisis, 344
states' rights and, 230–232
Nullification, 50
Nurse, Rebecca, 59

O

Octagon houses, 308, 312, *313*
Oglethrope, James, 73, 94
Old Hickory, 250
"Old Hickory." *See* Jackson, Andrew
Old Lights, 75, 94
Old Northwest, 154
border disputes in, *139*
settling of, 140–141
Old Southwest, border disputes in, *139*. *See also* Southwest
Olive Branch Petition, 107–110
Olmecs, 5
Olmsted, Frederick Law, 309, 364
Omnibus, 265
Oneida community, 299
On to liberty (Kaufmann), 385
Osborn, Daniel, 347
O'Sullivan, John, 319–320, 322
Otis, Elisha, 361
Otis, James, 98, 123
Ottoman Empire, 10, 311
Overland Trail, 316, 320, 338
Owen, Robert, 301

P

Pacifism, Quaker, 93
Paine, Thomas, 110, 115, 121
Paleo-Indians, 4–5, 32
Panic of 1819, 213, 219
Panic of 1837, 243, 320
Panic of 1857, 364
Panic of 1873, 424
Paper money, 137, 138
Paris, Treaty of (1783), 95, 118, 126, 140, 154, 169
Parker, Theodore, 349
Parks, 309–310
Parliament
colonial taxes enacted by, 98–100
control of colonial behavior by, 61
creation of Board of Trade by, 61
Parris, Samuel, 58
Path Where They Cried, 238
Patriots, 111, 126
Patterson, William, 144
Paxton Boys, 92, 93
Peale, Charles Wilson, 115, 124, 136
Peculiar institution, 294, 314
Peninsular Campaign, 382, 402
Penitentiaries, 288–289, 314
Penninsular Campaign, 382–383
Penn, Sir William, 50, 53
Pennsylvania, Constitution created by, 120
Pennsylvania State House, 70, *70*
Penn, William, 53, 63
The People the Best Governors, 121
Perfectionism, 299
Personal liberty laws, 347–348
Peru, 19
Philadelphia
Bible riots in, 267
growth of, 265
Philadelphia Convention, 155
conflict over slavery at, 145–146
large states *versus* small states at, 143–145
Philadelphia Penitentiary, 288–289, *289*
Philip II (king of Spain), 28
Phips, William, 59
Phrenology, 307, 312
Pickens, Fort, 370
Pickett, George, 392
Pickett's Charge, 392
Pierce, Franklin, 350, 351
Pike, Zebulin, 319

Pinckney, Charles, 145–146, 180
Pinckney, Charles Cotesworth, 181
Pinckney, Eliza, 68, 95
Pinckney's Treaty (1795), 170
Piracy, 138–139
Pittsburgh, 265
Pitt, William, 89
Pizarro, Francisco, 19
Plantations, 28, 32, 252, 274
    freedmen forcibily returned to, *407*
    slave burial on, *277*
Plow, steel, invention of, 361
Plymouth Plantation, 42–44
Pocahontas, 37
    ordeal of, 38
Poe, Edgar Allan, 306
Politics
    of annexation and Republic of Texas,
        327–328
    colonial, 70–71
    of honor, political slurs and, 191–193
    increased participation in, 220
    in Jeffersonian America, 190–193
    popular, in Revolutionary era, 119
    and race in Jacksonian era, 233–236
    republicanism and, 135–137
    third-party challenges to, 239–241
    of virtue: views from the states,
        131–132
    Whig vision of, 60
Polk, James K., 328
    expansionist views of, 328–329
Poll tax, 435
Polo, Marco, 11, 16
Polygamy, 324
Polytheism, 20
Pontiac's Rebellion, 92
Popular sovereignty, 338
    defined, 334
    focus on viability of, 366
Population
    explosion in California, 342–343
    growth and land scarcity, 86
Portraits, 69
Portugal
    Benin, and international slave trade,
        23
Pottawatomie Creek massacre, 356, 366
Powers, Hiram, 291, 292
Powhatan (chief of Indian
        confederacy), 36
Predestination, 285
Prescott, Samuel, 106

Pringle, Robert, 68
Printing press, 11, 32
Privateers, 28–29, 32
Proclamation of 1763, 92, 95
Prohibitory Act, 110
Prophet Tenskwataqwa, 199
Propietor, 40, 62
Proslavery
    cartoon, 294
    rhetoric, intensivitation of, 293–294
Prostitution, 268, 295, 342
Protestantism, 13–14, 42
Protestants, 13–14
Publishing, 258, 259
Publius, 148, 149, 150
Pueblo Bonito, 7
Pueblo Revolt (1680), 57
Pueblos, 7
Puritans, 44–47
    conflict between Indians and, 55
    town models of, *46*
Putney Association, 299

Q

Quakers, 48, 53–54, 55, 62, 93
    condemnation of slavery, 80, 290
    as force in Pennsylvania politics, 84
Quebec
    fall of, 95
    founding of, 27

R

Race riots, 416, *416*
Racism
    Andrew Johnson plays on white, 417
    attitudes to, 177
    against Chinese, 342–343, *343*
    intensification of, 232
    politics of, *421*
Radical Republicans
    control of Reconstruction taken by,
        417
Railroads, 256, 361
Raleigh, Sir Walter, 29
Ranchero system, 325
Randolph, Edmund, 147, 159
Randolph, John, 204
Randolph, John Hampden, 270
Reaper, invention of, 361
Reconquista, 15
Reconstruction
    abandonment of, 423–427

black churches during, 411
congressional, 415–417
emancipation test cases, 406–408
governments in South, creating,
    419–420
policy, divided opinions regarding,
    408
presidential, 412–413
Reconstruction Acts, 417
Redeemer rule, 428
Redeemers, 426, 436
Reformation, 13–14, 32
Reform(s)
    behaviors targeted by, 284
    clamor for, 282
    cult of true womanhood, and
        women's rights, 295–297
    Greek Revival and, in American
        architecture, 31–313
    Oglethorpe as champion for prison,
        73
    parks and cemeteries, 309–311
    revival movement and, 284–289
    schools, prisons, and asylums,
        287–289
Regulators, 119
Religion. *See also* Catholicism; Prot-
        estantism; Revival movement;
        Roman Catholic Church
    African, 21
    in New England, 84
    in post-revolutionary America, 133
    revival movement, 64, 76
    slave, 276–277
Renaissance, 13–14
Rendezvous, 318, 338
"Report on Public Credit" (Hamilton),
    161
Republic, America as, 128
Republicanism
    emphasis on virtue, 131–132
    women and, 134
Republican Party, 353, 365
    Lincoln becomes rising star in, 366
    in South, 418–419
    victory in election of 1864, 397–399
Republicans, 158, 186
    beliefs of, 160
    conflict between Johnson and con-
        gressional, 417
    Federalists, and politics of race,
        176–177
    Know-Nothings and, 354

Republican virtue, 131–132
Restoration, 62
Revenue Act, 98
Revere, Paul, 102, 104, *104*, 106
Revival movement, 64, 76. *See also*
    Religion
    market revolution and, 284–285
    reform and, 284–289
Revolutionary War. *See also* American
    Revolution
    campaigns in North, 114–117
    campaigns in South, 117–118
    debt incurred due to, 161–162
    end of, 118
    France and, 116–117
Rice, 54, 68, 79
The Rights of Man to Property! (Skid-
    more), 240
*The Rights of the British Colonies As-
    serted and Proved* (Otis), 98
Roads, 255–256
Roanoke colony, 29–30
Robinson, Frederick, 249
Rolfe, John, 37, 61
Roman Catholic Church. *See also* Ca-
    tholicism; Catholics
    influence Spanish America of, 25
    Luther's rejection of, 13
Roosevelt, Franklin, 205
Rosecrans, William S., 386
Rossiter, Thomas, 43, *144*
Ross, John, 237
Rowson, Susanna, 175–176
Ruffin, Thomas, 279
Rural cemetery movement, 310–311
Rush-Bagot Treaty of 1817, 209
Rush, Benjamin, 133
Ryan, Martha, 133
Ryan, Rev. Abram, 428

S

Sacagawea, 197–198
Salem, Peter, 109
Salem Village, 58–59
Samplers, 134
Sampson, Deborah, 123
Sandys, Sir Edwin, 39
Sanford, Nathan, 224
San Francisco Presidio, 325
Santa Anna, Antonio López de, 327
Santa Fe Trail, 326
Savannah, Georgia, founding of, 73

Scalawags, 418–419, 436
The Scarlet Letter (Hawthorne), 304
Scott, Dred, 358–359, *359*
Scott, Winfield, 330, 350, 357
Seabury, Samuel, 112
Secession
    election of 1860 and, 367–369, *368*
    preventing, of Border States, 379
Second Amendment, 159
Second Bank of the United States, Jack-
    son's war on, 244
Second Battle of Bull Run, 383
Second Confiscation Act, 384
Second Great Awakening, 284, 302
Second War of Independence. *See* War
    of 1812
Secoton (White), 8, 30
Sectionalism, rise of, 347–348
Secular utopianism, 301–303
Segregation
    spread of, 434
Seneca Falls Convention, 296–297, 314
Separatism, 44, 62
"Seventh of March Address" (Webster),
    345
Seven Years War, 89
Seward, William, 341, 345, 365
Sexuality, controlling, 296
Seymour, Horatio, 420, *421*
Shakers, 298–299, 324
    furniture and buildings of, 311
    market economy and, 299
    reactions to gender roles of, 300
Shakespeare, William, 2
Shamans, 8
Sharecropping, *431*, 431–432
Shaw, Robert Gould, 392
Shays, Daniel, 141
Shay's Rebellion, 141–142, 154, 155
    court closings and major battles in,
    142
Sheridan, Philip, 401
Sherman, Roger, 111, 145
Sherman's March to the Sea, 400, 402
Sherman, William Tecumseh, 374, 392,
    398, 399, 409–410
Silver, 19
Sims, Thomas, 349
Singletary, Amos, 150
Sing Sing prison, 288
Skidmore, Thomas, 240
Slater, Samuel, 210, 260
Slave Codes, 272, 278

The Slave Market (Crowe), 275
Slavery
    abolishing, 408
    in Africa, 21–22
    African-American culture emerging
        from, 81–82
    in American literature, 306–307
    in Barbados, 50–51
    in colonial era, 77
    conflict over, at Philadelphia Conven-
        tion, 146–147
    controversy over, 340, *356*
    election of 1848 and, 337
    idea of colonization as solution to,
        290
    Jefferson and, 192
    and the law, 278
    northern, 80–81
    Portuguese justification for, 21
    questioning of, 64
    southerrn, 79–80
    varied systems of slave labor, 274–
        276
    in Virginia, 56
    Wilmot Proviso and, 334
Slaves
    African culture/traditions preserved
        by, 82
    as contraband of war, 384
    freed during Revolution, 112
    fugitive, 347–348
    life in quarters of, 276
    marriage and, 82
    marriages between, 275
    religion and music of, 276–277
    resistance of, 81, 176–177, 277–278
    "saltwater," 79
    "seasoning'" of, 79
Slave trade
    Atlantic, 77–79
    Benin, Portugal, and international, 23
    international, 2
    Islamic, 22
Slidell, John, 329
Small, John, 111
Smith, Adam, 61
Smith, John, 37
Smith, Joseph, 301, 322
Smith, Margaret Bayard, 229, 231
Smith, William, 135–136, *136*
Society(ies)
    advanced, Mesoamerica, 5–6
    African, 21

Society(ies) (*continued*)
American, on eve of European contact, 9
destruction of fabric of southern, 384
Eastern Woodlands Indians, 8–9
French multiracial, 87–88
mound building, 7
Puritan, 44–47
two visions of government and, 248–249
Society of Friends. *See* Quakers
Songhai Empire, 20
Sons of Liberty, 101, 103, 106
Soto, Hernando de, 25
South. *See also* Confederacy; Lower South
advantages and disadvantages of, 376–377
antebellum, 274
economy of, 252, 340
free black communities in, 272
Lost Cause and, 428–429
lower, 274
mobilization of, 378
naval blockade of, 391
and North, divergent philosophies of, 364–365
planter class in, 270–271
Republican Party in, 418–419
supremacy of cotton in, 362–363
upper, 274
white culture in, 273
yeoman and tenant farmers, 271
South Carolina, 54
harsh slave codes of, 82
nullification crisis and, 230–232
Southwest. *See also* Old Southwest
American expansionism into, 325–326
early civilizations in, 7
Spain
in Americas, crumbling empire of, 209
Black Legend of, 24
Mexico declares independence from, 325
North American presence of, 139, 325
as sovereign nation-state, 15
Spanish Armada, 29
Spanish Inquisition, 15, 32
Special Field Order No. 15, 400, 402, 410

Specie Circular, 242
Spenser, Lilly Martin, 295
Spirituals, 277, 280
Spoils system, 229, 250
Stamp Act, 100–101, 102, 126
Stanton, Edwin, 417
Stanton, Elizabeth Cady, 297
"The Star Spangled Banner" (anthem), 205
States' rights, 183, 186
nullification crisis and, 230–232
State v. Mann, 279, 280
St. Augustine, Florida, 73
Stay laws, 137
Steamboats, 256
Steen, Jan, 42, 43
Steinway and Sons, 266
Stephens, Alexander, 369, 387
Stevens, Thaddeus, 415
Stiles, Ezra, 132
Stiles, Hannah Stockton, 256
Stinebuagh-Bradford, Mary, 389
St. Louis, 265
Stone Age, 4
Stono Rebellion, 81, 82
Story, Joseph, 212, 310
The Story of Margarwetta (Murray), 176
Stowe, Harriet Beecher, 348
Strictures on the Modern System of Female Education (Moore), 176
Strikes, 263
at Lowell mill, 262
Stuart, Gilbert, 179, *180*
Stump Speaking or the County canvas (Bingham), 220, *231*
Stump speech, 220
Stuyvesant, Peter, 53
Suffrage. *See also* Voting
changes in requirements for, between 1800 and 1828, *223*
for white men, 233
Sugar Act, 98, 105, 126
Sugar production, 50
Sumner, Charles, "Crime Against Kansas" speech, 356
Sumter, Fort, 370
Supreme Court, authority of newly created, 146–147

T

Tallmadge, John, 213
Tammany Hall, 420

Tar and Feathering Committee, 103
Tariff Act of 1832, 232
Tariffs, 231, 232
Taylor, Zachary, 329, 335–336, 337, 343, 344
Tea
boycott, 101–102
Tea Act, 96
The Tears of the Indians (Las Casas), 24, *25*
Technology, 252
film, 332–333
improvement in print, 258–259
transportation, 255–256
Tecumseh, 202, 206
Tejanos, 325
Telegraph, 258, 280
use of in Mexican War, 332
Temperance, 285–286, 314
reform and its critics, 287
Tenant farms, 431–432
Tender laws, 137
Teniers, Abraham, 39
Tennent, Gilbert, 74, 76
Tenochtitlán, 6, 7, 32
Ten Percent Plan, 408, 436
Tenth Amendment, 159
Tenure of Office Act, 417
Territories
Kansas-Nebraska controversy, 351–353
slavery question in, 334
Terrorism, post-Civil War, 422, 424–426
Texas
annexation of, 327–328
clash of interests in, 326–327
Mexican policy toward, in 1824, 325–326
Thackery, William Makepeace, 275
Third Amendment, 159
Thirteenth Amendment, 408, 412
Thomson, Charles, 133
Thoreau, Henry David, 282, 304
civil disobedience of, 331
Tilden, Samuel J., 426
Timbuktu, 20
Tippecanoe, battle of, 246
Tituba, 58
Tobacco
agriculture and political reorganization, 37–40
cartoon mocking, 39
society and, 41

Tocqueville, Alexis de, 222, 287, 304
Toltecs, 5
The Topsy-Turvy World (Steen), 43
Townsend, Richard, 54
Townshend Acts, 101, 102–103
Townshend, Charles, 101
Trade
  in Africa, 21
  Aztec, 6
  and commerce quit, *256*
  fur, 27
  networks along Mexican American
    border, 326
  piracy disrupts, 138–139
  routes to East, control of, 10
  triangle, *67*
Trail of Tears, 238
Transcendentalism, 282, 304, 314
Transportation
  advances in mass, 265
  improvements in, 255–256
The Travels of Marco Polo, 11
The Tree of Liberty, 252, 253
Trent Affair, 380, *380*, 402
Trent (ship), 380
Triangle trade, *67*
Trumbull, John, 107, 108–109
Truth, Sojourner, 392
Tubman, Harriet, 347
Tweed, William "Boss," 420
Twelfth Amendment, 184
Twenty Negro Law, 391
Tyler, John, 246, 328

U

Uncle Tom's Cabin (Stowe), 348
Underground Railroad, 347, 372
Union
  according to Calhoun, 231
  advantages on eve of Civil War, *376*
  secession from, 369–370
United Daughters of the Confederacy,
  429
United Kingdom, 61
  North American presence of, 139
United States. *See also* America
  changes brought by Civil War to, 374
  early migration to, 4
  immigration to, 353
Upper South, 85, 274
Urbanization, 267–268
  among ancient peoples, 5

  in Europe, 11, *26*
  in Spanish America, 25
  trade, commerce and, 10–11
Utopianism
  locations of experiments in, *303*
  radical, 299
  religious, 298–299
  secular, 301–303

V

Van Buren, Martin, 228, 230, 328, 335,
  337
  economic crisis and presidency of,
    242–245
Vance, Zebulon M., 378
Vanderlyn, John, 123
Vaux, Calvert, 309
Venice, 10
Verplank Room, Metropolitan Museum
  of Art, 66
Verrazano, Giovanni, 27
Vesey, Denmark, 215–217
Vespucci, Amerigo, 2, 3
Vicksburg, siege of, 392
View from Mt. Holyoke (Cole), 308, *308*
Vikings, 16
A Vindication of the Rights of Women
  (Wollstonecraft), 176
Virginia
  founding of, 29
  immigrants in, 40
  slavery in, 56
Virginia Company, 36
Virginia Company of London, 39
Virginia Company of Plymouth, 42
Virginia Declaration of Rights, 131
Virginia Plan, 143–144, 154
Virgin Queen. *See* Elizabeth I (queen of
  England)
Virtual representation, 71
A Visit from the Old Mistress (Homer),
  404, *404–405*
Voting. *See also* Suffrage
  for the first time, *419*
  property requirements for, 224

W

Wade, Benjamin, 408, 417
Wade-Davis Bill, 408
Walden (Thoreau), 304
Walker, David, 290–291
Walker, Mary Richardson, 320

Walking cities, 265
Waltham System, 261, 280
War correspondents, 332
Ward, Nathaniel, 49
War Hawks, 204–205
Warner, Susana, 305
War News from Mexico (Woodville),
  316, 317
War of 1812, 203–206, 218
  consequences of, 208–211
  economic and technology innova-
    tion, 210–211
War of Jenkins' Ear, 88
Warren, James, 123
Warren, Joseph, 128
Warren, Mercy Otis, 123
Washington, George, 88, 104, 142, 143,
  239
  as American Cincinnatus, 130–131,
    131
  Continental Army and, 114–115
  farewell address of, 179–181
  as nation's first president, 158
  Stuart's portrait of, *180*
  Whiskey Rebellion and, 172–174
Washington, Lund, 106
Wayles, John, 65
The Way of Good and Evil, 283, 306
Webster, Daniel, *231,* 231–232, 241, 245
  "Seventh of March Address" of, 345
Webster Replying to Hayne (Healy), 231
Wentworth, Charles, Marquess of
  Rockingham, 101
West
  Jefferson's vision of, 140–141, *141*
  trails to, *319*
West, Benjamin, 89, 90, 108
Westover Plantation, 68
Westward expansion, as threat to
  Mexico, 325
"Westward the Course of Empire
  Takes its Way" (Leutze), 350–351,
  351
Wheatley, Phillis, 410
Whigs, 60, 62, 120–121, 250, 346
  appeal of, gender and social class,
    247–248
  Bank War and rise of, 242
  Democrats and, 248
  Democrats and: two visions of
    government and society, 248–249
  election of 1840, 246–247
  election of 1848 and, 337

Whigs, (*continued*)
poor performance of, 350
shattering along sectional lines of, 334–336
temperance issue and, 288
Texas issue and, 327–328
Whiskey Rebellion, 186
Washington's decision to crush, 172–174
"Whiskey Ring" scandal, 423
White Brotherhood, 422
Whitefield, George, 64, 72, 75
White, John, 8, 12, 29
White supremacy, 426
redeemer politics and, 428
Whitgift, John, 42
Whitman, Walt, 304
Whitney, Eli, 210
The Wide, Wide World, 305
Wilderness, battle of the, 398
William and Mary, 57–58
William of Orange, 57
Williams, Abigal, 58
Williams, Roger, 47, 49, 62
Wilmot Proviso, 334, 338, 348
Wilson, James, 148, 150, 151
Wilson, John, 273
Winnemucca, Sarah, 322

Winslow, Anna Green, 101
Winthrop, John, 44–45, 47
Witchcraft, hysteria in Salem, 34, 58–59, 63
Wolfe, James, 89–90, *90*
Wollstonecraft, Mary, 176, 263
Women
Archaic Era, 5
Aztec, 6
during Civil War, 388–389
in colonial era, 68
of Eastern Woodlands societies, 9
factory system and, 260–261
Gold Rush and, 342
middle-class ideal of, 295
"outwork" performed by, 361–363
republicanism and, 134
revolutionary movement and, 123–125
rights of, reform, and cult of true womanhood, 295–297
role of, in Indian diplomacy, 38
Western migration and, 320
Whigs and, 247–248
witchcraft trials and, 58–59
work and, 261–262

writers, 305
Women's Central Association for Relief, 388
Wood, Jethro, 254
Woodmason, Rev. Charles, 86
Woodville, Richard Caton, 316, 317
Woolens Act, 61
Woolman, John, 81
Worcester v. Georgia, 236
Workies, *241*
Wright, Francis, 303
Wright, Paulina, 296
Wyatt, Francis, 35

X

XYZ Affair, 181–182, 186

Y

Yale University, 84
Yates, Robert, 147
Yorktown, battle of, 117–118, 127
Young America, 350–351, 372
Young, Brigham, 324

Z

Zouaves, 378, *378*

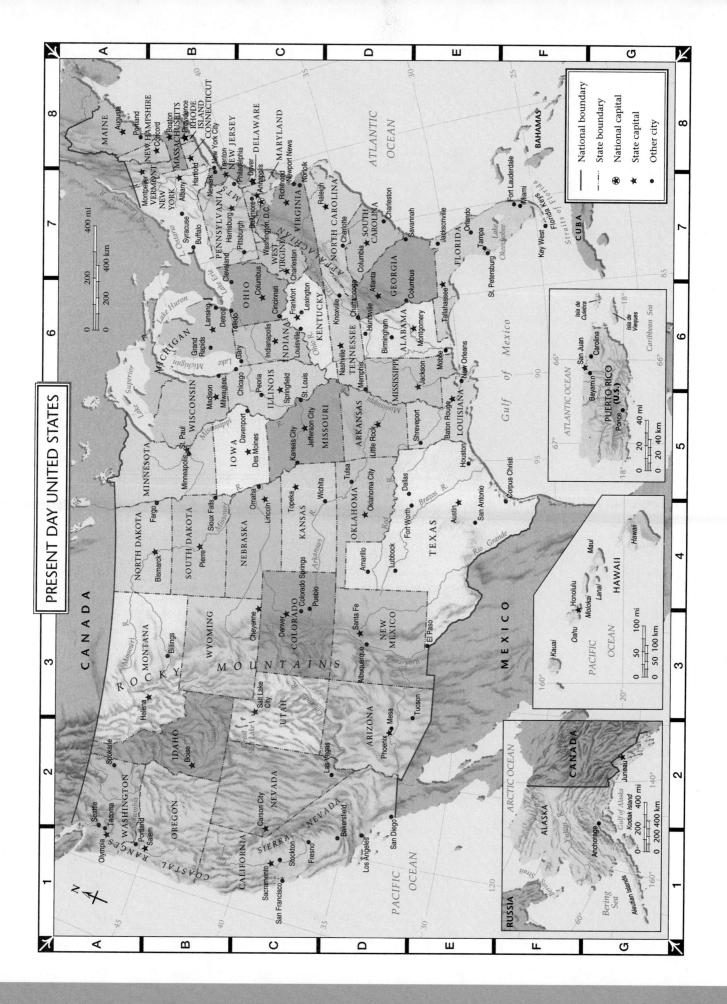

PRESENT DAY UNITED STATES

M-1

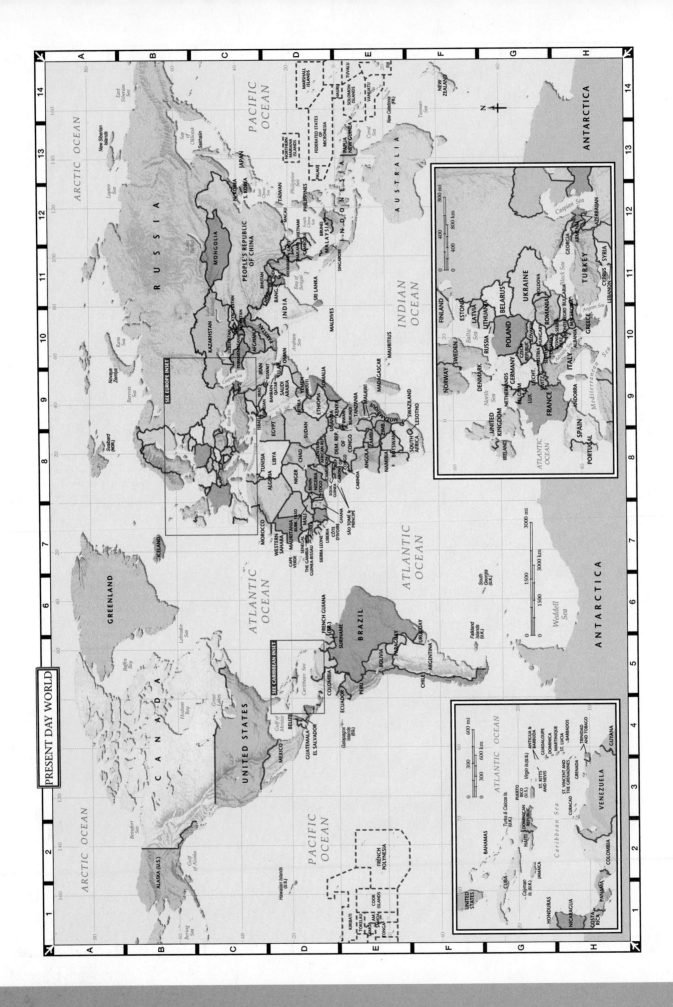

PRESENT DAY WORLD